AN AFRICAN TRADING EMPIRE

The Story of Susman Brothers & Wulfsohn, 1901–2005

HUGH MACMILLAN

I.B. TAURIS
LONDON · NEW YORK

New paperback edition published in 2017 by
I.B.Tauris & Co. Ltd
London • New York
www.ibtauris.com

First published in hardback in 2005 by I.B.Tauris & Co. Ltd

Copyright © 2005, 2017 Hugh Macmillan

The right of Hugh Macmillan to be identified as the author of this work has been asserted by him in accordance with the Copyright, Designs and Patents Act 1988.

All rights reserved. Except for brief quotations in a review, this book, or any part thereof, may not be reproduced, stored in or introduced into a retrieval system, or transmitted, in any form or by any means, electronic, mechanical, photocopying, recording or otherwise, without the prior written permission of the publisher.

Every attempt has been made to gain permission for the use of the images in this book. Any omissions will be rectified in future editions.

References to websites were correct at the time of writing.

ISBN: 978 1 78453 678 7
eISBN: 978 1 78672 121 1
ePDF ISBN: 978 1 78673 121 0

A full CIP record for this book is available from the British Library
A full CIP record is available from the Library of Congress

Library of Congress Catalog Card Number: available

Typeset by JCS Publishing Services Ltd, www.jcs-publishing.co.uk
Printed and bound by CPI Group (UK) Ltd, Croydon, CR0 4YY

Contents

List of Illustrations   vii
Abbreviations   viii
Maps   x
Diagram of Main Companies in the Susman Brothers & Wulfsohn Group, 1966   xii

1. From Lithuania to Barotseland: The African and Baltic Backgrounds   1
2. Barotseland Beginnings, 1901–4   16
3. Settled at Sesheke, 1904–8   34
4. Life at Lealui, 1904–8   51
5. King Lobengula's Treasure   67
6. From Sesheke to Livingstone via Palestine, 1909–14   83
7. Sesheke, War and the Barotseland Cattle Trade, 1909–31   101
8. From Ngamiland to the Congo, 1912–36   120
9. From Livingstone to the Copperbelt via South Africa, 1914–39   139
10. Harry Wulfsohn: From Latvia to Livingstone, 1930–44   167
11. Susman Brothers & Wulfsohn: The Development of the Stores Network, 1944–56   188
12. The Susmans, Woolworths and Marks & Spencer   209
13. Susman Brothers & Wulfsohn: Partners and Politics, 1953–74   221
14. Susman Brothers & Wulfsohn Stores: People   256
15. Werners: The Copperbelt and the Central African Cattle Trade, 1944–75   276
16. The Gersh Brothers: A Copperbelt Conglomerate   300
17. Primary Industry: Zambesi Saw Mills, 1948–68   318
18. Secondary Industry: Northern Rhodesia/Zambia Textiles, 1946–2003   340
19. Farms and Ranches, 1945–93   353
20. From Conflict to Concorde: Rhodesia, Zimbabwe, Botswana and the United Kingdom, 1963–2003   373

21 Emerging Markets? Trans Zambezi Industries (TZI) 395
22 Conclusions 411

Acknowledgements and Note on Sources 421
Notes 437
Index 479

List of Illustrations

1	The treasure hunters, including Elie Susman	80
2	The wedding of Harry Susman and Annie Grill, July 1910	94
3	Advertisement for the Pioneer Butchery, Livingstone, 1909	96
4	Oscar Susman crossing the Zambezi, 1913	104
5	Elie Susman crossing the Lualaba River, 1927	115
6	Harry Susman with a herd of Ngamiland cattle, Northern Rhodesia or Bechuanaland, early 1930s	135
7	Litunga Yeta III and Harry Susman with the future Litunga, Imwiko, Livingstone, 1925	141
8	Harry Susman with workers stringing tobacco at Kabulonga Farm, Lusaka, 1927	154
9	Harry Wulfsohn and his future wife, Trude Wiesenbacher, Lusaka, 1939	180
10	Harry Wulfsohn, 1950s	225
11	Elie Susman, portrait by Neville Lewis, 1950	233
12	Harry Wulfsohn, Max Barnett, Mike Pretorius and pilot, with De Havilland Rapide aircraft, Livingstone or Barotseland, early 1950s	279
13	Maurice Rabb with President Kenneth Kaunda at the opening of Zambia Spinners, Livingstone, 1981	349
14	Harry Wulfsohn and Jack Tuffin on Kafue River, Nanga Ranch, Zambia, 1967	357
15	Harry Wulfsohn unveils the Wulfsohn History Gallery, Rhodes–Livingstone Museum, Livingstone, 1956	380
16	Trans Zambezi Industries, board of directors, *circa* 1995	398

Abbreviations

AE	Agricultural Enterprises
Afcom	African Commercial Motors
AGM	Annual General Meeting
BNA	Botswana National Archives
BP	Bechuanaland Protectorate
BSA	British South Africa
CAMS	Central African Motors
CBC	Campbell Booker Carter
CDC	Colonial/Commonwealth Development Corporation
CMCB	Cattle Marketing and Control Board
CS	Chief Secretary
CVO	Chief Veterinary Officer
DC	District Commissioner
GG	Governor-General
GS	Government Secretary
HC	High Commissioner
Indeco	Industrial Development Corporation
LM	Livingstone Museum
MMD	Movement for Multi-party Democracy
NAZ	National Archives of Zambia
NIEC	National Import and Export Company
Nortex	Northern Rhodesia Textiles
NR	Northern Rhodesia
NRG	Northern Rhodesian Government
NTC	Ngamiland Trading Company
PP	pleuro-pneumonia
RC	Resident Commissioner
RHL	Rhodes House Library, Oxford
RM	Resident Magistrate
RMH	Rhodesian Mercantile Holdings

RP	Rabb Papers
RST	Rhodesian Selection Trust
SA	South Africa
SB	Susman Brothers
SBA	Standard Bank Archives
SB & W	Susman Brothers & Wulfsohn
SP	Susman Papers
SR	Southern Rhodesia
TZI	Trans Zambezi Industries
UDI	Unilateral Declaration of Independence
UFP	United Federal Party
UNIP	United National Independence Party
WP	Wulfsohn Papers
ZA	Zimbabwe Archives
ZANU	Zimbabwe African National Union
ZAPU	Zimbabwe African People's Union
ZCBC	Zambia Consumer Buying Corporation
ZRC	Zambesi Ranching Corporation/Zambesi Ranching and Cropping
ZSM	Zambesi Saw Mills
ZCCM	Zambia Consolidated Copper Mines

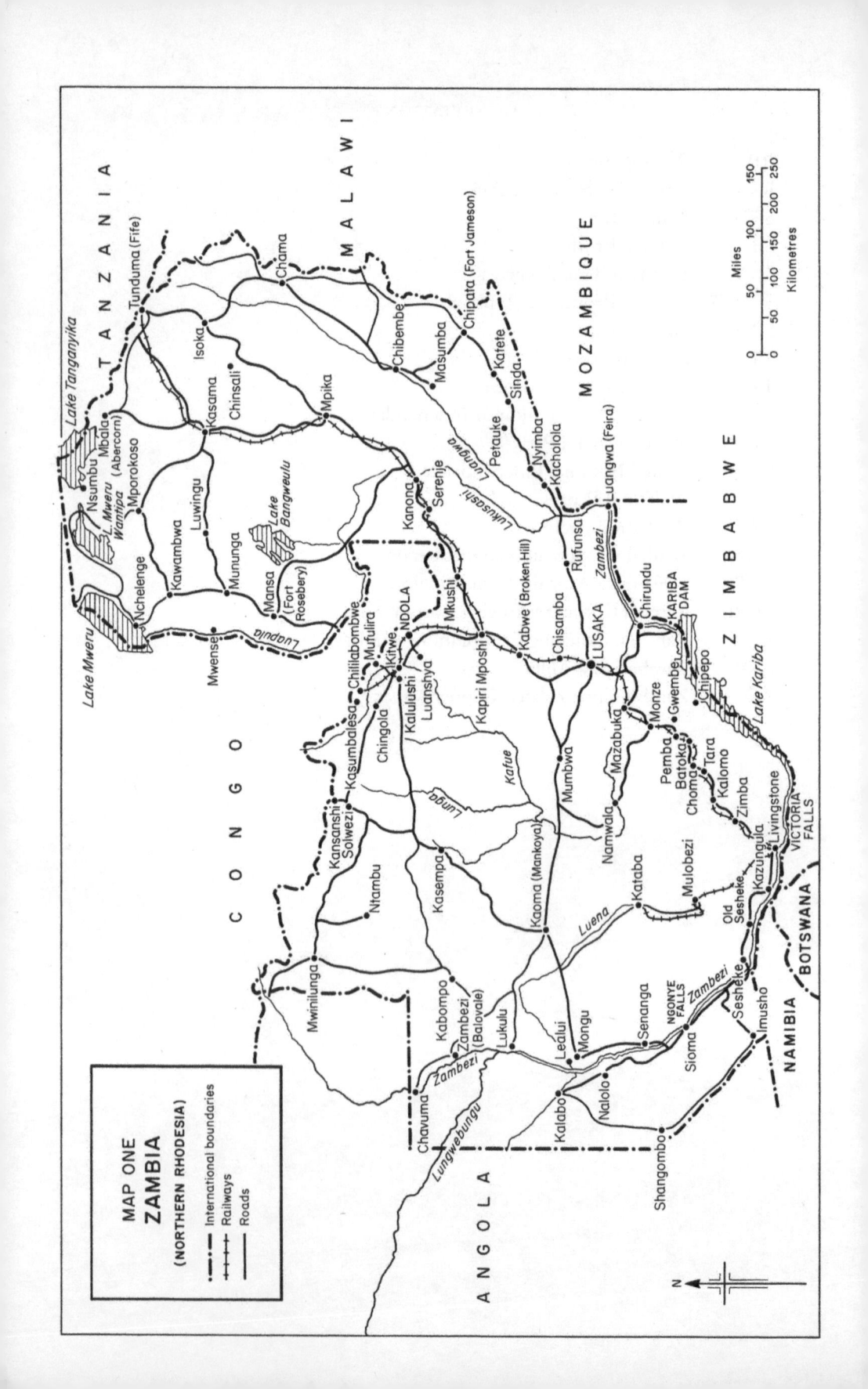

MAP ONE
ZAMBIA
(NORTHERN RHODESIA)

International boundaries
Railways
Roads

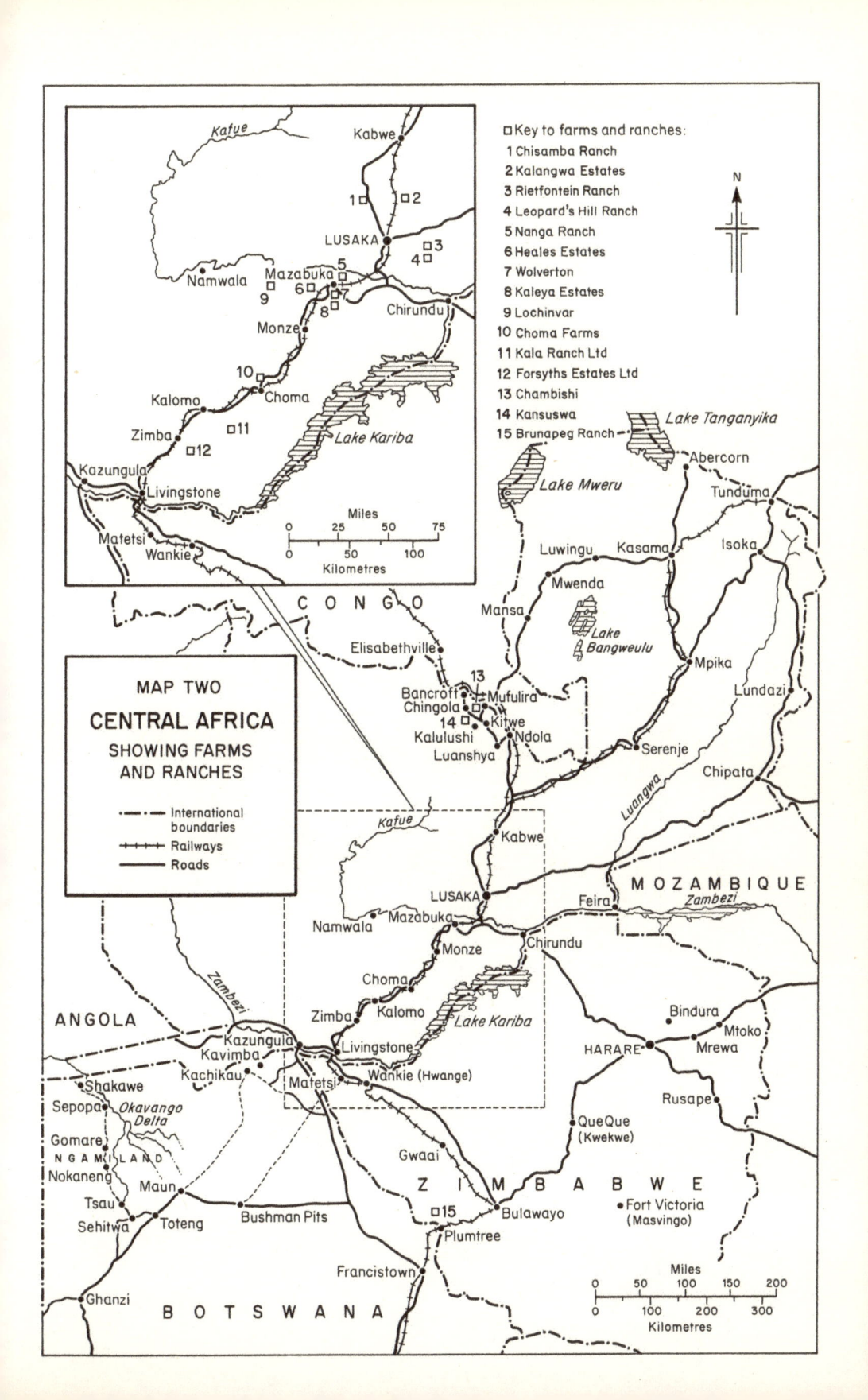

MAP TWO
CENTRAL AFRICA
SHOWING FARMS AND RANCHES

Key to farms and ranches:
1 Chisamba Ranch
2 Kalangwa Estates
3 Rietfontein Ranch
4 Leopard's Hill Ranch
5 Nanga Ranch
6 Heales Estates
7 Wolverton
8 Kaleya Estates
9 Lochinvar
10 Choma Farms
11 Kala Ranch Ltd
12 Forsyths Estates Ltd
13 Chambishi
14 Kansuswa
15 Brunapeg Ranch

— · — International boundaries
+++ Railways
— Roads

DIAGRAM OF MAIN COMPANIES IN THE SUSMAN BROTHERS AND WULFSOHN GROUP, 1966

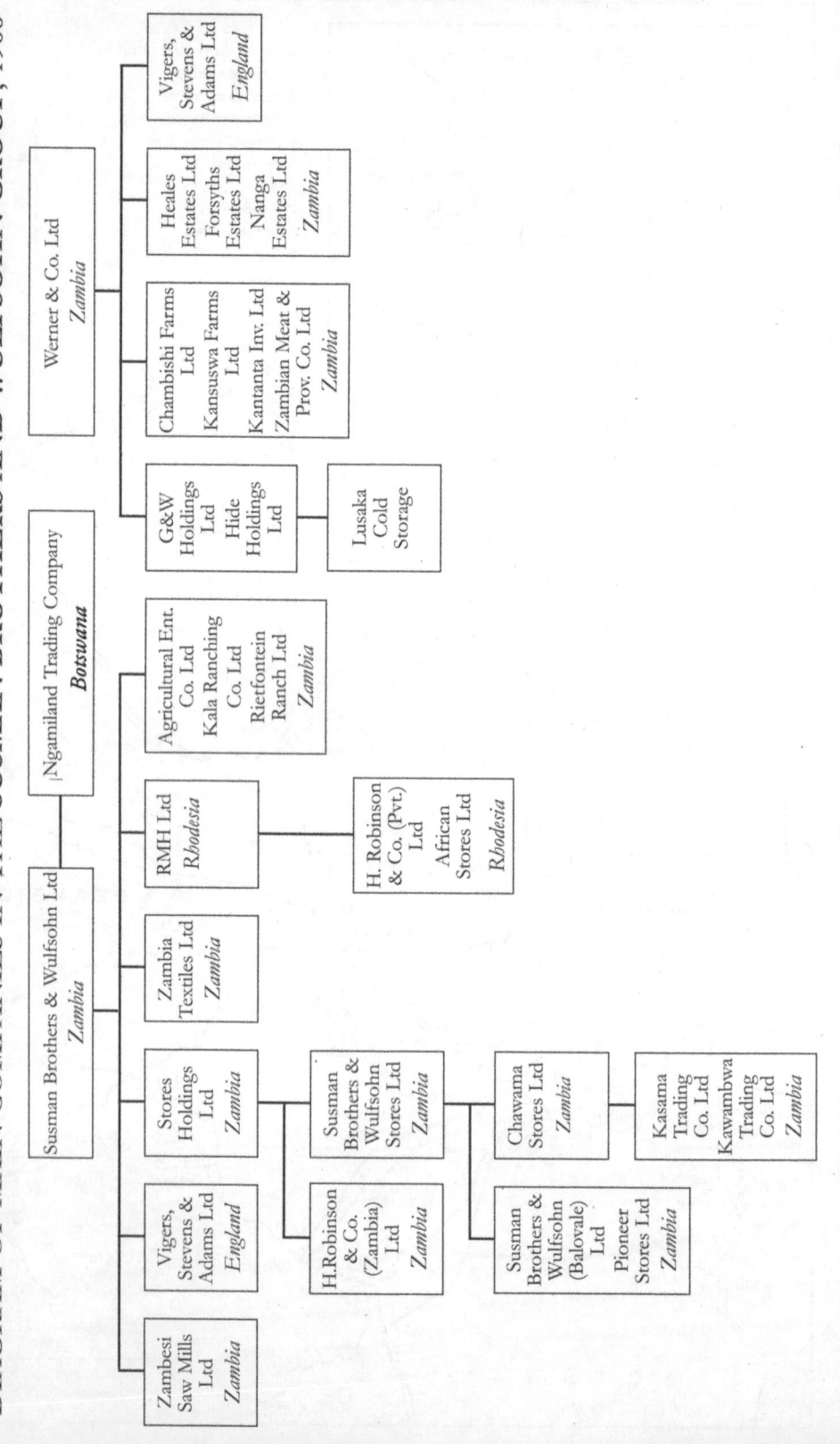

- **Susman Brothers & Wulfsohn Ltd** *Zambia*
  - Zambesi Saw Mills Ltd *Zambia*
  - Vigers, Stevens & Adams Ltd *England*
  - Stores Holdings Ltd *Zambia*
    - H. Robinson & Co. (Zambia) Ltd *Zambia*
    - Susman Brothers & Wulfsohn Stores Ltd *Zambia*
      - Susman Brothers & Wulfsohn (Balovale) Ltd Pioneer Stores Ltd *Zambia*
      - Chawama Stores Ltd *Zambia*
        - Kasama Trading Co. Ltd Kawambwa Trading Co. Ltd *Zambia*
  - Zambia Textiles Ltd *Zambia*
  - RMH Ltd *Rhodesia*
    - H. Robinson & Co. (Pvt.) Ltd African Stores Ltd *Rhodesia*

- **Ngamiland Trading Company** *Botswana*
  - Agricultural Ent. Co. Ltd Kala Ranching Co. Ltd Rietfontein Ranch Ltd *Zambia*
  - G&W Holdings Ltd Hide Holdings Ltd
    - Lusaka Cold Storage

- **Werner & Co. Ltd** *Zambia*
  - Chambishi Farms Ltd Kansuswa Farms Ltd Kantanta Inv. Ltd Zambian Meat & Prov. Co. Ltd *Zambia*
  - Heales Estates Ltd Forsyths Estates Ltd Nanga Estates Ltd *Zambia*
  - Vigers, Stevens & Adams Ltd *England*

CHAPTER 1

From Lithuania to Barotseland: The African and Baltic Backgrounds

This is the story of a family business. It has operated in many countries, and under many different names, but it is best known as Susman Brothers & Wulfsohn. The main focus of its activities has always been in south-central Africa. The story begins in the heyday of imperialism and touches several European empires: the Russian, the British, the German and the Portuguese, as well as a Eurasian one, the Turkish and, more importantly, an African one – the Lozi. It could start at any one of several different places and times: in Russia in 1876, in Cape Town in 1896, or in Francistown, Bechuanaland, in 1900. But the really decisive moment occurred just over a century ago, in April 1901. It was then that two brothers, Elie and Harry Susman, crossed the Zambezi in dugout canoes and landed on its north bank at Kazungula in what is today Zambia. What is special about Kazungula? Who were the Susman brothers? Where did they come from? How did they get to Kazungula? Why were they there?

Kazungula is not a conventional beauty spot, but it has its own charms. Colin Harding, first commandant of the British South Africa Company's Barotseland Police, spent three weeks at Kazungula late in 1899 waiting for boats to take him up the Zambezi to Lealui. He provided this most evocative pen-portrait of the place:

> Kazungula is by no means a sanatorium, but though unhealthy, the beauty of the 460 yards of water that divided us from the opposite bank was very great. The sunsets were glorious, lighting up the river as evening drew on with a glow of colour of exquisite variety and beauty. Occasionally we would sail out to pass an hour or two down the reaches in a welting flood of crimson and gold in the west. The far-off cry of some wild bird alone breaking the glowing silence of the evening, while, in spite of the scene of romance and dreams around, we would practically replenish our larder with the large tiger-fish

which abound at this point, and make an excellent dish for the hungry traveller eaten under the dim light of the stars and the brighter one of our own cheery camp fire.[1]

Someone standing on the river bank at Kazungula in Zambia today, and looking south across the Zambezi, can see, in midstream on the right, a reed-fringed island with low bush which is the eastern tip of Namibia's Caprivi Strip. On the other side of the island, the Chobe River, a major tributary, enters the Zambezi and separates Namibia from Botswana. Straight ahead on the south bank of the river is the boundary between Zimbabwe and Botswana. This is the only place where Botswana touches the Zambezi River. It is the only place in the world where four countries meet at one place – an imaginary point in the middle of the Zambezi. The boundary of a fifth country, Angola, with Zambia and Namibia, lies not much more than 100 miles to the west.

This political and geographical peculiarity is one of the many strange consequences of the late nineteenth-century Scramble for Africa in which the major Western European powers, Great Britain, France and Germany, and some smaller ones, carved up the continent between themselves. In a deal done with Britain in 1890, without reference to local rulers or people, Germany acquired a pan-handle of territory, much of it periodically flooded, which gave its colony of South West Africa at least nominal access to the Zambezi. This became known in German as the Caprivi Zipfel and in English as the Caprivi Strip. It was named after the little-known chancellor who succeeded Bismarck. Its anomalous existence – it was described by the eminent geographer Frank Debenham as 'the ridiculous Caprivi Strip, that enormity of political geography' – is the reason for Kazungula's uniqueness.[2]

Kazungula, which is thirty-five miles upstream from the Victoria Falls, just above the Katombora Rapids, and just below the gentler rapids at Kambove, has been for more than a century, and is still today, an important Zambezi crossing-point. It is the main point of entry for trucks carrying goods from South Africa to Zambia, the Congo and Malawi. Some return empty, but others carry copper and cobalt from the Copperbelt of Zambia and the Congo, or tea and tobacco from Malawi. As there is no bridge, trucks and their trailers are carried across the river on a motorised pontoon. Although bridges have been built across the Zambezi further downstream at the Victoria Falls, at Chirundu and within Mozambique at Tete, Kazungula has retained its significance. It is the most important point of direct contact between the countries of the South African Customs Union and those to the north. The existence of this river-crossing allows trucks to travel between the north and the south without entering Zimbabwe.

One hundred years ago, the Scramble for Africa was virtually complete on paper, but not nearly complete on the ground. An up-to-date atlas of the world would have indicated that Kazungula was, at least in theory, the meeting place of four countries: German South West Africa, the British protectorates of Bechuanaland, 'Barotseland–North-Western Rhodesia', and Southern Rhodesia. The last two territories were under the control of the British South Africa Company, better known as the Chartered Company. The Germans had not yet occupied the Caprivi Strip and were in the end to do so for only five years – between 1909 and 1914. It remained under the effective control of King Lewanika, the ruler of Bulozi, an African kingdom, almost an empire, which the British called Barotseland. The British had not yet taken control of the northern part of the Bechuanaland Protectorate, nor had their surrogate – the Chartered Company – taken effective control of Barotseland.

For many years the Kazungula crossing was the only way into the Lozi kingdom from the south. From about 1874 until his death in 1888, the keeper of this gate to Barotseland was George Westbeech, an English ivory trader who had befriended King Mzilikazi and his son and heir, Lobengula, at Bulawayo in the 1860s. He went on in the 1870s to befriend Sipopa, king of the Lozi, and his eventual successor, Lubosi Lewanika, who seized power in Bulozi in 1877. Sipopa had latterly ruled from Sesheke in the Zambezi valley, but Lewanika returned the capital to the central flood plain, 250 miles to the north. He made his headquarters at Lealui. Lewanika valued Westbeech for his links with Lobengula, and for his ability both to prevent Ndebele attacks and to keep out undesirable white traders. Westbeech made his base at Pandamatenga, about fifty miles south of Kazungula, but he also had stores at various times at Lishoma, ten miles to the south of the Zambezi, at Sesheke and, for a while, at Kazungula itself. In return for services rendered, including the supply of guns and powder, Lewanika granted Westbeech the exclusive right to hunt elephants in the Linyanti-Chobe marshes – the future Caprivi Strip.

Kazungula became the terminus of Westbeech's Road, also known as the Old Hunters' Road. Westbeech developed it as a wagon route in the 1870s and 1880s. It was a continuation of the Missionaries' Road, which led northwards from Shoshong in Khama's Ngwato kingdom. The road bypassed Lobengula's Ndebele kingdom, leaving its boundaries to the east, but also avoided the tsetse-fly belts of the Kalahari, and the Makgadikgadi saltpan, which lay to the west. A succession of traders, travellers and explorers, including Serpa Pinto, Emil Holub and Frederick Courtney Selous, as well as aspiring missionaries, all passed this way in the 1870s and 1880s.

Westbeech eased the way into Barotseland for François Coillard, representative of the Paris Mission, and obstructed the way for the Jesuits, who had reached Kazungula in 1880. The Paris Mission was French, Protestant and evangelical, but drew many of its missionaries from Switzerland and Italy. Coillard had worked for many years in Basutoland. His wife was Scots, and he was sympathetic to the extension of British influence in south-central Africa. In the years after 1885, his mission established stations at Sesheke and Lealui, the upper and lower capitals of the kingdom, as well as at Senanga, Sefula and Kazungula itself. Lewanika wanted missionaries because he realised the benefits that might flow from Western education and technology. He also sought a British protectorate, like the one established for the benefit, more or less, of Khama, and other Tswana rulers, in Bechuanaland in 1885.[3]

Lewanika was never very securely established in the kingdom where he had seized power. He had to deal with two major rebellions within the first decade of his reign. In one of them, in 1884, he was forced to flee his capital and it took him more than a year to regain his throne. Westbeech thought that the Lozi kingdom was like a republic and that Lewanika lived in 'mortal dread' of being overthrown by the chiefs. Alfred St Hill Gibbons, hunter and explorer, who passed through the kingdom in 1895–6 and again in 1898–9, described it as '… a heterogeneous regime embracing a score of "quondam" independent tribes, speaking many different languages, each retaining and influenced by its own tribal customs and characteristics, some governed directly by the king, others through satraps or governors selected by him from among the members of his family, and others again by subject chiefs'.[4] The kingdom had many of the characteristics of a nineteenth-century European empire. It was large, extending over 250,000 square miles, the same size as the then German Empire, though with a very much smaller population. It was also polyglot and multi-ethnic. The ruling Lozi, or Luyi, people made up a minority of the population, even within the historical heartland of the central plain. Many of the outlying peoples, such as the Luvale, the Kaonde, the Ila and the Tonga, paid tribute to the king, but were not directly ruled by him. The effective language of government was Silozi, a variant of a South African language, Sesotho, which had been imported into Bulozi in the 1840s and had become the lingua franca in this multi-lingual area. This was the language of the Kololo invaders from the south who took power in the

Zambezi valley from the Luyi ruling group between the 1840s and the 1860s.

Until the end of the nineteenth century, ivory was the most valuable export from the Lozi kingdom. Lewanika's control over ivory was vital to his economic survival. Many of the guns, and much of the powder, which were essential for elephant hunting, came from the south, but Portuguese and Ovimbundu, or Mambari, traders also imported these commodities from the west. There were also contacts with Arab, Swahili and Nyamwezi traders from the north. Lewanika did not himself engage in the slave trade. He refused, for example, to sell slaves to a Portuguese trader who visited Lealui in 1895, but slave caravans were encountered on the northwestern frontiers of his dominions until the eve of the First World War. These slaves were usually bought by Ovimbundu traders and were destined for use on plantations within Angola. They were no longer exported from the continent of Africa. Although Lewanika did not engage in the slave trade, forms of slavery or serfdom were essential features of production in Bulozi. Lewanika's armies continued to raid neighbouring and subject peoples, such as the Ila and Tonga, for captives and cattle until well into the 1890s. Slave, captive and tribute labour was essential for agricultural production at royal headquarters such as Lealui, Sesheke, Nalolo and Libonda, as well as for the construction of mounds and canals in the plain. Although slavery was formally abolished in 1906, some people continued to work as slaves into the 1920s. The memory of slave status lasted much longer.[5]

Even though Lewanika controlled a state that had depended on raiding to increase or replenish supplies of labour and cattle, he continued to live in fear of attack by his more militaristic neighbour, Lobengula, and his Ndebele state. Westbeech's death in 1888 left a power vacuum on the southern boundaries of the Lozi kingdom. Fear of the Ndebele led Lewanika in 1890 to sign an agreement with Frank Lochner, a representative of the British South Africa Company, encouraged to do so by François Coillard. The Lochner Concession became the basis of the company's claims to control Lewanika's territory. The British South Africa Company was financed by Cecil Rhodes and Alfred Beit from the profits that they derived from the exploitation of Kimberley diamonds and Witwatersrand gold. It had been granted a royal charter by Queen Victoria in 1889, which authorised it to occupy and control, on behalf of Great Britain, the region between the Limpopo and Zambezi rivers. The charter was extended to the north of the Zambezi in 1893, but the company had to fight two wars against the Ndebele and Shona peoples to establish its control in the south, and it was slow to move into the north. Lewanika always distrusted the company and hoped for a protectorate that would be administered directly by the Colonial Office in London. He knew that Khama, whom he saw as a role model, enjoyed a considerable degree of autonomy under Colonial Office rule in the Bechuanaland Protectorate.[6]

Robert Coryndon, one of Cecil Rhodes's protégés, a man of only twenty-seven, arrived at King Lewanika's capital, Lealui, in October 1897 as the company's first resident representative. Lewanika gave Coryndon a frosty reception, refusing to believe that he could represent both the British government and the Chartered Company. He only softened his stand after intervention by Adolphe Jalla, an Italian member of the Paris Mission. An order-in-council, signed by Queen Victoria, was promulgated in November 1899 and provided for the establishment of company rule in 'Barotziland–North-Western Rhodesia' under the supervision of the British high commissioner in South Africa. Coryndon was appointed administrator in September 1900. The Lewanika Concession, negotiated in October 1900, drew an internal boundary between the two parts of the British protectorate at the Machili River, about thirty miles west of Kazungula. Effective control of Barotseland remained with King Lewanika and was only gradually taken from him in the ensuing decade, but the company gave itself a free hand in the area that it designated as North-Western Rhodesia.[7]

The government of the Bechuanaland Protectorate was also slow to establish control over its northern boundary area. Real power there remained for some years – at least until he was deposed by the British in 1906 – with Chief Sekgoma Letsholathebe, ruler of the Batawana people. British officials were sent from Bechuanaland and North-Western Rhodesia in 1902 to settle a boundary dispute between King Lewanika and Chief Sekgoma, ignoring the existence of the German sphere, which was supposed to separate the two. This question of Barotseland's western boundary with the Portuguese colony of Angola was referred by Great Britain and Portugal to the king of Italy for arbitration. Until his decision was announced in 1905, the international boundaries on the west bank of the Zambezi remained unclear. In reality King Lewanika continued to control an area that extended from the upper Zambezi for some distance westwards into what is today Angola. The arbitration award removed from Bulozi the dominions claimed by King Lewanika west of the Kwando River. The settlement of the boundary line about sixty miles west of the Zambezi did not please Lewanika, but it allowed company officials to operate freely for the first time on the west bank of the river. They had earlier feared that the Zambezi might be declared to be the western boundary of Barotseland.[8]

Kazungula lies at the centre of some very complex political geography, but of some even more complex physical geography. David Livingstone, one of the area's first explorers, compared the upper Zambezi basin to a saucer tilted from northwest to southeast. The Zambezi itself rises in northwestern Zambia and flows through Angola, re-entering Zambia above the Chavuma Falls. As it flows through Zambia two major rivers then join it, the Kabompo from the east and the Lungwebungu from the west. The latter river is navigable for several hundred miles into Angola.[9]

The Zambezi then flows for 120 miles through a vast flood plain which is up to thirty miles wide, and has been for three or four hundred years the heart of the Lozi kingdom. Impermeable clay lying beneath the Kalahari sands that cover much of western Zambia, as well as Botswana and eastern Angola, creates the flood plain. The floods begin to rise soon after the beginning of the rains in December, but the delayed arrival of water flowing from the north ensures that they reach their highest point in May, two months after the end of the rains. When the floods subside in July they leave pools of water, some of which remain until the next rainy season. They also leave areas of moist mud, providing fertile gardens.

Most of the Lozi people now live permanently on the margins of the flood plain, though they continue to cultivate and to graze cattle in the plain. Only a minority today live as their ancestors did, spending one half of the year on mounds in the plain, and the other half on the slightly higher bush margins. Cattle are still moved twice a year, from the lush grasslands of the plain to the poorer grass of the bush margins and back again. Livingstone, who first saw Bulozi in 1851, was greatly impressed by the rich food resources of the plain, whose people could draw on apparently abundant sources of fish, meat, cereals, vegetables, pulses and tubers. He compared the beneficial impact of the annual flood with that of the Nile in Egypt.[10]

The central plain narrows and comes to an end south of Senanga. The Zambezi, which is navigable from Chavuma southwards, is then broken by falls at Sioma and by a series of rapids and cataracts near Katima Mulilo. It flows for most of 200 miles from Sioma through semi-arid bush country and teak forests, until it reaches the Chobe flood plain, or Sesheke flats, which terminate at Kazungula.

The most peculiar consequences of Livingstone's tilted saucer are to be found to the south and west of Kazungula. Two very unusual rivers, the Kwando (which becomes the Chobe or Linyanti) and the Okavango, rise to the west of the Zambezi in Angola and flow southwards parallel to it for several hundred miles. The Kwando flows to the west and south of the Zambezi, but then takes a sharp turn to the east and north and enters the Zambezi from the south at Kazungula. It does not, however, always flow into the Zambezi. If the floodwaters of the Zambezi rise first, the Chobe can flow backwards into its own swampy flood plain. The course of the Okavango is even stranger. It flows into Ngamiland, a region of northern Botswana named after the now dry lake that was the object of Livingstone's early explorations. The southeasterly flow of the river is stopped by a wall of Kalahari sand and it feeds the extraordinary inland delta of swamps that take their name from the river. While floodwater from the Okavango can reach the Zambezi by way of the Makwegana spillway and the Chobe, water from the Chobe does occasionally flow back by the same route into the Okavango. Water from the Okavango also flows, by way of the seasonal Botletle and Thamalakane rivers, through Ngamiland into the true desert of the Makgadikgadi saltpan.

The area centred on Kazungula was, in 1901, a frontier zone in several senses. It was a place where remaining pre-colonial African states met; where the spheres of influence of several European powers met; and where several embryonic protectorates and colonies met – at least on paper. It was a place where pre-colonial African states and European protectorates uneasily co-existed. It was also a frontier zone in a wider sense. It was a place of contact and interaction between black and white people; of white penetration, occupation and settlement; and of black accommodation, collaboration and resistance. Above all, it was a place where aspects of the environment – navigable stretches of river broken by falls and rapids; malarial swamps and seasonal flood plains; Kalahari sands, with bush and forest; mosquitoes, tsetse flies and snakes; crocodiles, lions and hippopotami; extremes of summer heat and winter cold, all provided real obstacles to travel, trade and communications.

The Kazungula axis, including Sesheke-Mwandi, forty miles to the west, and Victoria Falls-Livingstone, a similar distance to the east, was for many years to be central to the business whose history is the subject of this book. The business was based at first on Sesheke and latterly on Livingstone. In the early decades of the twentieth century its activities extended over 300 miles to the north through the upper Zambezi valley and over 300 miles to the south through the Kalahari to Ngamiland. It operated as a trading and transport business in two of the most remote, inaccessible and logistically difficult regions in southern Africa.

The Baltic Background

Who were the Susman Brothers? The founders of this business, Elie and Harry Susman, started their lives as Elias Jacob and Hirsch Leib Zusmanovitz in the small market town, or *shtetl*, of Riteve on the western frontier of the Russian Empire. Riteve was about thirty miles east of Memel, a Baltic sea port that lay at the northern tip of the kingdom of Prussia and, from 1871, of the German Empire. Kovno *Gubernia*, the province in which Riteve lay, was once part of the Grand Duchy of Lithuania, and was attached to the kingdom of Poland. As a result of the French Revolutionary Wars, and the Third Partition of Poland, the area became in 1795 a part of the Russian Empire. It was also a part of the Pale of Settlement, the western border area of the Russian Empire in which the vast majority of its Jewish population was confined. The Susman brothers were, like the majority of the people of Riteve, Jews. Elie, the younger brother, but the senior partner in what he called the 'Barotseland trading expedition', had just passed his twenty-first birthday when he crossed the Zambezi at Kazungula in April 1901. Harry, the elder brother, but junior partner, was twenty-five. Riteve's existence depended to a large degree on cross-border trade and so, in moving from a Baltic province of the Russian Empire to central Africa, the Susmans had exchanged one frontier zone for another.[11]

According to the Russian census of 1897, Riteve had a population of 1,750. Of these almost 1,400 were Jews. Perhaps one-third of Riteve's economically active population was engaged in trade, another third were craftsmen. The remaining third included people who made a living from transport with horses, wagons and boats, as well as a handful of professional people, and an even smaller number of people who were engaged in agriculture. Riteve was just one of a large number of predominantly Jewish market towns that were scattered throughout the Pale of Settlement. Nearby towns of this kind included a rather larger centre, Telz, as well as Plungyan, Vorne, Salant and Gorzhd. Riteve was not in itself an important centre, and its inhabitants tended to think of it as poor and isolated. But it was close to Memel, a significant Baltic port, and it was on main roads from Memel to Plungyan and Shavl, and not far from the main road between Memel and the provincial capitals of Kaunas (Kovno) and Vilna. It was also on a river, the Yureh, which was a navigable tributary of the Niemen. River transport was important for timber, which was cut in neighbouring forests and transported to Baltic ports.[12]

Riteve was a centre for the timber industry and for the production and export of flax. It was also unusual for a *shtetl* in that it was one of the principal seats of the Oginski family, who were the most powerful of the Polish nobles in the former grand duchy of Lithuania, and who were comparable in influence in Poland itself with the Radziwills, the Potockis and the Poniatowskis. The Oginskis were also major landowners in the neighbouring centres of Plungyan and Salant. A branch of the Oginski family, probably the main branch, was resident at Riteve for most of the nineteenth century. Accounts of Riteve, written in the twentieth century by former Jewish residents, reveal an ambivalent attitude towards the Oginskis.

On the one hand, these accounts recall anti-Semitic incidents in which the *poritz, graf,* or duke, Irenaeus Oginski, is alleged to have driven pigs into the *beit midrash*, or prayer house, and in which his sons dug up the Jewish cemetery. They recall Duke Irenaeus's suicide on the eve of the festival of Purim in 1859. He was a Polish nationalist and was about to be arrested by a troop of Cossacks for treason, a few years before the second great Polish nationalist uprising. The Jews are said to have celebrated in later years their double liberation from Haman, whose plot to kill the Jews is described in the book of Esther, and Duke Irenaeus.

On the other hand, the accounts also recall with a degree of pride Irenaeus's liberation of the Lithuanian serfs in 1835, nearly thirty years before their emancipation by Tsar Alexander II in Greater Russia. They recall the beauty of the Oginski Park, and their free access to its lake, gardens and greenhouses. They remember the beauty of the Oginski Palace, which, according to one distinguished Jewish native of Riteve, 'could take its place on the Champs Elysées, Piccadilly or 5th Avenue, New York'. They recall the beauty of the Catholic church, which was built by the Oginskis and completed in the 1870s. Its tall spire was a local landmark and could be seen for three miles by returning residents – both Christians and Jews. They also recall that Duke Irenaeus paved the road to Memel in the 1850s; that Riteve was in 1882 one of the first towns in Lithuania to be connected to the outside world by telephone; and that in 1892 it was the first town in the region to have electric street lights. They also remember the Oginskis' establishment of an agricultural school in the 1880s, and of a professional music school, which provided this small town with a sixty-piece orchestra.[13]

The main role of the Jews in this part of the Russian Empire was as middlemen between the Polish nobility and the Lithuanian peasants. The peasants of Riteve were freed from serfdom and the village commune, or *mir,* was typical of Russia but not the norm in Lithuania. While the nobility owned large estates, the peasants farmed on individual plots. Wednesday was market day in Riteve and peasants came into the town to exchange their produce, such as grain and flax, for manufactures. Business on other days was slow, and many of the Jews were peddlers who spent the whole week walking from village to village, and from farm to farm, hawking haberdashery, cotton reels and cloth. They often exchanged goods for produce, anything from eggs to pig bristles. They slept at the farms of their customers and returned home for the sabbath and for high days and holidays.[14]

The nobility and the Jews were controversially linked through the noble monopoly of inns and taverns, preserved until the 1860s, and their control over the manufacture and sale of alcohol. The nobles usually leased their taverns to Jews, for whom inn-keeping was a staple activity, often combined with petty trading. The Jews themselves were thought to be abstemious, but were frequently accused of profiting from the drunkenness of the peasantry. In Riteve the main source of income for the Zusmanowitz family was a wayside inn on the road to Memel. This was one of the more important inns in the town, and must have brought the family into direct contact with their noble landlords, the Oginskis.[15]

The Jews of the Lithuanian provinces of the Russian Empire, Kovno and Vilna, were known for their devotion to Orthodox Judaism. The influence of Elijah ben-Solomon Salmon, the Vilna *gaon* – genius – of the eighteenth century, was strong. He was not opposed to secular learning, which he saw as necessary for the understanding of the Torah, but he was profoundly opposed to the mysticism of the Hassidic tendency. This mysticism made little progress in the region. The leaders of Orthodox Judaism were also opposed to the Jewish 'Enlightenment', or *Haskalah* movement, though this did make some progress in the Lithuanian provinces in the nineteenth century. Orthodox Judaism almost certainly gained strength during the century as Jews reacted against the official policy of Russification, and the evangelism of the Russian Orthodox Church. These policies of Church and State also targeted Christian minorities in the region: the Catholic Poles and Lithuanians, and Protestant Germans. The Jews of Riteve took great pride in the large number of rabbinical scholars who emerged from their small town in the course of the century. Daily life, for the men anyway, revolved around the *beit midrash*, with morning and evening prayers, and study of the Torah and Talmud. The Vilna *gaon* had hoped to be able to go to live and work in Jerusalem. Some of his followers did go to the Promised Land in the first decade of the nineteenth century and others followed in the 1860s. The leaders of Orthodox Jewry were, however, suspicious of the rise of the

Zionist movement, which began in the 1880s as Chibat Zion – a spiritual movement whose followers were known as the Chovevei Zion. It is unlikely that this movement, or the secular Zionism of Theodor Herzl, had much impact in Riteve before the end of the nineteenth century.[16]

Not a great deal is known about the life of the Susman brothers in the Russian Empire before their departure for Africa in 1896. We do know that their father Behr Zusmanowitz (also known as Zusmanovitz, Susmanowitz and Susmanovitch) was born at Riteve in April 1853. He was the son of Joel Zusmanovitz, described in one source as Rabbi Joel, probably an honorific rather than a professional title. Behr married Taube (Tova) Diamond in about 1874. They had five children, three sons and two daughters, all born at Riteve within the ensuing twenty years. Behr Zusmanowitz was a man of strong character who grew into a stern patriarch. His religion was strictly Orthodox, but he was not, in the words of his grandson, Maurice Gersh, 'a *yeshivah bocher*' – a seminarian. He had some of the characteristics of the 'wandering Jew' and was able to earn his living as a tailor. On several occasions, he left his wife and family to manage the inn while he went off to seek a fortune overseas. He travelled first to America in the early 1880s and seems to have spent time in New York. He was shocked by what he saw, regarding the country as 'immoral and unethical'. Unable to come to terms with the modern world as he saw it in the United States, he preferred to return to Riteve.[17]

In seeking his fortune in the United States, Behr Zusmanowitz became part of a large-scale emigration of Jews from the Russian Empire in the 1880s. This was triggered by the wave of anti-Semitic pogroms, which broke out after the assassination of Tsar Alexander II in 1881. The pogroms were largely confined to the southern parts of the Pale of Settlement and did not occur in the northern provinces, though there were isolated incidents of arson aimed at Jewish businesses there. Emigration was also encouraged by the generally anti-Semitic tendency of government policy; its continued threat to remove Jews from border areas; and to reduce their involvement in rural trade and in the production and distribution of alcohol. Other factors encouraging emigration included: the worldwide depression in agriculture in the 1880s; the effects of railway-building on older modes of transport; and the adverse effect of the moves towards freer trade on cross-border smuggling. This latter development must have had an effect on the local economy of Riteve, which was just thirty miles from the German border at Memel – precisely the distance from the border to which, throughout the nineteenth century, the Russian government threatened to remove the Jews.[18]

The second most popular destination for Jewish emigrants from the Lithuanian provinces of the Russian Empire was South Africa. It is usually estimated that three-quarters of the 50,000 or so Jews from the Russian Empire who reached South Africa in the late nineteenth century came from these provinces. This has been attributed to reports reaching them in the mid 1880s, before the discovery of the Witwatersrand, of the spectacular success of a few Jews from the area – in particular the good fortune experienced at Kimberley and in the Transvaal Republic by Sammy Marks, who formed a close alliance with President Paul Kruger. Reports of his success were carried in the Hebrew paper that circulated in the Russian Empire – *Hamelitz*. Another factor may have been the efforts made to advertise South Africa by Sir Donald Currie and his Castle Line shipping company. It sought steerage passengers to fill its ships and advertised in *Hamelitz*. Currie helped to sponsor the Jews' Temporary Shelter in the East End of London. This provided accommodation between ships for emigrants from the Baltic, who usually landed at Hull but then left the country for the United States or South Africa from London. The predominant share of Jewish immigrants to South Africa coming from a small area within the Russian Empire could be further explained by the workings of the extended family in tight-knit communities. New immigrants worked hard to save money to pay for passages for their brothers, sisters, parents and grandparents – and, ultimately, aunts, uncles and cousins.[19]

It would be a mistake to exaggerate the similarities between the frontier zone in the Russian Empire from which the Susman brothers, and other Jewish emigrants, came, and the African frontier zone to which they moved. Emigration and immigration are painful and difficult at any time. Although experience of a multi-lingual society may have been an advantage to migrants moving from Russia to southern Africa, it must be easier as a general rule to move to a place, such as the United States, where the official language is also the lingua franca. Jewish immigrant traders in Africa faced a peculiar difficulty, which they shared with missionaries from countries in Europe where English was not spoken. They had to learn to function in new official languages at the same time as in several African ones.

As the immigrants worked their way through the Cape Colony, the Orange Free State and the Transvaal in the years before the Anglo-Boer War and the creation of the Union of South Africa, they had to deal with two official languages: English and Dutch. They also had to learn some words of Afrikaans, Zulu, Sotho or Tswana in order to deal with their customers. While this must have been very difficult, it was not an entirely unfamiliar situation to people from the frontier of the Russian and German empires. They had already had to contend as peddlers and petty traders with two official languages, Russian and German, and with customers who spoke Lithuanian or Polish. They were also used to a situation in which the peasants spoke dialects that had not yet been reduced to writing or which deviated markedly from the written standard.

Although Jewish immigrants faced huge linguistic and cultural difficulties, including widespread and rampant anti-Semitism – especially in the English-speaking white population and the official classes – there were one or two points of linguistic and cultural contact. There were some quite strong similarities between Yiddish and colloquial Afrikaans, which was still not a recognised or written language. It was not very difficult for Yiddish-speakers to learn to communicate in Afrikaans. Jews on the frontier also found that they had something in common with Afrikaners and Scots, who were also over-represented there. They were both 'peoples of the Book' whose Bible-based and Calvinist form of Christianity had a good deal in common with Orthodox Judaism – including an emphasis on the Old Testament. It was, of course, suggested by the controversial German economist, Werner Sombart, that Max Weber's 'Protestant ethic' was in reality a 'Jewish ethic'.

While the climates of Lithuania and central Africa might seem to be very different, there are some surprising environmental similarities between the two regions. Accounts of Riteve frequently refer to plains, forests, rivers, lakes and seasonal swamps, to winter mud and summer dust – only the latter an inversion of the central African norm. Many Jews made their living as polers on river barges. Accounts speak of long journeys at night in tented wagons, drawn by horses instead of oxen. Riteve was not an important centre for the cattle trade, though nearby Telz was a centre for the dairy industry. The Jews of Lithuania and Poland had, however, been involved for centuries in the supply of cattle by way of long-distance trails to Germany, and to the Black Sea regions of the Ottoman Empire. Very little is known about the life of the Susman brothers before they left Europe. It is, however, known that Elie Susman, as a boy of fourteen or fifteen, peddled haberdashery to the farms and villages around Riteve. He would take orders for cotton thread from peasants' or farmers' wives and return with them in the following week. Peddling and petty-trading skills were certainly transferable from one environment to another, as were the skills of cattle and horse traders, transport riders and butchers.[20]

There were also some similarities between the social structures of the Russian and Lozi empires. The official abolitions of slavery or serfdom in the two empires were separated by only forty years. Lozi kings, queens and chiefs may not have been able to compete with the Russian royal family, or nobility, in terms of material splendour, or the grandeur of their palaces, but they could keep their end up in terms of the complexity of court ceremonial and ritual. The Zusmanowitz family almost certainly had a close, if feudal, relationship with the Oginskis at Riteve. The Susman brothers established a close and mutually advantageous relationship with King Lewanika and his successors. The Lewanikas shared with the Oginskis a reputation for capriciousness, as well as for modernising tendencies. The Susman brothers' ability to deal with Lozi kings, queens, princes and chiefs, as well as with commoners, or peasants, was an important aspect of their ultimate success. It was, like peddling and trading, a skill that they transferred across continents and cultures.

CHAPTER 2

Barotseland Beginnings, 1901–4

According to the official gazette of the Cape Colony for 28 February 1899, Hirsch Zusmanovitz (*sic*), later known as Harry Susman, paid £3 (about £150 in modern money) in Cape Town in January 1899 for a divisional hawker's licence for the year – a general hawker's licence would have cost him £10. This entitled him to work as a peddler – a *smous*. He had probably been doing this in the Boland, the country areas around Cape Town, for at least two years. Other records may exist, but this is the earliest documentary evidence, discovered so far, for the presence of any member of the Susman family in Africa.[1]

From later accounts, it is fairly certain that Behr Zusmanovitz and his two elder sons, Hirsch/Harry and Elias/Elie, were in southern Africa at the same time, though probably not in the same place, between 1896 and 1899. Behr was in Johannesburg and Bulawayo in these years. He apparently reached Bulawayo after the end of the rebellion of 1896 but returned to Russia in 1899 – not long before the outbreak of the Anglo-Boer War. According to family tradition, he was employed on the construction of a public park, a measure of poor relief, in Bulawayo at this time. He so impressed the Chartered Company official in charge of the project with his piety that he was given an exemption from work on the sabbath – to the annoyance of other workers. Elie arrived in South Africa in 1896 at the age of sixteen. He did not voyage to Africa with his brother, but he may have travelled with his father. He spent two years at the Cape, and then moved north to Johannesburg and Bulawayo in 1898. Again, according to legend, he sold ginger beer on the Bulawayo station platform soon after the arrival of the railway, which was in 1897. Harry joined Elie at Francistown, in the Bechuanaland Protectorate, in 1900. He joined Elie in a business that the latter had already started. This seems to be one of the reasons why Elie, the younger brother, was always the senior partner.[2]

The nearest thing to a personal memoir of these events comes from the slightly embroidered report of an interview which Elie Susman gave over fifty years later to the *South African Jewish Times* in 1952:

> He was a lad of 16 when he came out to Africa, 'the finstere medina'. Two years later, in 1898, he travelled up to Johannesburg, storm centre of Kruger's Republic. In that year, thirsting for reckless excitement, he gave ear to the famous advice of Cecil Rhodes and believing that for him and for his older brother, Harry, 'the hinterland lay north', trekked on to Bulawayo. Within a short time, Susman Brothers was established north of the Limpopo, in an obscure trading town, called Francistown. Here the foundations were laid for what was to be a long, adventurous and profitable association between the two brothers.[3]

There is a good deal of uncertainty, and contradictory evidence, about this sequence of events. Three things do, however, seem to be almost certain: Harry Susman reached South Africa before Elie did; Elie Susman got to Bulawayo and Francistown before Harry did; and their father was in Johannesburg and Bulawayo on his own for at least two years while his sons were at the Cape. The following explanation would resolve most of the contradictions. Harry Susman travelled alone to the Cape and then sent for his brother. His adventurous father decided to escort his sixteen-year-old son, Elie, to Africa. He left him in Cape Town with Harry and went north on his own. Two years later, Elie travelled north, stopping to work for some time on the Witwatersrand, and joined his father in Bulawayo. His father then returned to Russia, and Elie went on to Francistown where Harry joined him.

This chronology might also help to explain the major difference between the two brothers. Harry was never able to read or write in English, and his spoken English was fluent, but idiosyncratic – as were his Silozi and Afrikaans. Elie was much more articulate. He spoke with a distinctive accent, but could hold his own in English at a public meeting. He kept a diary in English and was able to compose business letters and memoranda. Elie certainly did not learn to read and write in English at Riteve, where the only education available to the two brothers was a religious education in Hebrew at a *cheder* school. One source suggests that Harry brought Elie out to Africa and paid for his education. It seems likely that Elie received some kind of education, perhaps business training, in Cape Town in the two years that he spent there before moving north to join his father.[4]

The Barotseland Cattle Trade

A month or so before he crossed the Zambezi at Kazungula with his brother, Elie Susman had, on 8 March 1901, obtained a licence 'to trade beyond the land boundaries of Southern Rhodesia'. He received the licence from a representative of the Chartered Company, the civil commissioner at Bulawayo. He paid £3 for this privilege. The licence, number 32, was issued in terms of a government notice of 1899. It permitted Elie Susman 'to proceed through and beyond the land boundaries of Southern Rhodesia for the purposes of Trade in terms of Ordinance 81 of the Cape of Good Hope', but it carried a note stating that 'this licence does not permit the holder to trade in Southern Rhodesia, nor does it purport to authorise the [sic] dealings in trade in countries beyond the land boundaries of Southern Rhodesia against the wishes of the persons and Chiefs controlling or administering such countries.'[5]

This complex legal language concealed the real purpose of licences of this kind. They were not intended to promote trade to the north, but to control the movement of traders into an area that was still beyond the effective control of the Chartered Company. There was no police or border post at Kazungula. There had been a small British South Africa (BSA) Company police post there between 1898 and 1900, but then it was moved eastwards, to the Victoria Falls. There was a Paris Mission station at Kazungula, but there was no strong representation of the Lozi kingdom. King Lewanika's eldest son and eventual heir, Prince Litia, had been established as chief at Kazungula in 1894, but he moved his village and court, which was known as Mwandi, to Sesheke in 1898. According to one tradition, his father moved him in order to reduce the risk of conflict between Litia and the administration. When the Susman brothers crossed the Zambezi in April there was no legal provision for the Chartered Company to licence traders in the north. Provision for licensing was only made in a proclamation in August 1901. On their arrival they needed the permission of King Lewanika to trade in his kingdom. They may have been able to get permission from Prince Litia to trade at Sesheke, but they had to wait for permission to travel north to come down from King Lewanika at Lealui.[6]

The Susman brothers crossed the Zambezi in April 1901 in order to buy cattle. A combination of environmental and political factors had produced a dearth of cattle in southern Africa as a whole and prices had reached unprecedented heights. The main environmental cause of the cattle shortage was the rinderpest epidemic, which swept through the region between 1895 and 1897. Rinderpest killed ninety per cent of the cattle in its path and an equally large proportion of game such as antelope and buffalo. The epidemic swept through the region like a bush fire. It killed game and cattle, but did not linger or become endemic. Alfred St Hill Gibbons, hunter and explorer, travelled south from Kazungula in March 1896 and left a graphic description of the impact of rinderpest in central Bechuanaland:

> All along the road the putrefying carcasses of oxen were strewn, and especially thickly round the few waters. It was indeed a pitiful sight, but the smell, which was something more than that emitted from mere decomposing flesh, was more indescribably and disgustingly repulsive than can be imagined; through night and day it was always there and only varied in degree.[7]

According to one account there were 4,000 abandoned wagons and 64,000 dead oxen on the road between Gaberones in southern Bechuanaland and Bulawayo at this time.[8] The political factor that compounded the prevailing cattle shortage was the Anglo-Boer War that broke out in October 1899 and lasted until May 1902. The war between Britain and the Afrikaner republics not only disrupted existing lines of communication throughout the region, but also created a large new demand for trek oxen and for beef.

There were good reasons why traders were attracted to Barotseland at this time. Rinderpest had passed through the southern part of the kingdom in March 1896, killing almost all the cattle at Sesheke and Kazungula. For reasons which remain obscure, but which may relate to its isolation, the epidemic bypassed the central Barotse plain. King Lewanika and his people were, therefore, left in possession of the largest untouched stocks of cattle in southern Africa.[9] The Lozi kingdom had probably been exporting cattle to the west for some time. When a Portuguese slave trader reached Lealui in 1895, he had been told that he could not buy slaves, but he could buy cattle. There was, however, no tradition of exporting cattle to the south: when a lone trader visited Sesheke in 1895, looking for cattle to buy, he was sent away empty-handed.[10] It was the exceptionally high prices produced by the outbreak of the Anglo-Boer War that led traders to consider seriously the possibility of trekking cattle from central Barotseland to Bulawayo, which the railway had reached in 1897. This would involve a trek of 6–700 miles through inhospitable and semi-arid terrain.

Since the time of David Livingstone's first visit to the central Zambezi plain in 1853, it has been noted that there are two basic types of cattle in Barotseland. These are the large Barotse – and similar Ngami – cattle, which are said to be a cross between longhorn humpless and another type of humpless Zebu stock, and the smaller Ila/Tonga cattle which are of shorthorn Sanga stock. As a result of pre-colonial raiding, and trading, these two types co-existed in Barotseland, but also became interbred. In the Ila/Tonga areas, which became the Southern Province of Northern Rhodesia/Zambia, the smaller type of cattle continued to predominate, while in the Ngamiland area of northern Bechuanaland the larger big-boned and long-horned type of cattle remained dominant. Many of the young bullocks that were the staple of the Barotseland trade, and of the later Ngamiland trade, were very small with a weight of 350–400 pounds.[11]

The cattle trade was not a royal monopoly, but cattle ownership was concentrated in the hands of the ruling family and other aristocrats. Members of the ruling group loaned many cattle to commoners through the system known as *mafisa*. This system, which was common among pastoral peoples in southern Africa, gave the people who looked after the cattle some rights in relation to their use – milk was an important part of the diet – but the natural increase in stock belonged to the owner. King Lewanika used *mafisa* as a means of restocking the southern part of his kingdom after the rinderpest epidemic. He used it to strengthen his political position in an area that was peopled by members of the Subiya and Totela ethnic groups.[12]

The Chartered Company in Bulawayo wrote to King Lewanika in March 1900 to tell him that they were sending a trader, Robert Granger, to buy cattle in his kingdom. Granger was Jewish and was, with his brothers, a founder of the Bulawayo Hebrew Congregation. A number of freelance Jewish cattle buyers followed him in his progress northwards. Granger himself had a frustrating time and his temper was not improved by serious illness. He complained that Prince Litia had treated him with 'scant courtesy' at Sesheke, and that King Lewanika himself had been polite, but unhelpful. Other traders were able to buy 300 head of cattle at Sesheke, but he trekked south from Lealui at the end of July with about 150 cattle – he had paid more than £6 each for them. He complained that Lewanika refused to sell more, claiming that he had none. Some of the traders who followed him north may have been more successful, as they arrived later and were prepared to stay longer.[13]

Colin Harding, the acting-administrator, who was then at Lealui, thought that Granger's apparent failure was due to the difficulty that Lewanika had in getting cattle back from the plains. They would have been moved from the plains to the bush margins in February, but returned to the plains in June before the end of the floods. Granger had also had to compete with traders from Bihé in Angola who brought 'gunpowder, arms and calico which are bartered for cattle more readily than gold ...'. Harding noted in February

1901 that there was then so much gold in the country that owners refused to sell cattle unless there was a proportion of goods involved in the deal. He also noted that local prices had risen with 'gigantic strides' in the previous year from £4.5.0 to £6.15.0 per head.[14]

Robert Coryndon had other explanations for Granger's apparent failure. In his view Granger had been treated with inadequate respect because the missionaries had treated Lewanika, Litia and the indunas (chiefs or councillors) 'too familiarly', and 'a bad class of low-down Jew trader ... have not impressed these natives favourably ...'. He regretted that he did not have 'the power to sit on evil-doers or to carry out a "bluff"' – a coded reference to the use of force. As Granger was almost certainly the first Jewish trader to reach Lealui, Coryndon's anti-Semitic remark may have been aimed at him personally, and at the Chartered Company's use of a Jewish intermediary.[15]

A number of other cattle traders did reach Lealui during 1900. Among them were Robert Gordon and Fishel Levitz. They did well enough to return in the next and subsequent years. They were both Jews from the Baltic provinces of the Russian Empire, and were among the four partners in the firm of Lesser, Levitz and Co., storekeepers and traders, at Francistown. The senior partner was Samuel Lesser. It is probable that it was through Gordon and Levitz that the Susman brothers became involved in the Barotseland trade. It is indeed possible that Elie Susman's investment in a Francistown business venture – he reckoned in July 1902 that it had accumulated profits of £150 – was a stake in Lesser, Levitz and Co. It was later suggested by one of their backers that Robert Gordon and Elie Susman were close friends. They certainly developed a close business relationship. Robert Gordon disappeared in 1905, as will become apparent, but Fishel Levitz continued to be involved in Barotseland trade, and with the Susman brothers, for another thirty years.[16]

The Barotseland Trading Expedition

It is possible with the help of later memoirs, and the accounts of contemporaries, to get some idea of the Susmans' journey to the north. After acquiring their licence in Bulawayo early in March, they set off for the north from Plumtree, a stop on the railway about seventy miles southwest of Bulawayo and close to the Bechuanaland border. Although they had been living in Francistown, about fifty miles south of the border, Plumtree was the base for their expeditions to the north in 1901 and 1902. A number of Jewish traders were settled there, the most important of whom were Edward

Kollenberg and Abraham Grossberg, partners in the firm of Kollenberg and Grossberg. They were Latvian Jews who had started business at nearby Mangwe, and moved to the siding at Plumtree after the building of the railway. They were the agents at both places for Julius Weil and Co., of Mafeking and Bulawayo, the ultimate backers of many of the Jewish traders in south-central Africa at this time. Another important Francistown firm was that of Lewis Braude and Co.[17]

Elie Susman later recalled that the journey from Plumtree to Lealui took four months. When asked in an interview: 'What provisions did you take?' Elie replied: 'We lived on our guns.' According to his nephew, Maurice Gersh, the brothers could not afford the £100 needed to buy a wagon, and had to hire one. They are said to have travelled with a number of other traders in a convoy of eight wagons. Not all of their companions reached Lealui. Some may have turned back before they reached the Zambezi, others may have travelled no further than Sesheke. Wolf Levin and Joseph Finkelstein, who was to remain in Barotseland for over forty years, were two of their companions who went all the way. Suggestions that a large number of the Susmans' group perished en route must be apocryphal: any significant mortality of white men at this time would have left some trace in the archival or literary record.[18]

Their route from Plumtree to Kazungula followed the Old Hunters' Road. This road became the boundary between the Bechuanaland Protectorate and Southern Rhodesia and is today followed by the main road through Botswana from Francistown to Kasane, the border post on the south bank of the Zambezi, opposite Kazungula. About forty-five miles out from Plumtree, the road crosses the Nata River, which flows, when it flows, westwards into the Makgadikgadi saltpan. The road continues for 100 miles beyond the Nata through Hendrick's Pan to Deka and Pandamatenga, Westbeech's old headquarters. South of Deka at Makalaka the brothers would have passed the village of Klaas Africa, allegedly the son of a Jewish father and a Griqua mother. He had hunted with Selous and acted as a guide to many later travellers, including Gibbons. North of Pandamatenga they would have travelled a further sixty-five miles to the Zambezi, passing through the Gesuma Pan, swampy when wet and deep sand when dry, before reaching Lishoma and the Zambezi.[19]

Full-size loaded wagons, capable of carrying between three and four tons of goods, and drawn by sixteen to eighteen oxen, would have taken at least three weeks to complete the 250-mile journey from Plumtree. A smaller wagon carrying 3,000 pounds was thought by Gibbons to need ten oxen to draw it through the Kalahari sands. Most people travelled at night to spare their oxen and themselves the pain of moving in the heat of the day. Nocturnal journeys also reduced the risk of cattle being bitten by tsetse flies and infected with trypanosomiasis – sleeping sickness. The Old Hunters' Road was supposed to be free of fly at least as far as Pandamatenga.[20]

Oxen were temperamental creatures, with their own names and characters – lazy or hardworking, good-natured or bad-tempered. A good transport rider knew how to train them, match them in pairs and encourage them to work without undue coercion. Even so, individual oxen sometimes went on strike, sat down and refused to move. Stories were told of wagon 'boys' resorting to a variety of strategies to make them get up – from biting their tails to lighting fires under them. Not all travellers used oxen and wagons. Some people used carts drawn by donkeys, which were unaffected by tsetse flies, but unable to draw such heavy loads.

Gibbons left an account of this route as it was in March–April 1896. He travelled south at the same time of year as the Susman brothers journeyed north. His description gives some idea of what their experience must have been.

> I will spare the reader an account of the daily monotonous hard work, which was enhanced by the groaning struggles of the poor oxen as they gallantly forced the cart through the deep sand which rose all round them as they disturbed it with their hoofs, half choking and parching them, thus rendering the long treks from water doubly trying.
>
> Trekking went on all night at intervals – three hours trek, one hour grazing – from an hour before sunset to an hour before sunrise, while during the day the oxen slept and grazed at their own sweet will … when the oxen were compelled to spend the day without drinking the mouths of the poor creatures became so parched that they could not eat and they strayed in all directions in search of a pool.[21]

It is not clear whether the Susman brothers took their wagon across the Zambezi or left it on the south bank. The Paris Missionaries had developed a dry-season wagon road to Lealui in the late 1880s. Crossing the Zambezi with wagons and oxen was not a simple matter. Mathilde Keck Goy, widow of Auguste Goy, a Paris Missionary who died at Sesheke in 1896, left a graphic account of this process:

> Everything must be carried over in canoes, box after box, even to the smallest parcel. The wagon must be taken to pieces, and the parts separately ferried to the other side. It was an interesting sight to see the tent of the wagon resting on four or five canoes, and the men rowing with all their might, trying to cross the river.

> But what a terrible loss it would be if the canoe should capsize and one of the precious parts of the wagon should go to the bottom! To get the oxen across is a difficult matter. Each ox is caught by the horns with a strong *riem* or leather thong. One man in the canoe holds it, while three or four others are rowing, and so the poor animal is dragged to the opposite bank quite exhausted. To carry a wagon and its load, together with a span of oxen ... across usually takes two or three days when it is calm; but when there is wind, the work goes very slowly.[22]

Gibbons noticed that local cattle were used to crossing the river and would follow their leaders with little difficulty into the Zambezi, but trek oxen from the south were reluctant to make the crossing.

> In such cases each ox is secured with a reim [*sic*] passed over the horns. A boy sitting in the centre of the canoe holds on to the other end, while the beast is driven, sometimes with much difficulty, into deep water. He is then drawn to the side of the canoe, and his head held and secured so as to render his struggles powerless to upset the unstable craft, and in this position he remains until his feet strike the shallows of the opposite bank. Occasionally a crocodile, more venturesome than his fellows, deems the opportunity too tempting to be wasted, but in the vast majority of cases no mishap occurs.[23]

If the Susman brothers did not take their wagon across the Zambezi, they would have had to rely on boats and paddlers supplied by King Lewanika, by Prince Litia at Sesheke, or by the Mulena Mukwae (queen or princess) at Nalolo. At this time the boats in question were dugout canoes, which could carry only a few hundred pounds weight of goods. The going rate charged by the Mulena Mukwae for the hire of a boat from Sesheke to Nalolo in 1902 was between £3.10.0 and £4.10.0 for a one-way trip. It is not clear whether this price would have included the wages of paddlers or their provisions. An account by Frank Worthington, an administrative official, suggests that it did not. At a later date traders used wooden barges, which were capable of carrying several thousand pounds of cargo.[24]

Travelling westwards by boat from Kazungula, the Susman brothers would have had to ascend the rapids at Kambove, their paddlers straining to make headway against the strong flow of the river. They would then have followed the river's gently meandering course westwards for most of 100 miles with the wide expanse of the Chobe flats to their south, and the more clearly defined bank of the Zambezi on the north. They would have passed, and certainly stopped at, Prince Litia's newly established capital at Mwandi, and the older established, and neighbouring, capital of Akanangisa Atangambuyu, the Mulena Mukwae, at Sesheke. Atangambuyu was a junior queen, the daughter of Lewanika's sister. Her mother, the Mulena Mukwae

Matauka, was the second most powerful person in the kingdom, a dual monarch controlling the southern part of the central Zambezi plain from Nalolo.

The party would have encountered a further series of rapids beginning at Katima Mulilo, a name that translates as 'fire extinguisher'. After Katima Mulilo they would have travelled northwards against the stream and through more wooded country for a further 100 miles, passing several rapids, to the falls at Sioma. Here there was an unavoidable portage where goods and canoes had to be dragged for several miles around the falls. It was then a further forty miles before the beginning of the plain at Senanga, and fifty miles beyond that to Matauka's capital at Nalolo. From there it was only about thirty miles through the plain to Lealui. Whether they travelled by wagon or by boat, the journey from Kazungula to Lealui was over 300 miles and would have taken them three or four weeks.

The Susman brothers regarded their first two trips to Lealui, in 1901 and 1902, as trading expeditions from their base of operations at Plumtree in the south. In 1901 they probably spent six months, from April to October, north of the Zambezi and only a few months at Lealui. They seem to have stayed rather longer at Lealui in 1902, as they did not leave the area until late November or early December. Apart from their initial licence, the only surviving document from the Susman brothers' first 'Barotseland trading expedition' is a letter to Elie from the district commissioner at the Victoria Falls, Frank W. Sykes, dated 11 October 1901. He understood that Elie was ill and that his 'boy' was on the way south with 110 cattle. He asked him to return to the Victoria Falls to get a trading licence from the administrator, Robert Coryndon. Elie almost certainly was ill. According to family tradition, he had developed blackwater fever and was evacuated from Lealui by boat with paddlers provided by King Lewanika. This was not necessarily a privilege as the Lozi royal establishment had a monopoly of boat transport on the Zambezi at this time. In spite of his illness, Elie must have returned to the Victoria Falls. Trading and gun licences are stamped on the back of Sykes's letter.[25]

Little more is known about their second expedition than about the first. Only two relevant documents have survived. One of them does shed some light on the Susman brothers' activities and their network of contacts. It is a will, which Elie wrote at Nalolo on 29 July 1902 while suffering from blackwater fever, and apparently on the point of death. The witnesses to the will were two other Barotseland traders, Aaron Barnett Diamond and N. M. Human. A. B. Diamond was an older man who was born in 1854 – he was about the same age as Elie's father. He was a Russian Jew who had been naturalised in Ireland and had served in the Anglo-Boer War, which had ended only two months previously. A founder member of the Bulawayo Hebrew Congregation, he was a close friend of its first rabbi, Moses Cohen. Diamond was also a founder of Chibat Zion, the early Zionist movement in Bulawayo, and was later to be a founder of the Chevra Kadisha, a Jewish burial association, which was the precursor to the Hebrew Congregation, at Elisabethville in the Congo. In 1902 he was on his first expedition to Barotseland, but he was to become a major figure in the trade of the region, pioneering cattle trails to Lobito Bay in 1905, and to the Congo in 1909. Several members of his family joined him in Barotseland and Northern Rhodesia. The other witness was N. M. Human, an Afrikaner trader who also remained in the region for many years. It is likely that he had fought on the other side during the Anglo-Boer War. Frank Worthington had encountered him at Sesheke early in June 1902. Human said then that he had been waiting for three months to get a boat to take him north, he protested bitterly about the Jewish traders who had arrived later, but had obtained boats from Litia before him.[26]

The executors of the will were David Landau and Elie's brother, Harry. David Landau was about the same age as Elie. He was one of three brothers who had moved from Manchester, England, by way of Port Elizabeth, to Bulawayo, where they established a successful wholesale business. The first of them, Louis, had reached Bulawayo in 1896, while Morris and David came later. They were backed at first by the old established Port Elizabeth wholesalers, Mosenthal and Company. According to Rabbi Moses Cohen, the Anglo-Boer War, including the long sieges of Kimberley and Mafeking, broke the lines of communication and credit with the south and allowed the Bulawayo wholesalers to establish their independence of the Port Elizabeth merchants. The Bulawayo wholesalers opened new lines of communication with Beira and appointed their own agents in London, or, as in the case of Landau Brothers, set up their own London office. Elie Susman's appointment of David Landau as an executor is an indication that he was a close friend. It also suggests that Landau Brothers were, as is evident from other sources, the main backers of the Susmans' expedition. The Susmans would never have been able to enter the Barotseland trade without the credit in goods and cash that was provided by the Bulawayo wholesalers. It was, however, a symbiotic relationship: the fortunes of most of the Bulawayo wholesalers were closely tied to, and in some cases based upon, the Barotseland cattle trade.[27]

The second surviving document is a letter written by Robert Coryndon at Lealui on 1 August 1902, containing advice on the treatment of blackwater fever. It was apparently sent in response to a urgent message sent by Elie, or perhaps by Diamond or Human, to Coryndon who was then on a visit to Lealui. The letter is not addressed, but reads as follows:

> For blackwater patient
>   Take one calomel tabloid at once.
>   If vomiting put a mustard plaster on pit of stomach – plaster can be made with ordinary mustard and water. If you have no mustard put on cloth dipped in hot water and wrung out.
>   If pain in kidneys put mustard plaster, or hot fermentation (as above described) on kidneys.
>   When vomiting stops take one quinine tablet every three hours.
>   If patient is weak and you have champagne he should take a little every three hours.
>   Take no more calomel.
>   I send a bottle of champagne, also two letters and a present for Morena Magwai [i.e. the Mulena Mukwae].[28]

Apart from its possible interest as an example of antique medical practice, this letter does show that Coryndon, despite the anti-Semitic attitudes, which have already been illustrated, was prepared to help Jewish traders in an emergency. Anti-Semitism was, however, endemic among Chartered Company officials.

Anti-Semitism

The correspondence of Ferdinand Aitkens, who entered the country with Coryndon, and became district commissioner at Lealui in 1901, provides plenty of evidence of this. His annual report on the 1902 cattle-trading season, written at the beginning of December, is largely a diatribe against the allegedly underhand activities of Jewish traders. The following extracts are samples of his opinions as expressed in this report.

> Most of the traders have been Jews, many of them undesirable characters ... I consider the class of Jew trader that has been here this last season, in Lealui especially, as likely to cause bad feeling, and that the natives will lose what little respect they have for the white man if nothing worse.
>   I am strongly of opinion that many of the Jew traders have traded ammunition in part for cattle.
>   If a native can obtain for an ox the same amount of goods plus the cartridges from a Jew trader he will not go to any other store ... It is in this way only that I can account for the Jew traders being able to buy 20 head of cattle

a day while the more respectable trader can do practically no trade. Either the undesirable trader must be kept out of the country, or the respectable trader be permitted to bring in cartridges, if this is not done then this is a blow [?] for a respectable law-abiding trade, for it is impossible to catch a Jew in the act of selling cartridges or obtain information against him since all the natives side with him.

There is I regret to say a certain insolence about the natives towards traders, other than Jews, making it difficult to maintain the peace and the respect for the white man is not what it should be ...[29]

He reckoned that 2,500 cattle had been exported to the south from the central Zambezi plain during the season. Ovimbundu traders also exported many cattle to the west. Aitkens had no control over these traders because the western boundary of Barotseland had not yet been defined. There were also unlicensed African traders in the valley from Bulawayo, Gwelo and Palapye, including Ngwato from Khama's kingdom, and 'Shangaans' (Tsonga) from Mozambique. The latter seems to have been a very loose category, including people with Afrikaans names.

Aitkens sought to explain the apparent success of Jewish traders in the face of strong competition with 'respectable traders' – those who were white, but not Jewish. He was convinced that the success of Jewish traders was due to their willingness to include ammunition as part of a deal in trade goods and cash. He believed that Jewish traders brought in large quantities of ammunition, ostensibly for their own use, but proceeded to use cartridges as trade goods. He complained that Jews were not sportsmen and did not need more than forty cartridges for their own use.

In fairness to Aitkens, it must be said that he had a difficult time during the 1902 season. Lewanika was away on a six-month trip to Great Britain for the coronation of Edward VII. When asked by François Coillard whether he would not be embarrassed at his first interview with King Edward VII, Lewanika had replied rather grandly: 'Oh No, when we kings get together we always find plenty to talk about.' Aitkens had himself escorted Lewanika to Cape Town, where Colin Harding had taken over for the trip to England. Aitkens had returned to Barotseland in time for the trading season, but Lewanika did not return to Lealui until 1 January 1903, after a very successful trip. A crowd of 6–7,000 people greeted him on his return. His prime minister, the Ngambela, accompanied Lewanika on his journey to England. He had left his kingdom in the hands of a regent, but there had evidently been a partial breakdown in law and order at Lealui during his absence. Aitkens had intervened to punish 'boys' – it is not clear whether they were young or old – who threatened Robert Gordon. He also believed that he had prevented the burning or looting of Gordon's store. Some of Gordon's cattle had been stolen at Lealui, and it was believed that a prominent induna, Namayamba, was involved in the theft.[30]

Aitkens had also had to deal with a large number of disputes between traders. In some cases these were disputes between Jewish traders, as over an alleged assault by Hermann Hepker on A. B. Diamond, and in other cases they were disputes between Jews and Gentiles. He had little power to deal with disputes between traders and the Lozi population because traders took these to the *kuta*, the royal court, which was presided over by the Ngambela or his deputy. Aitkens alleged that traders were afraid to bring these disputes to his attention, as they feared a Lozi trade boycott if they took cases to the district commissioner. Disputes over jurisdiction continued for a number of years. The district commissioners sought to establish their control over all cases involving traders, and objected strongly to traders taking their cases to the Lozi rulers' courts, and to the imposition of fines on traders by the *kuta*s at Lealui and Nalolo.[31]

Aitkens was fed up with the frequent disputes between traders, and thought that these lowered the prestige of whites in the eyes of the local people. He recommended that there should be a reduction in the number of licences issued for trade in the Barotse valley and that the district commissioner should have the power to vet licences issued at the Victoria Falls. He refused to renew A. B. Diamond's licence for 1903. He was, however, well disposed towards Robert Gordon. In forwarding his application for a licence, he noted that 'the Chief (Lewanika) has no objection and says Mr. Gordon is a good man'. He stated his own opinion that: 'He has been here a number of years and is well able to supply the wants of the people, and is not likely to run short and would be excellent competition to the BTA [Bechuanaland Trading Association] and anyone else.'[32]

There is one reference to the Susmans in Aitkens's report. He said that Induna Moi-Moi (Muwi-Muwi) had been to see him at the end of November 'ostensibly to say that traders Susman [probably Elie] and Lewis [probably Levitz] had asked him to look after their goods as they did not wish to remain over the wet season. He said he did not wish to take care of their goods and asked me if he was bound to do so.' Aitkens advised him that he was under no obligation to look after the goods and could do as he liked. If he did undertake to look after the goods, he should not accept liability for them. Muwi-Muwi was a prince said by Lewanika to have been his 'brother', though he may have been a cousin in English terminology. He was, in any case, a senior member of the royal family who was almost certainly acting as regent in the absence of Lewanika. He acted many years later as master of ceremonies at Lewanika's funeral. This glimpse of the Susmans at Lealui in 1902 shows that they were about to leave to go south at the end of November and that they had not sold all their trade goods. It also suggests that they were already on close enough terms with leading members of the royal family to seek to entrust them with their possessions.[33]

The Susman brothers did not return to Barotseland in 1903. Their personal expenses were low and they may have accumulated as much as £2–3,000 in two years' trading. They could have made this money through the purchase and sale of 5–600 cattle, spread over that time. This calculation assumes that they could buy cattle in Barotseland for £6–7 per head with a combination of trade goods and cash, and could sell cattle in Bulawayo for twice that amount.

Embakwe and Sesheke

Elie's two brushes with blackwater fever, and Harry's similar experience, may have discouraged the brothers from a return to Barotseland. It is also possible, though less likely, that they failed to obtain a licence to return in 1903. In any event they did not return, and Elie Susman became a partner in July 1903 with John Austen in a general dealer's and hotel business at Embakwe (later QueQue, now Kwekwe) in Southern Rhodesia. Embakwe was on the new railway line between Salisbury and Bulawayo and was the site of the Globe and Phoenix Mine, one of the largest and most highly capitalised gold mines in Southern Rhodesia. Elie Susman was to be 'the active managing partner' and was to run the business. The proposed investments were to be very unequal. Elie Susman was to invest £5,000 'forthwith', while John Austen invested only £200. Austen's role was to provide the premises and the licence, while Elie Susman provided the capital and the management. He told the Standard Bank in December 1903 that he had invested £3,000 in the business. The bank's inspector described the partners as 'respectable and energetic people', and noted that Elie Susman had taken over the business as a going concern. The contract anticipated the building of a new store and hotel on a new site. This was evidently acquired: among Elie Susman's surviving papers is a lease in his name from the Chartered Company for a stand of one morgen in the new township of Embakwe. The lease was issued at Salisbury on 5 February 1904, running from 1 January 1904, and the annual rent was £50. Harry Susman was not a partner in this business, but he worked in the bar that was a part of it.[34]

It was while he was at Embakwe that Elie Susman made contact with a number of people who were later his business partners, including Philip Sussman (no relation) and Willie Hepker. Elie played in an all-Jewish football team – predictably called the Wanderers – at Bulawayo in 1904. Among the other players were S. S. Grossberg, the young son of Abraham Grossberg of Plumtree, and H. B. Ellenbogen. They were both to become important Bulawayo wholesalers, and the latter became a close friend. The short time that Elie spent at Embakwe was important for the establishment of contacts and the construction of a network that stood him in good stead for many years. John Austen was involved at both Embakwe and Sesheke. In 1902 he had been responsible for the establishment and construction, on behalf of Lesser and Co., of their store at Sesheke. This was the first permanent store built anywhere in Barotseland – at least since the days of Westbeech. Traders at Lealui and Nalolo came only for the season, moving south with their cattle before the floods rose and before the annual movement of the royal capitals from the plain to the *mafulo* – the margins of the plain. Frank Sykes, the district commissioner at the Victoria Falls, noted that the establishment of Lesser's store would be 'of considerable convenience to the district'. There were, of course, a few stores established at the Old Drift, the commercial settlement near the Victoria Falls, but they were not in Barotseland proper, but in North-Western Rhodesia.[35]

Frank Worthington visited Sesheke in June–July 1902 and again in October 1903. He was not greatly impressed with what he saw. On the first of these visits he described Sesheke as 'the filthiest native town I have ever been in, which is saying a good deal, as no native regards sanitary matters'. On his later visit he described it as 'almost the hottest and dirtiest place I know'. He commented: 'I don't mind how seldom I see it'. He did, however, explain that his reaction was in part due to the fact that both Litia and the Mulena Mukwae lived rather well in large new houses, which compared very favourably with the huts at the disposal of visiting officials.[36]

Worthington found John Austen at Sesheke in June 1902 and interceded with Prince Litia and his prime minister, the Lashimba, to get him a better site for the store that he was about to build. He was not, however, happy with the prices that Austen charged for the goods in his store, which was completed by the end of July 1902. He complained that he had to pay a total of £2.10.0 (about £125 in modern money) for thirty pounds of meal, five pounds of sugar and five bars of soap. In a private letter to Austen, he complained about his business methods, and advised him to get rid of his Jewish partner, Robinson.[37]

Worthington's diaries are, like the letters and reports of his boss, Coryndon, and his colleague Aitkens, littered with anti-Semitic comments. His racism was not, of course, confined to Jews, but extended also to the African population. A not untypical diary comment reads: 'I am getting to hate niggers more and more. They are such infernal liars.' Like Aitkens, he was concerned about the alleged sale of ammunition by Jewish traders, though he privately acknowledged that cattle purchases would have been almost impossible at that date without the inclusion of some cartridges as part of the deal. He was also concerned about the export of cows from Barotseland, which was, he noted, contrary to Lewanika's ban on the export of breeding stock.[38]

In spite of Worthington's criticisms of his business methods, John Austen prospered as trader, farmer and mine owner in Southern Rhodesia. He was also involved in the early days of mining in Northern Rhodesia and the Congo, and was a regular visitor to both countries in the years before 1910. His firm, J. A. Austen and Co., had stores in 1908–9 in the Ndola District, probably at the Kansanshi Mine, and also at the Star of the Congo Mine, which was over the border in the Belgian Congo. He became the first mayor of QueQue (Kwekwe). When he died in 1942 at the age of eighty, he left £50,000 to the Royal Navy as a contribution towards the construction of a destroyer to be named HMS *QueQue*.[39]

Samuel Lesser, who was at least nominally Austen's senior partner, was at Sesheke himself in 1903. He attempted to sell the store to Percy Clark, later the author of *Autobiography of an Old Drifter*. Clark, whose book is full of anti-Semitic remarks, pulled out of the deal when he found that he was supposed to work with an unnamed Jew. This must have been another of Lesser's partners, Robert Gordon, who took over the business at this time in the name of Gordon and Levitz. Lesser was paid out in cattle for his share in the business at this time – he was also about to lose his licences at Lealui and Nalolo. Ferdinand Aitkens refused to renew them for 1904 because of disputes between the partners as to who should trade where. His Francistown business went bankrupt a year or two later and he died in Johannesburg in 1927 at the age of sixty-three: in contrast with John Austen, he had not become a wealthy man.[40]

Elie Susman returned to Barotseland in July 1904. He then bought the Sesheke store from Robert Gordon. He undertook to pay £819.8.0 in four instalments of £204.17.0 each for the premises and goodwill of the business, the first instalment was due on 1 September 1904. Elie would not gain full control of the business until the last payment was made on 1 June 1905. He also paid £683.13.7 for the stock in trade. The stock list survives and gives a good indication of the variety of goods that were then in demand in Barotseland. These included not only the staples, piece goods, beads and salt, but also blankets, Dutch prints, handkerchiefs, jackets, moleskins, khaki suits, overcoats, waistcoats, shirts, boots, as well as two dozen cups and saucers, four dozen kettles, four concertinas, 100 gross of buttons, a large quantity of sickles and a great variety of other goods.[41]

It is not entirely clear what the real nature of the links between Samuel Lesser, Robert Gordon, Fishel Levitz, John Austen and Elie Susman was. The first three men were partners in a Francistown business in 1900. It was probably through them that Elie Susman became involved in the Barotseland trade. Austen was a partner with them at Sesheke in 1902 and with Elie Susman at Embakwe in the following year. It cannot have been a coincidence that Elie Susman withdrew from a partnership with Austen at Embakwe in 1904 in order to take over from Robert Gordon the Sesheke business that Austen had founded two years earlier. This was apparently a deal done within an established network of business associates.

From July 1904 onwards, Sesheke was to be the centre of the Susman brothers' business until the First World War. It was the place from which their business 'took off' from small beginnings. One or other of the Susman brothers was to be permanently resident north of the Zambezi for the next forty years. For the first three years the business traded as E. Susman and Co.; it was not until 27 March 1907 that the name was changed to Susman Brothers. From the photograph of their store that survives from 1909, it is clear that it had by then become a substantial brick building with large verandas and a corrugated-iron roof. It had become a major centre for the cattle, grain, hides, skins and curio trades, as well as for wagon and river transport. It was largely as a result of the presence, energy and resourcefulness of the Susman brothers that Sesheke became, for a while, an important commercial centre.[42]

CHAPTER 3

Settled at Sesheke, 1904–8

Sesheke, which means 'place of sand', is not where it once was. Modern Sesheke is forty miles to the west and up the Zambezi River from the old double capital of Sesheke-Mwandi. The district headquarters, or *boma*, moved there in 1945. Old Sesheke, now known from its surviving *kuta* as Mwandi, is today a pretty place, but rather a sleepy one. The main centres of activity are the headquarters of Senior Chief Inyambo Yeta, and the United Church of Zambia's mission hospital. Chief Inyambo is the son of Litunga Yeta IV, and grandson of Prince Litia who became Litunga Yeta III. He is the great-grandson of King Lewanika. A lawyer who studied at the University of Zambia, he has been involved in politics as a leading member of the United National Independence Party (UNIP), the party that was formerly led by President Kenneth Kaunda. The Mwandi *kuta* still functions and is presided over by its chief councillor, the Lashimba. Its main preoccupation today, as with the *kuta*s at Lealui, Nalolo and Libonda, is with the allocation of land.[1]

The United Church of Zambia is the successor to the Paris Mission. It is no longer linked to France. Its hospital and church receive funds from the Presbyterian Church in the United States. The hospital is spacious, spotlessly clean, and in 2001 had two doctors, a husband and wife team who trained at the University of Zambia. It had a well-equipped operating theatre, and received an annual visit by eye specialists from the United States. The hospital administrator was a woman, an ordained minister of the United Church of Zambia, the Reverend Elizabeth Mulonda Silishebo.[2]

Mwandi is no longer a thriving commercial centre. The Susman Brothers & Wulfsohn store, which may have been built on the site of the Susmans' original store, stands empty, though not derelict. It retains its roof, its shelves and its safe. Although there are a few small shops and market stalls which sell basic items, there is no longer a general dealer's shop, as there was a century ago, or even thirty years ago, selling everything from clothes to agricultural implements. The road from Livingstone is nominally tarred, but is, unless recently rebuilt, in such a poor state that it is an impediment to good communications. Old men can still point to 'Likamba laSusmani', Susman's Harbour. There are canoes there, which carry people across the Zambezi to Namibia, but there is no long-distance river traffic.[3]

Sesheke-Mwandi in 1904 was a much more vibrant place than it is today. It was, unusually, the site of two royal capitals – Sesheke for the Mulena Mukwae Akanangisa Atangambuyu (then known to the white population as Akanangisa, or 'the Little Mukwae', but better known today by the second of her two names), and Mwandi for Prince Litia – each with its own *kuta*. There was also a Paris Mission station with a doctor and the beginnings of a hospital. The Mwandi *kuta* and the mission church and hospital are the only institutions that have survived until the present day. The doctor, Dr Reutter, arrived in 1902 and built for himself the first mosquito-proofed house in North-Western Rhodesia. The theory of the transmission of malaria by mosquitoes had only recently been discovered. He remained at Sesheke-Mwandi for most of the next thirty years. The head of the mission was the Reverend Eugene Béguin who had arrived in 1894 and who also remained for many years.[4]

Sesheke was also the site of a sub-district with its own small *boma* and an assistant district commissioner, F. W. Dawson, who was appointed in 1903. The *boma* building in 1904 was probably built of wattle and daub, though a few years later it was said that the *boma* possessed the only brick-built government buildings outside the capital, Kalomo. Dawson was unusual, if not unique, among district officers at that date in that he had attended an English public school and Oxford University, but was forced out of his job in the following year. Apart from his superior education, his offence – in the eyes of Coryndon – appears to have been an inability to get on with Prince Litia and the Mulena Mukwae, and an inclination to take the side of the people against their rulers. Coryndon accused him of undermining what he claimed to be a basic principle of administration in North-Western Rhodesia – indirect rule through the chiefs. Coryndon's own idea of indirect rule through chiefs was that chiefs should do what he told them.[5]

Dawson was also accused of a general inability to handle 'Natives'. The high commissioner, Lord Milner, a supremely competent civil servant, told Coryndon that the charges against Dawson were too vague to justify dismissal and that a proper civil service could only be established in North-Western Rhodesia, or anywhere else, on the basis of job security for its members. He did, however, agree that Dawson could be transferred from

Sesheke. Coryndon noted caustically that if Dawson's public school and Oxford education had not enabled him to get on with such an intelligent and relatively well-educated 'Native' as Prince Litia, there was little chance of his being able to get on with 'ordinary Natives'. Dawson's successor, F. C. Macaulay, was more to Coryndon's liking. He had served as a sergeant major in the British South Africa Police and had driven the last coach to leave Bulawayo during the Ndebele Rebellion in 1896.[6]

Prince Litia

The Susman brothers' relationships with the two local rulers, as well as with King Lewanika and the Mulena Mukwae at Nalolo, were of great importance to their business success. Prince Litia was born in the early 1870s. During the palace revolution at Lealui in 1884–5 he made a dramatic escape with his father, Lewanika, and took refuge with him in the Mashi River area. He had spent some time at the school which Frederick Arnot had run at Lealui in 1884 and also attended the Paris Mission school there in the later 1880s and early 1890s. He set out to attend the London Missionary Society's senior school at Tigerkloof in the northern Cape in 1891, but does not seem to have got any further than Khama's capital at Serowe. He studied English, but was never able to speak it fluently. He was baptised by the Paris Mission and married by Christian rites, though, like most chiefs, he found that monogamy was difficult to reconcile with his chiefly status.

Litia was, like his father, an artist in wood, but he also worked with metal and ivory. The Susman family still owns a beautiful ivory crocodile, which he is said to have made. He was also an architect and carpenter, and built a splendid rectangular house with large verandas at Mwandi in 1898. He was given a camera by a trader and pursued an interest in photography; he already had his own darkroom and was developing his own photographs when Percy Clark, a professional photographer, visited Sesheke in 1903. Clark gave Litia some lessons in photography and Litia tried to persuade him to stay but thought that Clark's proposed fee – payment in cattle to the value of £30 a month – was too high. Some of Litia's photographs of the arrival of his father at Sesheke were published in a glossy Christmas supplement to the *Livingstone Mail* in 1910. It seems likely that he also took a photograph of the Susmans' store that appeared as part of an advertisement in the same number. The editor, Leopold Moore, commented that Litia had not only taken the photographs, but had developed and enlarged them himself in his own darkroom. By the 1930s he had become interested in cinema photography and made his own home movies, which were spliced together with wartime information films and shown with great success to Lozi audiences. His interest in technology began with bicycles and progressed to motorcycles and cars. On the advice of his councillors he did not, however, accept an offer of a lift in an aeroplane at Lealui in 1932; he had travelled by train to Cape Town in 1903, and went by ship to London for the coronation of King George VI in 1937.[7]

Alfred St Hill Gibbons left an attractive pen-portrait of Litia as a young man on a bicycle in 1899.

> Litia has a bicycle, he also has his suite – his A.D.C.s, equerries, and so forth, called by different names, no doubt, but in a comparative sense victims to the same privileges and responsibilities as are those who attend the sons of kings in Europe. Now to see a black man neatly attired in European costume and riding a bicycle is not in itself very extraordinary, but to see that same man of colour gliding along under a hot sun at the rate of eight miles an hour, unaffected by either heat or exertion, and then to glance from him to his sweating retinue, middle-aged men, members of the aristocracy of the country, puffing and blowing and panting in the dusty wake of the royal bicycle in their praiseworthy and successful effort to do their duty, produces an effect at once novel and comical.[8]

For all his modernising tendencies, Litia could be hot-tempered and autocratic, nor was he initially inclined to forego his feudal rights. He appears to have argued in 1905 that the produce of his people was his own and that they had no right to sell anything without his permission. It was only in the following year that the Chartered Company administration decreed, and had King Lewanika proclaim, the end of slavery in the Lozi kingdom.

Litia's neighbour and cousin, the Mulena Mukwae, was a more difficult person. She was thought by Gibbons to have been about twenty-three in 1895, and was described by him as both 'capricious and comely'. She had succeeded her brother in the Sesheke chieftaincy on his death in 1893. Gibbons's view of her character was shared by members of the Paris Mission and, ultimately, by many of her councillors and subjects: 'Pleasant in address, friendly and accommodating to those in whose favour she is predisposed, she has on many occasions proved herself vindictive and unscrupulous in her dealings with those with whom she is not in sympathy, or whose existence has not been convenient to her'.[9] She was believed to have been responsible for the murder of a senior councillor, Ratau, and of a number of young women who were alleged to have been her husband's lovers.

King Lewanika may have moved Prince Litia to Sesheke in 1898 in order to keep an eye on the Mulena Mukwae. She does seem to have been restrained by Litia's presence at Mwandi. This restraint ended with his move to Lealui following the death of his father in 1916. The existence of two chieftaincies and courts in one place was a prescription for conflict. There are different views as to the territorial distribution of power between the two rulers. By one account, the Mwandi *kuta* had power in the southeast of the district while the Sesheke *kuta* ruled to the southwest. According to another view, the subordinate villages of the two *kuta*s were not territorially divided, but scattered throughout the district. There was continuous trouble between her and Litia's successor, his brother, Imwiko. She survived her immensely long-lived mother, the Mulena Mukwae Matauka, of Nalolo, but she was eventually rejected by the Nalolo *kuta*, after a short trial period, as her mother's successor.[10]

In order to reduce conflict it was essential for traders to maintain close relationships with the ruling group. At Sesheke the trade in grain, probably maize and millet, was important in the early years. Grain was grown by slave, tribute or otherwise forced labour in gardens in the flood plain at Sesheke-Mwandi and across the river in the extensive flood plains of the Caprivi Strip. Some was produced on behalf of Prince Litia and the Mulena Mukwae. The rulers also sought to control the sale of grain produced in individual gardens. It was carried by wagon in the early years to supply the local demand in the Victoria Falls-Livingstone area. Later it was transported by wagon to supply government employees at Mongu. The Sesheke-Mwandi area was not as rich in cattle as the central Zambezi plain, though at this date the Lozi had free access to grazing on the Caprivi Strip, but it was an important staging point on the wagon route to Lealui, which left the river and turned inland from there. It was also the point at which the cattle trail from Lealui, which followed the same route, reached the Zambezi. The area was an equally important staging point on the Zambezi River route between Lealui and the Victoria Falls.[11]

Jews, Scots and Afrikaners

The Lesser–Gordon–Susman store was the first in the district, but a number of other traders, river transport contractors and transport riders – almost all Jews, Scots or Afrikaners – made the place their base of operations in the next few years. Among the traders and transport riders who were there in 1904, or who arrived in the next few years, were several who were to have continuing links with the Susmans. Among the Jews, Max Kominsky, who had a general dealer's licence from about 1906, was Elie Susman's closest friend. Kominsky's business partner was Bora Danzig, from the Lithuanian *shtetl* of Wilkomir, who was accidentally drowned while crossing the Sinde River near Livingstone in December 1908. Kominsky remained at Sesheke until his marriage in 1911. Fishel Levitz worked for the Susmans as a storekeeper at Sesheke after being bankrupted by his partner, Robert Gordon. The story of that incident is told below. There were also a number of Jews who were recruited to work for the Susmans at Sesheke in the years before the First World War. Their careers will be dealt with in a later chapter.[12]

Among the Scots, J. A. Chalmers, described in 1906 as a 'cartage contractor', was at Sesheke at this time. King Lewanika complained that Chalmers, a German as he thought, was farming at Linyanti on the south bank of the Zambezi in the still unclaimed Caprivi Strip. He seems to have remained in the area until 1909, and then worked for many years as the manager of the Susmans' cattle post and farm on the Gwaai River in Southern Rhodesia. He was one of a number of people who later claimed to have discovered the grave of Lobengula. D. Currie may have worked on his own as a transport rider, but eventually worked for the Susmans as a transport conductor between Sesheke and Livingstone. The firm of Thomson and Bissett, in which the partners were C. M. Thomson and S. Bissett, was also a transport business. Its wagons provided some competition with the Susmans, but C. M. Thomson, one of several brothers, died of blackwater fever in August 1909. George Findlay was a cattle trader who opened a general dealer's store and had a licence to deal in arms and ammunition. He and his brother, James, later ran barges on the river, as did George Buchanan who was to be closely associated with the Susmans as a cattle drover and dairy farmer for many years. Sam Haslett also spent time at Sesheke, where he was originally in partnership with A. S. O'Connor. They had a store there from 1903, but moved on to Lealui. Haslett was to remain a prominent figure in the cattle trade for over forty years.[13]

The Scots were sufficiently numerous to be able to hold a St Andrew's Night dinner at Sesheke in November 1908 at which twenty people, not all Scots, sat down. C. M. Thomson was the chairman and made the toasts to the patron saint, to the king, and to the district commissioner, F. C. Macaulay, and his wife, who were going on leave. George Findlay proposed the toast to 'Trade and Commerce', and J. Todd to 'absent Scots'. Kail soup, roast duck and whisky were on the menu. Haggis was withdrawn from it as, owing to the chef's lack of a recipe, it was said to have turned out like 'boiled bagpipes'. Messrs Wilde, Findlay and Levitz, on the accordion, violin and flute, provided the music. The assistant district commissioner, W. T. Daniell, and George Findlay won the horse races, which were run in the afternoon.[14]

Among the Afrikaners, A. T. 'Braam' Dreyer had been trading at Lealui in 1903, but became a transport rider in the Sesheke District. He eventually became a partner with the Susmans in a transport business associated with the Zambesi Saw Mills. Barend Cristoffel 'Rooi' Labuschagne crossed the Zambezi in June 1903 after serving in the Anglo-Boer War, and was trading at Sesheke before the end of the year. He was also a hunter and was reported to have killed thirty-one hippo on an expedition in October 1906. His knowledge of the Sesotho language had enabled him to act as interpreter at negotiations between King Lewanika and the Chartered Company in the previous year. His daughter attended the Paris Mission school at Sesheke. He eventually sold his business to the Susmans and later farmed at Zimba and Kalomo. Like J. A. Chalmers, Labuschagne claimed to have found the grave of King Lobengula in the vicinity of the Gwaai River. Other Afrikaners at Sesheke included members of the Erasmus and Peltzer families, and a blacksmith with a Scots name, Elliott, who seems to have been an Afrikaner. Although there were never more than a handful of families, they built their own Dutch Reformed Church, probably of wattle and daub. It was opened in June 1907.[15]

The rise of the Susman brothers to a dominant position in the trade of Barotseland did not come easily or at once. Landau Brothers, his main backers, took Elie Susman to court in January 1905 when he failed to honour a bill of exchange, or promissory note, for £204.17.0. He had drawn the bill for goods supplied to the firm of Gordon and Levitz, and Robert Gordon endorsed it on behalf of himself and the firm. Elie said that he had paid the money to Gordon, who should have redeemed the bill. He also said that he would be unable to pay the same bill twice, as he owed money on other bills that were outstanding to Gordon. Elie was at this time in the process of taking over the Sesheke store from Gordon and Levitz – a process that would only be complete with the payment of the last of four instalments. Landau Brothers were not happy with his explanation and suggested that he and Gordon were good friends and acting in collusion.[16] The magistrate, Henry Rangely, then at Kalomo, found for Landau Brothers, but he was sympathetic to Elie's case. He negotiated with Landau Brothers for a stay of execution of the order that he had granted against Elie's 'movables' and also wrote to Gordon, then in Francistown, demanding that he refund the money that Elie had paid him on account of the bill. Elie was certain that Gordon was financially embarrassed and that he would be unable to pay.

This was a very unusual, but crucially important, example of a Chartered Company official doing a legal favour to one of the Susman brothers in their early years.[17]

Later in the same year, Elie applied for a licence to open a store at Nalolo. Aitkens, who was still the district commissioner at Lealui-Mongu, seemed to be favourably disposed towards his application. The Mulena Mukwae was also happy with the proposal and told Aitkens that she liked 'Mr Susman'. Aitkens made routine enquiries with the assistant district commissioner in Sesheke, F. W. Dawson, and was told that Elie Susman was suspected of selling ammunition. This related to the sale in Sesheke of cartridges, which were alleged to have been part of a consignment of government stores, and to have disappeared from the Susmans' wagons on the way to Mongu. An alternative allegation was that the ammunition had been brought into the country on the Susmans' wagons under the cover that they were government stores. There does not appear to have been any truth in these allegations. Although Aitkens urged further investigation, no action was ever taken against Elie in relation to them. Dawson's successor, F. C. Macaulay, who was a fully-fledged district commissioner, issued him with a licence to trade at Sesheke on 4 January 1906, apparently without difficulty. The licence, which still exists, obliged Elie to keep in stock £400 of 'whitemens' provisions' and £100 of other provisions.[18]

Aitkens had, however, changed his mind about the Nalolo licence and informed Elie in a curt note that his application had been rejected. The allegation of gun-running thwarted any plans that the Susmans may have had to expand into the central Barotse plain. It reflected the almost paranoid preoccupation of Chartered Company officials with the involvement of Jews in the trade in arms and ammunition. They tended to explain what they saw as the relative success of Jewish traders in competition with 'respectable', and non-Jewish, traders in terms of the willingness of the former to deal in arms and ammunition. In fairness, it must be said that they were equally concerned about the continuing sales of guns and powder by Ovimbundu traders from Angola.[19]

These allegations against Elie Susman coincided with a boycott by Prince Litia of the traders at Sesheke, and Dawson's final transfer to Senkobo in June 1905. He refused to accept the transfer and left the Chartered Company's service. He protested against his treatment and made a great deal of his success in settling what he claimed to have been a serious dispute between Prince Litia and the traders over grain trading. He claimed that F. V. Worthington had written to Litia, threatening to send in the Barotseland

Native Police to protect the traders. He also said that Worthington had given him verbal instructions 'to get a clear case of violent assault by Letia's [sic] police on natives wanting to sell grain, and then take action in the matter'.[20]

Coryndon dismissed the whole affair as a storm in a teacup. He wrote, rather typically:

> Personally I was unaware of any serious dispute between the Chief Letia [sic] and the traders; I have no doubt it was of a nature quite common in places like Sesheke, Lealui, Palachwe [Palapye], Linchwe's and Kanye where it is, or was, physically and politically impracticable to draw a hard and fast line between the arbitrary and ignorant actions of the native chiefs and the bribery and frequently illegitimate methods brought into use by low class traders; such disputes are of frequent occurrence and are seldom of any importance.[21]

From the annual report of the Paris Mission station at Sesheke for 1905–6, written by the Reverend Eugene Béguin, it appears that Litia imposed a ban on grain sales for most of the year. This affected the Paris Mission, which normally bought its supplies for the year at harvest time in May and June. According to Béguin, the boycott arose from the administration's imposition of hut tax and Litia's insistence that traders, and the mission, should pay in cash, meaning gold and silver, instead of goods, for grain supplied. This would have increased the price of grain considerably. It may be that it was at this time that King Lewanika's council decreed that traders should pay cash for at least half the value of their purchases. It was natural for Coryndon to play down the significance of a conflict that had its origins in his administration's own actions. It is possible that Dawson's allegations against Elie Susman were part of the fallout from this conflict at Sesheke. It is likely that in a conflict between Litia and the administration, Elie would have taken Litia's side.[22]

Gordon and Levitz

During 1906–8 Elie Susman was also peripherally involved in the aftermath of the mysterious disappearance of Robert Gordon. In September 1906 Lewis Braude and Co. of Francistown, and Sabrin Jacoby of Bulawayo, secured an injunction against the firm of Gordon and Levitz, restraining them from selling 250 cattle that Elie Susman was keeping for them at Sesheke. The injunction also applied to Elie who said that he had already sold nearly half of them to Max Kominsky, a close friend. He produced a letter of authorisation to sell the cattle from Gordon and Levitz in Francistown. The letter, which still exists among the four volumes of documents in the National Archives of Zambia relating to the bankruptcy of Gordon and

Levitz, was written, as were many of the relevant accounts, in Yiddish. Elie Susman looked after the balance of the herd on behalf of the High Court for a further year and was eventually paid for his services.[23]

Robert Gordon had disappeared from Lealui in September/October 1905 with about 600 cattle. In the absence of his partner, Fishel Levitz, who had gone south to buy goods for King Lewanika, he had sold the firm's entire stock. He exchanged it for cattle with David Wersock, another Lealui trader, who had previously worked for their firm. He set off for the west coast on a route to Lobito Bay, which had been pioneered by A. B. Diamond. In addition to the cattle that he bought from Wersock, he also took with him sixty-nine of King Lewanika's, and a smaller number belonging to the Mulena Mukwae at Nalolo, and to Egnatz Snapper, a trader at Lealui. Robert Gordon was at first reported to have died, but was later said to be alive and well and living at Bihé in Angola. He was still there in the early months of 1907, but nothing is known of his ultimate fate. He left his firm and partner bankrupt and with debts amounting to several thousand pounds. The cattle left in Elie Susman's care were the firm's only surviving assets. Their eventual sale enabled the trustee in bankruptcy to pay a dividend of two shillings in the pound to the firm's creditors. The trustee had wanted to take action against David Wersock for the recovery of the goods sold to him, but was restrained from doing so, probably on account of the cost of legal action, by the creditors themselves.[24]

The story of Robert Gordon's disappearance is an extraordinary one and is remarkably well documented. It is a dramatic story of intrigue, fraud and betrayal involving several key players in the Barotseland cattle trade. The evidence given in the bankruptcy proceedings by Fishel Levitz, Egnatz Snapper, David Wersock and Samuel Peimer sheds a good deal of light on the workings of the trade. Peimer's evidence, for instance, makes it clear that the prices paid for cattle were not as high as they appeared to be, as payments were usually made partly in goods, on which the traders made a profit, or were made in cash, much of which found its way back into the trader's store. By 1907–8 the average price of cattle at Lealui had fallen by as much as a half from the boom days of 1901–2.[25]

By 1907 the three main partners in the Francistown firm, which had dominated the Barotseland cattle trade in 1900–3, had either disappeared or gone bankrupt. Samuel Lesser and Fishel Levitz were bankrupt and Robert Gordon had vanished, leaving a trail of commercial devastation behind him. Elie Susman had clearly had a close relationship with all three of them, but especially with Gordon and Levitz. There is no evidence that he was involved in any impropriety in connection with this case, but he was clearly fortunate to be able to extricate himself, and his business, from what was clearly a complex imbroglio involving partners and friends. It is precisely at this time that he begins to emerge not only as a survivor in a very difficult business, but as the major player in Barotseland trade.

In April 1907 the inspector of the Standard Bank's Bulawayo branch described Elie Susman as 'a respectable man who is doing a good trade in North Western Rhodesia as a storekeeper. Keeps a satisfactory account with us, average credit balance £200. Informs us that he has a Capital of £3,000 invested in his business and livestock.' By February 1908 the business had changed its name to Susman Brothers and the inspector noted that Elie and Harry Susman were doing well as traders and cattle dealers in North-Western Rhodesia. He quoted a balance sheet, dated 23 June 1907, which indicated that the firm had assets of just over £10,000, liabilities of about £4,000 and a surplus of £6,000. About a third of the assets consisted of merchandise, another third of cattle, and the balance was made up of outstanding bills, buildings and grain.[26]

Leopold Moore and the *Livingstone Mail*

It is from about the same date that it is possible for the first time to get a real insight into Elie Susman's understanding of the Barotseland trade. This comes from the report of an interview with him that was published in the *Livingstone Mail* on 2 November 1907. The interview was with the editor, Leopold F. Moore, who had founded the paper in the previous year. Plots in the new township of Livingstone were sold early in 1905, and the capital of North-Western Rhodesia had been moved there from Kalomo in the course of 1907. Moore was to be a major player in settler politics in North-Western/Northern Rhodesia until his death almost forty years later. He came from England and worked his way as a pharmacist through Mafeking and Bulawayo to the Old Drift – the malarial settlement on the banks of the Zambezi that preceded Livingstone as the commercial centre of North-Western Rhodesia. Moore was a rumbustious character who had made pre-siege Mafeking too hot for himself, and had gone bankrupt in Bulawayo in 1903 before moving north with his young wife. A populist politician, and a stern critic of Chartered Company rule, he was a member of the Advisory Council set up under the Chartered Company in 1918 and of the Legislative Council from 1924. He had opposed the move from the Old Drift to Livingstone, and used his paper to campaign against Belgian rule in the Congo, the influence of missionaries, the imposition of municipal rates and income taxes, the Colonial Office doctrine of 'Native Paramountcy' for territories north of the Zambezi, and, at least until the late 1930s, the amalgamation of Northern and Southern Rhodesia. He would have a good claim to be Northern Rhodesia/Zambia's first nationalist. He was a white supremacist, but his paper was relatively free of colonial racism. He was knighted in 1937 and died in 1945. Probably Moore's greatest achievement was to produce a readable weekly newspaper for nearly forty years in what was, for most of the time, a very difficult economic and an often impossible logistical environment.[27]

Moore was widely believed to be of Jewish descent, though also to be anti-Semitic. The latter characteristic may have loomed large in the eyes of Livingstone's small Jewish population as a consequence of his opposition to the immigration of German Jewish refugees in the 1930s, and of his consistent scepticism about Zionism. It did not prevent him from becoming at an earlier date a good friend, as well as bridge partner, of Elie Susman. Moore's wife, who was also thought to be of Jewish descent, was an equally remarkable person. She frequently acted as editor, and manager, of the paper. She was the usual editor of its 'Notes and Memos' column, which kept a close eye on, and recorded, the movements of the Susman brothers, and even infant members of their families, for the next forty or fifty years.[28]

Moore's interview with Elie Susman sheds a bright light on the contemporary commercial scene and on the latter's understanding of the market. It also does more than any other document to explain his exceptional long-term success as a trader. Even allowing for some embellishment by Moore, it is clear that he had subjected the Barotseland trade to an exceptionally sophisticated and sociological analysis. It reveals him to have been, in the phrase of the Italian socialist and political theorist, Antonio Gramsci, 'an organic intellectual' – in other words a thinking man's businessman. It is not clear where, or how, Elie Susman acquired this ability both to think, and to articulate his thoughts, about the market so clearly.

It may have been in discussion with his colleagues during the long dark evenings at Sesheke. There were some exceptionally well-educated people among the Jewish traders on the frontier in North-Western Rhodesia. Elie Susman's closest friend in these early days, Max Kominsky, was never a business partner in the strictest sense, but he lived and worked with the Susmans at Sesheke between 1906 and 1911. Born in Memel, not far from Riteve, in 1872, he studied Commerce at a German university before moving to the University of Moscow, where he studied Chemistry to a postgraduate level.

Despatched by his father, he reached Southern Rhodesia in 1898, but failed in his mission to save a sister from the disgrace of a divorce. After his marriage in 1911 – Elie Susman was his best man – he moved to South Africa, and turned his attention once again to science. During the First World War, he developed the Kominsky Process for recycling cyanide from waste water – slimes – on the gold mines, and worked on the metallurgy of chrome. After the war he went back into the Congo cattle trade, and died of blackwater fever in 1926.[29]

Leopold Moore's interview with Elie Susman is a unique document and is reproduced below in its entirety:

No. 84.   THE LIVINGSTONE MAIL   November 2nd 07.
THE NATIVE TRADE IN BAROTSELAND
INTERVIEW WITH MR. E. SUSMAN

In the course of a long and interesting interview with Mr. E. Susman, the well-known trader of Sesheke, and head of the firm of Susman Bros., we learned several new and somewhat startling facts. Considerations of space compel condensation, but the gist of the matter is included in the following summary.

Mr Susman asserts that the indiscriminate granting of licences – all restrictions against which are to be removed after Jan 1st. 08 – has already resulted in such keen competition, more particularly by the small traders with little capital, that the old-established firms in the Barotse valley are threatened with extinction. Traders who have been there for years, have built large camps and substantial stores, carry heavy stocks of trading goods, etc, are handicapped by the expenses of maintaining their establishments. The small traders, often supported by speculative firms in Bulawayo but having little capital of their own, live and trade mostly in their own wagons, making no attempt to build permanent stores, to live and behave as befites [sic] white men, and assume none of the responsibilities of legitimate traders.

These men, Mr Susman asserts, content with very meagre fare and comfortless lives, are satisfied with a far lower rate of profit than will enable the established trader to live in modest comfort and decency, and pay his way. They are able to cut the trade to pieces by underselling, caring nothing for established prices, and only anxious to obtain custom and cattle by any means. Having secured their grain, or cattle, or both, sold out their small stock of goods, they load up their wagons with the spoil and transport it to the nearest market. They may return or be succeeded by others, but the result is the same – total demoralization of the natives and all round reduction in prices.

GRAIN. Conditions are rapidly changing; the price of grain and the rate of transport are such that business in this commodity can no longer be profitably undertaken. He supplied the following figures:

Mealies can only be bought from the natives at a cost, in trade goods, averaging 5/6 per bag; to this must be added about 1/- for the cost of the grain-bag, the proportion of the wages of the white man employed in the business etc. Transport is 6/6 per bag of 200 lbs from Sesheke to Livingstone, which enables the transport-rider to make about £10 on the round trip, which takes 17 days. The mealies cost 13/- a bag, landed in Livingstone. Even if business could be done at this price – and to-day it cannot – there is no margin of profit, and the consequence is that grain trading is likely to be indefinitely suspended in districts remote from the railway.

CATTLE. There is great competition in the cattle trade. Cattle cost from 50/- to 60/- per head, and can rarely be bought except for cash. By the time the expenses of herding, transporting the stock to Livingstone have been discharged there is no more profit than in the grain trade. Cattle at the Bulawayo Market fetch from 40/- to 42/6 per 100 lbs, but 27/6 is the average price realised in Livingstone: a trifle over £4, per head on an average.

The small native cattle owners have been almost completely bought out and they are now even selling their cows: native-cattle dealers will appreciate the significance of this. The indunas, who hold the bulk of the stock, sell only a proportion of their stock, probably less than their increase – which is said to average 65% per ann. – and are steadily accumulating herds.

The natives' standard of living has improved to a remarkable extent during the last eight years, and their purchases have extended both in range and quality, some of the wealthier indunas even buying farming machinery. The men must find the money to supply the increasing demands of their families – for there are emulation and rivalry even amongst the Barotse – and the result is that, their stocks of grain and cattle being exhausted, an ever growing proportion of them will have to seek work in the mines or towns.

Conditions will doubtless right themselves in the course of time, but meanwhile, Mr Susman foresees, the established trader is going to have a very anxious time.

Elie Susman's analysis may be divided into several sections. The first of these deals with what he sees as unfair competition from undercapitalised wagon traders. The references to 'established' and 'legitimate' traders may seem a little presumptuous, coming from a man of twenty-seven who had started life as a hawker, and had only been a settled trader at Sesheke for three years. The Susman brothers were also to be beneficiaries, at least for a year, from the liberalisation of policy on trade licences that enabled them to open stores at this time at Lealui and, for a short time, at Nalolo. As traders at these centres were still transhumant, moving seasonally between the flood plain and the bush margin, the Susmans' Sesheke store must have been one of a handful of permanent stores in Barotseland. Elie's statements on this issue do, therefore, contain an element of special pleading. Underlying that, however, there was a valid point – that only permanently settled traders could establish well-stocked stores, respond to the changing demands of the market and provide continuity of service. They required a reasonable rate of profit to be able to do that.

It is, of course, also the case that the narrow margins in the cattle and grain trades, to which Elie referred, did not prevent the Susman brothers from making substantial profits. This was indeed the time when they established their dominant position in these trades in the face of intense competition. They were only able to do so through hard work, good credit, efficient trading and a superior understanding of the market.

The most interesting thing about the interview is Elie Susman's application of a kind of class analysis both to the traders themselves, between the capitalised and the undercapitalised, and to the people with whom they were trading. This is made most explicit in his last section where he not only analyses the consequences of the uneven distribution of cattle ownership on cattle sales, but also looks at the rapidly changing nature of the market, the demand for new kinds of commodities and the consequences of 'emulation and rivalry' among the Lozi.

There is no other contemporary analysis of the market in south-central Africa which factors into the equation issues such as the distance of grain producers from the Line of Rail, the skewed distribution of cattle, the introduction of agricultural machinery, or the links between class formation, class differentiation and the beginning of labour migration. These elements give his analysis a very modern ring. Some of these issues are not only still current almost a century later, but were identified as new issues by development economists and sociologists within the last twenty or thirty years. It would be hard to find another document produced at any time in the last 100 years that raised all of these issues. Nor, it must be said, did Elie Susman ever again provide such a frank breakdown of the commercial environment in which he worked.

The last sentence in his analysis points to an issue which occurred to academic observers of Northern Rhodesia at a much later date – in the 1930s. That is the notion of Northern Rhodesia as a society in a state of disequilibrium, which, optimistically speaking, will right itself. It is not often noticed by academic or lay observers that an understanding of the market requires an understanding of society, and the changes that are taking place in it. This shows that Elie Susman had a quite exceptional understanding of the changes that were taking place in a society in which he had lived for most of six years.

His interpretation of the market and society did not go without some contemporary response. This came from Joseph Finkelstein, a trader at Lealui who had travelled to Barotseland in the same party as the Susman brothers in 1901. In a cryptic editorial note appended to Finkelstein's response, Leopold Moore commented that 'we seem to have heard some of this before. Can it be that the hands are the hands of Esau, but that the voice is the voice of Jacob?' He clearly believed that Finkelstein was a mouthpiece for someone else – possibly for the official point of view, represented at this time by William Hazell, district commissioner at Lealui, with whom the Susmans were soon to clash. Finkelstein made no reference to the finer points of Elie Susman's analysis. He extolled the virtues of competition, defended the small traders against the large, and made the indisputable point that 'old established traders' were also once 'young'. The main burden of the response was, however, a thinly veiled attack on the Susmans' business methods – with special reference to their closeness to, or familiarity with, the Lozi people and their rulers. Traders should not, Finkelstein argued, lower themselves to the level of the 'Native'. He wished that 'the old established trader [i.e. Susman] should alter his kind manner of dealing with the native and abolish the old trader's costume [custom] and habit ...'. This was, he implied, the practice of 'hearty hand shaking' with the people. He would not speak about this, but 'leave it to the judgement and *dignity* of every respectable trader himself!'[30]

This was coded language requiring 'deconstruction'. It was Robert Coryndon who insisted that Chartered Company officials should shake hands only with King Lewanika, Prince Litia and the Mulena Mukwae at Nalolo. Nearly thirty years later, Sir Ronald Storrs, governor of Northern Rhodesia in 1933–4, commented unfavourably on the persistence of this strange custom, which precluded the governor from shaking hands with any other black people in the whole of Northern Rhodesia.[31] Other white people, including traders, adopted this practice, which was seen as symbolising white superiority. A Lozi deputation to the administrator in the early 1920s complained that traders, even in Livingstone, were then demanding that Lozi people should take off their hats, kneel and clap hands when greeting all white people. It is clear from Finkelstein's letter that the Susmans continued to shake hands with their customers. Finkelstein was a British Jew, though able to interpret from Yiddish to English. His letter reveals an anxious desire to conform to what was becoming the frontier model of social distance between white and black.[32]

> My idea of a legitimate trader is one who does not forget that he is a white man when buying an ox of a native: who impresses upon him to have a little more respect for the trader and for the white man generally; every whiteman [*sic*] in Barotseland can testify to the fact that they are badly in want of it![33]

This was not then, nor was it later, Elie or Harry Susman's idea of 'the legitimate trader'.

CHAPTER 4

Life at Lealui, 1904–8

The Susman brothers had emerged as the major force in the trade of Barotseland before the end of 1907. For nearly three years they had worked hard to build their business at Sesheke, where they had clearly established a good relationship with Prince Litia. They had built their dominant position without being able to establish a base for themselves in the central plain at Lealui or Nalolo. Their attempt to open a store at Nalolo had been rebuffed, though they clearly had the support of the Mulena Mukwae Matauka. They had also established a good working relationship with King Lewanika himself, but the evidence for this is circumstantial. According to legend within the Susman family, they had won his favour by organising the importation for him of a four-wheeled cab, a 'growler', similar to those that he had seen on the streets of London on his visit for the coronation of King Edward VII in 1902. This had arrived and was in use by February 1904, when F. V. Worthington was transported in it across the plain to Lealui from Mongu. He found the journey to be hot, dusty and uncomfortable, and regretted that he had not travelled on horseback. As the journey is now difficult in a four-wheel drive vehicle, it is, perhaps, a miracle that he arrived at all. The Mulena Mukwae, at Nalolo also acquired a barouche at this time. It was still in use in 1959. There has to be some doubt about the Susmans' involvement in the import of King Lewanika's 'growler', as they were not in Barotseland in 1903 when it arrived; it may have been that it was the Mulena Mukwae's vehicle that they brought up from Kazungula, probably in pieces, on canoes and barges.[1]

Although they must have had contact with King Lewanika during their first stay at Lealui in 1901, and were certainly in touch with his regent, Prince Muwi-Muwi, at the end of 1902, there is no documentary evidence of a link with him before 1906. A letter written at Lealui by, or on behalf of, Prince Litia on 3 September 1906 survives in the Susman papers. It was addressed to 'Mr E. Susman' at 'Moandi', Sesheke, and reached him on 19 September. It is written in Silozi, with a touch of Setswana, and gives the consent of the 'Morena Lewanika' for the building of a new store at Sesheke. It is not clear whether this was erected on the site of the Gordon and Levitz store. The substantial brick building that appears in photographs from 1909 onwards was built with this royal permission in 1906–7.[2]

King Lewanika and the Traders

The Susman brothers' inability to establish themselves in the central Barotse plain does not seem to have done them much harm. It meant that they did not become embroiled in the triangular and long-running conflicts between the Lozi authorities, Chartered Company officials, and the traders, which were a feature of life at Lealui and Nalolo for several years. There was an ongoing struggle between the king, his council, and the traders, for control over the terms of trade, and between the king and the Company for jurisdiction over the traders, and over disputes between them and the Lozi people. King Lewanika had no illusions about the role of white traders or Company officials in his kingdom. In January 1898 he told the Lealui *kuta* in the presence of the missionary Adolphe Jalla that 'There are three types of whites: those of the government, traders and missionaries. Those of the government, fear them, they have the power; traders, eat them, for they have come to eat you. As for the missionaries they are ours, they are at home with us – chez nous.'[3]

Lozi kings had to be traders. For centuries their wealth had been primarily drawn from control over the trade in ivory. Like most African kings they claimed a monopoly over foreign trade and enjoyed various domestic perquisites. King Lewanika was a considerable entrepreneur. He followed the example of his mentor, King Khama, of the Ngwato, in seeking to involve himself in modern types of business. At the same time he tried to preserve old monopolies, such as his control over the ivory trade, river transport and the porterage at Sioma.

Lewanika did his best to exploit the traders for his own benefit, but he was not averse to joint ventures. His modern business projects included the unsuccessful attempt to build a canal and lock at the Sioma Falls and the importation of saw-milling machinery. He employed a Scotsman, J. Soane Campbell, to supervise the first of these projects, which proved in the end to be impractical. According to J. H. Venning, Lewanika paid Campbell £25 a month for his work, but was not much distressed by the lack of progress.

Lewanika commissioned another Scot, W. B. Simpson, whom he had previously employed on canal-building projects, to import the sawmill. The administration appropriated it for the Barotse National School, which was set up in 1906. Lewanika also bought wagons and entered the transport-riding business; he also continued to run canoes on the Zambezi.[4]

With the decline of the ivory trade, the cattle trade emerged as his major source of wealth. Lewanika moved to assert ownership and control of royal cattle herds by adopting the colonial practice of branding. He told the resident magistrate in 1908 that he was taking steps to have all his cattle branded. He also informed the administration of the names, or titles, of a small number of his officials who were authorised to sell cattle on his behalf. It was important for the rulers to keep control of the cattle trade so as to ensure that their own herds were not depleted by unauthorised sales. King Lewanika's sister, the Mulena Mukwae Matauka, initially insisted that traders could only buy cattle at her capital, Nalolo, and not in outlying parts of her area. She said that she did this in order to ensure that her own cattle were not sold without her knowledge.[5]

The assistant district commissioner in the Lukona Sub-district, later the Kalabo District, on the west bank of the Zambezi, reported in 1908–9 that through the practice of *mafisa* a proportion of all herds in the district belonged to King Lewanika. He noted:

> This custom lends itself to much abuse as at branding time (about February and March) when his servants come to brand the cattle they are very apt from excessive zeal to brand local-owned cattle as well, especially if they have any doubts as to the probity of the headman in charge of the cattle.
>
> On the other side any dishonest headman of which there are many will take care that any dead beast is reported as one of the Chief's.[6]

There had been a crisis at Lealui in the later months of 1903. In the absence of the district commissioner, Ferdinand Aitkens, who was absent on a long journey into northeastern Angola, the problems there had come to a head. The traders complained about high charges for river transport. Lewanika complained about the traders' high prices for goods. The traders were summoned to a meeting of the *kuta* and were confronted by Prince Litia and the Ngambela. When they refused to lower their prices, they were told that their stores would be closed. They complained to the administration that they had £20–30,000 of goods stockpiled at Lealui and threatened to take legal action against King Lewanika for interfering with their right to trade.[7] They also protested that '… it was the custom for the King or Queen in this country to suppress all complaints from traders by either closing their stores or refusing to allow their subjects to trade with them ...'.[8]

In the following year King Lewanika was compelled to give way, publicly if not privately, to the demand of Company officials that he abandon the right of jurisdiction over traders' disputes. The district commissioner at Mongu sent a circular to traders at Lealui in which he requested that all cases of 'native theft, insolence etc.' which had occurred during the year should be reported to him at once. He also indicated that the names of all the traders' employees, with the names of their indunas and villages, should be reported to the district commissioner's office. He proposed that a pair of handcuffs and leg irons should be left at 'Mr Levitz's' store', presumably for use on suspected miscreants. He further indicated that 'the object of these regulations is that the reports about injustice in Barotse may cease and that Chief Lewanika may be free from responsibility as regards whitemen's complaints'.[9]

Robert Coryndon reported to the Chartered Company on a trip to Mongu in October 1904:

> The whole system of trade and exchange was unbusinesslike; extortionate prices were charged by the traders for their goods, the chiefs insisted on a quite ridiculous cash price for their cattle, the traders combined in a half-hearted manner and bribed some of the head chiefs, who on their side persuaded Lewanika to commit various arbitrary acts, and to boycott the stores. I pointed out to Lewanika that he had no control over the traders, induced him to promise to prevent store thefts, arranged for a final reference to the D.C. in case of disputes, warned the traders and threatened Lewanika to refuse all licences for Lialui [*sic*], if the disputes continued.[10]

He also reported that he had arranged for a fixed tariff for canoe paddlers between Lealui and Kazungula, for the ferry at Kazungula and for the canoe porterages at Sioma and elsewhere.

Coryndon, Harding and Codrington

While Coryndon pursued a hard line in seeking to subordinate King Lewanika to Company control, and to remove rights of jurisdiction from him, Company officials did not all speak with one voice. There was a conflict between the two senior members of the administration, Coryndon, the administrator, and Colin Harding, the commandant of the Barotse Native Police. It revolved around their personal relationship with the king – a title that Coryndon deliberately denied Lewanika – and around the meaning of 'protection'. Lewanika had always distrusted Coryndon. He saw him, quite rightly, as a South African who was appointed by Cecil Rhodes and who owed his primary allegiance to the Chartered Company. Lewanika had a much better relationship with Colin Harding, a British officer, who had served with the Chartered Company in Southern Rhodesia, but owed his primary allegiance to the high commissioner. Harding had come to know Lewanika well when he acted as resident at Lealui in 1900, and their relationship was strengthened when he served as the king's official escort – he described himself as his 'bear-leader' – during the royal visit to England in 1902. Harding entertained Lewanika at his home in Somerset and returned to Africa with him. Coryndon was jealous of this relationship and thought that Harding was cultivating it in order to undermine Coryndon's influence. He accused him of encouraging in Lewanika 'a dangerous spirit of opposition to the constituted authority'.[11]

Harding was not a liberal. He did, however, believe that a 'protectorate' implied the protection of African interests. He believed that Lewanika had signed treaties with the Chartered Company that allowed him a measure of autonomy. He thought that Coryndon's imposition of hut tax in 1904–5 in outlying areas was premature – hut tax was not collected in the Barotse District until 1907 – and that the tax was levied at too high a rate. He refused to carry out the instructions of a political officer, William Hazell, then acting-secretary for native affairs, that he launch a punitive expedition against Chief Rabompo and his people. They were, in his view, not unwilling to pay tax, but were unable to do so because they had no money.[12] Harding withdrew from the field of operations, communicated with the high commissioner by telegram, and managed to get an instruction from him that the huts of tax-defaulters should not be burned. Coryndon had been trying to get rid of Harding since 1904, but the high commissioner, Lord Milner, resisted his efforts. Harding's role as a whistle-blower made his already precarious position untenable and he resigned in March 1906. A year later Coryndon was transferred to Swaziland. Robert Codrington, who was administrator of North-Eastern Rhodesia, succeeded him in North-Western Rhodesia.[13]

Both Harding and Coryndon had visited Lealui in the course of 1905. They provided contrasting assessments of Lewanika and of life at Lealui. Harding emphasised the relative prosperity of the Barotse plain, which he saw as 'teeming with inhabitants and alive with Barotse cattle'. He saw it as a place where '… the natives are, generally speaking, well fed, well dressed, and well to do, and form a striking contrast to the natives who live in the outlying districts of Kalomo'. Using an analogy drawn from contemporary London, he saw Lealui and the Barotse plain as the West End and Kalomo as Whitechapel. In his book, *In Remotest Barotseland*, which he published during 1905, though it must have been written a year or two earlier, Harding had commented that while Lewanika may at times in the past have been a tyrant and a Machiavelli, as well as a hero, he had become 'emphatically a statesman, and a far-seeing one, and has at heart the welfare of his country and people to an extent surprising in one brought up as he was in his youth'.[14]

While Harding implied that Lewanika's position had been weakened by the introduction of Company rule, Coryndon's view was rather different. He argued that Lewanika's position had been undermined by his own actions as much as by those of the Company, and that he would not have survived without Company support. After a visit to Lealui in December 1905, he wrote to the high commissioner, Lord Selborne:

> It may be that Lewanika's visit to England, his European clothing and manner of life, and his friendliness with white people have to some extent alienated the sympathies and respect of a people whose chief characteristic, in common with most African tribes, is suspicion; and perhaps that he is largely blamed for many of the irritating restrictions which have come with a white administration, among which are suppression of domestic slavery, the imposition of hut tax, the prevention of the promiscuous raiding and plundering by which the Barotse obtained and held their supremacy, and so on. Besides these reasons I have no doubt that, seeing that the days of his tyranny are coming to an end with the growth of our influence, he and one or two of his chief indunas have hurried through the execution of various works with practically slave or forced labour – many large houses in Lealui and Nalolo, a fleet of canoes, and a huge foundation [for a new house] measuring perhaps three acres and raised above the surrounding swamp area by thousands of unpaid workers.
>
> Lewanika is not naturally a strong man in the sense that Chaka, Umsiligaas [Mzilikazi], or Sebituane [Sebetwane] were strong men, and I do not think he would be Paramount Chief today had it not been for the establishment of a white Government which has consistently supported his authority.[15]

The Susman Brothers at Lealui

Coryndon's successor as administrator, Codrington, lasted for only eighteen months. He had a heart attack and dropped dead in the streets of London while on leave in December 1908. He was about to marry a Miss Bird, reputed to be the heiress to a fortune founded on the manufacture of custard powder.[16] Codrington was a man of few words, but he was decisive. In his short period in office, he moved the capital of North-Western Rhodesia from Kalomo to Livingstone. He also reversed the prohibition on the granting of new trade licences in the Barotse plain, which Coryndon had imposed in May 1906. The Susman brothers were given a licence at Lealui a few months before this change of policy came into effect on 1 January 1908.

On 6 September 1907 the newly appointed district commissioner at Lealui, William Hazell, addressed a letter to 'My Friend Katema'. Government officials wrote directly to only a handful of black people apart from King Lewanika himself. Katema was, presumably, a senior induna at Lealui. Hazell wrote to him: 'I am writing to tell you I have granted a Trader's licence to Mr Susman to have a store at Lealui. The Morena Lewanika met him at Nalolo and promised to give him a place to build a store on. So I have told Mr Susman to see you about it.'[17] When the administration did finally grant the Susman brothers a licence to trade in the Barotse plain, it was, therefore, at the request of King Lewanika himself. Not a great deal is known about the origins of the district commissioner, William Hazell. He had, while acting as secretary for native affairs, clashed with Harding in 1905. He must also have clashed with the magistrate at Kalomo, Henry Rangely, as he took him to court for hunting game without a licence – not a tactful thing for a relatively junior official to do. He was later criticised for the harshness with which he dealt with the aftermath of the murder of a white man in the Kasempa District to which he was transferred from Lealui. He ordered the public execution of three people convicted of the murder and, not surprisingly, acquired a reputation as a hard man. Theodore Williams, a Jamaica-born and relatively liberal company official, said of him: 'There is a great deal of powerfulness, if very little of principle, in his creed... .' He retired from the Chartered Company's service in 1916 – long before the end of Company rule.[18]

In granting the Susmans a licence to trade at Lealui, Hazell seems to have acted against his better judgement. He may have regretted that he did so under pressure from King Lewanika soon after his arrival at Lealui. He certainly watched them like a hawk. Several of his letter books for 1908 survive and contain a score of letters to them on a variety of issues. Some of these were circulars, such as one sent to all traders at Lealui telling them that they could move with King Lewanika from Lealui to the *mafulo* (the margin of the plain) in February, but that they could not keep stores open at both places. There is also a letter thanking Susman Brothers for sending in the annual return of the guns and ammunition in their possession. Then there is correspondence relating to a request from the Mulena Mukwae at Nalolo to buy from Susman Brothers a .350 rifle and a shotgun. Hazell questions their possession of the guns, which, he says, were not mentioned in their return. Their answer to this letter must have been satisfactory as he gave them permission for the sale, though only through the district commissioner – that is, himself.[19]

On the same day that he wrote about the guns, he wrote to say that a man, 'Mundiya', had come in to pay tax with a bright new farthing. Mundiya claimed that Induna Namayamba had given him the coin and had claimed that it was a half sovereign. The Induna claimed that Susman Brothers had given it to him in part payment for an ox. Hazell asked them to make enquiries about the matter, 'I want to know where the farthing came from.'[20]

The first hint in the letter books that the Susmans were in real trouble came in a letter written to King Lewanika himself on 22 February 1908. Hazell wrote as follows:

> It has been reported to me that a white trader in Lealui stabbed his servant in the back with a fish spear. This is said to have happened the day before I went to Lealui.
>
> I hear this matter was settled by the khotla [*kuta*]. If this is so I am surprised that I was not told about when I was in Lealui. Will you please tell me the facts of the case. If it is true that the man was stabbed, then it is my duty to hear the case and find out who is to blame. If the white man did stab a man, then he will be punished. Will you please tell me the names of all the people involved in this case, and if there is any truth in the matter all the witnesses should be sent to me.[21]

Lewanika complied with this request. A week later, on 29 February, Hazell wrote to inform him that '... the case against Mr Susman has been tried today, and Mr Susman has been fined £20 and the boy who was stabbed has been paid £1.15.0 and the two witnesses have been paid 15/- each'. The docket for this case – 'Rex versus Harry Susman', Criminal Case number 6 of 1908 – survives in the Zambian National Archives. The charge is that Harry Susman 'on or about the 20 February 1908 at or near Lealui ... did wrongfully and unlawfully and wilfully assault the complainant Muishebela alias Tungani by stabbing him in the back with a fish spear, thereby wounding and occasioning actual bodily harm.' The plea was not guilty, and the verdict was guilty.[22]

There was no dispute as to what happened. Harry Susman offered no defence and asked the witnesses no questions. He had bought an ox from people who came to the store to sell cattle. He had then travelled by canoe to Lealui, crossing from one mound in the plain to another. On his return to Lealui some hours later, he was annoyed to discover that his workers had not moved the ox according to his instructions. The story as told by 'Muishebela' was as follows:

I am working for the accused Mr Susman as a messenger – About 8 days ago I was in my hut at Mr Susman's store – My master called me. I did not hear. I am deaf. Mr Susman then came close to the hut with a 'Moyio' (fish spear). The walls of the hut were of reeds. My master (Mr Susman) pushed the spear through the walls of the hut. He did this twice – Masiakuluka was in the hut with me – He caught hold of the spear – Masiakuluka then let the spear go and ran out of the Hut. I was frightened and also ran out of the Hut thinking that the white man (Mr Susman) would kill me. As I ran my master (Mr Susman) threw the spear at me. The spear struck me in the back. When I got near the cattle kraal I pulled the spear out – Masiakuluka and Mbomwai were present when this happened – The wound caused by the spear caused me a lot of pain – Mbomwai took me away to Lealui by boat.[23]

The facts of the case are not as important as the size of the fine and its relevance to the question of jurisdiction. There was clearly no justification for Harry Susman's action, which was dangerous and potentially lethal. Incidents of this kind were, unfortunately, common at Lealui. A fine of £20 (about £1,000 in modern money) for an offence of this kind was exceptional, and almost certainly unique. In a later case, on 28 June 1908, Hazell fined John Horn £3 after he admitted that he had hit his wagon driver, Klaas, 'a Xhosa native', with his fists, had then hit him several times with a yoke, and had finally sjambokked him. The only matter in dispute was whether Klaas was concussed, as he said, or could get up after the beating, as Horn claimed.[24]

In a case in the following year, the resident magistrate, Barotse District, Charles McKinnon, fined F. D. Law £6 for an assault on 'Mobita'. Law had hit him with a hot branding iron after he had let the cattle out of the kraal. The magistrate noted that the letters 'B. I.' could 'clearly be read on his shoulder yesterday'. He rejected Law's defence that this was the result of an accident and that there was no malicious intent. He did, however, take into account his previous good character and the fact that it was a first offence. Law was then a trader working for Meikle Brothers. He was later a prominent citizen of Livingstone and a member of the Town Council.[25]

It is clear that Hazell imposed an exemplary fine on Harry Susman. About three-quarters of the fine related to the real offence in his eyes – Harry had ignored the district commissioner and had taken his case to the Lealui *kuta* where a fine of a cow is likely to have been imposed. It is not clear whether or not Harry Susman appealed against the size of the fine imposed by Hazell. There must, however, have been some complaint as Hazell was asked to send the file to Livingstone and to explain his action. In doing so he wrote to the legal department as follows:

> The accused in this case has the reputation of being a man of violent and ungovernable temper, and the seriousness of the offence is enhanced where natives like the Barotse are concerned who would not stop at incendiaryism [*sic*] or even murder in revenge for an act of unprovoked violence which in this case might very easily have resulted in death.
>
> I may mention that the Accused, when asked, pleaded 'Guilty' at first, but as it was evident that he was ignorant of the liabilities of such a pleading, it was explained to him and subsequently he pleaded 'Not Guilty.'[26]

There is no doubt that Harry Susman was hot-tempered and quick with his fists but there is equally no doubt that he was to acquire a reputation as the kindest and friendliest of men. It is not insignificant that all the witnesses who gave evidence for the prosecution in this case, including the injured man, described themselves as still in his employment. The consequences of this case were not slow in coming. Six weeks later, in the middle of April 1908, Elie Susman wrote to Hazell to complain about the employment of so-called 'native touts' by other traders in the district. 'Touts' were sometimes employed by traders to attract customers to their stores. They were also employed as unlicensed hawkers to peddle the traders' goods. Elie must have been taken aback by the response to his letter.

> I understand from the Chief Lewanika that this mode of trading was first resorted to by the Jewish traders of Lealui and he expressed the opinion it should be stopped. I agree with the Chief that this practice is undesirable. I am also aware that other more reprehensible practices are resorted to by *one* trader in particular in order to secure custom.
>
> These matters will be taken into consideration when the time comes to renew licences.[27]

What were these 'more reprehensible practices'? There are only two possibilities. One would be the sale of guns and ammunition and the other would be Harry's resort to the *kuta*. Susman Brothers made a number of sales of guns and ammunition to local notables at this time: to the Mulena Mukwae, to King Lewanika himself, and to Induna Namayamba. These sales were, however, always made with the permission of Hazell. It is extremely unlikely that he would have given this permission if he thought that they were carrying on an illicit trade in guns and ammunition. Hazell's reference must relate specifically to Harry Susman's resort to the Lozi courts, and, more generally, to the Susman brothers' closeness to the Lozi royal establishment and to the 'hearty handshakes' which had caused Finkelstein, perhaps with some prompting from Hazell, such annoyance. Hazell was, like Coryndon, a man who placed great emphasis on the status of 'the white

Exclusion

Robert Codrington visited Mongu-Lealui during July 1908. It is clear that a decision was made at this time to reverse once again the policy on trade licences in the Barotse District and to reduce the number of licences issued. The Susman brothers were told on 6 August that their licence at Lealui would not be renewed and that a licence at Nalolo would be refused. They appear to have been told on the same day that they would not be allowed to trade anywhere in the Barotse District. David Wersock, who had been implicated in the Gordon and Levitz bankruptcy, and H. A. Jacobson, who traded at Nalolo – they were both Russian Jews – were also told at this time that their licences would not be renewed.[29]

There is no doubt that this was an anti-Semitic decision. Hazell made this quite explicit. Referring to the refusal of a licence to W. Ullmann, one of several brothers who were based at Kapopo near the modern town of Ndola, he wrote on 18 August: 'It is inadvisable to increase the number of licences issued to men of his class (Jews) in the District.'[30] A couple of Scots traders, George Smith and George Buchanan, were also told in August that their licences would not be renewed, but in January 1909 they were. The administration was careful to cover its tracks on the issue at this time. It rushed out a proclamation during September, stating explicitly that it could grant or withhold licences as it wished, and that it did not have to give reasons for its decisions.[31]

The administration apparently felt that it could not refuse licences to all Jews. A licence was granted for 1909 to Egnatz Snapper who had been at Libonda since 1902. He became the first trader at Kanyonyo, which was close to the government offices at Mongu. Licences were also granted to Joseph Finkelstein and A. B. Diamond at Lealui, as well as to his son, Harry Diamond, at Nalolo. A. B. Diamond had been in and out of the district since 1901. He had been refused a licence for 1903 and his son had been refused one for 1908.[32]

The basis for discrimination between Jewish traders seems to have been an assessment of their degree of Britishness. Finkelstein appears to have been brought up in Britain. Snapper had family in London, while A. B. Diamond, his son Harry and brother Louis were regarded as Irish. Egnatz Snapper and A. B. Diamond had both served in the Anglo-Boer War with the Diamond Fields Light Horse. The Susmans were always described in district censuses at this time as Russian Jews, or 'Hebrews', though Elie was naturalised as a British subject in Southern Rhodesia in April 1903 and Harry in April 1908 – not long after getting into trouble with the law at Lealui.[33]

There may, however, have been a difference of opinion between officials as to how to deal with the Susmans. The resident magistrate, Charles McKinnon, a more senior official than Hazell, though he had only recently arrived in the district, allowed them to open a store in October at Nalolo, the headquarters of the Mulena Mukwae. This annoyed the traders who were already established there: Messrs Jacobson and Kiehl, and Harry Diamond. According to the assistant district commissioner at Nalolo, Jacobson had 'for some considerable time held Messrs. Susman Bros. in great business antipathy, and he resented very much them coming to Nalolo ... as he knew that with their big stock they could defy competition ...'. The licence for Nalolo was a short-term one and may have been intended to enable them to dispose of some of the stock that they had at Lealui.[34]

There is no direct evidence of a reaction by King Lewanika to the administration's refusal to renew the Susmans' licence at Lealui. Indirect evidence emerges from the notes of the first meetings between him and the new acting-administrator, Lawrence Wallace, in July and August 1909. Among the items that Lewanika had included on the agenda, when writing earlier in the year to request a meeting, was the need for 'a good store' at Lealui – something that the Susmans had provided. In discussions with the Ngambela and *kuta* in July and August, Wallace said, somewhat disingenuously, that no one would come to Lealui to live 'in a little house on an ant heap' at Lealui, nor would they invest thousands of pounds in a good store, without a guarantee of security of tenure. He also thought that no one would open a good store unless they were able to sell goods for cash. He did, however, undertake to look for someone to open a good store in the Barotse plain. He did not live up to his promise. It was not until 1916, shortly after the death of Lewanika, that the Susmans were able to get back to Lealui, and it was not until 1921 that they were able to construct the first substantial brick-built store at Kanyonyo, near Mongu.[35]

The Susman brothers' first response to the threat that their licence would not be renewed was to try to get a licence for one of their employees to trade at Lealui. An application from Gabriel Epstein, an Irish Jew, was, however, rejected. In the end they sold their store and remaining stock to A. B. Diamond. The latter inserted the following advertisement in the *Livingstone Mail* on 13 February 1909:

> Mr A. B. Diamond begs to announce that he has re-opened business as a *General Dealer* at Lealui having taken over the whole stock of Messrs. Susman Brothers with fresh supplies arriving monthly, including *Groceries, Gent's Outfitting, Drapery, Cutlery, Patent Medicines, Cigars and Cigarettes, Boots and Shoes, Tools etc.* This comprises the largest and best-selected stock in Barotseland.[36]

Although Diamond was to trade on his own account at Lealui, it is clear that the plan was that he would be an agent for Susman Brothers and they would supply him with goods for sale. This relationship did not work out well. Less than two years later, at the end of 1910, the Susman brothers took him to court for non-payment of bills amounting to about £1,000 – about half the price of the goods that he had taken over at Lealui. They dropped their action after he paid part of the outstanding amount and received the balance – paid out in cattle in the Congo – in 1912. Diamond had pioneered long cattle trails to Lobito Bay in 1905 and to the Congo in 1909. He spent most of his time on the trail and had left the Barotseland business in the hands of his brother, Louis, in 1909. He established a butchery business in Elisabethville in 1911, and returned to farm at Diamondale near Lusaka in the following year.[37]

Although the Susman brothers were not able to trade for themselves in the Barotse District for a number of years after 1908, and had to fall back on their base at Sesheke, it seems that they were able to maintain a dominant position in the Barotse trade as wholesalers supplying goods to other traders, and as the major cattle-buyers from the Barotse traders. In spite of Elie Susman's forebodings about the future of settled traders, and the series of difficulties and setbacks that Susman Brothers had encountered during 1908, it turned out to be an excellent trading year. This was illustrated by the success of what the *Livingstone Mail* described as 'The Great Cattle Sale' at Livingstone in June 1908 when Susman Brothers sold about 1,200 cattle for close to £5,000. It was noted that the success of the sale was enhanced by the arrival of many buyers from the south who were attracted by the relaxation of the prohibition on the export of breeding stock. Almost equal numbers of slaughter and breeding stock were sold. Among the buyers from the south were Theodore Haddon, manager of the Globe and Phoenix Mine, Embakwe, the Susman Brothers' old stamping ground, and J. Smith, of Selukwe. There were also Greek and Jewish buyers from the south, such as Malevris and Blumenthal. The *Livingstone Mail* understood that 'there

[were] many thousand of head of cattle coming forward for sale, and anticipate[d] quite a small boom in the local cattle trade'.[38]

Prices were about the same as Elie Susman had quoted in his interview in November 1907. There had been a recovery from the depressed prices that he had correctly anticipated as likely to prevail in the early months of the year. The *Livingstone Mail* had published an article in January 1908 about 'the crisis in the cattle market'. This had arisen as a result of the administration's ban on the export of breeding stock, and also from uncertainty about the policy on cattle-trading permits. The market seems to have recovered following the clarification of these issues. The *Livingstone Mail* noted in June that Susman Brothers, in particular, stood to benefit from these changes.[39]

Extraordinary evidence of Susman Brothers' predominance in the trade comes from the annual report for Sesheke for 1908–9. On 31 March 1909, at a time when all cattle bought in the previous season would have been brought down from the central Zambezi plain and the Barotse District, Susman Brothers had 3,552 cattle in their possession in Sesheke District. About one-third of these cattle were cows, heifers or female calves. The remaining two-thirds were bulls, oxen, yearlings and male calves. This amounted to almost three-quarters of the nearly 5,000 cattle held by white traders in the district. The second largest herd was that of Galanos, a Greek trader at Kazungula, who had just over 500 head. The number of cattle held by Susman Brothers was equal to about half of the total cattle exports from the Barotse District for the year. Susman Brothers not only had a dominant share of the cattle trade passing through Sesheke, but they also had more than half of the wagon transport business done during the year. Their wagons had carried 120,000 pounds of goods into or out of the district during the year, a good deal of this was probably grain exported from Sesheke District. Their only rivals were the Scots, Messrs Thomson and Bissett.[40]

More evidence of their success comes from the inspector of the Standard Bank branch in Bulawayo. He reported in October 1909 that Susman Brothers, traders and cattle dealers of Sesheke, was a 'respectable and trustworthy firm who are engaged in trading operations in North Western Rhodesia out of which they appear to be doing well. Old customers of this Branch whose dealings with us have always been satisfactory. The partners Elie and Harry Susman are hardworking men who give close attention to their business. Engagements are met fairly punctually.' According to a balance sheet submitted to the Standard Bank, and dated 31 August 1909, they then had assets of just over £30,000, liabilities of just over £14,000 and a surplus of just under £16,000. At this date they held about 3,250 head of cattle, 2,800 of them in Southern Rhodesia, and only 450 head in North-Western Rhodesia. They had exported most of their cattle from Sesheke to the south in the previous six months. In the two years since 1907 the scale of their business had increased quite dramatically. The surplus of assets over liabilities had gone up by £10,000 – from £6,000 to £16,000.[41]

A Joint Venture

Apart from hard work, shrewd trading and understanding of the market, there was another explanation for this success. This was the special relationship that the Susmans had developed with King Lewanika and other members of the Lozi royal family. It would have been impossible for them to achieve such a dominant position in the Barotse cattle trade without privileged access to royal cattle herds. Although much of the evidence for this is circumstantial, and comes from oral tradition on both sides, there is some harder evidence that emerges from a most unusual agreement made between Susman Brothers and King Lewanika in September 1909.

The agreement reads as follows: 'We the undermentioned Susman Bros. of Sesheke have sold to the Chief Lewanika our camp situated in Sesheke, North Western Rhodesia consisting of: – 1 brick store, 2 dwelling houses, and stable, huts and cetera fenced in, for £1,000 of which £500 we received in cash and the balance to be paid in 12 months.' The agreement was signed on 27 September 1909 and witnessed by the Ngambela, and by Induna Ntyekwa. It was also counter-signed by the resident magistrate, Charles McKinnon, on 29 September. There appears to have been another agreement under which Susman Brothers agreed to pay Lewanika an annual rent of £120 for the use of the premises.[42] There was a minor misunderstanding about this when, two years later, Lewanika said that he had not received the promised rent. It then became apparent that he had not paid the £500 that he owed as the second instalment of the transaction. This matter seems to have been resolved in 1912 when Lewanika paid the balance minus the rent due, though with some allowance for interest on the overdue amount, and for improvements that the Susmans had carried out in the previous two years.[43]

It is difficult to explain this transaction except in terms of a joint venture. The Susmans did not need the cash but, if they had, £120 a year was a high rate of interest on £1,000. On the other hand, if Lewanika wanted to increase his income, there was nothing to stop him increasing the ground rent that he charged on all stores in Barotseland. It looks as if this sale was a device that was intended to insure the Susmans against the non-renewal of their trade licence at Sesheke. They were no doubt aware that the 1908 proclamation on trade licences stipulated that, in the event of the non-renewal of a licence, a store had to be dismantled within three months. Failing that, the Company gave itself the right to put the premises up for sale. This proclamation assumed that traders' stores were made from wattle and daub or were corrugated-iron sheds. It made no provision for the substantial brick structure that the Susmans had built at Sesheke. In the event that their licence was not renewed, they would, presumably, have attempted to carry on the Barotseland business as Lewanika's agents. It is clear that many people already saw them as acting on his behalf.

CHAPTER 5

King Lobengula's Treasure

As if the story of the Susman brothers' life at Lealui in 1908 was not exciting enough, Elie Susman became involved during the year in another drama that requires a chapter to itself. Although this led him into a brush with the law and a fine, it does not seem to have had any long-term repercussions on his reputation or on the business. In all probability, Elie's role in this drama did more to enhance than to diminish his standing in the eyes of colonial society, even though it might have been expected to undermine his reputation as a shrewd businessman and judge of the market. Before the events described here unfolded, the brothers had been told that they would not have their licence renewed at Lealui – so there were no consequences in that direction. It has to be said that while the archival record places Elie at the centre of this drama, family tradition gives a more prominent role to his brother, Harry.[1]

The best way into the story is to quote in its entirety an article that appeared in the *Livingstone Mail* of 2 January 1909 under the heading 'A Treasure Hunt'. This is the way that people in Livingstone at the time would have had their first news of a drama, the main episodes of which had occurred most of 600 miles away to the northwest. It is almost certain that the account given there was written by Leopold Moore and that his major informant was his friend Elie Susman – one of a handful of people who would have known the whole story, or most of it.

A Treasure Hunt

Under the most commonplace circumstances, fragments of quite an interesting and adventurous enterprise were recently communicated to us. Two Transvaalers, aggrieved at the decision of the Magistrate at Lealui – who fined them ten pounds for flogging a native – related that they had been engaged in a search for the treasure said to have been carried away by Lobengula in 1892.

It would take many columns to tell the whole story; but, briefly, we understand that a certain native preacher – the Rev. John Jacobs, with a Lovedale education and a taste for fermented liquor – confided to a Mr. Spinner that he had been charged with the transport and burial of the treasure referred to above, while acting as Lobengula's private secretary. He alleges that he has letters from both Dr. Jameson and the late Mr. Rhodes, requesting him to discover it. He, however, appears to have had a wholly unaccountable objection to trusting the Chartered Company, and preferred to communicate his secret – on terms – to a Dutchman.

To cut a long story short, an expedition was made up, and, after many vicissitudes, reached Sesheke – the journey he had originally taken (*via* Lake Ngami) being deemed impracticable. Here, two of the expedition turned back; and Messrs. A. Spinner and J. Monckts proceeded by waggon – with his reverence – into the heart of the Balovale District, at the head-waters of the Zambesi.

Much time was consumed in endeavouring to locate the two hills their guide described as the landmarks he sought; and some confusion in the names of streams and rivers led them far out of their path. Circumstances necessitated their return to Lealui; and there they were detained by the sickness of their guide. Supplies ran short; and at this juncture, Mr. E. Susman appears on the scene. He was willing to render assistance; but he claimed their confidence and – subsequently – a share in the enterprise.

Freshly equipped, the expedition started for the neighbourhood of the alleged treasure, which is about three hundred miles north-west of Lealui; and after some adventures that might possibly be done justice to by R.L. Stevenson or Rider Haggard, their guide still failing to make good, relations appear to have become strained. At one time, Jacobs indicated a spot, and set them all digging; at another, he declined to confide his secret to anyone but Susman. Ultimately, long-smouldering suspicion of his reverence's bona-fides seem to have hardened into conviction, and twenty-five [lashes] were administered. This brought the treasure seekers before the local authority; and Monckts and Susman were fined ten pounds a-piece – which Monckts appears to think excessive.

Now the officials have got hold of John Jacobs, and he professes to be only too eager to afford the Company all the information in his power.

How much of the affair is a hoax, a fraud or a fact, we do not pretend to say; but if the Chartered Company takes up the search for the treasure, all we can say is that we wish they may get it.[2]

Apart from some confusion about nationalities, this appears to be a reasonably accurate summary of events that occurred between Sesheke, Lealui and the extreme northwestern corner of the Balovale (now Zambezi) District between March and December 1908. Although at least one 'Dutchman', possibly a Transvaaler, does appear to have been involved in the story, none was charged in connection with it. Sprinner (not Spinner) and Monckts were Germans – Monckts was probably a Swiss German. Furthermore, it was not Monckts who appealed against the judgement of the magistrate at Lealui, William Hazell. It was Elie Susman.

A further, and more speculative, article, 'More about the Treasure Hunt', appeared in the *Livingstone Mail* three weeks later on 23 January 1909. It did not add a great deal to the story given above, though it was more specific about the nature of the treasure and about King Lobengula's plans for retreat into an area that was then believed to be in the Portuguese sphere of influence. From the tone of the article it appears that the author, again presumably Leopold Moore, may have interviewed John Jacobs himself.

> He [Lobengula] accordingly had a number of new sails cut up and made into bags of a convenient size. These he filled with specie, 400 diamonds and some bars of gold, had packed into three large iron chests of varying sizes – the largest of all being about 'the size of a door.' Ten waggons were loaded up with these cases and the chief's best ivory, and, under an escort of three indunas, and a hundred and fifty men, the private secretary set out for the country. Lobengula had decided to retire to.[3]

According to this account, Jacobs and this large party travelled through Ngamiland. They took their wagons across the Chobe-Linyanti-Kwando River, avoiding the necessity of crossing the Zambezi. They then made their way up the west bank of the Zambezi until they reached its headwaters. 'Having selected a spot which might be easily identified in future, he had holes dug, and the chests, ivory etc. buried. The expedition then returned.' Jacobs was apparently evasive on the subject of what happened to the other members of the party, suggesting that they were killed in the subsequent war with the Chartered Company. When pressed further, Jacobs said: 'Don't ask me.' The reporter was prepared to use his own vivid imagination to fill in the gaps.

> The slaves who dug the holes were probably buried in them – with the treasure. The diminished impi, [troop or platoon of warriors] which returned with the waggons, was probably met at some little distance from home by another impi, with definite instructions. The three indunas were certainly knocked on the head; and if any were spared, their ignorance of what they had been doing was what saved them. Moreover, it is highly probable that any survivors were killed in the subsequent war.
>
> Jacobs, we can quite understand, was spared until he should have communicated the exact spot to the chief. This he probably did, for it is known that Lobengula was travelling in that direction when he died.

Before examining in more detail Elie Susman's role in this story, it is necessary to say something about the earlier history of John Jacobs (alias Witbooi). He may have been a professional conman, and an exceptionally talented and persuasive one, but there is one element of truth in his story. He was private secretary to King Lobengula in the last months of the king's life. Sprinner and Monckts were not the first people to encounter him, nor were they the first to believe that he knew where Lobengula's treasure was buried.

The official who knew most about him was Hugh Marshall Hole, a long-serving Chartered Company employee, who acted as administrator of North-Western Rhodesia for some months in 1903. In his retirement, he wrote a number of books about south-central Africa, including *The Making of Rhodesia*, *The Passing of the Black Kings* and *Lobengula*. In a memorandum to the board of directors of the Chartered Company, written in October 1907, he said that he had little doubt that Lobengula's treasure was buried somewhere and that John Jacobs knew where it was. A few months later, Sidney Paxton Willson contacted the Chartered Company saying that he was in touch with a 'native' who knew where Lobengula's treasure was buried. Willson was said to be 'a not very reputable hanger-on at the Charter Hotel' in Bulawayo, Hole seemed to be fairly certain that the ultimate source of his information about the treasure was Jacobs. The Company eventually agreed to allow Willson to retain as his share thirty per cent of any treasure that he might find.[4]

Given the date of this correspondence, January 1908, it is probable that it related to the Sprinner–Monckts expedition. Willson may well have been one of the treasure hunters who started out with them, but turned back from Sesheke. It is also probable that their expedition had initially some kind of official sanction. Jacobs himself was, however, *persona non grata* north of the Limpopo. He had been arrested and deported at Tuli while on his way into Southern Rhodesia on a treasure-hunting expedition in February 1905. At that stage he claimed that the treasure was to be found in the vicinity of the Bembesi River in Southern Rhodesia.[5]

In letters and memoranda that he wrote to a senior Chartered Company official in 1907–8, Hole recalled that during the Ndebele War of 1893–4 John Jacobs

> was sent up from Bulawayo as a prisoner of war, and was detained in gaol at Salisbury for a long time; being eventually released by order of the judge for there was no warrant for his detention and no charge against him... . [He] offered to conduct me to a spot where rough diamonds were hidden if I would procure his release from Salisbury gaol in 1894. I do believe that Loben [*sic*] had a lot of uncut diamonds and he must have hidden them somewhere, but whether they have been unearthed long ago or are still there is a doubtful question.

Hole appears to have believed then that the treasure was most likely to be found in the neighbourhood of the Umguza River north of Bulawayo, though he later gave equal weight to the theory that it had been carried north of the Zambezi. He later wrote that Jacobs had been found in possession of a small quantity of uncut diamonds when he was taken prisoner in 1894. Jacobs claimed then that he had been given these by Lobengula, who had kept them in a paraffin tin. He also claimed to know where the remainder was hidden. Hole also recalled that a thorough search had been made of the burnt-out ruins of the royal quarters at Bulawayo at that time, but this had produced only some half-burnt sporting rifles, a silver model of an elephant and a signet ring.[6]

In his later books, Hole supplied more information on John Jacobs's background and role in the last days of Lobengula. Other information comes from a statement which Jacobs made to an immigration officer in Southern Rhodesia in 1917 – it survives in the Zimbabwe National Archives – and from an interview with him that was conducted by the writer, Hedley Chilvers, in Johannesburg in April 1930 – not long before Jacobs's death. According to Hole, Jacobs was the illegitimate son of a Fingo (Mfengu) mother – 'the offspring of a chance intimacy with a Dutch *bywoner* [squatter]'. He was taken in by a missionary couple who taught him to read and write in English. He moved to Kimberley where he became involved in 'I.D.B.' – illicit diamond buying and was eventually sentenced to a term of six years' imprisonment with hard labour, which he served at the Breakwater – a Cape Town prison. He was released and worked as a police trap, 'but his crooked instincts made him untrustworthy even in that degraded profession, and one conviction followed another'. According to Hole, Jacobs received a sentence of lashes for 'a gross assault on a woman', but another account says that he was given thirty-six lashes in 1895 for cattle theft: he had apparently appropriated cattle in Southern Rhodesia, claiming that he had been sent by Dr Jameson to collect unbranded animals.[7]

According to his own account of his life, Jacobs was born in 1842 and educated by the London Missionary Society at Hankey, near Port Elizabeth. This date of birth is most improbable, and may indeed be a misprint for 1862, which is a more likely date. Chilvers thought that he was a well-preserved seventy-year-old in 1930. Jacobs claimed that he had fought at the Battle of Isandhlwana in 1879, that he had served with the British in the First Boer War in 1881, and later with President Kruger's Transvaal Republic forces. He had then worked as a missionary for the Church of England, which sent him as a teacher to Kanye and Palapye in Bechuanaland in the late 1880s. A black police sergeant recalled, however, that he had first seen him tied up with rope at Palapye in 1888; he had, apparently, helped himself to a white man's goods. He claimed at different times that he reached Bulawayo in 1888 or 1890. In his last interview with Chilvers in 1930, he added a new dimension to his colourful career, he said then that Lobengula had sent for him while he was a student at Lovedale, 'for he had heard that I could write English and Dutch, and he knew that I had been to Scotland to be educated'.[8]

Hugh Marshall Hole believed that Jacobs had only become involved with Lobengula after the departure of traders and missionaries from Bulawayo during the rebellion in 1893, and became useful to Lobengula in the absence of his usual interpreters and intermediaries. Jacobs accompanied Lobengula on his retreat northwards from Bulawayo after the defeat of the Ndebele army by Dr Leander Starr Jameson and a volunteer force at the Bembesi River at the beginning of November 1893. When Dr Jameson sent a message to Lobengula asking him to return to Bulawayo for talks, it was Jacobs who wrote Lobengula's response. In this letter, Lobengula said that he would return, but asked what had happened to his three indunas, who had been sent with a message to the high commissioner, Sir Henry Loch. Lobengula knew very well that two of them had been killed at Tati (Francistown) when they attempted to escape from the custody of the Bechuanaland Police. He also complained that, as Bulawayo had been burnt on his own instructions, there would be nowhere for him to stay.[9]

Lobengula did not return to Bulawayo, but continued northwards towards the Zambezi. On his way north he may have met a large *impi*, which he had recalled from a raid into Barotseland – probably into the Batoka country. According to one of Hole's published accounts, Jacobs deserted Lobengula soon after writing the letter to Dr Jameson, and handed himself over to the Company's forces. In a later more colourful and, perhaps, more imaginative account, Hole suggested that Jacobs remained with Lobengula until the end. He also suggested that Jacobs had by then established a liaison with Lobengula's favourite wife, Queen Losikeyi, and that they made a plan together to secure the treasure for themselves – a plan which was foiled at the last minute by Lobengula's most senior and loyal general, 'Mjaan', commander of the Imbezu Regiment.[10]

It may well be asked: how did Elie Susman get mixed up with this plausible rogue? No documents relating to this episode survive among the Susman brothers' own papers. The correspondence of William Hazell, district commissioner at Lealui, does shed some light on the origins of this affair. It is apparent from this source, and from the record of the later trial, that Elie Susman first met Sprinner and Monckts at Sesheke when they were on their way into the country. This was not later than the beginning of March 1908, as they were already at Lealui on 7 April 1908. On that day William Hazell wrote to 'Mr E. C. Monk, c/o Susman Bros., Lealui', to tell him that he noted his intention to proceed up the Zambezi 'on a pleasure trip, and also for the purpose of some bird shooting, further that your absence may possibly be of two weeks duration and that the limit of your trip will be the Lafisi River'.[11]

This letter refers to the first of Sprinner and Monckts's two trips up the Zambezi. It was after the failure of this expedition that Elie Susman became involved in the venture. It was only then that he was let into the secret purpose of the journey and agreed to provide wagons in return for a sixteen and a half per cent share in the proceeds. On 6 August, Hazell wrote to 'Mr E. Spinner' to say that 'Mr Susman' had asked for permission to take a wagon into Portuguese West Africa (Angola). He said that as the law stood this permission could not be granted. He asked him to call and see the resident magistrate – he was himself acting in that capacity – at Mongu before proceeding. Two days later Hazell wrote to say he had no objection to his 'proceeding with two wagons up the west bank to a point ... close to the kraal of Shonandala which is situated on the east bank of the river. ... seven miles south of the Sepuma [Chavuma] cataracts – beyond this point cattle may not be taken'.[12]

It seems probable that Sprinner, Monckts and Jacobs, who was accompanied by his two young sons, had travelled up from Sesheke by boat, possibly in company with Elie Susman. Their first expedition from Lealui was probably conducted by boat or on foot. Elie Susman's major input into the second expedition, apart from his own personal involvement, was the provision of two wagons. They must have set off from Lealui on the long journey to the north in the middle of August. According to J. H. Venning, the district commissioner at Balovale, their wagons were the first to travel up the west bank of the Zambezi and to cross the Lungwebungu River, a major tributary with its own flood plain. Travelling during the dry season, they were spared the possibility of floods, but must have had to contend with the Kalahari sands. The journey from Lealui to Chavuma was about 200 miles as the crow flies; it must have taken most of a month for wagons travelling through what was then uncharted territory.[13]

The only surviving narrative of what happened next comes from the record of the proceedings of the case of 'Rex versus Julius Monckts and Elie

Susman', which took place at Mongu on 15 December. This was Criminal Case number 34, 1908, in the court of the magistrate at Mongu-Lealui in the district of Barotse. Monckts and Susman were then charged with assault and occasioning actual bodily harm to John Jacobs 'on or about the 17th day of October at or near Lukosi'. The magistrate was the Susmans' old sparring partner, William Hazell – technically he was then 'acting assistant magistrate'. In an unusual departure from normal legal practice, Hazell acted as both prosecutor and judge. Both the accused pleaded not guilty. The Crown's case against them arose from a letter written on 8 December by John Jacobs to 'His Excellency the Right Honourable Resident Magistrate of Mongu'. His semi-literate letter, which is attached to the docket, suggests that he cannot have been a very competent secretary to Lobengula. The letter was his response to a civil action for theft, which had been brought against him by Sprinner and Monckts. The most interesting thing about the letter is that he clearly saw himself as a 'parner' – a partner in the venture. He was offended by the accusations made against him by his fellow partners. This case was heard as Civil Case 31 of 1908 in the Barotse District Court. The record of the case does not appear to have survived, but Jacobs was, presumably, acquitted.[14]

From Elie Susman's defence statement in the criminal case it appears that he did not accompany the wagons on their journey to the north, but that he travelled north by boat and joined the party at Balovale in the middle of October. It is, however, also possible that he had travelled up with the wagons and that he then made a quick return trip to Lealui. There is, however, no way that he could have reached Balovale from Lealui in five days, as is suggested below, unless he travelled by boat. It must be said that there is some confusion in the record about dates. It is not entirely clear whether the events described took place in September/October or October/November. According to Susman's statement the crisis point was reached some time in November, but the date on the charge sheet is 17 October.

Elie Susman's statement is reproduced below with the original spelling as recorded by William Hazell.

> Eli Susman one of the accused being duly cautioned elects to make the following statement:–
>
> On the 14th Oct. I left Lealui for the west [sic] to join the party and arrived at the wagons at Malovala [Balovale] on the 19th Oct. The next day we arranged to start off for their destination. Jacob was taken [taking] them to a place where Lobengula's treasure was buried. He said it was at the headwaters of the Lukosi River. We arrived at the headwaters of the Lukosi and outspanned near a village. Jacob said: 'We will find the place tomorrow, but we

have to make another trek till we come to some place where we can get water for the cattle.' When we came to the water I thought he appeared quite lost and that the whole affair was a swindle but he did not say so, he said 'we have another 15 or 20 miles to do and then we'll find the place.' Sprinnner, Jacobs and myself started off and we were away three days but came back to Lukosi with the wagons and after this Mr Sprinner and Jacobs, then I and Mr Sprinner and then I and Jacobs went out in all about 15 days but could find nothing. I believe we returned to the wagons about the twelfth of November. After stopping four days Jacobs said he could no nothing but he told me that he does not want to give it up to Sprinner and Monckts and he'll show me the place near a clump of trees and said 'here is the place where the ivory gold and diamonds are buried.' Then he took me to another place and said 'here is also something buried.' I tried to persuade him to open it but he would not have it. I went back to the wagons and told everything to Mr Sprinner though I personally did not believe in it. Then Sprinner Jacobs and myself took three boys and we dug for about three or four feet and found nothing. I then showed that it was all a swindle and that he [Jacobs] took me up there knowing absolutely nothing about it. I said to Sprinner if he likes he could dig some more but that I was going to have nothing more to do with it. Jacobs turned round and said 'You must give me a show, let us dig somewhere else and see if we can find it.' So Mr Sprinner said 'Mr Susman does not wish to go but I will go with you tomorrow, I do not wish you to say we did not give you every chance.' Next morning Sprinner Jacobs and 10 natives started off for the place, they dug up to three o'clock but returned with nothing. Mr Monckts was sick with fever. On their return Mr Sprinner and I told Jacobs to clear away from the wagons. Mr Monckts was so sick that he could not say anything.

As to the events, which led to criminal proceedings, John Jacobs's accusation was as follows:

Mr. Susman drove me away from the wagons one day last month (about 17th November) at Lukosi south of Mr Venning's camp at Nampama and then sent his boys to go and call me back, and when I came back flogged me. Mr Monckts gave me eleven lashes with a rhinoceros hide sjambok with his own hand. Mr Susman said 'I will not touch him he is an English dog.' Mr Susman called Kleinboy his servant to flog me. Kleinboi gave me 10 lashes. Mr. Susman then called Manoela and Manoela gave me 10 lashes. He called his Barotse boys to hold me but they did not wish to hold me. Then he told me to clear from the wagons saying 'if you dare to come back I'll shoot you, you dog.' Then Mr. Susman took my things and my children's, clothing, watch, portmanteau and two blankets. So I went without food till I met Mr. Venning and Mr. Venning assisted me. My children can witness to the same.

In cross-examination, Jacobs stated that he had declined to reveal the real location of the treasure as he had overheard his partners plotting to kill him after its discovery.

In his defence statement Elie Susman had described these events in the following terms:

> A few minutes after Jacobs left Monckts got better and he asked me to send for Jacobs. I told him he had gone. He said 'Tell some boys to go and call him, I want to give him a hiding and he deserves it too.' As Mr Monckts cannot speak the language I interpreted to the boys for him and those natives were all in Sprinner and Monckts' employ from Lealui. Even my own boys were paid by Sprinner and Monckts. When Jacobs returned Mr Monckts told me to tell the boys to take all his things and put them in the waggon. I did so and then Mr Monckts gave him 10 with the sjambok. After giving him 10 Mr Monckts collapsed and he asked me to take the sjambok and give him another ten. I said 'I would not dirty my hands with a dog like him.' So he asked me to tell Manoela to do it for him and I did so. And that was the finish.

The evidence of Julius Monckts tended to confirm Elie Susman's line of defence, which was that he had not flogged Jacobs, or instructed anyone to flog Jacobs, but that he had simply acted as an interpreter, a role that he had performed throughout the journey. The evidence of Monckts was as follows:

> On the 21st Oct we started from Mr. Venning's camp to the Balovale. Jacobs had orders to go with us to the Balovale, instead of going to Balovale he went up the river to the kaffir village. We waited, Jacobs did not fulfil his promises. Mr. Susman fetched him and he came. Then we came as far as he wanted us to and Mr. Susman asked whether I, Jacobs and Mr. Susman should go back and look for the treasure. They came back and afterwards I took no notice of the whole expedition. I never spoke to Jacobs any more. I declared to Messrs. Susman and Sprinner that it was all a swindle. I wanted to get back to Johannesburg as quick as possible as I am ruined. Mr. Susman said I should still stop a few days to give fair play. I got fever badly. Mr. Sprinner asked me to come and dig holes as Jacobs [said] that was certainly the place as the things were buried. I told Mr. Sprinner I would have nothing more to do with such nonsense. I told Mr. Sprinner to make a plan to inform the Government officials, so that if Jacobs ruined us he would not have the chance to ruin others. Afterwards we started with the wagons to come back to Lealui. I was very bad with the fever and I see Jacobs was leaving the wagons and I was awfully excited and asked Mr. Susman where Jacobs was. He said he was going away. I said if there was only a chance to get him back I would give him a lesson. So Jacobs came back and I jumped out of the wagon and took a small bit of a sjambok and Jacobs was laying down and I gave him a few lashes, I don't know how many. Everytime I hit him, it shook my head and I asked Mr. Susman 'it's useless for me to flog him it's like a match falling on my foot.' I asked Mr Susman to flog him he was a strong man and I thought Jacobs would feel it better. Mr. Susman refused it saying that he would not put his hand on such a dirty brute. So I spoke to a boy Manoela he did not understand so Mr. Sus-

man interpreted for me and than another boy came and Mr. Susman interpreted to him and I said these youngsters of Jacob are playing the gentleman yet and the natives laugh at the whitemen [*sic*]. I saw their things in their hand – portmanteaux – and I said to the boys 'Chuck them on the wagons' and as the boys did not understand Mr. Susman interpreted for me. Then I laid down we travelled further. I did not see anything of Jacobs till I hear Mr Venning had him.

Jacobs's two sons, Vincent and Antonie, Elie Susman's cook, Manoela, described as 'a Portuguese native', and Sprinner all gave evidence. Although there were some minor inconsistencies as to the details of who said what to whom, and who did what to whom, there was no real argument about the facts of the case. In his judgement, William Hazell took the view that the accused had committed 'an unprovoked and premeditated assault while they were actually in the commission of, or attempting to commit, a felony'. He rejected Elie Susman's defence. He held that 'the fact of his knowledge of the objects of the Expedition and the assistance he rendered in the search, proves him to have been one of the partners in the Scheme, and also a Principal in the assault, and not merely a servant or interpreter'. He felt that his view was borne out by the evidence given in the civil case to the effect that Susman stood to gain a percentage share in whatever was found.

In a gloss on his judgement, Hazell added that

a native acting under the order of his master and committing an unlawful act might be held guiltless himself as an irresponsible person acting under orders, but it is held that a responsible whiteman [*sic*] could not put forward such a plea in his defence, unless the unlawful act were committed under compulsion or bodily fear, and there is no evidence of the latter construction.

He seems to have been consistent on this point. No action was taken against Elie Susman's servants, Kleinbooi and Manoela, for their role in these events.

The accused were fined £10 each, or one month's hard labour in default, and were given twenty-four hours in which to pay the fine. The judgement seems fair, but Elie Susman was clearly unhappy with it. That is hardly surprising given his personal knowledge of William Hazell, the magistrate, and of the anti-Semitic prejudice that he had shown towards the Susmans, and some other Jewish traders, at Lealui. He had, it seems, conducted a vendetta against the Susmans and it is not improbable that he had prompted Jacobs's complaint against Susman and Monckts. E. Knowles Jordan, Hazell's assistant as native commissioner at Mongu in 1908, recalled many years later the interest that the case aroused at the time and his own view that Jacobs, 'an arrant scoundrel', had been given 'a severe flogging ... which, I have no doubt, he richly deserved'.[15] Elie Susman took the case on appeal to the newly constituted Appeal Court in Livingstone, but the appeal was rejected on 24 April 1909. According to Leopold Moore, it was 'notorious' that the appeal judge, Mr Justice Vincent, 'had never found the Company in default'.[16]

This detailed account of what happened, miraculously preserved in the Zambian Archives, leaves many questions unanswered. Where, for example, did these events occur? The main action took place in the vicinity of the headwaters of the Lukolwe River. It would be difficult today to find a more remote place in Zambia, or indeed in Africa. In 1908 it was most of two months' journey from Livingstone; even today it would take three days to get there from Livingstone in the dry season with a four-wheel drive vehicle. The headwaters of the Lukolwe River lie on the west bank of the Zambezi within fifteen miles of the northern and western boundaries of Zambia with Angola, north of the small lake at Chinyama Litapi, and south of the Kashiji plain. The place is so remote that government officials rarely visited it in the colonial period, and are even less likely to visit it today. To get there at all in 1908 was a considerable achievement, and to get wagons up the west bank of the Zambezi as far as Chavuma was an amazing feat. It could only have been done at the driest time of the year, but this was also the hottest time of the year. October was known among white settlers in colonial Rhodesia as the 'suicide month'. Daytime temperatures in the shade are likely to have been in excess of 100° Fahrenheit. This, together with the effects of fever, would have been enough to explain the frayed tempers of some of the main actors, though that is not to excuse their resort to violence.

Some interesting sidelights on the story come from the contemporary notes and later recollections of J. H. Venning who was the first district commissioner at Balovale. He took up his post and established the *boma* there in the second half of 1908, after spending some time as assistant to William Hazell at Lealui. He gave refuge to Jacobs and his sons, though they may also have been in his custody. According to the account which he recorded in the Balovale District Notebook in 1909, the treasure was said by Jacobs to consist of 'two safes of gold (money), two boxes of raw gold, one box of rough diamonds and a great quantity of ivory; altogether thirteen wagons came up loaded'. He noted that:

> After a prolonged search, the party found nothing, Jacob [*sic*] stating that he overheard plans they had made to kill him, and clearing to Portuguese Territory. Jacob insists that the treasure is here and that he would be able to find it – personally, I don't think there is any truth in the yarn; as natives that have

been here years declare that the first wagons to cross the Lungwebungu were Mr. Susman's, whose wagons this party brought up.[17]

In a letter that he wrote to the editor of the *Northern Rhodesia Journal* in September 1954, Venning recalled:

> I doubted at the time if Jacobs had actually been secretary to Lobengula, he appeared to be rather too young for it was about fourteen years after Lobengula's death. I had him in my office and questioned him. He seemed to know little about the country and in course of conversation he admitted that he had not come up with the treasure, but that he had met a driver in Matabeleland who told him that he had helped to bury the treasure and had described the locality to him in such detail that he felt sure he would be able to find it.
>
> Jacobs probably deserted the party because he feared he would be roughly handled if, unable to find the treasure, they found out that he had not been north, but had only heard about it.[18]

In his later memoirs Venning recalled that these 'Boers' did not know much about the country as 'they brought me a large dish of what they said were duck eggs and they had been using them to beat up in coffee in place of milk. They had rather a shock when I told them that they were crocodile eggs which could be found and dug up in hundreds at that time of the year.' He also recounted that

> on their return, quite disillusioned about the treasure, they told me that the people in the north were all cannibals for they had found numbers of human bones quite near to the villages. They did not know that the people disposed of their dead by putting them up on platforms in the trees. Vultures soon disposed of the bodies and as the bones dropped to the ground they were mostly eaten by hyaenas. It was quite possible that if one fossicked about one might come on a human bone.[19]

Venning's insistence that Jacobs had deserted the party and gone on his own into Angola is intriguing. There is not much evidence of that in the court proceedings, though Elie Susman did apparently go to get him back from a village up the river, and also suggested in cross-examination that Jacobs was in fact at a 'native village' ten miles away on 17 October. There are some other unexplained issues. The court record suggests that Elie Susman supplied two wagons, but there are three wagons in a photograph of the treasure hunters that was taken by Venning at Balovale. One of them may have belonged to a 'Boer', Rulf, who, like Elie Susman, was present at, but declined to participate in, the flogging of Jacobs. He is, presumably, the fourth white man who appears in the photograph standing on his own to the right. He seems to have vanished from the scene after this event. His

1 The treasure hunters, including Elie Susman, with their wagons on the west bank of the Zambezi at Balovale, 1908. Photo by J. H. Venning.

presence helps to explain Venning's recollection, fifty years later, that the treasure hunters were 'Boers'.[20]

Another curious angle on the story is the suggestion of Maurice Gersh, Elie Susman's nephew, that King Lewanika supplied an armed guard for the expedition. Sprinner did, apparently, have twenty-four 'Barotse boys' in his employment at the time, which King Lewanika may have provided as an escort. It is an open question as to whether the king was aware of the objects of the expedition, or whether he had a stake in it. There is no evidence to support the later suggestion that Elie Susman lost his wagons, though it is possible that he ended the day out of pocket to the tune of £500.[21]

What happened to the key players? John Jacobs continued to make a living of sorts as a source of information about Lobengula's treasure until his death over twenty years later. He was deported from North-Western Rhodesia on 26 January 1909, but returned in August 1917. On that occasion he came with a party that included Solomon Glass, a Jewish butcher from Pretoria, and three friends. The party included Bishop S. J. Brander, the leader of an African independent church, the Ethiopian Catholic Church in Zion, which was founded in 1904. It is possible that the Reverend John Jacobs, who was using this title in 1908, had been ordained into this church. Another member of the party was James Makue whose role was to recruit Glass for the expedition. This unlikely group travelled together by motorcar from the Transvaal, arriving in Livingstone on 24 August 1917. They must have been among the first people to arrive in Livingstone by this means of transport. The story then goes that Harry Susman spotted Jacobs in the streets of Livingstone, alerted the police, and also warned Solomon Glass about him. Jacobs was deported to Southern Rhodesia on 28 August 1917, leaving the country in the company of Bishop Brander and John Makue. He apparently assured the secretary for native affairs on this occasion that the treasure was to be found west of Lealui. This was the third time that Jacobs had been deported from either Northern or Southern Rhodesia. It was not, however, to be the last. After several further attempts, he was given a three-month prison sentence in Southern Rhodesia on 4 August 1922 for giving a false statement to an immigration officer. He was again deported. He was still talking about the treasure when Hedley Chilvers interviewed him in Johannesburg in 1930; he swore then that he was present when it was buried.[22]

What of the other treasure hunters – Sprinner and Monckts? Andreas Sprinner seems to have vanished from the records, but Julius Monckts makes at least two more appearances. He was, it seems, an incurable treasure hunter. In October 1910 he was charged in Johannesburg with receiving from Jack II, 'a Coloured person', six ounces of 'an unwrought precious metal' – an amalgam of gold worth £6.7.3. This was in contravention of Section 113 of Act 35 of 1908 of the Transvaal Colony. The outcome of the case is unknown, but he was clearly the victim of a police trap. Monckts died on 12 July 1935 in Johannesburg General Hospital at the age of sixty-nine, and was buried on the same day in a pauper's grave; he was described as Swiss, and as 'an ex-engineer and fitter'. He had been living in a corrugated-iron hut on the farm Grasfontein 240 at the Lichtenburg diamond fields. His estate was valued at £30.18.5. It included two water tanks, a digger's windlass, a digger's sorting table, a toolbox, some old underclothes, and £1.5.9 in a post office savings account.[23]

Monckt's major creditor was Dr S. M. Molema, a well-known doctor in Mafeking, to whom he owed £17 for treatment provided in 1933 and 1934. Dr Molema was the son of Chief Silas Molema of the Barolong tribe, a founder of the South African Natives' National Congress – the precursor to the African National Congress. Unlike the Reverend John Jacobs, he really was educated at Lovedale and in Scotland, where he graduated from the University of Glasgow with a degree in Medicine in 1921. He was also the author of *Bantu – Past and Present*. In 1949 he became the national treasurer of the African National Congress.

There is one more twist in the tale of the Reverend John Jacobs and Lobengula's treasure. It is now widely believed, and it was apparently common knowledge among Chartered Company officials, that King Lobengula did not die south of the Zambezi early in 1894. Instead, he may have crossed the Zambezi and died in the north, possibly many years later, while living with King Mpezeni, of the Ngoni people, in what is today the Eastern Province of Zambia. It is possible that John Jacobs's extraordinarily persistent attempts to cross the Zambezi were linked to this belief. The real object of his journeys north of the Zambezi may have been the discovery of King Lobengula himself.[24]

CHAPTER 6

From Sesheke to Livingstone via Palestine, 1909–14

The exclusion of the Susman brothers from the central Barotse plain may have been a setback in the short term. In the longer run it almost certainly did them a favour, because it compelled them to look to Livingstone and the newly opened Line of Rail for the expansion and diversification of their business. The railway had reached the south bank of the Zambezi at the Victoria Falls in 1904 and was extended northwards to Kalomo even before the completion of the remarkable bridge over the Zambezi in 1905. It reached Broken Hill, the site of the recently opened lead and zinc mine, in 1906. At that point the money ran out and the railway did not resume its northwards progress to the Congo until 1909. The first train crossed the Congo border in December 1909, though the railway line did not reach Elisabethville for another year. This last town became the centre for the development of the Belgian side of the Copperbelt – this preceded significant mining development on the Northern Rhodesian side of the border by a decade.[1]

The completion of the railway bridge over the Zambezi made the river-crossing at the Old Drift redundant. Coryndon decided to move the commercial centre six miles from the river to a healthier spot on the sand belt. The town of Livingstone was laid out in February 1905. By 1906 the businesses at the Old Drift had either closed down altogether or had moved to the new town. Among the first businesses to move was F. J. 'Mopani' Clarke's Zambesi Trading Association, the main supplier of goods to the white population; Clarke had reached the Zambezi in 1898. Leopold Moore was the last to move. Livingstone became the capital of North-Western Rhodesia in 1907, and of the united territory of Northern Rhodesia in 1911. It remained the capital until 1935 when it was replaced by the new town of Lusaka.

On Saturday 27 February 1909 the *Livingstone Mail*'s gossip column, 'Notes and Memos', announced that 'Mr. E. Susman (Susman Bros.)' had arrived in Livingstone from Sesheke on the previous Monday and that he left for Broken Hill on Saturday. He probably went there in connection with the supply of cattle to the mine, and to the contractors who were about to resume the construction of the railway. On 6 March the paper reported that a 'wire' had been received from Broken Hill to say that Mr Susman was laid up there with blackwater fever. It added optimistically, and surprisingly, that 'he has had several attacks recently so there is little danger'.[2]

Elie Susman may not have shared Leopold Moore's optimistic view of his state of health. The illness prompted him to write his second will – the previous one was written at Nalolo in July 1902. The new will, which was a more professional effort than the last one, was drafted on 1 March 1909, but was not actually signed until 7 March. The witnesses were Dr Dundas S. MacKnight, the Broken Hill doctor, and Joseph R. Rollnick, a Jewish trader who had been at Lealui in 1903 and had then worked his way up with the railway to Kalomo, Lusaka and Broken Hill. He was probably the first resident trader in each of these places and followed the railway all the way to the Congo where, at a later date, he was to be the Susmans' agent in Elisabethville.[3]

In this will Elie provided for the liquidation of Susman Brothers in the event of his death, and for the division of his assets between his parents, then at Jaffa (Haifa), Palestine, and his brother, Harry, whom he named as his sole executor. He also left £750 each to his married sister, Esther Deborah (Dora) Girchowitz (*sic*), then in Jerusalem, and to his younger brother, Oscar, whom he described as being 'at present on his way to South Africa'. He left £50 each to the Bulawayo Hebrew Congregation and to the Livingstone Hospital, and a total of £300 to the Jewish National Fund.

Palestine

The connection with Palestine, then part of the Turkish Empire, began in 1905 when Elie's father and mother had moved there from Riteve with their three younger children, Dora, Oscar and Marcia. According to family tradition, one of the brothers travelled to Europe in 1905 to persuade his parents to come to Africa. He failed in that objective, but the family moved to Palestine. It is unlikely that either of the brothers travelled to Europe at that date, though they may have tried to persuade their parents to come to Africa. Their emigration came in the wake of the Russo-Japanese War, and the First

Russian Revolution, events that were accompanied by renewed pressure on the Jews. The fear that their youngest son, Oscar, would be conscripted may have persuaded them to leave Russia at this time. Many years later, Leopold Moore provided a unique glimpse of the impact of the Russo-Japanese War on Jews in North-Western Rhodesia. He recalled that he had witnessed a fight over the war at Pieters's Bar at the Old Drift: '... a young Russian Jew burst into tears about a Japanese victory and a compatriot jeered. He was not enthusiastically pro-Russian since some soldiers had visited their village. The lad explained that the defeat would involve his brothers being called up.'[4]

Behr Susman (as he was later known) did not move to Palestine as a Zionist, but as a religious Jew who saw it as his obligation to live and work in the Promised Land. He did, however, take part in the Land Lottery on 11 April 1909, which allocated the first plots in the new town of Tel Aviv. A surviving photograph of this event shows a large crowd standing in the middle of the desert. He later built a house on this plot in Lillienblum Street, one of the first twenty houses to be built in the future capital of Israel. He and his family occupied the house intermittently until his death over thirty years later. It remained in the possession of the family until recently, when it was exchanged with a commercial bank for part of a property on the other side of the street. Lillienblum Street had, meanwhile, become Israel's Wall Street.[5]

The Susman brothers' sister, Dora Gersh, recalled the journey by camel across the desert from Jaffa to Jerusalem.[6] Oscar also spent time in Jerusalem where he attended a *yeshiva* school – a seminary. He did not complete the course, but chose to join his elder brothers in Africa. He reached Northern Rhodesia during 1909 and was to spend most of the next six years at Sesheke where, in the later years, he was often the only resident member of the family. It is possible that he spent some time in Cape Town studying English, he wrote the language more fluently than Elie. Oscar remains something of a dark horse, but he became a full partner in the business in 1914 and, by the time of his premature death in 1920, he had a substantial stake in it. He had a strong commitment to Zionism and his first-hand knowledge of Palestine made him unusual among Southern African Zionists.[7]

His elder brothers probably acquired their own interest in Zionism, as revealed by Elie's 1909 bequests to the Jewish National Fund, while they were in central Africa. Zionism was already well established in Bulawayo where the minister of the Hebrew Congregation, the Reverend Moses Cohen, was an enthusiast, though he tended towards the views of Israel Zangwill and was an advocate, in the early years of the century anyway, of a

Jewish National Home in Africa. Max Kominsky's daughter recalls that her father and Elie Susman were prepared to trek north in 1904–5 to take part in the ill-fated Uganda Scheme, which split the Zionist movement at this time and contributed to the premature death of its founder, Theodor Herzl. Elie Susman's son, David, doubts that his father would ever have contemplated such a move.[8]

Elie was, however, soon to make his own first journey to Palestine. According to the *South African Jewish Times*, he was one of the first Zionists to travel to Palestine from southern Africa. He left Livingstone on 4 May 1910 for Bulawayo, where he was expected to stay for a few days 'prior to his departure for Europe on an extended holiday'. The always well-informed *Livingstone Mail* understood that he intended 'visiting in a leisurely manner places of interest from Jaffa to St John's Wood, and we hope that he will have a good time'.[9] A couple of weeks before he set off on his long journey to Europe and Palestine, Elie Susman had one more near-death experience. It was not blackwater fever this time, but a brush with rapids on the Zambezi not far from Livingstone. His companion in this adventure, H. E. van Blerk, was an Old Drifter who had worked for A. and I. Pieters. He eventually moved to Lusaka where his descendants still farm.

> Messrs. Susman and Van Blerk had an adventure last Sunday evening which they will remember all their lives. They had been over to the south bank of the river inspecting some of the latter's cattle, and set off on the return journey about sundown in a small dugout with a crew of two natives. The current was strong and they got too near the rapids, but with the greatest difficulty they managed to negotiate them when the crazy craft bumped a tree stump and promptly turned turtle. One boy swam the rapids and landed. The two white men and the other boy managed to hang on to a small tree growing on a submerged rock, and for some time attempted to right the canoe, but without success. It was now almost dark and the prospect of clinging to that frail tree was not alluring enough to one of them, recently over an attack of blackwater, so they decided to chance the rapids and land further down. Stripped to the 'buff' they emerged dripping and shivering – they had left all their clothes hanging on the branches of the tree – and, the horses having cleared, they had to walk a matter of two and a half miles to the nearest kraal. There they got some blankets and dispatched a messenger to Mr Van Blerk's house for clothes. Their clothing and some papers and effects of value were recovered the day following, a big canoe with a strong crew being requisitioned. When we saw Mr Susman on Monday night he was apparently none the worse for an experience which might easily have been a tragedy.[10]

Not a great deal is known about the journey that took Elie Susman away from Africa for most of a year. He did not return to Livingstone until March

1911. Apart from the desire for a rest after ten years' hard work, frequent ill health and not infrequent exposure to personal danger, he may have been persuaded to undertake the journey by news of the illness of his sister Dora's Lithuanian-born husband, Rabbi Emmanuel Girshowitz. (The name was later changed to Gersh.) They had married in Palestine in 1905 and had two young sons, Moshe (Maurice) and Hirsch (Harry). Girshowitz appears to have contracted tuberculosis; Elie travelled with him, Dora and their children from Palestine to Vienna in search of the best doctors, but their journey was in vain. The patient died and was buried in a Vienna cemetery. Many years later, in 1937, Elie travelled again to Vienna with his wife and daughters. He was then disappointed by the decline of the city, which he had first seen at the height of its power as the imperial capital of much of eastern and central Europe. By the time of his second visit it had become the capital of a small country and was under the shadow of Hitler and the forthcoming *Anschluss*.[11]

On this visit to Palestine Elie attempted once again to persuade his parents to come to Africa. His father again refused, but decided to return to Riteve and the Russian Empire with his wife, two daughters and two grandsons, making that journey in 1911. Elie himself was unable to return to, or to visit, Russia as he had left the country illegally in 1896. It was not until 1913, with the prospect of war looming in Europe, that Harry Susman was able to persuade his parents to come to Africa. He then paid a visit to Memel in Germany, as he was also unable to enter Russia, and organised the departure of his parents and their family from there. His parents travelled separately to Cape Town, arriving on different ships in September 1913. Behr Susman made a quick visit to Palestine before setting off for Africa. The immigration authorities at Cape Town were reluctant to give permission for Taube Susman to remain permanently in South Africa because, they asserted, she was illiterate and 'of a poor type'. The authorities in Pretoria were more sympathetic and were impressed by an assurance from the Standard Bank that her sons in Livingstone were well able to support her. She was eventually allowed to stay, not permanently, but on a permit which had to be renewed annually. It is a reflection of contemporary attitudes that, in the section of her husband's immigration form, which asked whether he was European, Asiatic or African, the word 'European' was scratched out and replaced by 'Hebrew'. The Susman parents and their younger daughter, Marcia, Dora Gersh and her two sons all spent the war years in Cape Town. Marcia married Louis Rubinstein in Cape Town in 1915.[12]

A Public Profile

It was in the year or so before his long sabbatical that Elie Susman began to emerge as a public figure not only within the small Jewish community in Livingstone, but in settler society as a whole. Although none of the Susman brothers seems to have been permanently resident in Livingstone before 1912, Elie began to spend more time there following his enforced retreat to Sesheke from the Barotse plain at the beginning of 1909. In May of that year, he had represented the Jewish community in negotiations with the Livingstone Church Council on the reservation of plots for a future synagogue, involving an exchange of plots with the Anglican Church. The plots originally designated for the synagogue became the site of St Andrew's Church. The Livingstone Hebrew Congregation was set up in 1910 at the time of Harry Susman's marriage, which is described below. Elie was abroad at the time. It was to be nearly twenty years later that he laid the foundation stone for the synagogue, which was finally built in 1928.[13]

In April 1909 he took part in the founding meeting of the North-Western Rhodesian Commercial Association. Max Kominsky proposed and Elie seconded a resolution that the association should appoint a deputation to interview the acting-administrator about the delay in issuing permits for the purchase of cattle in Barotseland. He was a member of the deputation and some relief was obtained. In July 1909 the association met to discuss the introduction of copper coinage. The main speaker was F. V. Worthington, the secretary for native affairs, who said that this was the first occasion on which the administration had consulted the traders on an issue of policy. Elie supported A. B. Diamond in opposition to the proposal. Diamond maintained that the 'Natives' were then unwilling to accept any coin smaller than a shilling and that they preferred gold. Elie argued that it would be impossible to work with pennies, as the 'Natives' already refused silver. He thought that the introduction of copper coins would result in a rapid reduction in profits. There would be price-cutting and the loss would fall on the trader. Fishel Levitz argued that the 'Native' knew the difference between a trader and an official. 'He might not haggle with the latter, but he would not deal with the former unless the customary "bursela" [*basela* – something extra given by a trader on the conclusion of a deal] were forthcoming.' Resistance by traders succeeded in delaying the introduction of copper coinage until the mid 1930s. Even then it was said that traders priced their goods in three-penny units and were reluctant to deal in pennies.[14]

In October 1909 a public meeting was held in Livingstone to consider the composition of a public address to be presented to the high commissioner, Lord Selborne, on his forthcoming visit to the town. Elie was elected a member of this committee, which was chaired by Leopold Moore. The other members were A. A. Willis, a lawyer and farmer, J. T. Fisher, a clearing agent, and M. Bloch, a Jewish trader in Livingstone. In the following month Elie was a member of the deputation that presented the address. The election of Elie to a deputation of this kind implied recognition of the brothers' commercial success, and also represented a triumph for them over the anti-Semitism of the officials who had tried hard to clip their commercial wings.[15]

The Susman brothers were fully aware at this time, and later, of the value of good public relations. Elie's presentation of a challenge cup to the North-Western Rhodesia Rifle Association in January 1910 was a stroke of public relations genius. The cup became known as the Susman Cup and was awarded in subsequent years to the best marksman in the country. The visiting Duke of Connaught, son of Queen Victoria, presented a second cup later in the year, but the Susman Cup retained its premier status. The rifle association had been set up in 1908 as an informal voluntary reserve force. The *Livingstone Mail* described it in December 1910 as 'the largest and most important organization in the country' with a membership of 300 out of 600 white males. Elie Susman was elected a vice-president of the association a few months after this presentation; the president was the administrator, Lawrence Wallace. The other vice-presidents were all senior members of the administration: they included Lieutenant-Colonel John Carden, the police commandant and acting-administrator, his deputy, and F. V. Worthington, secretary for native affairs. Elie Susman was the only outsider in this group, which was drawn from members of the elite of colonial society. He also presented a cup to the Sesheke branch of the North-Western Rhodesia Rifle Association, which became the Northern Rhodesia Rifle Association in 1911. These presentations seem to have opened the way for Jewish membership of what had been in its first years an entirely Anglo-Saxon association. Harry Susman, Oscar Susman, who was a good shot, and two of their employees, S. H. Saperstein and Gabriel Epstein, became members of the Sesheke branch.[16]

It would, however, be a mistake to conclude that official anti-Semitism was a thing of the past. When a public meeting in Livingstone in February 1911 appointed a two-man deputation, led by Leopold Moore, to go to Cape Town to lobby the high commissioner against the levying of municipal rates, the administrator, Lawrence Wallace, wrote to the high commissioner to point out that 'The deputation to your Lordship was voted for by seventeen persons including several alien Jews who cannot be said to be representative either of the better element or even of a majority of Livingstone residents.' The meeting in question was attended by twenty-eight people. Ten of them, including Oscar Susman, were Jews.[17]

Two Marriages

The wedding of Harry Susman and Annie Grill in Livingstone on 26 June 1910 was the first Jewish wedding to be held in the country. It was also the first wedding of any denomination to be celebrated in style in the new town, and the major social event of the year, apart from those connected with the visit of the Duke and Duchess of Connaught in November. The wedding clearly did a great deal to raise the profile of the Susman brothers in a town in which they were just beginning to do business and had not yet come to live. It took place in the absence of Elie Susman, who was on his grand tour, but Oscar Susman was there. The greater part of the *Livingstone Mail*'s account of this event is reproduced below.[18]

> Last Sunday was a red letter day in the history of Livingstone, for the first Jewish wedding was not only solemnised but was also celebrated in a style that will long be remembered.
>
> By 2.30 o'clock the North-Western Hotel presented an animated scene. No less than 80 guests, in festal attire, thronged the verandah and, on the arrival of the bride, Miss Annie Grill, second daughter of Mr. and Mrs. M. Grill, entered the Assembly Rooms. Here, under a red velvet canopy, which was supported by friends of the happy pair, stood the Rev. M. I. Cohen, wearing a Jewish *Shashi* and a velvet cap. All, ladies and gentlemen, it should be noted wore their hats throughout the ceremony, which, being unfamiliar to most of our readers, we will briefly describe.
>
> The bride and bridegroom, the former wearing an elegant white Roman satin dress, beautifully ornamented with silver and pearl trimmings and orange blossoms and embroidered veil for headdress, and the latter, in addition to ordinary morning dress, a praying *Shashi*, stood before the rabbi, supported by the nearest relatives of the bride. The rabbi sang the prayer of Isaac when he met Rebecca in the veldt, and the usual questions having been asked and answered the bridegroom then affixed the ring on the bride's finger. Then followed more chanting in Hebrew and a glass of wine was handed to the rabbi, who gave it to the bridegroom, and he, having sipped it, passed it to the bride, whose veil had to be lifted for the purpose of partaking. The rabbi then addressed them on the foundations of the Hebrew religion and its relations with the family life of the nation. A wineglass, wrapped in paper, was brought in and the bridegroom firmly trod upon it, breaking it in pieces. A glass of

wine was again brought in and passed this time to the bride first and then to the bridegroom. There was another Hebrew chant and the marriage contract was read in Hebrew and in English, the ceremony concluding with the blessing of the rabbi.

Thereafter there were congratulations from all present and the guests adjourned to the next room where long tables had been spread with light refreshments and confectionery. Champagne was the only drink, and it was lavishly supplied. Everyone was in the best possible humour and it seemed as if all were talking at once. Presently the rabbi, seated at the bride, rose to propose the health of the bride and bridegroom. He said this was the first Jewish wedding to be celebrated in North-Western Rhodesia, but was sure it would not be the last. Many friends of both parties had come up by train from Bulawayo to be present and the day might not be far distant when the journey would be done by aeroplane. Livingstone, he was happy to see, was growing, and the country might so develop that it might yet become a suburb of Bulawayo. He, on this occasion, represented many friends in Bulawayo who would have liked to be present, but whose sympathies were to-day with their coreligionists. The country was rapidly being opened up and had progressed far since the day when the bridegroom first entered it as a pioneer. He (the bridegroom) had suffered many hardships, but had won through and was to be congratulated on his success. He noticed, with a professional eye, that there was any amount of material for future weddings. (Laughter). There were plenty of young men and women present and he exhorted them to do their duty by the State and play the game. The bride was one of a large family of sisters. He had the pleasure of celebrating the marriage of her elder sister a few years ago, and he was sure that the husband looked back to that day as the happiest in his life, and he felt certain the bride would make as good a wife. Marriage, like Mercy, blesses alike him that gives and him that receives, and he hoped that Mr. and Mrs. Grill would confer many similar blessings in the future. He wished long life and happiness to the young couple whose health he proposed.

The speech was punctuated with laughter and applause and the toast was drunk with enthusiasm.

Further speeches were given by Marcus Grill, the father of the bride, by F. V. Worthington who proposed the toast to the bridesmaids, and by Dr Aylmer May, the senior medical officer, by Leopold Moore and by Max Kominsky. A group photograph was taken and 'in the evening many of the guests returned and an informal dance was held, merrymaking continuing until the lights winked'.

The *Livingstone Mail* did not list the names of all those who attended this event, but it gave a detailed list of the wedding presents and the names of the donors. From this it is possible to reconstruct the mainly Jewish commercial networks of Livingstone and Bulawayo. It appears that rather more than half the people who attended the wedding, or sent presents, were Jewish and that half of them came from Bulawayo. These included representatives of most of the prominent Jewish wholesalers, the Landaus, Braudes, Pieters, Messrs Freedman and Grossberg, Jack Goldberg and Aaron Jacobs of the Matabeleland Trading Association, as well as another prominent Bulawayo trader and rancher who was not Jewish, Tom Meikle. Jacobs and Meikle were to play important roles on opposite, and not necessarily predictable, sides in a major crisis in the Susman brothers' business lives some years later. Among the Barotseland traders represented were A. B. Diamond and George Findlay. The Livingstone traders included Isadore Aberman, Max Taube, Paul Kopelowitz, who had begun to visit the town two years previously as a trader in giraffe's tails, the Jacobs brothers and Messrs Wersock and Peimer.

Harry Susman did not marry into the Jewish elite of Bulawayo, but he did marry into a very large family, which became centred on Livingstone and spread itself in the following fifty or sixty years through much of south-central Africa. His bride was Annie Grill, daughter of Marcus Grill. The arrival in Livingstone of Marcus and Faiga Grill with their ten children in the previous year had come close to doubling the Jewish population of the town and had made a not insignificant contribution to the size of its white population, which was still less than 200. The links between the Susmans and the Grills went back to Lithuania. Marcus Grill had run a mill at the tiny settlement of Medingyan not far from Riteve. According to tradition on the Grill side of the family, Behr Susman and Marcus Grill, who was ten years or so younger than Behr, had left Russia together in 1895, had worked their way through England to Cape Town, reaching Bulawayo together. Marcus Grill had remained in Bulawayo when Behr Susman returned to Russia. He had struggled to make a living as a small trader with a shop made from old planks and managed to bring his wife and the first five of his children out to Africa in 1900. The second half of his large family was born in Africa. He eventually kept a boarding house in Salisbury, but went bankrupt there in 1909. It was a loan of £200 from Harry Susman that enabled the family to move north later in that year. Marcus Grill then set up a small draper's shop in the town. He was not a great businessman, but he became a Livingstone character, noted both for the extent of his family and for his idiosyncratic use of the English language, displayed in frequent interventions at public meetings. He died in Cape Town in 1935, but his widow, Faiga, lived for another thirty years, dying in Bulawayo at the age of ninety-nine in 1969.[19]

Members of the Grill family remained in Livingstone for sixty years and made a varied contribution to the life of the town. Their most notable achievement was in the realm of the cinema. Marcus Grill opened the first open-air cinema in 1917. A more permanent, though corrugated-iron, structure, Grill's Kinema, was opened in 1919. His eldest son, Solly, and eldest daughter, Gertie, were responsible for the construction in 1931 of the splendid Capitol Cinema, which still stands in Livingstone's main street. It was designed for the showing of the then new 'talkies' and can seat 500 people. It was on the occasion of the opening of Grill's Kinema that Leopold Moore pointed out that the Grill family was not only capable of supplying the cinema with its proprietor, manager, projectionist, box office staff and ushers, but also with a very respectable audience.[20]

Gertie Grill had married Jacob Rabinowitz, or Merber, who was then working with the Susmans at Sesheke, in August 1909. Following their marriage, the Merbers had moved to Umvuma in Southern Rhodesia, but soon returned to Northern Rhodesia. Jacob Merber was then involved in a short-lived partnership with Solly Grill at Mazabuka, but this was dissolved early in 1914. He joined the British army soon after the outbreak of the First World War and was posted missing in action on the Western Front. At one stage he was reported to be alive and well and a prisoner-of-war in Germany, but he never returned to Africa. His widow remained a formidable presence in Livingstone for a further forty years. At the end of the First World War, she was trained in police work and may have provided Livingstone with a one-woman criminal investigations department. At various times she owned and managed a garage and a furniture factory, as well as the cinema.[21]

After their marriage Harry and Annie Susman returned to live and work at Sesheke, which continued to be the headquarters of the Susman Brothers business. It was not until after the birth of their first child, Joe, in April 1911, that they began to establish a home in Livingstone. It was probably during the visit of the new high commissioner, Lord Gladstone, to Livingstone in September 1911 that the baby was presented to King Lewanika. According to legend, he took the child in his arms and proclaimed: 'this child is going to be your trader. You can always trust a Susman ... The man who does not know Susman is not a Barotse.'[22]

It was not until the eve of the First World War that Elie Susman followed his brother's example and married. The *Livingstone Mail* clearly looked forward to another exciting Livingstone marriage when it welcomed the announcement of his engagement to Bertha Lewison, daughter of Mr and Mrs Lewison of Johannesburg, in April 1913. It commented: 'There can be no reason for a long engagement and we hope shortly to dance at his wedding.' The wedding did not take place until July 1914 and was then celebrated at the President Street Synagogue in Johannesburg, with a reception at the Langham Hotel. In the meantime, Bertha Lewison and her parents made a number of visits to the Victoria Falls Hotel and to Harry and Annie Susman's house in Livingstone. Fears of further delay must have arisen in May 1914 when it was reported that Elie had been involved in an accident at Kambove in the Congo. It was believed that 'a train or part of one' had run over his feet, injuring his toes. The reports of this accident were apparently exaggerated. His fiancée thought that this was a case of pre-marital nerves – or cold feet.[23]

The *Livingstone Mail* reprinted an account of the wedding from the Johannesburg *Star*. The bride's dress, indeed the three dresses that she wore at various stages of the proceedings, were described professionally and in great detail, but the account of the wedding lacked the vitality, personal interest and local colour of Leopold Moore's description of Harry's marriage four years earlier. Harry and Annie Susman were present, and performed the role of *unterführers*, but they may have been the only representatives from Northern Rhodesia. The Susman brothers' younger sister, Marcia, was a bridesmaid, but the main parts, including that of best man, were played by the bride's four brothers and three sisters. The newly married couple spent their honeymoon at Durban and the Victoria Falls.[24]

2 The wedding of Harry Susman and Annie Grill,
North-Western Hotel, Livingstone, July 1910.

Bertha Lewison was born at Ferreirasdorp, Johannesburg, in 1890. Her father was a pioneer of the Johannesburg Gold Rush and was then keeping a canteen or bar. He was described at the time of the engagement as 'formerly' of Londiiana (now Londiani), in the British East African Protectorate – now Kenya. He was, however, still running a hotel there in 1916 when Elie Susman sought permission from the authorities for a wartime visit to East Africa for himself, Bertha, their eldest child, Bruna, and her nurse, Miss Louise Brattle. Londiiana was strategically placed on another Line of Rail, the so-called Uganda railway, most of which lay within the borders of British East Africa. It was, at 8,000 feet above sea level, close to the summit of this great railway. It was less than 100 miles from Lake Victoria, 200 miles northwest of Nairobi and almost exactly 500 miles from Mombasa. It was in the 'White Highlands' of Kenya, and not far from Nakuru or Eldoret. Mr Lewison may have been one of a handful of Jews who were inspired to travel to Kenya after 1904 by Joseph Chamberlain's promise, and Theodor Herzl's apparent acceptance, of this area as the site for a Jewish National Home. The Lewison family did not have the impact on Northern Rhodesia that the Grill family did, but at least two of Bertha's brothers worked for the Susmans in Barotseland in the years following the First World War. They also maintained a presence in Kenya for many years.[25]

Livingstone and the Line Of Rail

It was not until 1914 that the two elder Susman brothers were permanently based in Livingstone. It was only in January 1912 that the advertisements for their business in the *Livingstone Mail* began to state that it was based in Livingstone as well as Sesheke. They had by then acquired stands and were in the process of building business premises in the new town's main street, Mainway. Their first move into Livingstone and the Line of Rail had come in July 1909 when they bought the premises and goodwill of George Smith's Pioneer Butchery and Bakery. They paid £850 for the business. Smith was a Scot who had also been involved in the Barotseland cattle trade. He had set up his Pioneer Butchery in 1906, but was drowned while trying to cross the Maramba stream on horseback in May 1909. The new business was a partnership with Fred Davis, who had been a butcher in the town for some time. Their butchery was dependent for cold storage facilities, as were the other butcheries in the town, on the North-Western Rhodesia Cold Storage plant. It had been set up by Paulings, the railway contractors, and was then taken over by the Chartered Company. The *Livingstone Mail* welcomed the

Susmans' move into the town. It noted that they intended to develop the business 'with their customary energy', and that 'they are, perhaps, the largest cattle owners in the country, and thus will be in a position, in a few weeks, to supply the finest beef procurable'. In their own advertisement the Susmans emphasised 'that no one in the country is able to compete with [us] in the supply of fat cattle, and that beef, of a quality hitherto unprocurable, will always be obtainable at current market prices'.[26]

Their partnership with Davis lasted until April 1910 when it was dissolved by mutual consent. The *Livingstone Mail* announced that Davis had left for the south and, in one of its cryptic asides, noted that 'considerable curiosity is being generally manifested as to his precise destination'. Susman Brothers took sole control of the business and the place of Davis seems to have been taken by A. Hirschberg. He was given power of attorney to run the Susmans' business in Livingstone during Elie Susman's long absence in 1910–11. The Pioneer Butchery seems to have had no serious competition until February 1910, when J. J. Hantche, described as an 'Ottoman Greek', a

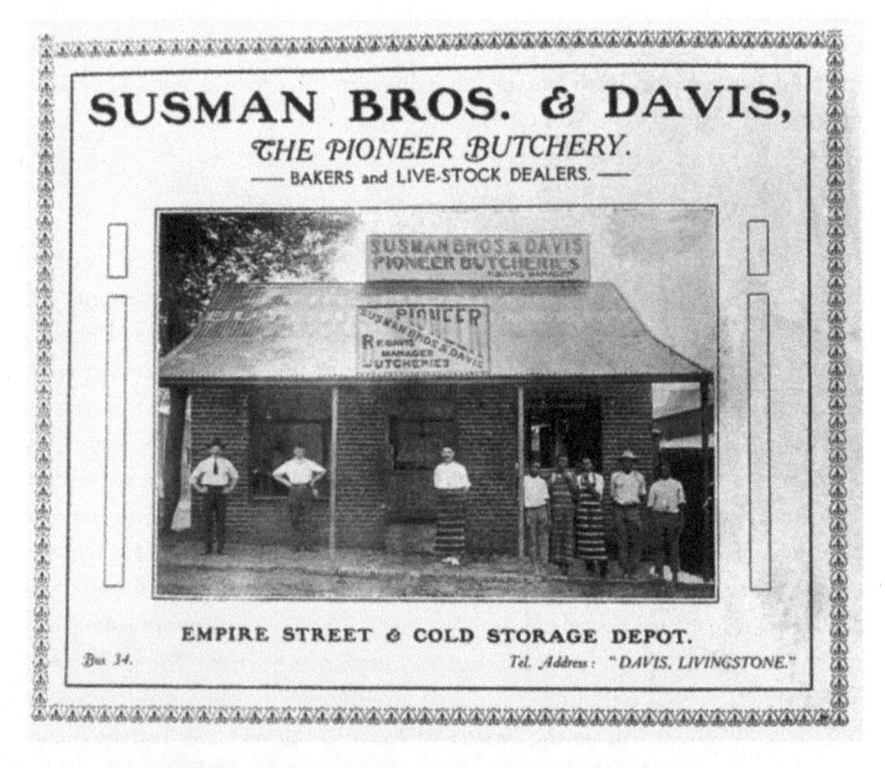

3 Advertisement for the Pioneer Butchery, Livingstone, 1909.
Harry and Elie Susman are on the left of the picture.

Greek from the Turkish Empire, announced his establishment of the Livingstone Butchery and Bakery.[27]

The Susman brothers' next venture into the butchery business was at Elisabethville in the Congo. Elie Susman travelled by rail to the Congo for the first time in July 1911, a few months after his return from Europe and Palestine. The object of his journey was to investigate the possibility of setting up a cold storage and butchery business there. This would help to create a market for Barotseland cattle at a time when the market in Southern Rhodesia had been under threat for two years. He returned to Elisabethville late in August 1911 and indicated before his departure that he expected that the erection of the firm's cold storage plant would be completed before the end of the year.[28] It is not clear whether this project went ahead as planned. In June 1912 Elie returned from another trip to Elisabethville and announced that he had taken over the Ullman brothers' butchery business there. They had been based at Kapopo, near the modern town of Ndola, and had run wagons between Broken Hill and Elisabethville before the completion of the railway; they had also been involved in the rubber and ivory trades. Elie then believed that business at Elisabethville had 'touched bottom', that it would 'speedily re-establish its credit, and that the period of depression will not be protracted for more than a few months'. The butchery business in Elisabethville was intensely competitive at this time. The Susmans' butchery remained open for some years, but seems to have closed down soon after the outbreak of the First World War. The most successful of the Congo butchers was Barnett 'Bongola' Smith who reached Elisabethville in 1911. He features later in this story as the Susman brothers' major partner in the Congo cattle trade during the 1920s.[29]

Farming

It was in 1909–10 that the Susmans made their first ventures into farming. One of these was to the north, and the other to the south of Livingstone. During 1910 they established their old friend from Sesheke, J. A. Chalmers, as manager of a farm, Lynwood's, which they acquired from the Chartered Company in Southern Rhodesia. The farm, actually two 'volunteer' farms, with an area of about 8,500 acres, was on the Gwaai River, about 100 miles south of the Zambezi. The farms were close to the Ngamo railway siding and were in an area, the Ngamo flats, which was used by Barotseland cattle traders for many years as a holding ground for cattle for the Bulawayo market. Cattle sales certainly took place there and were attended by the

Bulawayo ranchers and butchers. The Susmans seem usually to have had 1,000 head of cattle at the Gwaai, but this increased to 2,000 or more at certain times of the year, when they leased additional grazing land. Chalmers built a comfortable house on the farm and grew mealies, and smaller quantities of wheat and barley. He also produced butter there, which was sent north for sale at the Susman Brothers' butchery in Livingstone. In later years it was sold as 'Lynwood's famous' butter. Although he was originally an employee, Chalmers eventually became a partner in the farm, and seems to have taken it over on his own account during the 1920s.[30]

By 1918–19 the Gwaai River farm was threatened by the spread of tsetse fly and the Susman brothers sought to exchange their land there for a farm in an area that would be further from the tsetse belts. They were unable to exchange their land, but were offered a 50,000-acre ranch in the Bulilima-Mangwe District, not far from the Bechuanaland border in the vicinity of Plumtree. They undertook to buy this land in 1919, but they were unable to stock it before 1921 because of the spread of another cattle disease, East Coast fever. This ranch was named Brunapeg in honour of Elie Susman's two eldest daughters, Bruna and Peggy. The brothers kept up to 4,000 head of cattle on the ranch in the mid 1920s, but they sold it to 'Bongola' Smith's Congo–Rhodesia Ranching Company on its establishment in 1929.[31]

The Susmans' second farm, though it was probably acquired at about the same time, was at Bowood Siding, ten miles north of Zimba, in the Kalomo District of North-Western Rhodesia. This was about seventy miles north of Livingstone. The intervening area was thought to be unsuitable for commercial farming. While the farm on the Gwaai River was well placed for the Bulawayo market, the farm at Zimba was better positioned for the new market for cattle that was beginning to develop at Broken Hill and in the Congo. The *Livingstone Mail* reported as early as April 1909 that the future for the cattle market lay to the north. The farm consisted of about 5,000 acres and was placed under the management of a Mr A. Waters. Like Chalmers at Lynwood's, he produced butter, and also grew potatoes, onions and vegetables for the Livingstone market. Waters had passed through Livingstone in June 1910 with 200 breeding stock and 240 oxen for Bowood, where Susman Brothers were said to be ranching on a large scale. The Susmans' farming neighbours in the Kalomo District included the American, George Horton, who established the much more extensive – 50,000 acres – Lion's Kop Ranch at about the same time. Another of their Sesheke colleagues, George Buchanan, also began to farm in the same district, though on a smaller scale, at this time.[32]

The Susman brothers' most dramatic move into farming and ranching in the years before the First World War came in the Lusaka District where they negotiated in 1911-12 to buy land on the Luimba River, a tributary of the Chongwe River, and ultimately of the Zambezi, about forty miles south of Lusaka, in the direction of the Zambezi escarpment. This was the nucleus of Leopard's Hill Ranch. It was added to by stages, in 1914-15, and again in 1927, and eventually extended over 56,000 acres of rolling grassland and fertile soils — some of the most beautiful farming country in Zambia. The brothers had the choice of good farming land all along the Line of Rail from Livingstone to Broken Hill, and it took a good deal of research to find this stretch of land which was 300 miles north of Livingstone and several days' trek by wagon from the then unimportant railway siding at Lusaaka. They had wanted to establish a ranch close to the Line of Rail at Pemba, but were told by the administrator that they could not establish a ranch within twenty miles of the railway. At a later date the government's policy was to reserve most of the land within twenty miles of the Line of Rail for settler farmers and to push African peasant farmers beyond the twenty-mile line. Harry Susman recalled that he made his first visit to Leopard's Hill on a bicycle, and that on his way back he spent several hours up a tree waiting for a lion to clear off. The name of the ranch derived from the leopard-like shape of a neighbouring hill, but it continued to be famous for its abundance of lions until long after the Second World War.[33]

It is hardly surprising that the brothers' first manager at Leopard's Hill was better known as a big-game hunter than as a farmer. He was E. C., later known as 'Anzac', Mills, an Australian, who gave a succinct description of his arrival and of his first two years at the ranch — as well as a not entirely accurate, but plausible, report of the alignment of forces on the outbreak of the First World War.

> In July 1912, I took up the Leopard's Hill Ranch for the Susman Brothers of Livingstone. It was forty miles east of Lusaka. It was out in the wilds, and a fine bit of country. I took a couple of horses. It was amusing to see the natives running from their villages when I came riding along. The horse was a new sort of *nyama* [meat or game] to them, and they were afraid of them. In July 1914, I got three weeks leave to go to the lower Luangwa to do a bit of shooting. Had a good time and some good adventures. When I left the Ranch, things looked bad in Ireland. I got back to the Ranch on the 15 August. I met a Dutchman who said in the *taal*, 'There is War'. 'What, has it started in Ireland?' 'No, but America, England and France are fighting Germany, Austria and Russia.'[34]

Mills was, like many other settlers, determined to join the armed forces for action in German East Africa. It was not until November 1914 that he was able to achieve this ambition. He then took part in the Northern Rhodesia Regiment's long march to the northern border at Abercorn. Although the ranch was extended in 1915, there is not much evidence of activity there during the war, and it was probably not fully stocked with cattle until peacetime.

CHAPTER 7

Sesheke, War and the Barotseland Cattle Trade, 1909–31

Although the main focus for the expansion of the Susman brothers' business from 1909 onwards was on Livingstone and the Line of Rail, the core of the business remained the Barotseland cattle trade, and its headquarters remained at Sesheke. As the New Year began, the brothers returned to Sesheke and they were by no means despondent. On 1 February 1909, a day that they claimed as their joint birthday, they had a party for their friends at Sesheke, where they were famous for their hospitality to passing traders. The writer of the *Livingstone Mail*'s 'Sesheke Notes' provided a rare glimpse of the brothers relaxing with their friends during their bachelor years in Barotseland.

> Today being the anniversary of both H. and E. Susman's birthdays (they are 31 and 28 respectively) they invited all their friends to dinner, and as there are quite a number of traders passing through just now no less than fourteen sat down. After a most excellent repast the remainder of the evening was devoted to music. Songs were contributed by several of the guests, the gramophone filling in the intervals. Mr. Levitz, on the flute, and Mr. Epstein, on the violin, provided the instrumental portion of the programme, and quite a surprising amount of talent was brought to light. Toasts were numerous, and if good wishes count for anything the firm of Susman Brothers should prosper.[1]

The instrumentalists, Fishel Levitz and Gabriel Epstein, were among a number of Jewish traders whom the Susmans employed from 1907 onwards as they expanded their business to Lealui and, briefly, Nalolo. Fishel Levitz featured earlier as a pioneer of the Barotseland cattle trade. Gabriel Epstein was an Irish Jew who had moved to Bulawayo with his father in his youth. He joined the Susman brothers in 1908 and worked for them at Sesheke until 1911. S. H. Saperstein also joined at this time. He was probably British as he was able to write English well enough to become a contributor to the

Livingstone Mail. Among others who joined them in the years before the First World War were Shmerl Naparstock and M. J. Jacobs. Naparstock came from Lithuania, possibly Riteve, and remained with the brothers for many years as a cattle buyer in Barotseland and as a transport conductor in the Kalahari. M. J. Jacobs was a well-educated man who was almost certainly British. He was recruited as a clerk/accountant and performed the role of a manager, writing a fine copperplate hand and keeping meticulous accounts. He joined up soon after the outbreak of war, served in East Africa and with the Camel Corps in the Middle East. He ended the war as a captain and a staff officer in the British Army of the Rhine.[2] The Susman brothers also employed many Scots and Afrikaners as transport conductors and as cattle trekkers. Veterinary regulations required them to employ a white man to take charge of any herd of more than 100 animals. The brothers were fully prepared to entrust these herds to Lozi employees, and objected to regulations that involved them in what they saw as unnecessary expense.

The Coming of War

Germany finally occupied the Caprivi Strip in 1909. Captain Streitwolf arrived with a small force of soldiers in February and established his base at Schuckmannsburg, about three miles from the south bank of the Zambezi opposite Sesheke. His arrival ended the status of the Caprivi Strip as a no-man's-land, frequented by ivory poachers, outlaws and fugitives. Among them was the Greek Cypriot, Harris Johns, known as 'John the Greek', who had a long and colourful career in the border regions of North-Western Rhodesia, Bechuanaland and South West Africa, until his death in an affray at Sipango on the Mashi River in Angola in 1923.[3] The Zambezi at Sesheke became the front line between two competing empires. The British occupied the northern frontier region of the Bechuanaland Protectorate at about the same time and established a police post at Kasane opposite Kazungula. Both these occupations complicated the Susman brothers' trading relations with people in the two territories where trade had been unregulated. Their relationship with the deposed chief of the Tawana people, Sekgoma Letsholathebe, will be discussed in a later chapter.

In 1911 the Caprivi Strip was placed under civilian administration and Herr von Frankenberg replaced Captain Streitwolf. The new administrator had served for many years in the Cape Colony's survey department. He was said to speak English without a trace of a German accent. He not only was a customer at the Susman Brothers store, but also came over to Sesheke regularly to collect his letters from the post office. He was reputed to be a cousin of Count von Zeppelin, the inventor of the airship, and to be in regular communication with him. He was on close and friendly terms with the district commissioner at Sesheke, J. H. Venning, and with other members of Sesheke's small official population. He allowed them to hunt for hippo on the nominally German side of the Zambezi.[4]

In view of this relationship, it is not surprising that von Frankenberg was 'very put out' by the prospect of war between Germany and Great Britain in August 1914. The BSA Police intercepted messengers on their way to him from his superiors with news of the outbreak of war. He realised what had happened when Venning stopped his letters and, a little unkindly, his supply of malaria tablets. The occupation of the Caprivi Strip by the BSA Company Police on 21 September 1914 involved the capture of von Frankenberg, together with his sole white companion, Sergeant Fischer, and their removal as prisoners-of-war to South Africa. It also involved the first transfer of territory between the great powers in the First World War.[5]

'The Conquest of Schuckmannsburg', as described by the *Livingstone Mail*'s correspondent, possibly S. H. Saperstein, was conducted according to old-fashioned and gentlemanly rules of war. The BSA Police commander, Major Capel, crossed the Zambezi with another officer to discuss the surrender with von Frankenberg in the morning. They returned in the afternoon for the 'conquest' with eleven boats, a platoon of forty police and a Maxim gun. The arrival in Sesheke of the administrator, Lawrence Wallace, in a Ford motorcar on 4 October, after a journey of nine hours from Livingstone, was almost as sensational an event as the 'conquest'. This exploit, which was only possible at the driest time of the year, was not to be repeated for many years.[6]

Oscar Susman was the only one of the Susman brothers at Sesheke at this time. He was also the only one who became directly involved in the war, possibly encouraged to join up by his success as a marksman in the Sesheke and Livingstone branches of the North-Western Rhodesia Rifle Association. After a visit to his parents in the Cape, he joined the 2nd Rhodesia Regiment in Salisbury in August 1915. He served with his regiment in the East African campaign and was invalided out of the army at the end of 1916. He returned to Northern Rhodesia in January 1917 after treatment, probably for the after-effects of blackwater fever, at the Wynberg Military Hospital in the Cape. He worked in Barotseland between 1917 and 1919, but seems never to have recovered his health.[7]

4 Oscar Susman with paddlers crossing the Zambezi, 1913.

It was not until after the outbreak of the war that the Susman brothers made any attempt to get a licence to move back into the Barotse plain. Oscar Susman applied for a licence to trade at Lealui in October 1914. There does not seem to have been any objection to the application, but he did not move to Lealui, remaining in Sesheke until he joined the army. The Susmans were not entirely immune from the old prejudices or from pressure on their licence at Sesheke. The acting-assistant magistrate there contemplated the cancellation of their licence in February 1913 on the grounds that they had given credit of £20 to a 'Native'. He claimed that this was contrary to an endorsement on their licence and to a proclamation of 1908. He did not get much support from the legal department, which told him that there was no statutory prohibition against the giving of such credit. He was, however, told that he could warn Susman Brothers that the government disapproved of the practice and that its continuance might endanger their licence. These officials were probably unaware that in May 1912 Susman Brothers were owed a total of nearly £1,500 by at least twenty 'Natives'. The largest debtor on their books at that time was Prince Litia, who owed more than £750 – a substantial sum in those days. King Lewanika himself owed about £400, but part of that was an unpaid instalment for his purchase of their Sesheke store. Other debtors included the Ngambela or Sofie at Lealui and the Mulena Mukwae at Nalolo.[8]

The Barotseland Cattle Trade

Although the Susman brothers did not have stores in the Barotse plain between 1909 and 1916, they were able to get permits to buy cattle in the area. They continued to spend a good deal of time there during the cattle-buying season. At the end of August 1912, for instance, it was reported that Elie Susman had been detained in quarantine near Nalolo for fifteen days after the discovery of a case of smallpox among his, or his companion's, carriers. He was compelled to camp on 'a huge anthill' – probably a mound in the flood plain. Six weeks later, it was reported that 'he had come in from the Barotse Valley looking fit and well'.[9] The brothers also worked through partners and agents. The most important of their partners, and the largest cattle buyer in the valley in these years, was James, known as Jimmy, Dawson, a junior contemporary of George Westbeech who had been working and trading in south-central Africa since the early 1870s. After acting as secretary to King Khama, he had become close to King Lobengula, and was one of the few white men who did not leave Bulawayo at the onset of the rebellion in 1893. He remained at Bulawayo after the end of the rebellion, but moved north to Barotseland in 1906 and traded at Lealui and Kanyonyo. Other partners included George Buchanan and George Findlay. With their help, the Susman brothers continued to control at least half of Barotseland's cattle exports.[10]

Another of their agents was their former employee, Gabriel Epstein, who had a store at Nalolo from 1911. He was probably the only one of the Barotseland traders who lived in the plain with his white wife. Olga Hilda Crowngold came, as he did, from Ireland: she arrived at Nalolo as a bride of seventeen in 1912. Their first child, David, was born there with the help of the Paris Mission doctor and nurse in 1913. In later years, she described how the formidable Mulena Mukwae Matauka, elder sister of King Lewanika, arrived at her wattle-and-daub house at Nalolo soon after the birth of the baby. The Mukwae, who was already about eighty years old, did not come in her carriage, but in her royal barge dragged through the sand by oxen with bells ringing. She asked the teenaged mother: 'do you know how to bath the baby? I'll show you how to bath *petutu* [the little buck].' Soon after the birth of her second child, a daughter, Olga Epstein was advised by the Paris Mission doctor to leave the valley for reasons of health.[11]

From 1909 onwards, there were frequent interruptions to the cattle trade with the south. In the early months of 1909 it was estimated that 10,000 cattle were exported to beat a deadline for exports of 15 May. It was presumed that the administration imposed this ban in response to pressure from settler farmers in Southern Rhodesia. A veterinary officer from the south spent time in the north at this time. He made a visit to Sesheke, which was already thought to be the source of a peculiar fly-borne disease – later called 'Sesheke sickness'. There were outbreaks of anthrax in Barotseland in 1909 and 1910, which may have justified later border closures.[12]

The threat to the southern trade led A. B. Diamond to open a cattle-trekking route from Barotseland to the Congo in 1909. The demand for cattle was at the Étoile du Katanga Mine at what became Elisabethville. Government regulations forced cattle trekkers to remain within the borders of North-Western Rhodesia until they reached a border post near the Kansanshi Mine. The cattle trail followed a circuitous route in order to avoid tsetse belts, and passed close to the Christian Mission to Many Lands' mission station at Kalene Hill, in what is today the Mwinilunga District. Among those who drove 'mobs' for the Susmans from Barotseland to the Congo in the years before the First World War was George Sterling. He was a native of Vilna, Lithuania, who had served with the American army in the suppression of the Boxer Rebellion in China. He recalled the meticulous organisation and provisioning of these treks and the dangers that were encountered, including lions and wild dogs. According to one account, Harry Susman himself took cattle through to the Congo in 1913, and had problems with the Portuguese authorities in the process. The source of this information is not, however, a reliable one, and it is difficult to see how he would have had time to do the journey in a year in which he also travelled to Europe.[13]

The Susmans' business reached a pre-war peak in 1912. They estimated the total value of their assets in May 1912 at close to £60,000 and their capital at about £33,000. They owed over £20,000 in bills of exchange and on open account to a variety of people, including a number of Bulawayo wholesalers: the Matabeleland Trading Association, Landau Brothers, Meikle Brothers, I. Pieters and C. Salomon. They owed smaller sums to Mosenthals and to Dunnell, Ebden of Port Elizabeth, and W. Bolus of London. Their only debt to a bank was an unsecured overdraft of £2,000 owed to the Standard Bank in Livingstone. Their inspector noted in July 1912 that they were 'inclined to overtrade and their position must be carefully watched'. He presumably meant that their liabilities were too large for comfort – given the risky nature of their business. He may also have been referring to their tendency to expand and diversify their business at a rapid rate. In the following year the inspector referred to the problems caused by yet another closure of the Southern Rhodesian market and by the dearth of cash in Livingstone. In 1914 the inspector noted that the mainly Jewish traders of Livingstone were scraping a living, but not much more. There was a significant reduction in the capital employed in the Susman brothers' business between May 1912 and December 1914 – from £33,000 to £18,000. This reflected a general depression and lower cattle prices.[14]

The mysterious 'Sesheke sickness' had some adverse consequences for the business. The veterinary officer who investigated the disease in 1912 concluded that its source lay with their trek oxen, which had passed through fly belts and been infected with trypanosamiasis. They provided a reservoir of infection that could be transmitted, possibly by ordinary cattle flies, to other animals in an area where there were no tsetse flies. His efforts seem to have resulted in the elimination of this mysterious disease. In 1915 it was reported that there had been no cases for two years.[15] The Susman brothers had experienced a setback in November 1912 when the High Court judge, Leicester (later Sir Leicester) Beaufort, decided against them in what was seen as a test case with major implications for the local cattle trade. They had sued Ludwig Napoleon Papenfus, of Kafue, for his failure to honour a promissory note issued in part payment for six spans of oxen. They had previously used the oxen for two years on the road between Sesheke and Livingstone. According to the *Livingstone Mail*: 'the shabby and scantily furnished structure in which the High Court sits was well filled when the Judge took his seat. Nearly every cattle man in the country was present and quite a number of them were there in the capacity of witnesses.'[16]

Papenfus said that he had withheld payment for about a third of the cattle because they had died within a few months of purchase. His lawyer argued that there was 'an implied warranty' – that they had been sold with a guarantee that they were healthy. He argued that they were in fact fly-struck and suffering from 'Sesheke sickness'. A medical doctor, not a vet, testified that he had found 'tryps' in the blood of one of the dead oxen. The Susmans' case was that they had only guaranteed that the trek oxen were experienced and trained. They had not guaranteed, and could not guarantee, the health of working oxen. Their witnesses testified that there were no tsetse flies on the wagon route from Lealui to Livingstone. Their lawyer argued that the deaths among them were due to 'poverty' – the cattleman's euphemism for starvation – and to the hard way in which their new owner drove them. He also suggested that the oxen had been driven through fly belts on their way from Livingstone to the Hook of Kafue – a journey of 300 miles. In finding for Papenfus, Beaufort cited an English case involving the sale of infected milk.

The Susman brothers were liable to compensate the purchaser for the loss of the cattle, whether or not it was possible for them to have known in advance that they were infected. The *Livingstone Mail* advised its readers that in future people selling cattle would have to require buyers to sign a declaration that they were buying without warranty, 'implied or expressed'.[17]

Bovine Pleuro-Pneumonia – The 'P.P.' Crisis

The Barotseland cattle trade continued to suffer from periodic closures, and was also affected by the collapse of the Congo market following the outbreak of the First World War. As early as February 1915, John Smith, the young vet who had been at Sesheke in 1913–14, told his parents that: 'The outlook for our market is rapidly getting worse. Yesterday, movements of cattle were stopped from Northern Rhodesia to the south, whilst the Congo market is almost non-existent, as most of the Belgians have left to go back to Europe, and those remaining are almost bankrupt. So the outlook for our traders is grim.'[18]

A few months later, a further blow fell when it was discovered that bovine pleuro-pneumonia, lung sickness, or the *snotsiekte*, had broken out in Barotseland. There was much debate as to how lung sickness, known colloquially as 'P.P.', was introduced into Barotseland. It was generally agreed that it came in from Angola and that that there was a link with the Anglo-Portuguese Boundary Commission that was drawing the boundary with Angola on the west bank of the Zambezi in 1914.[19] One of the explanations involved the Susmans. It was said that they had sold some spans of oxen to King Lewanika who hired them to the Boundary Commission. It had taken them into Angola and had been allowed, by an inexperienced junior official, to bring them back into Northern Rhodesia. J. H. Venning had another, and perhaps more convincing, explanation which also involved the Commission. He explained that the demarcation of the boundary led Lozi cattle-owners, including King Lewanika, to withdraw large numbers of cattle from Angola, where the disease was endemic, into Barotseland. According to Venning, the disease broke out in cattle on the west bank of the Zambezi in the Lukona, later Kalabo, District in September 1914, but this was not known to officials until March 1915. Meanwhile, King Lewanika, Chief Kalonga and other large cattle-owners, had suffered large losses. Venning said that the owners, knowing of the infection, sold cattle cheaply to traders who may, or may not, have been aware of the risk. He thought that the spread of the disease could have been stopped if there had been a veterinary officer stationed in Barotseland, and if action had been taken to prevent the movement of cattle from the west bank of the Zambezi. He also believed that the Lozi authorities would have co-operated with a scheme for the eradication of the disease by the killing of infected animals if compensation had been offered, but the Chartered Company was not prepared to pay.[20]

The view that Barotseland traders knowingly bought infected cattle and drove them south was also expressed, or implied, by the *Livingstone Mail*. It criticised them for their ignorance of cattle matters and blamed them for the spread of the disease to the Line of Rail. Gabriel Epstein disputed this view. He said that Barotseland traders might buy old, middle-aged or young stock if the price was right, but that they would not buy sick stock. He pointed out that 'the average trader in Barotse practically lives with his cattle'.[21] It was not until late April 1915 that news of the outbreak reached the administrator in Livingstone. He despatched the chief veterinary officer, A. J. Lane, to Barotseland early in May. Lane did not reach Mongu until June and then launched an inoculation campaign, which was administered by incompetent temporary stock inspectors and caused so many deaths that it set back the cause of inoculation, and of the Veterinary Department, among the Lozi for twenty years.[22]

Meanwhile, John Smith identified cases of 'P.P.' in cattle at Senkobo, on the Line of Rail north of Livingstone, on 8 May. Cases were soon afterwards found in trek oxen at Livingstone and in some cattle as far north as Kalomo. Smith immediately took steps to stop all cattle movements for trade and transport. He quarantined Barotseland cattle where they were and embarked on an energetic campaign of inoculation and slaughter. He eventually succeeded in his twin objectives of driving the disease out of the Southern Province and of preventing its spread to the large Ila cattle herds. The ban on ox-wagon transport caused considerable hardship in some areas of the Southern Province, which were dependent on it for the movement of grain supplies.[23]

John Smith was sympathetic with the traders. He wrote to his parents on 15 May:

> The traders whose cattle have been stopped are in a bad way, and I feel very sorry for them. They buy all their supplies 'on tick' and depend on selling their cattle as soon as they arrive down south to pay these bills. Now, the cattle are stopped and many may die, so there will be no funds to meet these commitments.[24]

Elie Susman was not in the country when the crisis broke. He left Livingstone with his new wife for Lynwood's, the Gwaai River farm, in the first week of April, and was away until 19 June. It must have been clear from the second week in May that the business was facing a major crisis, and it is surprising that Elie did not return at once. It is even more surprising that Susman Brothers had bought nearly 2,000 of the cattle in quarantine at Senkobo by 16 June. The firm had bought all but one of the herds that had been brought down by the Barotseland traders – Diamond, Dawson, Antonopoulos, Harrington, Epstein, Eden and Bennett. John Smith himself expressed considerable surprise at their action. He noted that 'this firm has made many complaints about our enforcing white supervision of their herds. These complaints had been made on the ground of expense and yet Messrs. Susman have not hesitated to purchase further herds well knowing that disease was in the Area and that the cattle were suspects.'[25] Robert F. 'Katombora' Sutherland recalled many years later that the Susmans bought 'infected or suspect' cattle at this time. Sam Haslett told him that he had met Harry Susman on the Machili River at this time, Haslett had 600 head of cattle and Harry offered him a price for the lot. Haslett claimed, somewhat improbably, that 'by evening they were all dead'.[26]

There are several possible explanations for the Susman brothers' actions at this time. They may have had a legal, or at least moral, obligation to buy cattle that had been brought down for them by business partners such as Dawson, Epstein and Buchanan. It is also possible that they bought at a heavy discount, and gambled on the survival of a proportion of the cattle. Another possibility is that they bought the cattle at a very low price for the value of their hides. Family tradition suggests that they survived the crisis through the purchase and sale of hides. Sutherland later recalled that 'at the height of the epidemic the country reeked of dying cattle. Boats and barges which had once been piled high with merchandise went hurrying down the river piled high with hides.' The Veterinary Department laid down strict regulations governing the purchase, packing and shipment of infected hides.[27]

Elie Susman's first comment on the crisis came in a long letter to the *Livingstone Mail* that he wrote on 24 June – less than a week after his belated return from the Gwaai. He argued against slaughter without compensation, and was confident that a market could be found for the infected cattle in the Congo and locally 'as neither the disease nor the inoculation is detrimental to the cattle for slaughter purposes'. He concluded that:

> It is only right that the whole question should be dealt with in such as way as to ensure the safety of the cattle not yet infected and also to lighten the burden of those unfortunates whose losses are not only already heavy, but who are bound to lose considerably in the future, to say nothing of the large extra

expense to which they have already been put in their efforts to prevent the disease from spreading.[28]

He does not appear to have included himself among the 'unfortunates'. His proposals seem to be sensible and one of them, that all suspect animals should be branded, had already been made by John Smith and was implemented. His suggestion that the quarantine area should be enlarged so as to provide adequate grazing was an important one, though it does not seem to have been accepted. In January 1916 it was reported that the Susman brothers had lost 800 cattle since the crisis began and that at least half of them had died of 'poverty'. At a public meeting with Sir Leander Starr Jameson, of the Chartered Company, later in the month, the administrator pointed out that Elie Susman had been reluctant to drive his cattle back towards the Machili from Senkobo because he believed that he could sell them to the Congo market. Elie did not dispute this point and appears to have agreed that an extension of the quarantine area would make the disease more difficult to control.[29]

The surviving accounts of the Susman Brothers business provide little evidence for the impact of this crisis. The Standard Bank's inspection reports do not suggest that the bank was initially concerned by its impact on one of its Livingstone branch's most important customers. In a report dated 30 June 1915, the inspector wrote:

> Business generally in Livingstone and throughout the Territory is at a low ebb and prospects appear gloomy. The recent outbreak of cattle disease has greatly accentuated the depression caused by the war, and the effects of this combination of disasters will be felt probably for years to come. ... Our own advances appear to be safe at date and the important liabilities – Susman and others – are being satisfactorily reduced.[30]

A year later their inspector reported that the cattle trade with the south was still closed, but that cattle could be taken to the northern border, slaughtered there, and exported as beef to the Congo. Of Livingstone, he reported: 'Local business remains dull, the position of traders having often been seriously affected by losses in cattle ... a despondent feeling prevails among the few shopkeepers of the place.'[31]

It was probably at this time that the Susmans experienced real financial difficulties. About a year after the crisis broke, the brothers were summoned to a meeting of their main creditors, the Bulawayo wholesalers. According to Hubert S. Whitehead, an old Barotseland trader, it was Aaron Jacobs, of the Matabeleland Trading Association, probably the Susmans' largest single creditor, who initiated this move. Writing to Elie Susman forty years later, he recalled: 'I don't think you ever knew that when you came down to Bulawayo in 1913 or 1914 [*sic*] to pacify your creditors (after the cattle sickness in Barotse) Old Aaron Jacobs – M.T.A. for whom I worked – hid me within earshot to take down notes of that Meeting. Well, you made good...'.[32] According to Susman family tradition, and Robert Sutherland's account, it was Tom Meikle, of Meikle Brothers, also one of the principal creditors and a major buyer of Barotseland cattle, who saved the day. Elie Susman recalled that the meeting was going badly when Meikle walked into the room and said: 'you can't break these boys. They're workers. They must have another chance. They'll come out on top if they get another chance.' He apparently backed up his words with a substantial cash advance. Elie Susman later recalled that they lost 5,000 head of cattle to 'P.P.'. This seems improbable, but their total losses over five or six years may have run to several thousand head, and a great deal of capital was tied up for a long time in immovable stock.[33]

The brothers had moved quickly to tighten their belts. They stopped their regular advertisements in the *Livingstone Mail* in May 1915 and did not resume them again until the end of the war. Elie Susman negotiated with Prince Litia in July for a reduction in the rent payable for their Sesheke store, saying that they were unable to pay because of the crisis. Litia agreed to a reduction until the end of 1915. He seemed at first to be reluctant to extend it beyond that date, but it is probable that the matter was resolved amicably. Harry Susman seems to have returned from Livingstone to live with his wife at Sesheke at this time. This may also have been an economy measure, though it enabled him to keep a closer eye on the Barotseland business.[34]

The 'P.P.' crisis was not only a major setback for the Susman brothers' business. It was also a major blow to the economy of Barotseland. The cattle trade had been the backbone of the economy since 1900 and was the main source of income for the payment of tax as well as for the purchase of goods. Cattle stocks were reduced by between one-third and a half, and lung sickness became endemic among those that remained. Labour migration increased dramatically from 1916 onwards as people sought alternative means of generating income for these purposes. The royal family and the aristocracy were particularly hard hit by the closure of the trade; their dominant position in Bulozi was seriously threatened. King Lewanika died at the height of the crisis in February 1916 at the age of seventy-four. His funeral was a great event and was attended by thousands of his subjects, as well as by officials, missionaries and traders. Prince Litia succeeded King Lewanika as Litunga, with the title of Yeta III, and moved up from Sesheke to Lealui. His brother, Imwiko, succeeded him in the Mwandi chieftaincy at Sesheke. The Susman brothers continued to maintain close personal and business links with both these rulers. Imwiko built up a substantial debt to the Susmans at this time, which was only gradually paid off by his brother, Yeta III, in the 1920s.[35]

None of the Susman brothers had been present at King Lewanika's funeral. It was only later in 1916 that they were able to get licences to re-open stores at Lealui and Nalolo. Elie Susman opened the store at Lealui himself. The Nalolo store was in the hands of a manager, but Oscar Susman moved there in July 1917, soon after his return from the war, and remained there for most of the next two years. The Susmans and other traders campaigned for the re-opening of the Barotseland cattle trade at the earliest opportunity. Harry Susman provided the *Livingstone Mail* with a glowing, and clearly over-optimistic, account of the condition of cattle in the valley in January 1916. He said that he had seen thousands of head of cattle in the Lueti (perhaps Liachi), Nalolo, Lealui and Lukona Districts and 'never before have they appeared in better condition'. He reported that 12–13,000 head had died from 'P.P.' before the beginning of the inoculation campaign. A few were still dying, but they were 'nothing worth mentioning'.[36]

In addition to the cattle that they had in quarantine on the Line of Rail and at Sesheke, the Susmans were left with nearly 1,000 cattle at various places such as Lealui, Lukona and Lukulu, which they were unable to sell between 1915 and 1918. They were given permission to concentrate their holdings at Senanga after re-inoculation late in 1917. After a meeting between Elie Susman and the administrator, Lawrence Wallace in June 1918, they were given permission to bring them down to the Line of Rail for export to the Congo. The cattle travelled south in two batches but 'P.P.' broke out in one batch at the Machili, and the cattle were quarantined there. The second batch had to return to Senanga. Permits were issued for cattle-buying in the valley and at Sesheke late in 1918, and there were exports from Barotseland to the Congo in 1919, 1920 and 1921. The Barotseland cattle trade to the south and to the Congo was finally closed in January 1922 after outbreaks of 'P.P.' among Barotse cattle in Livingstone, and among stock supplied by the Susmans to their partner, 'Bongola' Smith, in Elisabethville.[37]

The Susmans maintained their dominant position in the Barotseland cattle trade during the three years that the trade was, with interruptions, re-opened. Their position in the reduced trade was then stronger than ever because of the withdrawal of many traders from Barotseland after the initial outbreak of 'P.P.'. Gabriel Epstein went bankrupt after a mysterious fire at his store at Nalolo in October 1915 but was apparently enabled to open up again in Southern Rhodesia with the help of a bonus from the Susmans. George Findlay also went bankrupt in 1915. A. B. Diamond withdrew to his farm, Diamondale, near Lusaka, where he died in 1918. He had been fined £100 for a minor breach of the regulations on cattle movements in 1915. He was unable to pay the fine and was briefly imprisoned. The Susmans' one-time partner, Jimmy Dawson, got into financial difficulties as a result of the collapse of the cattle trade, and died tragically at the age of seventy at Kanyonyo in 1921. Many other traders left to join the armed forces during the war and only a few of them returned. The only cattle trader who provided the Susmans with any serious competition in the post-war period was the Greek, George Antonopoulos, who lasted through the 1920s, but died in 1929, leaving large debts to Landau Brothers.[38]

There was a good deal of opposition to the re-opening of the Barotseland cattle trade from settler farmers on the Line of Rail, and there were frequent debates about the issue at the meetings of the North-Western Rhodesian Farmers' Association. They were alarmed by the threat of the disease spreading into their areas, but they also sought to capture the Congo market from the Barotseland traders. The Susman brothers were traders and ranchers and so had an interest in both camps. They knew that the farmers would be unable to meet the demand from the Congo on their own and that there was still a need for an additional source of supply.

It was in the immediate post-war period that the Susmans were first accused of having a monopoly of the Barotseland cattle trade. Their accuser was Tom King, a Mazabuka farmer, and the former partner of H. C. Werner. He accused them of being able to use the quarantine regulations to block access for other traders to the rail transport that was now used for the Congo market. The *Livingstone Mail* suggested that he was acting as a mouthpiece for others. B. C. 'Rooi' Labuschagne wrote from Barotseland in the Susmans' defence:

> My employers Messrs. Susman Brothers seem to be the only old traders that have got any mettle left in them. Why don't these 'grumblers' take a sporting chance and employ agents to buy for them, or even better, come to Barotse and buy for themselves? 'Big capital is wasted on this outfit.' The field is open to all runners, and a good field too, without handicapping. Is all the sporting spirit dead in Northern Rhodesia?[39]

George Antonopoulos, with William Dempster, made a dramatic attempt to find a new outlet for Barotseland cattle to the north in 1922. He investigated a route from Barotseland to the diamond mines that had recently opened at Dundu in the northeast of Angola. He delivered the first batch of cattle to the Angolan mines in 1923. The Susmans entered the trade in the following year in partnership with George Buchanan, a Highland Scot from Argyll, and an old associate from Sesheke. In the three years that they were involved in this trade they exported well over 5,000 cattle from Barotseland to northeastern Angola – about half of the total exports. In 1925–6 they employed E. C. 'Anzac' Mills, their former Leopard's Hill manager, as their main cattle trekker. He has left a vivid account of the difficulties involved in trekking cattle over a route of 1,000 miles. He travelled up the east bank of

5 Elie Susman crossing the Lualaba River, in the Congo en route to Angola in a Morris Commercial truck, 1927.

the Zambezi with over 2,000 head of cattle. He had to swim the cattle across eighteen rivers, including the fast-flowing Kabompo, the Zambezi and the Kasai. He was proud of the fact that he managed to get the cattle through with only small losses. It was reported that George Buchanan spent nine months on one of these journeys. There were frequent problems with the Portuguese authorities and Elie Susman had on one occasion to travel into Angola to rescue Buchanan. The latter returned from the first of his trips in July 1925 by way of the Congo, but set off again for Angola with his family almost immediately. Prices paid for cattle at this time were low and the Litunga himself complained that Antonopoulos paid no cash for them.[40]

Trekking beasts to Angola proved to be the last gasp of the Barotseland cattle trade. After the closure of the Angolan market in 1926, there was to be no revival until the late 1930s, when the government embarked on a plan, with the co-operation of the Lozi authorities, to eradicate 'P.P.'. In the absence of a sustained level of cattle exports, the Susmans' business in Barotseland became dependent for survival on a variety of other activities. Government contracts for the supply of grain were important to them, as was the purchase of hides, skins, ivory, hippo teeth, hippo strips and curios. They also became increasingly reliant, as did their competitors, on store trade and the supply of goods to returning labour migrants. They obtained a licence for a store at Kanyonyo, the trading area at Mongu, in 1919. This was in addition to their Lealui store, which they soon transferred to Fishel Levitz.[41]

Mongu-Kanyonyo

The main role of the store at Kanyonyo in the eyes of the administration was to supply the official population with 'white man's' provisions. The Susmans' first manager at Kanyonyo was Jack Lewison, Elie Susman's brother-in-law, who was at Mongu with his wife in time for the Armistice Day celebrations in 1919. He remained in Barotseland until 1924. The administration was not pleased with the service that he provided: the Barotseland Annual Report for 1920–1 included the comment that:

> Messrs. Susmans' licence at Kanyonyo was granted upon condition that sufficient supplies of European goods should be maintained at prices to be approved by the Resident Magistrate; during the year stocks have not been at all well maintained, and of many articles the quality has been very inferior. The conduct of the firm's manager in Barotse District has given rise to some dissatisfaction, and he has only been allowed to remain under strict caution as to his future behaviour.[42]

Susman Brothers did better in the following year when it was reported that they had built 'a large and improved store of green brick with corrugated iron roof'. This was the first substantial building to be erected at Kanyonyo. Known then, and for many years afterwards, as 'Mongu Number 1', it survives until today as part of what grew into a large compound. Lewison was transferred to Nalolo and was succeeded as manager at Kanyonyo by A. L. Gesowitz who spent most, if not all, of the decade in Barotseland. He was clearly well rewarded for his work: on his return from a trip to Europe in 1928, he donated a silver cup to the Barotse Rifle Association and two spoons to the Kambili Golf Club. It was reported in 1930 that the Kanyonyo store 'caters for European as well as native trade. It is well stocked and ably managed and is a great boon to the white community.' By then the impact of the Great Depression was beginning to be felt, and traders had resorted to a variety of tactics to improve business. Some were offering biscuits as a *basela* to their customers. Messrs Shelton and Whitehead had opened a cinema at their store and had daily film shows for 'Native' patrons, and weekly ones for the white population. Whitehead was also the agent for R. F. Sutherland Ltd and, according to the ecologist Colin Trapnell, was the only trader who was socially acceptable to colonial officials.[43]

Although the Susman brothers made strenuous efforts to maintain the Barotseland cattle trade and their position as traders in Barotseland, their attention was increasingly diverted from 1916 onwards, as will be shown in succeeding chapters, to Ngamiland, the Congo and the Line of Rail. They continued, however, to make regular visits throughout the 1920s to their Barotseland interests. In 1920, for instance, Elie Susman took a ten-day trip, by boat, to Sesheke. He was pleased with the work of the manager there at the time, J. A. Frost, who went on to work in the Ngamiland business. Smerl Naparstock was still at Sesheke and was acting as a cattle buyer. On this visit Elie did not meet Chief Imwiko, though he did have a meeting with one of his councillors, 'Ishenakoma', and sorted out matters relating to the 'camp' with him.[44]

The brothers' visits to Barotseland were less frequent after the ending of cattle exports to the south, though Harry Susman spent three months in 1925 travelling with his family to Sesheke and Lealui. In August 1930 Elie Susman made his first flight to Barotseland – the first plane had landed at Lealui in the previous year. He flew with Captain Roxburgh Smith of the Rhodesian Aviation Company, the plane landed at Schuckmannsburg to refuel and then touched down at Lealui. He spent a week at Lealui-Mongu-Kanyonyo and met a number of old friends – almost certainly including his old associate, Prince Litia, now the Litunga Yeta III. This was to be his last visit for many years. Less than a year later, in May 1931, an advertisement in the *Livingstone Mail* announced that 'Susman Brothers have decided to liquidate their Barotse business and have instructed their manager at Kanyonyo to sell it as a going concern or to dispose of all their Barotse stock in trade, buildings etc. to best advantage.' In July they sold the business to P. C. Nicolai. He was an Englishman of German descent who had been in business in Barotseland, firstly at Sesheke, and latterly at Kanyonyo, for twenty-five years. The writer of the *Livingstone Mail*'s 'Mongu Notes' reported that 'Susman Brothers' grocery business was the only one of its kind in Barotse and we understand that Mr. Nicolai intends to keep this on in conjunction with his Native Stores.' In the following year it was reported that Nicolai had acquired a near-monopoly of local trade, both wholesale and retail. This was as a result not only of his takeover of the Susmans' business, but also of the deaths during the year of three veteran traders, Fishel Levitz, Egnatz Snapper and Harry Diamond, son of A. B. Diamond. Messrs Shelton and Whitehead also remained in business at Kanyonyo and provided some competition.[45]

It was the impact of the Depression that led the Susman brothers to sell their Barotseland stores. The suspension of labour recruiting from Barotseland from 1931 onwards meant that trade there was at a very low ebb. It reached its nadir in 1933 and only slowly recovered in the later 1930s. Payment for the stores was probably made over several years and may have helped the Susmans to reduce their overdraft at the Standard Bank from an average of £15,000 in 1931–2 to £5,000 in 1932–3. The sale of the stores did not mark a complete end to their involvement in Barotseland. In October 1917 they had taken a one-third share in the Zambesi Transport Syndicate, which took over the river transport business of George Buchanan. The other shareholders were Robert Sutherland and William Shelmerdine. Sutherland was, like Buchanan, a Scot who had been in Northern Rhodesia, mainly North-Eastern Rhodesia, for sixteen years. He probably came out to Africa to work for the African Lakes Corporation. He was not only a shareholder, but also the manager of the syndicate, which became R. F. Sutherland Ltd in 1924. The Susman brothers had a substantial share in the new enterprise, which eventually opened stores in Barotseland on it own account. By 1929 the company was running thirty-two paddle barges on the Zambezi, from its base at Katombora, and had a virtual monopoly of river transport. Arthur Harrington, a well-known Barotseland character, built the barges at Senanga where he had five sawpits and employed a large number of people. The barges were thirty-five feet long, four or five feet wide, and were each able to carry more than two tons of goods. They were flat-bottomed and oxen were used to drag them around the falls at Sioma. Among their more spectacular cargoes was a small Fordson tractor. This was carried up in 1926 for use by Harrington himself in the movement of timber.[46]

The Susman brothers did not, therefore, abandon Barotseland at this time, after thirty years of involvement. They retained an interest through R. F. Sutherland Ltd and, within a few years, they were investigating the possibility of getting back into the Barotseland cattle trade – something that they began to do shortly before the outbreak of the Second World War. It was, however, to be almost fifteen years before they got back into the stores business on their own account, buying back their old stores, and many others, under a new dispensation – Susman Brothers & Wulfsohn Ltd.

CHAPTER 8

From Ngamiland to the Congo, 1912–36

As the Barotseland cattle trade went into decline from 1915 onwards, the Susman brothers turned much of their attention to the development of a new source of supply for their Northern Rhodesian and Congo markets. This lay south of the Zambezi in the extraordinarily difficult terrain of the Kalahari and Ngamiland. The Susmans had begun to establish a presence in the northern part of the Bechuanaland Protectorate a few years before the crisis that threatened their Barotseland interests. They responded to a request for help from a controversial chief, Sekgoma Letsholathebe, the former ruler of the Tawana people. He had acquired a degree of fame, or notoriety, as a result of his dealings with Frederick Lugard, later Lord Lugard, Britain's most famous African proconsul. Lugard had spent time in Sekgoma's territory around Tsau and Lake Ngami in 1896–7 as the representative of the British West Charterland Company, which had a mineral concession there. The resident commissioner, Ralph Williams, deposed Sekgoma in 1906 after a vote by members of the Tawana royal family, but Sekgoma retained support at the grassroots, and among subject peoples: the Yei, Hambukushu and the Herero – the latter were refugees from German South-West Africa. His successor, Mathiba, was held to be the rightful heir, but he lacked Sekgoma's force of personality.[1]

Sekgoma fought his deposition as chief as far as the Privy Council in London. In its judgement in 1910 it claimed it had no jurisdiction, citing the Foreign Jurisdictions Act, which put arbitrary acts by the administrators of British protectorates beyond legal challenge. The prominent South African nationalist, author and journalist, Sol Plaatje, described Sekgoma as 'the Black Dreyfus'. Charles Riley was Sekgoma's 'attorney' in the early stages of this litigation, but it is unlikely that he had any legal training. He was a recently bankrupted farmer and hotelier from Mafeking whose origins lay on the Atlantic island of St Helena, where he was born in 1862. He was in

South African terms 'Coloured', though he had a white wife and his children were accepted as white. He had previously acted for a number of other Tswana chiefs. It is probable that he was pushed out from Mafeking to make his living in the Kalahari by the rising tide of racial prejudice.[2]

After the failure of Sekgoma's legal action, there was talk of settling him in the Cape, the Transvaal, or in the southern part of the protectorate. At one stage he applied to King Lewanika, with whom he had a somewhat uneasy relationship, for asylum in Barotseland. He employed the remarkable West African journalist, early Pan-Africanist, and occasional police informer, F. Z. S. Peregrino, as a go-between in his negotiations with Lewanika. Peregrino had previously acted for Lewanika and had secured a mineral concession from him, but Lewanika showed no interest in providing Sekgoma with a home.[3]

In 1912 the British authorities finally sent Sekgoma into internal exile at Kabulabula on the northern border of the Bechuanaland Protectorate. It was not much more than twenty miles from Sesheke across the Zambezi, the tip of the Caprivi Strip, and the Chobe-Linyanti River. It was also about twenty miles south of Kazungula. The majority of Sekgoma's people trekked north across the Kalahari from Ngamiland to join him there. They were confined within a fifteen-mile radius of the camp of the resident magistrate, Captain H. V. Eason, at Kasane. They had difficulty in finding food and had little means of paying for it, but Susman Brothers at Sesheke supplied them with grain and Sekgoma begged them to open a store at Kabulabula. In one of many letters which he, or his secretary, wrote to them, Sekgoma said that they were in need of 'kaffir corn, meal and etc. (sugar, tea and coffee) and clothing'. Sekgoma also begged Eason to allow Susman Brothers to trade in the protectorate.[4]

Susman Brothers & Riley

The resident commissioner, F. W. Panzera, was, however, unwilling to grant a licence for a store. He was also unwilling to grant a licence in Bechuanaland to any traders based in Livingstone, as they did not have 'vested interests in the country' — even though Susman Brothers said that they were prepared to invest £10,000 in it. He was only prepared to grant a hawker's licence to Charles Riley and expected him to bring in goods from George Haskins at Francistown. Eason denied that Sekgoma and his people were living in destitution at Kabulabula, but he acknowledged that it would be much cheaper to get supplies through Livingstone — he had a personal account with Susman Brothers at Sesheke. Acting on his own authority, he gave the Susmans permission to enter into a trading relationship with Charles Riley, who arrived at Kavimba on the Chobe River in December 1912. Susman Brothers then established a formal partnership with him under the name of Susman Brothers & Riley. Sekgoma died in 1914, but Charles Riley continued to represent the partnership at Kavimba for several years. He eventually moved south to Maun, the new settlement on the Thamalakane River, about 300 miles south of the Zambezi, which replaced Tsau as the tribal headquarters of the Tawana people, and as the administrative centre of Ngamiland, in 1915. Susman Brothers & Riley opened a branch at Maun in 1916 and also opened branches further south and west at Tsau and Gomare.[5]

The partners began to buy cattle in the northern part of the Bechuanaland Protectorate two or three years before the 'P.P.' crisis hit the Barotseland cattle trade. They were at first unable to export these cattle to Northern Rhodesia and sought a southern market for them. Evidence for their activities at this time comes from the diary of G. E. Nettleton, a young official who was then based at Maun. Nettleton travelled back to Maun from the Victoria Falls in June 1916, and camped at 'one of Susmans' cattle posts' at Kabulabula. A day's trek further south, he met and had tea with a 'Dutchman', Johannes Jacobus Louw, who was in charge of 1,000 head of cattle belonging to Susman Brothers & Riley. Louw had attempted to drive these cattle to Francistown en route to the Johannesburg market in the previous year, but he had been forced to turn back because of the scarcity of water. Lions were now troubling the herd and had killed some of the stock. Louw did not have 'a high opinion of the country and seemed thoroughly disgusted with everything. He said it was "Too blerry dry".'[6]

Nettleton travelled by boat on the Chobe River – looking out somewhat nervously for crocodiles and hippos – for the three-mile trip from the Kavimba Police Post to the store where he met Charles Riley. He alluded in one sentence both to Riley's legal exploits in defence of Sekgoma, and to his 'Coloured' origins. 'The Lord Chief Justice seemed darker than ever, no wonder it is remarked that he is sunburnt all over.' He also reported that Riley had a manager, 'one of the Lost Legion', an anti-Semitic reference, possibly to H. A. Jacobson who became manager for Susman Brothers & Riley at Maun.[7] Riley's elder son, Jim, who was then sixteen, was with him. His younger son, Charles Henry de Beauvoir Riley, known as Harry, was only twelve in 1916, but achieved fame as the founder of Riley's Hotel at Maun in the early 1930s.[8] Nettleton was not very impressed by the new settlement there: 'I get a worse impression of this camp every day. The mosquitoes swarm in the daytime especially in my office and the midges are here in their millions and seem to have great fascination for one's eyes.'[9]

A few months earlier, the *Livingstone Mail* had reported that Elie Susman 'looking very fit and well' had returned from a seven-week trip 'across the desert' to Ngamiland. This was the first time that either of the Susman brothers had crossed the Kalahari. They had already begun to look at Ngamiland as an alternative source of cattle for the Congo market, though they may also have been seeking to compensate for losses in Barotseland by gaining access to the South African market. As late as August 1920, Elie Susman met Charles Riley at Mafeking, and had consultations with him about 600 cattle that the latter had brought down from Ngamiland for sale on the Johannesburg market. Riley must then have trekked south by way of Ghanzi, Molepolole and Lobatse. The partnership with Riley was dissolved in 1924–5, and the Kavimba store was closed then. Its replacement was an R. F. Sutherland store at Kachikau, about five miles further south – a business in which the Susman brothers also had a share. Susman Brothers remained in business on its own account at Maun and other centres in Ngamiland.[10]

Maun and the Kalahari

Maun was, and remains, an exceptional place. Although it has grown enormously in the last ninety years, there is still debate as to whether or not it is a town. The first significant social gathering to be held there was a Christmas Sports, which was organised by the resident magistrate, A. G. Stigand, on 27 December 1920. According to an account by the Ghanzi settler, and later Maun resident, M. T. Kays, as many as forty white people were gathered together from a very wide area – a record for the settlement. There were, of course, also hundreds of black participants. Harry Susman was in Ngamiland at the time and may have been present. Among those who donated funds for the event were Charles Riley, R. B. Lock, an old Barotseland trader, and two of the Deaconos brothers, founder members of Ngamiland's Greek Cypriot community. Susman Brothers & Riley and Susman Brothers gave separate donations, as did Charles and Jim Riley. The only other trading firm represented at the settlement was the Bechuanaland Trading Association.[11]

Susman Brothers was heavily engaged in cattle trekking and transport riding across the Kalahari between Kazungula and Maun throughout the 1920s and early 1930s. A number of tracks were developed across the Kalahari. Jim Riley cut the first two of these in 1921 and 1924, and they were both known in turn as Riley's Road. A third track was cut in 1926 and was known as Susman's Road. By that time the Susmans were losing fifty cattle a month to trypanosomiasis in their herds at Kachikau-Kazungula, and it was thought that they had been infected on the way north. The alignment of the new road was to the east of the old tracks and it was significantly longer. It kept away from the rivers and avoided flooding, but required the sinking of wells, many of which turned out to be salty. Of one it was said that it was saltier than the sea, and of another that even donkeys would not drink from it.[12]

Nettleton has left a vivid account of a journey from Maun to Kazungula in June 1925, using Riley's Road. He travelled the first few miles by boat along the Thamalakane River. He then transferred to his Scotch cart and followed the track along the edge of the river. Although the main flood from the Okavango had not yet arrived, parts of the track were already under four feet of water. He eventually left the road and cut a new track for himself through the dry bush. After a couple of days he returned to the road and the river. It was at this point that:

> We met Susman Bros.' convoy of wagons on their way from Kazengula [sic] to Maun and on one I was pleased to see our long awaited bath. I ordered it some time ago as I considered it was time Maun had a decent bath if nothing else. There were six wagons in charge of a man called Terblanche [sic] I asked him about roads and have since discovered that when he said 'take the road on the right' he meant his right and my left as we were travelling in opposite directions – so much for his advice.[13]

After leaving the dry river, Nettleton entered the land of pans – pools of water – there were said to be tsetse flies on this part of the road. He reached Kachikau after ten days on the road. About twenty-five miles further north he met another representative of Susman Brothers: as he was going to sleep, 'a Scotch cart came along and I heard the melodious voice of Naparstock and he came along and decided to outspan there and he talked to me until 11 p.m., but I refused to get out of bed'.[14] On the following day he met 'another Ngamiland merchant prince on his way home'. This was L. G. Deaconos of Maun, who described in great detail an earlier experience with a lion on the road near the Mababe Flats. He spent two nights alone in his wagon with an angry lion pacing around it. The lion had taken one of his oxen and the rest had bolted. On the morning after the attack he had sent his wagon 'boys' off to look for the missing oxen. They did not return, but the lion did. Deaconos fired several shots at it, but failed to do more than annoy it. He was rescued from this ordeal by the arrival of other wagons on the afternoon of the third day.[15]

Harry Susman's son, Joe, had a terrifying experience while trekking cattle in this area. After lions stampeded his cattle, he left the road to look for them with his Lozi foreman. They became disoriented and were unable to find their way back to the road. A party of San (Bushman) hunters rescued them after five days: they not only saved their lives by finding them water, but also found their cattle and took them back to the road. Susman and his companion had become lost only a short distance away from it.[16]

This route was harder on animals than on men. Elie Susman reported an extreme case of hardship and cattle loss in July 1924:

> Some 520 head of cattle were being driven in from the interior of Ngamiland, and for five days were without water: nearing a native village, where wells had been sunk, the cattle smelt the water and stampeded; they fell down the wells – as many as thirty dead beasts choked one of them – while some rushed to the reedy bed of the dry river and went mad. Altogether 218 died: a heavy loss.[17]

Vivien Ellenberger, the assistant resident commissioner, commented on the rapid pace of change in the district. The first camel had reached Maun in 1921, the first motorcar in 1926, and the first aeroplane in 1931.[18] The first person to arrive in Maun by plane was L. G. Deaconos – on 28 August 1931. According to Ellenberger: 'When the aeroplane landed and its occupants stepped out the natives stood with their mouths open and shook their heads at this latest wonder (magic) of the white man.' He was no less amazed himself to be able to read the same day's *Bulawayo Chronicle* in Maun at 10 a.m. He had his own first flight near Maun in the following year and found it a thrilling experience, but was somewhat alarmed by the manoeuvres that the pilot made to avoid airborne vultures while landing. The 'aerodrome' at Maun was a widened bit of the Kazungula Road near Riley's Hotel.[19]

It was also in 1931 that Harry Riley established a land-speed record for the trip from Maun to Livingstone of fifteen hours for 310 miles. Speed corrugations had begun to appear on the road, and Ellenberger wrote of the need to separate wagon traffic and cattle from the motor track. J. A. Frost, who was Susman Brothers' manager at Maun, obtained a government contract during the year to run a fortnightly mail service to Livingstone. Ellenberger described the unaccustomed luxury of fresh fruit, vegetables, butter, and of potatoes, which had never been seen before in Maun. There were complaints about high prices as compared with Livingstone – the traders were permitted to charge three pence a pound for freight.[20]

Changes in the mode of transport across the Kalahari affected the Susmans' business. They reduced the amount of time spent on travelling and also made more frequent visits possible. Harry Susman crossed the Kalahari to Maun and Ngamiland by wagon for the last time on a three-month journey between October 1926 and January 1927. In February 1928 it was reported that he was travelling to Ngamiland by motorcar and would be away for six weeks. He travelled there again in September and was again away for six weeks. When the governor-general, Lord Athlone, came on a hunting expedition to Kavimba in September of the following year, the Northern Rhodesia government's chief secretary appealed unsuccessfully to Harry Susman for the use of the brothers' Dodge truck. Dodge and Chevrolet trucks, fitted with balloon tyres, and with a sleeping cabin or 'caboose' on the back, were just beginning to become the accepted mode of transport in the Kalahari. Motor transport had its own problems and dramas; it was to be some time before ox wagons fell into disuse.[21]

Chief Mathiba, Sekgoma's ineffective successor, was compulsorily retired in 1932 and died a year later. He had not welcomed the arrival of motor vehicles and had banned them from his reserve. His stand against the motorcar gained him a degree of international fame. The humorous magazine *Punch* published the following verses about him:

> When buses roll along the Strand
> With people bound for Samarkand
> I'll book to Bechuanaland
> Mathiba I will visit;
> And all my heavy trunks shall go
> From point to point by buffalo
> In Bechuanaland the slow;
> And by the way, where is it?[22]

The Susmans had clearly had a close relationship with Chief Sekgoma, but there is no evidence that they enjoyed a similar relationship with Chief Mathiba. They must have dealt with his councillors, some of whom had enormous herds of cattle. As in Barotseland, traders were unable to buy land and had to pay rent for store plots. There were two long-running points of contention between the Ngamiland traders in general and the tribal authorities. Complaints continued for forty years about the system of payment that prevailed in Ngamiland and some other parts of Bechuanaland. The common practice was for traders to pay half the price of cattle in cash and the other half in 'good-fors', which were credit notes that could be used only at the store that had issued them. Susman Brothers' manager at Maun, J. A. Frost, stated in 1931 that no 'Motawana' could then say that he was forced to accept 'good-fors'. The real issue was rather different. If a seller demanded cash, he was paid a significantly lower price – unless cattle were in short supply.[23]

The administration was concerned that people should have cash with which to pay tax, but it was never prepared to take effective steps against the system of credit notes, which was probably not illegal. It was more concerned about the common, but undoubtedly illegal, practice of paying cowherds in kind. The Susman brothers were unusual in that they paid their employees in cash. They aimed to sell cattle for twice the price that they paid for them. This sounds like a wide margin, but it did not guarantee large profits in an area where cattle often had to be held for long periods – in some cases for years – and where there were large risks, and costs, arising from drought, predators, long treks, cattle diseases, market closures, veterinary regulations and highly volatile cattle prices.[24]

The other long-running issue between traders and tribal authorities concerned grazing rights. There was competition for scarce grazing in a drought-prone country between the traders – who often accumulated large herds and held them over long periods – and resident cattle-owners. The Susmans collected cattle at Maun, where the traders had cattle posts in the Naraga valley and at points further south such as Sehitwa, and sent them north in batches. They usually kept large 'mobs' at cattle posts in the north between Kachikau and Kazungula. Other traders had cattle posts in the north around Tsotsoroga Pan, where there was competition between traders for grazing land. These cattle posts were not strictly speaking in Ngamiland and were, or became, part of the Chobe Crown Lands.

From Ngamiland to the Congo

From the later months of 1920 until the bottom of the depression in 1933 the major destination for the export of Ngamiland cattle was the Congo, though the development of the Northern Rhodesian Copperbelt from the late 1920s did provide an alternative market. The story of the Susmans' involvement in the Ngamiland–Congo cattle trade can be told in terms of their relationships with two men. These two men had little in common, but they were both called Smith, they both had an interest in cattle and they both became close personal friends of the Susman brothers. One was Barnett 'Bongola' Smith who had established a dominant position in the Congo cattle market by 1920. The other was John Smith who returned to Northern Rhodesia in 1921, after an absence of five years, as chief veterinary officer. 'Bongola' Smith provided the market and became the Susmans' most important business partner. John Smith had more influence than anyone else on the way in which the competition between Southern Rhodesia, Northern Rhodesia and Bechuanaland for the Congo and Copperbelt markets for beef was conducted.

The astonishing emergence from obscurity of 'Bongola' Smith has been described in some detail in another book.[25] He was Jewish and was born at Riga in what was then the province of Kurland, in the Russian Empire, in about 1870. After following his father to London, he worked as a trouser presser in an East End sweatshop and moved to South Africa at about the time of the Anglo-Boer War, working his way north as a peddler – a *smous* – and a wagon trader. By 1911 he had moved through the Rhodesias to the Congo and set himself up as a butcher and cattle trader at Elisabethville. Apparently unable to read or write in any language, he was a man of prodigious energy and of an explosive temperament. He used his knowledge of Afrikaans to form alliances with prominent Flemish-speaking Belgians, including a future bishop of Katanga, Monsignor de Hemptinne, and a future governor of the province, Gaston Heenen, and he became the dominant figure in a fiercely competitive environment. British colonial officials also held him in considerable awe – his naturalisation as a British citizen was rushed through in Northern Rhodesia in 1922.

Although a few competitors, such as J. J. Hantche, the Blumenthal brothers and Robert Granat survived in the butchery business in Katanga, Smith achieved a near-monopoly, securing beef contracts from the major mining company, Union Minière, the government and the railways. He also established his own ranch on the Biano plateau near Likasi and was the first person to keep cattle in any numbers in Katanga. In 1922 he bought the entire stock of the Lochinvar Ranch in Northern Rhodesia and had the cattle driven, or perhaps railed, up to the Congo. In 1925 he did a deal with Belgian banking interests, Baron Henri Lambert of the Banque Lambert, and his cousins, the Rothschilds. This resulted in the merging of his varied businesses in a new company, which became known as Elakat. It remained a major player in the butchery, ranching, trading and textile businesses in the Congo, in parallel with the later evolution of Susman Brothers & Wulfsohn, until after independence in 1960. Elakat set up a subsidiary in 1929, the Congo–Rhodesia Ranching Company, which acquired ranches and farms in the Rhodesias, including Smith's Lubombo Ranch near Mazabuka and farms in the Lusaka District. 'Bongola' Smith moved south to Bulawayo and continued to play a major role in the southern African beef and cattle markets until his death in 1941.[26]

Because of the closure, on veterinary grounds, of the railway through Northern Rhodesia for the transit of live cattle from Southern Rhodesia to the Congo, Smith was forced in 1920 to look for Northern Rhodesian suppliers. In a somewhat unusual advertisement under the heading 'alleged Shortage of Cattle', Susman Brothers informed the readers of the *Livingstone Mail* on 13 February 1920 that they were able to offer 'for prompt delivery at Livingstone, in quantities to suit purchasers, up to 3,000 head at current market prices, based on Sales by Public Auction'. The advertisement also carried a note to the effect that 'the rumour that sufficient slaughter stock for the Congo are unobtainable in N. Rhodesia is thus disposed of'. After complex negotiations through intermediaries, and visits by Elie Susman to Elisabethville and by 'Bongola' Smith to Livingstone, Susman Brothers entered into a contract to supply 800 head of cattle a month to the Congo at a price which worked out at about £10 a head. The Susmans saw this as a partnership and it appeared in their accounts under the heading: 'Susman Brothers & Smith'.[27]

It was their original intention to meet this contract with Barotseland cattle, but interruptions in supply due to 'P.P.' made that impossible. In October 1920 Elie Susman was able to persuade the Farmers' Association, of which he was a prominent member, to allow the import of cattle from Ngamiland to meet the shortfall. The actual decision rested with the administration, as advised by the Veterinary Department, but the farmers had an effective veto on policy under Chartered Company rule. The cattle began to flow north in the early months of 1921. The Susmans' contracts with Smith were renewed in subsequent years, though on a reduced scale from 1925 onwards. By that date the restrictions on the movement of Southern Rhodesian cattle through Northern Rhodesia had been lifted, and Smith obtained the bulk of his supplies from the south. By 1929–30 the flow of Ngamiland cattle to the Congo had virtually stopped, but there was a new demand for its cattle on the Northern Rhodesian Copperbelt, which was going through a construction boom.[28]

There was always some opposition to Ngamiland imports from Northern Rhodesian settler farmers, including the most prominent ranchers, George Horton, F. J. Clarke and Ben Woest. The inability of the settlers to meet the demand from the Congo, and then the Copperbelt, at a competitive price ensured, however, that these imports were allowed to continue until the low point of the Depression in 1933. At one meeting in July 1921, 'Mr Susman' – it is not clear which one – had agreed with Tom King's suggestion that he 'would not have gone to Ngamiland for cattle if he could get them here'. For some time imports from Ngamiland for the Congo were restricted to 6,000 head per year, and there were also some seasonal restrictions on their movement. All Ngamiland cattle had to spend a month in quarantine at Katombora and the size of the holding grounds put a limit on the number of cattle that could be imported.[29]

John Smith acknowledged in 1925 that there was 'a feeling in the district' that the Susmans, together with their partner, Robert Sutherland, had acquired a monopoly of the Ngamiland cattle trade. This was not quite the case, though they probably controlled more than three-quarters of its exports. There was competition for the purchase of cattle in Ngamiland with the Greek Cypriots. George Orphanides, who had traded as a hawker in Barotseland before the First World War, reached Ngamiland with one or more brothers during the war, as did the Deaconos brothers. Relations between the 'Jews' and the 'Greeks', as they were locally described, in Ngamiland were not always good. On the other hand, the Susmans frequently bought cattle from the Greek Cypriots in order to meet their own contracts, and the latter were sometimes able to sell directly to other traders such as H. C. Werner. The Riley brothers also acted independently in Ngamiland, sometimes dealing with the Susmans and sometimes with the 'Greeks'. By the early 1930s, if not before, Harry Riley had joined forces with Orphanides. The Susmans' strength came from their superior capitalisation – they had £30,000 invested in Ngamiland and its cattle by the mid 1920s – and organisation. Above all, their relationship with 'Bongola' Smith gave them privileged access to the Congo market.[30]

They also acquired a near-monopoly position for Ngamiland cattle in the Livingstone District. This was for local consumption through their own butchery, and as suppliers of slaughter and trek oxen to the Zambesi Saw Mills Ltd. This firm had emerged by the end of the First World War as the major extractive industry, and probably the largest employer, in Northern Rhodesia. After an outbreak of 'P.P.' in the Livingstone District in 1921, John Smith undertook a radical programme of action. In the following year he not only closed the Barotseland cattle trade and constructed a cordon between Barotseland and the Batoka Province, he also had the entire cattle population of the Livingstone District either slaughtered for local consumption, or exported as slaughter stock to the Congo. He replaced the cattle, compensating African owners on a one-for-one basis, with Ngamiland stock supplied by the Susmans. He also stopped the movement of cattle between Livingstone and the Southern Province, thus cutting Livingstone off from

Northern Rhodesian supplies, and creating an enclosed market for Ngamiland imports.[31]

John Smith's recently published memoir, *Vet in Africa*, shows him to have been an exceptionally energetic, observant, open-minded and competent civil servant. Not all of his actions benefited the Susmans' interests. They recognised, however, that his energetic measures did stop the spread of 'P.P.' in 1915–16 and again in 1921–2. He may have closed down the Barotseland trade, but he protected their interests as ranchers along the Line of Rail, facilitated the Ngamiland trade and provided them with a niche market in Livingstone. They undoubtedly established an unusual rapport with him at a time when anti-Semitism and snobbery made friendships with civil servants exceptional for members of Livingstone's small Jewish community. Smith and Elie Susman corresponded regularly until Elie's death – twenty-five years after Smith's departure from Northern Rhodesia. Smith addressed his letters in the early 1930s to 'Dear Elie', indicating an uncommon degree of familiarity at that date. His son, Tony, recalls the food parcels which his family received from the Susmans during the Second World War.[32]

Their friendship survived an extraordinary episode in 1923–4. This incident also threatened Leopold Moore with bankruptcy and the *Livingstone Mail* with closure. It began on 6 December 1923 with Moore's publication, in a leading article, of earlier correspondence between a lawyer acting for Susman Brothers, and the administration, as well as letters between himself and the administration, about fees charged for Ngamiland cattle using the quarantine camp at Katombora. Susman Brothers had pointed out that the Veterinary Department's charge of 6s. 6d. per beast resulted in a significant profit for the department at a time when depressed prices threatened the viability of the traders. They asked for a reduction in the fee and for a rebate of fees paid on the 3,500 cattle that they had imported during the year so far. It was pointed out that the government of Bechuanaland had already halved its 5s. levy on cattle exports in view of the depression. The administration declined the request, but conceded that there might be grounds for a reduction in the following year. There is no doubt that the Susmans had a case and that the fees, which had been increased since the conclusion of their current contracts with 'Bongola' Smith, contributed to the overall loss their business made during the year. In his annual review Leopold Moore wrote: 'The year 1923 will, we sincerely hope, be remembered as the least prosperous in the history of the country.'[33]

In his leading article, Moore, who combined his role as editor of the paper with that of leader of the unofficial members of the Advisory Council, went beyond the original issue of an unfair profit. He seized upon the fact that the veterinary surgeon who inspected the cattle received 6d. per head as a personal fee. He suggested that this gave the Veterinary Department an interest in encouraging the flow of cattle from Ngamiland to the Congo – to the detriment of settler farmers. John Smith took this as a libel on himself and his department. He demanded that Moore print and prominently display a retraction and apology. Moore declined to print an apology and intensified his attack in the following week's paper, implicitly calling for Smith's resignation. He also published a poem, under the title 'A Song of Sixpence', which was contributed by a pseudonymous author, 'Agricola':

> O sing a song of Sixpence,
> And Cattle for the Congo,
> And you can bet they'll pass the Vet,
> So send them all along O!
>
> A Sixpence is a Magic Charm,
> It negatives all thought of harm,
> And Risk to those who only farm,
> And don't pass Stock for Congo.
>
> The Okapi is rare indeed,
> And scarcer still the Bongo,
> But rarer yet, so says the Vet.,
> Are Rejects for the Congo.
>
> How very fortunate are we,
> For such a small indemnity,
> To keep our herds infection free,
> To quibble *must* be wrong O!
>
> And yet we think it would appear
> That those who gave the word 'all clear'
> To Cattle for the Congo
> Are also those who take the fee;
> Leaving the Risk to you and me;
> (Correct me if I'm wrong O.)
>
> The Super Mind, above desire
> Of Sixpences, we'd fain admire,
> And Celebrate in Song O.
> But now we lie awake o'nights
> Wondering what OTHER perquisites
> Are snaffled by our 'Guiding Lights,'
> On Cattle for the Congo.[34]

According to John Smith, the second article contained no less than eighteen libels. The case came to court in April 1924 and John Smith gave evidence for two days. His main witnesses were Elie Susman and Robert Sutherland. The court upheld the charge of libel in respect of both the article and the poem and Moore had to pay £100 in damages and Smith's costs of £240, in addition to his own. In an unusually plaintive article, Moore said that he had 'nursed the Livingstone Mail through years of depression because I considered that it served useful purposes and, also, in the hope of future prosperity'. He hoped that with the support of his friends he would be able 'to laugh and carry on'. Within forty-eight hours of the judgement, he received a cheque for £100 as 'the first instalment on account of Voluntary Subscriptions from the public of Livingstone'. He eventually received over £200 in contributions towards his costs. There is reason to believe that the first instalment came from the Susman brothers. Harry Susman told John Smith shortly after the conclusion of the case that they were glad that he had won, but that they would be making a contribution to Moore's costs. They had inspired the original article, though not the personal attack on Smith, and they clearly felt that they had an obligation to Moore.[35]

It is to the credit of all parties that this incident did not damage the Susmans' relations with either Smith or Moore. There was, however, an understandable coolness towards Smith in the columns of the *Livingstone Mail* during the years that he remained in the country. There were clearly many undercurrents to this case. Moore had been a thorn in the Chartered Company's side, and it may not be entirely coincidental that this storm blew up in the last months of its rule. The Colonial Office took over the administration from 1 April 1924 with a fanfare of fireworks. Smith continued to serve the new regime, becoming director of agriculture as well as director of animal health in 1926, and pushed ahead with the establishment of a major research establishment at Mazabuka. This was badly hit by retrenchments during the Depression, which prompted Smith's own departure at the end of December 1932.[36]

The Ngamiland cattle trade ran more smoothly under Colonial Office rule. The new governor, Sir Herbert Stanley, was not as susceptible to the pressure of settler farmers as the previous regime had been. There was, however, to be one more significant episode involving the Susmans and Smith. This demonstrated that an understanding, almost an alliance, had developed between them. It also provided evidence of governmental recognition of the Susmans' important commercial role. In April 1931 there was a foot-and-mouth outbreak in Southern Rhodesia. Smith immediately closed the border for the transit of Southern Rhodesian cattle to the Congo. He then asked the Susmans to accumulate Ngamiland cattle to fill the void in the Congo market, and they did so. Eighteen months later, Smith organised a conference on the cattle trade at the Victoria Falls. Representatives of Northern Rhodesia, Southern Rhodesia and Bechuanaland agreed that there would be a stop to movements of cattle between the three countries from July 1933 onwards, and for the duration of the Depression. This meant that Southern Rhodesia could send cattle to the Congo, but Bechuanaland could not send cattle to Northern Rhodesia. Smith told the conference that the Northern Rhodesian government had a moral obligation to take in some Ngamiland cattle and suggested that the Susmans should be allowed to bring in cattle for Livingstone after July 1933. There was an understanding that they would be allowed to bring in 3,600 cattle, which would supply Livingstone for a further two years.[37]

Foot-and-mouth disease broke out in Bechuanaland in January 1933, within weeks of Smith's departure, and this resulted in the closure of the border with Northern Rhodesia and a ban on cattle movements within the protectorate. The Susmans were left with 4,000 head of cattle in the Kachikau-Kazungula grazing grounds and were unable to cross them into Northern Rhodesia. When the border opened again, Smith, who had retired to Britain, supported the Susmans in their contention that the government had a moral obligation to take some of their Ngamiland cattle – in spite of the standstill agreement. After complex negotiations, ultimately involving direct talks between the governor of Northern Rhodesia, Sir Ronald Storrs, and the prime minister of Southern Rhodesia, Godfrey Huggins, a compromise was reached and it was agreed in December 1933 that the Susmans should be allowed to import 1,800 cattle into Northern Rhodesia for use in the Livingstone District in the course of 1934. Harry Susman played a major part in these negotiations, demonstrating that he was able to hold his own at the highest level. A number of tributes were paid to his integrity at this time. Smith's successor, J. P. A. 'Seamus' Morris, noted: 'I have always found Mr H. Susman very straightforward in his dealings with Government'.[38]

The fragile economy of the Bechuanaland Protectorate was entirely dependent on cattle exports. It was badly hit by the Depression, foot-and-mouth disease, the closure of the South African market and restrictions on its exports from Ngamiland. Its government acknowledged that Ngamiland had only kept its share of the Congo market as a result of the special relationship that existed between the Susmans and 'Bongola' Smith. There was recognition at a high level that they performed a useful role in the imperial

6 Harry Susman with a herd of Ngamiland cattle, Northern Rhodesia or Bechuanaland, early 1930s.

scheme of things by providing a market for Ngamiland cattle and income for the impoverished protectorate.[39]

Colonel Rey and the Depression

The resident commissioner in Bechuanaland from 1929 to 1937 was the outspoken, frankly anti-Semitic, but energetic, Colonel Charles Rey. He was full of ideas for the development of Bechuanaland, but had the misfortune to run the protectorate during the Depression. In a desperate move to get cattle from white farms in the Tati Block in eastern Bechuanaland to the northern markets, bypassing Southern Rhodesia, he had employed Jim Riley to survey the route from Francistown to Kazungula – along the line of the Old Hunters' Road. Riley managed to get through by car in spite of difficulties caused by rain, elephants and uprooted trees. He brought 1,000 head of cattle through in the early months of 1932. Rey got no encouragement from the Susmans, or from 'Bongola' Smith, for this scheme. After an apparently exhilarating conversation at Livingstone on 19 November 1931, Rey noted that Harry Susman was totally opposed to the scheme and said that it would 'ruin Ngamiland'.[40]

This conversation inspired Rey to write a memorable account of the politics and dynamics of the central African cattle trade, the impact on it of the Depression and the prospects for recovery.

> ... owing to the slump in the world price of copper, production has fallen off in the Congo and Northern Rhodesia, thousands of people have been dismissed and the consumption of meat has fallen. It all depends on a conference of copper producers sitting in New York now – so does the price of copper in London and New York affect the sale of cattle in Bechuanaland! And there are other factors too: all the meat contracts in the Congo (the Union Minière, the railways, and the other big mines) are controlled by my villainous friend Mr Bongola Smith. His directors sit in Brussels – Mr Carton de Wiart, Count Lippens, ex-Governor of the Congo, one of the Rothschilds etc., and they in their turn control the Congo Government! A dirty game – and a network of intrigue covering Cape Town, Salisbury, Bulawayo, Livingstone, Elisabethville, Brussels and New York.[41]

Ten days later, Rey visited Elie Susman at his South African home in Beach Road, Muizenberg, Cape Town. Elie was as strongly opposed to Rey's Tati Block scheme as his brother had been. In his view the northern market was already too small for Ngamiland's cattle output. He had been seriously considering the liquidation of the Ngamiland business, but there had recently been a slight improvement – presumably as a result of the re-opening of the

Congo market. He was strongly in favour of Rey's visionary scheme for a game reserve and hotel in the Chobe area – a precursor of the present Chobe National Park. He thought that it would need an investment of £15–20,000, and said that 'in normal times he would have got together a syndicate himself to run it, but times were too bad and too critical. He would certainly consider it later on.' At the same meeting he complained that the Greeks were doing a great deal of harm to the cattle trade, and regretted that they, either Deaconos or Orphanides Brothers, had been granted a trading licence at Tsau. He also asked for additional grazing grounds, and complained that his firm had been deprived of one of its grazing areas between Kazungula and Kachikau. 'He said that as his firm had done so much for Ngamiland trade they should be given some consideration.'[42]

Eighteen months later, in June 1933, Rey himself reported that he had encountered 5,000 of the Susmans' cattle in the care of their man, Engelbrecht, along the road between Kasane and Kachikau. These were the cattle that had been bought for the Congo market and which became the subject of high-level negotiations. He noted that the cattle were grazing along the Chobe River and seemed to be in good condition. Less than a year later Rey noted that one of the Engelbrechts – there seem to have been two, a father and a son – had been killed by a lion at Kazungula.[43]

In the later months of 1933, while negotiating about the fate of these cattle, Elie Susman said once again that he was trying to close down the Ngamiland business. He seems to have been unable to do so. On a visit to Maun and the branches in March 1933 he had closed the Gomare branch, but made arrangements to keep the others open. In March of the following year he was able to arrange for the 1,800 cattle, for which he had a special dispensation, to cross the Zambezi. These were the last cattle to make the crossing for at least five years. From then until the outbreak of the Second World War, the northern market for Ngamiland cattle remained closed. He found that business at Maun and Tsau at this time was 'fair'.[44]

From 1935 onwards there was a revival in the demand for, and price of, cattle in South Africa, and there was a shift to the south in the direction of the Ngamiland cattle trade. In the following year, Elie Susman supervised the arrival in Lobatse of thousands of cattle that had been trekked south from Ngamiland. Some of these cattle may have been slaughtered at the Lobatse abattoir that had been built in 1927, but which only functioned in 1935–6. Other cattle may have crossed legally on the hoof into South Africa, but there was also a thriving trade in smuggled cattle. In November 1936 Colonel Rey reckoned that cattle from Ghanzi and Ngamiland were being smuggled across the Lobatse border at the rate of 5,000 a month. An official report estimated that 250,000 cattle were smuggled across the border in 1935–8, significantly reducing the cattle population of the protectorate, which had already been depleted by drought. By 1936 the Susmans had transferred their Ngamiland interests to a new enterprise, the Ngamiland Trading Company. This was a partnership in which the junior partner was A. D. 'Chobo' Weskob. He will feature later in this story as the dominant figure in the Ngamiland cattle trade in the post-war era.[45]

At the same time that the Susman brothers were trying to wind down their Ngamiland cattle business in the face of the Depression, they were becoming involved in a new project in northern Bechuanaland. From 1932–5 they were engaged in negotiations about a timber project in the Kazungula-Kasane area. They had started extracting timber for sale to Zambesi Saw Mills from a concession on the south bank of the Zambezi, in Southern Rhodesia, in 1930. They now wanted to extend their railway line into Bechuanaland and to exploit valuable timber within the boundaries of the protectorate. Negotiations were slow and tortuous as they involved the governments of two countries: Bechuanaland and Southern Rhodesia. One cause of delay was the foot-and-mouth outbreak and the refusal of the Southern Rhodesian government to allow the movement of timber through its territory for so long as the outbreak lasted. Agreement was finally reached in April 1935. The railway line was extended and timber extraction was carried on for two years. The Bechuanaland timber project, which is described in more detail in the next chapter, was just one example of the Susmans' tendency to diversify their interests and undertake new ventures at times and in places that would have deterred most entrepreneurs.[46]

CHAPTER 9

From Livingstone to the Copperbelt via South Africa, 1914–39

Between the outbreak of the First and Second World Wars there were significant changes in the political and economic context in which the Susmans worked in Northern Rhodesia. The major political change was the transfer of the administration of the territory from the British South Africa Company to the Colonial Office in 1924. There was some talk of the amalgamation of Northern and Southern Rhodesia under Company rule during the First World War, but the majority of the settlers in Southern Rhodesia feared association with the 'black' north, and opposed this. The settlers in Northern Rhodesia also wanted to escape from Company rule and looked for direct rule from the Colonial Office in London as their best hope for the future. Similar views were held by the Lozi king, Lewanika's son and successor, Yeta III, formerly Prince Litia. In a series of petitions from 1918 onwards, Yeta demanded the end of the Chartered Company's control over Barotseland, the restoration of the Lozi kingship and other rights, the return of the Caprivi Strip to Lozi control, and the transfer of Barotseland to the Colonial Office. Yeta, and the relatively well-educated 'new men' who were attached to his court, were the only Africans who were able to speak out against amalgamation and for Colonial Office administration at this time.[1]

These 'new men' included Yeta's own sons, Daniel Akafuna and Edward Kalue and his brothers, Imwiko and Mwanawina, who had all been educated in South Africa or the United Kingdom. They were primarily interested in the restoration of the Lozi kingdom, and had no real sense of a Northern Rhodesian identity. It was not until the early 1930s that the first glimmerings of African nationalism were seen in Northern Rhodesia with the establishment of African Welfare Associations in such places as Livingstone, Lusaka and Ndola. Among the leaders of this movement was Nelson Nalumango, a man who was closely associated with the Lozi royal family, and also with Jewish traders in Livingstone, such as Jehiel Jacobs, a Barotseland trader and labour recruiter, for whom he worked for many years. There is circumstantial evidence of cross-fertilisation between early exponents of Zionism and socialism in Livingstone, such as Meyer Flax, a partner of Jacobs, and the emerging African intelligentsia represented by people like Nalumango. The Susman brothers were certainly in regular touch with Yeta and his brother, Imwiko, who was Chief at Mwandi-Sesheke from 1916 to 1945, and with other members of the Lozi elite, but these links are not easy to document. By the early 1920s the Lozi royal establishment had an efficient secretariat staffed by men with a good command of English. Their letters were typed and were properly filed. The loss, or perhaps inaccessibility, of its archives leaves a gap in the political and social record.[2]

Yeta and his men failed to attain most of their demands, but Company rule did come to an end and Northern Rhodesia as a whole was transferred to Colonial Office rule. Barotseland, however, remained a province and was not granted protectorate status until 1953. From 1924 onwards, the head of the government of Northern Rhodesia was the governor, who ran the territory with the help of the Legislative Council. The majority of its members were officials and there was a minority of elected members – all of them until after the Second World War were white, as was the electorate. The question of the future size and shape of Northern Rhodesia continued to preoccupy the council. The boundaries of the territory, which had only become a single entity through the combination of North-Western and North-Eastern Rhodesia in 1911, were not thought of as a permanent fixture. Communications between the western and eastern ends of the country remained very difficult until the completion of the Great East Road in the mid 1930s, and were not very easy after that. Various schemes for amalgamation with the south, association with the north and east, or dismemberment, continued to be discussed until the eve of independence fifty years later. Commissions were sent out to Africa from the United Kingdom in the late 1920s and late 1930s to consider these issues. In written evidence to the Hilton Young Commission in 1928, Elie Susman indicated that he was then opposed to amalgamation with Southern Rhodesia. He thought that amalgamation would result in an outflow of labour to the south, and that there was 'insufficient dissatisfaction' with the present regime to justify a change. It was not until the mid 1930s, in the wake of the Depression, that the majority of settler representatives, including Elie Susman's friend, Leopold Moore, declared themselves in favour of amalga-

7 Litunga Yeta III (seated) and Harry Susman with the future Litunga, Imwiko (standing), Livingstone, 1925 – on the occasion of the visit of the Prince of Wales.

mation. Elie Susman did not give evidence to the Bledisloe Commission in 1938, and it is not clear what his views on the subject then were.[3]

In economic terms the major event in Northern Rhodesia in the period covered by this chapter was the massive new investment in the development of the Copperbelt, which began in the late 1920s. This development was interrupted by the Depression, which had a delayed and relatively short-lived, though severe, impact on the territory. One consequence of the Depression in the whole of southern Africa was the beginning of a move away from the free market for agricultural products. Legislation was passed in Northern Rhodesia for the control of maize marketing in 1935 and of cattle marketing in 1937. Other changes of economic significance included improvements in roads and the introduction of the motorcar and aircraft. The responses of the Susman brothers to the changing economic, social and political environment are the subject of this chapter.

Family Life

By the time of the outbreak of the First World War in August 1914, Harry and Elie Susman were both married men. Harry and his wife, Annie, had two children, Joe and Ella. Elie and Bertha's first child, Bruna, was born in November 1915. By the end of the war Harry and Annie had three children, after the birth of Zelda, and Elie and Bertha had two daughters, after the birth of Peggy. Harry's family was completed by the birth of Oscar in 1922, and Elie's by the births of Osna in 1920, and David in 1925.

By the end of 1913, Harry Susman had built a substantial, but unpretentious, house on Government Road. It was, and still is, well placed with a fine view of the spray rising from the Victoria Falls about six miles away. Elie Susman does not seem to have owned a house in Livingstone until 1919, when he took over Maramba House from F. J. 'Mopani' Clarke. This was also a substantial house, which had been built on the site of the camp used by the engineers who built the railway. By the end of the First World War, the brothers had also acquired a holiday home, or homes, at Muizenberg, near Cape Town, and their families spent several months of the year at the coast, usually leaving in November or December and returning in January or February. Bertha Susman was away for six months from November 1918 to May 1919, and Elie was away for over four months from the end of December until the middle of May. The brothers may have taken turns to have long holidays – Harry Susman and his family were away for three months from the end of October 1919 to the end of January 1920.[4]

Livingstone was not an easy place in which to bring up children. There was a constant danger of malaria and water-borne diseases in a town that had no main drainage and relied on the primitive bucket system of sanitation. Summer temperatures were very high, and there was the possibility of frost in winter. Although the Susmans supplied fresh butter and vegetables to the town from their farms at Zimba and the Gwaai, there was no regular supply of fresh milk until the establishment of a dairy farm after the Second World War. None of the Susmans' children appears to have attended school in Livingstone. Like many other white children, they had nannies and governesses, and were sent off to school in Cape Town or Bulawayo at an early age. Within a couple of weeks of the birth of Bruna, her parents recruited an English nanny, Miss Louise Brattle, to help with the baby, she had come to Livingstone with the administrator, Sir Lawrence Wallace. Dr Ellacombe recommended her to Elie and Bertha, and also recommended them to her, saying: 'they are Jewish, but they are a very nice family'. One of her later duties was to accompany the girls on long train journeys to school in Cape Town. They did not eat in the dining car, but carried hampers of provisions, which were replenished by friends in Bulawayo and Kimberley. Miss Brattle stayed with the family for thirty-seven years. She served as a companion to Bertha when the children had grown up, and she died at Bruna's home in Johannesburg in 1952.[5]

Before they went to school in Cape Town, the girls also had a governess in Livingstone, Miss Becker. She was Danish and was a good pianist – her name appears in the *Livingstone Mail* as the accompanist to the songs sung at a Burns' Night dinner. She was an adventurous young woman who scandalised Livingstone's polite society by taking long trips 'alone' on the Zambezi in *mokoro*s (dugout canoes) – she was accompanied, of course, by Lozi paddlers. Bruna and her husband visited her in Denmark after the Second World War. Harry and Annie Susman had a housekeeper, Miss Moody, who was famed for the quality of her cakes. Their elder son, Joe, attended school at the South African College School in Cape Town and at Milton in Bulawayo. Their elder daughter, Ella, was sent to school in Bulawayo at the age of seven, as were her younger sister and brother.[6]

The Jewish Community

Annie Susman's parents and many of her numerous Grill siblings lived in Livingstone. She was more at home in the town than Bertha and lived there for thirty-six years – much longer than Bertha's fifteen years. Harry and

Annie's daughter, Ella, thought that her parents sought to recreate the *shtetl* in Livingstone. This may not be a far-fetched idea: Joseph Roth, in his book *The Wandering Jews* provided a description of a typical Jewish *shtetl* in Europe in the 1920s and 1930s. It would do quite well as a description of Livingstone and other towns along the Line of Rail in Northern Rhodesia at the same time.

> The little town lies in the middle of a great plain, not bounded by any hill or forest or river. It runs out into the plain. It begins with little huts and ends with them. After a while the huts are replaced by houses. Streets begin. One runs from north to south, the other from east to west. Where they intersect is the market place. At the far end of the north–south street is the railway station. A passenger train calls in once a day. A passenger train pulls out once a day.[7]

If the physical attributes of a *shtetl* were already there, it was the social aspects that were in need of re-creation. It was, perhaps, because of Annie's large family in the town and Harry's extrovert personality that it was their home, rather than Elie and Bertha's, that became the social and religious centre for Livingstone's Jewish community. This grew to about 100 souls before the construction of a synagogue, or *shul*, in 1928. For many years all religious services, festivals, weddings, and possibly even funerals, were conducted at their home. The *Livingstone Mail* frequently noted that an 'interesting little ceremony' – a *bris* – had taken place at the house. None of the Susman brothers had inherited their father's strict orthodoxy. Ella recalled with some amusement that when they visited their grandparents in Tel Aviv in 1934, her father leapt out of bed in the morning to put on *teffilin* (phylacteries) for morning prayers at the sound of his father's imperious knock on the bedroom door. This was not something that he was in the habit of doing in Livingstone. Both brothers were 'traditional' Jews, meaning that they followed some, but by no means all, of the precepts of Judaism. They did not keep strictly kosher homes – something that would have been difficult, if not impossible, to do in frontier conditions.[8]

Both brothers served their term as president of the Livingstone Hebrew Congregation, which was established in 1910. It was in that capacity that Elie laid the foundation stone for the synagogue on 8 July 1928. This fair-sized building was opened by the chief secretary, the Hon. H. A. Northcote, and consecrated by the Reverends Moses Cohen and A. Weinberg, just over two months later. On that occasion Cohen 'paid a warm tribute to Mr E. Susman and the other splendid workers who had given the Livingstone Jewish community so fine a name'. The Susmans were major contributors to the building fund.[9]

Harry Susman's house was also the preferred meeting place for the Herzl Zionist Society, which was formed in 1912. Elie was the first president and Harry was the first treasurer. His house was the venue for most meetings of the society. From the early 1920s onwards many leading personalities in the Zionist movement visited Livingstone as their last stop on southern African fund-raising tours. Among the distinguished visitors were Nahum Sokolow, chairman of the Zionist Executive in 1926, and again in 1934, and Colonel Frederick Kisch, head of the Zionist Executive in Palestine, in 1928. Chaim Weizmann, the charismatic leader of the Zionist Movement came in March 1932, he had been compelled to step down as president of the World Zionist Federation in the previous year. He came to southern Africa at this time to combat the growing influence of Vladimir Jabotinksy's Revisionist movement – it never had many sympathisers in Northern Rhodesia. Weizmann, who was accompanied by his wife, arrived on Friday 25 March. He spent Saturday at the Victoria Falls, where he enjoyed a boat trip and a short flight. He addressed the assembled crowd of Livingstone Jewry and other well-wishers at a Sunday morning tea party at Harry and Annie's house. He and his wife were then escorted to Government House for lunch with the governor, Sir James Maxwell. After lunch, a large crowd accompanied them to the railway station.[10]

Oscar Susman, the youngest of the three brothers, had forged a link between the family and the leaders of the World Zionist Federation. He died at the age of thirty on 21 March 1920 in London, while waiting to get a visa to re-enter Palestine where he had lived with his parents for four years. His death was a family tragedy, but the Reverend Moses Cohen, the most prominent Zionist in central Africa, saw it as a blow to the movement in the region as a whole. In an obituary notice, which was published in London in the *Zionist Bulletin*, he wrote:

> He came here ten years ago from a Jerusalem Yeshiva. He soon mastered the English language and became a practical man of affairs, a real pioneer of Barotseland. Life to him in the Zambesi valley was but a means to an end. He dreamt ever of the time when he should be able to return to Palestine, and help to build up our land. He was a most ardent Zionist and the movement in Rhodesia owes much to his support. When the war broke out he felt it was his duty as a Jew to go to the front. His kit bag did not lack a prayer book, and [in] all he did and suffered he strove to uphold the honour of our name ... A most promising life has been tragically cut short. We mourn his loss and cherish his memory.[11]

When Oscar left Northern Rhodesia in company with Captain M. J. Jacobs, a former Susman Brothers employee, in September 1919, it was reported that he was going to Palestine and that he would be away for at least six months. Elie Susman, who was in Elisabethville and stranded by a railway strike, received the news of Oscar's sudden illness and death through telegrams on consecutive days. He was himself heartbroken and thought that the news would kill their mother. In reporting his death, the *Livingstone Mail* said that he been suffering for some time from 'nervous breakdown' – not necessarily at that time a psychological illness – and was travelling to Palestine in the hope of a recovery in health. It seems probable that he was suffering from the after-effects of blackwater fever and that he may have had a recurrence in London.[12]

While in London, Oscar was introduced by Maurice Abrahams, a leading South African Zionist, to both Weizmann and Sokolow. According to Moses Cohen, they were 'delighted to meet such a fine specimen of South African Jewry, ready to give his life to the great national cause'. He was himself convinced that 'the prospects for Zionism are very good ...' and felt that South African Jews, though unsuited to small-scale farming, might do well in Palestine in commerce. He seems to have decided to settle permanently in Palestine where his parents had a plot, if not a house. He had already made substantial donations to the Palestine National Fund, and had his name inscribed in the Golden Book of Palestine while in Livingstone. He also left the proceeds of an insurance policy to the fund.[13]

The Susmans' father, the much-travelled Behr Susman, spent several months in Livingstone in 1919–20. He went south with Bertha in February, just a month before the news of Oscar's death. He had come up from Cape Town and was soon to leave, with his wife, for Palestine. They lived in their house in Lillienblum Street, Tel Aviv, until their deaths – Taube died in 1937 and Behr in 1941. He was buried on the Mount of Olives. Harry, and some of his family, visited them in 1934; Elie did so with his three eldest children in 1937. Bruna Zacks recalls the visit to her grandparents, remembering her grandfather as a stern old man who was shocked when the visitors took his wife out to a fashion show – which she, a sweet old lady, enjoyed. The brothers had added a number of flats to the house in the hope of generating income for their parents. They found on their visits, however, that these were let to rabbinical students rent-free. At some stage, probably in the 1920s or early 1930s, the Susman brothers became the owners of a large area of land in Palestine at Beersheba. They gave this property to the National Fund after the recognition of the state of Israel, and it has become part of the centre of the modern city of Beersheba.[14]

The Susmans' sister, Dora Gersh, came on a long visit to Livingstone in 1921. Her sons, Maurice and Harry, who were born in Palestine, came to live with their uncles in 1924 and 1925. They had done their Junior Certificate exams at Cape Town Normal College. Maurice Gersh worked in the office in Livingstone until 1929 when he was transferred to the Copperbelt. While based in Livingstone, he worked closely with the Susmans' secretary/manager, Lewis Hochstein, and did much of the clerical work. He was on one occasion sent up to Leopard's Hill to help manage the ranch. He also travelled once by boat to Sesheke to sort out problems at the store there, and also went with his Uncle Harry by wagon to Ngamiland. His cousin, Bruna, recalls that Miss Brattle strongly disapproved of her taking rides on the pillion of his motorcycle. Harry Gersh did not work for long in the office. He set up his own stores in the Livingstone area from 1927 onwards and also on the Southern Rhodesian side of the river. He had a portable iron shed, which he moved around the forests on an ox wagon.[15]

The Wider Community

Although their families, both nuclear and extended, and the wider Jewish community provided the Susman brothers with much of their social life, the brothers also played a part in the social and political life of the town as a whole. Elie Susman was always more of a leader in settler society than Harry was. He continued throughout the 1920s and early 1930s to play a prominent part in the activities of the North-Western Rhodesian Farmers' Association. He had been elected in 1917 to the important cattle committee of the association, and was a committee member of the later Cattle Owners' Association. He did not have political ambitions, but he had been one of those who called for the establishment of an advisory council at a Farmers' Association meeting in 1912. He seconded the motion of thanks for the offer of an advisory council in 1917. At a meeting on the question of income tax in 1920, he said that he was not opposed to income tax in principle, but he was opposed to taxation without proper representation. In the following year he was elected as a member of the reception committee for the visit of the governor-general, Prince Arthur of Connaught. He later nominated candidates for the elections to the Legislative Council in 1924 and to the new Livingstone Town Council in 1929.[16]

The great social event of the 1920s was the visit of Edward, Prince of Wales, later King Edward VIII, in July 1925. On that occasion the Susman brothers and their wives, as well as their young nephews, Maurice and Harry

Gersh, were invited to the dance that was held in the grounds of Government House. The tennis court was converted into a dance floor and was decorated with thousands of flowers. The Prince of Wales enjoyed himself so much that he declined to leave at midnight, and asked that the clocks should be put back by an hour.[17]

These invitations might suggest that by the 1920s official anti-Semitism was on the wane. There is some evidence to support this view. During the war Lady Wallace, the administrator's wife, Mrs Beaufort (wife of the judge), and Mrs Marshall, wife of a senior official, had joined Annie Susman in support of appeals for the Polish Russian Jewish Relief Fund.[18] The Susman brothers' growing wealth and economic importance may also have helped to break down barriers, but prejudice and snobbery were still real issues in a highly stratified settler society. Anti-Semitism was to rise again in the late 1930s when the arrival in Livingstone, and in Northern Rhodesia as a whole, of a relatively small number of German Jewish refugees raised passions in settler society. Sir Leopold Moore – he had by then been knighted for his services as leader of the unofficial member of the Legislative Council – was in the forefront of opposition to this influx. Livingstone was then in a depressed state and was less well able to support refugees than the Copperbelt towns or Lusaka. Harry Susman was clearly feeling the strain when he wrote in April 1939 to the Jewish Guild in Bulawayo: 'We are feeding three families already, and I myself have spent three to four hundred pounds in guarantees and money given to them. What can one man do for a community – it is heartbreaking.'[19]

The Susmans were almost certainly not members of 'the club' – the United Services Club – of which their friend John Smith was chairman. This was a club for men only, which was dominated by civil servants. Women were allowed in for occasional dances and were also permitted to use the affiliated golf and tennis facilities. Both Bertha and Annie Susman took up golf in the early 1920s and played with the wives of senior civil servants. A new source of entertainment for the better-off residents of Livingstone from the end of the First World War onwards was motoring. Elie Susman was an active member of the Livingstone Motor and Cycle Club, which was set up in 1918. The other major new source of entertainment in the town was the cinema. The Grill family opened their first cinema in 1917, and also played a major part in the organisation of amateur dramatics. Jazz bands began to visit Livingstone and other Northern Rhodesian towns from the early 1920s.[20]

Travel and Transport

Even when nominally living with their families in Livingstone, the Susman brothers spent a great deal of time on the road or – more precisely, at least until the late 1920s – on the railway. In 1916, something of a crisis year, Elie spent most of six months away from home, including four months in Barotseland. From the evidence of his diary for 1920, it is clear that he spent four months of that year travelling. In this fairly typical year, he made two lengthy business trips to Elisabethville, two week-long visits to the Lusaka farms, a ten-day trip by boat to Sesheke, two trips to Bulawayo, and a three-week journey to Cape Town. He did not travel in that year to Ngamiland. Each of the brothers made several three-month treks to Maun in the years before the development of a motor road in the late 1920s made shorter journeys possible. In 1925 Harry Susman undertook a three-month journey with his family to Sesheke and Mongu. In the latter part of 1927 Elie Susman made a three-month journey through the Congo and Angola, travelling 10,000 kilometres by train and car. During this journey he visited the Angolan diamond fields at Dundu in an apparently vain attempt to secure the re-opening of the Barotseland cattle trade. He commented on the superior quality of the roads in the two countries, 'but saw no land that he preferred to that of Northern Rhodesia either for cattle or ranching'. During 1929 Elie and Bertha Susman were away for five months, visiting Europe and the United States; on their return from this long journey, Bertha set up home at Muizenberg. Elie continued to spend six months of the year in Livingstone until 1935, while Bertha and their youngest child David visited for several months in the year.[21]

There were, of course, dramatic developments in transport in Northern Rhodesia during the 1920s. Elie Susman witnessed on 5 March 1920 the arrival of the first aircraft to reach Livingstone. This was a Vickers Vimy, the *Silver Queen*, piloted by Colonel Pierre Van Ryneveld and Captain Brand. It was taking part in a two-plane race from London to Cape Town. Van Ryneveld and Brand failed to reach Cape Town in the plane in which they set off, but their competitor did not arrive at all. Almost the entire population of Livingstone, black and white, turned out for the event. Chief Imwiko had made a special trip from Sesheke and presented the colonel with a fly-whisk. Elie made his own first flight over the Victoria Falls a few months later on 21 July 1920. He flew in a plane called *The Rhodesian* that was piloted by Lieutenants Rutherford and Thompson. Elie described his first flight as 'the event in my life ... It was beautiful and very exciting. I really cannot describe the sensation. The Falls was a sight for the Gods.'[22]

Owing to the lack of suitable roads, it was only slowly that motor transport became a serious competitor with the railway. In July 1924 it was reported as a newsworthy event that Elie Susman had succeeded in driving to Kazungula by car. He said that the road was too sandy for a Ford – no doubt a Model T – it was not until 1926 that he was able to drive to Lusaka and the Leopard's Hill Ranch. It was only in 1928 that the government provided a pontoon to carry cars across the Kafue River. This made road-travel from the south to the north of the country easier. In 1927 there were reckoned to be 240 motor vehicles in the Batoka Province, which included Livingstone, and many more motorcycles.[23]

The Livingstone Business

The Susman brothers tried to ensure that at least one of them was usually in Livingstone, but they also relied on a number of managers. The most important of them was Lewis Hochstein. He was the key man in the office from the early 1920s until his departure for the United States in 1935. He had come from England to Kalomo with his parents as a child in 1905. His father had a store in Livingstone for many years, before moving to Broken Hill in 1922. Lewis Hochstein did most of the firm's correspondence. This was something which Harry Susman could not do in English, though he did sometimes dictate letters from notes which he kept in Yiddish – a language which Hochstein would probably have spoken and certainly understood. According to one story, Harry Susman could not originally sign his name, he was said to know only one of the three Rs – the last one – but the manager of the Standard Bank in Livingstone was able to recognise Harry's mark, which consisted of a certain number of crossed vertical and horizontal lines. Hochstein made two trips to the USA in the late 1920s and returned from one of them with a wife from Akron, Ohio. According to Hymie Wolffe, who worked for the firm's auditors in the late 1920s and early 1930s, Hochstein was a very competent manager. After his departure, Robert Davidson, an Old Drifter who had worked for F. J. Clarke's Zambesi Trading Association for many years, acted as manager for a while. Elie noted in his diary in 1936 that he had given Harry's son, Joe, this 'billet'. Joe had inherited his father's charm, and is described as a perfect gentleman. He was also a sportsman, and a great fisherman, but he was never thought to be a deskman. After leaving school he had worked for a while at Leopard's Hill Ranch in 1929–30, but he then travelled to England on his own. He married his first wife, Lou Stanley, in Liverpool and returned to Northern Rhodesia from Liverpool with her in 1936. He joined the army soon after the outbreak of the Second World War and served as a staff sergeant.[24]

The most important of the firm's business interests in Livingstone was the Pioneer Butchery and Bakery. For long periods it was the only butchery in town. It was always difficult for anyone else to compete with the Susmans because of their control over the Ngamiland cattle trade. The *Livingstone Mail* reported in its review of 1923, a year of depression, that 'the first rumblings of the meat war' were heard in April when two new butcheries opened up and prices fell from one shilling to three pence a pound. A nephew of Egnatz Snapper, Sidney Diamond, who had recently come down from Barotseland, was the promoter of one of them. He went on to be the most successful trader in the Copperbelt town of Kitwe and a legendary figure. According to his widow, Molly, an unusually reliable source, he was knocked out of the competition when the Susmans' Pioneer Butchery lowered its price to seven pence a pound. This was less than the price at which he could himself buy meat.[25]

Max Taube, the owner of a successful hardware store and building business, and a prominent member of the Jewish community, set up another butchery with A. T. Dreyer in 1926. 'Braam' Dreyer was very close to the Susmans, probably getting his meat from them, and he continued to be a partner with them in another enterprise. He became a member of the new Livingstone Town Council in 1929, but died soon afterwards as a result of injuries received when he was accidentally shot while crossing the Sindi River in a truck. Another old friend of the Susmans, F. D. Law, ran the Victoria Falls Butchery. It was the only surviving competitor in 1934, but was said to have 'an arrangement' with Susman Brothers. There may have been rather more competition in the bakery business. The Susmans' long-serving employee, Herbert Rothkugel, joined Max Taube in 1925 to set up the Livingstone Bakery, Tea Room, and Frascati Restaurant. This establishment boasted that it did all the catering for the visit of the Prince of Wales. Rothkugel was bankrupt by 1930, though he seems to have remained in business in the town.[26]

The Susmans opened one new business in Livingstone in the early 1930s. When Elie Susman's family became more or less permanently resident at the Cape at the end of 1929, he kept a bungalow in Livingstone for his own use. The family home, Maramba House, was rebuilt and became the Windsor Hotel. The *Livingstone Mail* noted that 'many of the older residents cherish the recollection of the hospitality they received there when Mrs Susman was in residence'. It described the reconstructed hotel as having high ceilings and electric fans in the dining room and lounge, which opened on to a huge veranda. The *Mail* also mentioned the quality of the furniture, which had been made by Zambesi Saw Mills from local woods – including *mukwa*. A later advertisement made a feature of the hotel's tennis court, and its convenience for the golf course and cricket ground.[27]

Ranches and Farms

The Susmans continued to be heavily engaged throughout the 1920s and the 1930s in cattle buying along the Line of Rail. They bought cattle from farmers at auctions, but also had partners, such as Abraham Wacks and George Buchanan, who were involved in the early 1920s in cattle buying from the Ila people in today's Southern Province. The Susmans supplied ivory bangles, which were essential as trade goods in the Ila area, to Wacks. According to one source, Wacks, a Viennese Jew, had previously been involved in the design and import of bangles, which were made in Austria from an early form of plastic. This proved to be highly inflammable and did serious injury to a number of innocent users, so Wacks was prohibited from importing any more and had to fall back on the genuine article. The Susmans also dealt with the Cavadias, the Greek traders at Pemba and Namwala. They were close to the American rancher, George Horton, of Lion's Kop Ranch, but were never very close to 'Mopani' Clarke, another prominent rancher. He seems to have been a regular supplier to H. C. Werner, a competitor. The brothers declined to join the Livestock Cooperative Society, which was set up at the instigation of John Smith in 1931 in an attempt to bolster producer prices. They saw it, as did many other traders and ranchers, as an attempt to cut out the middleman. Elie Susman was also concerned by the threat posed by the society to their Ngamiland interests and feared that it might allow 'dumping' of cattle by Southern Rhodesia. The society eventually fell under the control of another competitor, Sam Haslett, who ran the butchery in Lusaka. The cattle industry was placed under statutory regulation in 1937 with the establishment of the Cattle Marketing and Control Board, the idea was to keep up prices for local producers and to regulate imports.[28]

Leopard's Hill Ranch, near Lusaka, was used as a holding ranch for cattle bought along the Line of Rail. The ranch was run as two units. Its long-serving managers in the 1920s and early 1930s were W. F. Elderkin and R. H. Wienand. The depredations of lions and leopards continued to be a serious problem on the ranch. It was reported in 1921 that 'a marauding lion entered a kraal and seized a full-grown cow. In spite of every effort on the part of the manager to trap the beast it was not until the casualties had numbered four head on four successive nights that Mr. Wienand's endeavours were crowned with success.' Ten years later it was said that eighty cattle had been lost to lions on the ranch and in the late 1930s leopards were reported to be a problem. By that time the manager was Paddy Drake, an Irishman and a well-known hunter. It was with him that the young David Susman shot his first leopard in 1938 – at the age of twelve. On his retirement Drake worked a small gold mine on the property – it is still known as Drake's Mine.[29]

Leopard's Hill Ranch had been enlarged after complex negotiations with the government in 1927. The Susmans said that they needed more land because the ranch was seriously overstocked. In the end they settled for an additional 14,000 acres in two blocks. This was much less than they had originally applied for. The Native Reserves Commission, which sat in the previous year, had allocated most of the land that they wanted to the Soli Reserve. As a result of the establishment of the reserve, the Susmans were told that they would not have to make provision for people who might be displaced from their new land. They reckoned that they had about 400 people, including 150 labourers, living on the original parts of the ranch.[30]

The Susmans were at this time bringing in pedigree breeding stock from England and South Africa. In October 1927 they brought in nineteen South Devon pedigree bulls and forty-two South Devon heifers. They then said that they expected to bring in a further 500 'well bred' breeding stock. The *Livingstone Mail* took this as evidence that the cattle industry was reviving and that 'local enterprise is being stimulated'. In the early 1930s there seem to have been an average of about 3,000 cattle on the ranch. In the early 1920s they planted up to 200 acres of wheat as well as mealies there, using bat guano from Leopard's Hill caves as fertiliser.[31]

During the 1920s the brothers bought and sold a number of other farms in the Lusaka District. They grew tobacco on Kabulonga Farm, which was much closer to the railway line, but they sold the farm after the collapse of tobacco prices in 1928. It later became the site of Lusaka's most exclusive suburb. They also owned a section of a farm, Villa Elisabetta, farm number 110a, which was on the railway line and close to the centre of Lusaka. They sold this land to David Shapiro who used it for brick making during the construction of the new town of Lusaka in the early 1930s. The farm is today the site of much of Lusaka's heavy industrial area. By the end of the decade they had also sold their Gwaai River and Zimba farms. At the same time, they took over Wolverton Ranch, on the Kafue River in the Mazabuka

8 Harry Susman with workers stringing tobacco at Kabulonga Farm, Lusaka, 1927.

District. It was named after its founder, Frederick Glyn, Lord Wolverton – one of a number of members of the House of Lords who became landowners in Northern Rhodesia. In the early 1930s the Susmans usually had about 2,000 cattle on this ranch, which is now part of the Nakambala Sugar Estate. In 1932 they owned a total of 12,000 cattle, spread over the ranches in Northern Rhodesia, their forestry concession in Southern Rhodesia and grazing areas in Bechuanaland. They were valued at the low point of the Depression at £36,000.[32]

Timber

From their base in Livingstone the Susman brothers became involved in the post-war years in a number of new enterprises involving partnerships. Some of these, such as those with Robert Sutherland in the Zambesi Transport Syndicate, and R. F. Sutherland Ltd, have already been mentioned. They were also involved in a partnership with A. T. Dreyer in the Mapanda Transport Company. This represented their first formal involvement in the timber business with which they were to have a continuing association. Zambesi Saw Mills Ltd became the major industrial enterprise in Livingstone, and in Northern Rhodesia, in the later years of the First World War. It had its origin in the Livingstone Saw Mills, which were set up in 1911 by Lewis and Michael Jacobs, Lithuanian Jews from Kipuski, and Hippocrates Troumbas, a Greek from the island of Samos. The business was taken over and transformed in 1915–16 by A. F. Philip and Company, who were based in Bulawayo. The Philips were descendants of the great Scottish missionary, and superintendent of the London Missionary Society, Dr John Philip. They began their business as timber importers in Port Elizabeth and extended it through Bulawayo to Livingstone where they had a branch by 1914. Their timber manager in Bulawayo was W. E. Tongue, and their manager in Livingstone from October 1915 was C. S. 'Charlie' Knight. These two men were to play important roles in the timber industry for over thirty years. They also became close friends and business associates of the Susman brothers.[33]

Charlie Knight also played an important part in the political and social life of Livingstone. He was a Londoner who had been a major building contractor in Port Elizabeth. He became the first elected mayor of Livingstone in 1929, and was twice re-elected. His popularity was certainly enhanced by his successful construction from timber of a floating crocodile-proof swimming pool, which was launched in the Zambezi, near the Boat Club, in 1930. Unlike Leopold Moore, he was an early advocate of the amalgamation of the two Rhodesias. He was succeeded as manager of Zambesi Saw Mills by Jimmy Mitchell, but then did most of the company's logging operations as a contractor through his own company – Knight and Folkestad Ltd. Knight's partner in this business was a Norwegian, Sofus Knutzen; the company was merged with Zambesi Saw Mills when Knutzen left the country in 1931.[34]

Zambesi Saw Mills had secured in 1916 a large contract for sleepers from Rhodesia Railways. These were to be made from Rhodesian teak, also known as redwood, or *mukusi*. At first they were cut at the Mapanda Mill in the forest about thirty miles west of Livingstone, and ten miles north of the Zambezi, and then taken on wagons to the Zambezi and shipped by barge to the railhead at Livingstone. This proved very expensive because of the need to trans-ship cargoes several times around rapids. Between 1917 and 1919 a wooden tramway was constructed from the forest to Livingstone and the sawmill was moved to the town. The tramway was financed by Rhodesia Railways, which then took a stake in the company. The completion of the narrow-gauge tramway required the construction of bridges across rivers, such as the Sindi – the first bridge there was built from huge timbers and was a remarkable feat of engineering. From 1919 until 1924 timber was carried to the mill on ten-ton bogies drawn by relays of oxen.[35]

This was where the Susman brothers, 'Braam' Dreyer, and the Mapanda Transport Company, came into the picture. Their oxen shifted large quantities of timber six days a week over a thirty-mile route. In 1924–5 the tramway was replaced by a normal-gauge steel railway and locomotives replaced the oxen, but large numbers of oxen were still required for hauling timber in the forest. The Susmans and Dreyer continued with this work, employing many labourers and as many as 1,000 oxen. By 1930 the main Zambesi Saw Mills railway had been extended for over 100 miles to the Machili concession on the east bank of the Machili River. In 1934 a new mill was constructed on this concession at Mulobezi, which was to remain a major centre of timber operations for many years. The Depression led to reduced demand and production for a few years, but the Livingstone mill was back to three shifts by 1934.[36]

The Susmans became more heavily involved in timber extraction in 1930, when they became the main contractors for the extraction of timber from a concession on the south side of the Zambezi in Southern Rhodesia. In order to get timber from here to the mill in Livingstone, Zambesi Saw Mills built an eleven-mile branch line to the Zambezi near Katombora from a junction on their new Malanda line about eighteen miles out of Livingstone. They also built an enormous pontoon from local mahogany, capable of carrying five bogie trucks laden with timber – a total weight of sixty tons – across the Zambezi. On the south bank Susman Brothers constructed a narrow-gauge railway into the Kazungula and Westwood forests. By 1934 this extended for twenty-two miles to the border with the Bechuanaland Protectorate and used three locomotives. Two of these, known as Cement I and II, had started life in the 1890s on the original narrow-gauge line between Beira and Umtali, and the third on a zinc mine north of Lusaka. From 1935 to 1937 the Susmans worked an adjacent concession in Bechuanaland – this required the construction of a further thirty miles of line. The technique of timber extraction involved the continuous movement of branch lines through the forest and the cutting of a swathe of timber for about a quarter of a mile on each side of them. Oxen – again as many as 1,000 of them – then hauled the cut timber along the branch lines to the main line.[37]

The logistical problems involved in laying track, servicing locomotives and running trains over sand and through vleis, or dambos, and seasonal floods were immense. It was fortunate for the Susmans that their concession area was fairly level – not more than undulating – and that they did not have to build bridges. They eventually abandoned the Bechuanaland concession when they came to a valley that would have been both difficult and expensive to bridge. It was, however, not unusual for locomotives to topple over and it required a huge effort to jack them back onto the track. The pontoon was sunk twice – once when a bogie ran off the end while a laden train was being winched down on to it, and once again in April 1934, when floods dislodged its cable and the fully laden pontoon was sunk seventy yards from the bank and settled fifteen feet below the surface of the Zambezi. On the latter occasion it took most of a year to raise it from the bottom of the river.[38]

R. T. 'Bob' Cooke was the Susmans' senior locomotive driver/fitter from September 1931 until November 1937 when they closed down the Bechuanaland concession. He recalled that they aimed to shift two trains of 100–120 tons of timber a day for six days a week. He also said that it was the high rate of royalties levied by the Bechuanaland Protectorate that 'knocked Susmans'. Their Southern Rhodesian operations may have been profitable, in spite of the fact that they were carried on at the low point of the Depression, but it is unlikely that they made anything out of the Bechuanaland concession. They found the good trees thinly scattered, but they were not allowed by the forestry department to 'cherry-pick' them. When Harry Susman was offered a further extension of the Chobe concession in 1936, his reply was an emphatic 'No!' This was not, however, the end of the Susman brothers' involvement with the timber industry. They continued to provide trek oxen and slaughter cattle to Zambesi Saw Mills and eventually came to control it.[39]

The Copperbelt

The development of the Northern Rhodesian Copperbelt began to take off with the reorganisation of the Bwana Mkubwa Mine, near Ndola, in 1922 and the granting by the Chartered Company of prospecting rights over a large area to the Rhodesia–Congo Border Concessions Company in 1923. The involvement of the Susman brothers pre-dated these developments: between 1916 and 1918 they owned two concessions, which covered part of what eventually became the Nkana Mine. They acquired these through a prospector, H. C. Winnicott, who worked for them, their names appearing on the original title deeds. The stories that the brothers bought them for £100, or acquired them in exchange for a grand piano, appear to be apocryphal. In fact, they seem to have spent about £400 on what they called the 'Nkana Prospects', and had to defend them in a case before the commissioner for mines against a charge by the Bwana Mkubwa Mine, which claimed that Winnicott had moved its pegs. They won the case and offered the claims to Bwana Mkubwa for £100, but their offer was turned down; the Susmans eventually sold the claims in 1918 to William Lee. The brothers seem, however, to have retained the trading rights on the concessions. Lee did further prospecting and the claims changed hands several times for larger and larger sums of money in the next few years, and they eventually became part of one of the richest copper mines in the world. It is not clear how the Susmans were drawn into mineral speculation. Elie Susman's old partner, John Austen, owned claims in the same area and it may have been through him that they became involved. It was the Susmans' misfortune to have owned these claims at the wrong time: their value did not lie in the exposed oxide ores, but in the massive underground sulphide ores. The existence of these ores was unknown in 1918, but anyway they would have been unworkable with the techniques then available. When travelling to the Copperbelt by train in 1936, Sir Ernest Oppenheimer, Chairman of the Anglo American Corporation, which had developed the mine, entered Elie Susman's compartment and introduced himself. He said that he had always wanted to meet the man who had owned the Nkana Mine and sold it for £100.[40]

The Susmans may have missed out on some more realistic opportunities in connection with the development of the Copperbelt. They allowed their rival, H. C. Werner, to establish a commanding position as supplier of trek and slaughter oxen to the mining companies in the development phase which began in the late 1920s. 'Wingy' Werner, as he was known, on account of a damaged arm, is usually described as Dutch, but was almost certainly an Afrikaner. He had been involved in the cattle trade since the early years of the century when he was in partnership with Tom King, and by the mid 1920s he was living in semi-retirement on his farm, Hereford's, at Lusaka. When mining development began, he realised that large numbers of trek oxen would be required for transport through dense bush before the roads and branch railway lines could be built. He supplied oxen and organised transport for the mining companies. This put him in a strong position to secure contracts for the supply of slaughter stock to feed the large number of workers who were employed in the next stage of the construction process. He secured the meat contracts for the two big mining groups, Rhodesian Anglo American and Rhodesian Selection Trust. The Susmans only had the contract for the older established Bwana Mkubwa Mine, but sold cattle to Werner to enable him to meet his other contracts. As their Ngamiland cattle were squeezed out of the Congo trade in 1928–9 by cheaper Southern Rhodesian stock, the Susmans had to fight to be allowed to bring in cattle from Ngamiland to supply the new demand from the mines. They succeeded in persuading the government to allow them to do this in the first months of 1930. The flow of Ngamiland cattle continued until early 1933 – by which time demand had fallen off dramatically as a result of the delayed, but still devastating, impact of the Depression putting a stop to construction work.[41]

The Susmans' first real move into the Copperbelt came when they took over the Bwana Mkubwa Hotel and Ndola Butchery and Bakery from Messrs Greenberg and Kriegler in September 1928. This was a relatively small investment, but it did not work out well. Elie Susman invited an old friend, Willie Hepker, to come up from Bulawayo to manage the hotel. He was one of the Hepker brothers, Latvian Jews who had established a strong position in the butchery business in Bulawayo and had gone on to establish a timber business which was similar to Zambesi Saw Mills. It supplied sleepers to Rhodesia Railways from *mukusi* forests between Bulawayo and the Zambezi.

Willie Hepker had fallen out with his brothers and was in financial difficulties, with debts of £5,000. Elie Susman offered him the management and a partnership in the hotel. Elie did this as a favour, but he was concerned that Hepker's creditors might have claims against a partnership, so he changed his mind about the partnership and set the business up as a company, Northern Suppliers Ltd, financed by loans from Susman Brothers. Willie Hepker and his wife, Rebecca, did a good job of managing the hotel, which became very popular, but he spent too much money on refurbishment and the hotel's profitability was threatened by the onset of the Depression. The Susmans decided to put the company into voluntary liquidation and to sell the hotel. They offered to share any proceeds from the liquidation with Hepker, but he challenged this decision in the courts, claiming that he was a partner and not an employee. He won the case on a technicality, but the liquidation went ahead; the Susmans' nephew, Maurice Gersh, was sent up to the Copperbelt at the end of 1929 to manage the business and act as one of the liquidators.[42]

A consequence of this failure was to bring new investors onto the scene. The business was sold to a new company, Northern Caterers Ltd, which was set up in 1930. The major investors in it were the Sussman brothers. They were Lithuanian Jews, but were not related to the Susmans. Philip Sussman had, like Hepker, been a friend of Elie Susman in Southern Rhodesia. He had gone on to establish himself in Kimberley as the major supplier of beef to De Beer's and was a close friend of Sir Ernest Oppenheimer. Willie Sussman, one of his brothers, was a rancher in Southern Rhodesia. He brought into the company his partner, Isadore Kollenberg, who was to play an important role in it over the next forty years. The Kollenbergs were, like the Hepkers, Latvian Jews. Isadore Kollenberg's father, Edward, and his brother, Henrie, had started trading at Lusaka in 1908. The Susman brothers were minority shareholders in this new company, which built hotels at Nkana and Nchanga, and set up bakeries and bottle stores in many of the Copperbelt towns. Elie Susman was actively involved in the management of the company – especially in the construction of the splendid Nkana Hotel, which was completed in 1932. It is still a fine building, even though it has seen better days. It cost £40,000 to erect – a fabulous sum at that time and place.[43]

There is a danger that the dry recital of company history may give the misleading impression that the Susmans and their partners were operating in a conventional business environment. This splendid hotel was built in a place which the geologist, J. A. Bancroft, described on his first visit five years earlier as 'a snake park'. He said that he saw more snakes in a few months at Nkana than he had seen in the previous nine years which he had spent prospecting in the Northern Rhodesian bush. The following is part of his description of the place as he first saw it in April 1927:

> Puff adders were very numerous, including some specimens of the gaboon adder type. Spitting cobras were common and occasionally green mambas made their appearance. The first night I occupied my rondavel I was wakened by an unusual noise which caused me to flash my electric torch on the floor. There two puff adders, each two to three feet in length, were emitting peculiar guttural noises. Stepping outside I found a stick and killed both of them. More interesting were the denizens of the surrounding forest. Rarely a night passed without hearing the roaring of lions in the distance and the subdued cough of prowling leopards in closer proximity.[44]

The Susmans also became minority holders in a second company, Copperfields Cold Storage Ltd, which was set up the following year by the same group of investors. 'Bongola' Smith took a minority share in this company, together with his son-in-law, Abe Gelman. The company appears to have taken over Smith's farming interests in Northern Rhodesia: there was an agreement that he would not compete with Copperfields in the Northern Rhodesian market and that it would not compete with his company, Elakat, in the Congo. Smith had been prepared to sustain heavy losses in order to break into the Copperbelt market and had sought a partnership with Werner. Under this new dispensation, Copperfields and H. C. Werner shared the Copperbelt market. Werner retained the Rhodesian Selection Trust meat contracts and supplied their mine towns – Mufulira and Luanshya. Copperfields secured the Anglo American meat contracts and dominated the butchery business at Nkana and Nchanga. Werner died in 1933, but his widow, Alberta Henrietta Werner, carried on the business with the help of her manager, E. W. Dechow. There were soon complaints from farmers, such as Hamish Forsyth of Luezi Ranch, Zimba, that Copperfields and Werners had set up a cartel and that this had a depressing effect on cattle prices. The Susman brothers may have had some sympathy with this view. Elie Susman did not get on well with Isadore Kollenberg, who became the manager of the company. In the course of the 1930s the Susmans reduced their stake in Copperfields, and in 1937 took a significant, though not yet controlling, share in Werners. This eventually became the vehicle through which they took on Copperfields and broke the cartel.[45]

The Susman brothers became involved in one more Copperbelt enterprise at this time. In conjunction with their nephews, Maurice and Harry Gersh, they set up in 1931 a company called Economy Stores Ltd. It established stores, which eventually became department stores, on the mine concessions at Nkana and Nchanga. Starting at the low point of the Depression it had a slow start, but became increasingly profitable with the recovery of the Copperbelt from depression in the later months of 1933. Harry Gersh had joined his brother on the Copperbelt in 1930 and set up his own store at Nchanga; he moved to Nkana early in 1931 when Elie Susman helped his nephews identify a store site. By 1936 he was able to report that the company had made pleasing progress. Maurice Gersh worked for some years with Copperfields Cold Storage and Northern Caterers, supervising their activities at Ndola, Luanshya and Bwana Mkubwa. After a few years, he was able to devote his entire attention to the development of Economy Stores. In 1935-6 he played a leading part in negotiations with the government, resulting in the establishment of the new town of Kitwe. The traders on the Nkana mine concession paid large premiums for sites at nearby Kitwe, but were given twenty years' protection against new competition. There was also a guarantee that no new township would be set up within twenty miles of the Nkana Mine's smoke stack. This was the first of the 'closed townships'. Similar arrangements were made later at Mufulira and Chingola. Maurice Gersh had a large share of his uncles' business acumen; Economy Stores was to serve as the base for an enormous proliferation of enterprises in the post-war years.[46]

Woolworths

The Susman brothers' response to the Depression may seem surprising. On the one hand they pulled out of Barotseland, at least partially, and tried to run down their Ngamiland business, but at much the same time they became involved in three or four new businesses. One explanation for this could be that the Depression hit the Copperbelt rather late. Until 1931 it seemed that Northern Rhodesia in general, and the Copperbelt in particular, might escape its worst impact. It failed to do so and the Depression was severe in 1932–3, when the Bwana Mkubwa Mine closed down and construction work was stopped at several others. The Nkana and Roan Antelope (Luanshya) mines began production at the lowest point of the Depression in the middle of 1932. Recovery began with the announcement of the re-opening of Mufulira in July 1933, and from 1934 onwards business on the Copperbelt was good, which had a stimulating effect on the rest of the Northern Rhodesian economy. The Susman brothers had also had to contend with the impact of Britain's departure from the gold standard in 1931 while South Africa remained on it. Elie Susman seems to have hedged against currency fluctuations by successful speculation in the shares of Northern Rhodesian copper mines and South African gold mines.[47]

It was as the recovery from the Depression in Northern Rhodesia and South Africa was nearing completion that the Susman brothers made their most momentous new investment. In December 1934 they agreed to take a share in Woolworths, a firm which had been started a few years previously in Cape Town by Max Sonnenberg. His links with the Susmans went back to their earliest days in Francistown. He went on to become an MP in South Africa and had a varied, but not wholly successful, business career. He bought a department store in Cape Town in 1929, which became the first branch of Woolworths in 1931. There was no connection with F. W. Woolworth; Sonnenberg was encouraged to pirate the name by a firm of London agents who were already supplying shops of the same name in Australia and New Zealand. From 1930 onwards, Elie Susman began to spend half the year with his wife and family at the house – 'Barotse' – which he built in Beach Road, Muizenberg. Max Sonnenberg moved there at the same time and they resumed their friendship. Sonnenberg suggested that Elie Susman should finance and manage the expansion of the business to Johannesburg and the Transvaal.[48]

An agreement was concluded in December 1934 under which Susman Brothers, of Livingstone, would invest £25,000 in Woolworths and take a twenty per cent share in the business. In fact, Susman Brothers, and Elie Susman on his own account, invested over £50,000 in the business in the next two years. Elie moved his family from Cape Town to Johannesburg and became a director of the original company in June 1935. He was then almost fully employed in supervising the finishing of the first store in Johannesburg, which opened later in the year, and Woolworths was launched as a public company in 1936. Elie not only became a director of the new company, but also had a contract as the manager of the business in the Transvaal. Most of the investment was in the name of Susman Brothers and the involvement with Woolworths was seen as a joint venture. Although Harry Susman was never involved in the management of the company, he continued to draw a half share of Elie's salary until July 1941. A letter survives from that date in which Harry formally released Elie from this obligation.[49]

It is not entirely clear how the Susmans were able to finance this large new investment. Some of the money came from the sale of stocks and shares. Some came from the sale of Ngamiland cattle at good prices on the Johannesburg market. A good deal of it must have come from an overdraft at Standard Bank in Livingstone, which was secured on the Susman brothers' assets in Northern Rhodesia. Their overdraft there in 1939 was over £50,000, though some of that must have been used in the financing of Northern Rhodesian businesses. Elie Susman was fifty-five years old when he began to work on a more or less full-time basis for Woolworths. This was an extraordinary challenge for a man in late middle age to take on after nearly forty years of hard work in extremely difficult circumstances. He continued to show exceptional energy and dynamism and played a leading part in the development of one of South Africa's most successful retail chains. Although he was unable to spend as much time as he had done previously in Northern Rhodesia, there was no lessening in his interest in the country. He continued to take new initiatives and to launch new enterprises, both north and south of the Zambezi.[50]

Livingstone – the Depression and After

Livingstone as a town did suffer from the Depression, but no more than anywhere else in the country. Its recovery was, however, thwarted by the movement of the railway workshops to Broken Hill in 1932, and by the decision to move the capital to Lusaka. The new capital was officially opened in 1935. Although some departments remained in Livingstone, there was an exodus of civil servants and a decline in the white population. Elie Susman's final departure from Livingstone coincided with this change. From 1935 onwards he was only able to spend one or two months a year in the country – he usually came up from Johannesburg twice a year. Harry Susman was then the main representative of the family in Livingstone until his retirement to a farm near Salisbury in 1945. He had become a much-loved character about whom innumerable stories were told – all of which relate to his good humour. The *Livingstone Mail*'s Lusaka correspondent typically noted in 1922: 'Mr Susman also paid us a visit and was his usual cheery self in spite of quiet times'.[51] There is only space here for a couple of anecdotes that give something of the flavour of the man. Both come from officials of the type who did not always give the Susman brothers an easy time in their younger days. Charles Murray, later secretary for agriculture in the Federation of Rhodesia and Nyasaland, recalled that he had been forced to go without food for twenty-four hours when travelling from Bulawayo to Kafue to judge cattle at the agricultural show in 1933. He was very relieved when:

> Thank goodness a wonderful man got on the train at Livingstone with a huge basket laden with enough food for at least four people, and as soon as the train pulled out of the station he opened the basket and – thank goodness – invited me to share it with him. We had a very pleasant day on the train together, and my companion became a very good friend: he was the great and well-liked Harry Susman, who had an exhibit of Afrikanders in the show that year.[52]

Malcolm Billing, the former resident commissioner in Barotseland, and minister for African affairs in the Northern Rhodesian government, remembered in an unpublished memoir:

> From time to time he travelled out to see his labour force, and he always insisted on sleeping for the night in one or other of his forests. He would arrange for his camp bed to be set up amongst the trees, and this was just a little risky because he would be out on his own in lion-country. It was a fact that on more than one occasion the next morning spoor showed that lions had been close to his couch. But they never molested him; our friend maintained that the sight of a mosquito net put them off. After many years in Rhodesia he decided to have a holiday in England. This he did, and on his return he was asked what he had enjoyed most during his visit. To this enquiry came the intriguing reply: 'There was one remarkable spectacle. I saw the Grenadier Guards manuring all over the Salisbury Plain.'[53]

Although Harry Susman was always the junior partner and lacked the entrepreneurial genius of Elie, he was no fool. When the young George Horton accompanied him to a cattle sale, he was asked to keep a note of Harry's purchases, but he found that his work was largely superfluous: Harry could remember every detail of the day's sale. His preference was for cattle dealing and ranching, though he was also much involved in the forestry work; he continued to pay regular visits to Ngamiland, and he retained a great love for Barotseland. When Abe Galaun, then a young Jewish refugee from Lithuania, told him in 1940 that he had got a job at Mongu, Harry immediately replied: 'You're a very lucky man. It's the best place in the world'. The brothers never despaired of getting back into the Barotseland cattle trade, which had been the source of their initial success.[54]

From 1933 onwards there was serious talk of a campaign for the eradication of bovine pleuro-pneumonia in Barotseland, and from 1934–5 there was talk of slaughtering cattle at Mulobezi and using the Zambesi Saw Mills railway to bring meat to Livingstone in refrigerated trucks. An alternative scheme, sometimes called the Susman Scheme, was to truck live cattle from Mulobezi to the abattoir at Livingstone. Seamus Morris, the chief veterinary officer, suggested that the Susmans should be involved in this project and the idea may in fact have come from them. Other traders feared that the government intended to give the Susmans a monopoly over a revived Barotseland trade. Harry and Elie travelled together to Senanga in 1935 to inspect cattle that had been bought on their behalf in anticipation of this scheme coming to fruition. The programme of vaccination and eradication of 'P.P.' by the identification and slaughter of 'lungers', did not, in fact, get under way until 1937. From that year onwards the Susmans were able to buy cattle in Barotseland for sale as trek and slaughter stock for Zambesi Saw Mills. In 1938 they bought several thousand head of cattle in anticipation of the opening, in January 1939, of the Livingstone abattoir to cattle railed down from Mulobezi.[55]

There was a link between the approach of war in 1939, the higher price of copper on the world market, higher levels of employment on the mines, and an increasing demand for beef. The re-opening of the Barotseland cattle trade after seventeen years of closure, and of the Ngamiland trade after five or six years of closure, provided the Susman brothers with great new opportunities in the two markets which had been the corner stones of their business. Their ability to respond was limited by Elie's preoccupation with Woolworths, and Harry's increasing age. The next generation of the family was not yet ready to take over. Joe Susman was old enough, but did not show much aptitude or inclination for business, Oscar and David were still too young. The Susmans' daughters were, however, beginning to marry and to bring sons-in-law into the family. In what was undoubtedly Livingstone's wedding of the decade, Ella Susman married Harry Robinson in June 1936 in the presence of 300 guests. He was a well-known sportsman and a Salisbury wholesaler who was just about to set up his own business. Three years later, Elie's daughter Peggy married Maurice Rabb in Johannesburg, he was a graduate of the University of the Witwatersrand and a junior executive at

Woolworths. Both men were to play a prominent part in this story in the post-war years, but they did not do so immediately.[56]

It was Harry Susman who befriended and recruited the young man who was to play an increasingly dynamic role in the continuation and development of the business during the war years, and for over twenty years after it ended. He was Harry Wulfsohn and his surname was soon to become inseparably linked with that of Susman. He was a young Jewish immigrant from Saldus, Latvia, who had arrived in Northern Rhodesia in 1930 to join his sister in Ndola. It was a shared love of cattle trading which drew him to Harry Susman, whom he came to love as a father. He almost certainly had earlier links with the Susmans, but a kind of partnership seems to have begun when they agreed in August 1939 to sell to Wulfsohn the Pioneer Butchery, which they had owned for thirty years. It is to the earlier life of Harry Wulfsohn that we will now turn.

CHAPTER 10

Harry Wulfsohn: From Latvia To Livingstone, 1930–44

Hozias (Joshua) Vulfsohns, later known as Harry Wulfsohn, was born at Saldus in what was then the Russian province of Kurland on 10 March 1911. The province became part of the independent state of Latvia in 1918. Harry Wulfsohn was a full generation younger than the Susman brothers and too young to remember the days of the Russian Empire. He may, however, have recalled the dislocation caused by the First World War, which broke out when he was three. The Russian government had been threatening for most of a century to withdraw the Jewish population from border areas. Soon after the outbreak of war most of the Jews of Kurland were forcibly removed into Greater Russia, and only a minority returned. The Wulfsohn family does not seem to have been affected by this move, but Saldus was occupied for a time by German forces. It was a small market town in the southwestern corner of Latvia, lying on the railway line about half way between the two main towns – Riga and Libau. The economy of Latvia was more highly developed than that of Lithuania and the town was more prosperous than the Susmans' Riteve. It had a significant Jewish minority, but there was no ghetto. There was one main synagogue, or *shul*, and two smaller houses of prayer. Although anti-Semitism was endemic, the inter-war years were a time of relative freedom for the country's Jewish population.[1]

Harry Wulfsohn was the fifth child and eldest son of Isaac and Chaya (Haja) Vulfsohns. His father was a butcher by trade and a stern disciplinarian, and his mother was a deeply religious woman. The family was not well off, but she went out every Friday with a basket of food to give to people who were poorer than she was. The family lived in a small house with two storeys on a street where most of the neighbours were Jewish tailors and workers. The family were Orthodox Jews and their home language was

Yiddish. One of the elder sisters, Hessie, recalled that they spoke Yiddish at home and Latvian at school, the younger children attending a Hebrew school run by a Mr Finkelstein. The family was influenced by Zionism, but of a religious and not a secular type. A younger sister, Josephine, was expelled from Mr Finkelstein's school when she became the secretary of a Zionist/socialist youth group.

The young Harry Wulfsohn was bright, but bored with school. According to his younger brother, Wulf, better known as Wulfie, 'he had the knack of making money from his bar mitzvah'. He learned about cattle trading from his father and was soon doing it on his own account. On market days, Thursdays and Fridays, he would go out to trade with peasant farmers who were on their way to market. In winter he would go out into the forests with his father's cart and bring it back laden with fox skins. His father had academic ambitions for the young boy, but his mother turned a blind eye to his truancy as his trading ventures increased the family income.

In 1929, when he was about eighteen, Harry Wulfsohn's aunt, Miriam Levenson – she was the widow of his mother's brother, Nathan Levenson – invited him to travel to South Africa with his sister, Marlie. Miriam was the licensee of the Grand Hotel (formerly the Masonic Hotel) at Barkly East, a small town in the Eastern Cape, which lies close to the borders of Lesotho (formerly Basutoland) and the Transkei. His aunt's invitation may have been prompted by the prospect of restrictions on Jewish immigration to South Africa. There was a rush of immigration from the Baltic states in 1929–30. This was in anticipation of the coming into force on 1 May 1930 of the Immigration Quota Act – an anti-Semitic measure that was associated with the name of the Afrikaner nationalist politician, Dr D. F. Malan.[2]

Harry worked for some time in the bar of his aunt's hotel, but did not stay long in South Africa. By 1930 he had followed Marlie to Ndola, where she married Abe Lowenthal, to whom she had been betrothed before she left Latvia. Marlie died tragically three years later. Her sister, Hessie, followed her to Africa and became Abe Lowenthal's second wife in 1934. Abe was born at Sabile in Latvia in 1904 and had reached Southern Rhodesia in 1924 and Northern Rhodesia in 1926. With his brother, William, he opened the Bijou Cinema at Ndola in 1929; another brother, Conrad, reached the country in 1932. Abe had been brought out to central Africa from Latvia by his Hepker uncles. The four Hepker brothers came from Goldingen in Latvia. They were somewhat older than the Susman brothers, but their business had followed a similar trajectory. The eldest brother, Hermann, had worked his way through South West Africa, the Cape and Bechuanaland to Southern

Rhodesia. He started the Charter Butchery in Bulawayo in 1896 and was actively involved in the Barotseland cattle trade in its early years. In 1911 he and his brothers founded the Rhodesian Native Timber Concessions Company, which extracted timber from forests around Nyamandhlovu in northern Matabeleland. One of the brothers, Willie Hepker, was on the Copperbelt in 1928–30, and has already featured in this story.[3]

Harry Wulfsohn arrived in Ndola after the onset of the Depression, but before it hit Northern Rhodesia with its full intensity. He knew little English and worked in his brother-in-law's cinema. He was dark in complexion and soon became known as 'Gandhi' or 'Gandhi's brother' – much to his annoyance. He probably did not stay long in Ndola, but soon moved south to Lusaka. He may have been encouraged to leave Ndola by the closure of the Bwana Mkubwa Mine in February 1931, which had a devastating effect on the economy of the town, and he may have been drawn to Lusaka by the presence there of his father's cousin, Samuel Barnett Wulfsohn. 'Tubby' Wulfsohn, as he was locally known, came from Froneberg, Kurland, and reached Livingstone before the First World War. He went on to trade at Kalomo, but moved north to the Congo before the end of the war; he did well there, but his business was hit by the Depression and he was back in Lusaka by 1930. 'Tubby' had married Floretta Glasstone, a Scots Jew, in the Congo. Her father, Reuben Glasstone, also moved north to the Congo through Northern Rhodesia before the First World War and had prospered for a while in Elisabethville.[4]

Lusaka

Another attractive feature of Lusaka was the government's decision to make it the capital of Northern Rhodesia. The Lusaka new town project was the only potential growth point in the country in 1931–3, when development work on the mines – with the exceptions of Nkana and Luanshya – came to a halt. Harry worked at first with David Shapiro, a young man who had reached Lusaka in the early 1920s from the pioneer Zionist settlement in Palestine, Rishon le Zion. Shapiro set up trading stores around Lusaka and profited more than any other local trader from the development of the new capital. In 1933 he won the contract to supply all the bricks and tiles for the new town project. According to family tradition, Harry lost his job – for which he is said to have been paid £5 a month – when Shapiro came on a surprise visit to an outlying store and found him sleeping on the shop counter. It may have been this experience that prompted Harry to set up in business on his own.[5]

There are a number of stories about how Harry Wulfsohn acquired his first capital. According to one of them, he had only one treasured possession, a gramophone, which he pawned for £1 with Lusaka's only pawnbroker who was either a Jew or a Scot – a Mr Levy in one version and a Mr Macpherson in another. He then walked for four hours into the bush and enjoyed a meal of *nsima* (maize porridge) and relish with a local chief or headman. After lunch he made a careful choice from among the headman's cattle and picked out a black cow, which he bought with his pound. He walked back to town with his cow and sold it to the local butcher, probably Sam Haslett, for £1.10s. His preferred field of trading activities was the newly defined Lenje Reserve, which was about ten miles north of Lusaka. After a while he saved enough money to buy a bicycle, which reduced the time he spent walking. He built his own wattle-and-daub hut on the outskirts of the town, but often spent the night at local villages on his trading trips.[6]

When Harry needed a loan of £50 to expand his business, he was advised to approach the town's only plumber, Jack Gerber. He approached the house nervously, hoping that he would be able to carry out the necessary negotiations in Yiddish. When the door was opened by Mrs Gerber, who was large and frightening, instead of her mild-mannered husband, Harry fled. He then tried the bank manager, who asked to see his balance sheet. Harry had to admit that he had no idea what a balance sheet was, but he impressed the manager with his enterprise and got the loan. His loan was obtained from Barclays Bank, which had recently set itself up in the town in competition with the Standard Bank. The latter's inspector commented rather acidly in June 1933: 'their Manager, who is particularly active, might well be described as a kind of "outdoor bank salesman" and it must be expected that he will make good use of their new building as an advertisement. I doubt whether the methods he adopts do him much good.'[7] Harry appears to have benefited from the manager's unorthodox approach, but these anecdotes illustrate how difficult it was for a young Jewish immigrant to get started in business in Northern Rhodesia at the low point of the Depression. Harry realised at this time that he must learn not only to speak, but also to read and write, English. He bought a batch of books at a sale – they included the Koran – and read his way through them. He never became a fluent writer of English, but he dictated remarkably lucid memoranda.

Lusaka was then not much more than a village. It had a white population of about 750 and an uncertain black population – probably several times higher. The town consisted of a railway station, a hotel and a dozen shops strung out along half a mile of one side of Cairo Road. Most of the shopkeepers were Jews and most of them still lived behind their shops, though a few houses had been built in the new suburb of Fairview. During 1931–2 two new buildings appeared in the town centre – the magistrate's offices or *boma* at the south end of Cairo Road, and a new post office in an underdeveloped parallel street. About £100,000 was spent during 1932 on the layout of the new capital site on the Ridgeway (now Independence Avenue) – a new road that had been built in an easterly direction across the railway line from the south end of Cairo Road. Barracks for the police and the military were built before work was suspended owing to the financial crisis. Construction began again in the latter half of 1933 on projects worth £500,000 – much of the money was provided by the Beit Trust. The mainly Afrikaner and 'poor white' sections of the population lived in Emmasdale, which was also less politely known as 'Blikkiesdorp'. Lusaka was notorious at the time for dust and wind in the dry season and for floods in summer.[8]

There appears to be no documentary trace of Harry Wulfsohn's early adventures in and around Lusaka. This is hardly surprising as he was not much more than twenty when he reached the town and only twenty-one or so when he set up in business on his own account. By 1934 he had his own headed notepaper. This described him simply as 'H. Wulfsohn – General Merchant, PO Box 96, Lusaka'. It proclaimed that he had slaughter and 'treck' (*sic*) oxen 'always on hand' and that he was a buyer of hides. By the end of the year this letterhead had been overprinted 'Dorsky and Wulfsohn', as he had by then formed a partnership with Harry Dorsky who had a concession store at Nchanga (later Chingola) on the Copperbelt and a 'Native eating-house' at Mufulira. Harry Dorsky was a Lithuanian Jew who had reached Northern Rhodesia in the mid 1920s. He had a formidable sister, Mrs Schatz, who became a leading figure in the Nkana-Kitwe Hebrew Congregation. According to Wulfie Wulfsohn, she took a close personal interest in the partnership's accounts. Harry Dorsky looked after the partnership's urban interests on the Copperbelt, while Harry Wulfsohn looked after the rural trading interests between Lusaka and Livingstone. The partners rarely met, but there seems to have been a symbiotic relationship between the two ends of the business. Wulfsohn may have supplied maize and cattle to Dorsky, who provided a captive market.[9]

The provincial commissioner for the Southern Province commented on the depressed state of the cattle trade around Lusaka in his annual report for 1934. He noted the low price of cattle and the high price of maize that had prevailed in the earlier part of the year – apparently an ox could be exchanged for a bag of mealie meal. This was almost certainly a consequence of drought and of a plague of locusts, which had devastated crops in 1933 and 1934. He also noted that:

> The implication is that the native is in the hands of the traders, but in fairness to the latter it must be recorded that they have reported that the natives will not dispose of their surplus stock. Two traders have recently stated that they are prepared to offer what appear to be reasonable prices. It remains to be seen whether they will be successful in obtaining such as they require.[10]

It is probable that he was referring to Wulfsohn and Dorsky, but the offer of better prices does not appear to have had the desired effect. In November 1934 Harry Wulfsohn, writing from Lusaka, informed the district commissioner for Namwala, in the Southern Province, that his firm had been advised by the Veterinary Department to go there to purchase cattle 'in view of the shortage of cattle here'. He asked about the possibility of obtaining a store site at Namwala. After consultations between the provincial commissioner, T. F. Sandford, and the district commissioner, J. Gordon Read, and between Sandford and Wulfsohn himself, he was eventually offered a store site, but he did not take it up at once.[11]

Namwala

Harry Wulfsohn had reached Namwala by the middle of 1935. His appearance on the scene had an immediate impact and was noted by the district commissioner. The arrival of competition had a stimulating effect on trade and increased the prices paid for cattle. The main established traders in the Namwala District were the Cavadias – their firm was known as Cavadia and Nephews. They were Greeks who had arrived in the country with the railway in the early years of the century. The senior partner was Pangos, better known as Pete, Cavadia. They were based at Pemba on the Line of Rail, but completed what was described as 'a palatial store' at Namwala in 1931. In 1935 they leased their Namwala store to Harry Wulfsohn, who also took over stores at Kantengwa and Mbeza, and employed an old Barotseland trader, Louis S. Diamond, as a manager. Although there is no doubt that Harry Wulfsohn was the prime mover in these activities, he initially operated there under the umbrella of the Northern Produce and Livestock Company. This company was set up in 1930 by Henrie Kollenberg, farmer and trader at Lusaka, and also involved 'Tubby' Wulfsohn, Harry's cousin. Henrie Kollenberg was a member of a Latvian Jewish clan, the son of Edward and the brother of Hermann, David and Isadore. They were all prominent in the trade of Northern Rhodesia, though the family business had begun in the south, and Isadore retained a base there. The larger partnership was dissolved in 1937 when Dorsky and (Harry) Wulfsohn emerged as the owners of the Namwala business. A few months later they sold it to the Cavadias. From then onwards, Harry Wulfsohn concentrated his attention on the store at Tara Siding, about ten miles south of Choma, which he acquired at about that time.[12]

It was through his energetic involvement in the Namwala cattle trade in the mid 1930s that Harry Wulfsohn first made his mark in Northern Rhodesia and came to the notice of officials. It was also through this trade that he began to accumulate capital, though this was by no means easy. He was operating in one of the most difficult environments in the country. Namwala was the administrative headquarters for an area that included much of the Kafue Flats and was dominated by the Ila-speaking people. Some of the Ila chiefs, such as Chief Mungaila, whose headquarters was near Maala, and Chief Mukobela, owned huge herds. Most of the cattle moved backwards and forwards seasonally between the flats and the neighbouring higher ground. In some parts of the district cattle keeping was impossible because of the prevalence of tsetse fly. Maize was also grown in some areas, but it was usually too far from the Line of Rail to be of any commercial value. A trader, probably Harry Wulfsohn himself, found it worthwhile to buy 1,000 bags of maize at Mbeza, in the southern part of the district, in 1936, but this was an unusual occurrence.[13]

The district commissioner, J. Gordon Read, took a personal interest in Harry Wulfsohn's progress and seems to have derived some of his information about the trade of the district from conversation with him. He commented in 1936 on the economics of the cattle trade in a district that exported about 2,000 head a year in the mid 1930s, at prices which averaged between £2.10.0 and £3.10.0 a head. He thought that Dorsky and Wulfsohn's costs were high, and that their profits were not as large as might appear: 'When one knows that traders have to pay grazing fees, [and] herd boys, build their own kraals at their own expense, suffer substantial loss from crocodiles and lions and by theft, the profits are not so large as many people believe.'[14]

This was one of the wildest areas in the country – much more so than the more densely populated region of Barotseland – and predators were a serious threat. Wynant Davis Hubbard, an American naturalist, lion catcher and filmmaker, has left a vivid account in his book *Ibamba* of the struggle between cattle owners and predators in the Namwala District at this time. He had first come to Northern Rhodesia in the early 1920s. He lived then at

Tara, later Harry Wulfsohn's base, where he hunted, captured lions and made a film *Wild Animals* – the first wildlife film ever made in the country. Between 1930 and 1934 he tried to run the isolated Ibamba Ranch near Namwala as an experimental station. He kept cattle and was interested in investigating the immunity of wild animals to some diseases that affected domesticated stock. He and his wife survived the Depression, but were finally forced to leave by locusts, which destroyed their crops, and lions, which threatened their stock. They left Ibamba in September 1934, not long before Harry Wulfsohn arrived in the district. On their last journey from Ibamba to Choma they passed through a locust swarm which was at least 125 miles wide. They were unable to take their pet lion cub with them because of an outbreak of foot-and-mouth disease, which put a temporary stop to all animal movements.[15]

The Hubbards had taken over the ranch from the Cavadias, who had leased it from the owner, 'Mopani' Clarke, and tried to run it as a holding ground for their cattle. According to Hubbard, the Cavadias had lost two or three cattle a week to lions and one or two to crocodiles. He thought that they could afford the losses, but the Cavadias evidently thought otherwise. Harry Wulfsohn is reputed to have lost many of the cattle in his first 'mob' because lions were able to get into an imperfectly constructed kraal. Hubbard described the process of building a lion-proof kraal. This involved sinking sixteen- to twenty-foot poles in a two-foot trench and lashing them together with green *mopani* bark or iron wire. He also described the hazards of the journey by motor vehicle from Choma to Namwala along a track that had been pioneered by the Cavadias' wagons:

> Transport ... over the rutty, sandy trail winding a hundred and twenty-five miles across the veldt – in which hard hidden stumps, ant-bear holes, and treacherous mud lay in wait for the unwary – presented a fearsome task. The track – it could not be called a road – to Ibamba and on to Namwala had originally been made by wagons drawn by eighteen straining oxen. Of necessity it wound around anthills, turned and twisted to avoid large trees and soft ground near waterholes and pans. Because the oxen required grazing every day, the track sought areas where grass was available; it led from village to village so that the drivers and the traders could barter for food, grain, hides, and skins. There was no place where gasoline or oil or tires or tubes could be obtained, nor were there any mechanics.[16]

Tara

After he moved his main base from Namwala to Tara in 1937, Harry Wulfsohn continued to be involved in the Ila cattle trade, trekking cattle to Pemba for export to the Copperbelt. He loved buying cattle and the excitement of bargaining and acquired an Ila soubriquet, which translated as 'good bargainer'. He was also heavily involved in maize trading and took on contracts to supply the government. Among his competitors in this business were a number of other traders including the Cavadias and their fellow Greek, Paul Zaloumis, who became a good friend; Wulfsohn and he used to play poker dice together at the Choma Hotel. The hotel was run by Hugh McKee, a Scot, who was later known as the proprietor of Kee's, a department store in Lusaka's Cairo Road, as a member of the Legislative Council and as Northern Rhodesia's first representative in London. On one occasion, when Harry Wulfsohn was hard pressed to meet a maize contract, he and Zaloumis played with bags of maize as chips. Harry won and was able to meet his contract. On another occasion they tossed a coin to decide who should bid for a bean contract. Maize traders, including Harry Wulfsohn, may have benefited from the setting-up at this time of the Maize Marketing and Control Board, which offered a guaranteed market and fixed prices for maize along the Line of Rail. It was intended to benefit settler farmers, but seems to have been of some benefit also to African peasant producers – though only to those who were within a reasonable distance of the Line of Rail.[17]

It was while he was living at Tara in the late 1930s that Harry Wulfsohn made a number of friends who were to be important to him for the rest of his life. They included Geoffrey Beckett and Robert Boyd. Beckett was born in Middlesex in 1903 and came to Northern Rhodesia at the age of twenty-one. He was recruited by 'Mopani' Clarke to work on the Demo Estate near Choma. After a few years he bought a nearby farm, Momba, where he grew tobacco and raised cattle. For many years Beckett was one of the most influential figures in Northern Rhodesian agricultural circles. He was the main architect of the Cattle Marketing and Control Board that the government set up in 1937 in an attempt to raise cattle prices for settler farmers, and to provide a mechanism for the control of imports. He was also president of the Livestock Cooperative Society and of the Farmers' Union. He became a member of the Legislative Council and was member for agriculture from 1949 to 1954.[18]

Robert Boyd was another cattleman. He was a tall and rather dour Scot who worked for 'Bongola' Smith in Northern Rhodesia and the Congo in the early 1920s. He then worked on farms in Southern Rhodesia and was recruited in 1937 by the governor of Southern Rhodesia, Sir Herbert Stanley, to manage the Duke of Westminster's Nanga Estate on the Kafue River near Mazabuka. Both Beckett and Boyd were to play major roles in the politics of cattle and beef in central Africa – especially through long-term membership of the Cattle Marketing and Control Board. They were both recruited after the Second World War to work with what had emerged as the Susman Brothers & Wulfsohn group of companies.[19]

According to Geoffrey Beckett's son, Mike, his father was often criticised for his closeness to Harry Wulfsohn and 'the Jews' in what was still a predominantly anti-Semitic settler society. Although Wulfsohn seems to have received some help early in his career from officials such as the district commissioner at Namwala, J. Gordon Read and the provincial commissioner, T. F. Sandford, anti-Semitism was still an issue with many officials. He clearly made a strong impression on Malcolm Billing, the district commissioner at Kalomo in the late 1930s, who eventually became resident commissioner in Barotseland and minister for African affairs. In his unpublished memoir, 'Crest of the Wave', Billing, looking back from the 1960s, left an ambivalent portrait of Wulfsohn that combines a measure of sympathy and admiration for his hard work and remarkable achievements with a not wholly successful attempt by Billing to overcome his own prejudices.

> I remember a young man named Wulfsohn who established a trading store on the border of one these reserves. When he arrived in the country he had virtually no funds of his own, and he was financed by one of his kith and kin. For five or six years he worked like a slave. He bought cattle on the hoof (there were no government sales in those days) and he sold his African customers a variety of goods, many of them basic items such as meal, sugar or paraffin that were required in village homes. In due course the young trader prospered exceedingly; he built and controlled more stores; he financed the establishment of a cold storage plant. Later he ran a timber export business, and he ended up owning blocks of valuable property in Salisbury. He had a great flair for business but, like many of his race, he was not a popular member of the community. Why are prejudices still so strong? Is it jealousy because of their commercial success? Or is it due to their frequent failure to shine in the world of sport?[20]

While Billing's conjectures as to the causes of anti-Semitism are not profound, he does provide evidence for its prevalence. It was clearly hard for some observers to understand the single-mindedness with which refugees and immigrants, such as Harry Wulfsohn, pursued their search for security, not only for themselves, but also for their families; Wulfsohn's first priority had always been to send money to his mother in Latvia. As the Second World War approached, the anti-Semitism of colonial Northern Rhodesia paled into insignificance in comparison with the real threat posed by the rise of Hitler in Germany and the approach of war in Europe. Harry Wulfsohn had a very strong sense of family and, with his brother-in-law Abe Lowenthal, he tried to get as many members of his family out of Europe as he could. Hessie Lowenthal returned to Europe in 1938 and stayed there for a year. She came back in 1939 with their youngest brother, Wulfie, who was then eighteen. Another brother, Paul, and sister, Josephine, were able to travel to the United Kingdom where they stayed at first with their aunt Miriam Levenson who had left South Africa with her children at the bottom of the Depression. Paul and Josephine went on to study at Manchester University. Their father, Isaac Wulfsohn, died before the outbreak of war, but their mother, Chaya, and a sister, Lena, with her husband and two children, were murdered after the Nazi occupation of Latvia in 1941. Another sister, Esther, who had married out of the faith and moved to the Soviet Union, survived the war. Her son became a prominent newspaper editor in Latvia.[21]

While Harry Wulfsohn, and some other members of his family were fortunate to leave Latvia before the war, Malcolm Billing provided an account of his providential escape from a near-death experience in Northern Rhodesia in the late 1930s:

> ... it was at this time that Wulfsohn's life nearly came to an abrupt close. With a friend he was inspecting a cold room in an abattoir which had been built in the days when safety measures were not entirely reliable, and warning lights did not always come on to show that someone was inside the freezing chamber. Wulfsohn and his friend entered and closed the door behind them. After a while they prepared to leave. Alas, the lock on the door held fast. Much shouting followed, but all to no purpose. Meanwhile the luckless pair were already cold and were getting colder all the time. Frantic knocking and still more shouting ensued, but half an hour later no one had answered their cries. Eventually they were missed, the premises were searched, and the cold room door was opened from outside. Two exhausted, very shaken and half-frozen figures staggered out – and they survived.[22]

Trude Wiesenbacher

In the year or two before the outbreak of the Second World War nearly 300 German Jewish refugees, as well as about 100 Jewish refugees from the Baltic states, reached Northern Rhodesia. It served as a refuge of last resort to people who were unable to get visas to enter South Africa or Southern Rhodesia. Only a few of the refugees stayed in Livingstone, which was still suffering from the transfer of the capital to Lusaka. They were encouraged to travel on to Lusaka and the Copperbelt. Harry Wulfsohn's cousin, 'Tubby', was actively involved in the committee that was set up by the Jewish community in Lusaka for the reception of the German refugees. His work for this committee was highly appreciated by the refugees. The committee organised a boarding house, ironically named 'The Arcadia', and also rented a farm at Lilayi from Henrie Kollenberg. A number of refugees were kept there out of sight of the somewhat hostile settler population.[23]

Among these new arrivals in Lusaka in August 1939 was a seventeen-year-old girl – Trude Wiesenbacher. After three years at a finishing school at Lausanne in Switzerland, where she had fortunately studied English as well as French, she had left her home in Stuttgart in July. Her father, Adolf Wiesenbacher, was a wealthy textile wholesaler who had protected himself against the hyperinflation of the 1920s and the slump of the 1930s by the purchase of urban property. Like many other German Jews, he was forced to look for a country of refuge by the pogroms of *Krystallnacht* in November 1938. His daughter still has a vivid memory of the destruction of Stuttgart's synagogue on that night. Her mother, Klara (Claire), had a brother in South Africa, Sam Weil, the co-founder of a clothing manufacturing business, Weil & Ascheim. With his help they were eventually able to get visas for Northern Rhodesia. Trude left Germany for Switzerland, with her parents and younger brother, on dummy Costa Rican visas in July. They went on from there to Genoa, where they boarded a German ship, the *Watussi*. They sailed down the east coast of Africa to Durban where Trude's aunt, Roselle Weil, collected them. She drove them home to Johannesburg, but they were not allowed to stay for long in South Africa.[24]

Leaving Germany at the age of seventeen, Trude was, she recalls, 'mature and ready to fight for my existence'. The transition from an affluent lifestyle in Europe, and a Swiss finishing school, to the Arcadia boarding house in Lusaka, where she shared a room with four married women, was shocking. At the same time she noticed the liberating effect which arriving in Lusaka had on her father. Trude soon began work for a minuscule wage at 'Floretta's', the small clothing and haberdashery shop that was kept by, and bore the name of, 'Tubby' Wulfsohn's wife. Thirty years later she had a vivid recollection of the fifteen-minute walk from the boarding house to Floretta's – from Fairview on the Great East Road to half-way down Cairo Road. She was particularly shocked by the queue of African men waiting outside Haslett's butchery (now the Lusaka Cold Storage Butchery) to collect meat for their white employers.

> I had never seen such badly dressed people, some only in loincloths held together by beads, some clad in torn khaki shorts and short loose *kansas*. Some natives wore white long *kansas* made of calico which to me looked like some kind of nightshirt. It flashed through my mind that the queue only consisted of black men. Where were their women folk? Grown-up men could not command much respect dressed in such a peculiar manner.

Within a few days Trude had left the Arcadia and moved into the Wulfsohns' home behind the shop. She now had to share a room with Floretta Wulfsohn's mother, the elderly Mrs Glasstone. Trude did not get on well with Floretta and even less well with her mother, and her attempts to tidy up the shop were not well received. It was, however, through the shop that she met Harry Wulfsohn, whom she was to marry before the end of the year, and before her own eighteenth birthday. She does not recall meeting Harry as a member of her employer's extended family, but as a customer who came to the shop. He came in one day to buy socks, and stayed to buy a tie. Within a day, or at the most two, he had taken her out to lunch at the Lusaka Hotel and for a drive and picnic at the Kafue River – accompanied by his servant, Moses. He soon returned to Tara and they kept in touch by telephone. Trude retained the services of a small boy to summon her to the post office when Harry's calls came through. Trude says this was a case of love at first sight. She had to overcome her parents' doubts, but by September they were engaged. The wedding took place on 17 December 1939 in a room at the Grand Hotel in Lusaka's Cairo Road, and was conducted by Cantor Feivel Metzger. They had to wait for the only *chupah*, or bridal canopy, in the country to be brought from Broken Hill where the last Jewish wedding had taken place several years previously. Cantor Metzger was a remarkable man who had arrived in Lusaka as a refugee from Germany in August 1939. He was recruited as spiritual leader for the German refugee population, and was the driving force behind the building of Lusaka's synagogue. This was completed at the low point of the war in 1942.[25]

The arrival of Trude Wiesenbacher in Lusaka, and Harry's sudden and unanticipated engagement and marriage, appear to have had dramatic consequences for his business life. The long-standing partnership with Harry Dorsky was dissolved in October 1939. Harry Wulfsohn retained control of the Southern Province businesses based on Tara and Pemba, while Dorksy retained the Copperbelt businesses based in Nchanga and Mufulira. Dorsky also got married at this time, and both families believe that the partners'

9 Harry Wulfsohn and his future wife, Trude Wiesenbacher, Lusaka, 1939.

marriages were the main cause of the dissolution of the partnership. According to Wulfie Wulfsohn, his brother realised that he could not expect his sophisticated young fiancée from Stuttgart to begin her married life in his little house beside the store at Tara Siding, where the nearest white neighbour was Mr Kruger, the railway ganger, who lived two miles away. He therefore decided that he needed an urban business and arranged to buy a Livingstone butchery. A company calling itself Premier Caterers Ltd announced in the *Livingstone Mail* on 12 August 1939 that it was taking over the Susmans' Pioneer Butchery and that the licence would be transferred when its new premises were finished. The new butchery – the Modern Butchery – began to advertise in the paper on 28 October. The same paper printed an advertisement for the Central Butchery, whose proprietor was Ben Robinson.[26]

Livingstone Cold Storage

On 3 February 1940 the *Livingstone Mail* carried an advertisement that announced that 'as from 1 March 1940 Premier Caterers and the Central Butchery will amalgamate under the name and style of Livingstone Cold Storage Ltd'. Harry Wulfsohn signed the advertisement on behalf of the new company – this was the first time that his name had appeared in the columns of the *Livingstone Mail*. Trude recalls that Harry had bought the butchery before they left for their honeymoon in the Cape in December. She also remembers that on their return in January they spent three days in Bulawayo where the wholesaler, S. S. Grossberg, a Latvian Jewish connection, failed to come up with promised finance for the business. This created a crisis. Financial salvation came a week or two later when the newly married couple visited Chris van der Spuy, a good friend of Harry's, at his farm near Mazabuka. He gave Harry an unsecured loan of £10,000, in two cheques, or bills, payable over six months. This was a huge amount of money at that time – equivalent to nearly £250,000 in modern terms. This loan enabled Harry Wulfsohn to consolidate his purchase of the Pioneer Butchery, his establishment of the Modern Butchery and the takeover of Robinson's Central Butchery.[27]

It is difficult to work out what the relationship between Harry Wulfsohn and the Susman brothers was at this time as few records survive from this date. Hymie Woolfe, who worked as an accountant for F. H. Lowe and Company until the end of 1935, thinks that there were links between them before he left Livingstone. Documents in the Botswana Archives suggest that Harry Wulfsohn may have done some work for the Susman brothers in connection with their Bechuanaland timber concession in 1936–7 and it is probable, but not certain, that he agreed to buy the Pioneer Butchery from them as a result of direct negotiations with Elie Susman in July 1939. If he did so, his intention to move into the butchery business must have pre-dated his engagement.[28]

Elie Susman spent most of July 1939 in Livingstone. It must have been then that he negotiated the sale of the butchery and a major reorganisation of the Livingstone business. Susman Brothers announced on 2 September 1939 that it was moving its office from the building in Mainway, where it had been since 1912, to Stanley House in the same street. It also asked that all payments should in future be made to its accountants, F. H. Lowe & Company, whose office was in the same building. The sole partner in this firm was J. W. A. 'Puggy' Parkhurst. He had arrived in Livingstone as a young accountant in 1936 and soon established himself as a major figure in the small town, becoming a town councillor in 1940 and mayor in 1952–4. He played an important role as an adviser to Wulfsohn in his takeover of the butchery businesses, and later helped to set up various partnerships with the Susman brothers. Parkhurst recalled an adventurous hunting expedition with Harry Susman to the 'tongue' of the Caprivi Strip in 1943. On that occasion they slept in the open and elephants strolled though the camp.[29]

The Susman brothers must have put a lot of thought into the sale of the butchery business. They had owned it for thirty years and it had always been the flagship of their business in Livingstone. They could afford to pick and choose their successor. In selling to Harry Wulfsohn, they identified him as a rising star in the commercial world. After the sale they seem to have withdrawn from cattle trading on their own account in Northern Rhodesia. They retained a small stake in Copperfields Cold Storage and a larger one in Werners. They also continued to control the Ngamiland Trading Company and retained the Leopard's Hill and Wolverton Ranches, but withdrew from the Barotseland cattle trade to which they had returned with vigour in 1938–9. When Harry Susman attended meetings with representatives of the government and the Copperbelt mining companies about cattle supplies in the early years of the war, he did not do so as a representative of the Northern Rhodesian butchers and graziers, but as a representative of the Bechuanaland cattle traders. There does seem to have been an understanding that, when Harry Wulfsohn took over the butchery, he also took over the Susman Brothers' role in local cattle trading.[30]

Although there was no formal partnership, it is probable that Harry Wulfsohn had some financial backing from the Susmans in the early years of the war. He was certainly close to Harry Susman and undertook cattle-buying trips with him in Bechuanaland. Trude Robins recalls them setting off together with a vanette loaded with £20,000 in silver half-crowns – enough to pay for several thousand cattle. The vanette later sank up to its axles in the sands of the Kalahari. Harry Susman, who was known for his great strength, though small stature, is reputed to have pushed aside all assistance and lifted the front of the vehicle out of the sand on his own.[31]

The first formal joint venture between the Susman brothers and Harry Wulfsohn was the establishment in May 1942 of the Kala Ranching Company. The new company bought a derelict ranch of around 20,000 acres on the Zambezi escarpment about forty miles southwest of Kalomo. In the first few years the company let the ranch to Wulfsohn who ran it on his own account. He intended to use this ranch as a holding ground for his butchery business, but it was too far from the Line of Rail to be ideal for this purpose.[32]

Soon after the establishment of Livingstone Cold Storage, Wulfsohn took an initiative that had significant consequences for the Barotseland cattle trade. In April 1940 he put forward a plan to the government for the construction of a modern cold storage plant in Livingstone to cater for the export of Barotseland beef to the Copperbelt. He offered to finance the construction of the plant in return for a guarantee of the right to buy 5,000 cattle a year from Barotseland. There was some irony in this proposal as the advertisements for the Livingstone Cold Storage Company which appeared in the *Livingstone Mail* from that month onwards proclaimed that it sold only 'highest quality farm bred cattle' and carried, as a footnote, a statement in large print which proclaimed: 'NO BAROTSE CATTLE'. This was a concession to the popular view, which can be traced back to 1900, and which is still current in Lusaka, that Barotse cattle are a tough breed.[33]

Harry Wulfsohn's proposal was followed by a counter-proposal along the same lines from Isadore Kollenberg and E. W. Dechow. They represented Copperfields Cold Storage and Werners who were acting as a cartel. They proposed that the government should build the plant and lease it to them. They wanted a guaranteed supply of over 6,000 cattle a year from Barotseland. Before investigating these schemes further the government carried out experimental shipments of Barotse beef to the Copperbelt in order to ascertain that the mining companies would accept beef that came from cattle killed as part of the 'P.P.' eradication campaign as suitable for 'compound' consumption. Lengthy negotiations followed, during which the government tried to get the competing interests to agree to co-operate in running a plant which the government would build. A later government report claimed that plans for this fell through 'at the eleventh hour'. According to John Hobday, who became chief veterinary officer on the resignation of 'Seamus' Morris in March 1943, negotiations broke down over the government's stipulation that the cold storage works should be run on a non-profit-making basis. The government felt obliged to insist on this because the cattle were compulsorily purchased in Barotseland and it was thought to be improper that private entrepreneurs should profit from the eradication scheme. Hobday, who had been chief veterinary officer in Bechuanaland, was to serve in this role for over a decade and was eventually employed for a while, like Beckett and Boyd, by the Susman Brothers & Wulfsohn Group.[34]

Although the entire correspondence does not appear to have survived, Harry Wulfsohn's own views emerge from a letter that he wrote to the secretary for native affairs, T. F. Sandford, in August 1941. He continued to argue that the plant should be built through private enterprise and also proposed that Barotse cattle-owners, whose stock was compulsorily slaughtered, should be paid only a proportion of the purchase price in cash. The bulk of it should be used for the purchase of replacement stock. His letter was expressed clearly and cogently argued. It is clear that by this time he was negotiating directly with senior government officials, including Sandford, Morris and Hobday, and that they took his proposals seriously. Although he was less than thirty when he put his initial proposals forward, the officials dealt with him on the same basis as they did with veterans of the central African cattle trade, such as Isadore Kollenberg and E. W. Dechow: he had come a long way in ten years.[35]

In the end the government decided in the latter half of 1942 to build the cold storage plant itself, hoping that production would begin in September 1943. It decided to go ahead on its own because of the greatly increased demand for beef on the Copperbelt. An army of workers had been recruited to sustain maximum production of copper for the war effort; Northern Rhodesia produced one and a half million tons of copper during the war. Copper production and beef consumption reached a peak in 1943. In that year the Northern Rhodesian public consumed a record 55,000 head of cattle. The majority of these came from within the country, but the equivalent of 18,000 head had to be imported. Large numbers came in on the hoof from Ngamiland, mainly through the Ngamiland Trading Company; many more were brought in by rail from eastern Bechuanaland and Southern Rhodesia. About half of total imports came in as chilled and frozen beef from Southern Rhodesia.[36]

The building of the new plant did not run smoothly. The cost of construction rose from an estimated £20,000 to an actual £60,000 and it came on stream eight months late, in April 1944. There were complications arising from wartime shortages and the decision to buy second-hand plant from the Lobatse Abattoir in Bechuanaland, which was nearly twenty years old. The compulsory purchase of infected cattle in Barotseland began in 1943. Purchases were organised through the provincial administration, Lozi indunas, and the Veterinary Department. The delay in opening the plant resulted in heavy stock losses – these were attributed to 'poverty', lions, crocodiles and hyenas.[37]

It was probably not a coincidence that the opening of the Livingstone Cold Storage plant coincided with the conclusion of a new and much stronger alliance between Harry Wulfsohn and the Susman brothers. In April 1944, they were involved in a joint takeover of Werner and Company from Mrs H. A. Werner and her manager E. W. Dechow. Susman Brothers already owned about forty-five per cent of the company and Elie Susman had been a director since soon after its flotation in 1937. After the takeover Susman Brothers and Harry Wulfsohn split the voting shares in the company between them on a fifty-fifty basis, but split the non-voting shares on the basis of sixty per cent to Susman Brothers and forty per cent to Wulfsohn. The purchase of the balance of the shares in the company was partly financed by a loan of £10,000, repayable in three years, from Mrs Werner to the Susman brothers in their individual capacities. At the same time Susman Brothers, the company, invested £15,000 in a new company – Harry Wulfsohn Ltd. The shares in this new company were split on a fifty-fifty basis between Susman Brothers and Wulfsohn. The Susman brothers' own shares in the latter business were split on the basis of thirty per cent to Elie and twenty per cent to Harry.[38]

In preparation for these moves the Susman brothers had dissolved their own partnership at the end of March 1942 and had replaced it with a private company, Susman Brothers Ltd. This was registered as Local Company number 141 on 14 October 1942. It had a nominal capital of £75,000. This made it, at least potentially, the second most highly capitalised local company in the country – second only to Northern Caterers. In fulfilment of a legal obligation the Susman brothers announced these changes, rather belatedly, in an advertisement in the *Livingstone Mail* on 24 September 1943.

> Notice is hereby given that the partnership heretofore carried on by Elie Susman and Harry Susman as merchants in Northern Rhodesia and elsewhere as

'Susman Brothers' has been terminated by mutual consent and ceased to exist on 31 March 1942.

The partnership was entered into in 1901 in the early pioneering days of the European occupation of Northern Rhodesia and has continued with complete harmony, co-operation and trust between the partners through many adversities until now when for business reasons the continuance of the firm is no longer necessary as their interests have been absorbed by a company incorporated for the purpose and known as 'Susman Brothers Limited'.

Dated this 17th day of September 1943. Signed: E. Susman. H. Susman.[39]

No documentary evidence seems to have survived relating to the negotiations that preceded the formation of this grand alliance between the Susman brothers and Harry Wulfsohn. From Trude Robins's recollections it appears that the deal may have been worked out in principle between Harry Wulfsohn and Harry Susman in Livingstone. Final negotiations, however, involved Elie Susman in visits to Livingstone and Harry Wulfsohn in visits to Johannesburg; Elie Susman spent about a month in Northern Rhodesia in July–August 1943 and made two further visits in March–April and August 1944. The Susman brothers contributed their good name and reputation, as well as money, to the partnership, but it did not involve any of their assets in central Africa, apart from their earlier investment in Werners. The Ngamiland Trading Company, Leopard's Hill and Wolverton Ranches, and their stakes in Northern Caterers, Economy Stores and R. F. Sutherland Ltd remained outside the deal. A consequence of their takeover of Werners was, however, that they were forced to part with their shares in Copperfields Cold Storage. The constitution of that company barred shareholders from owning or controlling businesses that were in direct competition with it. Harry Wulfsohn, on the other hand, contributed Livingstone Cold Storage Ltd and his stores based in Tara. He also contributed his youthful energy and proven entrepreneurial talent.[40]

The formation of this alliance was intended to solve the Susmans' problem of management in central Africa from which they had suffered since the departure of Elie Susman to Woolworths, and Lewis Hochstein to the United States, in 1935. Joe Susman was not a satisfactory successor and went off to join the army soon after the outbreak of war. The alliance gave Harry Wulfsohn access to capital for expansion and a link with an old established and reputable local business. Its formation certainly marked the beginning of a new phase in which the Susmans' central African interests, which had been in decline since the mid 1930s, took on a new lease of life. Expansion followed in three closely related areas: the cattle trade, the butchery business and rural trade. For the Susmans this involved a return in force to the scene of their earliest activities – Barotseland – as well as a strengthening of their position on the Copperbelt. As David Susman has observed: 'Harry Wulfsohn was an aggressive and very intelligent trader who drove the business very strongly after the war'.[41]

CHAPTER 11

Susman Brothers & Wulfsohn: The Development of the Stores Network, 1944–56

Harry Wulfsohn Ltd – soon to be known as Susman Brothers & Wulfsohn Ltd – and Werners expanded rapidly in the post-war years. They took over, or spun off, a variety of other businesses, including Zambesi Saw Mills and Northern Rhodesia Textiles. The name, Susman Brothers & Wulfsohn, was sometimes used to describe the partnership in all its ramifications, but was also used more specifically as the name of the network of trading stores that was developed to cover most of the western half of Northern Rhodesia in the immediate post-war years: it was extended into the Northern and Luapula Provinces in 1955. The main focus of this chapter is on the early development of that network. The story of Werners, Zambesi Saw Mills and Northern Rhodesia Textiles, as well as the subsequent history of the stores, will be considered in later chapters.

The colonial government of Northern Rhodesia anticipated that the end of the Second World War would be followed by an economic depression. Cuts in copper production before the end of the war encouraged this pessimistic view. In reality the post-war period was one of rapid economic growth. There was large-scale immigration of settlers from the United Kingdom and South Africa. There was also a renewed, and more vigorous, settler demand for amalgamation with Southern Rhodesia. Roy Welensky, the 'white labour' leader with a power base among the railway workers of Broken Hill, had introduced a motion in the Legislative Council in 1943 that called for amalgamation and received the support of the majority of the unofficial members. He continued to press for this in the years after the war, but was eventually persuaded by Britain's post-war Labour government to accept what he, and the Colonial Office, saw as the compromise goal of federation.

This militant settler nationalism was matched by the emergence for the first time of an African nationalist movement, which was, at least in part, a reaction to it. The Northern Rhodesian Congress, formed in 1948, grew out of a federation of African welfare associations. Among its prime movers were two members of the Lozi elite, Nelson Nalumango and Godwin Mbikusita Lewanika, a junior son of King Lewanika, its first president. The congress was at first moderate in its political demands and deferential in its approach to the colonial government. It took a more radical turn in 1951 when it became the Northern Rhodesian African National Congress, and Harry Nkumbula, who had studied at Makerere University College in Uganda, and at the London School of Economics, replaced Lewanika as president.[1]

As well as operating in a much more dynamic political, and a more buoyant economic, environment, the new partnership had to cope with a very different commercial context from the one in which the Susman brothers had functioned for the previous forty years. The move away from the free market had begun just before the outbreak of the Second World War with the establishment of the Maize Marketing and Cattle Marketing and Control Boards. These were intended to improve and stabilise prices in the interests of settler farmers. During the war the government intervened in much more dramatic ways. It suspended the London Metal Exchange and took direct control of copper production and prices. By 1942 it had set up a complex system for the control of imports, foreign exchange and prices. At the same time petrol and sometimes meat were rationed. The government not only controlled the prices of staple commodities such as maize and meat, but also periodically subsidised them. It was not until the mid 1950s that these controls were relaxed or abolished.[2]

It was also during the Second World War that the Colonial Office, and the government in Northern Rhodesia, began to think in terms of development planning and social welfare. Thousands of African men were recruited in Northern Rhodesia for the war effort and served in the army as far away as Burma. There was concern at the impact that their return after the war might have on African society. There was a well-grounded fear in official circles that African nationalism would be stimulated by the return of ex-servicemen with heightened expectations. All the district commissioners were asked to write five-year plans for their districts, with a view to identifying employment opportunities for these men. Many of them wrote in terms of co-operative marketing and of collective farms on the Soviet model. There was a good deal of hostility towards the involvement of private enterprise in African trade. A ten-year plan for the territory as a whole was approved soon after the end of the war.[3]

Livingstone

The town of Livingstone was always the centre of Susman Brothers & Wulfsohn's activities. Its recovery from the Depression was at first slow, but was accelerated by the war. The local economy was stimulated by the arrival of large numbers of Polish refugees in the town; by its use as a rest and recuperation centre for the Royal Air Force, which trained pilots in Southern Rhodesia; and by the increased demand for the output of Zambesi Saw Mills. After the war the opening of a new airport, which was intended to be, and for a while was, the main international airport for central Africa, also provided a stimulus. The town even made a bid in 1952 to be the capital of the new Federation.[4]

Harry and Trude Wulfsohn lived in Livingstone throughout the war and worked hard as they built a business and started a family. In the early years of their marriage Harry rose at three to work in the butchery and Trude got up at seven to do the accounts. She was involved in the business from the beginning and became a founding director of Werners in 1944 at the age of twenty-two. Their first child, Edwin, was born in June 1942, and their second child, Marlene, eighteen months later. Their family was completed by the arrival of twins, Miriam and Rosalind, in September 1948. The family had also been joined in Livingstone by Trude's parents, Adolph and Klara Wiesenbacher, and her young brother, Freddy, who moved south from Lusaka. Trude's father worked at first in the butchery, but from 1944 onwards he worked in the textile department of Susman Brothers & Wulfsohn. There had been a small influx of German Jewish refugees to Livingstone in the year or two before the war, and a much larger one of Polish refugees during the war. For several years Trude had help with her young family from Loda, a young Polish woman, who had reached Northern Rhodesia with several thousand others in 1943, by way of Siberia and Iran. For the first few years the family lived in a small rented house, and kept a low social profile. Soon after the war they moved into a larger house, where they were neighbours of the provincial commissioner. Anti-Semitism remained an issue, and colonial society remained stiff and highly stratified, but Trude taught herself to entertain according to its peculiar norms and etiquette. The family was able to establish a good relationship with the family of at least one of the provincial commissioners, Gervas Clay – his wife Betty was the daughter of Lord Baden-Powell.[5]

Issues of Succession

The business was centred on Livingstone, but Barotseland remained its commercial core. The eradication of bovine pleuro-pneumonia, the revival of the cattle trade, and the beginning of labour migration to the South African mines, all contributed during the war to the recovery of what had been since the early 1930s a severely depressed economy. The revival of the cattle trade had, of course, been the inspiration for the formation of the partnership in 1944. The Susman brothers' old friend, the Litunga Yeta III, had a stroke in 1939, not long after his return from the coronation of King George VI. He was unable to speak and was compelled by the provincial commissioner to abdicate in 1945. His successor was his brother Imwiko, another friend of the Susmans, who was transferred to Lealui from the chieftaincy at Mwandi. Imwiko himself died in 1948 in what were thought to be mysterious circumstances. His successor was another son of Lewanika, who took the title Mwanawina III. He was probably not as close to the Susman brothers as his predecessors had been: he had spent many years as the resident chief at Mankoya. There had also been changes, imposed by the colonial authorities from the late 1930s onwards, in the working of the 'Barotse Native Government', which had been brought into line with the Colonial Office policy of 'Indirect Rule'. Although the Lozi authorities, and the majority of the people, had always been opposed to amalgamation, Mwanawina was eventually persuaded to give his backing to the Federation by the recognition of Barotseland as a protectorate within Northern Rhodesia. By doing so, he incurred the hostility of most of his people.[6]

There were, of course, also issues of succession within the Susman family. A few months before the end of the war, Harry Susman left Livingstone and settled on a farm, Umritsar, near Salisbury in Southern Rhodesia. He engaged in tobacco farming and cattle production there, with the help of his younger son, Oscar. He continued to visit Northern Rhodesia regularly until his death in January 1952, but he did not play a major part in the development of the new network of stores. He did, however, perform an important role as the company's envoy to the Lozi rulers – the relationship with them remained vital to the success of the business. He flew to Mongu in June 1945 to commiserate with Yeta III after his deposition, and again in the following year to introduce Harry Wulfsohn to the new Litunga and to get his approval for the transfer of P. C. Nicolai's stores and licences to the company. Nicolai had died in 1944 and these stores included the ones at Lealui, Limulunga and Kanyonyo, which the Susmans had sold to him in 1931: they were bought back from his heirs. In his will Harry Susman left substantial legacies to a Livingstone children's charity and to the Paris Mission. Under the headline 'Death of an Old Livingstone Trader: A Pioneer Passes Away', the *Livingstone Mail* noted that 'a full history of this remarkable man's life would make good and exciting reading' and that 'his cheery greetings to his many friends in Livingstone on his frequent visits will be sadly missed'. His elder son, Joe, remained in the town until 1947, but he was not involved in the business, and moved to Salisbury where he developed his own business interests. Joe joined Susman Brothers & Wulfsohn in the late 1950s, but was never a very active participant in the affairs of the group. His main interests in life were in sport and fishing. He found his real metier late in life when he settled on the Zimbabwe side of the border at the Victoria Falls, and organised fishing expeditions. He then achieved international recognition as an eco-mystic and guru of the Zambezi River. He died there in 1990 in his eightieth year.[7]

Harry Susman had lived long enough to celebrate the fiftieth anniversary of the brothers' first crossing of the Zambezi in April 1951. Sadly, he did not live to witness the unveiling of the 'four-faced' tower clock that they donated to the Rhodes–Livingstone Museum to commemorate that event. The donation came as a result of a request from Jock Millar, the former mayor of the town, to Harry Susman in March 1951, not long before the opening of the new museum building. Elie Susman suggested that it should be called the Susman Clock, and that the donation should be linked to the anniversary of their arrival in the country, but there was a change of mind about the name. 'The Pioneers' Clock' was unveiled in September 1952 by Elie's daughter, Peggy Rabb. She regretted that her father could not be present, and that her uncle had not lived to be there as 'he was never happier than when in Livingstone or in Northern Rhodesia'. The Mayor of Livingstone, J. W. A. Parkhurst, noted that the gift of the clock was 'just one of very many instances of the openhanded and very often anonymous generosity of the Susman Brothers …'. The provincial commissioner, Gervas Clay, was glad that the clock had four faces – it was the first of its kind in the country: he asked the gathering to 'think how awkward it would have been for us if it had been a two-faced clock, and of the remarks that might have been passed!'[8]

Until his own death in January 1958, there was never any doubt that Elie Susman was, in spite of his absence in South Africa for most of the year, the senior partner and dominant personality in the business. He was the chairman of both the main companies and was certainly not prepared to take a back seat: it was not until the mid 1950s that his own son, David, began to take over some of his responsibilities. There was equally no doubt that Harry Wulfsohn was the man on the spot who really drove the expansion of the business. He was anxious to use the Susmans' name as it had an excellent 'brand image' – especially in Barotseland. Elie Susman was at first reluctant to allow this, but at a meeting in February 1946 it was agreed that the company should apply to the governor for permission to change its name from Harry Wulfsohn Ltd to Susman Brothers & Wulfsohn Ltd. This request was, however, turned down because of the similarity of the new name to that of the Susmans' own company – Susman Brothers Ltd. It was decided in August 1946 to apply to change the name of the latter company to E. and H. Susman Ltd, permission for this change was granted and Harry Wulfsohn Ltd was allowed to become Susman Brothers & Wulfsohn Ltd a few months later.[9]

Maurice Rabb

Elie Susman's change of mind about the name may have been prompted by Wulfsohn's suggestion that Elie's son-in-law, Maurice Rabb, should join the company as a working director, and take shares in it. Harry Wulfsohn had first met Maurice Rabb when Rabb and his wife, Peggy, visited Livingstone in July 1944 at the time of the formation of the Susman–Wulfsohn partnership. They met again on the beach at Muizenberg in February 1946. Rabb discussed the invitation with his wife and they eventually agreed to accept – provided that they could get a reasonable share of the equity in the two companies. At meetings in Livingstone in August 1946 he was elected as a director of both companies. It was then agreed that he would take a twenty-five per cent stake in Susman Brothers & Wulfsohn and a twenty per cent stake in Werners. Rabb was to be given non-voting shares in both companies so as not to disturb the fifty-fifty balance between the founding partners. The shares issued to him were to come from the capitalisation of profits, but would, nevertheless, reduce the proportions of shares held by the other partners. His association with the Susmans meant that shares issued to him, and his wife, tended to shift the balance of overall share ownership in their direction.[10]

At the annual general meetings of the two companies in August 1947 Harry Wulfsohn kept his promise to hand over ten per cent of Susman Brothers & Wulfsohn, but he declined to part with the five per cent share in Werners. Consequently Rabb secured a twenty-five per cent share in Susman Brothers & Wulfsohn, but only a fifteen per cent share in Werners. He was clearly upset by Wulfsohn's refusal to hand over the shares as promised, but he accepted the position. In a later memoir he said that he would have returned south there and then if had not already moved his family to Livingstone where they were settled in Harry Susman's old house. The structure of the companies was an uneasy compromise between an old-style partnership and a modern private company. The fifty-fifty split in the voting shares between the two major partners was a recipe for trouble – specifically for deadlock in the event of disagreement. This structure was common at the time, though Maurice Rabb said a few years later that 'it was against all modern conceptions of company practice'.[11]

Maurice Rabb arrived in Livingstone on 3 January 1947 and immediately began work. He collected his wife and three small children, Tessa, John and Anne, from Johannesburg six months later. He was to play a major role in the history of the Susman Brothers & Wulfsohn business for the next forty years. He was also to play a prominent part in the social and political life of Livingstone and of Northern Rhodesia as a whole. He came from a Lithuanian Jewish family, the fifth child and eldest son of Joseph and Golda Rabinowitz. Joseph came from Popolan and had studied for the rabbinate at the famous *yeshiva* in Telz. He set off for the United States in 1894, but ended up in Durban. There he served the small Jewish community of Vryheid as a rabbi for a few years and then began to work for a firm of general dealers, Baranov Brothers. After the outbreak of the Anglo-Boer War, Joseph was asked by General Louis Botha to buy saddles for the Boer Army and was then arrested by British forces and interned for two years. He subsequently moved to Johannesburg and ended a varied business career as a director of a major butchery firm – Rand Cold Storage; he also played a prominent part in Jewish communal life.[12]

Maurice Rabb was born in 1910 in Doornfontein, Johannesburg and was educated at the Hebrew High School in Wolmarans Street, and at Doornfontein High School. He went on to the University of the Witwatersrand, originally intending to study Medicine or Dentistry, but changed to Commerce. He worked his way through university and had set up a tyre business before he graduated. He was also very active in student organisations and became the third president of the National Union of South African Students

(NUSAS) in 1936, and was the leader of the 1934 NUSAS tour to Europe, during which he was introduced to Benito Mussolini, and also paid visits to Egypt and Palestine.

In May 1935 Max Sonnenberg invited Maurice to join the staff of Woolworths, which was just about to establish its first Johannesburg branch. He worked there as an executive under Elie Susman, the resident director in the Transvaal, until his departure for Northern Rhodesia at the end of 1946. He met Peggy Susman for the first time in 1936 soon after her return to South Africa from St Paul's Girls' School in London. She began work in his department at Woolworths, but resigned after he asked her father to transfer her to another department, and she then went to work as a secretary for the chief rabbi, Dr J. L. Landau. Despite this apparent setback, a romance developed between Peggy and Maurice Rabb and they were married in Johannesburg in April 1939. A planned honeymoon in Europe was cancelled after Hitler's invasion of Czechoslovakia. On the outbreak of war Rabb attempted to join the army, but Woolworths applied to retain him as a key worker; he was finally allowed to join up in 1942 and served at the South African Army's headquarters, Roberts Heights, Pretoria, for three years.

Harry Wulfsohn recruited Maurice Rabb in 1946 because of his knowledge of store management and merchandising systems. Wulfsohn had already realised that his own skills lay in doing deals and expanding the business rather than in management. He may also have calculated that the Susmans would have more confidence in the business if they had one of their own family members on the spot. Elie Susman told his son-in-law and daughter that he would not seek to influence them to go north, but he thought that the prospects were good; the two businesses should be able to produce combined profits of £40,000 a year within a few years. He clearly hoped that Rabb would accept the offer and become the family's representative in central Africa, expecting him to keep a watchful eye, and to be a restraining influence, on Harry Wulfsohn. In one of his first letters to Rabb after his arrival in Livingstone, Elie Susman asked him to use his diplomatic skills to smooth the ruffled feathers of two prominent Livingstone personalities with whom Wulfsohn had fallen out. They were H. J. (Jock) Millar, the mayor of the town, and A. A. Logie, the manager of the *Livingstone Mail.* Elie Susman commented that 'it always pays to be friendly with people of their standing'.[13]

His first advice to Rabb on how to deal with his new partner was less diplomatic. He suggested that Wulfsohn was 'rather an excitable man … you just have to handle him very gently, and I think you can do so by pointing out some of his errors'. He was sure that Rabb 'would have plenty to do to organise new systems at Livingstone and get the business to run efficiently and profitably. I have always told Wulfshon [*sic*] that the business are [*sic*] not properly looked after and we are not getting the results we should get and that he cannot look after everything by himself.' Elie Susman's comments reflected his opinion that Wulfsohn was inclined to be impetuous and that his entrepreneurial drive was stronger than his managerial ability. Susman himself seems to have combined entrepreneurial flair with an eye for detail. Rabb's long and detailed weekly letters to his father-in-law covered all aspects of the business and enabled him to keep a very close eye on it. From Harry Wulfsohn's point of view this may well have appeared to be a case of telescopic micro-management. He probably came to regret his invitation to Rabb, but their talents were complementary. The best summary of the differences between these two men comes from Tony Serrano, who knew them both well: he features later in this story.

> Wulfsohn carried the whole business in his head. Rabb carried the whole business on paper. You need a balance. There is no way that Maurice Rabb could have driven the business as Harry Wulfsohn did. There's no way that Harry Wulfsohn could have done the paper work as Maurice Rabb did. By the time he left a meeting Harry Wulfsohn had already worked out the future profit and was looking ahead to the next project. He had that kind of mind.[14]

The Stores Network

The business was still relatively small when Rabb arrived in Livingstone. Apart from the butchery and bakery in the town itself, there were only thirteen outlying stores. These included Tara store, near Choma, a number of stores in the Livingstone District, extending along the Zambesi Saw Mills railway line to Mulobezi, which had been taken over from H. A. Schenk, and the Nicolai stores in Barotseland.[15] From 1946 to 1950 Harry Wulfsohn's main lieutenant and field worker in the stores business was Jack Faerber. He was based first at Monze and then, from 1946 to 1948, at Mongu where he supervised the takeover of the Nicolai stores and began the process of building up a network of stores in the province. Faerber was born in Latvia in 1907 and knew members of the Lowenthal and Wulfsohn families before his departure for Africa in 1924. After serving with the Rhodesia Regiment during the war, he joined Harry Wulfsohn soon after it ended. According to Tony Serrano he had a good mind and was capable of adding columns of figures without the use of a ready reckoner – this was before the days of adding machines. In 1950 Faerber resigned from Susman Brothers & Wulfsohn and set up on his own at Monze, he bought the butchery there from the Butts family, and also had three stores in the Gwembe valley. In the same year he married Esther Emdin, a member of a well-known Cape Town family. Her sister, Sylvia, was the wife of Max Barnett, who plays a large part in this story. Her brother, 'Sonny' Emdin, became an MP in South Africa and also became associated with the Susman Brothers & Wulfsohn Group of companies. According to Esther Faerber, her husband went out on his own because he found it difficult to work with his friend and *landsleit* (home boy) Harry Wulfsohn.[16]

In July 1947 Faerber gave evidence in Mongu to a commission of inquiry into prices. Its members included Roy Welensky, then leader of the unofficial members of the Legislative Council, and Nathan Schulman, then general manager of Northern Caterers. Faerber's evidence sheds some light on the state of trade in Barotseland at that time. There was, he said, plenty of money in circulation. Much of this came from men who had been recruited by WNLA (the Witwatersrand Native Labour Association) to work on the South African mines, though only about 3,500 men a year were being recruited at this time, and recruitment had only begun in 1940. Cattle prices were relatively high, but sales were low. The firm was still experiencing problems in securing British cotton piece goods, which were in short supply. American goods were available, but were expensive. Sugar, soap and candles were also difficult to get. Susman Brothers & Wulfsohn's ability to import some goods directly from London merchants and Bulawayo wholesalers meant that they were able to sell some goods in Barotseland at prices which were lower than the average on the Line of Rail – in spite of the costs of transport and the loss of goods en route. A good deal of wholesale business was being done with the 350 African village traders and hawkers in the province to whom the company sold at a discount of over ten per cent. The provincial commissioner for the Barotse Province, Thomas Fox-Pitt, thought that the wholesalers, who included Susman Brothers & Wulfsohn, tended to keep the most popular lines for themselves, and only sold the slower-moving items to African village shopkeepers. The reports of the district commissioners point to some changes in popular tastes in these years. Sugar and flour began to compete with salt as staple commodities. Shirts began to replace singlets (vests) and a little later on rayon dresses began to compete with cotton prints. Bicycles became increasingly popular, and were sometimes used by women. In one place, almost certainly Mwandi, which had a WNLA depot, a district commissioner noted that the use of bicycles by 'women of the *demi-monde*' enabled them to move more rapidly from one assignation to another, thus increasing their turnover.[17]

Wulfsohn and Rabb, with some assistance from Faerber, initiated a number of moves in 1948 to expand the business beyond Barotseland. These included the purchase of the network of stores that had been set up by the Greek trader, M. S. Pentopoulos, based on Batoka, about ten miles north of Choma, and extended into the then inaccessible Gwembe valley. Of greater long-term significance was the establishment of a joint venture in 1948 with Antonio F. Serrano, a Portuguese trader who had reached Lukulu in Barotseland, travelling down the Lungwebungu River from Angola by canoe before the outbreak of the Second World War. The terms of the deal were that Susman Brothers & Wulfsohn took an eighty per cent share in a new company, A. F. Serrano Limited. The headquarters of this new subsidiary was at Balovale (now Zambezi) on the Zambezi, about fifty miles south of the Angolan border. Branches were taken over or set up in the Balovale, Lukulu, Kalabo, Kabompo and Mankoya districts and Serrano seems also to have had a base in Mongu. A chain of stores linked Balovale and Mongu, and also extended up the Lungwebungu River which was navigable by canoes for several hundred miles into Angola.[18]

'Ndonyo' Serrano

A. F. Serrano was a remarkable man who remained at Balovale, one of the remotest *boma*s in Northern Rhodesia, until his retirement in 1963. Known in Angola and Northern Rhodesia as 'Ndonyo', he was born in northern Portugal in the early years of the twentieth century and came to Angola in the early 1930s. He began trading at Luso on the newly opened Benguela Railway before moving down the Lungwebungu River to Lukulu. He may have been persuaded to move into Northern Rhodesia by the Capuchin missionaries who were established in the Lukulu District. He did well during the war through the import of salt from Angola, which he exchanged for hides. He also exported soap from Northern Rhodesia to Angola, his main supplier being the Livingstone wholesaler, Elias Kopelowitz.

The expansion of this business was closely tied to cross-border trade with Angola. The basis of the relationship with Susman Brothers & Wulfsohn was that they provided capital, and access to merchandise, while Serrano provided a large new market. A large warehouse was built at Balovale and a wholesaling department supplied traders in Northern Rhodesia and Angola. The district commissioner reported in 1952 that Serrano had £50,000 worth of goods in stock. The company's only real competitor in the district was B. P. Rudge, an English trader with links to the Christian Mission to Many Lands (the Plymouth Brethren), which was well established in the area. Large quantities of millet and rice, as well as groundnuts and fish, were imported from Angola in exchange for trade goods and salt; Portuguese wines were imported too. The firm also acquired contracts for the supply of grain and cassava meal to the government in Mongu. These were often bought in exchange for salt and the two commodities were measured out in paraffin tins. The cassava meal and grain were carried down-river in paddle barges. There was some concern that excessive exports of cassava were endangering food supply in the Balovale District and the exports were halted, at least temporarily, in 1952. Beeswax was also an important trade item in this area, it was brought in to the shops in large balls that were sliced to ensure that they did not conceal stones, and the slices of wax were then boiled for many hours in forty-four-gallon drums. Cattle and hides from the west bank of the Zambezi were also traded south. The cattle were sometimes used to supply the Susman Brothers & Wulfsohn butchery at Mongu.[19]

An observant visitor to Balovale in 1956, Frank Fraser Darling, the distinguished naturalist, was impressed by Serrano's 'up-to-date' store 'with showcases and all the rest'. He bought a bottle of Pedro Domecq Amontillado sherry there for eight shillings and sixpence and noted that five-litre demijohns of Portuguese wine were on sale at thirty-five shillings each. He commented: 'Balovale is quite a place, though I can't quite understand why'. Clearly, one explanation was Serrano's store, and the cross-border trade that it generated. Balovale was far from the attention of the Department of Customs and Excise, which does not appear to have caught up with the place until 1963, when it imposed a fine on A. F. Serrano and Company and made a substantial demand for back payments of duty for imports from Angola. This caused some embarrassment to the parent company, Susman Brothers & Wulfsohn. Its directors then encouraged Serrano to retire, which he did later in the year.[20]

Transport

Transport to and from Barotseland and Balovale was always difficult. At first it was by barge up the Zambezi; from the early 1920s onwards R. F. Sutherland Ltd provided this service. It closed down its transport business in 1944, while retaining barges for its own use. The closure was apparently because of the refusal of government to allow the company to raise its charges, and because of the difficulty it experienced in getting fuel in wartime, and in replacing the trucks that it used on parts of the route. The government was then compelled to set up the Zambesi River Transport Service. This also used barges on the river, while trucking goods around the rapids. Salt and blankets were always the bulkiest commodities that were imported by barge – they were later used as ballast on trucks. By the early 1940s there was a dry-season road from Lusaka to Mongu, but it could only be used for three or four months in the year, and could not replace river transport. By the late 1940s a road of sorts had been constructed from Solwezi to Balovale, providing an overland route of nearly 500 miles from the Copperbelt, but it was usually impassable during the rains. It was in connection with this new route that the Pioneer Trading Company was set up in 1952 as a subsidiary of A. F. Serrano. It was based in Mufulira on the Copperbelt where it had a large warehouse and some urban stores. It also took over, or opened, stores in the Solwezi and Mwinilunga districts.[21]

Several members of Serrano's family – his brother-in-law, Alex Pires, his son-in-law, Antonio Gonçalves, and son, Tony, who was nineteen – set up the Barotse Transport Company in 1949 to transport goods for the group to and from Barotseland and Balovale. This was a spin-off from A. F. Serrano Ltd, though it was an independent business and was not directly financed by it. Tony Serrano had arrived in Northern Rhodesia at the age of twelve in 1942, travelling with his mother by barge down the Lungwebungu River from Angola. He learned English in Mongu, where he stayed with Abe Galaun, and went to secondary school in Bulawayo, returning home to Lukulu once a year, by a combination of rail, road and river. He recalls that he helped his father, who did not speak English well, in the negotiations with Harry Wulfsohn that preceded the takeover. He thinks that the trade in hides, in which they both had an interest, may have brought Wulfsohn and Serrano together. Tony Serrano worked for a year as a stock-taker for Susman Brothers & Wulfsohn at Batoka before joining Barotse Transport. His father had helped the partners in the firm to buy second-hand six-wheel drive trucks. They were General Motors trucks of a type supplied to the American army and were fitted with balloon tyres for use on sand. Pires and Gonçalves cut a road for over 100 miles through the bush from the Zambesi Saw Mills railhead at Mulobezi by way of Luampa to the Lusaka–Mongu road west of Mankoya (now Kaoma). This route provided competition for much of the year with Zambesi River Transport Services. Susman Brothers

& Wulfsohn opened five stores along the Barotse Transport route between Mulobezi and Mongu.[22]

Hides and Cattle

Until 1950 hides were the most important goods exported by Susman Brothers & Wulfsohn from Barotseland and Balovale, as well as from the Southern Province. The use of salt in the curing of hides was one of the reasons why it was imported in such large quantities. Most hides were sun-dried, but this process often damaged them, so from about 1949 onwards the company encouraged producers to bring in wet hides, which were shade-dried centrally at the stores. Maurice Rabb commented that it would take time 'to educate the natives' in the new process. The same prices per pound were paid for wet as for dry hides, though the weight of a wet hide was twice that of a dry one. The Korean War resulted in an unprecedented boom in the market for hides; windfall profits were made at this time, but the boom was followed by a slump from late in 1951, and large losses were then sustained. Susman Brothers & Wulfsohn bought the bulk of the 24,000 hides that were exported from Barotseland in the latter year.[23]

Although the revival of the Barotseland cattle trade had been the major reason for the establishment of the trading business, it was not able to buy many cattle in the area before 1950 as most buying was still done by members of the Veterinary Department, acting on behalf of the Cold Storage Board. After a peak of 12,000 head in 1943–4, associated with the compulsory purchase of cattle infected with bovine pleuro-pneumonia, purchases dropped dramatically after the war, though prices doubled. In an attempt to boost purchases the Cold Storage Board decided to appoint Susman Brothers & Wulfsohn as their cattle-buying agents in Barotseland. The company took over this role in October 1950 and continued with it until the end of 1959. The idea was that the company would buy cattle at all its stores throughout the year. This proved to be a successful strategy. In its first year as agent, the company bought 6,000 head of cattle, three times as many as had been bought on behalf of the Cold Storage Board in the previous year. It expected to be paid a commission of about £2 a head by the board for these cattle. There was, of course, a close link between cattle purchases and store sales. Good quality and low prices for goods encouraged people to sell cattle, and money put into the hands of cattle sellers tended to come back to the stores. Cattle were collected at stores and then concentrated in holding grounds before being trekked to Mulobezi or Livingstone. The company also bought cattle on commission for Zambesi Saw Mills.[24]

The company was fortunate in being able to recruit Mike Pretorius to supervise their cattle-buying operations. He became the company's manager in Mongu and remained there until 1957. According to Rob Hart, the Kalabo trader, who knew him well, Pretorius was born on a scotch cart in the Ghanzi District of Bechuanaland. He joined the Veterinary Department as a stock inspector before the war and served with the Royal Air Force during it. Other members of his family were Afrikaner nationalists and supporters of the militant and pro-Nazi Ossewa Brandwag. Pretorius returned to the Veterinary Department after the war and was put in charge of cattle buying for the Cold Storage Board. His Lozi name is said to have been 'Bopula', which Rob Hart translates as 'Mr Thunder' – possibly a reference to his style of addressing his workers, though it could also have been a reference to his use of the Setswana greeting, '*Pula*! – Rain!' He was a fluent speaker of Silozi and is described by Rob Hart as a very helpful man. The directors of the company were certainly pleased with Pretorius's work. By October 1951 the turnover of the Barotseland stores had grown from about £10,000 to £14,000 a month.[25]

Mike Pretorius's assistant manager and bulk store manager in Mongu for much of this time was Ronnie Vos. Born in Cape Town in 1930, he now lives in Boksburg, South Africa and, after farming for many years near Livingstone and in Zimbabwe, makes a good living as a maker of wrought-ironwork. He started work for Frasers Stores in Basutoland at the age of eighteen and as a wool buyer he rode horses all over the country. He answered an advertisement for jobs with Susman Brothers & Wulfsohn and moved north in 1950, swearing that he would never again sit on a horse. He worked at first with Fritz Mannsbach, a German Jewish refugee, who left Mongu when Pretorius arrived late in 1950. He has vivid recollections of those days: when he was not stocktaking at remote stores, he spent much of the time buying cattle and hides at places like Liachi in the Senanga District. It was famed for its inaccessibility and also for its wealth in cattle. He recalls: 'We would get a message to say the cattle are so thin, they are now invisible – come and get them.' It was a difficult place to get to in the dry season, but easier to get to by boat when the floods were up.[26]

Another Susman Brothers & Wulfsohn employee at Mongu at the time was Dougie Christians who ran the European store. He went to Fort Rosebery as group manager in 1957, but died there a few years later. Thelma Shelton, wife of Eric Shelton, the WNLA representative, did the accounts.

R. F. Sutherland, which had become part of the Campbell, Booker, Carter (CBC) group, provided the main competition. Their manager was Jack Trollip, then in his seventies, and his assistant manager, Benny van Zyl, really ran the business, but the competition was one-sided. In Ronnie Vos's opinion, Sutherland's were not in the same league as Susman Brothers & Wulfsohn.

Vos recalls Maurice Rabb as rather quiet and subdued – an office man, and someone who found it hard to say no. He has more positive memories of Harry Wulfsohn.

> He was alive, hard – a man who knew what he wanted. He was dynamic. He really drove the business. It would have got nowhere without him. He was a man who sat down and listened. If he said, 'Next time I come I want to see this done', you damned well made sure you did it. He kept you on your toes. If you did your job you had no trouble with him. He didn't miss a thing.

Ronnie Vos enjoyed life in Mongu. He met his wife, Hester (Poppie), there. She was the sister of the *boma* doctor, Dr de Kock, and her sister, Marie, married Tony Serrano. When Ronnie and Poppie were married in 1952 the *Livingstone Mail* reported this event a little ambiguously as the first 'white' wedding in Mongu for twenty-two years. Their house in 'Susman Square', Kanyonyo, had a well-thatched roof, no windowpanes, but gauze and shutters. There were about forty 'people' at the *boma* – there were riotous Guy Fawkes parties, and all-night poker games. There was still something of a gulf between traders and officials. Ronnie Vos did not have much time for the resident commissioner, A. F. B. Glennie, whom he describes as 'dour', or for the district commissioner, Glyn Jones (later governor of Nyasaland), who fined him thirty shillings for punching a man who had, he says, attacked him with a *panga* (machete or cutlass).

Grain and Rice

Members of the provincial administration did not usually take much interest in trade, and were often snobbish about traders. District officers' tour reports provide very little information about the activities of Susman Brothers & Wulfsohn in these years, though their annual reports usually have some information on trade. An exception must be made for the district commissioner in the Mankoya (Kaoma) District, R. J. N. Mark, who wrote a comprehensive report on the activities of the company in the district, which is about 100 miles east of Mongu, in the mid 1950s. His report, which is recorded in the District Notebook, provides a uniquely detailed account of the growth of the business in a district that was becoming increasingly important to the company at this time. His account sheds a rare light on the catalytic role of the company in the trades in maize and rice from this district. The company was also involved in the purchase and hulling of rice in the Mongu District at this time, but their activities there are less well documented. There had been only five Susman Brothers & Wulfsohn or Serrano stores in the Mankoya District in 1950. Mankoya became an independent group in 1953 when stores previously controlled from Livingstone and Mongu were brought together. A wholesale outlet had been opened in 1952 and from 1957 the Serrano stores in the district were leased to Susman Brothers & Wulfsohn.

The district commissioner reported in 1955:

Since the last entry was made five years ago Susman Brothers & Wulfsohn have expanded their stores considerably. At Mankoya their group of fifteen stores in the district are supervised by Mr H. B. Holland (Canadian), manager, and Mr D. E. Speares (Rhodesian), assistant manager. The Mankoya establishment consists of two permanent European houses, a large retail store in two sections, a wholesale and bulk section, and a rice milling shed. [There is a] [W]holesale business supplying African traders, turnover £900 a month at present [May 1955]. Goods for Susmans at Mankoya are brought up by their subsidiary, Barotse Transport Ltd, who presumably give them advantageous back-load rates for produce produced in the district. Susmans themselves supply their 'out-stores' by lorry from Mankoya (They have one lorry and one vanette). The 'out-stores' are reasonable Kimberley brick buildings. The supervision associated with these stores is considerable. Stocktaking from time to time involves shortages which occasionally reach the courts. The advantage of employing a European supervisory staff is obvious when comparison is made with their competitors.

Messrs R. F. Sutherland have five sites near each of which Susmans have established stores. This firm manage their store from Mongu with occasional visits from one of their European managers. During 1955 a new burnt brick store has been built adjacent to Susmans, and a wholesale section has recently been opened. (£70 turnover in May.) The range of goods for sale is very small indeed and Susmans, with their European managers close at hand, are always able to adjust their own prices accordingly. The directors of Susmans and Sutherlands pay visits every two months to their establishments here in the Boma: the directors of both companies have been known to arrive in the same aircraft.

He also noted that:

Susman Brothers & Wulfsohn are apparently prepared to buy almost any produce offered to them for sale at their fifteen stores in the district ... [They] have this year a permit to purchase up to 2,000 bags of maize which they intend to export to Livingstone. They have also signed an agreement with the Government to purchase unhulled rice offered to them for sale at 2d per lb. With this in view they have purchased from Government rice machinery to the value of £2,000; the machinery will be set up at their Mankoya store in a building put up by them in 1954 ...

During the 1955 buying season Susmans have taken to employing established African traders as their agents. One or two traders have been quick to see that, although they make only a small commission, the cash which they hand out at their stores to producers (on behalf of Susmans) comes back to them in purchases which the producers evidently make. It is worth noting that many of these traders are supplied with wholesale goods by Susmans.[27]

From the evidence of the Mankoya District Notebook, it seems to be no exaggeration to say that Susman Brothers & Wulfsohn had in the early 1950s created markets for maize, beans, groundnuts, rice, cassava and millet. The district commissioner fixed the prices of these commodities. Susmans were the only buyers, and only suppliers to the *boma*, prison, hospital and schools, as well as to the local missions, until 1958 when the Mankoya Co-operative Union was set up with the district commissioner as chairman. District Commissioner Mark had been impressed by the enterprise of Susman Brothers & Wulfsohn and had seen their role as positive. A later district commissioner seemed to get some satisfaction from the suggestion that the Co-operative Union, if successful, would 'take food-buying out of the hands of Susmans'. The new union secured the right to buy maize from the Native Authorities and Susmans were excluded from maize buying, though they continued to buy rice. The establishment of the Co-operative Union coincided with a bad harvest and it began to import maize from the Line of Rail and to sell maize meal, which it ground in its own mill. Susmans responded by setting up their own mill and selling maize meal for the first time.[28]

Ivory

As well as cattle, hides, grain, rice and beeswax, ivory continued to be an important commodity exported from Barotseland. The Litunga retained the right to the ground tusk from any elephant killed in Barotseland and, therefore, controlled about half of all ivory exports from the area. Susman Brothers & Wulfsohn were the Litunga's preferred buyers for his stock of this commodity. Geoff Kates recalls frequent visits to Lealui and Limulunga to buy ivory in the days of Mwanawina III, who reigned until 1968. He would receive a message that the Litunga wanted to sell ivory, and would go up to Barotseland, always taking someone with him for the experience, and as a witness. They would be entertained to tea by the Litunga, who had been at Lovedale in South Africa. He spoke excellent English and they would make polite conversation with him while drinking tea, and eating scones, served on Wedgwood china. When it came to the question of bargaining over the price of ivory the Litunga spoke in Silozi. His prime minister, the Ngambela, was the interpreter.

> We would begin by saying that before we discussed a price we must know the weight of ivory for sale. The Litunga would reply by saying that the price he expected was so much, naming a figure that was fifty percent more than we were prepared to pay. We would then say that the ivory market was flooded, the world price was down, we were not really interested in ivory, we were only buying as a favour and for the sake of goodwill etc. Of course we wanted the ivory desperately. We would start by naming a price that was much less than we were prepared to pay and would end up paying the price that we originally had in mind.[29]

Merchandise

Geoff Kates played a key role as merchandising manager, or director, of Susman Brothers & Wulfsohn, and its successor companies, for almost twenty years. He was born in London in 1920 of Irish and French descent. He left school at fourteen and started work with a wholesale business in the City. He served in the Royal Navy during the war and became a chief petty officer. He served on the Arctic convoys and was on a converted banana boat in the ill-fated convoy PQ17 when it was ordered to disperse; his ship reached Spitzbergen, where it was stranded for three months. He was later on a ship that was sunk off the coast of Tunisia. On his return from the war he found that his previous employers had been bombed out of existence. They found him a job with a company, Dominion Shippers, which sent him to Southern Rhodesia. While in Bulawayo, he was headhunted by Kaufman and Sons for Susman Brothers & Wulfsohn. After flying up to Livingstone for an interview, he joined them in 1952. He soon became merchandising manager and was transferred to Salisbury in 1956 to join the new head office. He acquired an unrivalled knowledge and understanding of the African retail market in the region and was one of the most remarkable of the employees of Susman Brothers & Wulfsohn. Many of his contemporaries regarded him as a bit of a genius in his own field.[30]

His reminiscences shed a good deal of light on an important aspect of the business – the market and merchandise. He emphasises that Susman Brothers & Wulfsohn stores stocked anything and everything that the people wanted to buy: bicycles, sewing machines, agricultural implements, tools, textiles, clothing, groceries, cooking oil, paraffin etc. They also bought anything that the people had to sell. The basic idea was to create a market by putting money into the hands of the people. This is a view that was shared by Maurice Rabb.[31] From the late 1950s onwards, Kates made two trips a year to Europe, India, Japan, Taiwan, Hong Kong and China looking for goods for the central African market. As time went on Europe became less important as a source of goods, though he does recall visiting Jablonex, the main manufacturers in Czechoslovakia of glass beads for the African market. He would go to the Far East at the time of the spring and autumn trade fairs in China – in those days he could only travel in China with a 'minder'. In Japan the company worked with Gerbers, the Cape Town-based shipping company, which had offices in Japan, as well as London, New York and Salisbury, and did a great deal of business with Woolworths.

In many ways the most complex field of merchandise was that of textiles. Although basic white and blue cloth was in demand everywhere there were regional variations in demand for colour and material. Barotse cloth was of an unusual width – twenty-five inches. It took up to twenty-five yards of red and white cloth to make the 'traditional' Victorian-style dress with petticoats for a Lozi woman. German print was also popular. Dutch Java prints seem to have become popular relatively late in the day, and a similar type of wax print was made in Japan. On at least one occasion Kates became involved in the design of prints for the central African market. He sat with three Japanese artists for three days and used his knowledge of colour and design to help them produce 'border prints' that would suit the market. He recalled one design that was based on the idea of Hannibal crossing the Alps with elephants and another that was based on the Japanese lanterns that he found in his hotel room.

Kates's great gift was to know what would sell, and where. He knew that there was no point in sending Barotse cloth to Luapula or fine shirts to Sikongo, a small store on the border with Angola. He links the company's profitability with the high turnover and the low rate of pilferage. The company had few competitors in Barotseland. He agreed with Ronnie Vos that it had the edge over Sutherlands. He recalled: 'They did not have the same expertise in supplying the stores. They would be out of goods for longer periods. The Africans came to know that you could rely on our stores to carry a wide variety of stock and good quality products.'

Conclusion

Susman Brothers & Wulfsohn grew very rapidly in the post-war years. Figures are hard to come by, but the company made a profit of £7,300 in the year to March 1946. Five years later it made a pre-tax profit of £75,000 on a turnover of about £400,000. This did, however, include a windfall profit of £30,000 on hides – it was almost wiped out two years later by a loss of £18,000 on the same commodity. The business was profitable, but it was also undercapitalised. It was unable to pay out dividends and all profits had to be re-invested. A good deal of the profit went back into replacing stocks at higher prices. Debts remained high and the business was in effect 'overtrading'. Its overdraft at the end of 1951 was close to £100,000 – probably more than the issued share capital at that date.[32]

Elie Susman warned of the danger of over-rapid expansion. He advised against the opening of African stores in Mufulira in 1952 before the finances of the company were stabilised. He told Rabb: 'It is no good putting the cart before the horse as you will only get into deeper financial difficulties'. There was discussion of transferring the group's accounts from the Standard Bank to Barclays Bank, which was said to be offering finance of up to £250,000, though it would require a mortgage of all the assets and of the partners' shares. Elie Susman thought that the businesses needed £250–300,000 of new permanent capital, which could, perhaps, be raised by the issue of ordinary shares or debentures. He felt, however, that money was tight, and hoped that the forthcoming establishment of the Federation of Rhodesia and Nyasaland would ease matters. He expected that the association of the two Rhodesias would create a larger unit, with an improved credit rating, and better prospects for investment.[33]

CHAPTER 12

The Susmans, Woolworths and Marks & Spencer

The Susman family was involved in two major business developments in the post-war years that were distinct from, and outside, the partnership with Harry Wulfsohn. Both had their origins in the 1930s, but expanded rapidly after the war. The first was Woolworths in South Africa. The second was the Gersh brothers' Economy Stores. This grew, with the participation of their uncles, into a large and varied business on the Copperbelt – African Commercial Holdings – its history is considered in a later chapter. The involvement of the Susman family in Woolworths, and in Marks & Spencer, was significant for the central African business. From the mid 1950s onwards, Elie Susman's son, David, gradually took over his father's role in both the South African and the central African businesses. He played a major part in the transmission of the philosophy and methods of Marks & Spencer to Woolworths, and he was largely responsible for the percolation of some of these ideas and practices to the Susman Brothers & Wulfsohn trading network.

From 1935 until his death in 1958 Elie Susman was resident director of Woolworths in the Transvaal. He worked with a fellow director, Harry Saevitzen, to develop shops in Johannesburg and Pretoria, and in the Reef mining towns of Springs, Brakpan and Benoni. Within a few months of his arrival in Johannesburg he recruited Hymie Wolffe, who had recently qualified as a chartered accountant in Livingstone, to join him in Johannesburg. Wolffe had a special interest in accounting systems and ensured that the procedures followed in the Transvaal were more advanced than those in the Cape. Johannesburg and Cape Town were 1,000 miles apart and this allowed for a degree of detachment between the two halves of the business. The Sonnenberg and Susman branches developed on rather different lines, though they were both parts of one department store chain, and the Johannesburg end of the business could not entirely escape from the control of Cape Town. In spite of the disruption caused by the war, the company grew quite rapidly from three branches in 1936 to thirteen at the beginning of 1947 and sixteen by the end of that year. By that time turnover was running at about £3,000,000 a year and the profit after tax was about £150,000.[1]

Early in 1947 Max Sonnenberg travelled with his wife and daughters on holiday to England. They met and became friendly with Israel Sieff and his family. Sieff was a director of Marks & Spencer, the British retail chain, and introduced Sonnenberg to his brother-in-law, Sir Simon Marks (later Lord Marks), the chairman of the company. They got on well together and Sonnenberg mentioned the possibility of an exchange of shares between Woolworths and Marks & Spencer. The discussion of a share swap led to talk of closer co-operation. There was pressure on British companies at the time to generate exports as their own level of imports was linked to their export performance. The possibility of exporting goods to South Africa was of interest not only to Marks & Spencer, but also to the clothing manufacturers who were closely linked to it.

A deal was eventually worked out between the two groups. In terms of an agreement that was approved by its shareholders in October 1947, Marks & Spencer took an interest in Woolworths that was equal to rather more than ten per cent of its issued share capital. There was also a private arrangement whereby a group of British investors and a South African group exchanged options to buy blocks of shares in each other's companies. The British group included members of Sir Simon Marks's family, all the directors of Marks & Spencer and some close associates, including Chaim Weizmann, later president of Israel, Leopold Amery, a former colonial secretary and member of Churchill's wartime cabinet, and the maharajah of Jaipur. The South African group included Max Sonnenberg, his son, Richard (Dick), and Elie Susman. In addition to the agreement on shares there was an understanding that Marks & Spencer would supply Woolworths with a range of its own branded products. The basis of these arrangements was the rapport that had been established between Sir Simon Marks, Israel Sieff and Max Sonnenberg. This was backed up by a report by an accountant who had analysed Woolworths's balance sheets. It was not long, however, before Sir Simon Marks set off for South Africa to see for himself the business into which he had bought.[2]

He reached South Africa in January 1948 with a high-powered deputation on a tour of inspection. Apart from himself and his wife, the party included the finance and store operations directors, Bruce Goodman and Wilfred

Norris, with their wives; two nephews of Sir Simon, Marcus Sieff – later Lord Sieff – and Michael Sacher with his wife. Bobby Wessell, managing director of Marks & Spencer's largest clothing supplier, Corah's of Leicester, was also a member of the party. The group also included Ann Laski, Sir Simon's niece. She was the daughter of his sister, Elaine Blond, and of her former husband, Norman Laski, a director of Marks & Spencer. Elaine Blond's second husband was Neville Blond, who came from a family of Manchester textile manufacturers and had served with the RAF and the Ministry of Production during the Second World War. Ann Laski had recently been demobilised from the Royal Navy where she had served as a radio artificer with the Fleet Air Arm.

David Susman was at the time a young man of twenty-two. After education at Kingswood, a Methodist school in Grahamstown, he had spent a year at the University of the Witwatersrand, waiting for his eighteenth birthday when he would be old enough to join the army. He joined up at the end of 1943 and had a varied military career serving, with his close friend Jeff Perlman, in various regiments as a sapper, a gunner and, finally, as a trooper in the Natal Carbineers during the Italian campaign. He was demobilised in 1946 and returned to Wits to complete a degree in Commerce. He was still a student, though on vacation, at the time of the visit by the Marks & Spencer deputation. Work in the Johannesburg office of Woolworths had given him some insight into the business, and strong views as to how it could be improved. He provides a vivid description of the impact of the visiting 'Circus' on Woolworths in Cape Town.

> There can never have been a more effective and professional group of executives. Under the dynamic leadership of Sir Simon himself, the men worked sometimes for twelve hours a day, in the stores and in Head Office, critically analysing the figures, the goods and their composition, store layouts and fixtures, and the meagre control systems of the business. Simon was a small man, forthright, earthy and aggressive, and he did not even try to conceal his shock at the miserable state of the company into which he had bought. He described the merchandise as 'dreck' (rubbish in polite language), and the senior management as 'schmocks' (idiots, ditto). He walked the length of the haberdashery counter in the Cape Town store with his arm rigidly stretched out, and shovelled every single item on to the floor. He picked up random items of merchandise from the counters and threw them to the ground. ... He terrified store managers and buyers alike, reducing them to a state of gibbering incoherence. The other members of his team spent much time and calculated effort calming the atmosphere and counselling the victims.[3]

Marcus Sieff recalled that at the first store they visited Simon Marks told Max Sonnenberg: 'You really can't offer these goods for sale; they should be given to the Bishop for his charity garden party.' But at the next store they visited, he said: 'You can't even give this stuff to the Bishop for his garden party, you must burn it!'[4]

David Susman recalls that he heard reports of the bloodbath in Cape Town 'with wicked glee'. Even his father, though loyal to the Sonnenbergs, 'seemed to take a grim satisfaction in the come-uppance visited on the complacency and short-sightedness of Head Office'. Nevertheless, people in the Johannesburg office, including himself, awaited the arrival of the deputation 'with the same apprehension with which the Incas must have awaited the Conquistadors'. The visit went off surprisingly well. Hymie Wolffe recalls that the visitors were impressed by his accounting procedures and use of a primitive calculating machine, which ensured that the results of a stock-take were available within days rather than months. They insisted that he should be transferred to head office in Cape Town where he soon became the company secretary and, eventually, a director.[5]

Marks was fascinated by Elie Susman and pressed him for tales of his pioneering days in Barotseland. Sir Simon Marks's powerful personality and fascinating philosophy had a huge impact on David Susman.

> We dined with the Circus for night after night, with Simon holding forth on the romance of shop keeping, and the huge potential of Woolworths, if only it were to absorb and apply the principles and philosophies of M & S. I was completely mesmerised by him. He spent an inordinate amount of time with me, explaining, illustrating and asking my opinion about the business. Not even the most sycophantic of Father's employees had ever done that, let alone Max or Dick, and certainly not Father himself. With Simon's permission, I took Jeff [Perlman] with me for a drink with him one evening, in the suite at the Carlton Hotel where he was staying. He interrupted our breathless account of the shortcomings of the business, and said, peremptorily: 'Write me a note.' I was to learn later that he enjoyed challenging young people to express themselves clearly and articulately, and that he always sought their views in writing. Jeff and I rushed back home and spent the rest of the night writing and rewriting 'Woolworths (Pty.) Limited. A Brief Outline as a Basis to Future Policy.' Bearing in mind Simon's stricture to 'keep it short', we condensed it into three pages, typed by Father's secretary first thing next morning, and I handed it to Simon as he arrived at the office.[6]

In their paper they wrote of 'false economies, poor shop fittings, lack of trained staff, and unwillingness to dispose of bad stocks'. They proposed 'centralised buying, the establishment of a central distribution department, and standardised equipment'. They emphasised the need for head office to allocate counter space, feature lines and window displays, and to send out professionally printed price tickets so that store managers could concentrate on 'the ensuring of maximum service and attention to their customers'. David Susman now acknowledges that many of the ideas must have come from earlier discussions with Simon Marks, and other members of the deputation, but remembers that he was 'gracious and full of praise for our jejune work'. He believes that 'the foundation of his subsequent affection and support for me was laid at that time'. He has no doubt that 'Simon Marks's powerful personality, his uncompromising standards and his profound philosophical approach to his business has dominated my life, as has no other influence.'[7]

The visit of Sir Simon Marks and his party influenced the course of David Susman's life in two other ways. Contact with Marks, Marcus Sieff and Michael Sacher made him much more aware than he had been previously of recent events in Palestine, including the passing by the United Nations in November 1947 of a resolution on partition. The Susman family was itself close to Palestine and to Zionism, but members of 'the Family' were among the major international backers of Chaim Weizmann and David Ben-Gurion – they were soon to become first president and first prime minister of Israel. Marcus Sieff's father, Israel, had been secretary to the Zionist Commission that visited Palestine, under the leadership of Weizmann, in 1918. His mother, Rebecca, was world president of the Women's International Zionist Organisation. Marcus Sieff was himself about to pay an extended visit to Palestine and, at the request of Ben-Gurion, was to set up a logistical supply plan for the anticipated war of independence. When war broke out in May 1948, following the end of the British mandate and Israel's declaration of independence, David Susman was one of a number of young South Africans who volunteered for military service. He was wounded in the conflict and returned to South Africa for medical treatment.

A few months before he set off for Palestine David Susman had met Ann Laski at a party given by Dick and Cecilia Sonnenberg in Cape Town. Feeling themselves under some parental pressure to meet, they had avoided doing so until the last moment. They got on well together, but Ann was about to return to England with the Marks & Spencer deputation. They kept in touch by letter, but it was not until the following year that they met again. David Susman passed through London while on his way back to Israel after undergoing an operation in South Africa. Ann's mother described the ensuing events:

After two days they were engaged. I was surprised. I was even more surprised when they said they were to be married in three weeks. Of course, I told them it was quite impossible. I might as well have been talking to myself. Off they went to Israel for two years where David, who was among the brightest of his generation, shifted over from the military to the diplomatic corps. Under Teddy Kollek, his boss at the Foreign Ministry, his path to ambassadorial status seemed assured. But, emotionally, it was not easy for Ann and David to come to terms with the prospect of yet another cultural allegiance. Ann was English; David, a South African; both were Israelis by adoption. Now they had to think of resettling – yet again – in Washington.[8]

David and Ann Susman's eldest child, Simon, named in honour of Simon Marks, was born in Israel in May 1950. Elie and Bertha Susman visited them in Israel at that time; it was their first visit since 1937. Their youngest daughter, Osna, was also living there with her husband, Jack Wilton, at this time. Elie Susman told Dick Sonnenberg that he was impressed by the development of the country.

New farms are being established daily. Tenement buildings are going up everywhere. Road making, water pipe laying, is going ahead, and if one would not know that the finances of the country were in a very bad way, on the surface the country looks prosperous. Food conditions are very bad. No meat, excepting a few ounces weekly, but I must say I have not seen anyone starved or looking bad. ... To us coming from here [South Africa], which in comparison to Israel, is a land of milk and honey, it is very hard there.

I certainly would not like at my time of life to start pioneering again in Israel. The life is really very hard, and there are hardly any comforts there, but with all that, the country is developing. In the last two years they brought in nearly 400,000 immigrants. 300,000 are already placed on farms and in jobs, and only about 100,000 are still in camps waiting to be absorbed into jobs, which will be found for them shortly. The country requires a lot of capital.[9]

Elie Susman told Dick Sonnenberg in the same letter that David and Ann had decided to leave Israel in August. David intended 'to go into Marks & Spencer for training for a year or two, after which they will come out to South Africa'. According to Elaine Blond, his career path was not quite so smooth. She recalls that when discreet soundings were made with her brother, Sir Simon Marks, about a job for David in London, he responded: 'They didn't ask me about going to Israel so why should they ask me about coming to London?' He went on to ask why, if David wanted a job, he did he not say so himself. According to her account, David then made a direct approach to him, but he continued to show some resistance. David said in desperation: 'If you don't want me at Marks & Spencer, I'll go elsewhere.' Only then did Sir Simon offer him a job. Elaine Blond is sure that her brother 'had his eye on David as a likely saviour of Woolworth's South Africa' from the beginning, but that he was too shrewd to approach the matter directly.[10]

On his arrival in London in August 1950 David Susman was put through an accelerated version of Marks & Spencer's course for management trainees. He spent most of a year in the stores, beginning at the Pantheon in Oxford Street, the second-largest shop in the chain. He was also sent on the standard two-month tour of selected clothing and textile manufacturers. This took him through much of the industrial heartland of England and Scotland in what turned out to be almost the last days of the domestic textile and clothing industry. He learned the basics of fibres, yarns, fabrics and garments and developed a fascination for merchandise that has remained with him forever afterwards. He also spent time with a number of divisional superintendents who had responsibility for groups of stores. Most of his second year was spent at head office, though with a break in South Africa.

From the moment that he started to work in head office he became increasingly aware of the deteriorating relationship between Woolworths and Marks & Spencer. This had not gone according to the plan that had been drawn up in 1947. Max Sonnenberg became ill in 1949 and withdrew from the day-to-day management of the company. The main burden of running the company fell upon his son, Dick, who suffered under the strain. The value of the shares that Sir Simon Marks and his friends had bought had fallen dramatically in the four years since the original deal was done. Emissaries sent out from Marks & Spencer failed to inculcate the firm's philosophy into its new associate. An Afrikaner Nationalist government had come to power and was beginning to turn South Africa into an international pariah. Controls continued to restrict Woolworths's imports and the company was giving only a small proportion of its quota to Marks & Spencer's goods. Sir Simon Marks made it clear to David that his patience was exhausted. He had received an offer for his and the company's shares in Woolworths from Sam Cohen of OK Bazaars. He intended to take up the offer and recommend it to his friends. David leapt angrily to the defence of the Sonnenbergs and of Woolworths: 'You keep sending the wrong people. They need someone young and committed ... with lots of energy!' David Susman recalls what happened next: 'There was a longish silence, during which Simon glared at me with the worst of his black looks, and I rapidly simmered down to an apprehensive quiver. He rose, came around his desk, put his hand on my shoulder and sprung his trap. "*Exactly!*" He said.'[11]

It was in the light of this conversation that David Susman made his future plans. In a long letter on Woolworths business, which he wrote on 4 September 1951, just a year after his arrival in London, he told Dick Sonnenberg that he intended to travel to Cape Town for two months in April 1952. He would then return to Marks & Spencer for six months. He would like to take two or three of Woolworths's younger and more promising men back with him to London for training. They would come back to Cape Town as a team, possibly augmented by one or two people from Marks & Spencer's head office. He would himself stay with Woolworths for five or six years.[12]

He stuck closely to the initial stages of this plan and came out to South Africa for a visit in April 1952, and to stay with his team in October 1952. He did not, however, stay with Woolworths for the promised five or six years. He remained with the company for fifty years – as general manager from 1952, managing director from 1956, chairman from 1983 and president from 1993 to 2002.

There was some discussion of the possibility of his returning to England with his family in 1955. Elaine Blond was anxious that her daughter, son-in-law and grandchildren should return to England. Elie Susman reported a discussion of his son's future that took place in David's absence in Sir Simon Marks's office at 82 Baker Street on 13 June 1955. Apart from Sir Simon, Elie Susman himself and Dick Sonnenberg, the discussion involved Israel and Michael Sieff. Sonnenberg said that he was anxious that David Susman should stay with Woolworths. He agreed with Sir Simon's view that the organisation of the company had begun to improve following David's arrival with his team three years previously. Sir Simon made it clear that, regardless of his sister's wishes, he would not interfere: David must make up his own mind about his future. He did, however, suggest that David might spend three months a year with Marks & Spencer in London. Elaine Blond recounted another private meeting with Sir Simon at which Ann complained that she felt cut off in South Africa. He shouted to his secretary: 'Mrs Susman feels cut off. Arrange for her to get the *Illustrated London News*.'[13]

David Susman had arrived in Cape Town, with Ann, to take up his duties as general manager of Woolworths in October 1952 – on his twenty-seventh birthday. He found that the company was effectively 'rudderless'. Dick Sonnenberg was recovering from a series of nervous breakdowns. He was primarily an accountant and had little interest in merchandise; he and his right-hand man, Fred Kossuth, were more interested in cutting costs than in cutting profit margins. Although an attempt had been made to introduce

Marks & Spencer's checking and ordering systems into the business, these were being honoured more in the breach than the observance. Only one or two of the company's executives, such as Ernst Loebenberg, one of Elie Susman's key men in Johannesburg, were really committed to the implementation of Marks & Spencer's philosophies and methods. The usual refrain was: 'It may work with Marks & Spencer, but it can't work here.' The company had not taken advantage of its links with Marks & Spencer to strengthen its position in the key clothing and textiles branch of the business. The shops' counters were still clogged with slow-moving and unsaleable stock. David Susman saw his immediate task was to shift the emphasis of the shops away from slow-moving 'hard' goods towards the faster-moving clothing and textile lines, and to use the company's import quotas to bring in higher quality goods from Marks & Spencer. At the same time he had to establish Marks & Spencer-type relationships with South African suppliers in order to improve the quality of locally manufactured goods. This involved keeping a close eye on suppliers' labour relations and employment practices. Above all, he had to spread what he called the gospel of St Michael: 'No compromise on quality standards, close cooperation with suppliers, tight control of stock levels and ruthless slaughtering of slow sellers.'[14]

It took about four years of hard work by David Susman and his team to turn Woolworths around and to produce results in terms of higher profits and an increasing share price. It was then that he began to build up a personal stake in the company. Simon Marks showed his confidence in the transformation by increasing Marks & Spencer's stake in it in such a way as to reduce the average price of its shareholding. It was at this time – 1956 – that Marks launched his campaign: 'Operation Simplification'. This was an attack, masterminded by Marcus Sieff, on excessive bureaucracy and administrative costs in the business. David Susman moved immediately to launch a similar 'good housekeeping' campaign within Woolworths.

Recognition of the success of his efforts to transform Woolworths came in 1962 when Simon Marks himself appointed David Susman to the board of Marks & Spencer. He was then thirty-seven and was to remain on the board, with one short break, for over thirty years. He was proud to be appointed to the board by his mentor. Simon Marks himself told him that his appointment was 'a toe in the door'. David Susman saw it as a boon that gave him a good reason for regular visits to London and immediate access to new thinking at Baker Street. It also gave Woolworths privileged access to Marks & Spencer's suppliers, and above all it cemented the relationship between the two companies. In making the appointment Marks may have been influenced by internal 'family' politics, but he was also recognising the hard work that David Susman had done over ten years at Woolworths. It was a tribute to the growth of the company in the image of Marks & Spencer, and to the fact that he had done more than anyone else to rescue the investment that Simon Marks had made in 1947.

For the first two years David Susman's work at Woolworths in Cape Town took up all his energy and he had little time to spare for the central African business which still accounted for the greater part of his family's assets. From 1954 onwards he began to devote more attention to central Africa. By 1956 he had joined the boards of almost all the companies, sometimes as an alternate to his father. He played a major part, as will be shown below, in the establishment in 1955 of an enlarged central African stores business – Rhodesian Mercantile Holdings. Many of the ideas behind this new enterprise came from Woolworths and Marks & Spencer. A major objective was to provide centralised merchandising for a varied group of businesses operating in three countries. Many of the systems used in the business were transferred directly from Woolworths and were derived from Marks & Spencer. David Susman provided a personal link between central Africa and two of the most progressive and dynamic retailing businesses in Britain and South Africa.

While David Susman began to take on some of his father's responsibilities, Elie Susman continued to keep a close eye on Woolworths and the central African businesses until his death. In all probability his heart remained with the scene of his earliest adventures: his pocket diaries come alive with his twice-yearly visits to Northern Rhodesia, with their rounds of company meetings, and inspections of sawmills, factories, stores, butcheries, farms, ranches and, above all, cattle. The link between Woolworths and Marks & Spencer, and the family link created by David's marriage to Ann, added a new and exciting dimension to the last years of his life. Elie and Bertha Susman entertained directors of Marks & Spencer, such as Harry Sacher and Wilfred Norris, on working visits to South Africa. They also entertained David's parents-in-law, Neville and Elaine Blond, and Norman and Viola Laski, on their visits to the country.[15]

In turn Elie and Bertha travelled to London where they stayed at a hotel in Mayfair, but spent weekends at Gotwick Manor, near East Grinstead in Sussex, with Elaine and Neville Blond. According to David Susman, weekends at Gotwick were 'challenging to say the least ... Elaine Blond entertained lavishly and the house party was never less than eight or ten guests, each interesting and significant in their fields.' The guests might include senior British or Israeli civil servants, leading Zionists, doctors, historians, writers or musicians. They could also be enlivened by the presence of Neville Blond's son, Anthony, the author and publisher. Elie and Bertha Susman sometimes went with the Blonds to the races at Ascot and Epsom, while Elie sometimes had working lunches with Simon Marks, and other directors of Marks & Spencer, in Baker Street. On their last visit in 1955, they spent five days at Le Touquet, where Elie noted with some satisfaction that he won £80 playing *chemin de fer*, and they travelled widely in England and in Scandinavia. On one occasion they took John Cranko, the choreographer son of a director of OK Bazaars, to dinner at a Mayfair restaurant – Ann's sister, Simone Laski, was a backer of his musical revue, *Cranks*. These were a few moments of relaxation in an exceptionally hardworking life. Elie's origins were similar to those of Simon Marks, who was born in England, the son of a Yiddish-speaking immigrant from Poland, but the trajectory of his life was different. It is surprising that their paths ever crossed, but not surprising that Simon Marks should have been fascinated by the similarities and differences in their entrepreneurial and retailing careers.[16]

Elie Susman paid his last visits to Northern Rhodesia in 1957, travelling north three times. He spent a week in April on the Copperbelt, where he stayed with Maurice and Revée Gersh, attended meetings of Northern Caterers and Northern Bakeries, and visited the new Central African Cold Storage works. He also spent time in and around Lusaka, visiting the new bacon factory and Rietfontein Ranch. His last diary entry on 16 July recorded a visit to Swaziland with his daughter, Bruna, son-in-law, Sidney Zacks, and their daughter, Maxine – they slept at a hotel in Pigg's Peak. He returned to Northern Rhodesia in August and spent two or three weeks there, attending meetings in Livingstone and spending a few days at Lochinvar with Max Barnett and Harry Wulfsohn, who was accompanied by his wife, Trude, and their three daughters. He made what turned out to be his last visit to the country on 17 September, attending the annual general meeting of Zambesi Saw Mills with David, as he had done in the two previous years. In December 1957 he arranged to meet David in Johannesburg and to travel to Salisbury with him for a board meeting of Rhodesian Mercantile Holdings. David flew up from Cape Town on 7 January, intending to meet his father at his office in town and leave with him for Salisbury in the afternoon. Elie Susman's driver, Dickson, met him at the airport and told him that the 'Ou-baas' was at home and wanted him to go there. In David Susman's words:

I found Father in bed, looking frail and exhausted, while Mother and Barney Krikler, our family doctor, conferred anxiously in the sitting room. I sat with Father for all of that day as he slipped in and out of consciousness ... He was aware that his life was reaching its end, and, typically, wanted no fuss about it. When he sat up and sipped at a glass of water, I asked him how he felt. He nodded at me wryly, and whispered, 'Feeling better!' He died shortly afterwards.[17]

It was the end of an extraordinary life that had taken Elie Susman from Riteve on the frontier of the Russian and German empires in Europe to Sesheke and Livingstone on the frontiers of the British, German and Portuguese spheres of influence in Africa, and from there to Cape Town and Johannesburg. In his last years he became a respected elder statesman among Jewish businessmen in South Africa, and was called in to arbitrate in disputes between his peers. It gave him great satisfaction to know that his son, David, who was unanimously elected to the board of Woolworths on 16 January 1956, and who had joined the boards of most of the central African businesses at about the same time, was in a position to carry on his work and to build on the foundations which he had laid.[18]

CHAPTER 13

Susman Brothers & Wulfsohn: Partners and Politics, 1953–74

The Federation of Rhodesia and Nyasaland came into existence on 1 September 1953. In the view of the Colonial Office its establishment represented a compromise between white settler demands for the amalgamation of the two Rhodesias, and the official doctrine of the 'Paramountcy' of so-called 'Native' interests north of the Zambezi. The Federation was seen as a barrier against the spread of African nationalism from the north and Afrikaner nationalism from the south. Under the Federation's complex constitution, control of African interests in Northern Rhodesia and Nyasaland remained with the Colonial Office, but control of 'white' interests in the north was transferred to the federal government in Salisbury. The two northern territories retained their governors and Legislative Councils, while Southern Rhodesia retained its parliament and prime minister. A governor-general and Federal parliament were superimposed on the three territories.

Business interests in the north generally supported the establishment of the Federation, though spokesmen for the emerging African nationalist movement opposed it. Many colonial civil servants also had their doubts about the Federation, though few of them were ready to speak out against it. Elie Susman welcomed the establishment of the Federation because he thought that it would become easier for businesses in the north to attract capital. Other businessmen may have seen the Federation as providing them with a larger arena in which to exercise their talents, though Maurice Gersh was conscious of the possibly adverse effects of a federal tariff on secondary industrialisation in the north.

Elie Susman insisted that companies under his control should not make political contributions, though he did not object to directors doing so as individuals. Harry Wulfsohn, Max Barnett and Abe Galaun all made contributions in July 1953 to Roy Welensky's campaign fund for the election in the north. Maurice Gersh and Maurice Rabb may also have made contributions, as they became members of local committees of the United Federal Party (UFP). These donations were, of course, insignificant by comparison with the contributions that were made by the two Copperbelt mining groups, Rhodesian Selection Trust and Anglo American, through their chairmen Sir Ronald Prain and Harry Oppenheimer, who were, with the British South Africa Company, the main backers of the UFP. The donations did, however, indicate support for the federal idea in general, and for Welensky, an essentially Northern Rhodesian politician, in particular. Simon Zukas, who was one of the most active opponents of federation, recalls that Jewish businessmen were especially pleased to have someone whom they regarded as one of their own in a position of power. Welensky became federal minister of transport and development in 1953, and succeeded Sir Godfrey Huggins (Lord Malvern) as prime minister in 1956.[1]

Federation proved to be the great catalyst for the development of African nationalism in the north, though it took about five years for the movement to gain momentum. It was at first weakened by competition and conflict between the African National Congress (ANC), led by Harry Nkumbula, and the African Mineworkers' Union, led by Lawrence Katilungu. The union opposed the strike called by the ANC in 1953 in protest against federation. It also held aloof from the butchery boycotts, which were organised by the ANC in the early months of 1954: these were the congress's first successful attempts at direct political action. Among their targets, as will be shown in a later chapter, were shops owned by Werners and Lusaka Cold Storage, both members of the Susman Brothers & Wulfsohn Group. The economic depression, which began with the collapse of copper prices in 1956, provided an additional stimulus to the nationalist movement. The ANC split over participation in an election with a limited African franchise in 1958. Kenneth Kaunda, secretary-general of the ANC, emerged as the leader of the new and more radical Zambia African National Congress (ZANC), which was banned in 1959. After his release from detention in January 1960, Kaunda became the leader of the United National Independence Party (UNIP), the successor to ZANC. Nkumbula survived as the leader of the ANC, which was then largely confined to his home base in the Southern Province. Kaunda led UNIP through the break-up of the Federation at the end of 1963 to the independence of Zambia in October 1964. In Southern Rhodesia, the settler government made few concessions to African nationalism. The defeat of the UFP by the Rhodesian Front in December 1962 led, after the break-up of the Federation and Britain's refusal to grant independence before majority rule, to Ian Smith's Unilateral Declaration of Independence (UDI) in November 1965.

While the Federation appeared to many businessmen to be economically rational, it was politically flawed from the start. It lacked the support of the African majority, and the built-in predominance of the white settlers of Southern Rhodesia in the federal parliament ensured that capital expenditure and investment, much of it flowing from the taxation of Northern Rhodesian copper, was concentrated in the south. The classic example of this was the federal government's decision in 1955 to break an earlier promise, and to build the Kariba Dam, with its power station on the south bank of the Zambezi, in preference to the Kafue scheme, which would have been wholly in the north. Uneven industrial development ensured, as Maurice Gersh had feared, that the north became a captive market for the south.

Susman Brothers & Wulfsohn was a unique example of a Northern Rhodesian company that expanded southwards during the short-lived federal period. Its leading members had faith in the federal project, but their move into the south did not do them much good commercially or politically. They did not find Southern Rhodesia a favourable environment for rural trade and were unable to persuade the federal government to defend their vital cattle-trading interests in the north when these came into conflict with powerful vested interests in the south. Furthermore, their involvement in the south made it more difficult for them to defend their commercial interests in the north after Zambia's independence and Southern Rhodesia's UDI.

Conflicts and Animosities

The slogan of the Federation was racial 'partnership', but there was always some doubt as to what this meant. This chapter illustrates the difficulties of two kinds of partnership – in politics and business. The relationship between Elie Susman and Harry Wulfsohn was always tense, and there was frequent tension between Max Barnett, who was running Werners, and Wulfsohn. Overwork, rapid expansion and financial uncertainty caused stress and led to huge arguments between them. The pressure on Harry Wulfsohn was especially great, as he did most to drive the business and initially had all his assets tied up in it. There had already been two major crises. In the first of these Wulfsohn resigned as a working director in September/October 1950. He withdrew his resignation and was re-instated, but Elie Susman insisted that he write a letter to the directors asking for his job back.

There was another major crisis in 1952, the main issue then being whether to accept the terms of Barclays Bank – not the group's usual bankers – for a loan. Maurice Rabb was less assertive than his partners, but tended to get caught in the middle of their arguments. He thought at this time that there was a real danger that the business, though highly profitable, might become insolvent and be placed under judicial management.[2]

There were personal issues mixed up with the financial ones. Harry Wulfsohn wanted his brother, Wulfie, to have a share in the business. He thought that Elie Susman should accommodate him in the same way that he himself had made room for Maurice Rabb. Susman thought that Wulfie 'was quite a decent chap and I rather like him', but he did not think that he had sufficient experience to justify a place in the company alongside Rabb and Barnett. Relations between Wulfsohn and Barnett were also strained: Barnett thought that he should have a larger share in the business. In a hard-hitting letter, which he copied to Rabb, he accused Wulfsohn of being unable to work as part of a team, and of seeking to take all the credit for the group's achievements. Wulfsohn was distressed when Barnett took sides with Elie Susman against him.[3]

The tensions between the partners simmered on for the next two years, reaching a climax in the middle of 1954. Harry Wulfsohn indicated once again that he wished to resign as a working director and move to South Africa. There was some discussion of a division of the assets. Susman was shocked to learn in April 1954 that Wulfsohn and Barnett had not spoken to each other for four months. He commented: 'I know that there is no love lost between the two of them, but I never expected that they had not consulted each other in connection with our business.' He told Rabb that 'the only thing for you, Max Barnett, and Wulfsohn to do is to get together and work in harmony, and carry on as we are'. Wulfsohn did, however, leave for Johannesburg in September. Elie Susman told his son, David, that 'I am not concerned with him any more as I sent him a registered letter on 21st September telling him that as from the 22nd, the date he was leaving for Johannesburg, he will no longer be a working director.'[4]

While living in Johannesburg, Wulfsohn nevertheless spent a good deal of his time on the Copperbelt, and in Salisbury, dealing with the business of the group. To complicate matters further, Max Barnett had a mild heart attack in October 1954, and attempted to resign as managing director of Werners in January 1955. Elie Susman told him bluntly: '... I think you are acting very foolishly and to your own detriment'. He went on, however, to say that he,

Rabb and Wulfsohn 'would be very pleased if you would reconsider your decision'.[5]

It was at this stage that David Susman began to play an active part in the affairs of the group. He had already begun to show the benefits of his training as a diplomat in the service of the new state of Israel, and as a Marks & Spencer executive. He wrote to Max Barnett in a rather more emollient tone than that adopted by his father:

> Northern Rhodesia is on the threshold of great development, and although there may be temporary set-backs in the Butchery business, nevertheless we are too strongly entrenched in the territory to be seriously affected, whichever

10 Harry Wulfsohn, 1950s.

way things go ... I find it very hard to reconcile your decision with the fact that you have put your Heart and Soul into Werners over the past few years, and you must feel a great pride in what you have achieved. To let all this drop suddenly is like sacrificing your own child, and I do hope that you will do as Dad asks you, that is to decide to stay with the Companies.[6]

While these personal conflicts were taking up a great deal of the time and energy of the directors, they were simultaneously engaged in planning for a considerable expansion of the group's activities. Harry Wulfsohn was the prime mover in the expansion of the stores business and Max Barnett in the butchery business. Wulfsohn had the idea of establishing a new holding company in Salisbury. This would take control of the Northern Rhodesian stores business, of Harry Robinson's wholesale business and of African Stores Ltd, a network of rural stores in Southern Rhodesia belonging to a subsidiary of the Chartered Company. Barnett's scheme was for the construction of a large cold store in Kitwe to cater for the flow of chilled beef from the Lobatse abattoir in Bechuanaland. He also wanted to break the butchery cartel by challenging Copperfields Cold Storage in Kitwe and Chingola.

The idea for the enlarged stores business emerged from discussions in Salisbury between Harry Wulfsohn, Harry Robinson and his cousin, Julius Robinson. In the years following his marriage to Harry Susman's daughter, Ella, in 1936, Harry Robinson had built up a wholesaling business, Robinson & Schwartz, later H. Robinson and Company, in Salisbury. This became a substantial business that employed commercial travellers to sell goods to traders in both the Rhodesias and Nyasaland. Robinson was born in New York in 1901 and came to Southern Rhodesia in 1910. He went to school in Bulawayo and Salisbury and was a noted sportsman, representing Southern Rhodesia at rugby and swimming. A prominent member of settler society, Robinson was not a man of great vision, but he was known for his common sense, eye for detail and integrity. David Susman thought that he would be a useful addition to the group as he took 'an impartial and strong view of all our problems'.[7]

His cousin, Julius Robinson, was a more formidable businessman. He was based in South Africa and was a major financier. He was heavily involved in the import/export business and was also chairman of Charter Holdings; it was through this company that he acquired an option to buy a controlling interest in African Stores Ltd. He sought to trade this option for an agreement that his company, Goode Durrant & Murray, who were already shippers to African Stores, would become the shippers for the enlarged company. He was also prepared to provide substantial loan-funding for the new company.[8]

The first attempts to negotiate reconciliation between the partners, and agreement on terms for expansion of the business, took place at Elie Susman's house in Johannesburg early in March 1955, but they ended in failure. It was as a result of intervention by David Susman, with some help from Harry Robinson, that Wulfsohn was persuaded to attend a further meeting with Elie Susman and Maurice Rabb in April. In forwarding the minutes of the meeting to his son, Elie Susman noted that 'we have had several meetings with your pal Wulfsohn and a lot of worry and aggravation'. The end result was, in spite of a little later haggling, satisfactory to all parties. Each of the three managing directors, Harry Wulfsohn, Maurice Rabb and Max Barnett, were to be offered salaries of £6,000 a year. Barnett would have to sign a five-year contract, but would receive a share of the profits of the cold storage company that was to be set up in the Copperbelt. The offer to Harry Wulfsohn was conditional on his moving to Salisbury by 1 October 1955. It was made on the understanding that he would be allowed a few days a month to look after his timber interests in South Africa and Mozambique. It was also agreed that the two companies should pay regular dividends – something that they had not done in the past.[9]

There were also detailed agreements on the expansion of the business. A new company, Susman Brothers & Wulfsohn (Stores) Ltd, would take over the Northern Rhodesian stores business. Susman Brothers & Wulfsohn itself would then exchange its shares in the stores company for eighty per cent of the shares in a new holding company, which would also incorporate H. Robinson and Company and a majority interest in African Stores Ltd. It was further agreed that the new stores company would take over the Susmans' interest in the Ngamiland Trading Company. It was also confirmed that David Susman and Harry Robinson should be elected as directors of Susman Brothers & Wulfsohn, and that Harry Wulfsohn would have the opportunity to appoint two directors at a later date.

A further meeting in Mufulira in May brought Wulfsohn and Barnett together with Rabb. They had been delegated by the earlier meeting to work together to raise funds for the expansion of Werners. Harry Wulfsohn played the major role in this. Elie Susman, who was on holiday in England and Scandinavia, was pleased to hear that peace had broken out.[10] There were further meetings in David Susman's rooms in the Carlton Hotel in Johannesburg in June at which final agreement on most issues was reached. The partners unanimously agreed to vote a bonus of £4,000 to Wulfsohn for his work in raising capital for the expansion of the business. This payment was also compensation to him for the salary that he had lost when he left for Johannesburg in September.[11] David Susman told his father: 'I have always said that appeasement is sometimes necessary before one can get everything that one wants.' He thought that Wulfsohn's donation of half the bonus to the Livingstone Israel United Appeal Fund was a generous gesture.[12]

Rhodesian Mercantile Holdings

The statutory meeting of the new holding company, Rhodesian Mercantile Holdings, which was itself a subsidiary of Susman Brothers & Wulfsohn, was held in Livingstone on 29 July 1955. Elie Susman was in the chair and Wulfsohn, Rabb and J. W. A. Parkhurst were in attendance. The directors of the new company were to be Elie Susman, Harry Wulfsohn, Maurice Rabb, Max Barnett, Harry Robinson and his partner, Nathan Zelter. David Susman had indicated that he did want to be a substantive director, but that he would act as an alternate to his father. He joined the board in his own right in October 1956, Geoffrey Beckett joined the board at the same time and Joe Susman became a director a year or two later. Max Barnett stepped down at an early stage and was replaced by his brother-in-law, Sonny Emdin. The first issue of shares gave £375,000 out of £500,000 to Susman Brothers & Wulfsohn and the balance to Harry Robinson and associates. David Susman estimated the value of the company's assets at about £1,250,000. The Northern Rhodesian interests represented about two-thirds of the whole.[13]

A number of other acquisitions were made at this time. An agreement was finally reached with 'Chobo' Weskob for the takeover of the Ngamiland Trading Company. He was to retain twenty per cent of the business, but the Susman family's two-thirds interest was to be bought out over ten years. At about the same time the Ngamiland Trading Company took over Riley's Hotel, Service Station, and Stores, in Maun, in partnership with Aidan Riley. This followed the death of Harry Riley, Aidan's uncle, who had drowned in the Thamalakane River in April 1955, while attempting to cross the river with a truck on the pontoon during a flood. By 1958 the partnership was dissolved, and Ronnie Kays, son of Young Tom – who lived to be ninety-seven and died in 1990 – and grandson of Old Tom Kays, took over the partnership and the management of the business. Ronnie Kays succeeded Weskob, his uncle by marriage, as the uncrowned king of Maun, and has run Riley's Garage ever since.[14]

There was also to be some expansion of the trading network in the north. The group bought twenty stores from John Thom who had built up a trading network in the Northern and Luapula provinces of Northern Rhodesia over many years. These stores had become the object of a boycott by the African National Congress after their manager in Kasama had insulted the paramount chief of the Bemba. Kenneth Kaunda, then secretary-general of the African National Congress, described the new owners as 'more amenable' than their predecessors. These stores, which became known as Chawama Stores, gave the group a presence in an area where it had not previously worked.[15]

Administrative Centralisation

Rhodesian Mercantile Holdings now controlled about 200 retail stores and wholesale outlets in the Rhodesias and Bechuanaland. About two-thirds of these were in Northern Rhodesia, less than one-third in Southern Rhodesia, and about twenty were in Bechuanaland. Attention was paid from the beginning to the centralisation of administration, purchasing and distribution. Maurice Rabb and Nathan Zelter, Harry Robinson's right-hand man, drew up a memorandum on this subject in September 1955.[16] Although they made the first plans, it is clear that the new operating systems were derived directly from Woolworths, and ultimately from Marks & Spencer. David Susman led a meeting in Livingstone, really a managers' workshop, to plan 'the mechanics of the move to Salisbury' in February 1956. Hymie Wolffe, Woolworths's company secretary, and a director since the previous year, was also there. The minutes of the meeting spelt out the mechanisms for distribution, stock control, importation of merchandise, local purchasing, collection of information on sales etc. The emphasis was on the reduction of stockholding by the collection of accurate information from stores and groups on the sale of 200 basic lines in five departments: textiles, hardware, clothing, provisions and miscellaneous. All stores would have to check their sales using checking lists every two months. Information would be collected at the group level and forwarded to head office. It would be processed there using calculating machines and pegboards. Hymie Wolffe would provide a more detailed report on 'the basis of operating the new system'. The intention of these systems was to minimise stocks and increase the speed of turnover and the return on capital employed. The original target was to turn over stocks twice a year. In 1960 this was increased to two and a half times a year.[17]

The merchandising department was clearly central to the success of the whole business. The key man in the new head office was Nathan Zelter, the merchandising director, who was an unlikely partner for the highly conventional Harry Robinson. Zelter was born in Moldavia, Romania, in 1914 and, after a year studying Law at the University of Bucharest, went to Southern Rhodesia in 1935 to work for his uncle, M. Stein, the owner of a wholesale business. When Robinson and Schwartz took over this business in the following year, Zelter stayed on and became Robinson's adjutant. He combined a flair for merchandise with an interest in radical politics. He joined the Rhodesia Labour Party in 1940 and the Rhodesian Friends of the Soviet Union in the following year. When the Labour Party split into left and right wings, he went with the left wing; he was also associated with Rhodesia's Left Book Club and the country's minuscule Communist Party. He was later a sponsor of Guy and Molly Clutton-Brock's Cold Comfort Farm, a non-racial commune. He became a close friend of the novelist, Doris Lessing, and features in several of her memoirs. Asked at a later date how he reconciled his Marxism with his successful business career, he said that the conflict between 'serving Mammon and preaching his overthrow' had been 'the bane of my life!' He received some consolation from the journalist and historian Basil Davidson, who reminded him that Engels had supported Marx from the profits of his umbrella-silk business. Many of Zelter's colleagues had reservations about his politics, but none could deny his flair for merchandise, and he played a key role in the business until his resignation in 1963. He enjoyed a somewhat prickly relationship with his equally talented deputy, Geoff Kates, who moved from Livingstone to Salisbury in 1956.[18]

There was some overlap in functions between the merchandising department of Rhodesian Mercantile Holdings and H. Robinson and Company, though they were separate entities and had separate warehouses. Harry Robinson himself presided over the latter company and was assisted by Ralph Herzstein, a German Jewish refugee, as manager. Elton Joffe, who had married Harry Robinson's daughter, Esmée, succeeded him as manager of H. Robinson and Company in 1962. According to Denton Pitt and Colin Arnott, two men who began working with the company in 1956 and remained with it until it closed forty years later, Herzstein was a competent but excitable man. The company's commercial travellers visited Northern Rhodesia, Bechuanaland and Nyasaland, and its main competitor was Kaufman Sons and Company, which was based in Bulawayo. In 1960 the two groups set up a jointly owned company, Summit Trading Ltd, which acted as a buying cartel and obtained large discounts from manufacturers and suppliers through bulk orders.[19]

Major R. M. 'Bobby' Campbell emerged as the dominant force in the accounts department. He had served in the Indian Army, but was invalided out after contracting polio, which left him with some disability and he used crutches. He had trained as an accountant with Peat, Marwick, and came to Rhodesian Mercantile Holdings through African Stores Ltd – a company that was known for its military personnel. He was appointed chief accountant of the whole group in March 1958 and became company secretary in 1960, whereupon he immediately undertook a major reorganisation of the accounting system. He aimed 'to simplify the accounting procedures so as to provide management with the detailed information it requires for control purposes in the quickest way'. He was later credited with an ingenious simplification of accounting at the level of the individual stores. Goods were issued to the stores at sale price and the store managers – capitaos – had only to balance cash and stock. He was a disciplinarian and his military style did not endear him to all members of his staff, but there is no doubt that his reforms had, in the long run, a major impact on the profitability of the company. The company's auditors were Messrs Gelfand and Levinkind. Benny Gelfand was an accountant who had worked with Northern Caterers on the Copperbelt both before and after the Second World War. He attended most meetings of the board of directors by invitation and had a considerable influence on the affairs of the company. His deputy, Julius Levinkind, also attended some meetings.[20]

Elie Susman's Last Intervention

It was unfortunate that the establishment of the new holding company coincided with the recession that hit the Federation in 1956 and lasted for several years. The introduction of new systems and the creation of a single organisation out of a number of companies, operating in three countries with different administrative and political cultures, was never going to be easy. In what turned out to be the last year of his life, Elie Susman, the chairman of the new company, became convinced that there must be a stop to expansion and a period of consolidation. In the first full year of the new company's existence, 1956–7, it had a turnover of more than £2,000,000. He thought that it was reasonable to expect a net profit after tax of seven and a half per cent, or £150,000.[21] He was shocked when the preliminary accounts revealed a loss for the year of £9,000. In his last major intervention in the affairs of the business, he wrote a circular letter to the directors of Rhodesian Mercantile Holdings in May 1957. He had just returned from a visit to the Copperbelt where he had been told of plans for the opening of yet more new stores. In his letter he recapitulated his response to these proposals.

> In reply to these proposals I set out my views, viz. that the turnover in the native stores on the Copperbelt during the last 12 months had decreased from [by] 25 to 30%, and that times were not as good as they had been in the last few years. I advocated that the time had come for the consolidation of the Company's present interests, and that no consideration should be given to schemes for further expansion until the present interests of the Company had been consolidated and the Company placed on a sound basis, both from the point of view of finance and of organisation. In this view I am supported by the recent statements of both Sir Ernest Oppenheimer and Sir Simon Marks, who advise consolidation of businesses and curtailment of expansion in view of present business conditions.
>
> You are aware that the trading results of the Group for 1956 year were shocking. In addition, the Group has undertaken large commitments and the results so far achieved do not warrant the large investment of capital made in the Group by its shareholders. In view of our large liabilities our financial position is not good, and it is my view that by concentrating on the 200 odd stores presently conducted by the Group, it should be possible to improve our organisation to a point where a reasonable dividend on the capital involved could be achieved. Perhaps the fact that the Group's stores are scattered over an area of 2,000 miles has something to do with the deficiencies in organisation, and I do not think that this will be improved by the acquisition of new stores.
>
> After careful consideration, therefore, I have come to the conclusion that, for the benefit of all shareholders in the Group, the Group must adhere to a policy of consolidation of present interests and must restrict its expansion at least until such time as an annual dividend of 10% can be paid by the Company. When this state of affairs has been achieved, then will be the time to examine the possibility of further expansion and not before.[22]

He was probably right to suggest that a period of consolidation was necessary. The expansion of the business into Southern Rhodesia had proved to be especially problematic. African Stores Ltd was bought at a discount, but was difficult to turn around. It had never been profitable and its senior directors were military men whose business acumen was not outstanding. Maurice Rabb maintained that the chairman of the Chartered Company, Sir Ellis Robins (later Lord Robins), fell asleep during the meeting at which the purchase of the company was negotiated. The directors of Rhodesian Mercantile Holdings, with the exception of Harry Robinson and Nathan Zelter,

11 Elie Susman, portrait by Neville Lewis, presented to him by Woolworths to celebrate his seventieth birthday, 1950.

lacked experience of working in Southern Rhodesia, and found it an alien environment.[23]

In July 1959, after four years as a subsidiary of Rhodesian Mercantile Holdings, the managing directors of African Stores Ltd, Colonel John Hodges and Joe Leon, wrote a pessimistic report in which they recommended the sale of the stores and the liquidation of the company. They provided a long list of reasons why conditions in Southern Rhodesia did not lend themselves to 'the successful operation of multiple stores of this type'. They recommended the immediate disposal of the most saleable groups of stores, Mrewa, Pounsley (near Rusape), QueQue (Kwekwe) and Wankie (Hwange). Rhodesian Mercantile Holdings should take the remaining groups, Bindura, Gutu and Mtoko, under direct management until they could be sold. By the middle of 1961, only the group of stores around Gutu, which was about seventy miles from Fort Victoria (Masvingo), remained. David Susman had made it clear that he thought the sale of these assets was 'an admission of defeat by our Board'. He was not impressed by the managing directors' report, but commented that 'as I cannot do the job myself, I suppose the best thing would be to realise as good a price as possible'. According to Maurice Rabb, the shares in the company were bought for three shillings each, and the sale of the assets produced a capital gain of four shillings a share. This was some consolation for the failure to build the business in Southern Rhodesia.[24]

The expansion of the business into Copperbelt towns, such as Mufulira and Kitwe, also proved unsuccessful, as the company did not have much experience of retailing in urban areas and found it difficult to satisfy the sophisticated demands of urban customers. Stores in the predominantly rural areas of Solwezi, Kansanshi and Mwinilunga also proved to be unprofitable and were eventually sold. The store at Kipushi, close to the border with the Congo, and not far from Elisabethville (Lubumbashi), did very good business for a while – probably until the outbreak of civil war in the Congo soon after its independence in 1960. The stores in the Luapula Province, where there was a buoyant local economy based on the trade in fish, were eventually a success, but the stores in the Northern Province presented problems. Outlying stores at Chinsali and Isoka were, after some hesitation, sold to Asian traders, with whom there was increasingly intense competition. Stores at Abercorn (Mbala) and Mpulungu were also sold, but the stores in the Luwingu, Kasama and Nsumbu districts were retained.[25]

The core of the business remained in its historical heartland: Barotseland, the North-Western and Southern provinces of Northern Rhodesia, and in Ngamiland. Rhodesian Mercantile Holdings paid one dividend of ten per cent in 1958, but it paid no dividend in 1959, and dividends of only from four to six per cent between 1960 and 1963. The disposal of African Stores Ltd did at least allow it to reduce its debt. David Susman was convinced that the discipline of the checking list remained the key to success.[26] He told Maurice Rabb in April 1958 that '… we must place all priority on the provision of merchandise and sales records for individual lines. I do not believe that R.M.H. will ever prosper as a progressive Chain Store until such records are regularly available, and I believe that our control of buying leaves much to be desired because of this.'[27]

African Nationalism

It was not until the early 1960s that, with the end of the recession, the company began to achieve a measure of stability and regular profitability. It was at this stage that the Federation, which had been a raison d'être for the establishment of Rhodesian Mercantile Holdings, began to fall apart. From the time of the Federal Review Commission – the Monckton Commission – of 1960 it became unlikely that the Federation would survive. The pressure for the break-up came primarily from Nyasaland, with which Susman Brothers & Wulfsohn had little or no involvement, and secondarily from Northern Rhodesia. Pressure from within Northern Rhodesia began to build up from 1960 onwards with Kaunda and UNIP in the vanguard, and Nkumbula and the ANC adopting a more conservative approach. Susman Brothers & Wulfsohn had the majority of its stores in Barotseland, which turned out, despite its reputation for conservatism, to be a power-base for UNIP; the Southern Province, which was the stronghold of the ANC; and North-Western Province, which was split between the two.

The support of the directors of Susman Brothers & Wulfsohn for the Federation, and the involvement of some of them with the UFP, made it difficult for them to come to terms with the rise of African nationalism. Most of the directors were Jews, with personal experience of anti-Semitism. None of them would have subscribed to a racist ideology, but most of them tended towards paternalism. Nathan Zelter and David Susman were the only directors who showed much sympathy, from rather different perspectives, with African nationalism. Maurice Rabb was on the liberal wing of the UFP, but in July 1962 he joined Harry Wulfsohn in opposing David Susman's suggestion that the company should begin to recruit well-educated Africans for training as senior managers. While Zelter professed to be a Marxist, Susman was a supporter of Helen Suzman's Progressive Party in South Africa. He had associations with people who were much further to the left than he was, and was familiar with political developments in South Africa. His close friend, Jimmy Kantor, was one of the accused in the Rivonia Trial in 1963–4, together with Nelson Mandela, Walter Sisulu, Govan Mbeki and others. Kantor was not deeply involved politically, but suffered for his association with his brother-in-law, Harold Wolpe, another of the accused, who escaped, with Arthur Goldreich, from Pretoria Prison, and the trial. David Susman was primarily interested in the defence of Kantor, who was eventually acquitted, but he helped to raise money for the defence of all the accused in the trial. He recalls that he approached Harry Oppenheimer, who gave him a cheque for £5,000, and said: 'You can do what you like with it.'[28]

Seven years earlier, David had written to Maurice Rabb in connection with reports of a butchery boycott in Lusaka: '... I do hope it is not one of ours. Our good relationship with the African in Northern and Southern Rhodesia will always be the pivot of our business, and I think we should fall over backwards to maintain it.'[29] The majority of his fellow directors took a more conservative position. Harry Wulfsohn was, with his friend Geoff Beckett, close to Welensky. In July 1961 the Susman Brothers & Wulfsohn group of companies made a combined contribution of £1,000 to the UFP in response to a personal appeal from Welensky at a time of political crisis for the Federation. They made a smaller donation in November 1963 to the Welensky Fund – a retirement fund for the then outgoing prime minister. Harry Wulfsohn's brother, Wulfie, recalls that he embarrassed his brother in the company of people like Welensky and Beckett by his comparative radicalism. At one point, probably in 1962, Kenneth Kaunda asked Wulfie to stand for parliament on the UNIP ticket. Wulfie had by this time become a partner, with the help of his brother, in David Shapiro's Lusaka-based milling company. He declined Kaunda's invitation, saying that he was a miller and not a politician. The Wulfsohns' sister, Hessie Lowenthal, was also an early white member of UNIP in Ndola.[30]

Maurice Rabb and the Barotse National Party

Only one of the partners in Susman Brothers & Wulfsohn was actively involved in national politics. Maurice Rabb had attempted to resign as a director of the company in the latter months of 1953, saying that he wished to enter Northern Rhodesian politics and stand for the Legislative Council. He had hopes of ministerial office. He was already participating in local government and served as mayor of Livingstone in 1951–2, and again in 1956–7, becoming an alderman in 1959. His attempt to resign was summarily rejected by his father-in-law, Elie Susman, who enlisted the support of Max Barnett. Rabb did enter national politics in 1959, after his father-in-law's death. He was then elected unopposed as member of the Legislative Council for Livingstone and served for nearly four years. He took part in the constitutional talks at Lancaster House in 1960, and was then tipped as the future minister of finance – in the event that those talks had resulted in Responsible Government for Northern Rhodesia. He and his wife Peggy were very active in the public life of Livingstone, the territory and of the Federation: they both filled many voluntary positions. Peggy served for a decade on both the national and federal Education Advisory Boards and was federal president of the Women's Institutes. They also made charitable donations for the natural history gallery of the Rhodes–Livingstone Museum and for the hall at Livingstone's Hillcrest High School, which bears their name.[31]

The most controversial involvement of Susman Brothers & Wulfsohn in the pre-independence politics of Northern Rhodesia/Zambia came through Rabb's participation in the general election that was held on 31 October 1962. The story of this election demonstrates the difficulty that both he and the company had in coming to terms with African nationalism, and the continuing importance of their close relationship with the Litunga and the Lozi royal establishment. Although this cannot be documented continuously, it had lasted for most of sixty years. The elections were run according to the 'slide-rule' constitution, which was also known as the Macleod constitution, taking its name from the colonial secretary of the day, Iain Macleod. The extraordinary complexity of its provisions prompted Lord Salisbury to describe Macleod in a famous phrase as 'too clever by half'. There was a restricted franchise with an upper roll, which was eighty per cent white, and a lower roll, which was almost exclusively black, and there were also seven 'national' constituencies. Each of the latter constituencies was to elect two members, one black and one white. Candidates could only be elected if they scored a proportion of votes on both rolls. It was also necessary for white candidates to get at least ten per cent of the black votes, and for black candidates to get at least ten per cent of the white votes. There were in effect three separate elections, the predominantly white upper-roll election, the overwhelmingly black lower-roll election, and the contest for the national constituencies – the only seats for which candidates were compelled to seek the support of members of both races.[32]

Rabb agreed with his UFP colleague, Rodney Malcolmson, the Luanshya dentist, that they should 'have a go' at the national constituencies. Their participation would 'go a long way to prove that our partnership policy is sincere and that some of our leading party names are keen to represent both African and European'. He decided that he would not contest his own upper-roll seat in Livingstone, which he could easily have won, but opted instead to stand for the Zambezi national constituency, which covered Barotseland, Livingstone and part of the Southern Province. The problem that the UFP faced was how to ensure that its candidates got the minimum ten per cent of black votes necessary to ensure election. It solved this problem in several national constituencies by an unacknowledged electoral pact with the ANC. This would have been the best way of ensuring Rabb's election in the Zambezi constituency. There were, in the final analysis, twice as many registered voters in the parts of this huge constituency that fell within the ANC-dominated Southern Province as there were in Barotseland itself – although there were twice as many people in Barotseland as there were in the relevant bits of the Southern Province. The UFP preferred, however, to make an electoral pact for this constituency with a new party, the Barotse National Party (BNP), which was formed in June 1962. This seemed to make sense at the time, but proved to be a serious mistake. The UFP's electoral strategists misunderstood the ethnic composition of the constituency, underestimated the support for UNIP in Barotseland, and overestimated the political influence of the Litunga, and the strength of Lozi traditionalism.[33]

The pre-independence politics of Barotseland are mysterious and complex. The Litunga, Sir Mwanawina III – he had been made a Knight of the British Empire in 1959 – was both conservative and unpopular. His support for the Federation had alienated most of his subjects, and many influential members of the royal family – including the children of his two predecessors, Yeta III and Imwiko – had their own grievances against him. His opponents accused him at one time or another of witchcraft and murder. Mwanawina was deeply alarmed by the rise of radical nationalism, and campaigned from 1960 onwards for the secession of Barotseland from Northern Rhodesia and its recognition as a High Commission Territory along the lines of Bechuanaland. He and his Ngambela had visited London in April 1961 to press this demand, which was rejected by Iain Macleod. Macleod's cabinet colleague, Duncan Sandys, the minister for Commonwealth relations, had rather different ideas, and made a furtive visit to Lealui in February 1962. He appeared at the time to give encouragement to the suggestion that Barotseland might be allowed to secede from Northern Rhodesia, and remain in the Federation as a separate state. Godwin Mbikusita Lewanika, the founding president of the ANC, who had become a UFP member of the federal parliament and a parliamentary secretary to Welensky, accompanied Sandys to Lealui. He was close to the Litunga and a promoter of the plan for secession within the Federation.[34]

While campaigning for secession, the Litunga was determined to exclude nationalist politicians from Barotseland. The attempt to deport Nalumino Mundia, a leader of UNIP and a Lozi, from Barotseland in November 1961 had resulted in a riot at Lealui. Although Mwanawina was sympathetic to the UFP, he had not allowed it to campaign openly in Barotseland, which he tried to preserve as a party-free zone. It was not until the middle of May 1962 that he yielded to pressure from the administration and agreed to allow political parties to organise and the registration of voters to begin.[35] UNIP had been organising in Barotseland more or less clandestinely for some time. Its popularity there had been increased by the banishment of ZANC/UNIP leaders, such as Simon Kapwepwe and Justin Chimba, to Mongu in 1959. Its national leaders included a number of people who were very well educated, and who had close ties to the Lozi royal establishment. They included Arthur and Sikota Wina, the sons of Kalonga Wina, who had served as Ngambela to Yeta III and Imwiko. The Wina brothers were also grandsons of King Lewanika.

It is clear that UNIP's leaders identified Susman Brothers & Wulfsohn with the UFP and the Federation. They may also have associated the company with the Litunga and his secessionist views. The party's organising secretary in Mongu wrote to Lionel Dix, the divisional manager for Barotseland, in April or early May 1962, and accused the company 'of not allowing [its] staff to be concerned in any way with politics and of not helping the country in any way'. It was reported that 'a suitable reply to this letter was prepared and agreed to by the board'.[36] The full contents of these letters are unknown, but a journalist reported at the time that UNIP officials in Barotseland had given commercial firms 'their marching orders'. They had threatened to cancel their trading concessions and give them to Asians, who were 'friends of the people'.[37] UNIP had supporters and informants everywhere, and its officials probably knew that Welensky had, with Rabb's consent, used Lionel Dix as a channel of secret communications with the Litunga at the time of Duncan Sandys's visit. They must also have been aware that the organising secretary of the UFP in Barotseland was Henry Makiti Kutoma, who gave his address as 'c/o Lionel Dix, Susman Brothers & Wulfsohn, Box 1, Mongu'.[38]

Rabb must have originally intended to campaign in Barotseland under the UFP banner and to rely on Kutoma and others to bring in the votes. He was not responsible for the establishment of the Barotse National Party, though he became involved with it soon after its inception, and was closely identified with it. Godwin Lewanika denied that it was his idea, and gave the credit to Griffiths Mukande, who was Induna Mutwaleti at Lealui, and on the UFP's panel of election candidates. Lewanika saw the party as a response to the pressure from the British government to open Barotseland for political campaigning. Moves for the formation of a 'Litunga's party' began in May, and seem to have been well under way when the Litunga and council received deputations from all the competing parties on 4 June 1962. The UFP's representatives, Henry Kutoma and Prince Ngombala Lubita, told the

Litunga and council that they would support the UFP 'until Barotseland could afford to found her own national party'. A few days later they reported to the UFP in Lusaka that a Barotse Sicaba Party (*sicaba* means nation) had been formed and had been represented at the Lealui meeting. Its leader was Francis Suu, a trader who had been a councillor, and was later to be Ngambela. Mukande, and other UFP members, appear to have combined with Suu early in June 1962 to form the Barotse National Party, which was also widely known as the Sicaba Party.[39]

In spite of his denials, Godwin Lewanika was the link between the Litunga, Welensky and the UFP in Salisbury. The first indication of the UFP's involvement comes in a secret memorandum from Alf Adams, its general secretary, to Welensky, headed 'Operation Elephant', on 4 June 1962. This describes urgent plans to despatch Lewanika to Barotseland with three Land Rovers for the BNP. Ten thousand party cards and a similar number of 'elephant's head' lapel badges had been ordered. Adams was keen to involve Maurice Rabb and was going to Livingstone to see him. In an additional 'Note for Sir Roy only', he wrote: 'I would like to put Rabb fairly fully into picture as his organisation [Susman Brothers & Wulfsohn] could act as a watchdog for us apart from helping very directly with the BNP. Also if Maurice does become our National seat candidate for that area he should be in the picture right from the start.'[40] In his reply to this memorandum Welensky wrote:

> I am very anxious that we should get this one right if it's possible for us to do so. I believe it could have quite an important effect on the election results. The registration returns in regard to Barotseland are very poor indeed and will not justify much representation. I am certain it can be bettered. I take it you have brought Rab [*sic*] into the picture. I certainly have no objections.[41]

Welensky immediately arranged with Harry Grenfell and Sir Ellis Robins, directors of the BSA Company, for a subvention of £5,000 to cover the cost of the Land Rovers and the expenses of the new party. Adams reported on 18 June that the party had been registered, and that the Land Rovers were in use. Two organisers, Griffiths Mukande, who became president, and Mufana Lipalile, who became general secretary/treasurer, had been appointed. The Litunga agreed 'that Mr Rabb should stand for the National seat which includes Livingstone, as the Barotse in this area could be effective on Mr Rabb's behalf'. The Litunga had also discussed with Rabb the possibility of extending the period for registration from the end of June until the end of July. The Litunga and Rabb badly needed extra time for registration because very few of the BNP's potential supporters had registered for an election, which they had earlier been instructed to boycott. UNIP was well supplied with Land Rovers, and was far ahead of the BNP in the registration stakes, but it too sought an extension, which was not granted. Mukande and Lipalile had also written to Welensky to announce the party's registration. They assured Welensky that they would not deviate from the policy of the UFP, 'but for various reasons, perhaps well known to you, we want to fight the election under a different name'. They were determined 'that Barotseland becomes a separate state from Northern Rhodesia, and we hope you shall give us your support'.[42]

It was not until early in October that Rabb announced the election pact with the BNP at an apparently rowdy meeting in the Victoria Hall, Livingstone. He also introduced his running mate, Gore-Browne Mopani Chalinga, a compound manager for Zambesi Saw Mills, whom he had personally selected for this role. The other speakers were Godwin Lewanika and James Macmillan, Rabb's successor as the UFP candidate for the upper-roll seat in Livingstone. In an optimistic speech, Rabb told the meeting:

> Through my years in Northern Rhodesia and my connections with a very old family in Northern Rhodesia, I have had the opportunity of meeting Africans all over the Southern Province. I have come in contact with them through my day-to-day business and I feel if there is any candidate in this country who has a chance to get the co-operation of both races it is I.[43]

Rabb campaigned in Barotseland, but the BNP failed to make any political impact.

Its failure to register its voters was a major handicap. In the end there were only about 3,000 voters registered in Barotseland, and the great majority of them were UNIP supporters. A major problem was the failure of the Litunga to mobilise his own supporters – either to register or to vote. He had apparently wished to endorse the party, but had been told by the resident commissioner that he must not do so. He told Rabb that 'the Northern Rhodesian Government had prohibited him from taking any part in the elections despite the fact that according to Barotse Custom the people were waiting for him to do so'. Rabb told Welensky that in his canvassing in Barotseland he had 'come up against the same problem that people told me they were waiting for a directive from the Litunga'.[44]

Another problem was, of course, the incompetence and unreliability of the party's officials, and what Godwin Lewanika described as the superior 'underground' organisation of UNIP. According to an academic observer, the UFP failed to recognise that the BNP was 'a party in name only', which was unable to mount a 'recognisable election campaign'. There is not much evidence of a BNP campaign, though Lewanika referred to a meeting attended by 300 councillors and headmen at Lealui in August. A well-informed writer in the *Central African Examiner* observed that the BNP was 'widely regarded as a joke'. After the election, Lewanika said that it had been a mistake for Rabb to run in open partnership with the BNP, but UNIP had in any case no difficulty in identifying the BNP as a front for the UFP. Within weeks of the new party's registration, Arthur Wina was able to identify precisely the source of its Land Rovers and its funds, and to specify the sums of money involved. UNIP soon knew that the Land Rovers were registered in the name of Godwin Lewanika, and that the officials received their salaries from the UFP. In a letter to the *Northern News*, Sikota Wina claimed that Kenneth Kaunda had addressed a crowd of 6,000 people at a rally in Mongu in July. He described the UFP's belief that it could win in Barotseland as 'a self-delusion'.[45]

Sikota Wina was proved right, and Rabb's optimism was sadly misplaced. In the first round of the elections at the end of October, Rabb got over ninety per cent of the white votes, but less than two per cent of the black votes. Chalinga got nearly eighty per cent of the white votes, but just over two per cent of the black votes. The election for the constituency was aborted, as were the elections in all the national constituencies, except for the three where the UFP had an electoral pact with the ANC. In the two Barotseland lower-roll constituencies UNIP's candidates, Arthur Wina and Mubiana Nalilungwe, swept the board. The BNP's candidates Francis Suu and Griffiths Mukande scored sixty-five votes and forty-two votes respectively, and lost their deposits.[46]

Before the end of November, Francis Suu and two other founding members resigned from the party. They told the Litunga in a letter that they had discovered that: 'Some of the big people and masses of the people [had] joined UNIP one by one. Eventually found that wherever we went in Barotseland, people had become all UNIP members. Even in the Chiefs' villages, there were none on the side of freeing Barotseland from Northern Rhodesia.' They had wanted to free Barotseland from UNIP and the Federation, but had been 'shocked to find that some of us were trying to make our party a part of the Federal Party. It was not until the last moment when we realized this, for Mr Rabb of the Federal Party came and said all the material we used belonged to the Federal Party.'[47] It is possible that Suu really was unaware of the financial links between the BNP and the UFP.

By this time the UFP's election strategists realised that the pact with the BNP had been a mistake. They thought that the only prospect of ensuring

Rabb's election in the second round on 10 December was to form a new pact with the ANC, and to persuade Chalinga and the ANC's white candidate, W. J. Curtis, to withdraw.[48] Neither candidate withdrew, but Rabb came to an understanding with the ANC's black candidate, Job Michello, and ANC–UFP leaflets were distributed in the constituency. As a result of this deal, the white vote was divided between Chalinga and Michello, and the latter received a sufficient number of votes to ensure his election. Rabb was, however, still unable to get many more than two per cent of the black votes – about 300 votes – and the white seat remained unfilled.[49]

Rabb may have had ANC voters in mind when, at a poorly attended election meeting in Livingstone early in November, he said: 'I have never condemned African political parties outright. All I have said is that their record up to date is one that causes suspicion in the minds of the European. But if these parties can show over time their policy is a genuine one, then they will undoubtedly get support.'[50] He went on to argue that Northern Rhodesia should receive its fair share of federal revenues, and that there should be an increase in the purchasing power of local consumers in order to provide a market for local industries. He thought that universal suffrage was a desirable goal, but 'it was premature to bring this into effect now'. He resigned from the UFP soon after the second round of the elections. In his resignation letter he said that the party could no longer achieve anything for Northern Rhodesia, and that there was a need for a new party that would attract moderate elements from both population groups. He also expressed shock at the results of the elections in Southern Rhodesia, which had brought the Rhodesian Front to power.[51]

Rabb's failure to secure election must have been a great disappointment to him. A belief in 'partnership' had motivated to him to abandon his 'white' seat in Livingstone and to run for a national seat. He was not responsible for the formation of the BNP, or for the electoral pact with it, but he probably expected that a Lozi 'traditionalist' party could deliver the necessary ten per cent of the electorate. It is possible that open endorsement by the Litunga, and a more aggressive registration campaign, could have achieved this result in 1962, though it is, perhaps, unlikely. In the pre-independence elections of January 1964, which were held under a universal franchise, UNIP candidates, such as Arthur Wina, obtained ninety-seven per cent of the vote. By that time the BNP had dissolved itself, and its few remaining members had joined the ANC.[52]

Rabb was clearly close to the Litunga, and aware of the Susman family's history of friendship and co-operation with him and his predecessors.

However, both he and the UFP seem to have been unaware of Mwanawina's isolation within the traditional elite, and his lack of a popular power base. It is also open to question whether they were aware of the political danger of appearing to support a secessionist programme – at a time when the most prominent example of secession was Tshombe's regime in Katanga. In the run-up to independence in October 1964, Mwanawina continued to fight for secession and, failing that, for the recognition of the special status and privileges of the protectorate within independent Zambia. He appeared to have achieved this recognition when he signed the Barotseland Agreement with Kenneth Kaunda, then prime minister of the pre-independence government, in May 1964. This agreement had the backing of the British government and was intended to be perpetual. In the end it lasted for only five years, and turned out to be worth little more than the paper on which it was printed.[53]

There is no evidence that Susman Brothers & Wulfsohn gave funds, or other support, to Rabb's campaign or to the Barotse National Party. David Susman is sure that they did not, and points out that the company also resisted pressure from Joe Susman, a friend of Harry Nkumbula, to contribute funds to the ANC at this time. Rabb was, however, able to make several business-related announcements that were intended to help his campaign. He announced in October 1962 that Susman Brothers & Wulfsohn was setting up a Barotseland Trust Fund to commemorate the sixtieth anniversary of the arrival of the Susman brothers in Northern Rhodesia. The fund would provide scholarships of £100 per annum, tenable for three years, for university degrees in Agriculture. It was true, as he pointed out, that this proposal had been in the pipeline for over a year, but the announcement clearly had a political purpose. He was also able to tell the final meeting of the election campaign, which was held in the Victoria Hall, Livingstone, on 26 October, that Zambesi Saw Mills was considering a plan to extend its railway from Kataba to Senanga and Mongu. Welensky himself addressed this meeting, and said that he would give sympathetic consideration to this proposal. The federal minister of works, Rex L'Ange, discussed the matter in Salisbury a few days later with Sir Frederick Crawford, the BSA Company's resident director in Northern Rhodesia, and Harry Wulfsohn. The proposal was clearly a response to UNIP's promise that it would build a railway from Lusaka to Mongu.[54]

Rabb's participation in this election confirmed UNIP in its view that Susman Brothers & Wulfsohn was synonymous with the UFP, committed to federation, and opposed to African nationalism. The company was also seen, not entirely correctly, as a sponsor of the BNP, which Benson Kamitondo, a former employee and Lealui Induna, describes as 'Rabb's party'. He says that he, and many other employees, supported it. The company, on the other hand, may have been genuinely alarmed by UNIP's reported threats to its trading concessions in Barotseland, which was the core of its business. Rabb was eventually able to establish a good relationship with Arthur Wina, who now joined the government, but the 1962 election may have left a legacy of misunderstanding with lasting repercussions. Susman Brothers & Wulfsohn came under continuing pressure in 1963 to donate funds to UNIP, to advertise in UNIP papers, and, in one case, to rent a disused house in Mankoya to UNIP. These requests were all turned down, but by the end of the year the board yielded to pressure. It told Steve Nell, group manager at Fort Rosebery, that he could use his discretion to make small donations to political parties if the alternative was the threat of a boycott. It also gave way to popular demand, and commercial necessity, when it decided in November 1963 to stock UNIP *chitenges* and other clothing in its stores.[55]

Southern Rhodesia's UDI

By the early months of 1963 it was clear that the Federation was coming to an end, which it did on the last day of the year, and that Northern Rhodesia and Nyasaland were moving rapidly towards independence under African nationalist governments – Northern Rhodesia was to become independent as Zambia in October 1964. The future of Southern Rhodesia was less clear. In April 1963 the directors of Rhodesian Mercantile Holdings decided that it was necessary to make contingency plans in the light of these changes. Nathan Zelter and David Susman both argued that the head office should return to Livingstone. This was logical as the bulk of the business was in Northern Rhodesia, which was now scheduled to become independent as Zambia. Geoff Kates agreed with them and was prepared to go north at that time. Nathan Zelter, who had already taken an interest in a clothing factory in Lusaka – much to the annoyance of Harry Robinson – resigned over this issue and moved to Northern Rhodesia in July 1963. Both Harry Robinson and Harry Wulfsohn, who were comfortably settled in Salisbury, were totally opposed to a move. David Susman decided that they would not move and that it was not worth pushing the matter. Harry Wulfsohn resented his position on this issue and this was a factor in the cooling of relations between the two men. There was renewed discussion from this time onwards of the break-up of the business – a topic that will be considered in a later chapter.[56]

Although the board of the company was not ready in April 1963 to move the headquarters back to Livingstone, it did decide that it was necessary for the Northern Rhodesian business to be held through a holding company that was based in that country. They decided to sell the shares in Susman Brothers & Wulfsohn (Stores) Ltd to a new company, Stores Holdings Ltd, which would be set up in Northern Rhodesia. The shareholders in Rhodesian Mercantile Holdings would receive shares in the new company in proportion to their holdings in the parent company. At the same time a new wholesale company, Harry Robinson (Northern) Ltd was set up as a subsidiary of Stores Holdings Ltd. These were steps in the right direction, but they did not go far enough.

Under the new arrangements Maurice Rabb continued as the resident director in Livingstone. Harry Robinson and Harry Wulfsohn remained the effective managing directors of the business and stayed in Salisbury. A Stores Operations Executive was set up in Salisbury and two of its key members, Lionel Dix and Elton Joffe, were soon transferred to Livingstone. Dix moved south from Mongu to Salisbury at the end of 1963 and went north again to Livingstone at the beginning of 1965. Joffe moved north a little later. Maurice Rabb does not seem to have been as insistent on the need for a move in 1963 as Nathan Zelter and David Susman were, but Southern Rhodesia's UDI on 11 November 1965 certainly made him change his mind – if he had not already done so. Twelve days later, he 'raised the question of having a blue print of a plan of action should it become necessary to make the Zambian Organization completely independent of Rhodesian Mercantile Holdings. It was possible that political events may dictate such action and without a plan the Zambian organization could be left stranded without any records or personnel to carry out the work.' The first sign of problems came on 6 December 1965 when the overdraft of Susman Brothers & Wulfsohn (Stores) Ltd was frozen on the grounds that it was a foreign company. After intervention by Maurice Rabb it was unfrozen four days later.[57]

In spite of such warning signs, no action appears to have been taken in the following year to cut the company's links with the south. Although there was initially a feeling that UDI could not last – the British prime minister, Harold Wilson, spoke of 'weeks not months' – it is surprising that the directors allowed the matter to drift for so long. Geoff Kates recalls that he was concerned at the time that the company might be taken over without compensation because of its continued connections with Rhodesia. In October 1966 Rabb wrote to both Wulfsohn and Robinson insisting on the need to move the headquarters of the company to Livingstone:

You will recollect that I have brought up on previous occasions the question of administering our stores operations from Salisbury. I am convinced in spite of any patched up settlement which Britain makes with Rhodesia it will not improve relations between Zambia and Rhodesia, in fact these are more likely to deteriorate until Rhodesia attains a Government by majority of the people.

The statement by the President in regard to racial prejudices and the statement by the Minister of Labour in regard to Zambianisation cannot be ignored. To do so means burying our heads in the sand ... It is not a question of compromise amongst our directors it is a question of complying with Government policy in order to remain in business.

The time has come, if it has not already passed, when we must make a firm decision whether or not we wish to remain in business in Zambia. If the answer is yes then our policies must be shaped accordingly.[58]

Although no one anticipated that UDI would last for fifteen years, it is still amazing that Rabb's fellow directors were so reluctant to act. Harry Wulfsohn made it clear four months later that he was unwilling to contemplate the movement of the head office to Livingstone. He thought that Lionel Dix and Elton Joffe should be reinforced, but he was only prepared to consider sending an 'understudy' to Geoff Kates and setting up a 'shadow' accounting office in Livingstone. It was only in the latter half of 1967 that Geoff Kates and Major Campbell moved north, taking their merchandising and accounting skills with them.[59]

Economic Reforms

In April 1968 President Kenneth Kaunda announced the Mulungushi Reforms. Their declared object was the attainment of economic independence for Zambia. One way of doing this was to reduce the influence of what he called 'resident expatriate businesses'. These were businesses carried on by people, or companies, that were in, but not of, the country. An expatriate company was defined as one whose shareholders were not Zambian citizens. In furtherance of this policy, twenty-six companies – mainly the subsidiaries of multi-nationals – were 'invited' to sell fifty-one per cent of their shares to the Industrial Development Corporation (Indeco).[60]

At the same time Kaunda announced measures to limit the overdrafts of, and the remittance of dividends by, foreign businesses. Furthermore, trading licences were no longer to be granted to expatriate individuals or companies outside the centres of ten named towns. No new licences would be granted to expatriate individuals or companies in these centres. He announced that a number of retail groups, CBC Ltd, OK Bazaars, Standard Trading (the late

Sid Diamond's company), Solanki Brothers, and Mwaiseni Stores had been invited to sell fifty-one per cent of their shares to Indeco.

Kaunda also announced that two of these companies had already agreed to sell their shares and to share their management skills. He named one of these firms as Mwaiseni. He described it as wholly Zambian-owned. Its chairman and managing director, Andrew Sardanis, a young Greek Cypriot businessman, had built up a network of stores in the North-Western Province. It was based in Chingola and had grown up in competition with A. F. Serrano and Susman Brothers & Wulfsohn. Sardanis had become a Zambian citizen and was a member of UNIP. He was also permanent secretary in the Ministry of Commerce, Industry and Foreign Trade, and was the man who was driving the nationalisation process. He says himself that he probably drafted the paragraphs on retail trade in Kaunda's Mulungushi speech. The other company, which Kaunda did not name, was said to be foreign-owned, but to have done well in the Zambianisation process. This turned out to be CBC Ltd. The chairman of the parent company, Booker, McConnell Ltd, was Sir Jock (later Lord) Campbell. He had acquired experience of nationalist politicians, and of nationalisation, in Guyana.[61]

Only one company in the Susman Brothers & Wulfsohn Group was named in Kaunda's speech. It was Zambesi Saw Mills. Although he did not mention the fact, the company had asked to be taken over and, as Kaunda correctly said, it had threatened on several occasions in the past to close down. Susman Brothers & Wulfsohn was not named in the speech, but the implications were clear. From January 1969 it would not be able to get licences for its stores in the small towns and rural areas where most of them were situated. Only its stores in Choma and in Livingstone, where it had only a wholesale outlet, would qualify. There is no evidence in the minutes of Susman Brothers & Wulfsohn itself, Rhodesian Mercantile Holdings or Stores Holdings of the immediate response of the directors to Kaunda's speech.

The directors may have been knocked a little off balance by the sudden death in August 1968 of Harry Wulfsohn. His brother, Wulfie, and son, Edwin, believe that his death was not unrelated to the stress that events in Rhodesia and Zambia had caused him. They both believe that the Mulungushi Reforms contributed to his death at the early age of fifty-seven. The reforms not only threatened the rural stores network, but also had potentially serious implications for Werners. Its butcheries in the centres of the Copperbelt towns were safe, but its many butcheries in the African townships were under threat. Werners had already been adversely affected by the death of Max Barnett in 1965 and by the re-introduction of price controls.[62]

After the announcement of the Mulungushi Reforms the company had about eight months to prepare itself for the change. It does not appear to have approached the government, as would have been sensible, to ask for a special dispensation. It certainly did not do what the government may have hoped that it would do – offer itself for takeover. Although the majority of the directors were out of sympathy with UNIP, they were not without political connections. Maurice Rabb was by then on good terms with Arthur Wina, who was minister of education. Furthermore, a member of the Susman family, Maurice Gersh, had been on the board of Indeco until the previous year. He had left the board after objecting to the concentration of power in Sardanis's hands, and to his bringing decisions to the board to be rubber-stamped. He had also been critical of the takeover of failing companies without proper projections as to their future profitability. Although he was not a member of the board of Susman Brothers & Wulfsohn, and was no longer a member of the board of Indeco, he would have had a shrewd understanding of the way the wind was blowing. It is hard to believe that he was not consulted about a response to the reforms, or that he would have backed the strategy that the company chose to adopt.[63]

It sought, under the guidance of Maurice Rabb, to evade rather than to confront the reforms. Rabb drew up detailed plans to convert the company into a wholesale trader. The existing retail groups would be turned into co-operatives, with names like Mongu Retailers, in which the store managers would have shares. The company would continue to provide them with administrative, financial and logistical support. The individual stores would be sold to their managers over a period of years. Meanwhile the store managers would apply for licences in their own right. Harry Wulfsohn had apparently been sceptical about this scheme, and it certainly did not work out well. The licensing authorities at Balovale (Zambezi) refused to issue licences to the store managers, and there was 'a chain reaction', in the words of Rabb himself, as licences were subsequently refused in other districts. The managers were then instructed by the local authorities to close their stores. If they did not do so, the police would padlock them. According to Job Haloba, a senior Zambian employee, it was a store manager at Balovale, Willie Chinyama, who provoked the crisis. He told the district secretary: 'The whites are cheating us. This is not our store. It is theirs.'[64]

Haloba travelled with Maurice Rabb and Geoff Kates around the Southern Province, visiting Choma, Mazabuka and Maamba in a vain attempt to get licences in these areas. They had some difficult meetings with district governors. His most vivid memory of the journey is that Kates, who was always well turned out, travelled with three suits and changed before each interview. He is certain that the government intended to force Susman Brothers & Wulfsohn to beg to be taken over. He also believes, though there is no other evidence to support this view, that Sir Jock Campbell of Bookers advised Rabb to follow CBC's example and offer fifty-one per cent of its shares to the government.[65]

In the end the company had no choice. Maurice Rabb and Edwin Wulfsohn, who had returned to Zambia soon after his father's death to take charge of Werners, became involved in direct talks with Andrew Sardanis. Geoff Kates and Major Campbell may also have played a part. Legislation provided that companies should be taken over at book value with no allowance for goodwill. Rabb pointed out that this was unfair to the company as its policy was to write down the cost of new stores, which usually cost between £500–£1,000 to build, to £1 in the first year of their existence. It appeared that the government intended to buy 123 stores for £123. It was eventually agreed that the stores should be valued at cost with depreciation of two and a half per cent per year. Edwin Wulfsohn, in his first business meeting since leaving Wall Street, had suggested that the valuation should be on the basis of an earnings multiple rather than book value. He recalls that Sardanis's response was to summon his PA to 'bring the act', which he then threw down a long boardroom table, shouting 'read the act'. He then stormed out. Wulfsohn was shocked to find that the price eventually paid was 'a miserly multiple of less than one year's profit – nine months'.[66]

Zambesi Trading Company

The final agreement involved the sale of fifty-one per cent of the shares in Susman Brothers & Wulfsohn (Stores) Ltd to Indeco for 382,500 Zambian Kwacha (K), which was the par value of the shares. Indeco was to make a down payment of 'approximately fifty per cent' of the purchase price and the balance would be paid over four years. The purchase price would buy fifty-one per cent of the shares in a new company, the Zambesi Trading Company, which was to carry on the business of the old one from 1 February 1969. There was to be a further payment to Stores Holdings of just under K200,000. This represented the reserves of the old company and was the figure about which there had been argument. The total price to be paid was equivalent to approximately £300,000. The agreement also provided that existing staff should not be worse off, that expatriate staff would be given contracts of three to five years, and that Zambesi Trading should pay a consultancy fee of K2,500 a month to Stores Holdings. Until such time as Indeco had paid in full for its shares, Stores Holdings would have the right to appoint the key personnel after consultation with it.[67]

The board of Stores Holdings decided that sums received from Indeco should be used to pay the exceptionally large dividends that the company had declared in 1967 and 1968. These dividends had been declared with the proviso that they would be paid when funds were available. The dividend for 1967 was worth £150,000. The dividend for 1968 was K1.40 per K2 share and was of a similar value. These dividends were much larger than any that had previously been paid and were, presumably, declared in anticipation of a future takeover. The dividend for 1968 was not paid, or credited to shareholders in the books of the company, until March 1970.[68]

Geoff Kates became the managing director of Zambesi Trading and a number of other senior personnel remained with the new company. They included Lionel Dix, Steve Nell, Elton Joffe and Tim Payne. Indeco instructed the new company to close down its stores in the Luapula and Northern Provinces by the end of the year, and to confine its activities to its traditional core area. It also required that the company should begin to close all its stores with a turnover of less than K5,000 a month by the end of September 1969, and open supermarkets in Livingstone and Choma. The closure of the northern stores made sense, as they were remote from the company's headquarters in Livingstone, and were in competition with the CBC network. The closure of small stores was based on the premise that these stores provided unfair competition to Zambian traders. The management of Zambesi Trading was not enthusiastic about either of the latter instructions. It knew that the closure of small stores would have an adverse effect on people in remote areas and it thought that profitability, rather than turnover, should be the criterion for closure. In spite of reservations about the instructions, it did open successful supermarkets in Choma and Livingstone, taking over the premises of 'Sossy's' in the latter town. Its owner, Harry Sossen, was leaving the country.[69]

Remarkable testimony to the strength of the Susman Brothers & Wulfsohn tradition, and the continuing effectiveness of Zambesi Trading, comes from a report written by C. W. Catt, an Indeco consultant, in July 1970. He had been asked to write a report on 'shrinkage', which was believed to have grown since the Indeco takeover, but he interpreted his instructions loosely and his report provides comparative data on Zambesi Trading, ZCBC,

Mwaiseni and ZOK. He visited twenty out of 106 Zambesi Trading establishments (including wholesale outlets and bulk stores), twenty-four out of ninety ZCBC outlets, five out of eleven Mwaiseni stores and all three of the ZOK stores. His only visits to rural stores were in the Southern Province and the Western Province (formerly Barotseland).[70]

He met Geoff Kates, then managing director, and Steve Nell, stores operations executive controller, and was clearly impressed by the management of Zambesi Trading. The company had at the time 465 staff, including twenty-eight expatriates and had a turnover of K4,400,000 (about £2,000,000). He recommended that it should be given responsibility for the management of all rural stores and wholesale outlets in the western half of the country. He noted that the state of ZCBC stores compared badly with those of Zambesi Trading, whose stores were 'in an immaculate condition'. Susman Brothers & Wulfsohn's management systems were still in place, less than eighteen months after the takeover, and were clearly superior to those of ZCBC or Mwaiseni. Andrew Kashita, who became managing director of Indeco in 1970, confirms that Mwaiseni's results were always the worst in the group. According to Simon Zukas, who was also a member of the Indeco board, Sardanis was amazed at the relative profitability of Zambesi Trading, and attributed this to Kates's management skills; Sardanis himself confirms his high opinion of the latter's talents. Zukas describes Susman Brothers & Wulfsohn as a 'shoestring operation', which was able to maintain a high level of profits with a minimum of headquarters staff and wasteful expenditure.[71]

The company had been compelled to close forty-two stores, including stores in the Luapula and Northern Provinces and some stores with low turnovers in the west and south, and had opened eighteen others. It still had more rural stores than any other network. CBC had also had to close stores, but it never had as many rural stores as Susman Brothers & Wulfsohn, and they were more thinly spread over a larger number of provinces. What was remarkable about the Susman Brothers & Wulfsohn network, as inherited by Zambesi Trading, was the relatively high density of small stores, especially in Barotseland. It used to be said that when the first man reached the moon, he would find that there was a Susman Brothers & Wulfsohn store already there. Its great achievement had been to organise regular deliveries of a wide range of goods – as many as 400 lines – to these remote rural stores in a province that is still today a logistical and communications nightmare.

The policy of closing small stores began to weaken this network from 1969 onwards, but Zambesi Trading continued to provide a good service until the departure of the last of the key personnel from the old company in

1972, and, perhaps, for a year or two after that. Kates cited political interference, and pressure from district governors and ministers to employ unsuitable staff, as the main reason for his departure – he resigned when his wife began to receive abusive phone calls. Maurice Rabb concluded at about this time that the stores were not going to be run on business lines, as the government had begun to use its control over retail outlets as an instrument for the control of the prices of 'essential commodities', with obvious adverse consequences for profitability. Stores Holdings, which derived its income from Zambesi Trading, continued to pay reasonable dividends until 1973, but then they appear to have ceased. Zambesi Trading came to an end in 1975–6, when NIEC bought Stores Holdings' shares in the company, and the stores began to trade under its name. Stores Holdings transferred the debt owed by NIEC for these shares to Susman Brothers & Wulfsohn towards the end of 1976, but there is no evidence that NIEC ever paid the K450,000 that it owed for them.[72]

By 1975 the Zambian economy was in the throes of recession following the oil crisis and the collapse of copper prices. Kaunda certainly did not anticipate this in 1968, the year of the Mulungushi Reforms, or in 1969 when he announced the Matero Reforms, including the partial nationalisation of the copper mines. In his speech on the latter occasion he praised the directors of Susman Brothers & Wulfsohn for having the good sense to offer their company for takeover. He contrasted their behaviour with Solanki Brothers, an east African trading group that had resisted takeover. The economic reforms were carried out at the height of the unprecedented boom in copper prices which accompanied the Vietnam War. Zambia's leaders, and their economic advisers, seem to have temporarily forgotten the cyclical nature of the copper market and of the Zambian economy.[73]

The rights and wrongs of the Mulungushi and Matero Reforms can be debated endlessly. Edwin Wulfsohn thinks that the takeover was confiscatory. Many people in the Western Province and other provinces still regret the passing of the Susman Brothers & Wulfsohn stores, and wish that they would return. By the late 1970s people living in remote areas often had to travel great distances in order to find essential commodities. The closure of stores removed the incentive to produce from peasant farmers who were deprived of a source of goods and a market for their products.[74]

Andrew Sardanis is today unapologetic about his own role. He says that Susman Brothers & Wulfsohn had been around for a long time, and its directors were not powerless. They could have evaded takeover by putting the business into the hands of a family member who was a citizen, or had a claim to citizenship, such as Edwin Wulfsohn himself. He thinks that the valuation placed on their assets was reasonable. He still maintains that their rural stores, which were mainly built of Kimberley brick with corrugated-iron roofs, were overvalued. He compares regret for the passing of the Susman Brothers & Wulfsohn stores network with regret for the end of colonialism, and of the district commissioners, who, he says, did a good job in their own terms, while lording it over the people.[75]

Sardanis also argues that the commercial basis of rural trading networks had been undermined before the economic reforms. Traders operated on the basis of a two-way trade: they included the cost of transport in the selling price of goods, and subsidised the price that they paid for produce. The development of co-operatives in the late 1950s and early 1960s, both before and after independence, had taken the grain trade away from the traders and weakened their position. It is true that Susman Brothers & Wulfsohn did lose the grain trade in the Mankoya and Mongu districts in the late 1950s, and may have lost the rice trade in the early 1960s. There is no evidence, however, that this had any effect on their profitability. Sardanis acknowledges that there was political interference in the affairs of parastatal companies. He claims that he had designed mechanisms that were intended to limit this, but now admits that it was naive of him to think that they would work.

Andrew Kashita has a rather different perspective on these issues. He thinks that the Susman Brothers & Wulfsohn stores network was an accidental victim of a measure that was aimed at Asian traders. It was not a major target of the economic reforms. It was, however, impossible for legal draftsmen to design legislation that removed Asian traders from rural areas without affecting other expatriate businesses. He also regrets that businesses like Susman Brothers & Wulfsohn did not fight harder to defend the rights that takeover agreements and management contracts gave them as minority shareholders. He says that he was prepared as managing director to support the minority shareholders, but thinks that political interference increased after his own departure from Indeco in 1974.[76]

In spite of the major political changes and problems that came with the end of the Federation, Zambian independence and Rhodesia's UDI, the 1960s were the heyday of Susman Brothers & Wulfsohn as a trading business in its core areas. By the mid 1960s it was running well on lines that were derived from two of the most progressive retailing businesses in South Africa and the United Kingdom. It was at the height of its effectiveness and profitability. Although UDI created huge problems for the business, in terms of the location of the head office, the flow of imports and the recruitment of personnel, it was able to withstand this shock and to thrive. When older men and women in the western half of Zambia look back, as they frequently do, to the 'glory days' of Susman Brothers & Wulfsohn, they are looking back to the 1960s. This was a time when African spending power increased, and the company ran a large number of well-stocked stores in remote areas. It is to the nuts and bolts, and the all-important human base, of that business that we will now turn.

CHAPTER 14

Susman Brothers & Wulfsohn Stores: People

There seems to be general agreement that the secret of the success of the Susman Brothers & Wulfsohn business was its recruitment of the best available men for the job. Nathan Zelter recalled that he learnt from Harry Wulfsohn that 'the most essential thing in business is to delegate authority, and that it was of the essence to be sure that your top men were competent, talented and incorruptible people, whatever their eccentricities, whatever their views on things, [so long as these] did not threaten the best interests of the business.' David Susman and Edwin Wulfsohn would certainly concur with these sentiments. Geoff Kates would also agree that the success of the business depended on getting the right men for the job, and would add 'including me'. Denton Pitt and Colin Arnott would agree with him and add 'including us'. It was clearly important not only to get the right people at the top, but all the way down the line. This chapter takes a look at the kind of people, both black and white, who worked for Susman Brothers & Wulfsohn in the 1950s and 1960s. It draws on interviews with a few of the survivors from those days. The chapter does not pretend to be comprehensive in its coverage. The experience of a few people has to be taken as reflecting the experience of many more.[1]

Group Managers

Group managers were the people who ran the business in the field, or bush. The group system was in existence before the establishment of Rhodesian Mercantile Holdings in 1955–6, but it was then formalised. For a while there were also divisional managers in Livingstone, Mufulira and Salisbury. These divisions soon faded out, but in later years Mongu had a divisional manager who had a watching brief over the Mankoya and Balovale groups; the groups remained the building blocks of management. Until the appointment of James Kalufwelu as group manager at Batoka in 1966, all managers were white, or, in the language of the day, 'European'. At each group headquarters there was usually a manager and an assistant manager. It was the common practice that the wives of managers and assistant managers were employed in the business. They usually did clerical work and accounts, or worked in the European stores at places like Mongu and Fort Rosebery.

At the high point in the expansion of the business in the late 1950s, there were thirteen groups of stores, of which eight were in Northern Rhodesia, four were in Southern Rhodesia and one was in Bechuanaland. After the sale of the Copperbelt stores, and most of the Southern Rhodesian ones, the number of groups had fallen by the early 1960s to nine. Apart from Maun and Balovale, they were Mongu and Mankoya in Barotseland, Batoka and Livingstone in the Southern Province, Fort Rosebery and Kasama in the Northern and Luapula provinces, all in Northern Rhodesia, and Gutu in Southern Rhodesia. The Maun and Balovale groups were a little different from the others because their long-serving managers had shares in the business. Chobo Weskob dominated the Ngamiland Trading Company until his death in 1965. A. F. Serrano's position in the Balovale group, which he managed until his retirement in 1963, was similar to that of Weskob.

The core of managers at any one time was about twenty and the turnover was not high. Managers moved from one group to another, but often stayed in one place for long periods. The list below demonstrates this.

Mongu
  1950–7   Mike Pretorius
  1957–63 Lionel Dix
  1964–7   Steve Nell
  1967–9   Tim Payne

Batoka
  1957–65 Derek Speares
  1966–9   James Kalufwelu

Gutu
  1960–5   Tim Payne
  1965–   Derek Speares

Livingstone
  1950–7   Louis Fox
  1957–65 B. L. van Zyl
  1965–9   Lionel Dix

Fort Rosebery (Mansa)
  1956–7   Lionel Dix
  1957–61 D. C. (Dougie) Christians
  1962–4   Steve Nell
  1964–9   Steve Kuzniar

Steve Kuzniar and Keith Chick

Biographical information about the group managers and their assistants is not plentiful, and, sadly, few of them survive from the 1960s. The job attracted people of varied backgrounds and characters. There was probably no typical recruit, but all must have had in common a liking for what were still 'frontier' conditions and an ability to improvise. Stefan (known as Steve) Kuzniar now lives in Harare with his wife Patsy. The story of his life is certainly unusual. He was born in Poland in 1935 and became a child refugee with his sister during the Second World War. His father was an officer in the Polish army who managed to get his two youngest children onto a train that was taking refugees to Russia. Both Kuzniar's parents and his two elder brothers, who joined the partisans, were killed during the war, but he and his sister reached Persia by way of Siberia. The children were looked after by the British Red Cross and eventually reached Southern Rhodesia in 1943 under the auspices of the Middle Eastern Relief and Refugee Administration (MERRA). They were lucky enough to find an aunt in a refugee camp at Rusape and were brought up by her. Kuzniar was at school in Hartley and Bulawayo and did a course in Agriculture. He farmed for two seasons and then joined African Stores at Gutu. He also worked in the QueQue group before moving to the Rhodesian Mercantile Holdings head office in Salisbury, where he was a 'reserve' manager and trouble-shooter. He was sent from there to act on two occasions in 1963 as group manager at Mankoya and to sort out problems that had arisen there.[2]

Kuzniar spent only a few months at Mankoya, where he had eleven stores under his control. He recalls buying hides, lion, leopard and cheetah skins, as well as beeswax, but does not recall buying rice. He spent six years at Fort Rosebery (Mansa) where the market was more sophisticated. It was a rural extension of the Copperbelt and there was a good deal of money in circulation, much of which came from the fish trade. After the absorption of the Kasama group there were twenty-three stores in the group. There was not much produce-buying at Fort Rosebery, but there was a good deal of buying and selling of dried fish – *kapenta*. Although the company had sold off some of the outlying stores in the Northern Province, the stores in the group were still scattered over a very wide area. The most distant was at Nsumbu, at the southwest corner of Lake Tanganyika, about 250 miles from Fort Rosebery. There was competition in the area from CBC, and from Asian traders, but Kuzniar was able to boost turnover considerably during his time in the north. Like Barotseland and Ngamiland, this area was characterised by exceptionally difficult communications. There were wholesale stores at Luwingu, and at Samfya on Lake Bangweulu, where boats were used on the lake.

A great deal of the work of group managers related to stocktaking. This was supposed to be done at all stores on a monthly basis. It involved balancing the opening stock, and issues from stock, less credit notes and stock adjustments, against physical stock and cash. In other words, it was checking what was supposed to be there with what was actually there. A small shortage was acceptable, but if there was a large shortage it was necessary to close the store and lay off the store manager – the capitao. Prosecutions were unusual as convictions were difficult to obtain. A surplus was almost as bad as a shortage as it suggested that the store manager was overcharging customers to cover up theft. Tricks of the store manager's trade included folding one blanket to make it look like two, and stacking empty shoeboxes together with full ones. Denton Pitt and Colin Arnott recall stocktaking at Maun until midnight by the light of a candle after the electricity generator had been switched off. Marian Payne says that even today she cannot look at a bolt of cloth without remembering the time she spent measuring ends of rolls.[3]

There were also twice-yearly stocktakes for each group as a whole. These usually involved visiting directors. Steve Kuzniar recalled visits by Zelter and Kates among others. These visits by 'The Flying Circus' were events to look forward to, as managers had an entertainment allowance, and they were an excuse for a party. Patsy Kuzniar recalls serving Zelter, who was certainly not an Orthodox Jew, with venison stuffed with bacon. She apologised, but he told her not to worry: 'In the bush we eat anything'. These visits were also opportunities to get news of friends in other groups, to exchange information on merchandise, and to discuss common problems. Fort Rosebery was an out-of-the-way group and it was left alone for much of the time. Kuzniar has vivid memories of Harry Wulfsohn. He recalls that he had an amazing facility with figures. He would sit in a meeting and appear to be asleep. He would then wake up and come out with detailed percentages and projections. Kuzniar remembers Geoff Kates as hardworking, neat and meticulous. He knew the market and what would sell. He was envied for his frequent trips to the Far East. He made a few dud buys – goods that would not move – but these were unusual.

Kuzniar enjoyed life in the bush – hunting, fishing and game meat. This was the attraction for many of the men who worked for the firm. Managers had the personal use of a Land Rover. They were provided with a rent-free and furnished house, and they never paid a telephone bill – they had no telephones. The cost of living was low and conditions were generally good. According to Kuzniar, the company was tight with money, and people looked forward to their Christmas bonuses, but if you were sick or had other problems the company would look after you; it was a reasonably good employer. Kuzniar and his wife were in Zambia at independence and stayed on at Mansa until 1969, leaving when Indeco took over the company. Kuzniar later ran stores in the reserves in Rhodesia, but was forced out of them by the liberation war. He worked for many years for the Dairy Produce Board and retired in 2001 as manager of a food-processing firm.

Kuzniar's assistant manager for much of the time that he was at Fort Rosebery was Keith Chick, who was born in England in 1940 and moved to Southern Rhodesia when he was eleven. After leaving school at the age of fifteen, he began to work for Harry Robinson as a warehouse assistant. He has great respect for Robinson and is grateful to him for insisting that he do a Dale Carnegie sales course. As well as two stints at Fort Rosebery, Chick also worked with Jack True, opening a new warehouse for H. Robinson and Company on the Victoria Falls Road in Livingstone in 1964. The partnership with Steve Kuzniar at Fort Rosebery worked well and they greatly increased the turnover of the stores during their time together. Much of his time was spent stocktaking, but he also did a regular 'cash run', which involved visits to sixteen stores and a journey of 500 miles in a very long day. Travelling eastwards from Fort Rosebery they pass through Luwingu, north of Lake Bangweulu, to Kasama, and then northwards to Nsumbu at the south end of Lake Tanganyika, returning via Kawambwa on the Luapula. They only had time to stop, count the cash, leave a receipt and move on to the next store. Chick also recalls adventurous journeys travelling through the Congo on the Pedicle Road during the Katanga secession crisis. The road was not graded for three years and there were potholes so large, he claims, that an elephant could stand in them and only its ears would be visible. A gift of a bottle of whisky to the customs officials eased their way through – so much so that they were moved to the front of the queue.

Chick enjoyed hunting, and sometimes poaching, duiker on the Kapalala Plains. They gave shares to the police and to Father Tomas, of the White

Fathers. He got on well with the store managers: 'They were sensible people'. He stayed on after Zambian independence and left for personal, not political, reasons: his wife, Denise, became pregnant and there were complications which meant that she was advised that it was not safe for her to stay at Mansa. Chick asked for a transfer back to H. Robinson and Company in Salisbury, but his request was refused and he resigned. He was sorry to leave, but also disappointed that after ten years with the company his request for a transfer was declined. He later worked for Old Mutual in Zimbabwe and is now selling cars for Nissan Motors in Durban.[4]

Tim and Marian Payne

Marian Payne is the widow of Tim Payne, the last group manager at Mongu. She has written an unpublished memoir that gives a graphic account of their life together for the nearly twenty years that her husband worked for African Stores, Rhodesian Mercantile Holdings, Stores Holdings and Zambesi Trading. Tim Payne was born in England and joined the BSA police on a three-year contract in 1950. He was recruited by Colonel John Hodges to join African Stores at the end of his first contract in 1953. He had met Hodges while working for the CID on a case of theft of grain from the nearby Mrewa store. His starting salary with African Stores was £50 a month, rather more than the £35 that he got with the police, and so he started work with the Mtoko group, which was about ninety miles northeast of Salisbury. It was at Mtoko that he met Marian, his future wife, who arrived there in November 1954. She had been seconded to Southern Rhodesia by the British Post Office to help run the telephone system there. They were married in Salisbury in 1956.

In the following years Tim Payne worked at Gutu, about seventy miles from Fort Victoria, at Pounsley, near Rusape in Manicaland, and at the Steelworks Trading Company, QueQue, before returning to Gutu as group manager in 1960. Gutu was a mixed commercial and communal farming area, though most of the stores were in 'Native' Reserves and Purchase Areas. At the main store there was a bulk store, grain sheds and a mill. Grain buying was an important part of the group's business. There were nine stores in the group, including Baro, Basero, Basuto, Excelsior, Mungezi, Mushuku and Zavahera. Tim Payne was an extremely practical man – 'nothing fazed him be it electrics, woodwork, building, Rhodesian boilers, septic tanks, vehicles – or aeroplanes. A huge asset when one lived in the bush.' While at Gutu he built a new store at Basera, but this was petrol-bombed during 'an upsurge of African Nationalism', and burned to the ground within six weeks of opening – he had to rebuild it. It was while he was at Gutu that he learnt to fly – a skill that he was to put to good use in Zambia.[5]

Tim Payne moved to Livingstone with his wife and their four young sons early in 1965. He worked with Maurice Rabb, Jack True and Lionel Dix, eventually being joined by Elton Joffe, Geoff Kates and Bobby Campbell at the Livingstone office. Tim Payne spent a good deal of the time away from home, travelling by boat to stores at Sesheke and Senanga. In October 1966 he was asked to move to Mongu to work with Steve Nell and take over from him as divisional manager. This was a challenge and he was in his element. As divisional manager he was responsible for the overall supervision of approximately forty-eight stores in the Mongu, Mankoya and Balovale groups.

There were, as there always had been in Barotseland, huge logistical problems to overcome. The store groups relied on the Zambesi River Transport Service, Barotse Transport and on their own Land Rovers and trucks, barges and boats, and occasionally on *mokoros* – dugout canoes – for communications. Land Rovers and Bedford three-ton, or five-ton, trucks became standard issue as transport for the groups from the early 1960s. These were the same kinds of vehicles that were used by the provincial administration – the district officers and district commissioners. There was a sense in which Susman Brothers & Wulfsohn ran a parallel organisation to the administration. There were also two motorised steel barges – the *Iron Duke* and the *Nangweshi* – on the Zambezi at Mongu, as well as a number of speedboats. The *Iron Duke* was a fifteen-ton barge, and was capable of carrying a truck or a Land Rover. There was no telephone line from Mongu, though there was a telegraph line and the monthly turnover figures were sent by telegram in code. The line was often down and the figures went to Livingstone via Lusaka on the Barotse Transport truck.[6]

It was at the time of his move to Mongu that Tim Payne suggested to the directors that the company should buy an aircraft to facilitate contact with Mankoya, Kalabo and Balovale, as well as for travel to Livingstone for meetings of managers and for other business. Susman Brothers had, of course, been using aircraft for travel to Barotseland since the early 1930s, and had taken shares in Zambesi Airways in the late 1940s. Geoff Kates recalls that they used to charter a Rapide and he emphasises the value of aircraft in giving an element of surprise to stocktaking expeditions. The company had, however, always chartered aircraft and had never owned one until then. After doing a conversion course in Livingstone, Tim flew back to Mongu with the new plane – a Piper Cherokee 180-C with the registration number 9JRGB – in May 1967. There was no hangar so Marian had to sew a cover for the plane from yards and yards of heavy calico: 'It was a nightmare, particularly as I had just made a new windsock for the airstrip.' At the end of 1968 the government withdrew all private pilot's licences and Tim Payne was no longer able to fly the plane, but by that time the directors had realised how useful it was. They relocated the plane to Livingstone and employed a full-time commercial pilot – Ray Houghton.

Marian Payne recalls that for her family 'Mongu was magic'. Her children have happy memories of the place. Three of the four children were now of school age, and for the first year the two elder ones were at school in Salisbury. They later moved to a school at Pietersburg in the Northern Transvaal. Their journey to school involved a flight to Livingstone, train from there to Bulawayo, and bus for the last part of the journey. The third son spent a year at a primary school in Mongu before joining his brothers on their long journey south. Marian Payne worked full-time for the company in Mongu.

> I worked in the office doing stock control for each of the stores, checking stock sheets, checking and banking the cash as it came in. Each outside store had a runner, who with his little cashbox would bring the cash in twice a month, travelling miles across the bush, or in a *mokoro* along the river. An open invitation to muggers one would suppose, but until we left Mongu no one had ever been robbed. There was a branch of Barclay's Bank in the DC's complex and I would take the cash there unless, as frequently happened, the bank ran out of money. The money would come from Lusaka by Zambia Airways, but the pilots frequently 'lost' Mongu and would go back to Lusaka without delivering it, so I would get an SOS from the manager who would come to an office with his stamp and I would make up a deposit for him.

In May 1967 the Payne family moved from the entirely unsuitable house in which they first stayed to the divisional manager's house. This was in 'Susman Square', slightly off the main road, with houses making up one side and the Bulk Store and smaller stores making up the other. There was no hotel in Mongu, though one was soon to be built, and all company visitors, whether directors or buyers, came to stay with the Paynes. They had twenty-nine visitors during their last month – February 1969. 'There was a scruffy tennis court in front of the house and we scoffled the grass between the cracks in the cement and had some good tennis.' Marian found gardening in the Kalahari sands of Mongu a challenge and was never very successful at it. Their main entertainment came from the river and fishing. They would go for the day with the Barotse Transport barge as the guests of the manager, Mike Lyster, or with the company's barge, the *Nangweshi*, as it delivered goods to riverside stores. Marian remembers that some stores moved with the floods. This was probably still true of the stores at Lealui and Nalolo, which moved to the *mafulo* (bush margin of the plain) when the floods rose.

Housekeeping was difficult as supplies were erratic. As had been the case at the *boma*s on the Zambezi for many years, they frequently ordered meat and vegetables from Livingstone, and these were brought in on the Zambia Airways – formerly Central African Airways – Beaver. It was, she says, the only time that she bought baked beans by the case. 'Our own stores would stock basic supplies, margarine, cooking oil, flour, and some tinned goods, also liquor – beer (in cans) and a comprehensive selection of "hard tack" and liqueurs.' Susman Brothers & Wulfsohn had not previously sold alcohol, but did so from the early 1960s when liquor licences were granted in Barotseland for the first time.[7]

Marian Payne feels that Barotseland was still in a state of shock at this time after the end of the Federation and the loss of its special status as a protectorate within Northern Rhodesia. Among Tim Payne's duties as divisional manager was the maintenance of the company's special relationship with the Litunga, and he made regular visits to Sir Mwanawina III at Lealui and Limulunga. The Litunga continued to sell his ivory to the company and one of the divisional manger's duties was to negotiate with him for its purchase. The Litunga also controlled the granting of trading sites, and of licences, throughout Barotseland – the annual rent for a site in the 1950s was £23. He had refused to allow Susman Brothers & Wulfsohn to open a new store in Mongu District in 1962, saying that he wished to limit the number of stores in the province. The company then offered to close a store in the Mankoya District in exchange for permission to build at Kande. Marian Payne notes that Asian traders were excluded from Barotseland and that the company had enjoyed 'a trading monopoly for a considerable number of years'. It is still widely believed in Asian circles in Zambia that Susman Brothers & Wulfsohn influenced successive litungas to exclude Asian competition. There is no evidence of a conspiracy, but if there was one, the provincial administration must also have been involved. The only suggestion of anxiety about the penetration of Asian traders into Barotseland appeared in the board of directors' minutes in 1961. Maurice Rabb then opposed the suggestion that the company use an Asian transport firm to bring goods into Barotseland in competition with Barotse Transport. He was afraid that this might enable Asian traders to get a foothold in the province. When UNIP officials threatened in 1962 to cancel licences and give them to Asians, they may, however, have been touching a raw nerve.[8]

The Paynes were in Mongu during the last few years of the reign of Sir Mwanawina III. On two occasions they attended the *Kuomboka* ceremony, when the Litunga moves by barge from Lealui in the flood plain to Limulunga on the plain margin. It was the custom for Susman Brothers & Wulfsohn to give presents to the Litunga at this time. The paddlers of the royal barge, the *Nalikwanda*, wore new white vests and red berets, which were provided by the company. Marian Payne noted that there was a steep climb up from the plain to Limulunga and it was said that if the Litunga could not climb the hill he was no longer fit to be king. Mwanawina was about eighty years old and was surrounded by a large entourage, who may have given him a helping hand. He died in November 1968 and Tim Payne attended the funeral ceremony. Godwin Mbikusita Lewanika, whose earlier career has been outlined, was quickly chosen as his successor in a controversial election. There was some doubt as to whether the government would recognise his election – he was anathema to it because of his involvement in federal politics – but it did so. The day before the installation ceremony, which was set for 15 December, Payne was if he would take President Kaunda over to Lealui in the company boat, as all the government boats were out of action. He had to wait for the president, who was late 'as usual', and missed the ceremony. According to Marian the ceremony went ahead without the president. Other sources say that the president was present, but did not make a speech on this occasion 'because of the rain'. There were banners all over Lealui, reading 'Long Live King Lewanika.'[9]

These events occurred during the run-up to the first post-independence elections, which took place on 19 December 1968. Nalumino Mundia had broken away from UNIP and founded an opposition party, the United Party (UP) in 1966. Mundia's action was provoked by ethnic conflict within UNIP. His power base was in Barotseland and his party exploited the widespread unhappiness in the province at the government's breaches of the pre-independence Barotseland Agreement, its abolition of the Barotse National Council in 1965, and its deeply unpopular suspension early in 1966 of recruitment by WNLA of labour from Barotseland for the South African mines. The UP was banned in October 1968, but Mundia and his supporters quickly transferred their allegiance to the ANC and contested the elections under its banner, winning the majority of the seats in Barotseland.[10]

The death of Mwanawina III, the installation of the new Litunga as Lewanika II, and the general elections, coincided with the crisis over licences, the Indeco takeover, and the establishment of the Zambesi Trading Company.[11] Marian Payne's view of these events is as follows:

> We tried all ways to get around this problem including trying to get licences in the names of the individual store managers but it was obvious that the government had other things in mind and we learned that they were arbitrarily acquiring 51% of the company. SB & W would continue to run the operation and government would 'pay' for their shareholding from future profits. They also required the company to 'Zambianise' the managerial staff in Mongu, so we were to move back to Livingstone. We were devastated, but that's life!

The Paynes left Mongu in February 1969. Tim's new job was to run Stores Holdings's warehouse, which was the main holding point for imported goods and had apparently grown into 'an enormous set up'. The country's trade had been redirected to the north and there were a couple of 'big rigs' – including a thirty-ton truck – which went up to Dar-es-Salaam to pick up loads from the ships. Despite the management's reservations about it, the Livingstone supermarket worked out well. Its manager was a young Englishman, John Dobbin. 'It was a well-planned project and such a pleasure to shop in.' The Paynes remained happily in Livingstone until 1972. Tim Payne found the ban on private flying a nuisance, but busied himself with the restoration of an old boat. Marian Payne's mother came on a visit from England in 1971, but developed cerebral malaria, which was misdiagnosed and, sadly, she died. The border with Rhodesia was still open and Marian Payne gave birth to her fifth son at the Victoria Falls towards the end of the year. When the government announced in 1972 that it intended to close the border with Rhodesia, the Paynes 'thought long and hard' about the consequences of this for the education of their children, but decided to leave Zambia and return to Rhodesia. Tim Payne asked for a transfer back to H. Robinson in Salisbury, but, as had been the case with Steve Kuzniar, there was no vacancy for him in what was by then a much smaller business.

African Staff

The real basis of the business lay with the African labour force. They were the frontline troops who had day-to-day contact with the customers over the counter. The great majority of them worked in remote rural locations with only monthly visits from managerial staff. In Barotseland, especially, some of them worked in places where they could be cut off for months on end by floods, or where sand made access even more difficult in the dry season. The number of African employees in the field for the group as a whole remained static at about 600 between 1960 and 1963. The great majority of the African staff was employed at that date in Northern Rhodesia. It was estimated in 1963 that African wages constituted the largest single item of the company's annual expenditure. This came to £64,000 a year, or just over £100 per head as an annual wage. There are no precise figures, but about 150 of these employees would have been store managers – also known as capitaos. In 1956 there had been an attempt to change the basis on which they were paid. At that time the practice was, as it had been for many years, that store managers were paid a nominal wage, with rations, and their main income came from a commission which was payable after stocktaking. The commission was paid after the deduction of shortages – there was an allowance of about one per cent for acceptable 'shrinkage'. It was realised in 1956 that this system was unsatisfactory as there were often gaps of several months between stocktakes and the store manager 'was supposed to subsist on his meagre wages, which are totally inadequate for the purpose, and quite unrelated to the scale of remuneration obtainable by an African of similar capabilities in other types of employment'. It was thought that 'the present system is tantamount to encouraging the Capitaos to supplement their income illegally in order to satisfy their day-to-day needs'.[12]

Under the new system it was proposed that store managers should be paid a higher basic wage, which would be based on the average monthly wage and commission paid in the previous year. A commission would then be paid as a percentage of any increase in turnover subsequently achieved, and a bonus of a month's wages would be paid every six months, subject to a satisfactory stocktaking. Shortages of up to £5 or one per cent of turnover were to be regarded as negligible, but shortages of more than this were to be seen as a danger signal. The new system did not work well in all groups, and after a few months' trial the Mongu and Fort Rosebery groups reverted to the old one. At the first conference of group managers in September 1960, the managers recommended an increase in African wages that would have cost £19,000 a year. Discussion was deferred to a full meeting of the board. but Nathan Zelter insisted that, for political reasons, there must be an immediate increase in wages for staff in the Northern Province, and this was granted.[13]

In 1961 Sutherlands, a subsidiary of CBC, and the main competitor in Barotseland, increased its basic monthly wage, paying Livingstone wages to its Barotseland staff. Consequently, the basic monthly wage of store managers in the Mongu group was increased from £5 to £9.5.0. A commission of two and a half per cent was payable on turnover above £200. By the end of 1963 the basic monthly wage of store managers in Barotseland had increased to £13.10.0 with the same rate of commission. Geoff Kates recalls that the average rate of shrinkage was between one per cent and one and a half per cent. This was, in global terms, a very low rate and reflected well on the honesty of the staff. Capitaos who worked in Bulk Stores and wholesale outlets were paid a bonus rather than a commission. Staff were also able to get a discount on goods bought in the stores and could sometimes profit from reselling goods.[14]

Apart from capitaos, the most numerous African employees were tailors. There may, indeed, have been more tailors than there were capitaos as each store employed one or two of them. It had been the custom for many years that the tailoring of cloth bought at a store was done free of charge by the tailor who sat outside it, working on a hand-powered sewing machine. Tailors in Southern Rhodesia seem to have used treadle machines. Most of the tailors were men, but in Barotseland some were women. As the independence of Zambia approached, there were compulsory wage increases in terms of minimum wage legislation, which increased the cost to the company of African labour. Major Campbell suggested in April 1963 that the only way to cut the wage bill was to reduce the number of staff. He said that it was not the policy of the company to lay off staff in large numbers, but he hoped that a reduction of 100 employees could be achieved through natural wastage. Tim Payne, then group manager at Gutu, suggested that a reduction could be achieved by ending the provision of free tailoring. Doubts were expressed as to the wisdom of the policy. It was feared that if tailors became self-employed they might charge too much for their services and frighten away customers. It was, nevertheless, agreed that the policy could be tried as an experiment at Gutu. Lionel Dix thought that the application of this policy would save £5,000 a year in Barotseland alone, but it was agreed that it could only be applied there if Sutherlands agreed to introduce it at the same time. There must have been agreement on this as the tailors were laid off, but in November 1963 the now self-employed tailors started a boycott of the stores – this was, allegedly, organised by the United Trade Union Congress. They had returned to work by January 1964, but only after the two companies had agreed to pay gratuities based on the number of years that the tailors had worked for them.[15]

Among the other African employees of the company were runners, drivers and boat crews. Runners were employed until the late 1960s to carry messages and to bring in cash. Mrs McKillop, who worked in the Susman Brothers & Wulfsohn accounts office in Livingstone from 1960, recalls that runners would bring in money in cash boxes. The boxes were carried in cloth bags that were run up by the tailors from off-cuts and ends of rolls, and it was not uncommon for there to be 100 multi-coloured bags waiting to be opened and counted. Runners often carried cash to the group headquarters and it was sometimes taken by plane or truck from there to Livingstone. The Fort Rosebery group was too large and the stores there were too scattered for runners to be employed.[16]

It is difficult today to find store managers, or capitaos, who worked for Susman Brothers & Wulfsohn in the 1960s. Interviews with a small sample of these men give some idea of their backgrounds, experience and attitudes to their work. They were generally people who had finished primary school and held Standard VI certificates. Very few Africans in Northern Rhodesia had any secondary education before the 1960s. In Barotseland the capitaos had usually been educated at Sefula or other schools within the Paris Mission network, and they had often worked in Southern Rhodesia, or for other employers in Northern Rhodesia, before joining the company.

Joel Mubiana Liswaniso still lives in the suburbs of Mongu in a house on an eight-acre plot, which he bought from Zambesi Trading on his retirement in 1974. He not only has a good memory, but is also a keeper of records. He was born in the Senanga District in 1918. He moved to Livingstone as a youth and finished Standard VI at Chikuni Training Centre in 1943. He worked as a pupil teacher, at the hospital at Mulobezi, and for the Forestry Department, before joining Susman Brothers & Wulfsohn in Livingstone in July 1948. He became a senior capitao in the Bulk Store there and was transferred to Mongu in 1957. He was clearly ambitious and did a storekeepers' course with the International Correspondence Schools in London, his certificate dated 10 November 1961 indicates passes in Mathematics, Retail Accounts, Business Correspondence, Stores Accounts and Control. A testimonial from his group manager in Livingstone, B. L. van Zyl, describes him as 'hard-working and honest'. His group manager in Mongu, Lionel Dix, insisted that he should have a gun and recommended him for a licence. In his letter of recommendation he wrote:

> The position he holds is one of trust and apart from being a hard and willing worker we have always found him to be reliable and honest. He is of sober habits and is now one of the senior Africans in our employ. We understand that he wishes to acquire a shotgun and we therefore have no hesitation in recommending that he be granted the necessary permission.[17]

Liswaniso recalls working with B. L. van Zyl, Mike Pretorius, Lionel Dix, Steve Nell and Geoff Kates, as well as with Job Haloba under Zambesi Trading. He was retired 'on company policy' in 1974 and has not worked since his retirement, but farms in the flood plain. He has had two wives and sixteen children. Of his career with Susman Brothers & Wulfsohn, he says now that 'I was not rude. I was sober to everyone, to all my bwanas, even to Haloba. But I was very cheeky to those working with me. I said: "If you steal you spoil my name". They were very afraid of me.' He says that he lived well in those days: the cost of living was cheap, he had his wage and his bonus, and he could buy goods at a discount from the wholesale department and sell them to his friends for a small profit. All his bwanas were good to him, but Zambesi Trading 'did not respect us. We left one by one.'[18]

Ernest Mukwendela Kutoma also lives in Mongu and joined Susman Brothers & Wulfsohn in 1947 – at the age of eighteen. He was born at Nalongo in Barotseland in 1925 and completed his Standard VI at Kambole Government School. He worked as a store capitao at Libonda in Kalabo District, at Kabongola, Sitoti, Senanga and Mongu. When he started work, probably as a store assistant, his wage was thirty shillings a month with a commission on turnover of sixpence in the pound. At Libonda and Sitoti he also bought cattle and was paid a commission of two shillings and sixpence a head. He also bought cattle at Liachi, in Senanga District. It was well known as a store that did good business in spite of its difficult location. Among the directors he remembers Wulfsohn, Robinson, Kates and Joffe. Among the managers he recalls Pretorius, Dix and van Rensburg. He also remembers Ted Silley, a stock-taker and assistant manager who stayed with the company for many years. Kutoma says that he always made a point of selling goods at the prices that were set by his bosses. Some capitaos charged more, but they were taking money from the people, and were in danger of running up a surplus, which was as incriminating as a shortage. He recounts meetings for store managers in Mongu at which they were addressed by Rabb and Kates and told how to talk to people and how to get business. 'They talked to us in a friendly way, in a good manner. They were our parents.' On his retirement from Zambesi Trading he was given a store at Namushakende, but, as he says: 'I failed to run it. No money. No goods. No transport.' He still owns the store, and his daughter lives there, but he is no longer trading. He was pleased to hear from the late Litunga Yeta IV that he had met the Susman family at the Victoria Falls in 1999 and that they wanted to come back and do business. He now says: 'Tell Mr Susman. They should come back.'[19]

Benson Kamitondo was not a store manager, but worked at a somewhat higher level. He lives on the outskirts of Mongu on the Limulunga Road in a good house, which he built in the late 1960s on the advice of Maurice Rabb and Elton Joffe who both visited it on its completion. Born in 1922 and educated at Sefula, he worked for many years from 1948 with the Model Dairy in Bulawayo. After his return to Mongu in 1962 he began work with

Susman Brothers & Wulfsohn in the wholesale department and retains a good knowledge of the merchandise that was sold and of the discounts that were offered in the wholesale department. He worked closely with Nell and van Rensburg, and remembers Rabb and Kates as visiting directors. He feels that he was well treated by his employers and recalls that he was flown to hospital in Livingstone on the Central African Airways Beaver at the company's expense; his employers told the hospital to look after him, as he was a useful man. Like others who had worked with Susman Brothers & Wulfsohn he was not very happy with Zambesi Trading, the successor company, and resigned a few years after the takeover. Like Liswaniso and Mukwendela, he wishes that the Susmans would come back.[20]

Kamitondo is a Lozi traditionalist and became an induna at Lealui in 1991, with the title Mutwaleti. His role was to walk in front of the Litunga. During the 1990s he made a number of visits to Lusaka with the Litunga in an effort to get the government of Zambia to reinstate the Barotseland Agreement of 1964, which was abrogated in 1969, and to recognise once again the special status of Barotseland, which had then become known as the Western Province. When the Litunga, Yeta IV, and many indunas, went to meet the Susman family for their centenary celebration at the Victoria Falls in 1999, Kamitondo was asked as an old employee to say something about their contribution to Barotseland. He emphasised their roles as shopkeepers, as providers of transport, by road and river, and as buyers of cattle and hides. He also thought that their stores network and communications system supplemented the role of the post office in the delivery of letters, as they often had stores in places where there was no post office.

'African Advancement'

David Susman first raised the issue of training African staff for management positions in August 1960. Nathan Zelter then pointed out that CBC Ltd, the company's only real competitor in Northern Rhodesia, was employing Africans in more senior positions and had started a training school. He was also concerned that the reorganisation of CBC's merchandising department might result in stronger competition, especially in the northern part of the country. Discussion of 'African Advancement' was, however, deferred to a later meeting.[21] Two years later Susman suggested that the company should establish a training programme for African managers. He expressed the opinion that:

> ... as time went on it would be increasingly difficult to obtain European Staff who would be prepared to live in the bush, and in the interests of the organization the Company should lay down a two or three year training programme for say 6 Africans who had obtained a high standard of education, with a view to their obtaining the status of Assistant Group Manager or even Group Manager, if their merit warranted such a position.

He also suggested that they should start at a much higher salary than was usually paid. He did not get much support from his fellow directors who did not appear to understand his proposal. Maurice Rabb thought it would be impractical to employ people at a high salary who would be working as part of their training under store capitaos who were less well paid. Harry Wulfsohn thought that 'the progressive point of view was commendable', but that attention should rather be paid to the improvement of the housing of African staff. Promotion should come from within the company and he did not think that 'new employees should be introduced to higher positions'. Susman offered to draw up a memorandum on the subject, but the subject was not followed up.[22]

When, six months later, Nathan Zelter recommended that a second African stock-taker should be appointed to the Mongu group, Harry Robinson told him that Lionel Dix, the group manager, had assured him that 'there were no suitable Africans for this training'. Zelter and Major Campbell were then asked to produce a report on the subject of African advancement. At this point Zelter, whose political differences with Harry Robinson had reached a point of crisis after twenty-seven years, left the company. His successor, Geoff Kates, produced a report on the training and appointment of African supervisors to replace European stock-takers, which was adopted by the board. The first training course for African supervisors took place in January 1964, overseen by Rabb, Kates and Dix, and lasted for two weeks. Elton Joffe came up from Salisbury to take part in a second course later in the year. It was also agreed that there should be training of store managers within the groups.[23]

The emphasis was still on promotion from within the company. Steve Nell, the group manager in Fort Rosebery, identified one African employee in his group who had the ability to be promoted to a managerial position. James Kalufwelu was doing the job of a European and was promoted to the post of principal stock-taker, and was allowed to move into a house that had previously been occupied by a European member of staff. Kalufwelu, who was from the Northern Province, was the first Zambian member of staff to be appointed as a group manager. He took over the Batoka group on the departure of Derek Speares in 1965–6. It was not until the latter year that it was agreed that Maurice Rabb would seek to recruit 'suitable qualified and educated Zambians to be trained in supervisory capacities'.[24]

In his chairman's report to the Annual General Meeting of Stores Holdings, which was held in Livingstone on 28 October 1966, Harry Robinson had stated that:

> One of the biggest worries that the Directors have is that of staff. It is now becoming increasingly difficult to transfer European staff to Zambia or to get permission to engage new staff from outside it. We are trying to build up a staff of trained Africans who will be capable of taking over work previously done by Europeans, and training courses both on the trading and administrative sides of the business have been held. We do, however, require more of such staff than we already have, but it is not easy to get suitably educated Africans with the necessary capabilities for our kind of business.[25]

It is not clear what the results of this recruitment campaign were. A number of relatively well-educated Zambians did join the staff in senior positions in the following year or two. One of them, perhaps the most significant, was Job Kanenga Haloba. He was born in Bulawayo in 1940 to Tonga-speaking parents from Northern Rhodesia, and his father worked on the railways. Job did his primary education in Bulawayo and was then taken by a missionary family to Uganda where he completed his secondary education in 1964. He is proud of his Grade One passes in Cambridge O Level History and Maths, and still displays a remarkable knowledge of British constitutional history. He returned to Zambia, his 'home' – although he had not previously lived there – in 1965 and worked for two years with Zambia Railways.[26]

Haloba joined Susman Brothers & Wulfsohn as a senior stock-taker early in 1968, based at first in Livingstone, travelling to outlying stores in several groups, and then posted to Mongu in January 1969, succeeding Marian Payne as chief cashier there. He worked for only a year with the company in the days of its independence, but in the four or five years that he spent working closely with Lionel Dix, Steve Nell, Elton Joffe, Tim Payne and Geoff Kates he not only learnt a great deal about retail trade, but also developed a passionate loyalty to Susman Brothers & Wulfsohn and a belief in its ethos. He made it clear, when first interviewed in Livingstone in 2001, that he was prepared to talk about his days with the company, but only on condition that his evidence should not be used to its detriment. He was able to recall accurately, and without prompting, the names and numbers of almost all the stores in the Western, North-Western and Southern Provinces. He was also proud to be wearing a shirt and trousers that he had bought from

Zambesi Trading. The shirt was one of a dozen that he had bought from a consignment that had been ordered by Geoff Kates from London in the early 1970s. It was still in remarkably good condition.[27]

Job Haloba's account of his experiences in the late 1960s and early 1970s is not significantly different from that of the other managers who have been quoted. He has recollections of stocktaking, arriving in remote places by plane, Land Rover and boat. He recalls that produce buying was still going on, though it was usually only done at group headquarters. He bought rice, beeswax (in Mongu East and Kaoma), crocodile skins, ivory, rhino horn, leopard and lion skins. He remembers going to buy ivory from Chief Lukama, a son of King Lewanika, at Kaunga Mashi on the Angolan border in Senanga West. Runners were still employed to bring in cash boxes, which they carried in sacks, but this practice was stopped after a runner from Kalongola stole the money and claimed that he had been robbed. Porters were still used occasionally to carry goods between Mongu and Sefula when the roads were impassable during the rains.

In Haloba's view, Susman Brothers & Wulfsohn, with its vehicles, motorised barges and aircraft, was ahead of its time. He has no doubt that the economic reforms were a disaster. By 1973 he was stores operations manager for Zambesi Trading in the Western and North-Western Provinces. He resigned in 1977, soon after the takeover by NIEC. Like Maurice Rabb, he regretted the politicisation of the company and felt that it was not run on proper business lines. The managing director of NIEC Stores was General Sakala. Haloba asks, rhetorically, what a general would know about trading. Would he know that you cannot sell red and white cloth in Luapula Province, or that in some places it is necessary to stockpile goods before the annual floods make them inaccessible? He feels that the new management was suspicious of people, like himself, who had worked closely with the white managers of Zambesi Trading. He recalls that in about 1973 Dr Rajah Kunda, then minister of commerce and industry, summoned him to Lusaka to explain what 'the Susmans' had done with Zambesi Saw Mills' machinery. Kunda apparently believed that the failure of Zambesi Saw Mills was the result of industrial sabotage, and that Haloba, as 'a friend of the Susmans', should be able to explain what was going on.

Susman Brothers & Wulfsohn had a remarkable ability to inculcate loyalty into its staff, whether black or white. The example of Job Haloba suggests that they would have done well to begin the process of 'African advancement' and 'Zambianisation' when it was first mooted in 1960, if not earlier. The company also attracted a remarkable degree of loyalty from its customers, but that is rather more difficult to document. The end of Zambesi Trading coincided more or less with the impact of the severe recession that was associated with the oil crisis of 1973–4 and the subsequent collapse of copper prices. The collapse of retail trade, and the economic regression of the rural areas of the Western Province, which was painfully evident to visitors by the mid 1980s, may have been primarily a consequence of the recession, but it is clear that it was also the consequence of the disintegration of management, and the politicisation, of parastatal retail chains such as NIEC. It was easy for the government and its advisors to underestimate the difficulty of running retail stores in a very difficult environment. The collapse of produce buying and cattle buying also had serious consequences for the economy of remote rural areas. Simon Zukas recalls that when he was elected as MP for the remote Sikongo constituency in 1991, one of the first requests of his constituents was that he should arrange to 'bring back Susman Brothers & Wulfsohn'. Ten years later this was still a popular refrain. The establishment of a branch of the South African retail chain, Shoprite Checkers, in Mongu in the late 1990s had done nothing to restore rural trading networks, but made life difficult for the small class of local shop-keeping entrepreneurs. Some of them had learnt their trade with Susman Brothers & Wulfsohn and had taken over stores from its successors.[28]

CHAPTER 15

Werners: The Copperbelt and the Central African Cattle Trade, 1944–75

The other half of the twin businesses taken over or established by the Susman brothers and Harry Wulfsohn in 1944 was Werner and Company. While Susman Brothers & Wulfsohn built up an extensive rural trading network, Werners was primarily a Copperbelt business with close links to one of the two large copper-mining companies. Almost all of its retail outlets, and all of its cold stores, were in the Copperbelt towns, Lusaka and Livingstone, but as a company that traded in cattle and beef, it had strong rural roots and connections. The disappearance, for the moment anyway, of most of Werners's own records make it difficult to tell the story of the retail butchery business, and its relationship with its customers, in any detail. The main focus of this chapter is on Werners's involvement in the complex politics of the central African cattle trade. As was the case in the 1920s and 1930s, this not only involved Northern Rhodesia, but also Southern Rhodesia, Bechuanaland and the Congo. This chapter also deals with the impact of the Federation of Rhodesia and Nyasaland, and of the Colonial Development Corporation in Bechuanaland, on the regional trade in cattle and beef. The story of the farms and ranches is told in a later chapter.[1]

When the Susman and Wulfsohn partnership took control of Werners in 1944, its main activity was the supply of beef on contract to the Rhodesian Selection Trust mines at Mufulira and Luanshya. It also had retail outlets in those towns and a butchery at Ndola. The latter was the only place where Werners was in direct competition with Copperfields Cold Storage, which supplied the Anglo American mines at Nkana and Nchanga. These two companies operated more or less as a cartel, dividing the market between them, and also co-operating to keep down the price of cattle. Harry Wulfsohn became the managing director of Werners and his main lieutenant on the Copperbelt was Eric Speck, who acted as secretary/accountant of the company.

Speck was born in Wales in 1910 and came to Northern Rhodesia in 1921 with his father, who worked as a hotel manager in Lusaka and Mazabuka. Eric started work as a clerk with Rhodesia Railways and stayed with them for ten years. After a short time back in Wales he returned to Northern Rhodesia and joined Werners in 1939, working under E. W. Dechow, Mrs Werner's Australian manager. He stayed with the company for most of thirty years, becoming general manager in 1953. A sportsman who played rugby for various local teams, he was also a prominent Mason and became chairman of the Mufulira Township Management Board. He was a good accountant, but he did not have the overall understanding of the politics and dynamics of the cattle industry that was needed to take the company forward. Harry Wulfsohn had that understanding, but he was not able to devote all his time and energy to Werners.[2]

When Maurice Rabb arrived in Northern Rhodesia in January 1947, he noted that the profits of Werners were unsatisfactory. He must also have seen that there were problems with the management of the company. In the later months of the year the *Livingstone Mail* gave a great deal of prominence to a long-running case in which Werners and two of its butchery capitaos were charged with various offences under the price control regulations, and the weights and measures legislation. The alleged offences were committed at African butcheries in Mufulira. The case arose from a well-planned 'sting' operation in which meat was bought and immediately weighed. The company was eventually found guilty on five counts and fined a total of £1,000 – the two capitaos were fined £1 each. The magistrate did not think that they should take much of the blame, as their work was largely unsupervised. Neither Speck nor his senior butcher, C. J. Davies, came out of the case well. The standard of cleanliness was poor and the scales had been faulty for some months.[3]

Harry Wulfsohn, who was only able to visit the Copperbelt every month or two, realised that the company needed stronger management. He proceeded, with the help of Elie Susman, to recruit Max Barnett to Werners. Barnett was undoubtedly the best man for the job. He had been on the Copperbelt since 1929 and had worked for Copperfields Cold Storage since its inception. He was induced to move by the offer of ten per cent stakes in Werners, and Susman Brothers & Wulfsohn. He may also have been encouraged to leave Copperfields by the arrival on the Copperbelt of Len Pinshow, son-in-law of his long-time boss, Isadore Kollenberg. Barnett started work for Werners in January 1948, moving with his family from Kitwe to Mufulira.[4]

Max Barnett was born at Laingsburg in the Karoo in 1905. His father, Hyman Barnett, was a Jewish trader there, but moved to Kimberley: his mother was a Dorman – her family was involved in the crayfish business at Hout Bay in the Cape. Barnett was educated at the Christian Brothers' School in Kimberley – he had no more than a junior secondary school education, but his letters and memoranda indicate that he had a first-class mind. He acquired an exceptionally clear understanding of the complexities of the central African cattle industry and the ability to articulate his views on them.[5]

In the early 1930s Barnett worked under the direction of Isadore Kollenberg and Elie Susman, and in partnership with his near contemporary, Maurice Gersh, in the establishment of Northern Caterers and Copperfields. He was given responsibility for Nkana, Nchanga and Mufulira, and ran the butcheries, bottle stores and tearooms belonging to the two companies in those towns. He was closely associated with the construction of the hotels at Nkana and Nchanga. In 1934 he married Sylvia Emdin, a member of a prominent Jewish family in Muizenburg. The Barnetts played an active role in the social life of Kitwe and Mufulira for many years. Barnett was not only a cattleman, but also a lover of horses. In the post-war years he was a co-founder of both the Kitwe Polo Club and the Mufulira Gymkhana Club.

Barnett worked for eighteen years with Isadore Kollenberg. This was quite an achievement and was an indication that he was capable of tact, though he did not always use it. Kollenberg was not an easy man with whom to deal, as his son-in-law, Len Pinshow, would testify. Elie Susman compared him to a gramophone – 'he goes on and on'. Barnett's switch of allegiance from Copperfields to Werners was a blow to Kollenberg and did not contribute to harmonious relations between the two groups. The Copperbelt butchers' cartel was probably doomed from the moment that Barnett changed sides, though it did survive for some years. The relationship between Elie Susman and Isadore Kollenberg was never good, but that between Max Barnett and Len Pinshow, who succeeded him in the management of Copperfields, was worse.

Pinshow was ten years younger than Barnett. A chartered accountant with a degree from the University of the Witwatersrand, he had served with Montgomery's 8th Army during the war. He was sent home for political reasons and was later associated with the progressive war-veterans' organisation, the Springbok Legion. Barnett had served in the Northern

Rhodesian Defence Force, a kind of home guard, but had not done full-time military service. Barnett was a forceful character and had, through long residence and hard work, become a part of the Copperbelt establishment. Recognition of this came when he was made an OBE (Officer of the Order of the British Empire) in 1957. Pinshow took some pride in his reputation for abrasiveness, and did not fit so easily into the colonial social scene. He devoted much of his considerable energy to the organisation of sports on the Copperbelt and to involvement in national politics at the local level. He received a lesser honour – the MBE (Member of the Order of the British Empire) for his services to sport in 1959. It was no doubt difficult for Pinshow that Barnett, after his change of allegiance to a firm that was closely linked to Rhodesian Selection Trust, continued to enjoy a close relationship with the other side, the managers of Anglo American, with whom he had worked for most of twenty years.[6]

Barnett succeeded very quickly in turning around Werners's business on the Copperbelt. The existence of the cartel, and the 'closed township' regulations in Kitwe, Chingola and Mufulira precluded the expansion of either group into the other's territory there. It was for this reason that Barnett's first target for expansion was Lusaka – the still relatively new, but rapidly

12 Harry Wulfsohn, Max Barnett, Mike Pretorius and pilot, with De Havilland Rapide aircraft, Livingstone or Barotseland, early 1950s.

growing capital. Abe Galaun had quickly established himself as the dominant figure in the butchery business in Lusaka in the post-war years. Until his death in August 2003 he remained a major figure in Lusaka: he was the last survivor in the country of a generation of energetic Jewish immigrants and entrepreneurs who made their mark on the Northern Rhodesian/Zambian business scene in the twentieth century.

Galaun's remarkable life story has now been told several times. He was born at Vorne in Lithuania in 1913, the son of a butcher. He followed three brothers to southern Africa. He was not allowed to stay in South Africa and reached Northern Rhodesia in February 1939. After a short time in Livingstone, where he stayed with a cousin, Max Taube, he became involved in the collection of scrap iron for sale to the mines. His first real break came when he got a job as a store manager and labour recruiter in Barotseland, working for the reclusive Jehiel Jacobs. He spent most of the war years in Mongu and benefited from the revival of the Barotseland cattle trade. Having accumulated some capital, he moved to Lusaka at the end of the war, buying a share in a butchery from Tubby Wulfsohn. The other partner was E. W. Dechow – the former manager of Werners. Galaun soon bought out Dechow and then took on Sam Haslett, a Scots veteran of the Barotseland cattle trade, who still controlled the Livestock Cooperative Butchery in Cairo Road. By January 1946 he had taken over Haslett's business and established Lusaka Cold Storage Limited.[7]

According to Abe Galaun, the merger of his business with Werners in 1948 resulted from a clash with Max Barnett over cattle supplies. The cattle in question belonged to Fanie van Rensburg at Leopard's Hill Ranch. Galaun had established a good relationship with him when they stayed together at the Lusaka Hotel in 1945. As was often the case with Jews, Scots and Afrikaners, they found that they had a common interest in theological debate. According to Galaun's account, he agreed to buy 300 cattle from van Rensburg on credit, intending to pay for them after selling them. Barnett thought that Werners had a first claim to the Leopard's Hill cattle and tried to stop the sale by suggesting that Galaun would be unable to pay. Van Rensburg then asked for cash, and Galaun persuaded a bank manager to come up with a substantial unsecured loan. Galaun claimed that Barnett then threatened to close him down by cutting him off from sources of supply. The other side of the story may, of course, be that Galaun was short of capital and Werners could supply it. In the course of 1948 Lusaka Cold Storage became a subsidiary of Werners, which took a sixty per cent share in the company. Galaun retained the management and the voting shares were split, as with Werners itself, on a fifty-fifty basis. This arrangement was to be the source of much trouble and strife in later years. It was probably Barnett's intention to buy out Galaun and take complete control of the company. Elie Susman was, however, pleased with the new subsidiary's performance and suggested that Galaun should be left in place. Werners was able to acquire through Lusaka Cold Storage a dominant place in the butchery business of the growing town.[8]

Ngamiland and the CDC

Werners also had a close relationship with the Ngamiland Trading Company, which controlled at least half of the Ngamiland cattle trade. The Susman brothers held two-thirds of the shares in this business. Their managing partner, who owned the other third, was Alf 'Chobo' Weskob, and Werners was the sole importer of their exports. Weskob was the dominant figure in Ngamiland from the mid 1930s until his death in 1965. He was born in Doornfontein, Johannesburg, in 1900. His father was a Polish Jew and his mother an American Jew. He was certainly not 'observant' and would, in any case, have had little opportunity to practise his religion in Maun. He married Mary Kays, daughter of Old Tom, and sister of Young Tom. According to his brother, Cid, 'Chobo' had joined the army during the First World War, and moved to New York soon after it, working for the Yellow Cab Company, but left in a hurry after a brush with the New York Police. He seems to have moved to Bechuanaland in the early 1920s and worked his way from Serowe to Ngamiland. By the mid 1930s, he had become the Susmans' key man in Ngamiland. Alex Vlotamas who worked for him, and also in competition with him, says that he was well known to everyone in Ngamiland 'from the smallest baby to the oldest granny'. He was a fluent speaker of Setswana, and was also able to communicate with the Damara in their language, and with the Kalahari Bushmen, or San, in at least one of their many languages. His nickname 'Chobo' reflected his size and solidity, coming from a Setswana word for the part of the trunk of a tree from which a maize mortar is carved. According to his brother 'he was a bushman, he hated town life'. Like Harry Wulfsohn, his real love was cattle trading; he would happily spend an hour and a half buying an ox.

Cid Weskob joined his brother in Maun in 1944 and stayed for eighteen months. Life in wartime Maun was not easy. He recalls it as dominated by malaria, mosquitoes and lions. He claims that the ruts in the tracks within the village were so deep that it was possible to drive a truck from the

Ngamiland Trading Company's headquarters to Riley's Hotel without touching the steering wheel. Social life revolved around the hotel where 'Chobo' and others played tickey dice with the Greeks. 'Chobo' went there every evening, but his dog took him home at seven o'clock.[9]

The export of cattle from Ngamiland to Northern Rhodesia began again in 1939 after a lapse of five or six years. Large numbers of cattle were trekked north and swum across the Zambezi at Kazungula in the war years to supply the country's expanded demand for beef. Wartime exports reached a peak of 8,000 head in 1943, but were reduced to about 6,000 by a foot-and-mouth outbreak in the following year. In the post-war period, exports from Ngamiland via Kazungula reached a peak of over 10,000 head in 1950 and 1951. Records for the Ngamiland Trading Company are sparse, but a balance sheet for 1946–7 suggests that it had become a profitable business. In that year it had six bases of operations, at Maun, Tsau, Tholomore, Gomare, Sepopa and Shakawe, and made a gross profit of £24,000, or forty-four per cent of turnover, and a net profit before taxation of about £14,000. Most of the profits came from the sale of goods and only a small proportion came from the sale of cattle. This may, of course, have been an accounting device.[10]

The smooth running of the cattle trade from Ngamiland to Northern Rhodesia was threatened from 1951 onwards by the arrival on the scene of the Colonial (later Commonwealth) Development Corporation (CDC) with its visionary scheme for the development over eighteen years of a 16,000-square mile ranch, divided into eighteen units, in the Chobe Crown Lands in northern Bechuanaland. This was intended to produce 69,000 cattle a year from a herd of 360,000 animals. It was in connection with this project that the writer Laurens van der Post had his first contact with the Kalahari. He later claimed that Harry Susman had introduced him to the region.[11]

The idea was that cattle from this vast ranch would be supplied to the abattoir that the CDC planned to build at Lobatse. Nothing much came of the ranching scheme, but the CDC acquired monopoly control over all exports of cattle from Bechuanaland. Representatives of CDC, visiting Lusaka in September 1951, made it clear that they were not keen on the Kazungula route as it passed through their projected ranch, but they acknowledged that they would not be able to take control of cattle exports until 1953. The flow of cattle through Kazungula, though not from Ngamiland as a whole, soon came to an end, at least for a while – only 2,000 cattle were crossed in 1953 and very few in 1954. The intervention of the CDC had a more dramatic effect on exports of cattle from the eastern Line of Rail region of Bechuanaland. Exports to the north from this area were running at over 20,000 a year in the early 1950s. They were organised through the Northern Cattle Exporters' Pool, which involved Werners, Copperfields and Elakat, the Congo cattle conglomerate. Although intended to keep down the price of cattle, this pool paid premium prices in the early 1950s – above the Johannesburg price – in order to secure supplies in a highly competitive market. Some cattle from Bechuanaland were slaughtered at Livingstone and sent up to the Congo as chilled beef. From the latter half of 1954 onwards, cattle from eastern Bechuanaland were no longer exported northwards on the hoof, but were diverted to the south for slaughter at the newly opened Lobatse abattoir.[12]

In anticipation of the changes which would result from the opening of the Lobatse abattoir – originally planned for the end of 1952 – Susman Brothers & Wulfsohn proposed to the government of Northern Rhodesia in March 1952 that it should take over the Livingstone Cold Storage Works. It intended to use it as a central store and distribution centre for the chilled beef that was expected to flow from Lobatse. It clearly had the Congo and Copperbelt markets in mind. The government was reluctant to sell the works to the Susman group on its own and suggested that it consult the other butchers with a view to joint action, but the group rejected this proposal. Barnett and Wulfsohn, who had represented the group at meetings with Welensky and other representatives of the government, were correct to anticipate the need for a central cold store to cope with the import of large quantities of chilled beef.[13]

The Federation

In addition to the advent of the CDC and its plans for Bechuanaland, a further complication for Werners was the establishment of the Federation in 1953. There were marked differences in the way in which the cattle and beef markets operated in Northern and Southern Rhodesia. Cattle marketing in Northern Rhodesia had been controlled since 1937 by the Cattle Marketing and Control Board, which had statutory powers. It was composed of representatives of European farmers, butchers and the mining companies that were the main consumers. The director of veterinary services chaired the committee and another member of the Veterinary Department represented the interests of African producers. The main purpose of the Board was to protect the European ranching industry, which had suffered from low prices and low demand during the depression. It was originally intended to fix minimum prices for the sale of cattle and to limit imports until internal supplies were exhausted. The coming of the war created a massive demand for copper and for beef to feed the greatly enlarged workforce. The Board then sought to fix maximum prices for the sale of cattle and to keep down the price of 'compound' beef for the mining companies. The importation of Ngamiland cattle was one way of achieving this objective.[14]

In the post-war years the beef market in Northern Rhodesia remained largely in the hands of the two dominant groups, Werners and Copperfields. They operated within a highly regulated environment, which included retail price controls and, at times, meat rationing and subsidies. The butchers had, through the Cattle Marketing and Control Board, some influence over these regulations and were able to make good profits within this regulatory framework. Werners had a stronger voice on the Board than Copperfields, as their men, Max Barnett and Robert Boyd, sat on it for many years as the representatives of, respectively, the butchers and the cattle producers. Their ally, Geoff Beckett, was a founder member of the Board, and an advocate of the marketing system, which he had designed. He was the Legislative Council's member for agriculture for five years from 1949, and rejoined the Board in 1956. The long-serving director of veterinary services, John Hobday, was chairman of the Board from 1943 to 1954. He had a close association with the Susman group going back to his days as chief veterinary officer in Bechuanaland. By the early 1950s, Werners and Susman Brothers & Wulfsohn had become the main allies of the government of Northern Rhodesia in the management of country's cattle and beef industries. As a later government report indicated: 'The willingness of private enterprise to establish the necessary cold storage and handling facilities and to ensure continued supplies from outside the Territory was of great assistance to Government at a time when it was hard pressed to keep abreast of economic development...'.[15]

The demand for beef in the early 1950s was so great that the system of maximum prices began to break down. Butchers were prepared to pay higher prices for cattle, and to accept lower profit margins, within the system of price controls. The maximum price system was replaced in 1953 by a system under which the butchers undertook to adhere to 'fair indicated prices'. These were based on an estimate of producer costs and a reasonable margin between them and controlled retail prices. Price controls on meat were not abandoned in either of the Rhodesias, or South Africa, until 1956.[16]

In Southern Rhodesia the industry was controlled by the Cold Storage Commission, which was set up in 1938. This was an institution of the state and controlled the wholesale beef market. It did not simply make policy, but bought and sold cattle, becoming the major player in the market. It took over the Imperial Cold Storage business in Southern Rhodesia, together with its manager, Abe Gelman, who, as will appear in later chapters, became a partner of Susman Brothers & Wulfsohn in Zambesi Saw Mills and Northern Rhodesia Textiles. He had learnt the beef business in the Congo from his father-in-law, Barnett 'Bongola' Smith, and was a shrewd and tough operator. He set up the Commission and it continued to run on lines that he had devised. It was, together with Liebigs, the monopoly buyer of cattle from the African reserves. With the help of compulsory de-stocking policies, it was able to get African-owned cattle at very low prices. It ran a 'grazier' scheme under which it sold African cattle to European farmers who fattened the stock and sold them back to the Commission. Geoff Beckett told Welensky in 1957 that 'The Northern Rhodesian Government has for many years been of the opinion that the Cold Storage Commission has ridden on the back of the native cattle producer and in fact the native has subsidised European production.'[17]

It has been alleged that the policies of the Cattle Marketing and Control Board in Northern Rhodesia had a similar effect to those of the Cold Storage Commission in Southern Rhodesia, in so far as they pushed up the price of prime stock, mainly produced by settler farmers, and kept down the prices of 'compound' stock. In fact, Northern Rhodesian settler farmers produced very few prime cattle, and shortage of stock tended to push up the price of all grades of cattle. Prices were generally higher in Northern than in Southern Rhodesia. When the Southern Rhodesian grading system was applied to Northern Rhodesia in the early 1960s, it was found that both European and African-produced cattle were downgraded to a similar degree. It is probably true, however, that the price of low-grade stock would have been higher if it had not been for imports from Ngamiland.[18]

On the establishment of the Federation, the Cold Storage Commission made no immediate move to enter the Northern Rhodesian market. It had no surplus for export at that time. Nor was there an immediate attempt to establish a federal Cold Storage Commission. Northern Rhodesian interests hoped for the establishment of a federal Cattle Marketing and Control Board on their model. They also hoped that John Hobday would be transferred to the federal government to help manage the marketing of cattle on a federal basis. Such a move would have strengthened the position of Northern Rhodesia and Bechuanaland, where he had also served, as against Southern Rhodesian interests. Geoff Beckett was disappointed that this did not happen and Hobday was, instead, seconded to the CDC in

Bechuanaland for a year to help with the establishment of the Lobatse abattoir. Under pressure from the Northern Rhodesian Cattle Marketing and Control Board, the federal minister of agriculture, J. M. Caldicott, did agree in May 1956 to recommend the establishment of a federal Cattle and Beef Advisory Committee. This did not have the statutory powers of the Board, and it appears to have been unable to resolve the conflicts that developed between Northern and Southern Rhodesian interests.[19]

The impact of the CDC on Bechuanaland's exports, and on the local trade in beef, became apparent when the Lobatse abattoir came into full production in the second half of 1954. Chilled beef from Lobatse replaced cattle on the hoof from eastern Bechuanaland as Northern Rhodesia's main source of imported beef. The Veterinary Department reported on the effects of this change:

> While this method of handling has some advantages, it is more expensive and creates problems for a meat trade which hitherto has been organised to handle live cattle. In the past it was a normal practice of the trade to maintain a relatively large reserve of imported slaughter cattle on ranches and on holding grounds near the main consuming areas, thus ensuring that any interruption of railway services did not interfere with meat supplies. Owing to the lack of extensive cold storage facilities reserves of imported chilled meat cannot be so held, and the meat supply has therefore become more liable to interruption.[20]

This change had other consequences for the butchers. With chilled beef they lost the 'fifth quarter', composed of hides, heads, tails and offal, which was a major source of their profits. Furthermore, offal was the most popular type of meat among African consumers and was unavailable with chilled beef. It has been suggested that by forcing chilled beef onto a reluctant market in Northern Rhodesia, the CDC prepared the way for Southern Rhodesian chilled beef and unintentionally undermined its own market. Bechuanaland's change to chilled beef exports also had adverse consequences for the Cold Storage Board's Livingstone abattoir. It was no longer able to slaughter stock from eastern Bechuanaland, which had provided a good deal of its turnover.[21]

In the early months of 1955, the Cattle Marketing and Control Board debated the question of whether the new cold stores, which were required to handle chilled beef from Lobatse, should be built by state or private enterprise. It decided in favour of the latter. This was an issue that divided the two big butchery groups. Max Barnett and Werners favoured private enterprise, while Copperfields, which was not directly represented on the Board, favoured state enterprise. There had apparently been a vote on this issue in the recently established association of butchers, the Federation of Meat Distributors, in which Werners and its allies outvoted Copperfields. The latter company favoured the extension of the activities of the Southern Rhodesian Cold Storage Commission to Northern Rhodesia. Its chairman, Isadore Kollenberg, lived in Bulawayo, was a rancher there, and was in close touch with Southern Rhodesian cattle interests. Copperfields soon established an informal alliance with the Cold Storage Commission and withdrew from the Federation of Meat Distributors.[22]

Meanwhile, Werners undertook, with the authority of the Cattle Marketing and Control Board, and the support of the Northern Rhodesian government, to raise funds for the building of a large new cold store at Kitwe. It was, of course, Max Barnett who was the driving force behind this development. The building of the central cold store was only part of his project for the expansion of the company. His second project was to break the Copperbelt butchers' cartel by competing directly with Copperfields in the towns that were their preserve – Kitwe and Chingola. There were a number of reasons for this move. There was an element of retaliation involved. Copperfields had apparently initiated the battle by applying for licences in Livingstone and Lusaka, though there is no evidence that they obtained them. At the same time the Anglo American Corporation had been embarrassed for some time by Copperfields's near monopoly of the butchery business in Kitwe and Chingola. It encouraged Werners to move into these towns and to provide real competition. It was prepared to offer part of its mine meat contracts as an inducement, but it did so with the warning that these contracts were about to be phased out. In the course of 1956 Anglo American and Rhodesian Selection Trust both ended the supply of rations to most of their workers and replaced them with an inclusive cash wage. This was as a result of pressure from the African Mineworkers' Union. The importance of the mines' meat contracts consequently declined, but the distribution of meat through retail butcheries became more important.

Another factor behind the breakdown of the cartel may have been the need to enlarge the market for the planned Kitwe Cold Store. Disagreement over the role of the Cold Storage Commission contributed to the souring of an already poor relationship, and added to the real antagonism that existed between the two groups. Although Werners was already doing more business than Copperfields, as a result of its move into Lusaka's growing market, it could only establish real dominance in the butchery business if it took on Copperfields on its home ground.[23]

These expansionist moves involved an investment of about £200,000 in the erection of the cold store in Kitwe, which was built by a new subsidiary, Central African Cold Storages Ltd. They also involved the takeover or construction of new butchery premises in Ndola, Luanshya and Chingola, as well as in Kitwe and its compounds: Mindola, Wusikili and Chamboli. Elie Susman reckoned that Barnett's schemes required £350,000 in new capital. Harry Wulfsohn, with whom Barnett continued to enjoy a prickly, though creative, relationship, played the major part in raising this new money. Elie Susman was concerned that 'they had bitten off more than they could chew'. He was especially worried that they would have difficulty getting the right personnel. They apparently solved this problem by increasing salaries and poaching staff from Copperfields. Elie Susman was also anxious that the group as a whole had too much capital tied up in cattle and land. He reckoned that it had more than £350,000 invested in 15,000 head of cattle, valued at about £14 each, and about 140,000 acres of land valued at £1 an acre. He thought that they should reduce their cattle holdings by a third and use the capital released in the running of the business. David Susman was also concerned that they were 'radically over-trading' and that it might be necessary to bring in new equity capital.[24]

The construction of the new cold store, butchery and offices in Kitwe took over a year to complete. It was a substantial complex with eighteen chilling and freezing rooms in two blocks, together with a three-storey office block. A fine house for the managing director was built at the same time. In a reference to his equestrian activities, Max Barnett named it 'Tally-Ho'; it remains a landmark in Kitwe's Parklands suburb. On completion of the complex, the head office of Werners moved from Mufulira to Kitwe. In July 1955 the company recruited Frank Collins from Rand Cold Storage in Johannesburg to supervise this work and to run the cold store on its completion. At the same time there was expansion in Lusaka, where a bacon factory and associated cold store were completed early in 1956 in the name of Neill's Food Products, a subsidiary of Lusaka Cold Storage.[25]

In the following year Werners achieved a long-standing objective. It was able to buy the Livingstone Cold Storage Works and abattoir from the government. It set up a new subsidiary, the Zambesi Cold Storage and Export Company, to take over the abattoir and appointed the retiring director of veterinary services, John Hobday, to run it. By the date of this takeover, 20 July 1957, Werners had control of all the large cold storage facilities in the country and a dominant position in the wholesale beef business. The company also had, for a while, complete control of the Barotseland cattle trade, though it was soon to lose its position as monopoly buyer of cattle in that protectorate. In taking control of the Livingstone abattoir, Werners had defeated a bid from the Cold Storage Commission, which wanted to put pressure on Werners by opening up in the north. The federal minister of finance, Donald Macintyre, had told the Commission not to bid, but it went ahead anyway. He argued that it should not bid, as it was the policy of the federal government to support private enterprise. In rejecting its bid, the Northern Rhodesian government took account of the views of the Cattle Marketing and Control Board. The Board was convinced that the Livingstone abattoir should remain in the hands of 'a Northern Rhodesian interest', and that its ownership by the Cold Storage Commission would not be beneficial to Livingstone or the Barotseland cattle trade. Three of the five members of the Board present at this meeting, Barnett, Beckett and Boyd, were directors or employees of Werners or Susman Brothers & Wulfsohn, and it has to be acknowledged that they all had an interest in the outcome of the sale.[26]

Werners *Versus* the Cold Storage Commission

Meanwhile, a commission of inquiry had been set up to investigate cattle marketing in Southern Rhodesia. Its report, the Turner Report, was published in 1956, and was strongly critical of the Cold Storage Commission, especially of its exploitation of African producers. The government accepted its recommendations for liberalisation. As a result the Commission lost its monopoly of the African cattle trade and it was also exposed to competition in the market for cattle raised by settler farmers. This enabled Werners to intervene in the Southern Rhodesian market. It was able to buy cattle from African and settler producers, and, by doing so, to bid up the price of cattle from both sources in Southern Rhodesia – much to the annoyance of the Commission. In retaliation the Commission inspired a press campaign, which impugned Barnett's personal integrity, and was critical of Werners's continued imports of allegedly inferior stock from Ngamiland. The Commission also sought to increase its sales of chilled beef to Copperfields Cold Storage and other butchers on the Copperbelt.[27]

By this stage there was an all-out battle going on between Werners and the Commission. As the Horwood Report, looking back from 1963, described the situation:

> Soon after Federation a commercial battle for supplies had developed between the private enterprise butchers established in Northern Rhodesia and

the Cold Storage Commission; for markets; for export and import rights; for trading rights and the right to buy cattle, especially in Southern Rhodesia ... The Cold Storage Commission... claimed monopoly rights of import and export; the butchers claimed that they had embarked on heavy capital development at Government's request to ensure an even and adequate flow of beef to consumers and needed in return access to the cheapest supplies ... and to exports.[28]

Werners's position in this battle was weakened by the recession on the Copperbelt, which began in the middle of 1956, and lasted for several years. The market for beef may also have been affected by political boycotts. The butcheries in Lusaka and on the Copperbelt had since January 1954 been the object of boycotts, which were organised by the African National Congress. These had a political purpose as protests against the imposition of federation, but their immediate targets were discriminatory sales practices, including segregated shops and the sale of meat through 'hatches'. African nationalist leaders, including Harry Nkumbula and Kenneth Kaunda, also attacked the poor quality of meat sold by some butchers. Abe Galaun was the major protagonist in this conflict on the side of the butchers in Lusaka, where the boycott went on for two months. The dispute there was eventually resolved after late-night talks between Nkumbula and Galaun. On the Copperbelt the boycott was very short-lived. Max Barnett gave way to pressure gracefully and undertook to abandon discriminatory sales practices before the boycott started. He thus wrong-footed the organisers, and earned the praise of Kaunda, then secretary-general of the ANC. Copperfields was also a target of boycotts and was compelled to reorganise its shops. Occasional butchery boycotts, mainly over prices, continued for some years, and the eating of meat became a political issue. Kaunda stopped eating red meat in 1954 and has remained a vegetarian ever since.[29]

In spite of the recession, and the after-effects of the boycotts, Werners's turnover in the later months of 1957 was still about £120,000 a month. The Cold Storage Commission was also affected by the recession, and Werners's intervention in the Southern Rhodesian market forced up prices and damaged its position on its home ground. At the end of 1957 the two sides reached an uneasy truce. They negotiated a seven-year contract under which Werners undertook to get all its imports from Southern Rhodesia through the Commission, which, in its turn, undertook not to open depots in Northern Rhodesia. The agreement, which came into effect in January 1958, did not affect Werners's right to import cattle directly from Ngamiland, the Pandamatenga area of northern Bechuanaland, and the Caprivi Strip.[30]

This compromise arrangement between Werners and the Cold Storage Commission did not last long. Werners soon found that its activities, and the usefulness of its cold stores, was affected by the decision of the federal government to give the Commission monopoly control over all imports and exports of cattle and beef. This was an extraordinary decision, which demonstrated the dominance of Southern Rhodesian over Northern Rhodesian interests within the Federation. The federal government gave control over imports and exports to a Southern Rhodesian entity on which there was no representation of the north, and a quota on imports of cattle from Bechuanaland (including Ngamiland) was unilaterally imposed. There can be little doubt that the Commission intended the latter move to put pressure on Werners. At the same time the Commission refused to allow Werners to export chilled beef to the Congo from its Kitwe cold store. The Cattle Marketing and Control Board argued, on the other hand, that Werners should be allowed to export, so long as the local market was satisfied. Chilled beef had become available for export because the recession had caused the consumption of beef to drop by nearly a quarter in the first half of 1958. Werners was frustrated by its inability to import from Bechuanaland or to export to the Congo, but the Cold Storage Commission was equally frustrated by the refusal of the Cattle Marketing and Control Board to allow it to deal directly with Northern Rhodesian butchers. The Board insisted that the Commission could only send beef to its customers in the north, including Copperfields, under permit from itself, and it blocked some shipments.[31]

At the end of July 1958 Werners's directors wrote to the Commission offering to sell their three cold stores to it. This was a radical decision and a major change of tack. Max Barnett had fought a bitter battle with the Cold Storage Commission, and it is not certain that he was fully supportive of this move. As late as 19 August 1958, three weeks after Werners had made its offer to the Commission, he continued to argue eloquently, and at length, in the Cattle Marketing and Control Board against allowing the Commission to operate in Northern Rhodesia. He produced a string of arguments in favour of the current system and against the Commission, but by then the tide was turning against him. The Northern Rhodesian butchers had, as a result of the recession, failed for the first time to buy all the local cattle on offer. This undermined the confidence of the settler farmers in the system. It was, however, Copperfields that had declined to buy all the cattle offered to it by local suppliers, and this may have been a move calculated to discredit the system and to weaken Werners. Later in the year a meeting of farmers at Mazabuka voted in favour of inviting the Commission to enter Northern Rhodesia.[32]

Werners offered its cold stores for sale for £760,000. About £300,000 of this sum was for goodwill and was based on a generous estimate of the profits that would be lost in the three years subsequent to the sale of the cold stores. In its memorandum on the subject, Werners pointed out that it controlled more than sixty per cent of the market for meat in the country. It did so through its three cold stores and its thirty-six retail butcheries, twenty-nine of which were on the Copperbelt. The remainder were in Lusaka, Livingstone, Mongu and Fort Rosebery. It made it clear that its main reason for wishing to sell was its inability to make full use of its cold stores because of the restrictions on imports from Bechuanaland and exports to the Congo. It made a good deal of its historical role as a representative of private enterprise, its construction of cold stores at the request of the Northern Rhodesian government, and the impact on its business of two government-backed bodies, the CDC in Bechuanaland, and the Cold Storage Commission in Southern Rhodesia.[33]

In seeking federal government support for a takeover of Werners's cold stores, the Commission stated that it had given an undertaking to the Northern Rhodesian government not to operate in the country, but it anticipated that an invitation would soon be forthcoming. It feared that it would continue to experience difficulties in the Northern Rhodesian market so long as it had to compete with Werners. Its difficulties might, indeed, increase as the economic benefits of Werners's control of the cold stores became more apparent. It anticipated further pressure from Werners to block imports from Southern Rhodesia. At the same time the Commission listed numerous benefits for Northern Rhodesian producers that, it claimed, would flow from its own establishment in the north. These included the extension of its controversial 'grazier' scheme and its method of grading cattle 'on the hook' rather than 'on the hoof'. Ironically, while demanding monopoly control of the slaughter of cattle, it enumerated the advantages for 'private enterprise' that would result from its takeover of the cold stores. These would include the dismantling of Werners's 'near monopoly' and the encouragement of smaller butchers. It dismissed Werners's price for its assets as grossly inflated, and said that its claim for goodwill was groundless. It asserted that the cold stores were, in all probability, making substantial losses, and suggested that Werners might be forced into liquidation, in which case it should address its claim for compensation to the Northern Rhodesian government. The Commission also pointed out that control of the Kitwe cold store would facilitate its own access to the Congo market, and suggested that Northern Rhodesian producers might then be allowed a share of that market, which it currently monopolised in the interests of Southern Rhodesian producers.[34]

The federal minister of agriculture, J. M. Caldicott, supported the further investigation of Werners's offer. He pointed to the problems that had recently arisen as a result of Werners's attempt to export to the Congo, and the Cattle Marketing and Control Board's blocking of Southern Rhodesian exports to the north – 'to the great embarrassment of certain Northern Rhodesian butchers and of the Cold Storage Commission whose intake was organised to meet the requirements of the Northern Rhodesian contracts'. He made it clear that Werners was, through its large market share, and its domination of the Cattle Marketing and Control Board, performing much the same function as the Cold Storage Commission. It had long been recognised that it was difficult for 'the two systems ... to exist alongside each other'.[35]

It was a matter of some embarrassment to the federal government, as it acknowledged to itself, that it was the policy of the United Federal Party to support private enterprise. The takeover of Werners's cold stores by the Commission, a statutory body, amounted to nationalisation. The alternatives were that Werners should be forced into bankruptcy, which was politically unacceptable, or that it should be allowed to compete with the Commission on equal terms. It was probable that it would then obtain its imports from Bechuanaland, instead of Southern Rhodesia, and compete with the Commission in the Congo market. 'It had always been thought that the [Congo] market would be prejudiced if the Werner Group were allowed to enter it with inferior quality beef.'[36]

Negotiations on Werners's offer dragged on for well over a year and became very complex. The matter was discussed on several occasions by the federal cabinet, which referred it to its Economic and Development Committee. There were several meetings between representatives of Werners, including Max Barnett, Harry Wulfsohn and Maurice Rabb, and of the Commission, including its chairman, A. L. Bickle, and chief negotiator, Leon Levy. Although there does not appear to be a record of it, there was also a meeting involving the prime minister, Sir Roy Welensky, the minister of finance, Sir Donald Macintyre, and Max Barnett, Maurice Rabb and David Susman. According to the latter, Macintyre said that he thought that Werners's arguments in support of its claim for goodwill were 'pretty specious', but Welensky gave them some support. There is, however, a record of a meeting in June 1959 between Barnett, Wulfsohn, Rabb and Abe Galaun, and four members of the cabinet, including the ministers of finance, economic affairs, commerce and industry and agriculture.[37]

The Commission was determined to minimise the price to be paid and to ensure that the federal government paid as much of the price as possible. It maintained for the purposes of its initial negotiations with both Werners and the federal government that the Kitwe Cold Store, the most valuable asset, and two-thirds of the Lusaka Cold Store, were redundant for its purposes. The argument in relation to the Kitwe Cold Store was certainly false, as it had earlier acknowledged that it would be useful for the Congo market. It maintained that the Livingstone Cold Store was the only useful asset, and that the other cold stores would be purchased only for political reasons and for the sake of 'federalising' the cattle and beef market. It was also determined not to countenance any claim for goodwill. During the first round of serious face-to-face negotiations between the two sides in March 1959, Leon Levy argued that, in view of the recession, the sale of the cold stores was being negotiated at 'a most inopportune time'. Harry Wulfsohn said that he agreed with 'practically everything Mr Levy had said', but maintained that:

> Although trade during the last two years had been difficult, the Company had weathered the storm extremely well. The representatives of the group had come to the meeting with the intention of being reasonable but they had no intention of being talked out of their legitimate rights. There was no intention to give away for nothing that which had been built up over 30 to 40 years and in his opinion there could be no question of selling the works at their book value.

Max Barnett argued that in spite of the recession, and the loss of the mine contracts, Werners was still doing a big trade and supplying large quantities of meat through its retail shops. He was 'confident that the future was bright'. The prospects for the export of beef to Southern Rhodesia and overseas justified a claim for goodwill. Leon Levy responded that 'the Group were not selling a bright past but a black future. He could not under any circumstances recommend a payment for goodwill which did not exist.'[38]

Werners's strongest card in the negotiations was the threat to withdraw the offer of sale, and to remain in business in competition with the Commission, while demanding that it should be allowed to do so on equal terms. In the end the Cold Storage Commission increased its best offer from £400,000 to £435,000 and Werners reduced its price to £515,000, and the matter was referred to arbitration. In its own minutes Werners fixed its minimum price at £450,000, which was also the price favoured as a maximum by the federal minister of agriculture. It is not clear what the final price was, but it was probably close to £500,000. This price did include an element of compensation for loss of the wholesale business. The arbitrator was also asked to take into account the question of compensation for the cancellation of Werners's seven-year contract with the Commission, under the terms of which the latter had undertaken not to open cold stores in the north. The federal cabinet feared that consideration of this factor could push the price up to and beyond their limit. David Susman thinks that the final deal saved Werners, as its solvency was threatened by the recession and its inability to make full use of the cold stores. There can be no doubt that the viability of its investment in the cold stores was seriously undermined by its inability to import from Bechuanaland or export to the Congo. It may not have got the price that it asked for, but it did get more than it expected for its assets. The Cold Storage Commission took over the three cold stores and began to operate in Northern Rhodesia on 1 January 1960.[39]

The agreement with the Cold Storage Commission marked the end of Werners's short-lived control of the wholesale beef market in Northern Rhodesia. It was a setback for Max Barnett's vision of control by private enterprise. It was another example of the way in which the Federation of Rhodesia and Nyasaland, which the leaders of Susman Brothers & Wulfsohn had welcomed, worked against their own interests, and, arguably, against the interests of producers in Northern Rhodesia. Werners's position of almost complete control, which it had established by 1956–7, lasted for less than three years.

The recession also forced them to make some alterations to the retail business. It was found that some of the butcheries, which had been set up in the Kitwe 'compounds' and run by a subsidiary, the Rhodesia Meat and Provisions Company, were making losses. Werners obtained the permission of Anglo American to subdivide the shops. In some cases parts of the shops were leased as groceries to Kaldis and Company. Plans to build a new European butchery on a prestigious site in Coronation Square, Kitwe, were abandoned and the lease was offered for sale. Other plots and butchery premises in Kitwe and Mufulira were also sold or leased, in some cases to Asian traders. The sale of the cold stores improved Werners's financial position and it was able in 1960 to redouble its assault on Copperfields, which was already in a weakened position. Its chairman, Isadore Kollenberg, reported that Werners had made things 'hot for us'. His company was forced to the verge of bankruptcy and appealed to Welensky for compensation. The federal government, however, took the view that Copperfields was a retail chain and that its business was unaffected by the sale of the cold stores. Copperfields eventually made a new deal on supplies with the Cold Storage Commission and returned to profitability in the early 1960s.[40]

In 1962 Werners and Susman Brothers & Wulfsohn entered into a new long-term contract with the Cold Storage Commission for the supply of beef. In the terms of this contract the group agreed to take all its beef supplies from the Commission. It also agreed to bind its tenants and sub-tenants to do the same. It undertook, furthermore, not to compete with the Commission at government-organised cattle sales, though it could do so at privately organised sales. The Commission undertook in return to give substantial discounts to the group. The Horwood Report in 1963 was critical of this deal, which it saw as another example of the Commission's monopolistic 'all or nothing' approach. At the same time, Werners's Copperbelt butcheries were leased to the general manager, Eric Speck, who set up his own company, E. Speck and Co. This was not a subsidiary of Werners, but Werners received rent for the butcheries, based on a percentage of turnover. Werners was thus able to withdraw from direct involvement in retail trade and to become a ranching and rentier company.[41]

At about the same time an agreement was reached with Abe Galaun under which he leased the Lusaka butcheries and ran them independently. Werners retained its majority shareholding in Lusaka Cold Storage, and Galaun was unable to establish his full independence until the mid 1970s. The relationship with Galaun had always been a stormy one. He had been a reluctant seller of the Lusaka bacon factory and cold store, and David Susman recalls that he was 'a very difficult partner'. Abe Galaun, on the other hand, had a low opinion of partnerships in general. He told his biographer: 'The most detestable thing about partnerships is that you spend a lot of time in boardroom arguments when you should be getting things done out in the field. You also waste time planning how to outwit your partner's tricks of the trade.' He always saw his relationship with Werners and the Susman Brothers & Wulfsohn group as an unequal one. He protested that they were partners in his business, but he was not a partner in theirs.[42]

From 1962 onwards, Max Barnett's main activity as managing director was the supervision of the company's cattle-trading activities and farms. Although Werners's agreement with the Cold Storage Commission precluded it from operating as a wholesale butcher, it was not prevented from engaging in the cattle trade. It could raise, fatten and deal in stock, but was prevented from selling slaughter cattle directly to other butchers. The company's farming interests included Kansuswa Farm, near Mufulira, which had begun as a holding ground for cattle, but which became a major producer of pigs, and Chambishi Farm, which supplied Kitwe with most of its milk.

Independence

Werners had only managed to control the wholesale beef business of Northern Rhodesia for three years, but the federalised Cold Storage Commission did not last for much longer. By April 1963 Max Barnett was able to tell Harry Wulfsohn that 'the political and economic break-up of the Federation is now under way'. He turned his fertile mind to a scheme for regaining control of the wholesale beef market. He considered that there were three possible alternatives for the future organisation of the business. A Northern Rhodesian Cold Storage Commission could take over the assets of the federal Cold Storage Commission and continue on the same lines. The Northern Rhodesian government could set up a producers' co-operative which could perform the same functions. A third possibility was that the government could sell or lease the Cold Storage Commission's assets, which he valued at £500,000, to private enterprise. In spite of the large financial commitment that would be involved, he thought that this alternative had the best potential for Werners. It would enable it to safeguard the retail business of Speck and Company and its own stake in its profits. He reckoned that there was a potential turnover of £1,000,000 a year. A move of this kind would also enable the company to safeguard its cattle-trading and ranching activities. This was 'quite apart from any prospective profit-earning potential in enlarged cattle and meat trading activities brought about through the possession of Cold Storage works and free trading rights'.[43]

He also suggested that the government should be asked to lease the assets of the Cold Storage Commission to a joint venture between Werners and the Northern Rhodesian Industrial Development Corporation. Werners would have a management contract and the new company would provide a guaranteed market to producers in exchange for control over imports and exports. He argued that:

> In this way Government will secure the services of people experienced in the marketing of cattle and beef in Northern Rhodesia and be enabled to establish an organisation in which the interests ... of cattle producers are safe-guarded. We in return will benefit through the control at source of supplies to the retail shops and share in what could undoubtedly become a substantial profit-making venture.

Nothing came of this scheme, and on the dissolution of the Federation the government of Northern Rhodesia set up its own Cold Storage Board – it became the Cold Storage Board of Zambia at independence in October 1964. Werners's contract with the old Cold Storage Commission was unaffected by the independence of Zambia and the establishment of the new board. The new government drew upon Max Barnett's expertise, but he survived for less than a year under the new dispensation. He died on 9 October 1965 at the age of sixty. Unknown to his partners, he had been ill with leukaemia for some time. His death was a blow to Werners, but also to Susman Brothers & Wulfsohn as a whole. His readiness to envisage joint ventures with the new government suggests that his advice could have been useful in the transitional period.

Following the death of Max Barnett, Jack Tuffin was appointed as general manger of Werners and took up his appointment in January 1966. The lease of the butcheries to Eric Speck was renewed in 1967, but at that time Werners took a fifty per cent share in his company. When the government re-imposed price controls on meat on 1 January 1968, after a lapse of twelve years, the butcheries almost all began to make losses. Edwin Wulfsohn thought that price controls had exposed the weaknesses of Speck's style of management. The butcheries made profits, but there was poor supervision and little control of pilferage. Speck was reluctant to pay good salaries and did not attract the best block men. He also economised on maintenance and most of the cold rooms were in a poor state of repair. Werners took complete control of the business in October 1968 and Speck retired six months later – after an association with Werners that had lasted for thirty years.[44]

The Mulungushi Reforms of April 1968 threatened the butchery business in much the same way as they did the stores business, though there was some dispensation in relation to licences for businesses involved in the supply of food. Following the death of his father in August 1968, Edwin Wulfsohn returned to Zambia with the primary purpose of restoring the profitability of Werners. He negotiated a new deal with the Cold Storage Board of Zambia. Its chairman, Oliver Irwin, a chartered accountant who had arrived in Northern Rhodesia in 1950, had a close association with the butchery business as a friend of Len Pinshow, and as auditor to Copperfields Cold Storage. He was also close to President Kaunda. He decided that, as a result of the Mulungushi Reforms and the pressure that it put on expatriate businesses, there was a need for the Cold Storage Board to become involved in the retail market. He reached an agreement with Edwin Wulfsohn under which the Cold Storage Board would lease seventeen butcheries from Werners for a period of five years from 1 April 1970.[45]

Edwin Wulfsohn hoped that the Cold Storage Board would eventually buy the butcheries. It was, however, adversely affected by the recession, which hit Zambia from 1974 onwards, and it was unable to do so. Werners gradually sold off its large portfolio of shops and other properties on the Copperbelt – a process that was not completed until the 1980s. The endgame for Copperfields Cold Storage was very similar. Len Pinshow left the country in 1969 and Gerald Kollenberg presided over the winding down of that company. Werners's dominance of the Northern Rhodesian cattle trade had proved to be short-lived. Susman Brothers & Wulfsohn's links with Welensky and the UFP could not protect its cattle-trading interests against the Southern Rhodesian interests that dominated the Federation. It was not as strongly committed to the retail butchery business from which it withdrew for the first time in 1962, and again in 1970. Nevertheless, Werners survived for many years as the holding company for the farming and ranching enterprises of the group, which continued to be directly involved in the raising of cattle throughout the 1970s and 1980s. It was to come back into the butchery business in the 1990s through its indirect involvement with Zambeef. This company was to achieve an even more remarkable dominance of the cattle trade and retail butchery business of Zambia than had been achieved by its predecessor in the 1950s.[46]

CHAPTER 16

The Gersh Brothers: A Copperbelt Conglomerate

While Werners was the main Copperbelt business of the Susman Brothers & Wulfsohn Group in the post-war years, a branch of the Susman family built up another large business there, which was independent of that partnership. The Susman brothers' nephews, Maurice and Harry Gersh, were the representatives of the family on the Copperbelt from its beginning as a mining, industrial and commercial centre. Over a period of thirty years they developed a business that was almost as large and diverse as Susman Brothers & Wulfsohn itself. Maurice Gersh was an outstanding entrepreneur – as remarkable in his own way as his uncle, Elie Susman, his cousin, David Susman, or Harry Wulfsohn. He was also heavily involved in local government, and was the most articulate spokesman, whether on paper or by word of mouth, for the Copperbelt's commercial and industrial sectors. His brother, Harry, did not have the same entrepreneurial drive or intellectual weight, but he made his own contribution to the development of a large business.

Maurice Gersh worked for several years with Copperfields Cold Storage and Northern Caterers, but left those companies because of his inability to get on with Isadore Kollenberg. For several years, he combined this work with the leading share in the management of Economy Stores, the company that he set up with his brother in 1931. Their Susman uncles then owned half the shares and they both had seats on the board. From slow beginnings in the early 1930s, this company began to take off in 1936 with the recovery of the Copperbelt from the Depression, and the beginning of the pre-war re-armament boom. Economy Stores began with a mine concession store in a portable shed, made of wood and iron, at Nkana. They soon had a similar store, the Nchanga Trading Company, at the mine of that name.

Economy Stores and the Closed Townships

Maurice Gersh played the leading role in the negotiations with the government that resulted in the establishment of the new township of Kitwe in 1935–6. The government wanted to establish a township that would be outside the control of the mine, but it did not wish to finance the development itself. It also wanted to promote Ndola as the main commercial and industrial centre on the Copperbelt, and was anxious to limit the growth of competing centres. The traders themselves were not keen to move from the Nkana Mine. A compromise was worked out under which the Nkana traders agreed to move to Kitwe and to pay for the development of the town in exchange for a twenty-year monopoly. They would be protected against new competition until 1956. In the end only four general dealer's licences were issued. Economy Stores, Sid Diamond's Standard Trading, E. Kollenberg and Sons, and Campbell Brothers' Kitwe Stores, became the 'monopoly' traders of Kitwe. There is no doubt that the exclusion of Asian traders was a factor in the establishment of Kitwe as the first of the Copperbelt's 'closed townships'. Each of the traders paid £2,000 as a premium for their store site and then had to spend another £5,000 to build a store to the required standard. A limited number of licences were also issued for butchers, bakers, garages and other services. Closed townships were also established at Mufulira in 1937 and at Chingola (Nchanga) in 1945. Economy Stores undoubtedly benefited from these arrangements at Kitwe and Chingola, as did the other traders. Northern Caterers and Copperfields Cold Storage were also major beneficiaries of this system.[1]

Maurice Gersh was a nominated member of Kitwe Township Management Board from the date of its establishment and was elected as the first mayor of the town in 1954. He was re-elected in the following year. He also served as president of the Northern Rhodesian Municipal Association, as president of the Kitwe Chamber of Commerce and Industry, and of the Northern Rhodesian Association of Chambers of Commerce and Industry. No one made a greater personal contribution to the development of the town of Kitwe than he did. It was primarily for his services to Kitwe that he was awarded the OBE in the New Year Honours of 1957.[2]

By the outbreak of the Second World War in 1939 both Maurice and Harry Gersh were married and living in the new town of Kitwe. Harry Gersh had married Gertie Baron at the Bulawayo Synagogue in 1933. In the following year they travelled together to Palestine to visit Harry's grandparents, Behr and Taube Susman. The main object of this journey was to collect the *sefer torah* (biblical scroll) that had been written for them by the family scribe, Moshe Epstein. As the first married couple in the Jewish community in Nkana-Kitwe, they played an important role in the establishment of a Hebrew Congregation. When this was formally established in 1935, Maurice Gersh became the first president – a role that he filled for many years. He was eventually elected as a life president. Harry Gersh served for many years as a *chazan* (cantor) and *baal tefilah* (reader of prayers). Harry and Gertie Gersh's elder children, Jacqueline-Wendy and Errol, were born in 1936 and 1938 and were the first girl and boy to be born to Kitwe's Jewish community. Their younger daughter, Brenda, was born in 1944. Maurice Gersh married Revée Melamed in Johannesburg in 1938. She was born in the *shtetl* of Vorne in Lithuania and had arrived in Johannesburg with her mother and siblings in 1919. The remarkable story of the life of her family in Lithuania and South Africa has been told by her nephew, Dan Jacobson, in his book *Heshel's Kingdom*. Their children, Bernard and Rayna, were born in Kitwe during the war.[3]

In the year or so prior to the start of the war, Maurice Gersh was chairman of the local assistance committee that sought to provide relief for the German Jewish refugees who arrived on the Copperbelt in significant numbers at that time. Each of the Jewish-owned businesses provided jobs at low wages to at least one of the refugees. The task of resettlement was made more difficult by the initial refusal of the mines to give jobs to German citizens regardless of their ethnic origins. Maurice Gersh was especially proud of his role in finding employment at the Nkana Mine for a German Jewish doctor, Dr Dublon, who was stranded with his family and a number of other refugees at Beira in April 1939. Dr Dublon worked at first as a hospital orderly, but later retrained and served in the colonial medical service in Northern Rhodesia for twenty years. On the outbreak of war both Maurice and Harry Gersh joined the Northern Rhodesian Defence Force. Maurice Gersh was a commissioned officer and spent some months in 1944 with the King's African Rifles in East Africa.[4]

Maurice Gersh was also involved in the official system of import and price controls as an assistant controller of supplies, with responsibility for piece goods and clothing for the African market. He was regarded as an expert on these issues and gave substantial evidence to the Cost of Living Commission that was set up in 1947 in response to the African boycott of Asian shops in Luanshya. He suggested in his evidence that both prices and turnover had increased during the war, but that the rate of turnover had slowed down. As a result of shortages and the irregularity of supply, traders had to keep larger stocks and had to employ more capital in their businesses. They were also adversely affected by the tightening of credit by wholesalers and discount houses. Before the war, traders were usually given 90–120 days in which to pay for goods, but it was now common for suppliers to demand cash payment or payment in advance. The system of price controls worked through the limitation of wholesale and retail profit margins. The tendency was to hold down prices by squeezing margins. He said that a group of traders in Kitwe, presumably including Economy Stores, had made an average gross profit on turnover in the year to March 1946 of twenty-two per cent and a net profit of six and a half per cent. The profit was insufficient to finance the replacement of stocks at higher prices. He also made the general point that, under a system of price controls, the maximum prices permitted by government tended to become the minimum prices charged by traders. He suggested that the price of piece goods and clothing for the African market had increased more rapidly than most other prices and that government could make a contribution to the reduction or stabilisation of the African cost of living by abolishing import duties on these commodities.[5]

Price controls remained in place for many years after the war. In a memorandum written on behalf of the Associated Chambers of Commerce and Industry in 1951, Gersh made it clear that the chambers were not then opposed to their continuance. Traders thought that they had helped to restrain the price increases that resulted from the devaluation of sterling in 1949 and from the Korean War boom of 1950–1. They saw price controls as a necessary evil for so long as there continued to be a shortage of commodities. In spite of Gersh's earlier complaints, it is clear that price controls did not prevent Economy Stores from making good profits. Elie Susman noted in 1945 that the company had had a record year. Its profitability may have been helped by its position as one of the 'monopoly' traders in the 'closed townships' of Kitwe and Chingola.[6]

There was strong political pressure on these 'monopolies' from within the white labour and trade union movements in the post-war period. The government appointed a Closed Townships Commission in 1948 to examine them and to consider not whether, but how, they should be ended and what compensation should be paid to the affected traders. Among those who gave evidence to it were Frank Maybank, the communist trade unionist, who had been deported from Northern Rhodesia after allegedly inciting workers to strike in 1942, and Sarah Taylor Zaremba, a spokeswoman for the cooperative movement. They pointed to apparent anomalies such as the ability of Economy Stores to sell Hudson cars on a general dealer's licence, and the fact that some traders carried on more than one business in Kitwe, in apparent contradiction of the terms of their leases. Nathan Schulman, general manager of Northern Caterers, was originally appointed to the Commission as the representative of commercial interests. When he became ill, Maurice Gersh was himself appointed as a member of the Commission. It was almost certainly due to his determined and articulate advocacy that the Commission decided that there was no need to interfere with the system, as there was sufficient flexibility built into it to allow for the granting of additional licences where demand could be proved.[7]

'Monopoly' was, perhaps, too strong a word to describe the position of Kitwe's 'closed township' traders, though their ability to keep out new competitors, and Asian traders, created a kind of cartel. Economy Stores had strong competition in Kitwe from two main sources. Sid Diamond was a first-class trader who built up Standard Trading into what many people thought was the finest department store in central Africa. Campbell Brothers Carter (CBC)'s Kitwe Stores was also a well-run store. It was part of an international group with a base in London and a large central African network. Economy Stores also faced competition in Chingola from B. I. Menashe's B. I. Stores. He was a Sephardic Jew from the island of Rhodes who built up a very successful department store in the town. He also had a number of stores in the mine compounds. He had links with the Amato brothers and was a director of their company, Rhodesia Congo Oil and Soap Industries. By the early 1950s Campbell Brothers Carter had merged with Bookers, a company with West Indian connections, to become Campbell, Booker, Carter. This firm also had a branch in Chingola that operated under the name of Bookers.[8]

Maurice Gersh was fully aware of the possibilities that were presented by the expansion of the Northern Rhodesian economy in the post-war years. Together with the Susman brothers he became involved in a number of new ventures. He was not a director of Susman Brothers & Wulfsohn or Werners, but did become involved, with his brother, his Susman uncles and Harry Wulfsohn in Northern Rhodesia Textiles in 1946 and in Zambesi Saw Mills in 1948. He was an active director of both these companies in the early years, and returned later to their boards. He also started a number of new businesses in conjunction with the Susman brothers, but independently of Susman Brothers & Wulfsohn. Most of these focused on new service industries. Some of these, like garages and cinemas, catered mainly for the Copperbelt's affluent white mining population. Others like a Coca-Cola bottling plant and a bakery may have been aimed originally at a white market, but also helped to create a black one.

Cars and Cinemas

Central African Motor Services (CAMS), a motor distribution and services company, was set up in 1946. The Gersh and Susman brothers, through Economy Stores and as individuals, owned about sixty per cent of the shares in this company on its establishment. A significant block of shares was held by CBC in an unusual example of co-operation between the two groups. Their local managing director, Hugh Leishman, became a member of the board, as did his successor, W. H. McClelland. CBC declined an invitation in the same year to become founder shareholders in Northern Rhodesia Textiles. CAMS originally operated in the Copperbelt towns of Ndola, Mufulira and Chingola – it was excluded from Kitwe by the 'closed township' regulations until 1956. It set up a subsidiary company, CAMS (Midlands), to take over Kee's Garage, which belonged to CBC, at the south end of Lusaka's Cairo Road in 1951–2; this garage survived until recently, as Motor Holdings. Branches were also established in Broken Hill and Livingstone. The company also took over Kee's manager, Eric Angier, who became general manager, and later managing director of CAMS. In these years CAMS held the agency for the British manufacturer, Rootes Motors – the makers of Hillman and Humber cars and Commer commercial vehicles. This was probably not the most sought-after of agencies, though the Humber Hawk and Super Snipe sold well at the top end of the market. They also had the agency for a number of British motorcycle manufacturers. The issued share capital in these two companies was more than £200,000 in 1952.[9]

The direct importers of British cars faced increasing competition from the early 1950s onwards from German and Italian cars. Volkswagens and Fiats were assembled in South Africa and driven up to Northern Rhodesia. Attempts to get the abolition, or a reduction, of import duties on British cars failed, but CAMS remained profitable until the depression in copper prices hit the country in 1956. CAMS began to import small numbers of Fiat cars from 1957, but the company's future was insecure until the acquisition of the Rover franchise in 1958. At that time sales of Land Rovers in the country were running at 500 a year. The government of Northern Rhodesia, as distinct from the Federation, had a fleet of 2,000 Land Rovers – one of the largest in the world.[10]

Maurice Gersh had a personal interest in flying. He flew as a passenger in one of the first Imperial Airways flights from Europe to central Africa in 1932 and was one of the first people to hold a commercial pilot's licence in Northern Rhodesia – he held licence number 7. In the year of its establishment CAMS took a twenty-five per cent interest in Thatcher Hobson Airways, one of the earliest aviation companies to be set up in the country, a few years later it became a constituent part of Central African Airways. In a separate move Susman Brothers & Wulfsohn had taken an interest in Zambesi Airways, an air charter company operating out of Livingstone, in 1948.[11]

Another realm into which the Gersh brothers moved immediately after the end of the war was that of the cinema. Northern Theatres was set up in 1946 and it was followed by a wholly owned subsidiary, Northern Rhodesian Cinemas. The flagship of this company was the Astra Cinema in Kitwe, which was opened in 1950. Cinemas were also established in Chingola and Ndola, and in 1957 at Bancroft – the Vega. The Astra Cinema had an associated bar and restaurant which was an important Kitwe social centre. It proved very difficult to find managers for these facilities and they were eventually leased to C. Kaldis, a Greek businessman in Luanshya. The Astra Cinema Restaurant was the scene of a notorious racial incident involving the African nationalist leaders, Harry Nkumbula and Kenneth Kaunda in 1957, but it was not under the direct control of Northern Theatres at the time. All cinema facilities in the country were racially segregated until 1960. Northern Theatres opened an African cinema in Kitwe's Bauchi Township in 1954. A related investment was the forty-nine per cent stake which African Commercial Holdings took in the mid 1950s in the Northern Rhodesian branch of Radio (Limited), a branch of a business which Harry Robinson and his brother founded in Southern Rhodesia. It specialised in the sale of radios, gramophones and, eventually, of televisions and other electrical equipment.[12]

Almost all the Gersh brothers' enterprises were based on the Copperbelt and were distinctly urban in nature. Apart from their investment in Zambesi Saw Mills, the most obvious exception to this was their purchase in 1949 of Kaleya Estates, 22,000 acres of good farming and ranching land at Mazabuka. This had been one of the first farms to be established in the Mazabuka District. Attempts to grow tobacco there were not successful, and it was never very profitable. There were several attempts to sell it, but it proved to be an investment of long standing.[13]

African Commercial Holdings

It was clearly difficult to find capital for all these new enterprises. This is where Maurice Gersh had a stroke of good fortune, though it was one that was based on recognition by others of his outstanding talent as an entrepreneur and manager. It was through his close friend, Charles Savage, a partner in the Ndola office of the law firm, Ellis and Company, that he was able to find a source of international capital. Sir Ernest Guest, a lawyer, politician and former minister in Southern Rhodesia, was asked, with a colleague, Bill Underwood, to look for suitable opportunities for investment in Northern Rhodesia for the British company, Cable and Wireless (Holdings) Limited. This was an embryonic investment trust that held the international assets, including the cables and other facilities, which were not taken over when Cable and Wireless was nationalised by the post-war British Labour government in 1947. There was an agreement that these assets would be sold to the Commonwealth countries in which they were situated. The policy of the holding company, which survives today as the Electra Trust, was to reinvest the proceeds of their sale in these countries.[14]

Cable and Wireless established a Northern Rhodesian company, Electra (North) Ltd, as the channel for the investment of these funds in Northern Rhodesia. A similar company, Electra (South) Ltd made larger investments in Southern Rhodesia. Electra (North)'s initial investment was in a new company, African Commercial Holdings Ltd, which was set up in 1949. This company issued £200,000 of its own shares in exchange for the issued share capital of Economy Stores. Cable and Wireless, through Electra (North), subscribed for a further £50,000 of ordinary shares, and £100,000 of preference shares in the new company.[15]

The Gersh brothers owned about fifty per cent of the new company, and the Susman family about twenty-eight per cent, while most of the balance of the ordinary shares went to Electra (North). The founding directors of the new company were the Gersh brothers and the Susman brothers, with Sir Ernest Guest and Bill Underwood as the representatives of the new investors. Maurice and Harry Gersh were joint managing directors. Maurice Gersh was instrumental in securing an investment on a similar scale by Cable and Wireless in Zambesi Saw Mills in 1951–2. Guest and Underwood also joined the board of that company and had a significant influence on its affairs. Revée Gersh recalls tours of inspection to the Copperbelt by Sir Edward Wilshaw, the governor of Cable and Wireless (Holdings); the last of his visits was in 1958, by which time he was almost eighty. He was a formidable and flamboyant character who had continued to arrive at his office in the City of London in a carriage drawn by four horses until the early years of the Second World War. Although the Gersh brothers' business owed a great deal to Cable and Wireless, Maurice Gersh told Roy Welensky in 1952 that he had found British investors were very conservative in their approach to investment in 'new developing countries'. They wanted 100 per cent guarantees for their investments. He suggested that American capitalists might be more adventurous.[16]

The same group of investors was involved in the establishment of another new business, the Rhodesian Bottling Company Ltd, in 1949. This was not originally a subsidiary of African Commercial Holdings Ltd, but was controlled by the Gersh and Susman families with a significant investment from Electra (North). The initial capital employed in the company was £40,000 and its major asset was, or soon became, the Coca-Cola franchise. Its long-serving managing director was Jack Price, a prominent member of Kitwe's Hebrew Congregation. Through its policy of leasing refrigerators to African tearoom and café proprietors this company had a significant influence on Copperbelt social life. The company continued to make good profits through the depression of the late 1950s, justifying a substantial investment in the latest plant and machinery that had been made in 1955, but it faced some competition from Pepsi-Cola from the early 1960s. Maurice Gersh's most remarkable recruit for Coca-Cola was Neville Isdell who joined Coca-Cola Zambia in 1966 and beame chairman and chief executive of the Atlanta-based Coca-Cola Corporation in 2004.[17]

The main role of African Commercial Holdings was to provide capital for the development of existing enterprises. Additional capital continued to flow from Electra (North) through the issue to it of preference shares. This was used to rebuild Economy Stores's outlets in Kitwe and Chingola, and for the development of stores (both European and African) at a new mine at Bancroft (now Chililabombwe) in 1955–6. Capital was also used for property development in Kitwe, including the building of Afcom House, and for the development of the other businesses. David Susman recalls Maurice Gersh's fascination with the latest technology and his determination that Afcom House should be energy-efficient – at a time when the concept was almost unknown. Loans from African Commercial Holdings to its subsidiary companies were usually converted into ordinary shares in those companies. The issued capital of the company was gradually increased to £600,000 and it also had overdraft facilities of up to £400,000.[18]

African Commercial Holdings was the main backer of two new businesses that were set up in 1952–3. It was the largest investor in Raine Engineering, which opened a foundry in Ndola in 1953. It started with about twenty-five per cent of the shares and eventually owned about forty per cent. Its eponymous promoter was E. R. Raine, the Bulawayo foundry man, who was also a founding director of Northern Rhodesia Textiles. Among the other investors, apart from Raine himself, were J. D. H. Hobson, the manager of the Ndola foundry, T. C. H. Osterlick, its pattern maker, and L. A. Fletcher, who was also a director of the textile company. This proved to be a successful business which provided an important service to the mining companies. It was merged with Scaw Metals, and Scaw-Tow Foundries, in 1964.[19]

The other development was the establishment of a bakery in Kitwe. African Commercial Holdings subscribed the bulk of the shares in Fuller's Bakery, which began production in November 1953, an unusual example of a Gersh–Susman enterprise starting up in competition with Northern Bakeries. The latter company had been spun off from Northern Caterers in 1951. The Susmans still had a substantial stake in both companies and Elie Susman continued to sit on their boards. Maurice Gersh recruited Arthur Fuller, who was then working in the Orange Free State, to start the bakery that took his name. He had learnt the bakery business by working with Premier Milling and Tiger Oats in South Africa after war service with a cavalry regiment.[20]

African Commercial Holdings invested about £40,000 in the new bakery, which was one of the most modern and best equipped in Southern Africa. According to Fuller, it was the first bakery in the region to sell sliced and wax-wrapped bread. He did not regard Northern Bakeries as offering serious competition. He found that he could legally undercut them by selling a twenty-eight ounce loaf for one shilling in competition with their thirty-two ounce loaf, which sold at one shilling and two pence. The smaller loaf was both more popular and more profitable and Northern Bakeries was compelled to change the size of its loaf in order to compete. Fuller recalls that he was sent, through the good offices of David Susman, on a two-week tour of Marks & Spencer's bakery and confectionery suppliers in the United Kingdom, and that Fuller's became the agents for Hovis in Northern Rhodesia. Fuller's proved to be a very successful business. It was sold for a substantial profit to Spiller's in 1958, when the £1 shares were sold for more than four times their nominal value. Fuller stayed on as managing director for five years with the new owners.[21]

Maurice Gersh was generally recognised as a very astute businessman. He kept tight control over all aspects of his multifarious and increasingly extensive business empire. Although he was a director of the company until his death, Elie Susman attended very few board meetings. He seems to have trusted his talented nephew totally, and there is no evidence that he involved himself in the detailed management of this group of companies as he did in the affairs of Susman Brothers & Wulfsohn. David Susman succeeded his father as a director, but did not attend board meetings regularly either. Maurice Gersh's brother, Harry, seems also to have become a somewhat marginal figure in the business. He resigned as joint managing director of African Commercial Holdings in 1954, retaining a seat on the board, but pursuing his own relatively minor business interests on the Copperbelt. He came back, with some show of reluctance, to manage Economy Stores for a couple of years from 1958, but he resigned from the board of African Commercial Holdings and left the country in 1962. Like many Jews in central Africa, he was fascinated by Masonry and became a prominent member of the Scottish Lodge. Maurice Gersh was also a Mason, but he was not so actively involved in the movement. In the general direction of the companies, Maurice Gersh relied heavily on his friend, Charles Savage, the Ndola lawyer, and on his most trusted lieutenant, Hugh Berry, a chartered accountant, who succeeded E. F. R. Jutzen as secretary of the companies in 1951. Berry became a director of African Commercial Holdings in 1960 and managing director in 1967.[22]

While African Commercial Holdings consumed large quantities of capital, Maurice Gersh had to defend the company against the charge levelled by his fellow director, Sir Ernest Guest, that increasing capital investment and profits seemed to be matched by increasing costs. Gersh explained the problems of operating on the Copperbelt in the boom conditions of the early 1950s. He emphasised the difficulty of securing competent managerial staff and a reliable labour force in competition with the mining companies.

> ... Northern Rhodesia was a growing country – growing too fast, in many respects and ... Commerce was forced to compete with the Mining Companies for labour, whose cost of production bore no relationship to the selling price of copper. The Group's activities likewise were expanding and developing at a rate in excess of its personnel establishment. Many of its subsidiaries were also in their infancy and it must be appreciated that a settled efficient and permanent staff can only be established by trial and error over a period of time.[23]

The profits of the company were adversely affected by the recession that hit the Copperbelt in 1956. Two of the largest businesses, CAMS and Economy Stores, were particularly badly affected, and did not fully recover until 1961. African Commercial Holdings passed its dividend in 1958, in spite of the continued profitability of some of its subsidiaries. The profits of Economy Stores suffered as a result of the closure for a year or more of the new Bancroft Mine in 1958. A substantial investment had been made in a new subsidiary, the Bancroft Trading Company. The department stores were merged in 1963 with those of CBC Limited – African Commercial Holdings ending up with twenty-eight per cent of a new holding company. This minority interest was sold to CBC in 1965 for a price in excess of £300,000. There had apparently been a difference of opinion over policy between the two groups.[24]

CAMS also recovered in the early 1960s. Ron Woolf succeeded Eric Angier as general manager in 1961, and later became managing director. He had arrived to work for Northern Motors, a rival concern, but resigned within months. Woolf was a Londoner who had served in the RAF during the war and in the administration of the British zone in Germany after the war. He had then worked as sales manager for Colborne Motors in Surrey, the first Volkswagen agents in the United Kingdom. He was a co-founder of the Volkswagen Owners' Club of Great Britain and it was through his connections that the company was able to secure the important Volkswagen franchise in 1964.[25]

Another development at this time was the establishment of the Land Rover assembly plant at Ndola. The decision to build this plant came in response to competition from the Willis Jeep, for which a local assembly plant had been established earlier, but more especially from the arrival on the market of the Toyota Land Cruiser, which began to make inroads into the market in the early 1960s. Woolf recalls that sales of Land Rovers were temporarily boosted in 1960–1 by sales to Moise Tshombe's secessionist regime in the Congo. These sales were financed by the Belgian mining company, Union Minière, and were paid for through Swiss banks. African Commercial Holdings sold its controlling interest in CAMS to Tiny Rowland's Lonrho in 1966. Maurice Gersh continued for a while as chairman of the new board, but Ron Woolf did not last long with the new regime. He did, however, remain with African Commercial Holdings until it too was taken over by Lonrho.[26]

The Politics and Economics of Federation

The heyday of the Gersh brothers' business empire on the Copperbelt was the period of less than twenty years between the end of the Second World War and the independence of Zambia in 1964. For just about half of that period – from 1953–63 – Northern Rhodesia was part of the Federation. Maurice Gersh was more politically active than any leader of the Susman Brothers & Wulfsohn Group, with the exception of Maurice Rabb. By the time that the Federation was established, he had been involved in local government for most of twenty years. Like most white businessmen, and almost all Jewish businessmen, he was a supporter of the federal concept in general, and of the United Federal Party and its Northern Rhodesia-based leader, Sir Roy Welensky, in particular. Welensky usually stayed with Maurice and Revée on his visits to Kitwe. Although he became chairman of the Kitwe branch of the UFP in 1953 and campaigned for the party's candidate, Rex L'Ange, in the first federal elections, he does seem to have had some reservations on policy.[27]

Maurice Gersh told Welensky within a few months of the establishment of the Federation that the business community had hoped that this would make Northern Rhodesia more attractive to international capital. He reminded him that he wrote as someone who had a special relationship with a 'London finance house' and expressed regret that Federation seemed to be having the opposite to the desired effect. The equalisation of income tax between Northern and Southern Rhodesia had resulted in an increase in company income tax in the north. The continued prevalence of ninety-nine-year leasehold tenure in Northern Rhodesia's Copperbelt towns and Lusaka made investment there less attractive than it was in Southern Rhodesia where freehold tenure was the norm – this was not extended to the Copperbelt and Lusaka until 1959. He also argued, as he had done previously, that commerce and industry should pay a lower rate of company tax than the mining companies. He thought that the mining companies enjoyed unfair tax breaks on capital investment, and complained at this date, though he had not done so earlier, about the continuation of price, as well as rent, controls in the north.[28]

Maurice Gersh continued throughout the federal period to be the most articulate spokesman for commerce and industry in Northern Rhodesia. He was unusual among businessmen in being a compulsive writer. Many of his numerous memoranda survive in the voluminous papers of his friend, Sir Roy Welensky. He was neither progressive nor original as a political thinker, but he was the best-informed and most articulate advocate for secondary industrialisation in Northern Rhodesia. Not only did he advocate it, but he also took practical steps to promote it. His involvement with Zambesi Saw Mills, Northern Rhodesia Textiles, Rhodesian Bottling, Raine Engineering, Fuller's Bakery, Lion Tile (a tile-manufacturing business) and the Land Rover assembly plant, and as a founding director in 1959 of the state-sponsored Northern Rhodesia Industrial Development Corporation, later known as Indeco, gave him unrivalled experience in this field.

He listed his directorships in 1960 as involving 'retail distribution, farming and ranching, engineering and foundry, lumber and sawmills, cinemas, real estate, motor engineering and distribution, textile manufacturing and other industrial concerns'. He estimated the capital invested in his group, and associated companies (probably including Zambesi Saw Mills and Northern Rhodesia Textiles, but excluding Susman Brothers & Wulfsohn and Werners), at £1,500,000. He was able to say truthfully that 'I have practically no investments outside of Northern Rhodesia and the earnings of our various enterprises have all been ploughed back into this Territory.'[29]

His views on secondary industrialisation, and on the political situation in the Federation, were summarised towards the end of the federal period in two papers that he wrote in 1959–60. The first of these was written to represent the views of the Kitwe Chamber of Commerce and Industry, while the second – his evidence to the Federal Review Commission, the Monckton Commission – was written in his individual capacity. His position on the Copperbelt and his involvement in urban commerce and industry, as well as in urban local government, gave him a somewhat different perspective on Northern Rhodesia's political economy from other leaders of the Susman Brothers & Wulfsohn group of companies. Max Barnett, a close friend, was the only other one who was based on the Copperbelt, but he was also more heavily involved in agriculture than Gersh ever was.

Maurice Gersh's political position in relation to African advancement, and African participation in politics, was not very different from that of Maurice Rabb or Harry Wulfsohn. They would all have subscribed to the paternalist policies of the UFP – its political philosophy was derived from nineteenth-century Cape Liberalism. Power should remain for the indefinite future in 'responsible' white hands, and be gradually shared with a small number of educated Africans. Gersh summarised his own political views in 1960 as follows:

> My background as a businessman and industrialist has trained me in realism and hard facts, and my long association with local government and working

with Africans in many fields convinces me that it will be many years before the African can take a much larger share in the Government of this country, that is, if it is to be responsible, efficient and stable government.[30]

He was, however, more critical than either Rabb or Wulfsohn would have been of the Colonial Office and the provincial administration. He saw Colonial Office rule from London, which he described as paternalist, and the presence of an expatriate civil service, as major impediments to foreign investment and the development of secondary industry. He compared the situation in the north unfavourably with Southern Rhodesia, which had been granted responsible government under settler control in 1923. The other leaders of the Susman Brothers & Wulfsohn Group did not share this view. They usually worked in rural areas and co-operated closely with the provincial administration in Northern Rhodesia, and with its counterpart in Bechuanaland.[31]

Maurice Gersh began to develop his ideas on these subjects while he was a member of the Federal Tariff Commission. He recalled that he was then able to study economic conditions in each of the Federation's three territories. He said that the Northern Rhodesian representatives on this Commission, including himself, had gone along with the introduction of a tariff wall around the Federation in the knowledge that consumers in the north would be the main losers in the short term, as a result of the increased price of imports. They hoped that in the longer run there would be a development of secondary industry in Northern Rhodesia. Writing in 1959 he noted that this had not happened. Industrialists were 'gregarious' by nature, and most new development had been attracted to Bulawayo and Salisbury.[32]

He also noted that the Copperbelt was the second-largest centre of employment in the Federation, after Salisbury, and that the value of its copper production was £120,000,000 per annum. This was equal in value to the gold production of the Witwatersrand – about half of South Africa's gold production after the development of the Orange Free State mines. He thought that:

> An industry of that magnitude should have been able ... to engender, at least, some ancillary secondary industrial economy to replace in time a wasting mining asset, as has taken place on the Reef and in other parallel situations in other parts of the world. Why, therefore, has Northern Rhodesia in general, and the Copperbelt, in particular, lagged behind in secondary industrial development, particularly in the post-war years and since the advent of the Federation?[33]

Apart from the issue of Colonial Office rule, he attributed this failure to Northern Rhodesia's position at the end of a long haul on the railways, and to railway rating policies that had for a long time favoured Bulawayo as a distribution centre for Northern Rhodesia as opposed to Livingstone, Lusaka or Ndola. Rhodesia Railways had also used rating policy to render the Benguela Railway uneconomic for Northern Rhodesian importers and exporters from the late 1930s until 1956–7. This railway offered a shorter route to and from the coast and a shorter ocean voyage to and from Europe. He also blamed the policy of allowing duty-free imports from South Africa and Southern Rhodesia until 1953, and from Southern Rhodesia – within the Federation – after that date. This had made the development of secondary industry in the north impossible. Among the other factors that he mentioned were the high wage structure – especially for skilled workers – on the mines, and legislation that required employers to provide housing for all employees: he described this as an example of colonial paternalism.[34]

He was certain that industrial decentralisation could only be achieved by government intervention. He continued to suggest, as he had done in 1953, that lower rates of company taxation should be levied on commercial and industrial firms than on the mining companies. He suggested that the South African model of differential taxation of individual mines should be introduced and that taxation of the mines should be used to fund industrial development. He argued that it was only through secondary industrialisation that jobs could be created for the growing number of African school-leavers who were coming on to the labour market. He also recommended that greater efforts should be made to train Africans for administrative posts in the civil service.[35]

Independence

Maurice Gersh was clearly not in sympathy with Northern Rhodesia's rapid move to independence in 1964. In a letter written to Welensky early in 1962, he had mentioned the possibility of partition. The Copperbelt and Line of Rail, and possibly Barotseland, would remain within the Federation. He gave the somewhat unfortunate example of Palestine as an example of partition between two antagonistic racial groups. Although he had little sympathy with African nationalism, he did remain in Zambia for seven years after independence, and continued as chairman of African Commercial Holdings for two further years. This company was not a target of the economic reforms of 1968. Gersh continued as a critical member of the board of

Indeco for several years after independence. He had no difficulty in dealing with Zambian politicians and businessmen and was widely respected for his contribution to the building of Kitwe and as an industrialist. Zambian civil servants, such as Edward Shamwana and Andrew Kashita, who sat with him on the boards of the Standard Bank or Indeco, remembered him with respect, if not affection. In the opinion of his son Bernard, he was not sentimental about the country, or the business that he had built up. Beginning with the sale of Fuller's Bakery in 1958, he presided over its orderly dismantling. CBC absorbed Economy Stores in 1965. Raine Engineering had gone to Scaw-Tow in 1964 and control of CAMS to Lonrho in 1966. Kaleya Estates was merged with the farming interests of Susman Brothers & Wulfsohn as the Zambesi Ranching Corporation (later Zambesi Ranching and Cropping Ltd) in 1967–8.[36]

By the late 1960s the main assets of African Commercial Holdings were Copperbelt Bottling (formerly Rhodesian Bottling), Northern Theatres, Radio (Limited), Afcom Properties, and minority stakes in CAMS and the Zambesi Ranching Corporation. Copperbelt Bottling, which had by now become a subsidiary, was the main attraction for Tiny Rowland and Lonrho. They saw it as a potential 'cash cow'. Lonrho took control of African Commercial Holdings in two stages. The first of these was completed in March 1971 when Maurice Gersh left the country. The second stage was completed in 1973 when he stepped down as chairman. The Lonrho takeover was completed soon after the Mufulira Mine disaster, which was a major setback for the economy of the Copperbelt and Zambia. Gersh was relieved that Tiny Rowland completed the deal in spite of this event. Gersh's lieutenants, such as Ron Woolf and Hugh Berry, had reservations about the sale of the remainder of the business to Lonrho. They were unable to work for long in a company that they saw as having a different ethical base from that to which they were accustomed. Lonrho was, however, well adapted to survival in the new economic and political climate. Many of the businesses that the Gersh brothers had founded endured intact for thirty years until the disintegration of Lonrho itself, following Tiny Rowland's loss of control of the company and subsequent death. Some, like Copperbelt Bottling, survive under new owners today.[37]

Maurice Gersh retired to Cape Town where his brother, Harry, had been living since 1962. Harry Gersh died in December 1992 and was survived by his widow, Gertie. In the same year Maurice and Revée Gersh moved to the United States, where they lived near their daughter, Rayna, in Massachusetts. Maurice Gersh died there in December 2002 at the age of ninety-six. He had

had an exceptionally long and active life, which had taken him from birth in Jerusalem under Turkish rule, through Vienna under Habsburg rule, to Lithuania in the last days of the Russian Empire. He had reached South Africa within three years of the establishment of the Union and arrived in Northern Rhodesia in the year of the transition from British South Africa Company to Colonial Office rule. He had been, with his brother, a founder of the Copperbelt. He had become a successful entrepreneur and had set up, with the help of his brother and the backing of his uncles, a large business. Not the least of his achievements was the clear-headed way in which he organised its dismantling in the late 1960s and early 1970s – ensuring the survival of most of its constituent parts.

CHAPTER 17

Primary Industry: Zambesi Saw Mills, 1948–68

Susman Brothers & Wulfsohn also took over, or started, two rather different enterprises in the post-war years. They were both based in Livingstone – Zambesi Saw Mills and Northern Rhodesian Textiles. The first of these involved a return by the Susman brothers to a field in which they were involved in the 1920s and 1930s. Although they had worked as contractors to Zambesi Saw Mills from the end of the First World War until 1937, they were never shareholders in this Bulawayo-based company. They were, however, close to the two dominant figures in it, Charles (known as Charlie) Knight and W. E. Tongue. (For the earlier history of Zambesi Saw Mills, see above, pp. 154–7.)

It was through Tongue that they became involved in 1944 in a new, and rather different, timber project. It took them from the upper to the lower reaches of the Zambezi River and to a country in which they had never previously worked – Mozambique. The new project was on the Zangue River, a tributary of the Zambezi. The Zangue River Bridge is 138 miles north of Beira on the Trans-Zambezia Railway – the line that was built in 1920–1 to link Beira with the Zambezi, and, via the Central African and Shire Highlands Railways, with Nyasaland (now Malawi). It is not far from the Zambezi River Bridge, once the longest railway bridge in the world, which was completed in 1935. The new timber project involved a partnership with two Portuguese entrepreneurs, Antonio Frões and Victor Portela, in a company called Serracões da Zambesia – Zambesia Saw Mills. The company acquired a timber concession from the government of Mozambique, which took control of this part of the country from the Mozambique Company in 1942. According to one authoritative source, the attraction of the forest was the quality, relative density and accessibility of the trees, and their suitability for the manufacture of railway sleepers. The high level of wartime demand for them made the project attractive – in spite of the imponderable hazards of doing business in Mozambique. Another purpose of the company was to supply timber for the repair of ships in Durban during the war.[1]

Elie Susman set up a South African company, Zambesia Holdings Ltd, in 1944 to take a half share in this business. After an initial investment of £15,000 by himself and members of his family, he made a further direct investment of £9,000 in Serracões da Zambesia in 1946. He made his first visit to the area in July 1945, travelling to Beira with Tongue and Jimmy Mitchell, the former manager of Zambesi Saw Mills. They took an overnight train to Zangue and then spent two days there. He travelled for about forty miles through the forest by truck and was impressed by 'the lovely and marvellous trees'.[2]

Elie Susman's involvement in this Mozambican project led, by a somewhat circuitous route, to Susman Brothers & Wulfsohn and associates taking control of Zambesi Saw Mills in 1948. This company had operated at maximum capacity throughout the war in an attempt to meet the demand for sleepers. It had then employed an average of 100 white workers and 4,000 African workers to cut about 3,000,000 cubic feet of timber a year. The company moved about 1,000 logs a day by rail to its mills at Mulobezi and Livingstone and produced about 1,000,000 cubic feet of processed timber a year. Extraction methods were labour-intensive: all tree felling was by axe and manual labour was used to lift logs onto railway trucks. The company began to use Caterpillar tractors in the forests shortly before the Second World War, but until then it had used oxen for all movements of timber through the forest to the railway. It was the difficulty of feeding and watering oxen during the dry season that led to this change.[3]

The wages paid to its African workers were low and working conditions were poor. The lowest wage in 1943 was thirteen shillings and sixpence a month, though this was supplemented by a ration of maize meal, meat and beans. A strike by the workforce in January 1943 appears to have been provoked by adverse changes in the rationing system that were demanded by the government at a time of austerity. It ended after the intervention of Paramount Chief Yeta III. The strike prompted the government to implement minimum wage legislation and to insist on the establishment of a system of worker representation by so-called Tribal Elders. The provincial commissioner for the Southern Province said at the time that the government had been fighting since 1934 to get improvements in working conditions.[4]

Members of the Forest Department were consistently critical of what they saw as the company's wasteful methods of timber extraction. These resulted in large quantities of wood – canopy and slash – being left in the forest. This provided fuel for forest fires that destroyed young trees and retarded natural regeneration. It was only from 1935 onwards that there was any attempt by the Forest Department to ensure the future life of the forests. The ten-year licence that the company signed with the government and the Lozi authorities in 1937 placed it under a legal obligation to prevent fires and secure forest regeneration. The company resented what it saw as the bureaucratic interference of the Forest Department, its insistence on firebreaks, and its restrictions on the cutting of young trees. It had secured a royalty of less than a halfpenny per cubic foot in 1937 through the simple expedient of threatening to close down if it was asked to pay more. This was the first time that it had to pay a royalty based on the volume of timber extracted, as opposed to the area exploited. In 1940 it attempted to get, and probably obtained, a further reduction.[5]

The company then claimed that its profitability was affected by the cost of extending its railway line across the Machili River, by the transport of timber over long distances and by Forest Department controls. It threatened once again to close down. The government was worried that closure would reduce employment in Barotseland and Livingstone. It was also alarmed by the possible closure of the company's railway. This had become an important way into and out of Barotseland for passengers. By 1939 a branch line extended for about sixty miles to the southwest of Mulobezi, through Yeta's forests, and came quite close to Katima Mulilo. Members of the provincial administration used it as a convenient way into that part of Barotseland. The line from Mulobezi was also used during the war for the export of cattle from Barotseland as part of what was known as the 'Susman scheme'.

Matters came once again to a head when Zambesi Saw Mills applied in 1946 for an extension of its licence to cut timber in Barotseland. This was due to expire in the following year. The Northern Rhodesian government recruited two heavyweight forestry men, W. A. Robertson, forestry adviser to the Colonial Office, and J. D. Keet, the Union of South Africa's timber controller, to advise them on the renewal of the company's licence. They visited Northern Rhodesia in October–November 1946 and spent three weeks touring the forests and mills. They summarised their conclusions at a meeting with C. J. Lewin, the director of agriculture, and Colin Duff, the chief conservator of forests, representing the government, and with Tongue, and the general manager, Tom Jager, representing the company. They made it clear that Rhodesian teak was far too valuable a hardwood to be used for railway sleepers. These should no longer be made from naturally durable woods, but from cheaper woods that could be preserved with creosote. Teak should be used for building timber and, especially, flooring. In their reports to government they were scathing in their criticisms of the company's 'wasteful', 'primitive and ill-organised' methods of logging and milling. They also pointed out that production costs were higher than in either Southern Rhodesia or Mozambique. The company's defence was that it was operating in uniquely remote and difficult conditions and that its methods should not be compared with those used in other countries. The advisers became aware that the company was selling a third of its output to Rhodesia Railways, the major shareholder, at cost price. Other timber was sold to A. F. Philip and Company in Bulawayo, the other major shareholder, which sold timber on with a very high mark-up.[6]

It was estimated that Zambesi Saw Mills had in the previous ten years produced £5,000,000 worth of timber at current prices on which a royalty of £500,000 could have been paid. In his advice to government, Duff, the chief conservator, recommended that a royalty of not less than sixpence per cubic foot should be charged. This was the minimum amount necessary to finance the regeneration of the forests and the long-term future of the forestry industry in Barotseland. Duff took a strongly environmentalist, and a surprisingly nationalistic, line. He was certain that 'these forests should not be cut at all unless the cutter replaces the trees felled, or pays the Forest Department sufficient to replace them'. He pointed out that Zambesi Saw Mills' shareholders 'who derive the full benefit from the low charge on timber in this country all live outside its boundaries and have so directed their company's sales policy that Government also loses heavily in income tax'. He felt that it was possible that the company would be unable to

a) Alter its policy of sawing Rhodesian teak into cheap railway sleepers instead of sawing it into high-priced building and constructional timber
b) Break its tradition of wasteful logging in the forests
c) Modernise its sawmilling practices
d) Accept a royalty of 6d per cube – eighteen times what it pays now and
e) Stomach closer control over its logging and fire protection by Government officials

He was, however, certain that 'the threat of closure should not stampede the Government into parting with this large forest asset (belonging to the Barotse people) at a very low price'. He was clearly determined that the government should call the company's bluff. In the event of closure the government should buy the railway and Mulobezi Mill and offer a new agreement to another company. He was sure that 'the timber famine' in South Africa would encourage a better-equipped and financed company, such as Rhodesian Native Timber Concessions or Continental Timber Products, to offer good terms for Barotseland's proven reserves of 18,000,000 cubic feet of Rhodesian teak.[7]

Colin Duff was deeply suspicious of the company's intentions. He was seriously concerned that it might carry out its 'dispersal plan'. He alleged that the company intended to take most of its machinery and equipment, and 'send it down to Tongue's ... sawmills which he owns in Portuguese East Africa'. He thought that it would be necessary 'to rush through emergency regulations almost immediately to prevent the export of sawmill machinery, woodworking machinery, tractors, water boring equipment, telephone equipment, rails, sleepers and track-laying equipment, railway engines, rolling stock etc'.[8]

Whether or not Tongue had any such plan, it seems that this is where the link was made between Zambesi Saw Mills and the Mozambican project. Out of the threatened liquidation of Zambesi Saw Mills, the idea emerged that Susman Brothers & Wulfsohn should take over the company and use its resources to rescue Elie Susman's unsatisfactory investment in Serracões da Zambesia. It was thought at the time that the Barotseland teak forests would be cut out in six to eight years. An association between Zambesi Saw Mills and Serracões da Zambesia would be mutually beneficial. It would not only allow for the immediate pooling of management and technical expertise, but might also allow for the prolonging of the life of Zambesi Saw Mills through the gradual transfer of its activities to Mozambique. According to Maurice Rabb, it was Harry Wulfsohn who had the idea. Abe Gelman, son-in-law of 'Bongola' Smith, and a major figure in the Southern Rhodesian and Congo cattle trades, was also involved. He was an old associate of Elie Susman, but also established a close friendship with Wulfsohn at this time.[9]

The idea was attractive to the Southern Rhodesian owners of Zambesi Saw Mills for political reasons. Although the Susman Brothers & Wulfsohn Group was at first referred to rather mysteriously as 'the Johannesburg group', it clearly had impeccable Northern Rhodesian credentials. The simultaneous nationalisation by the Southern Rhodesian government of Rhodesia Railways, and the feeling that it would be inappropriate for the nationalised company to continue to hold one-third of the shares in Zambesi Saw Mills, was another factor. The basis of the eventual deal with the Southern Rhodesian owners was that the Susman Brothers & Wulfsohn Group would buy Rhodesia Railways' shares and that a new company would be floated in which it would hold at least fifty per cent of the voting shares and assume effective control.

A deal between Zambesi Saw Mills and the government was hammered out at a stormy meeting at Government House, Lusaka, on 12 May 1947. The meeting was chaired by the governor, Sir John Waddington, and was attended by senior civil servants, including Duff and his deputy, by Roy Welensky and Geoffrey Beckett, representing the unofficial members of the Legislative Council, by two representatives of Rhodesia Railways, Sir Henry Chapman, and E. Rice, the chief engineer, and by three representatives of Zambesi Saw Mills, Tongue, Knight and Jager. Sir Henry Chapman spoke for Zambesi Saw Mills and said that the company was not prepared to pay a royalty of more than two pence. It was, however, in touch with people who were prepared to take over the company and pay fifty-five shillings a share for it. They were also prepared to pay a royalty of three pence a cubic foot if the licence was renewed for ten years. Failing agreement on these terms the company would begin the process of liquidation on 31 May 1947. After an adjournment a compromise was worked out under which the government took a four-month option to buy out the private shareholders at fifty-five shillings a share. If it did not exercise the option to buy, it would renew the licence for ten years with a royalty of three pence and allow the company to sell to the other group. The government insisted that the new company must give priority to Northern Rhodesia's interests in the marketing of timber. It had in mind the diversion of output from railway sleepers for Rhodesia Railways to the production of mining timber for the Copperbelt.[10]

It is unlikely that the government ever intended to nationalise the company. It was interested in control of the railway and may have hoped to sell the timber business to another party. There was a suggestion that the United Africa Company was interested in securing the railway for transfer to a planned groundnut project in the Mumbwa District. This was a part of the British Labour government's visionary 'Groundnuts Scheme', there was talk at the time of putting 500,000 acres under groundnuts in Northern Rhodesia – most of it in the Mumbwa District.[11]

In any event the government did not exercise its option. The Susman Brothers & Wulfsohn Group took effective control of the company early in 1948 when Harry Wulfsohn and Abe Gelman joined the board. The old company was then placed in liquidation and sold its assets to Zambesi Saw Mills (1948) Ltd, which took over in November 1948. Susman Brothers & Wulfsohn, and associates, including Abe Gelman, and the Gersh brothers, bought slightly more than fifty per cent of the voting shares in the new company. The balance was allotted to members of the Philip and Knight families and to a variety of smaller shareholders. The new company issued £100,000 of voting shares in the first instance. A proportion of the interest of the old shareholders was taken care of by an allocation of preference shares. The Susman Brothers & Wulfsohn Group took effective control through a subscription of £50,000 of new capital. The Standard Bank, the group's usual bank, was not prepared to back this venture. Finance of up to £200,000 was obtained from Barclays Bank through the good offices of Abe Gelman. The bank put a proportion of its funds into preference shares.[12]

From the point of view of the Northern Rhodesian government, the Susman & Wulfsohn takeover had the advantage of repatriating the company. Harry Wulfsohn insisted that the new company must be registered in Northern Rhodesia and Elie Susman expressed his satisfaction at this decision. There were tax advantages, but there was also a political dimension to this decision. According to Maurice Rabb, the government's consent for the final dispensation was obtained at a private meeting with the governor at which he and Harry Wulfsohn explained that Elie Susman was the leading member of the 'Johannesburg group'.[13]

One of the key players in the history of Zambesi Saw Mills, and of Serracões, W. E. Tongue, died soon after the decisive meeting in May 1947, as did Sir Henry Chapman, the company's chairman. Tongue played no part in the transitional process. The chairman of the new company was Charles Knight, another of the founders of the company, but he became ill in 1950 and played only a small part in its affairs before his death in 1954. His son, Sidney, was a long-serving director, though he was thought to be only a pale reflection of his energetic and feisty father. Tom Jager continued as manager until 1952, when he too died. He had given Harry Wulfsohn a hard time over a cattle contract in the days of the old company, but remained in place in the new one. The company secretary, Walter Simpson, succeeded him. Simpson, and his eventual successor as secretary, and ultimately as manager, Bill Olds, both remained key members of the management team into the 1960s. Simpson resigned as managing director in 1963, but continued as a director until 1965. He had joined the company in 1935, and had a distinguished war record. He served with the South African forces in East Africa and rose to the rank of lieutenant colonel. He was also prominent in the municipal government of Livingstone. Olds succeeded Simpson as managing director in 1963, but left the company in 1966. He had also served as mayor of Livingstone.[14]

Serracões da Zambesia

An essential part of the 1948 agreement was the takeover of the management and financing of Serracões da Zambesia. This decision was implemented when Wulfsohn and Gelman joined the board in February

1948. The shares in Zambesia Holdings were exchanged at a discount for non-voting shares in Zambesi Saw Mills. The company proceeded at once to authorise the purchase of second-hand machinery and equipment from Rhodesian Native Timber Concessions for shipment to Zangue. In June 1948 the company appointed Maurice Smith to take over the management of Serracões. He was a civil engineer by profession and his job was to supervise the construction of the mill and the layout of the railway, which would carry timber to it. Smith was the son of 'Bongola' Smith and the brother-in-law of Abe Gelman. His family lived in Bulawayo and he commuted to Beira and Zangue by plane. The company demurred at his request that it should buy a plane for his use. Smith remained in the job at a high salary for eighteen months, but the mill was still not in full production when he left at the end of 1949. His successor as manager was John Henry, who divided his time between Beira and Livingstone. Henry remained with the company as mill manager until the 1960s.[15]

Wulfsohn and Gelman made frequent visits to Beira and Zangue, but the Mozambican business continued to present serious problems. These included foreign exchange and bureaucratic difficulties, the supply of labour and the provision of food and water to the labour force once it had been recruited. These were in addition to the elementary problems of language and communications. There seems also to have been some doubt as to the reliability of the company's Portuguese partners, Frões and Portela.[16]

The directors of the new company devoted a great deal of their time to the affairs of Serracões da Zambesia. It proved, however, to be a bottomless pit into which huge amounts of money were poured. Zambesi Saw Mills had committed £100,000 to Serracões by July 1948 and £200,000 by the end of 1951. The mill does not seem to have begun to produce sleepers before the middle of 1950. It was producing 7,000 sleepers a month in March 1951, but this was less than the target of 10,000. The company experienced a chronic cash-flow problem. Money frequently had to be sent in to pay outstanding arrears of salaries and wages. Attempts were made from an early stage to find new Portuguese partners or to sell the business. Liquidation was frequently discussed and the company was kept going from month to month. In the early months of 1952 liquidation was postponed for a while because of the prospect of large orders of sleepers for the new Lourenço Marques railway line that Rhodesia Railways was then building.[17]

It was at this stage that Harry Wulfsohn was sent to Beira to look for a partner or buyer for the business. If he could not find a partner or a buyer, he was to place the company into liquidation. He later insisted that his own account of what happened next should be recorded in the minutes of Zambesi Saw Mills (1948) Ltd.

> On his arrival in Beira, he was met by many creditors and employees demanding immediate payment of outstandings, and generally found things most unsatisfactory. In point of fact, after two days, he decided to see the Company's solicitors and arrange the liquidation. However, he was fortunate enough to meet a gentleman, who introduced him to Mr Riva, who has timber interests in Beira, including a sawmill. Mr Riva, in turn, introduced Mr Wulfsohn to Mr Barreto, who likewise has many interests in Beira, and, in particular, timber. After several days' discussions he was able to arrange the Partnership, on the conditions already stated.
>
> He explained to the Shareholders that if this Partnership had not been arranged, the Company would have been placed in liquidation, and from his knowledge of the Portuguese and their laws, there would have been very little from the salvage for the creditors, and consequently Zambesi Saw Mills (1948) Limited would have been liable for the majority of the liabilities.
>
> On his return to Livingstone, he advised Mr Simpson of the Partnership negotiations, and Mr Simpson stated that it would have been better if a complete sale had been arranged, as Zambesi Saw Mills (1948) Limited would then have been rid of the Beira liability. He advised Mr Simpson that if that was the feeling of the Directors and Shareholders, he had faith in the new Partnership, and that it may be possible for him to arrange a complete sale at a later date, but he pointed out that in arranging the sale it was likely that he would be an interested party. He did not himself suggest this sale and on the matter being put clearly to the Directors at their previous meeting, they agreed that an option could be granted him to arrange the sale of our interests in Zambesia Holdings (Proprietary) Limited.
>
> He wished to make it quite clear that he acted as a Director of this Company, and in the interests of the Company, but in view of the Shareholders' lack of confidence in Serracões da Zambesia Limitada, he had agreed to see what could be done to relieve this Company of all its liabilities in Serracões da Zambesia Limitada. He further wished it to be recorded that in making any future arrangements regarding the sale, it was being done with the full support of the Shareholders of Zambesi Saw Mills (1948) Limited, although he may make a personal gain. The Shareholders expressed [the view] that should Mr Wulfsohn make a fortune from this venture, they wished him good luck.[18]

The directors agreed to sell the business to Wulfsohn and his new partners for £250. Zambesia Holdings had by then a paid-up capital of £50,000. The buyers were also to take over £50,000 of the debt owed to the bank and about £30,000 of other debts. Another £150,000 of debt was to be written off. By November 1952 the deal was complete and Zambesi Saw Mills in general, and Elie Susman in particular, were rid of a disastrous investment.[19]

The partnership between Harry Wulfsohn and Henry Victor Riva turned out to be a very successful one. They were able to turn around Serracões, pay off the debt and make good profits over many years. They produced large quantities of sleepers for Rhodesia Railways and in the later 1950s they bid for contracts to supply the railways with 2–300,000 sleepers a year. Riva was the son of an Italian father and an English mother. Although he was born in Beira he was interned for some time during the war as an Italian. His mother managed to secure his release from an internment camp when she obtained both British and Portuguese passports for him. On his release from the camp he was immediately conscripted – to his great annoyance – and served for some time in the British army in North Africa. He gained experience of the timber business in Tanganyika and ran his own sawmill in Mozambique – Serracões da Machave. He had a half-brother, Reg Tully, who helped him in the business. Tully had served during the war with the Royal Engineers and was able to solve the numerous engineering problems that occurred in the mills and forests on a daily basis.[20]

The ultimate success of Serracões depended on the adoption of a new milling strategy. Soon after they took over, Riva decided that the large central mill was uneconomic. It was also plagued by labour problems, which he saw as having ethnic origins. He decided to break up the mill into three parts. He also divided the labour force along tribal lines. The mills were moved through the forest as the timber was cut. This was the origin of the 'bush mill' strategy of which Harry Wulfsohn became an enthusiastic exponent.[21]

According to Victor, Henry Victor Riva's son, his father and Harry Wulfsohn had a harmonious working relationship. He describes Wulfsohn as a man who was full of ideas. He frequently phoned Riva in the middle of the night to explain them. Riva was a diplomat and coped well with Wulfsohn's enthusiasms and insomnia. The success of the partnership may also be explained by the fact that Wulfsohn needed Riva badly. There was no way that he could run the business without him – he described Riva as 'the most honest and able sawmilling man' that he had ever encountered.[22]

Wulfsohn's gamble, as it seemed to others at the time, paid off handsomely – no doubt due to Riva's and his own hard work. The success of Serracões was very important to him because it provided him with his only significant source of funds outside the partnership with the Susmans. He was able to use his assets in Mozambique, and the income from them, to finance other independent ventures. Some members of the board of Zambesi Saw Mills were jealous of this success, but they appear to have forgotten how grateful they were to be relieved of the burden of Serracões. Bill Underwood and Sir Ernest Guest, the representatives of British investors, the Electra Trust, were especially critical, but they joined the board after the sale of Serracões. They took the view that Wulfsohn should not pursue independent timber projects and remain on the board of Zambesi Saw Mills. Wulfsohn himself thought that their hostility emanated from anti-Semitism. Elie Susman and other members of the family acknowledged that the deal was entirely in the open and they did not resent Wulfsohn's good fortune in this venture.[23]

Zambesi Saw Mills

Although much of its time and energy was directed towards Mozambique, the new directorate moved quickly to change the way things were done at Zambesi Saw Mills itself. Harry Wulfsohn and Abe Gelman were the driving force behind the modernisation of the company. Most of the moves that they initiated were in the direction that had been advocated by the government's advisers. There was an immediate increase in the price charged for railway sleepers to Rhodesia Railways, cuts in the output of sleepers and commensurate increases in the output of timber for mining, building, flooring and other purposes. In 1948, the first year of the new regime, the proportion of sleepers in the company's output was reduced to one-fifth of output, while mining timber increased to about a half of output.[24]

The directors also increased the wages of the African labour force, and overhauled the system of compound management and labour supervision. African wages in Barotseland continued, however, to be below the national average. The old regime had begun to introduce tractors, but had experienced problems with maintenance. Maurice Smith was responsible for setting up a tractor repair unit and insisted that tractors needed daily maintenance. Cranes and hoists were immediately brought into the Livingstone factory, but it was a few years before they began to be used in the forest. It was then found that one crane did the work of sixty men. Chain saws were introduced into the forest in 1954, but there were problems with maintenance and they were soon abandoned in favour of a return to the axe. A tougher breed of chain saw was introduced in 1960, but still proved expensive to maintain. Their main advantage was that they made possible a more efficient use of the timber felled.[25]

In the long term, mechanisation resulted in a reduction in the labour force. Unskilled workers made way for the semi-skilled. In the first ten years of the new regime, the African workforce fell from 3,000 to 2,000. The European labour force was also cut from 100 to about fifty. About 2,000,000 cubic feet of timber were cut in the forests and the output of processed timber was about a third of that. The new company seems to have enjoyed relatively harmonious relations with the Forest Department. The department noted at an early stage that the company was making better use of branch wood and leaving less timber in the forest. The company ran quite profitably until the depression of the late 1950s. Milling operations at Livingstone were then phased out and were concentrated at Mulobezi. About £100,000 was spent on the modernisation of the plant there in 1960–1.[26]

The company negotiated a new twelve-year timber licence covering the Kataba Forests in 1957. This came into effect in the following year. A major preoccupation of management between 1956 and 1958 was the extension of the railway line for sixty-five miles to the north from Mulobezi to Kataba, where a new logging camp was built, about 170 miles from Livingstone. Nearly 200 men were employed on the construction of the line. Extraction of timber then began from forests that extended northwards towards the boundary of the Mankoya District. The long haul to Kataba required more powerful locomotives, which were, like almost all the company's other locomotives, bought second-hand from Rhodesia Railways. There was some discussion of the possibility of moving the mill from Mulobezi to Kataba, but in the end it was decided that the mill should remain at Mulobezi.

At the same time that it was investing in three new mills at Mulobezi, the company began to move into a loss-making situation. This arose from the weakness of the market for parquet blocks in South Africa and from competition from other sources for the supply of timber to the Northern Rhodesian mines, and of sleepers to Rhodesia Railways. The directors also became concerned in 1961 that there were only four or five more years of proven reserves in the Kataba Forests and, perhaps, a few more years around Mulobezi. David Susman suggested that the company should prolong the life of the forests by reducing the amount of timber extracted by half. He also suggested that with the new and more efficient mills at Mulobezi it should be possible to increase the rate of recovery of sawn timber so as to produce the same net profit of £60,000 a year. After taxation this would allow for the payment of a ten per cent dividend on shareholders' capital. Sales at the time were running at about £500,000 a year. A subcommittee of directors under the chairmanship of Bill Underwood was appointed to investigate these suggestions. It concluded that a fifty per cent cut in output with the same recovery rate would result in a profit of only

£15,000 a year. Recovery of sawn timber would have to be increased from twenty-six per cent to thirty-two per cent to get the required rate of profit. It was not possible to estimate recovery rates until the new mills were in production. It was decided to maintain the same high rate of cutting until these were known.[27]

At the same time the company asked the government to carry out detailed surveys of the forests that fell under the licence, and of other forest reserves in Barotseland. Aerial and land surveys were made in 1962–3. The government also investigated the finances of the company. Its consultant took the view that a saw-milling business needed to make a net profit before taxation of twenty-five per cent to remain viable. He calculated that the net profit of Zambesi Saw Mills, after making allowance for unprofitable subsidiaries and including revenue from the railway, was about twenty per cent. He questioned whether the large scale of operations at Mulobezi was really necessary, and also wondered whether some of the prices quoted for timber were economic.[28]

In the course of 1961 the government also indicated that it was willing to offer licences for the exploitation of two blocks of teak forest in remote areas on the west bank of the Zambezi. The Mashi Forests were situated about sixty miles west of Katima Mulilo in the Sesheke District, while the Senanga Forests were situated at Kanja, a similar distance from Sioma in the Senanga District. These forests were close to the border with Angola. Zambesi Saw Mills appeared to be better placed to exploit the first of these, but it could only do so when it had finished with the exploitation of the Kataba Forests and was able to relay the railway line towards Katima Mulilo. This would be in about seven years' time. The company was also interested in taking control of the Zambesi River Transport Service in connection with this project. Harry Wulfsohn and Henry Victor Riva had become interested in the Senanga Forests and had apparently made a direct approach to the Litunga, Mwanawina III, about their exploitation sometime before August 1961. They saw them as ideal for the application of the 'bush mills' strategy. David Susman and Walter Simpson seem by this time to have been persuaded of the virtues of the bush mills, which had proved so profitable in Mozambique. Susman was inclined to encourage Wulfsohn and Riva to go ahead with the Senanga project. He thought that Zambesi Saw Mills might take a small interest in the project and that this would enable it to gain experience of the bush mills approach. This knowledge might later be applied to the Mashi Forests. There was also room for co-operation in the use of the now largely redundant Livingstone Mill. Maurice Rabb was not keen on the

Wulfsohn—Riva project and thought that Zambesi Saw Mills should assert its right to the exploitation of all forests in Barotseland.[29]

In the end Zambesi Saw Mills did not push its bid for the Mashi Forests and did not oppose Wulfsohn and Riva's bid for the Senanga Forests. With the encouragement and participation of Geoff Beckett, Wulfson and Riva acquired the Senanga licence and formed a new company, Barotseland Saw Mills Ltd, in 1962. Their licence entitled them to cut up to 10,000,000 cubic feet of timber over five years. They also had a contract to supply Rhodesia Railways with 750,000 sleepers. It was estimated that two-thirds of the output of the Senanga Forests would be sleepers and one-third would be parquet blocks. After what the Forestry Department described as 'innumerable teething difficulties', production from these forests got going in the later months of 1963, by which time two bush mills were in operation. Some of the difficulties related to the transport of sawn timber, which had to be carried by truck to the Zambezi, and then by barge and truck to Livingstone. Riva worked in the Senanga District with the bush mills and successfully extracted about 6,000,000 cubic feet of timber between 1963 and 1967. The rate of recovery of sawn timber was high. It was well over one-third of the timber extracted – a much better rate than was being achieved by Zambesi Saw Mills at Mulobezi at this time.[30]

Subsidiary Companies

The company had a number of subsidiaries. In 1949 it became the major shareholder in Rhodesia Wood Industries. This company produced plywood for the Southern Rhodesian and South African markets. It used *mukwa*, which was acquired from concessions in the Katima Mulilo area, and also from the Caprivi Strip. Difficulties in getting adequate supplies of peeler logs led the company to become dormant by the mid 1950s. *Mukwa* was also used in the manufacture of furniture. Fire destroyed the furniture factory at Livingstone in 1951, but fortunately it was well insured and was rebuilt. The market for furniture seems, however, to have weakened before the establishment of the Federation and was further damaged afterwards. The omission of *mukwa* from the list of woods prescribed by the Federal government for furniture put an end to the business. The factory was closed down in 1956 and its machinery was exported.[31]

The increasing importance of parquet flooring to the company's business had resulted in the establishment of a South African subsidiary, Zambesi Flooring Ltd, in 1955. This was originally a joint venture with Forest

Products Ltd, a company in which Harry Wulfsohn was a partner with Tom Robson. Wulfsohn had formed an alliance with Robson during the year that he spent in Johannesburg in 1954–5. Robson was a mechanical engineer and wartime squadron leader in the RAF, who had taken control of a diverse family business, Sturrock and Robson, in 1951. He had a variety of interests: in anthracite, coal, timber and locomotive engineering – to name a few. Among his other joint ventures with Wulfsohn was the Jessievale Sawmill in the vast pine forests of the Eastern Transvaal (now Mpumalanga) between Ermelo and the Swaziland border. Robson was widely respected for his honesty, bluntness and mechanical expertise, as well as for his useful links with South African and Rhodesian Railways. He became a director of Zambesi Saw Mills in 1960.[32]

The idea behind Zambesi Flooring was to establish a factory in South Africa for the processing of blocks and to create a captive market for the output of Zambesi Saw Mills. It succeeded in creating a market for some years, but it was never profitable and accumulated substantial losses. There were technical difficulties in cutting parquet battens from Rhodesian teak because of its exceptional hardness. The South African market for parquet flooring collapsed during the recession that followed the Sharpeville Massacre in 1960. Large quantities of parquet blocks and battens began to accumulate in Livingstone and Johannesburg. The factory was kept going for some years, but was eventually leased and finally sold to Hunt, Leuchars, and Hepburn, a large South African timber firm.[33]

The directors of Zambesi Saw Mills then decided that it was essential to find an alternative market in the United Kingdom and Europe. They thought that the best way to do this was to take over a British manufacturer of parquet flooring. Harry Wulfsohn and Walter Simpson identified Vigers Brothers in London as ideal for the purpose. Its proprietor, Fred Vigers, was nearing retirement and wished to sell the business; he was prepared to sell for £300,000. It was agreed to buy the company and that the shares should be split three ways between Zambesi Saw Mills, Barotseland Saw Mills and a third group that included Rhodesian Mercantile Holdings, Werners and some smaller investors. This last group would pay cash for its shares, but the purchase of shares by the two milling companies would be financed by overdrafts in London and Livingstone. These would be guaranteed by Susman Brothers & Wulfsohn. The overdrafts would be paid off by the export of parquet battens from Livingstone and Johannesburg and the companies would receive shares as payment. There was also an agreement that Vigers

Brothers would import parquet blocks in the proportion of two-thirds from Zambesi Saw Mills and one-third from Barotseland Saw Mills.[34]

The Federation of Rhodesia and Nyasaland had only just introduced exchange controls and the central bank initially rejected these proposals. The bank changed its mind after an interview between Maurice Rabb and the federal minister of finance, Sir Donald Macintyre. Rabb recalled that his intervention with Sir Henry McDowell, the secretary to the treasury, an old university friend, had helped to sway the argument. The decisive points related to the continued viability of Zambesi Saw Mills, which began to lose money in 1961–2, and to the foreign exchange saving which would result from Barotseland Saw Mills becoming the major source of sleepers to Rhodesia Railways in place of Mozambican suppliers. In presenting the case for the purchase of Vigers Brothers to the board of Zambesi Saw Mills, David Susman made it clear that the main issue was the survival of the company. It was essential that it should have control of a manufacturer and not rely on agents. The acquisition of an overseas asset was not a major issue for him, though Harry Wulfsohn and Geoff Beckett had been looking for some time for a suitable overseas investment as a hedge against political changes in the Federation. Within a year of the acquisition of Vigers Brothers, the group bought a second London-based flooring company, Steven and Adams, paying about £200,000 for the company. The merged company became known as Vigers, Stevens and Adams.[35]

Zambesi Saw Mills Railway

Although it was not a subsidiary, Zambesi Saw Mills Railway took on something of a life of its own. The story of the railway is undoubtedly romantic. It has been the source of innumerable stories, myths and legends. It also survives as part of the Zambia Railways network and as the basis of the Livingstone Railway Museum. After the extension of the line to Kataba in 1958 it ran for 170 miles from Livingstone and was said to be the longest private railway line in the world. Technically it was a logging tramway – a legal definition that allowed for less exacting standards of construction than those required for a railway. There were suggestions at various times that the line should be extended to the Zambezi above Sioma, to Mankoya, or to Mongu itself.[36]

Running the railway was an important part of the company's activities. The new regime introduced passenger wagons for the first time. Passengers had previously used open trucks and there was a danger that flying sparks would ignite their blankets, if not their clothes. A proper system of ticketing was also introduced at this time. Under the old regime passengers paid the engine drivers in person and this provided a substantial, though probably unofficial, source of additional income for them. According to Rob Hart, it was not unknown for trains to stop to allow the driver to engage in a bit of hunting, with the encouragement of the passengers. It was also usual for passengers to get out and forage for wild fruit while the train slowly climbed up towards Mulobezi. When the train reached the summit of its climb, the driver blew the whistle and the passengers scrambled back on board.[37]

In the late 1950s and early 1960s the company acquired nine second-hand passenger saloons from Rhodesia Railways. The oldest of these, known as 'RR1' was built in England in 1900 and was reputedly used by the colonial secretary, Joseph Chamberlain, on his tour of South Africa in 1901–2. David Susman recalls that it had six or seven comfortable bedrooms and a real bathroom. The directors used it on occasion for visits to the Mulobezi Mill. It served in the original Zambesi Express of 1905 and may have been one of the first carriages to cross the Victoria Falls Bridge. In the late 1950s and early 1960s revenue derived from passenger traffic provided a concealed subsidy to the logging activities of the company of more than £20,000 a year.[38]

The company, in both its old and new dispensations, retained the loyalty of some long-serving employees. George Wilson, the locomotive foreman, retired in 1964 after thirty-nine years' almost continuous service. He had first worked for the company in 1919. He presided over a collection of about sixteen, mainly antique, locomotives, the oldest of them dating back to 1901. He was so closely identified with the railway that it was said that it should be known as the 'GWR' – not the Great Western, but the George Wilson Railway – there were many stories told about him. He had certainly 'driven an engine over a track laid on bush poles which were invisible [and] submerged under a foot of water', and had occasionally had to jack up toppled engines to get them back on the rails. Wilson was also responsible for maintaining water pumps, and the telephone system, which ran parallel with the line. Marauding elephants frequently damaged this line.

Driving engines on the Zambesi Saw Mills Railway required exceptional skills and attracted an unusual breed of men. Wilson had a team of six engine drivers and a number of fitters and machinists to maintain the locomotives. Among the long-serving engine drivers was Attie Pretorius, brother of Mike Pretorius, Susman Brothers & Wulfsohn's Mongu manager. Bob Cooke, who had worked for the Susmans in the 1930s, returned to work for Zambesi Saw Mills in the 1960s. A typical Zambesi Saw Mills Railway story concerns a driver, Charlie Gosman, who was 'propelling six-eight trucks of steel sleepers and rails' from Bombwe up to Mulobezi.

> Late one afternoon the coupling between his engine and the heavily loaded trucks broke on a steep down grade and [they] ran away from the engine ... These trucks raced down the slope, tore across the embankment and up the other side, almost into Mulobezi, but they just did not make the grade on the flat country and so back they raced. For the best part of the late afternoon they seesawed backwards and forwards until finally they came to rest on the embankment. Here, next day, Charlie Gosman decided to couple up again and push them into the Camp but he had not taken into consideration the pounding the track had suffered from the mad chase backwards and forwards. The inevitable once again happened – he had hardly moved more than a few yards when over his engine went – and another major job of jacking took place![39]

The construction of the railway was in itself a remarkable feat of engineering. An impressive bridge was constructed over the Ngwezi River about fifty miles out of Livingstone in the mid 1930s. It was washed away in February 1950 by a flash flood: the river had flowed six feet over the level of the old bridge. It took eight months to rebuild the bridge, but a temporary 'corduroy' structure was in place after five or six weeks. The break in service affected the output of timber, but also disrupted supplies to Barotseland. The completed bridge is about 398 feet in length and is supported by fourteen timber trestles. Over fifty years later, it still carries locomotives weighing up to 125 tons.[40]

It was not only the railway that commanded the loyalty of many long-serving employees. The company's philosophy of 'make and mend', and its application of improvisation and intermediate technology, appealed to adventurous spirits. It also attracted people with an interest in hunting and the bush. Bob Beaton, the son of Donald Beaton, one of Livingstone's earliest residents, was a compound manager for many years. He was a noted African linguist, and the examiner of many civil servants in their language exams. He ended his career as the African Affairs manager for the Livingstone Municipality. Saws used for the cutting of hardwood could not be used for more than a few hours at a time. The saw doctor, Charles Buffé, had done twenty-five years' service in 1960. He worked with, and succeeded, his father who had also worked for the company for over twenty years at the time of his death in 1947. Buffé reckoned that they had to service 100 saws a day to keep the timber flowing from the forests and through the mills. J. F. van Staden also served the company for about thirty years and was in charge of its mechanical workshops. He was responsible for the maintenance of the company's growing fleet of Caterpillar and other tractors.[41]

Endgame

With the coming of independence it was, however, increasingly difficult to retain or attract the kind of artisan staff on which the company had for so long relied. While the company was compelled to double the low wages paid to African workers, it had to increase the wages of white artisans in the same proportion and transfer them to more attractive, but expensive, contract employment. It was reported in 1965 that there had been a 200 per cent turnover in engine drivers in one year. The general manager stated that there was no shortage of drivers, but 'most applicants lacked the essential qualities required to drive on the Company's system'. He did not specify what these qualities were, but resourcefulness was probably one of them. Harry Wulfsohn suggested that the company should seek to recruit Portuguese, Greek and Italian drivers as they were, in his view, better suited to roughing it in the bush. There were frequent hold-ups in the forest, at the mill and on the railway due to the shortage of technical staff.[42]

By this time it was clear that Zambesi Saw Mills Ltd was reaching the end of its natural life. The most accessible forests were almost worked out and the railway technology on which it was based was becoming uneconomic. The company had modernised its logging practices in the forest, but it was increasingly clear that the mobile bush mill was better suited to the environment in which it worked than the large static mills of the type that it had at Mulobezi. It was, nevertheless, able to increase the recovery rate of sawn timber in 1964–5 after the government insisted that it reduce its extraction of timber to the level permitted by its licence. The recovery rate was increased over two years from twenty-five to thirty-eight per cent and the company produced a profit for the first time in four years. This suggests that David Susman was on the right track in 1961 when he proposed that the company should aim to remain profitable by reducing the quantity of royalty timber extracted and increasing recovery rates.[43]

Although the company had greatly reduced its African labour force, which was only 1,300 in 1964, it was under increasing pressure from the government, and from the trade unions, to improve wages and working conditions. As a result of minimum wage determinations and the application of Copperbelt wage scales to Barotseland, the labour bill increased by fifty per cent in the two years between 1964 and 1966. By this time it was £300,000, and equal to about three-quarters of the value of output. The company had been embarrassed to find in 1964 that Harry Wulfsohn's Barotseland Saw Mills was paying a minimum wage of 150 shillings for a thirty-day ticket when the Zambesi Saw Mills had only recently increased its minimum to ninety shillings. Harry Wulfsohn had raised the question of 'African advancement' in November 1960. He 'considered it a matter of paramount importance that Africans be immediately advanced to positions of consequence and paid accordingly'. The general manager, Walter Simpson, indicated that 'he had already started a campaign along these lines on a small scale'. There is no indication that much progress was made. The company was in any case restricted in its ability to recruit African artisans by the fact that white labour policies and restrictive practices prevented the training of black people in most skills.[44]

The majority of the directors were eventually convinced that bush mills were a part of the answer to their problems and that the large central mill at Mulobezi should be closed down. Harry Wulfsohn had been campaigning for bush mills for many years. He had backed the recruitment of Henry Victor Riva and his brother-in-law, Reg Tully, to Zambesi Saw Mills, and the adoption of bush mills in 1960–1, but nothing had then come of the proposal. The majority of the directors were only convinced of the value of bush mills in 1965, by which time it had become impossible to recruit the technical staff necessary to run the Mulobezi Mill and railway. They finally realised that bush mills had the great advantage of simplicity, and bought several bush mills from Barotseland Saw Mills, which was beginning to wind down its operations in the Senanga District. Wulfsohn then proposed a merger between Zambesi and Barotseland Saw Mills and the recruitment of Henry Victor Riva as manager of the combined company. The managing director, Bill Olds, supported these proposals, but Bill Underwood, representing Electra Investments, opposed them. Olds resigned in June 1966, and Harry Wulfsohn recruited a new general manager, J. W. Griffiths, from Rhodesia. Such movements of staff were still possible for some time after UDI. In October 1966 it was noted that the majority of the directors of the company were still Rhodesian residents, and several were encouraged to resign. J. B. Philip had already resigned as chairman of the company, and had been replaced by Maurice Rabb. Maurice Gersh had also been invited to rejoin the board after a long absence from it.[45]

In November 1965 the directors decided, on the advice of Maurice Gersh, to approach the government with a view to securing a loan, or direct investment, of £250,000. As a result of this approach, a group of directors met with Andrew Sardanis, managing director of Indeco, who sent an analyst to examine the books. According to Sardanis, the company had made an approach to President Kaunda through Arthur Wina, then minister of finance. Sardanis says that he rejected their request. The company limped on through 1966 and reached another crisis at the end of the year. It then decided to close the Mulobezi mill and to retrench workers in order to cut losses, which were running at £10,000 a month. The retrenchments could only be carried out with the consent of the minister of labour. At a meeting in Livingstone on 7 January 1967 between Rabb, Gersh and Griffiths, on the one hand, and civil servants from the ministries of Commerce and Industry, Finance, Transport and Labour, on the other hand, Gersh was the main spokesman for the company. He stated that the present crisis had been caused by declining markets for the company's products, by wage increases and by the burden of ancillary activities, such as the maintenance of the railway and the township and hospital at Mulobezi. The company asked the government to take over the railway. Gersh stressed that it could be extended for ninety miles to Mankoya (Kaoma) at a relatively small cost. The company also asked government to suspend the timber royalty, and to allow the company to retrench 400 workers. Some of the retrenchments were linked to a shift in logging operations to new licence areas in the Kalomo and Sesheke districts. Government representatives asked if an order for railway sleepers would help to keep the company going. Gersh said that it might enable the company to reduce retrenchments, but pointed out that some of the directors favoured liquidation. He said that this would be 'a last desperate measure'.[46]

Three weeks later the company received a letter from the local labour officer giving it permission to retrench about 170 workers. The managing director then sent a telegram to Lusaka, threatening liquidation if the company was not allowed to retrench 400 workers by the end of February. There were further talks with representatives of government. These resulted in an agreement in March 1967 that the company would approach Indeco and ask for it to form a new company, which would take over the working assets of the old one. Indeco would hold fifty-one per cent of the shares in the new company, and Zambesi Saw Mills (1948) Ltd would hold forty-nine per cent.[47]

Negotiations continued throughout the year. President Kaunda announced that Indeco would take a fifty-one per cent share in the company in April 1968 as part of the Mulungushi Reforms. In doing so he made no reference to the fact that the company had asked to be taken over. He said that he had decided to take it over because it was an important employer in the Western Province and had frequently threatened to close down. The terms of the deal were finalised in May 1968 and were similar to those that had been agreed in principle in March 1967, though it was thought that they were rather more favourable than Indeco's earlier offer. The old company, which changed its name to Redwood Investments, retained its overseas assets, including its shares in Vigers, Stevens and Adams, and in Zambesi Flooring. It also retained its extensive property interests in and around Livingstone. It was to receive £250,000 for the assets that it sold to the new company, and was to reinvest just under half of that amount in it. It reckoned that there were sufficient funds left over to pay off its overdraft and the unpaid dividends on its preference shares. Its cash-flow problems had been eased by an order for sleepers from Zambia Railways. It was hoped that the new operating company, Zambesi Saw Mills (1968) Ltd, might benefit from an order for sleepers if the Tanzania–Zambia (Tazara) Railway was built. It took over all buildings, plant and machinery connected with the logging operations, including the railway. Redwood Investments somewhat reluctantly agreed to guarantee its share of the new company's overdraft of K300,000. This was eventually written off and in 1972 Redwood Investments sold its minority stake in the new company to Indeco for K721 – a very small sum. By that time, four years after the takeover, Zambesi Saw Mills (1968) Ltd had effectively ceased to function. The company was refinanced in 1973–4 and survived for a decade or so on a reduced scale, but the 'old' company came to an end when the last logging train left Mulobezi in June 1972.[48]

Edwin Wulfsohn now feels that Zambesi Saw Mills took up more of the partners' time than it was really worth. Although it was based in Livingstone and operated in Barotseland, and helped to provide a market for cattle and goods, it did not have much in common with the group's other activities. By the late 1950s, if not earlier, the railway and milling technology on which it was based was outmoded, and it was slow to modernise. Harry Wulfsohn was almost certainly right that the company should have moved over to bush mills in 1960–1. It would then have operated more profitably, though it is unlikely that its life could have been extended for long, as this depended on the teak forests of Barotseland, which were a wasting asset. It is also sad to relate that, in spite of the best efforts of Colin Duff and the Forest Department, and of Zambesi Saw Mills (1948) Ltd, there was no significant regeneration of these forests. They were in the late 1960s on the path to recovery, but, as Duff had foreseen, this was always going to be a long-term project, which would have required decades of dedicated care and maintenance. The failure to ensure the regeneration of this valuable resource appears to be the result of the relatively recent breakdown of controls on settlement, hunting and, above all, fire.[49]

CHAPTER 18

Secondary Industry: Northern Rhodesia/Zambia Textiles, 1946–2003

While Zambesi Saw Mills was involved in a primary industry and in the extraction of timber, Northern Rhodesia Textiles (Nortex) was the first major venture into secondary industry in Northern Rhodesia. It not only was the first major venture, but it is still today, nearly sixty years later, one of the few surviving – though precariously surviving – examples of manufacturing industry in the country. In 1944 the Northern Rhodesian government commissioned a distinguished South African economist, W. J. Busschau, to do a report on the possibilities for the development of secondary industry in the country. His report was produced in 1945. He was generally sceptical about the possibilities. He made no reference to textiles and concluded that 'the existence of a large measure of uncertainty is at present, and is likely to remain, a factor retarding investment in secondary industries in Northern Rhodesia'. Busschau's report was strongly influenced by then unfashionable free-market principles. It aroused an angry response from Roy Welensky because of its rejection of colour bars, its suggestion that white settlers in Northern Rhodesia were temporary residents, and its opposition to government intervention in support of industrialisation.[1]

Abe Gelman had the original idea for the establishment of a blanket factory to compete with the Consolidated Textiles factory, which opened in Bulawayo in 1945. The prime mover behind this business was Phillip Frame. He was born at Memel, Germany, in 1904 and trained as a textile engineer in Poland. He reached South Africa in the mid 1920s and soon made his mark on the textile business. He became one of South Africa's most colourful and controversial Jewish entrepreneurs. Gelman was heavily involved in the Congo and probably had that market, as well as the Northern and Southern Rhodesian markets, in mind. He shared his idea with Harry Wulfsohn, who persuaded him that the company should be set up in Livingstone, where the recently established stores business would provide a growing market. In moving to establish a secondary industry of this kind, Gelman and Wulfsohn were flying in the face of expert opinion, though they themselves had an unrivalled knowledge of the market. The demand for blankets in Zambia is, of course, seasonal, with several months in the year when temperatures on the high plateau fall towards freezing point. Nights in the Western Province (formerly Barotseland), where the Kalahari sands have little ability to retain heat, can be very cold and frosts are common.

The company was incorporated on 6 October and the first meeting of the directors was held in Livingstone on 26 October 1946. Those present were Abe Gelman, who took the chair, Harry Wulfsohn, Maurice Gersh, Geoff Beckett and E. R. Raine. The latter was a Bulawayo-based foundry man who made the looms for the new company. He was later to establish an engineering business – Raine Engineering – on the Copperbelt with the backing of Maurice Gersh. Another founding director was L. A. Fletcher, the manager of a Bulawayo textile mill. A prominent member of the original consortium was J. van der Westhuizen, a farmer in South West Africa. The plan was to raise £60,000 through the issue of 240,000 shares at five shillings each. One-third of the shares were to be taken up by the companies in the Susman Group. The bulk of the group's shares were issued to Susman Brothers & Wulfsohn with some going to the Gershes' Economy Stores. Shares issued to allies of the group, such as Abe Gelman, Geoff Beckett and Stewart Green, ensured it overall control. According to Maurice Rabb, Wulfsohn rapidly lost interest in the project. He did not want to be involved with a venture that he expected to fail and handed over his place on the board to Rabb. Maurice Gersh seems also to have lost interest at an early stage, although he and his brother continued to be major shareholders. Gelman maintained his interest in the company and remained chairman until ill-health forced his resignation in 1957. Geoff Beckett was then chairman until his death in 1965. Rabb succeeded him and was chairman until 1974, remaining on the board until his death. No one showed a greater long-term commitment to the company than he did.[2]

There were a relatively large number of small shareholders in this company. They included Jack Faerber, and his wife Esther, Paul Zaloumis, friend of Harry Wulfsohn, H. H. Field, compound manager at the Mufulira Mine, and Godfrey Pelletier, the Copperbelt importer and distributor. Shares were also offered to Campbell Brothers, Carter (later Campbell, Booker, Carter, and better known as CBC Ltd), but they declined the offer. Through R. F.

Sutherland, which became their subsidiary in 1948, they were to become the main competitors with Susman Brothers & Wulfsohn in Barotseland.[3]

The company recruited Willem J. van der Merwe as manager. He had worked for Frame in Bulawayo. Known as 'Lang Willem', he was, according to Chris Myburgh who worked with him for many years, impossibly difficult and exacting, but was a man with 'a good heart'. He remained with the company for nearly thirty years, retiring in 1965. He was almost literally the builder of the business and left a lasting impression on it. According to Myburgh the loom upon which all Nortex looms was modelled was 'stolen' or, perhaps, 'relocated' from Consolidated Textiles in Bulawayo. Van der Merwe had worked for eighteen years for Frame's mills in South Africa and Southern Rhodesia. Whatever the source of his model, E. R. Raine succeeded in making nine looms and they were installed in a prefabricated building on Livingstone's Katembora Road by the beginning of 1948. The building had been bought from an RAF base near Bulawayo. The problem then was to secure a reliable supply of raw materials, both warp and weft. Consideration was given to the possibility of spinning Northern Rhodesian cotton, but this proved impracticable.[4]

Gelman decided that the solution lay in an alliance with Reuben Amato, an old colleague from the Congo. Amato, a Sephardic Jew from the island of Rhodes in the former Turkish Empire, was in many ways an even more controversial character than Phillip Frame. He and his brothers – they set up Amato Frères – had made their fortune as contractors for Lever Brothers in the palm oil business in the Congo. They had moved on from there to challenge their former patrons and other competitors, such as Premier Milling and Tiger Oats, for control of the vegetable oil market in South Africa. Not content with taking on this battle they had also challenged Frame in the textile business. Amato wanted to take control of the company as a condition for coming to its aid. He was, however, persuaded to accept a one-third share in the company. The nominal share capital was increased to £100,000 and 120,000 shares were issued to him. He proved to be something of a disappointment. He was slow in paying for his shares and he did not come up with raw materials – especially the much-needed weft. He eventually paid three shillings and sixpence as a deposit on his five-shilling shares, but ultimately sold most of them to Susman Brothers & Wulfsohn, which consequently obtained a controlling interest in the business.[5]

The directors were, meanwhile, faced with the problem of how to get hold of a reliable supply of warp and weft. According to Maurice Rabb, supplies were eventually obtained from India, France and Holland. Production with the first nine looms began in 1948. A profit was made in 1949–50, but after the deduction of taxation and preliminary expenses it was insufficient to pay a dividend. It was hoped that a profit of £20,000 would be made in the following year but it was not until 1951 that a reliable supply of raw materials was found. Rabb visited France and Italy with David Yager, of Stenham and Company, the London confirming house. They eventually found a supplier in Prato, the blanket capital of Italy, who could provide them with the raw material that they required. They established a good relationship with Mauro Paoli, the young manager of this firm. This stood them in good stead later on, as he became the 'Blanket King' of Prato. Once a regular supply of material was secured, the number of looms was increased from nine to twenty-seven, and then again by stages to fifty-four. Capacity and output doubled in 1954–5. By the end of the latter year the company was running two shifts and was producing about 10,000 blankets a week – or about 500,000 blankets a year.[6]

Although the establishment of the Federation resulted in the reduction of tariff barriers against imports from Southern Rhodesia, the company still had some protection because of the bulky nature of blankets and of transport costs. Nortex produced only the cheaper varieties of blankets and was not in direct competition with Frame's Consolidated Textiles across the whole of its product range. According to Rabb, Frame priced his cheaper blankets above Nortex prices. He allowed Nortex to maintain a niche market, but discouraged it from producing a wider range of products. Susman Brothers & Wulfsohn and Economy Stores were the major buyers of blankets, but competitors, such as R. F. Sutherland Ltd and its parent company, CBC Ltd, were also customers, as were the copper-mining companies. Exports to the Congo and to Mozambique were also important. Members of the Kaufman family, major wholesalers in Southern Rhodesia, became shareholders and also placed orders. Basil Kaufman became a director in 1955 as a representative of his family's interests. The company also sold blankets to Asian traders in the Eastern Province of Northern Rhodesia and in Nyasaland. There was some discussion of the possibility of opening a factory in Nyasaland, but nothing came of this project; it was decided that the £50,000 that would be required would be better spent in Northern Rhodesia. This was the closest that the Susman Group ever came to making an investment in Nyasaland.[7]

Further investment in Northern Rhodesia increased capacity in the later 1950s. The factory continued to concentrate on the cheaper end of the market. There was discussion in 1960 of moving upmarket and there was also criticism from Geoff Kates, merchandising manager of Rhodesian Mercantile Holdings, and soon to become a director of Nortex, of the quality of its printed blankets. Nathan Zelter, merchandising director of Rhodesian Mercantile Holdings and a director of Nortex from 1957, had earlier asked why the company did not produce more printed blankets. The company was adversely affected by the collapse of the Congo market after the independence of that country in 1960. The collapse was not immediate, but was complete by 1963. This left the company with unsaleable stock and unusable raw materials, as it had made a larger type of blanket specifically for the Congo market.[8]

As the Federation moved towards its end, the company was also confronted, almost for the first time, by industrial action. It was reported in September 1962 that 160 machine operators, probably the bulk of the workforce, had gone on strike for a day. D. J. Nyirongo, the organising secretary of the Union of Commercial and Industrial Workers, claimed that this followed the dismissal of John Nalubutu, who was attempting to unionise the workers. The management asserted that Nalubutu had been dismissed because he was an unsatisfactory worker, and not because of union activities, to which it had no objection. According to the *Livingstone Mail* there was a meeting between the management and union representatives, as a result of which the strike was called off, but Nalubutu was not reinstated. The labour force did, however, become unionised, and there was a go-slow at the height of the blanket season in 1963, which resulted in a substantial loss for the year.[9]

In September 1962 it was reported that Phillip Frame, who was maintaining his old season's prices, 'now saw his way clear to break Nortex'. In March 1963 he told Harry Wulfsohn that he was interested in a complete takeover of the company. The directors were then asking for ten shillings a share, though their confidential minimum price was then seven shillings and sixpence. Frame must have thought that the price was too high, but he feared that the end of the Federation might result in the erection of a tariff barrier that would keep out his products. He investigated the possibility of starting a factory in Lusaka at this time – probably as a way of putting pressure on the directors of Nortex. Maurice Rabb went to see him in Durban and argued that there was no room in the country for two competing blanket factories. Frame insisted that he wanted at least fifty-one per cent of the shares and effective control. The directors of Susman Brothers & Wulfsohn, which now controlled seventy-five per cent of the shares, were not then prepared to give way to his demands. They wanted to retain control of Nortex because of its close relationship with their stores network, which took as much as sixty per cent of the factory's output.[10]

A compromise was eventually worked out under which they would share control with Consolidated Textiles. Susman Brothers & Wulfsohn would sell half its shares and control would be vested in a new jointly owned company, Livingstone Industrial Holdings. Frame agreed to pay seven shillings a share – slightly less than the minimum that the directors of Nortex had had in mind. It was not until May 1964 that these negotiations were completed. In the meantime, Maurice Rabb had lobbied the government to ensure that Northern Rhodesia preserved the old federal tariff against textile imports. Under the new dispensation there were to be three executive directors, Maurice Rabb, Willem van der Merwe and Joe de Haas, Frame's manager in Bulawayo, who was in overall control. There was an agreement that Consolidated Textiles would provide raw material as well as technical expertise. Chris Myburgh became secretary of the company at this time. He was born in South Africa to an Afrikaner father and a German Jewish mother and started work as a warehouseman at Consolidated Textiles' blanket factory at Harrismith, in the Orange Free State, during the Second World War. He moved north, joining Zambesi Saw Mills in 1952. He worked for a few years in charge of the large saw, cutting parquet blocks, but transferred to Nortex in 1955.[11]

According to Myburgh, de Haas looked upon the staff at Nortex, which became Zambia Textiles, or Zamtex, in November 1964, as 'second-class citizens'. He thought that the company suffered from a lack of a clear command structure and that too many directors had been involved in the management. He was certain that control should be concentrated in Bulawayo, and exerted pressure for an increase in output from 18,000 blankets to 20–25,000 blankets a week. He also argued that the company should improve the quality and variety of blankets that it produced. If it did not do so it would find it difficult to justify its tariff protection and there would be pressure for a reduction. This would, of course, benefit Consolidated Textiles's Bulawayo factory. Myburgh felt that de Haas and Frame wanted 'to squeeze us out'.[12]

Willem van der Merwe had soon had enough. Pressure from de Haas and Consolidated Textiles, combined with a lack of sympathy with the new political order and ill health, made him feel that it was time to go. In a letter to the directors, written in April 1965, he indicated that he would be retiring at the end of the year. He had been ill for seven weeks, but he also felt that 'living conditions at present are far from pleasant and can only contribute to declination of one's health'. This was, he said, not an easy decision to make after thirty-nine years in textiles, eighteen of them with Frame, 'and nineteen with this firm which I have built up from the very first brick, to what it is today …'.[13]

Rhodesia's Unilateral Declaration of Independence in November 1965 reduced the pressure on Zamtex from Consolidated Textiles. It soon became impossible for Zamtex to get its raw materials from Bulawayo, and by 1968 it was impossible to get them from South Africa either. Zamtex had to re-open its old lines of supply from Prato in Italy. At times it also obtained supplies from Japan and Kenya. UDI did have the advantage of providing Zamtex with an exceptional degree of protection against competition from the south, which continued to be the case until the independence of Zimbabwe in 1980. The company increased production and made good profits in the late 1960s and early 1970s. By 1970 it had, however, to contend with the resurrection of an old adversary, the price controller. Post-war price controls had lasted until the mid 1950s. There was a relatively brief interlude before they were re-introduced by the government of independent Zambia in the wake of UDI. Although the company continued to make reasonably good profits, these were limited by the refusal of the controller to allow price increases. One way around the controls was to introduce new product lines. Zamtex does not seem to have been targeted for nationalisation in the late 1960s, but there was discussion of the possibility of Indeco taking shares in the company in the early 1970s. The board welcomed this proposal, but it was not implemented. In a move towards greater Zambian participation, Arthur Wina was elected to the board in 1975, but he does not seem to have attended meetings.[14]

The relationship with Consolidated Textiles continued to be an uneasy one. Some kind of crisis was reached in 1974 with the removal of Joe de Haas from the board, and the dismissal of a recently appointed general manager. It is surprising that de Haas, with his Rhodesian connections, had been able to remain on the board for as long as he did. It was at this time that Jack Tuffin took over from Maurice Rabb as chairman of the company. He held the position for ten years and was succeeded by Denton Pitt in 1985. Chris Myburgh took over as general manager and remained in the post – through fifteen very difficult years – until 1990. He was assisted latterly by A. A. Sabzwari, as assistant general manager (technical) and by W. T. S. Fonseca, as assistant general manager (financial and administrative). Fonseca, an accountant from Sri Lanka, eventually succeeded Myburgh and has remained with the company as managing director until the time of writing.[15]

By the mid 1970s the company began to be affected by the impact of the global recession on Zambia and by foreign exchange shortages. In March 1976 it was reported that the profitability of the company was threatened by the failure of the Bank of Zambia to release relatively small amounts of money to pay port charges at Beira and Durban. As a result of this, supplies of yarn were held up at the ports. By this time the Bank of Zambia had established a 'pipeline', or queue, of unpaid foreign exchange bills. Payments of £800,000 from Zamtex to its shippers, Stenham, which was by this time also a part of the Susman Brothers & Wulfsohn Group, were stuck in this pipeline. Stenham continued to finance Zamtex's imports of yarn and kept the factory running, but two years later Zamtex had £2,400,000 of payments to Stenham in the pipeline. This was a very large sum of money and these debts threatened the solvency of Stenham itself. It was resolved that it should never again expose itself to such a great extent to one company, and that advances to Zamtex should be limited to £1,200,000. Maurice Rabb thought that if this sum could be turned over twice a year it should be enough to keep Zamtex supplied and the factory running. The subsequent withdrawal of support for Zambia by the British Export Credit Guarantee Department compelled Stenham to terminate its involvement with Zambian trade.[16]

Zambia Textiles was protected for some time by its good links with Stenham, and its overseas suppliers, but it was forced to begin short-time working in April 1978 and in November 1979 the factory closed down for three weeks because of a shortage of raw materials. There was a further six weeks' closure, which ended in February 1980. The company continued to pay the workers during these closures in order to keep the labour force intact. It was able to get back to full-time working with two shifts in April 1980, but by that time it had lost workers through natural wastage, and only three-quarters of the looms were in operation. The company continued to be troubled by foreign exchange shortages, and now had to contend with devaluation, inflation and the intensification of price controls. At one stage, price increases were granted and then withdrawn on the ground that blankets were 'essential commodities'. Conditions were increasingly difficult and in 1981 it was reported that the company had failed to return a profit for the first time in many years.[17]

The independence of Zimbabwe in 1980 did mean that there was an end to the serious transport difficulties that had been an issue for fifteen years and reached a crisis point in the later 1970s. On the other hand, the re-opening of the Zambian market to producers from the south created new problems and resulted in renewed pressure on management from the joint owners, Consolidated Textiles. The continued shortage of foreign exchange provided an additional incentive for the company to open its own spinning plant – something which it had had under consideration for many years. It was not proposed to spin yarn from local cotton, but rather to reclaim yarn from textile waste that could be collected in the country. Consolidated Textiles proposed that it should sell Zamtex second-hand machinery from one of its South African factories. After some discussion it was agreed to accept this offer and to set up a subsidiary company, Zambia Spinners Ltd, to carry on this activity. New capital of about K500,000 (then about $500,000) was required for this project. This came from local reserves, and as a loan from the Development Bank of Zambia. The project was delayed by the inability of the Bank of Zambia to provide the foreign exchange that was needed to pay for the purchase of the plant in South Africa. This was eventually released after a direct appeal to President Kaunda.[18]

The plant was up and running by July 1981 and was officially opened by the president in November of that year. The opening was televised and the new development was a public relations success for the company. It was hoped that by the end of 1981 Zambia Spinners would be producing twelve tons of yarn from textile waste a week. This was about a fifth of Zamtex's requirements. The supply of textile waste from within Zambia proved to be less plentiful than was expected and it was necessary to import some waste materials, but this still resulted in a saving of foreign exchange. At the time of the opening of the new plant, Zamtex expressed 'its willingness to fulfil its role as the sole blanket manufacturer in ... supplying the country's needs, provided that it receives foreign exchange for its materials and economic prices for its products'. Foreign exchange problems continued, as did delays in the arrival of raw materials, but there was some relaxation in the activities of the price controller. Substantial increases in blanket prices were made and the company returned to profitability in 1983.[19]

The company benefited from the introduction by the Zambian government of the foreign exchange auction system at the end of 1985, under pressure from the International Monetary Fund and as part of a Structural Adjustment Programme. During the period of eighteen months or so that it lasted, the company was able to bid for foreign exchange for the import of raw materials and machinery, and was no longer dependent on administrative allocations of scarce foreign exchange by the Bank of Zambia. It was at this time that the company achieved its maximum output of close to 1,500,000 blankets a year. It also finished about 500,000 blankets a year,

13 Maurice Rabb with President Kenneth Kaunda at the opening of Zambia Spinners, Livingstone, 1981.

which were imported from Czechoslovakia in a 'loom-ready' state. At its peak levels of production in the mid 1980s the company employed 650 workers and had at least 120 looms working three shifts and producing 30,000 blankets a week. By this time the looms and weaving technology in use were already antiquated, though they have continued in service until the present day. In the view of Peter Green, a former director of the company, they represent a form of intermediate technology. They are relatively cheap and easy to maintain, and are well suited to the Zambian environment. Chris Myburgh summed up his explanation for the survival of the company through the great difficulties of the 1970s and 1980s with one word – 'perseverance'. The company's best year was probably 1987 when the combined profits of Zambia Textiles and Zambia Spinners were more than K12,000,000. There were strict limitations on the amount of money that could be paid out in dividends and most of this profit was reinvested in the business.[20]

Consideration had been given in 1984 to the possibility of importing machinery from Italy for the establishment of a plant to spin yarn from local cotton. This would, however, have required $5,000,000 and there was little prospect at that time of raising such a large sum in foreign exchange. The introduction of the foreign exchange auction made this project appear to be practicable. The company made a successful bid in January 1986 for $2,000,000 for the import of machinery for the first stage of the construction of a cotton-spinning plant, and was able to finance this from its own resources. The machinery arrived and was set up in the early months of 1987. As a result of this investment, and the later import of machinery from Consolidated Textiles in Bulawayo, the company was eventually able to produce forty per cent of its own requirements of yarn. The foreign exchange auction did not, however, last long. By the middle of 1987 the government had become alarmed at the rapid devaluation of the kwacha and had abandoned the auction. There was a substantial revaluation of the currency and a new system of foreign exchange allocation by the Bank of Zambia, known as FEMAC, was introduced. The company's bids for foreign exchange were repeatedly rejected, and the supply of raw materials again became erratic. By 1988–9 the company was unable to meet local demand and a black market in blankets developed. The shortage resulted in adverse publicity for the company, though it could not really be blamed for it. The government was eventually persuaded to provide sufficient funds for raw materials, but did so on condition that there should be no further price increases. The company accepted this condition with some reluctance. It then gave serious consideration to raising from donor funds, or soft loans, the $4,000,000 that would be required to import more spinning machinery from Italy and free itself from the need to import yarn. It does not appear to have been able to raise the money at this time.[21]

There was some discussion of the sale of the company in the late 1980s. Among interested parties were said to be the SAAR Foundation (which had the backing of a Saudi Arabian prince), Lonrho and Enock Kavindele. Another Zambian businessman, H. M. Phiri, put in a bid of more than $3,000,000 for Susman Brothers & Wulfsohn's and Consolidated Textiles's controlling interests in 1989, but this fell through, possibly as a result of reluctance on the part of the latter company. In the early 1990s Consolidated Textiles was itself dismantled and its share in Zambia Textiles passed to Victor Cohen, a Zimbabwean businessman who had begun his career in clothing manufacturing in Livingstone after UDI. He eventually became the dominant force in Zimbabwean textile manufacturing and also took over Frame's Waverley blanket factory in South Africa. He maintains that the interest in Zambia Textiles was thrown in as part of a job lot when he took over Waverley. Victor Cohen attended board meetings for some time, and would have liked to play a larger part in the management of the business. He did help with the provision of second-hand spinning machinery from Bulawayo, but he appears to have lost interest when his ideas on the management of the business proved unacceptable to the majority of board members. In 1993 there was a suggestion that Zambia Textiles might be sold to Trans Zambezi Industries, together with Zambesi Ranching and Cropping, and other parts of the Susman Brothers & Wulfsohn Group, but this idea did not happen. It was apparently too small to be of interest to that company.[22]

The coming to power of the Movement for Multi-Party Democracy (MMD) government in 1991, and the rapid liberalisation of exchange controls that followed that event, should have signalled a new dawn for Zambia Textiles. Liberalisation also resulted, however, in the sudden removal of tariff barriers in 1992, and a situation where the company had to contend with competition and dumping from a wide variety of countries including Zimbabwe, Kenya, Pakistan, India and China. While virtually the whole of Livingstone's clothing and textile industry was wiped out by this onslaught, Zambia Textiles survived, but did so mainly because its long-term owners were prepared to allow it to remain in business without paying dividends, so long as it did not require additional capital. The last straw, however, was the economic collapse in Zimbabwe that began in the late 1990s. The Zambian kwacha emerged as a relatively hard currency, and there were large-scale imports of Zimbabwean blankets by cross-border traders at prices that were below the cost of production. At the same time the South African Shoprite chain seemed to be reluctant to stock Zambian blankets. By 1999 the company was making losses, and by 2000–1 production was down to 600,000 blankets a year, about half of possible output. Fifty-five looms, less than half the total available, were working two shifts, and the labour force had been reduced to about 350 people. The variety and quality of blankets being produced, from the cheapest Vanguard to multi-coloured prints, was, however, impressive. The sale price of blankets averaged K34,000 (then $10) and the company's turnover was about $6,0000,000.[23]

Simon Zukas, who took over from Denton Pitt as chairman of the company in 1996, hoped in 2001 that dumping from Zimbabwe would come to an end when that country's surviving blanket factory ran out of the foreign exchange that it needed to fund the import of raw materials. He also hoped that the Zambian government would take steps, as it was entitled to do under COMESA rules, to stop dumping. The government was, however, slow to act, and three years of losses had brought the company to the verge of bankruptcy. It was placed in provisional liquidation at the end of 2002 and was refinanced in the early months of 2003. The business survived, but Susman Brothers & Wulfsohn lost its stake after forty-seven years of involvement.[24]

The story of Northern Rhodesia/Zambia Textiles has been a story of survival through 'perseverance' against the odds. It was set up in 1946 against the implicit advice of the economist who advised the Northern Rhodesian government on secondary industrialisation. Its history demonstrates the difficulty of running a manufacturing industry in a land-locked country with a small domestic market and limited export opportunities. It has survived, so far, by overcoming problems relating to: the supply of raw materials, continuous pressure from Consolidated Textiles, the impact of the world recession, transport difficulties, foreign exchange shortages, and, finally, liberalisation, globalisation and dumping. It would not have survived so long, certainly not through the last decade, without the somewhat indulgent long-term support of its founders.

CHAPTER 19

Farms and Ranches, 1945–93

The Susman brothers' first major step into ranching and farming had been their acquisition of the Leopard's Hill Ranch near Lusaka in 1912. At about the same time that Harry Susman left the country, they put the ranch on the market, having owned and developed it for over thirty years. Elie Susman agreed to sell it to 'Fanie' van Rensburg at a meeting in Johannesburg on 22 June 1945. The buyer was a large-scale farmer in the Free State and the Transvaal. He was an Afrikaner, but a supporter of General Smuts and the United Party. According to his daughter, Edwardina Neethling, who still lives on a neighbouring farm, her father was a religious man who wanted a farm that would be big enough for his whole family to work together – something which he was never able to achieve. In her view Leopard's Hill Ranch was the most beautiful farm in Northern Rhodesia. Elie Susman told van Rensburg that he and his brother were only selling the ranch because of the difficulty that they had in finding good managers. There had been heavy stock losses and it was alleged that the Susmans' fine cattle were being 'swapped' for inferior stock. On the brothers' last visit to the ranch as owners in July 1945, Elie noted that the condition of the cattle there was 'not bad', but predators continued to be a problem. Van Rensburg shot dozens of lions in his first years there. Their skins decorated the veranda, which surrounded the ranch house. The family remained on the ranch until the late 1970s when they were compelled to abandon it. It was close to the Zambezi escarpment and was on an infiltration route for ZAPU guerrillas returning to Rhodesia. It was also on a route used by Rhodesian commandos who raided in the opposite direction. The ranch became the site of a resettlement scheme in the 1980s and the ranch house is now a clinic.[1]

The Susman brothers may have had other reasons for the sale in 1945. They had bought the neighbouring Rietfontein Ranch from the widow of Ben Woest, an early settler and transport rider, in the previous year. Its

12,000 acres made it easier to manage than Leopard's Hill's 56,000 acres. It was also closer to the Line of Rail, and better suited to mixed agriculture. The sale of the larger ranch may have been intended to release capital for the expansion of the new Northern Rhodesian businesses. It appears that only £15,000 in new capital was subscribed by the Susman brothers for Harry Wulfsohn Ltd in 1944. The other half of the initially paid-up capital of £30,000 represented the assets that Harry Wulfsohn put into the company. The initial expansion of the business was largely funded by loans from Susman Brothers Ltd. These were financed by an overdraft, which was secured on that company's assets in Northern Rhodesia, Bechuanaland and South Africa.[2]

Lochinvar and Other Ranches

The main purpose of Leopard's Hill Ranch had been the fattening of cattle for the Congo and, later on, the Copperbelt markets. Cattle imported from Ngamiland for these markets were usually sent to ranches at two–three years of age and sold at four–five years. They were held for sale in the last quarter of the year when cattle were scarcest and prices highest. Ngamiland cattle put on weight rapidly in the relatively lush pastures of the north. Werners, in conjunction with Copperfields, bought a number of ranches as joint ventures in the post-war years. The largest and most dramatic of these was Lochinvar, a 105,000-acre ranch on the Kafue Flats, which had been started in 1912–13 by an Australian, Robert Gordon, representing the Rhodesian Land and Cattle Company. The latter company had kept about 5,000 cattle on the ranch, but they were all sold to 'Bongola' Smith in 1920–1. He bought the ranch through the Congo–Rhodesia Ranching Company, a subsidiary of Elakat, in 1929, but it was sold again in 1933 to L. J. Vaughan, a conservationist, who kept it as a private game reserve. Vaughan had first seen the ranch in 1921 and later described it as it was then:

> The fantastic quantity of wildlife defies description, thousands, tens of thousands, and hundreds of thousands of animals roamed over the Kafue Flats and the savannas along its edges … [travelling along the Flats from Mazabuka] to Namwala and beyond you would never have been out of sight of countless herds of game all around you. Buffalo, Eland, Roan, Wildebeest, Zebra, Hartebeest, Lechwe [Kafue lechwe, a sub-species of semi-aquatic antelope and a relative of the red and black lechwe which are also found in Zambia], Puku, Reedbuck and the rest, while the savanna country was equally full of the browsers such as Sable, Kudu and Eland with the Buffalo using the dense *masitu* areas, lions were everywhere, the rivers full of hippo.[3]

In 1937 he reckoned that there were 20,000 lechwe, 5,000 zebra, 3,000 wildebeest and hundreds of buffalo, eland, roan and sable antelope, and kudu on the ranch. By that time it had become a minor tourist attraction. The district commissioner reported in 1938 that seventy-seven cars had visited it in the course of the year. Vaughan sold the ranch in that year to John Oliver and F. J. Summerton. Werners and Copperfields bought it at the end of 1948 from Oliver and his then co-owner, Herbert Smith. He was the father of Wilbur Smith, the popular novelist, who acknowledges that life on the ranch in the 1940s was the inspiration for many of his novels. The price paid for the ranch in 1948 was about £15,000.[4]

Lochinvar was never ideal as a ranch. About forty per cent of the surface was usually flooded. Another forty per cent was poorly drained. Only twenty per cent was suitable for year-round grazing. The title deeds of the ranch gave the local Ila people the right to trek their cattle annually across the ranch to the north bank of the Kafue, and they had the right to conduct regular ritual hunts for lechwe. There was also competition between cattle and game for grazing. Cattle stocks peaked at 12,000 in 1950 and averaged 5–9,000 during the remainder of the 1950s. Towards the end of 1951, Maurice Rabb reported that the management of Lochinvar was in a mess, and a large number of cattle had gone missing. The manager was unable to cope, and his deputy, 'Van' van Zyl, was reluctant to take over. When he was eventually persuaded to do so, Rabb reported that he had 'found' 800 missing cattle, and that search parties were still out. In the end it was reported that 600 cattle had died during the year and that 250 were 'lost or strayed'. Van Zyl remained at the ranch until his untimely death in December 1961. His deputy, Austin Fuller, succeeded him and remained on the ranch until its sale in 1966. Lochinvar was, and remains, a very beautiful place. The directors and staff of Werners and Copperfields frequently used the ranch house there for holidays, for the entertainment of important guests and for board meetings. They became very attached to the ranch and were reluctant to part with it when pressed to do so by the colonial government of Northern Rhodesia and, later on, by the independent government of Zambia.[5]

From 1956 onwards it began to be internationally recognised that Lochinvar was acting as an informal game and bird sanctuary. The distinguished naturalist and authority on the red deer of Scotland, Frank Fraser Darling, was commissioned by the Game and Tsetse Control Department to do a survey of wildlife in Northern Rhodesia as a whole. He visited Lochinvar in October 1956, and described the view of the lagoon from his camp at Chunga:

> The edge of the lagoon is lined with hundreds of pelicans, spur-winged geese, knob-nosed ducks, whistler and pink-billed ducks, saddle-bill and open-bill storks, marabou storks, and some wattled and crested cranes. Spoonbills, egrets and ibises are common; there are some cormorants and anhingas, white herons, blue herons (like ours), Goliath herons and squacco herons. The flats themselves show what you would expect, wattled and blacksmith plovers, coursers, pratincoles, pipits and larks, and on the anthill edge are the wheatears. Out there in front of us over the lagoon are miles and miles of flats and water, and the impression is of the great ocean.[6]

In the book that resulted from this project, as well as in his journals – which were published much later – he paid tribute to the role of the ranch in the conservation of the lechwe. It was thought that 16,000 of the 25,000 surviving animals in Northern Rhodesia were at Lochinvar. Darling stated that: 'The world has the Lochinvar Ranch – a commercial cattle-grazing enterprise – to thank for the sanctuary given to the most persecuted species of antelope in Northern Rhodesia. How far the owners' action will go in saving the red lechwe from the present senseless trend to extinction remains to be seen.' Darling was critical of the provincial administration's failure to stop the ritual hunts that were conducted by the Ila people four times a year, and which resulted in the slaughter of thousands of lechwe. He supported the plan to buy the ranch and set it up as a formal game sanctuary, though he thought that this would be of no use without a conservation plan. Sir Alfred Beit, co-owner with Colonel R. A. Critchley of Blue Lagoon, a ranch on the north bank of the Kafue, offered to put up £25,000 of the purchase price which was then expected to be £50,000. Darling thought that: 'It may well be that one of the best things I shall ever do in Northern Rhodesia will be to get the lechwe acknowledged as the animal best fitted to use the flats, get aerial patrol established and a conservation policy accepted.' He wanted a five-year period of absolute protection for the lechwe, and suggested that, later on, the ritual element of the hunt could be combined with a game management scheme and a scientific cull of surplus rams.[7]

Darling's suggestions were not followed up until four years later, after the visit of Sir Julian Huxley, another distinguished naturalist, who came on a UNESCO mission to east and central Africa. He visited Lochinvar with his wife in August 1960 and provided a lyrical description:

> Never have I seen such an abundance and variety of water, marsh and shore birds as on the flats of the Lochinvar Ranch – ducks, geese, pelicans, spoonbills, ibis, storks, cranes, terns, skimmers, plovers, stilts, ruffs and small waders. With groups of lechwe eating their way into the water, grazing amicably together with zebra on the unsubmerged part of the flats, and moving like

animated friezes across the horizon, the scene reminded me of a Breughel painting of the Creation, but greatly magnified and without the Creator.

He recommended the drawing-up of a wildlife management plan for the Kafue Flats as a whole, and the acquisition of Lochinvar as a National Park. He pointed out that the ranch could have been acquired for a few thousand pounds after the war, but the price had now multiplied five-fold. He cited this as an example of a penny-wise and pound-foolish attitude to wildlife conservation. It was as a result of Huxley's recommendations that Dr W. L. Robinette, an American naturalist, undertook a survey of the area in 1961–2 and made a detailed plan for game management and the commercial cropping of the red lechwe.[8]

Werners and Copperfields jointly acquired a further 80,000 acres of ranching land in 1946–8. The largest of these ranches was Forsyth's Estates, 47,000 acres on the Luezi River in the Zimba District, south of Kala Ranch. Hamish Forsyth had bought much of this land from George Buchanan soon after the First World War, and worked the ranch until his death in September 1946. He suffered heavy losses to predators, which were recorded with unfailing regularity in the 'Notes and Memos' column of the *Livingstone Mail*. In January 1947 the consortium bought the Nanga Ranch of 20,000 acres,

14 Harry Wulfsohn and Jack Tuffin
on Kafue River, Nanga Ranch, Zambia, 1967.

on the south side of the Kafue at Mazabuka, from the Duke of Westminster, paying £18,500 for it. Hugh Grosvenor, second Duke of Westminster, known to his friends as 'Bend'or', was the richest man in Britain. He had owned and developed the ranch since 1909, but had only visited it once. He had bought it because it was thought that it was suitable for large-scale cotton production. His managers included Ben Woest, his old hunting guide, and Major H. F. Darling, an Australian Anglo-Boer War veteran. Robert Boyd, who had been manager there since 1937, joined Susman Brothers & Wulfsohn as a result of this purchase. He was a close friend of Harry Wulfsohn who regarded him as the best rancher in the country. At about the same time the consortium bought the neighbouring Heale's Estates, another 11,000 acres on the south side of the Kafue.[9]

Although its history and scenery were not as dramatic as Lochinvar's, Nanga Ranch played a significant part in the agricultural history of Northern Rhodesia. It was chosen in 1956 by the Dutch advisers of Sir Ronald Prain and the Rhodesian Selection Trust as the site of the Kafue Flats Pilot Polder project. Leonard Tracey, an agricultural expert in Southern Rhodesia, had the idea that the Kafue Flats could be used for the commercial production of wheat, sugar and rice through the construction of a Dutch-style polder – a system of dykes and embankments which would protect the land from summer floods while providing for winter irrigation. Rhodesian Selection Trust leased about 1,500 acres from Nanga Estates for the experimental polder. The owners eventually donated this land to the Kafue Flats Pilot Polder Trust, which Rhodesian Selection Trust set up in 1960. The mining company spent a huge amount of money on this project and eventually produced a plan for a polder of 28,000 acres. This was modelled on the Gezira Scheme in the Sudan and would have involved an investment of £5,000,000 and a settlement scheme of 1,650 plots, supporting as many as 14,000 people. Rhodesian Selection Trust did not undertake to fund the next stage. The pilot polder was handed over to the government at independence and was soon abandoned. Tate & Lyle had, however, taken an interest in the project and the research done at Nanga laid the basis for the development of the Nakambala Sugar Estate near Mazabuka. This eventually made Zambia both self-sufficient in, and an exporter of, sugar.[10]

These ranches were very profitable during the boom years of the early 1950s. Their profitability depended on the weight, perhaps 200 pounds a year, which was added to cattle during the two years that they spent on the ranches. One observer calculated in 1962 that the weight gained by 4,000 cattle at Lochinvar would produce a gross income of £22,000 a year, from which all the expenses of the ranch, including cattle losses and transport costs had to be deducted. In the early years the ranches did not pay dividends, but they did issue bonus shares to their joint owners. The profitability of the ranches was closely tied to the flow of cattle from Ngamiland. This began to slow down when the Lobatse abattoir came into production in the latter half of 1954. It came to a complete halt in 1958 when a combination of economic recession and imports of chilled beef from Southern Rhodesia stopped the flow of live cattle from Bechuanaland.[11]

The movement of cattle across the Zambezi at Kazungula had already stopped in 1954. Restrictions imposed by the CDC on the export of underweight cattle, and the eastward spread of tsetse flies had already resulted in a reduction in the flow. A new route was developed which led eastwards to the Southern Rhodesian Line of Rail at Matetsi, passing through the CDC ranch at Bushman Pits. This ranch was leased to the Ngamiland Cattle Exporters' Association in 1954. The plan was that underweight cattle would be fattened there before export. 'Chobo' Weskob was chairman of the association, but he soon became doubtful about the economic viability of the scheme. Trekking on the Kazungula route began again in 1961 after an outbreak of foot-and-mouth disease cut Ngamiland off from the rest of the protectorate, but it came to a final end in 1967 when the new government of independent Botswana insisted that all Ngamiland cattle should be sent to Lobatse for slaughter.[12]

As a result of these changes in the pattern of trade, the owners began in the early 1960s to think of alternative uses for the ranches. It was decided that Lochinvar would continue to be used as a holding ranch, pending the outcome of negotiations about its sale to the government. There were 8,500 cattle on the ranch in October 1961, but this number had fallen to 3,600 a year later. The directors had by then begun to introduce a game management scheme along the lines suggested by Robinette. It was decided that the balance of Nanga Estates should be sold or leased, Heale's Estates should be used for crop production, and Forsyth's Estates should continue to be used for stock breeding.[13]

Negotiations over the sale of Lochinvar were protracted. The companies would have been well advised to conclude a deal with the colonial government before independence, but they failed to do so. After discussions in 1954–6 came to nothing, the government made a fresh approach through Maurice Rabb in 1961. Negotiations in the following year involved Isadore Kollenberg, Max Barnett, Harry Wulfsohn and the mediation of Colonel

Critchley. He suggested a price of £105,000, while the government was apparently prepared to offer £65,000.[14]

In June 1964, on the eve of independence, the owners informed the commissioner of lands that Lochinvar was for sale at a price of £202,000, or roughly £2 an acre. Max Barnett told David Susman that the directors of Lochinvar Estates had all agreed on this price. He thought that they would have to come down, but that it 'was a good opening gambit'. The directors emphasised the potential value of the ranch for tourism, game cropping and, possibly, the production of sugar. They were still sticking to this price in April 1965. By holding out for such a high price, Werners and Copperfields lost the credit that they had received from Fraser Darling and Huxley for saving the red lechwe. Errol Button, then an adviser to the Ministry of Lands, but famous as an eccentric district commissioner and the builder of Lundazi Castle, commented in a memorandum: '… I personally feel a sense of shock at anybody adopting this attitude over an obvious national asset when they themselves are incapable of protecting the asset and depend largely on Government to do so'. He said, a little unfairly, that the owners had in the past been reluctant to do anything to preserve the game. They had only recently agreed to employ six game guards – as a result of pressure from their manager, Austin Fuller. President Kaunda, who had a strong personal interest in conservation, responded to this memorandum: 'I agree with you and we must take over this place soon. I am writing from Lochinvar itself and I am shocked by the number of lechwe limping because they have been shot at. Please go ahead with your Appendix B memorandum to Cabinet.' This seems to have suggested an offer of £50–£65,000 backed up with the threat of compulsory purchase.[15]

Max Barnett, who was terminally ill and was to die within a few months, and Len Pinshow had a meeting with the permanent secretary, L. P. Mwanza, and other officials at the Ministry of Lands, in June 1965. According to the minutes of this meeting: 'Mr Barnett seemed rather reluctant to name a figure and considerable discussion took place before he finally stated that the lowest figure his Board was prepared to accept was £130,000.' The permanent secretary emphatically rejected this figure, pointing out that his minister, Solomon Kalulu, did not see why the government should pay more than the £15,000 that the owners had paid in 1948. The minister also took the view that the Chartered Company had no right to sell, or lease, the land in the first place. Max Barnett's explanation that the price was made up of £100,000 for the land, and £30,000 for the 'natural assets' on it, was not helpful, as it appeared to put a price on the lechwe. Barnett and Pinshow left the meeting saying that they would recommend a price of £100,000 to their partners.[16]

The minister of lands visited Lochinvar in October, and had a meeting with Harry Wulfsohn in Lusaka on 8 November 1965, three days before Rhodesia's UDI. Wulfsohn began by saying that he did not like bargaining over Lochinvar. He put forward a number of reasonable alternatives: that the company should be allowed to crop the lechwe under the terms of the Robinette Report; that the government should offer land in the Zimba or Mazabuka districts in exchange for the ranch; and that the price should be submitted to an independent arbitrator. The minister rejected game cropping and arbitration, but said that he might be prepared to consider an exchange of land. Following this meeting, Maurice Rabb wrote to President Kaunda on 14 December 1965 asking for arbitration or an exchange of land. The response was an offer of £28,000, which was rejected by the board of Nanga Estates in April 1966. The government came back with an offer of £40,000 – slightly less than the official valuation of £41,950. This was their final offer and was the price paid. The World Wildlife Fund, whose president, Prince Bernhardt of the Netherlands had expressed an interest in Lochinvar, contributed £2,000 towards the purchase price. Harry and Edwin Wulfsohn and Jack Tuffin were present when the ranch was handed over to government on 17 October 1966. It was, Edwin Wulfsohn recalls, 'a very sad day'. Lochinvar was gazetted as a National Park in 1972, and has proved to be an enduring and popular tourist attraction.[17]

Werners also had two smaller farms on the Copperbelt. Kansuswa Farm, near Mufulira, was originally used as a holding ground for slaughter cattle. When the flow of live cattle slowed down, Max Barnett developed piggeries there, and the farm became the Copperbelt's main supplier of pork. At much the same time Barnett developed the Chambishi dairy farm near Kitwe. The Copperbelt was a difficult area for dairy farming because of the high rainfall and leached soil. Costs were high because of the need for supplementary feeding, but at one stage this farm supplied sixty per cent of the fresh milk supply of Kitwe. Neither of these enterprises was ever very profitable. One of Edwin Wulfsohn's tasks on his return to Zambia in 1968 was to turn these farms around. He succeeded in doing this through the recruitment of an excellent manager, Doug Wylie, from Rhodesia in 1970. The two farms were sold together as a unit in 1975. Susman Brothers & Wulfsohn also owned a small dairy farm, Livingstone Jersey Farm, at Livingstone. Maurice Rabb and Harry Wulfsohn set this up soon after Rabb's arrival in the town in 1947, but it was too near the centre of the town and was closed down in 1963.[18]

Agricultural Enterprises Ltd

Susman Brothers & Wulfsohn, as distinct from Werners, also started a new farming venture soon after the war. Agricultural Enterprises Ltd began to farm in October 1946, though it was not formally established until March 1947. It consisted of a partnership between Susman Brothers & Wulfsohn, which subscribed half the issued share capital of £25,000, and Geoffrey Beckett and Stewart Green who each subscribed one-quarter. Beckett, who has already featured in this story, was a close friend of Harry Wulfsohn. He was, from 1948 onwards, a member of the Legislative Council. In the following year he became a member of the colonial government as member for agriculture. Stewart Green was a friend and neighbour of Beckett, farming side-by-side with him in the Choma District. Green was highly regarded as a tobacco farmer. He had, like Beckett, arrived in Northern Rhodesia from England as a young man in the mid 1920s. The idea behind Agricultural Enterprises was that the company should carry on mixed farming in tobacco, maize and cattle on a number of farms belonging to the partners. Susman Brothers & Wulfsohn contributed its Rietfontein and Kala ranches. Geoffrey Beckett contributed two developed farms, Momba and Shingororo, and two undeveloped farms, Duba and Nkanga, while Green contributed his Chenga farm. The five farms in the Choma District formed a block of about 20,000 acres and were thought to be well suited to tobacco production, with some maize and cattle. Rietfontein was felt to be primarily suited to maize and cattle production, while Kala Ranch consisted of about 19,000 acres of ranching land. The idea for this project probably came from discussions between Geoff Beckett and Harry Wulfsohn, though Elie Susman was also involved in the planning stage.[19]

This partnership lasted until 1953. After three years, however, it was apparent that there were problems with it. The fundamental difficulty seems to have been a clash of personalities and interests between Stewart Green, the managing director, and Robert Boyd, the cattle manager. Green thought that Boyd and Wulfsohn were only interested in cattle and uninterested in tobacco, giving priority to the Rietfontein and Kala ranches and neglecting the Choma farms. Boyd and Beckett, on the other hand, thought that Green was exclusively interested in tobacco and that he was a weak managing director. Boyd felt that Green should be a tougher disciplinarian with the young white men, many of them inexperienced ex-servicemen, who were recruited as farm managers. Green considered Boyd to be harsh, bad-tempered and parsimonious. Beckett also doubted Boyd's ability to get on with the managers 'owing to his very hasty temperament'. Both he and Wulfsohn were disappointed by the profits of the company at a time of high tobacco prices. Dividends were declared for three or four years, but these were credited to the accounts of the shareholders as the company lacked the cash to pay them out.[20]

Writing to Elie Susman in 1951, Beckett indicated a concern that the farms were not being run with due regard to the environmental concerns that they both shared. '... I think it is indisputable that the methods of land usage employed have been a long way from what you and I have always desired, with proper protection of the lands against erosion and proper rotations and use of manures to keep them in good heart.'[21] In an earlier letter to the directors he had been very critical of the poor standards of maintenance on his own farms, and had also been critical of the company's lack of concern with the welfare of its African employees. It was important that the company should ensure that its farms were popular places of employment. Robert Boyd attempted to resign in 1949. Stewart Green attempted to withdraw from the company two years later. The question of liquidation was first considered in 1949, and was seriously discussed in 1952. A decision to liquidate was taken in April 1953, but was rescinded in October of the same year. It was then decided that Susman Brothers & Wulfsohn would buy out the other shareholders and that the company would remain in business. In the final settlement Stewart Green exchanged his shares for his own farm. Beckett reclaimed Momba and Shingororo, while Duba and Nkanga were transferred to Susman Brothers & Wulfsohn.[22]

Stewart Green's son, Peter, who started work for Agricultural Enterprises in the last year of the partnership, still farms at Chenga with his sons. He has a diary of his first year's work. Looking back over fifty years, he is struck by the primitive methods of production, low yields, and 'shocking' labour relations, which were a feature of settler farming in those days. Tobacco yields are now four times what they were and curing is many times more efficient. He recalls nights spent sleeping at the barns, with an alarm clock, in an attempt to supervise the curing process. If the temperature was not right, a barn of tobacco could turn black in an hour. He remembers maize being carried in from the fields in *machilas* (cloth hammocks) and people working on the harvest until nine or ten at night. He feels that his father had little to show in the end for the seven or eight years of hard work that he put into the company. He regained his farm and received some cash, but the value of improvements to the farm was not great.[23]

Susman Brothers & Wulfsohn also made little profit out of this venture. It may, however, have served a useful purpose in training a number of farm managers who remained with the company. The alliance with Geoffrey Beckett, who had a great deal of influence in the agricultural life of the country until the end of the colonial period, was also of considerable value to the company. It was not without costs to Beckett himself. His son, Mike, who continues to farm alongside the Greens at Momba and Shingororo, recalls that anti-Semitism was still a factor in settler society in the 1950s, and that his father was criticised by other farmers for his alliance with 'the Jews'.[24]

After the dissolution of the partnership, Agricultural Enterprises remained in existence as the main farming subsidiary of Susman Brothers & Wulfsohn. The company continued to own the Choma group of farms and to manage the Kala and Rietfontein ranches. The latter became the company's show farm under the management of Hermanus Cloete from 1951 onwards. Elie Susman was pleased to note that the ranch's herd of 2,500 crossbred Sussex Afrikanders won all the fat-stock prizes at the Lusaka Show in 1955. A year later the ranch was credited with 'the finest commercial crop of maize standing in Northern Rhodesia'. This was expected to produce a then record crop of twenty-five to thirty bags an acre, and a profit of £10,000. Harry Wulfsohn, who was a great admirer of Cloete, sought to buy the farm from his partners in 1957. Elie Susman said that he had no objection to such a sale, but Maurice Rabb and David Susman opposed it. The latter felt strongly that directors should not be encouraged to make bids for prize assets, saying that offers from directors of Woolworths to purchase individual stores would not be countenanced. Cloete was an outstanding manager, though he was not an easy man to work with. It was said that in 1957 he was the only white employee on the ranch. This may have been due, not so much to liberal employment practices, as to the difficulty he had in retaining white subordinates. He did, however, provide training to Benford Nkobo, who later became a farm manager. Cloete resigned suddenly in November 1963 after twelve years at Rietfontein. Barnett and Boyd made strenuous efforts to persuade him to stay, but he was determined to leave. He returned to South Africa and died a few years later.[25]

Max Barnett took over the management of these farms when Robert Boyd retired in 1963. He differed with Harry Wulfsohn over the desirability of making further purchases of farms in the Choma area. He took the view that the farms were not yet profitable and that 'we are too prone to mix speculation with straight farming operations ... The ownership of undeveloped land always lands us in more and more capital expenditure, and cattle ranching, by companies, necessitating remote control, is at best a marginal enterprise'. Resistance to new acquisitions ended with Barnett's death in October 1965. Jack Tuffin had taken over from him as general manager of the farms a few months earlier. He was a mechanical engineer who answered an advertisement from the north of England. At the time of his appointment as a farm manager in 1960 at Choma, he had no experience of farming or of Africa. He proved to be hardworking and highly competent. He also succeeded Barnett as general manager of Werners and remained with the group for a further twenty years.[26]

Zambesi Ranching and Cropping

In spite of Barnett's reservations, Susman Brothers & Wulfsohn added considerably to its farming interests in the years before and after independence in 1964. A number of farms were bought in the Choma District. These were adjacent to Duba and Nkanga and created a block of over 80,000 acres. The best-known of these farms was Demo Estate, which was bought in 1962. Demo had a colourful early history. Its principal founder in 1909 was the actor Marmaduke Wetherell, who stayed at Demo for only a few years, but returned to Northern Rhodesia in 1924 to play Dr David Livingstone in the silent film *Livingstone*, which was made in that year. The farm's later owner was F. J. 'Mopani' Clarke. In 1968–9 it was reported that the farms in this group constituted the largest ranching unit in Zambia. In 1967 another group of farms was acquired in the Mazabuka District. Sikalozia Estate consisted of three farms and about 22,000 acres. It was bought from N. J. Strudwick, who continued to work as a manager on the farms for several years. The two neighbouring farms, known as Kangila, with about 14,500 acres, were bought from two partners, Peter Wroth and R. J. (Bob) Shenton. The latter continued to work as crops manager for the company for many years.[27]

In October 1967 the farming interests of Susman Brothers & Wulfsohn were merged with those of African Commercial Holdings to form a new company, Zambesi Ranching Corporation (ZRC) – the name was changed to Zambesi Ranching and Cropping Ltd in 1984. Susman Brothers & Wulfsohn held three-quarters of the shares in the new company, but Maurice Gersh, whose company held the remainder of the shares, became chairman. The merger added a further 24,000 acres of land in the Mazabuka District to the 36,500 that had been bought earlier in the year. This land belonged to Kaleya Estates, which the Gersh brothers had bought in 1949. The new company took over debts of £300,000 owed by the farming companies to Susman Brothers & Wulfsohn. A large proportion of these funds had been channelled from the profits of the trading business into the development of Rietfontein Ranch and the Choma farms. In addition to the Choma and Mazabuka groups of farms, the new company also took over the Kala and Rietfontein ranches. A further 47,000 acres of ranching land was added to the group by the purchase of Copperfields's share of Forsyth's Estates at Zimba in 1971. At about the same time Heale's Estates and the balance of Nanga Estates, both jointly owned with Copperfields Cold Storage, were sold to a parastatal company, the Rural Development Company, for a relatively small sum – less than K150,000.[28]

The acquisition of Kaleya Estate brought Chris Lowe, who was thought to be the best cattle manager in the country, into the service of the new company. He placed great emphasis on meticulous and methodical record keeping and scientific pasture management. He had arrived to work for Maurice Gersh in 1958–9 and remained with the new company until 1975. He then moved to South Africa where he is still an active farmer in Kwa-Zulu-Natal. Another man who came with the merger, and who proved in the long run to be an even more important asset, was Rodney Clyde-Anderson. He and Lowe had attended the same school – Jeppe Boys' High School in Johannesburg – an unlikely source for two first-class ranchers. Clyde-Anderson arrived at Mazabuka railway station with a battered suitcase and £5 in his pocket on 31 December 1961. He worked with Lowe for a year or two, but was retrenched after drought and a disastrous season. Maurice Gersh said that he could not afford to keep him on, but offered him a job at Werners's Kansuswa Farm on the Copperbelt. Clyde-Anderson preferred instead to work for Bob Burton at Kabwe, where he remained for four years. He returned to Kaleya as ranch manager in 1967 – not long before the merger. He became assistant general manager with special responsibility for cattle in 1983, and general manager in 1985. Over forty years after his first arrival at Kaleya he remains with ZRC as chairman, with his office at Sikalozia Farm.[29]

Jack Tuffin was the first general manager of the new company. His subordinates saw him as nitpicking and pedantic. Edwin Wulfsohn acknowledges that he lacked humour, but he says that he was an exceptionally competent and loyal company servant. Tuffin clearly had a capacity for constructive and critical thought. When he became chairman of the company in 1971, Chris Lowe took over as general manager. After Lowe's departure, Eric King, a retired government agricultural officer, was recruited as general manager. During the 1970s Tuffin, Lowe and King devoted themselves to the gradual improvement of the farms and ranches under their control. This involved fencing the land, the creation of pasture by the planting of grasses and the improvement of cattle herds by the import of Boran, Afrikander, Sussex and Hereford bulls from Kenya, South Africa and Great Britain. The acreage under maize increased from about 2,000 acres to 4,500 acres between 1967 and 1973.[30]

After UDI and the end of imports from Botswana, there was a serious shortage of beef in the country. The Cold Storage Board sought to alleviate the shortage by flying in beef from South Africa, paying seven times its value in freight charges. This was a luxury that Zambia could clearly not afford – certainly not after recession struck in 1974. ZRC had soon established itself as the major producer of cattle in the country, and this role gave it some protection against political pressures. Although President Kenneth Kaunda's 'Watershed Speech' in July 1975 abolished freehold title, replacing it with ninety-nine-year leases, and threatened the confiscation of under-utilised land, this was not a major threat to ZRC. Only a minority of its farms was held in freehold tenure, and its land was more likely to be over-stocked than under-used. Tuffin expressed concern in 1977 that, with one cow for every nine acres of grazing land, there was a serious danger of over-grazing. The company, nevertheless, sought assurances from the government that its land was regarded as fully utilised. It also decided to lower its public profile and reduce the size of the notice boards outside its farms. The Southern Province Land Commission, which took evidence in 1981 and reported in the following year, seemed to pose a threat to the company's land holdings: a soil survey suggested that its ranches in the Mazabuka District were suitable for peasant agriculture. In the end the report proved to be innocuous.[31]

In 1980–1 a part of Kaleya Ranch – about 4,000 acres – was compulsorily purchased for an out-growers scheme, which was sponsored by CDC and Barclays Bank. The out-growers were to produce cane for the Zambia Sugar Company's Nakambala Mill. Negotiations with the Zambia Sugar Company and CDC had been going on since 1975. Tuffin was reluctant to part with the land, which included some of the company's best maize-growing areas. He did not demand financial compensation, but held out for compensatory improvements to the remaining land. Edwin Wulfsohn thought that compulsory purchase was an embarrassing outcome to these long negotiations, as it gave the impression that the company did not support the out-growers scheme. After President Kaunda opened the new Zambia Spinners plant in Livingstone in 1981, Tuffin and Wulfsohn were able to organise a meeting with him in Lusaka. The meeting began inauspiciously when the visitors arrived two hours late – owing to confusion over the twenty-four hour clock. They eventually met the president at about midnight. He treated them with great courtesy and they received an assurance that ZRC's existence was not under threat.[32]

The company came through the tensions of the liberation war in Zimbabwe more or less unscathed, though Edwin Wulfsohn, Maurice Rabb and Jack Tuffin had a frightening encounter with some of Joshua Nkomo's ZAPU guerrillas at Kala Ranch in 1978. This ranch, like Leopard's Hill Ranch, was close to the Zambezi escarpment and was on a route for guerrillas infiltrating Rhodesia from Zambia across the river. The company was not, however, immune from the general consequences of the recession that began in the mid 1970s. This affected the availability of foreign exchange for the import of breeding stock and machinery, as well as for the remittance of dividends and the salaries of expatriate employees. From 1976 onwards, dividends were placed in the 'pipeline' or queue for foreign exchange. For five years from 1982 ZRC did not declare a dividend and reinvested its profits. Dividends from earlier years were also withdrawn from the pipeline and invested in the company. Some profits from Zamtex were also channelled through Susman Brothers & Wulfsohn to ZRC.[33]

In an article on 'Cattle Ranching in Zambia', which was published in 1980, Dina Wulfsohn, wife of Edwin, reported that the company was running 23,000 cattle on 220,000 acres. The annual off-take from the herds was close to 7,000 cattle. About two-thirds of these went to the butchers, but one-third were yearling steers that were sold to other ranchers. A major customer was the Anglo American ranch at Chisamba. The company was 'embarking on a major intensification programme which aims at doubling the current carrying capacity of one beast per nine acres, by reducing paddock size, multiplying watering points, bush clearing and possibly establishing legumes in the veldt, planting further Star and Rhodes grass pastures and intensifying management to cope with this development'. In spite of tropical and tick-borne diseases, and the prevalence of predators, annual stock losses were kept down to three per cent. The Boran herd was concentrated on the Choma farms. Rodney Clyde-Anderson was managing the crossbred Hereford/Afrikander stock at Kaleya, while the Sussex/Afrikander crossbred herd was kept at Sikalozia. The company had imported nearly 300 pedigree cattle, mainly Hereford and Sussex stock, from the United Kingdom in the previous five years at a cost of £225,000.[34]

Although the owners derived little or no income from ZRC for many years, they showed a degree of reluctance either to sell or to liquidate the business. In 1973 Lonrho had acquired a quarter share of ZRC through its takeover of African Commercial Holdings. There were direct talks at that time between Edwin Wulfsohn and Tiny Rowland about the possibility of Lonrho buying a half share in Werners, which was then the Zambian holding company for ZRC. The directors of Concorde Investments (Jersey) Ltd, which was set up as an offshore holding company for the central African assets of the group in 1973, were not enthusiastic about this proposal. They were more interested in an outright sale of the ranches, and were prepared to contemplate a sale of all the central African interests. Rowland, however, made it clear that he would only be prepared to buy the assets with foreign exchange at a substantial discount.[35]

There was renewed discussion of a Lonrho takeover of ZRC in 1976. The suggestion then was that shares in ZRC should be exchanged for shares in Lonrho to the value of about £2,000,000. David Susman put forward an alternative suggestion that Concorde Investments should sell half of its shares to Lonrho. An approximate value of £4,000,000 was placed on the group as a whole. In the following year there seems to have been agreement in principle for the sale of the ranches to Lonrho for £1,000,000, but the deal did not go through. At the same time Lonrho proved unwilling to sell its minority stake in ZRC. It did not wish to be seen to be disposing of agricultural assets in Zambia at a time when it was under pressure to increase them. It was not until 1978 that a settlement with Lonrho was worked out, under which it gave up its shareholding in ZRC in exchange for Rietfontein, the most highly developed ranch, and a share of the company's cattle herds. Vernon Mwaanga, Zambia's former foreign minister, was then working for Lonrho and took part in the negotiations. He contrasted Tuffin's conservative approach to farming with Lonrho's more dynamic style. Edwin Wulfsohn recalls that at one point in the negotiations he threatened to deliver Lonrho's share of the cattle – about 6,000 of them – to their offices in Lusaka's Cairo Road. Mwaanga recalls that he was 'a tough negotiator'.[36]

Bookers, the international trading group that had operated in Zambia as CBC Ltd, was also interested at one stage in taking a share in ZRC. There was a suggestion that it should buy one-third of the business and that another third should be sold to Zambian institutional investors. A few years later, Vernon Mwaanga, in partnership with Alex Chikwanda, the former minister of agriculture, expressed an interest in buying a half share in the company. Enock Kavindele, later vice-president of Zambia, also negotiated for the purchase of a half share. These talks fell through because of a problem with the overseas funding. Edwin Wulfsohn recalls that Kavindele conducted these negotiations 'impeccably'. There was also talk of a merger of the company with the agricultural interests of the Anglo American Corporation. The latter proposal fell through because Anglo was not prepared to pay any part of the purchase price in foreign exchange.[37]

In the end the only significant change in the ownership of the company in the 1980s was that Simon Zukas, a Zambian citizen, acting through the Zukas family trust, bought the Barnett family's share in Concorde Investments. Zukas became a director of ZRC in 1982 and took over as chairman of the company on the resignation of Jack Tuffin in the following year. He had arrived in Northern Rhodesia from Lithuania at the age of thirteen in 1938. He served with the King's African Rifles during the war and then studied Civil Engineering at the University of Cape Town. On his return to Northern Rhodesia Zukas became actively involved in the opposition to the establishment of the Federation and was imprisoned and deported to the United Kingdom by the colonial government in 1952. He returned to Zambia after independence and established a successful civil-engineering business. He had a link with the Susman family through his marriage to Cynthia Robinson, daughter of Julius Robinson, and cousin of Harry Robinson. Although he had not held political office, Zukas was a director of a number of parastatal companies, including Indeco, and had been a member of the governing party, UNIP. He was more closely in touch with political and commercial developments in Zambia than any other member of the board, and he was to play a leading part in the return of the country to multi-party democracy in 1990–1. His subsequent political career is outlined in a later chapter.[38]

There were few changes in the nature of the business during the 1980s. The cattle population remained fairly stable. ZRC participated in 1984–5 in the construction of a dam on the Kaleya River, which made possible the irrigation of several hundred acres of Dimba Ranch. The company had its own land development unit, which constructed smaller dams on the estates. There were some difficult years in the mid 1980s as a result of drought, and outbreaks of cattle diseases, including corridor disease and foot-and-mouth, which periodically limited cattle movements and sales. In the first half of the decade, the bulk of cattle were sold on contract to the Galauns' Lusaka Cold Storage and Galaunia Farms. In the middle of the decade new links were forged with Oliver Irwin's Kyundu Ranch and his emerging butchery business. At the same time, new foreign exchange incentives were introduced for the production of export crops, encouraging the growing of fruit and vegetables for export. At the same time it became possible for the first time in ten years to remit dividends.[39]

There was resistance to the Zambianisation of management from the existing white, and expatriate, farm managers during the 1970s. This continued in the Mazabuka area into the late 1980s. The first Zambian farm manager was Joshua Mwaanga who was identified as having potential in 1969. Three years later it was reported that he had proved to be very successful as the manager of the outlying Kala Ranch. Benford Nkobo, who came from Botswana, became manager at Sikalozia in the early 1980s. It was at that time that the company set up the Duba Training School, which provided short courses for assistant managers. From the mid 1980s there was increased pressure for localisation, as it became more difficult to obtain foreign exchange supplementation for expatriate staff. By the early 1990s all the farm managers were Zambian citizens; expatriates continued to fill management positions at the group level and in specialist roles.[40]

Among the most remarkable and indispensable of these was 'Rama' Rama Krishnan. He came from Madras, India, and had worked in Somalia for two years before joining the University of Zambia as chief accountant. Simon Zukas recruited him from there in 1983. He took over as company secretary and chief accountant in 1987 – posts that he filled until his return to India in 2001. He was based at the company's headquarters at Sikalozia, near Mazabuka, which replaced Livingstone as the registered office of the company in 1982. 'Rama' was an accountant of exceptional energy and dedication who formed an improbable, but apparently harmonious, partnership with Rodney Clyde-Anderson. He thought at first that he would find it difficult to gain acceptance among the members of Mazabuka's famously introverted settler farming community, but he soon became an essential adjunct to it. He is proud of the fact that he never wrote a bouncing cheque, though there were some occasions in the late 1990s when he had to delay payments.[41]

In terms of acreage, cattle population and annual off-take, the company remained remarkably stable from the late 1970s until the early 1990s. Some directors, including Edwin Wulfsohn, expressed frustration in the late 1980s at the apparent failure of plans for the intensification of production. He felt that more effort should be put into the production of crops for export, such as cotton and tobacco, as well as into the development of feedlots and the export of beef. He also thought that renewed talk of selling the company, or part of it, discouraged management. There was discussion at this time of a merger with Galaunia Farms, and of a merger with Lendor Burton, another major cattle producer. The parastatal mining company, Zambia Consolidated Copper Mines (ZCCM), showed some interest in buying a half share in the company, as did the Bata Shoe Company, which had a special interest in the purchase of hides, but none of these suggestions came to fruition.[42]

The growth of the company in these years was steady, but unspectacular. Investment in the improvement of the ranches and the cattle built up assets of substantial value. At the time of the talks with ZCCM in 1989 a value of $11,000,000 was put on the company. This growth in the value of the assets was achieved during a turbulent decade in the economic history of Zambia when management had to deal not only with natural phenomena such as drought and cattle disease, but also with the generally downward trend in the economy, and bewildering fluctuations in tax and foreign exchange regimes. These culminated in several attempts at Structural Adjustment, which were accompanied by massive devaluations and hyperinflation. It was a time when the maintenance of stability, and even stagnation, was a considerable achievement, and growth of any kind was difficult. More than twenty-five years of hard work by management and workers, with minimal returns to the shareholders, ultimately produced an asset that was in 1993 to form the basis of an entirely new enterprise – Trans Zambezi Industries.

CHAPTER 20

From Conflict to Concorde: Rhodesia, Zimbabwe, Botswana and the United Kingdom, 1963–2003

The end of the Federation, the independence of Zambia and Botswana, and UDI in Rhodesia, were events that had long-lasting consequences for the business. They were accompanied, or followed, by the deaths of three of the major protagonists: 'Chobo' Weskob, Max Barnett and Harry Wulfsohn. The main focus of this and the following chapter is on Edwin Wulfsohn's role in carrying the business forward to the turn of the millennium. In order to understand the later history of Susman Brothers & Wulfsohn in its new guise as Concorde Investments it is, however, necessary to return for a moment to the discussion of the break-up of the business that took up so much of the time and energy of the partners in the mid 1960s. Although this appears to have resulted from a clash of personalities, it is clear that political uncertainty and doubts about the future were important ingredients in a long-running saga. Harry Wulfsohn first suggested the division of the business to David Susman in the middle of 1962. Susman welcomed the suggestion and sought the advice of the group's auditor, Benny Gelfand, about the value of the two main businesses. He made his own back-of-an-envelope calculation of what they were worth, placing a value of £600,000 on Werners, and of £800,000 on Susman Brothers & Wulfsohn, which had become a holding company. It controlled Rhodesian Mercantile Holdings and held shares in Zambesi Saw Mills and Northern Rhodesia Textiles, as well as in some farms and ranches. Cattle were excluded from these calculations. Their inclusion would have brought the grand total to well over £1,500,000.[1]

The matter was brought to a head a year later in September 1963. In a letter to David Susman, Harry Wulfsohn complained that he had, since the death of Elie Susman, tried to work with his fellow directors as members of a team and as friends. He had, however, noticed that there was 'increasing friction between us ... emanating mainly from yourself'. He pointed out that the group had faced a serious crisis at the time of Elie Susman's death as a result of the loss of the mine contracts and 'political upheaval'. It was mainly as a result of his own 'foresight, drive and good name in financial circles in Rhodesia and London [that] we have emerged as one of the strongest and wealthiest groups in central Africa with a good name second to none'. He took issue with David Susman's recommendation that the head office of the trading business should be transferred back to Livingstone. He felt that the suggestion was 'unsound' and insulting to himself and Harry Robinson. They had, he said, taken every precaution to safeguard the company's position. He proposed that he should take over his share of the assets – thirty-six per cent of the whole – in the two main companies. He hoped that the break could be achieved in 'a friendly and amicable manner'.[2]

In his response to this letter David Susman wrote: '... I have felt for some time that your interests and the interests of my own immediate family no longer coincide, and this, of course, is the root of the difficulties that you feel have arisen between us'. He said that he was 'in complete agreement with your suggestion that we break up, as indeed I told you when we discussed it a year ago. It will be a difficult egg to unscramble, but since I have faith in your goodwill and fairness – and I am sure you have the same in mine – I believe it can be done.' He agreed that a split must take into account not only the value of assets, but the income derived from them, and suggested that the best way to achieve a break would be 'to split away entire businesses into one camp or the other'. His initial suggestion was that Wulfsohn should take control of Zambesi Saw Mills and Vigers, together with part of Werners and some of the farms.[3]

After a meeting with the other major partners, Max Barnett, Maurice Rabb and Harry Robinson in Johannesburg in October, David Susman told Wulfsohn that while 'the other directors may be in agreement with the principle that we should split and go our own ways, I regret very much that I was unable to persuade them that such a split should be made at this time'. He was personally sorry about this and said that he 'could see many further disagreements between our two camps in the future'. He felt, however, that 'the boys on the spot had a right to approach things their way, and I accordingly did not wish to force any issues'. Barnett, Rabb and Robinson had all indicated their opposition to the proposal in letters to Susman. Barnett thought that by courting Robinson, Wulfsohn was trying to drive a wedge between the families of Elie and Harry Susman. Maurice Rabb had a similar view, but also thought that Wulfsohn 'has made up his mind that Rhodesia is a write off and he is wanting to make his dispositions so that he is assured of a ready made business in UK without having to be answerable to his erstwhile colleagues'. He doubted that any break-up could be achieved amicably and thought that it would be 'a bitter battle all the way'. He also thought that it would be impossible to break up individual businesses.[4]

Over the next year the question of the break-up generated a great deal of correspondence. David Susman sought the advice of Johannesburg accountants and lawyers on how to value the assets. It was clear that valuation would be a complex and expensive business. The accountants noted that the economic and political uncertainties accompanying the break-up of the Federation presented particular problems. They took the view that most of the stores in 'the Native territories' were held on annual leases and were of little value. They also thought that the recent profits of the trading and butchery companies showed a downward trend and were insufficient to justify an allowance for goodwill. Harry Wulfsohn produced a memorandum in which he presented his own views on the proper basis for valuing the companies. He also gave an indication of the assets in which he was particularly interested. These included Zambesi Saw Mills, Vigers, Werners, and Northern Rhodesia Textiles.[5]

It seems to have been agreed that each side should appoint a valuator and that they should then agree on a neutral umpire. The former federal minister of finance, Sir Donald Macintyre, and the Chartered Company's resident director, Harry Grenfell, were mentioned as candidates for the latter role. In the end nothing happened. Harry Wulfsohn had second thoughts in August 1964 and suggested, through Harry Robinson, that the partners might be able to carry on without a rupture if their spheres of influence were more clearly defined. There were various suggestions as to how this could be done. Wulfsohn indicated that he wished to avoid contact with Max Barnett and did not, therefore, want to be involved with the farms. David Susman still thought that it would be better to go through with a complete break.[6]

The matter seems to have held fire during 1965, but was back on the table again in the middle months of 1966. This was in spite of the death of Max Barnett in October 1965, and of Rhodesian UDI in the following month. Harry Robinson told Maurice Rabb that the break would be better for all concerned and that December 1967 was his preferred date. Wulfsohn expressed a stronger interest than before in the farms and ranches, and in the Ngamiland Trading Company. David Susman indicated that he had no preference as to assets, though he predicted that 'in years to come the cattle and farms might not only be more profitable, but also more easily liquidated should this be necessary'. He was, however, reconciled to the idea of taking on the trading businesses in which Rabb and Robinson were most interested. He suggested that these could be valued on the basis of their profits in the past five years and without reference to the value of their assets.[7]

The Death of Harry Wulfsohn

The break-up did not take place at the end of 1967. The sudden and unexpected death of Harry Wulfsohn in August 1968 put an end to the debate. It is not entirely clear why the relationships between the partners had become so bad that a break had been thought to be necessary. The relationship between Harry Wulfsohn and Max Barnett had been difficult for years, though people who were close to them say that they had a fundamental respect for each other. They were both hard workers with strong views and strong principles, and they frequently clashed. There were times when they did not speak to each other for months, and when they could not be in the same room together, but they were also able to work together creatively for much of the time. Wulfsohn had a close and warm relationship with Harry Susman and looked upon him as a second father, but he was never so close to Elie Susman. There were tensions between them, but there was never really any doubt that Susman was the boss in spite of the fifty-fifty split in the voting shares in the two main companies.[8]

After Elie Susman's death Wulfsohn had a right to expect that he would, as the senior surviving partner and the main driver of the rapid post-war expansion of the businesses, inherit his mantle. There was instead a power vacuum in which he, Barnett and Rabb were nominal equals as managing directors of the Northern Rhodesian businesses, drawing equal salaries, while Harry Robinson had his own smaller fiefdom in Southern Rhodesia. Barnett had day-to-day responsibility for the management of Werners, and Rabb had, with Nathan Zelter, the same responsibility for Susman Brothers & Wulfsohn. Harry Wulfsohn was the real entrepreneur, dealmaker, and financial brain of the organisation, but he did not have as strong a power base in either of the main businesses as Barnett and Rabb did. He sought recognition as the leader and boss, but his partners were reluctant to concede this. Barnett, Rabb and Robinson looked to David Susman for leadership. He was a much younger man and he was not on the spot. He was also deeply involved in the building of another, larger, business. His control of the other half of the voting shares meant that he stood between Wulfsohn and what the latter saw, with some justification, as his rightful position. It was hardly surprising that an institutional conflict, originating in the division of the voting shares, came to be seen as a personal one.

Barnett's death removed one source of conflict, but it did not solve the problems between the partners. While David Susman had originally acted as a mediator between his father and Wulfsohn, his own relationship with the latter deteriorated over time. The initiative for a break came from Wulfsohn, but Susman welcomed the proposal and expressed regret when it was postponed. Looking back over nearly forty years, he now says that neither he, nor his father, ever had any doubt as to Wulfsohn's honesty and integrity. They had trusted him with the greater part of their family's wealth. He was bright, had driving ambition, and was a very hard worker. He was also determined, a lateral thinker, and a problem-solver. He had done more than anyone else to build the businesses after the war. He had made a great deal of money for the partnership and the business was largely free of debt. There was, however, a down side.

> The differences between Harry and me arose largely from our aspirations for the businesses, and secondarily, from an inevitable clash of personalities. Harry was a gung-ho expansionist, and I felt, as did my father before me, that we should consolidate and ensure that good management was in place before we undertook further ventures. It was, admittedly, easier for me to take that stance. The Susmans were not solely reliant on the SB & W stable to build up our wealth – our Woolworths interests, and various other investments, were flourishing. More importantly, however, I had serious doubts about Harry's actual ability to manage the businesses he was so keen to acquire.
>
> Harry was touchy and quick to take offence. He craved admiration, constant recognition of his undoubted business acumen, and speedy approval of each of his often risky proposals. When all of these were not instantly vouchsafed, he became confrontational and personally offensive. I could live with this, but Max Barnett and Maurice Rabb found it increasingly hard to do so, and they were key players in the day to day running of the businesses.[9]

It is, perhaps, unfair to Wulfsohn that his views are consistently underrepresented in the records, and he is no longer able to speak for himself. Alternative views of him come not so much from his partners as from those who worked under him. They all agree on his prowess as a businessman, his speed of thought and action, his decisiveness and his absolute honesty and integrity. They also tend to concur, as do some members of his family, that he was impatient with people who were slower on the uptake than he was.

Geoff Kates, who worked very closely with him in Susman Brothers & Wulfsohn and Rhodesian Mercantile Holdings, was a great admirer. He recalled:

> What a fine man! He had little or no education, but was such an astute businessman ... He spoke English with a heavy accent and would ask me to draft letters for him. But when I showed him the draft he would say: 'No, I don't want that word, what about this one?' We would end up with a really good letter. He was very decisive and could not stand people who could not make up their minds. He did not suffer fools gladly.

In response to the suggestion that he was impetuous, Kates says that impetuousness and decisiveness are two sides of the same coin. 'You say impetuous: I say decisive.' Wulfsohn would fight for what he thought was right. If he thought that something was wrong or unfair, 'he could be belligerent'. Kates had personally found him a very good man to work for – an excellent, and caring, employer. 'He was a private man. He enjoyed a joke and was a good mixer. He was never boastful, though he had a great deal to boast about.' Kates also sheds some light on his relationship with his partners. He thinks that Maurice Rabb had rather a superior attitude towards Wulfsohn on the basis of his own university education. Wulfsohn, on the other hand, thought that Rabb was too cautious and indecisive. In Kates's view, Rabb was a competent day-to-day manager, but there was no doubt as to who was the superior businessman.[10]

Denton Pitt, who worked closely with Wulfsohn in Rhodesian Mercantile Holdings, is also an admirer. He emphasises Wulfsohn's honesty and his decisiveness. He was a man who never went back on his word. Pitt would say: 'Make the decision. Take the loss. Don't look back.' He found him to be 'genuine, polite, straightforward'. He was, however, more of a trader than a manager. He would go around a shop and say: 'These goods have been here a long time. Cut the price by fifty per cent.' Harry Robinson would come around later and say: 'Nonsense. Cut them by ten per cent.' While Robinson would look at the profits, Wulfsohn would look at the downside. 'Where are the missing calves? What about the remainders?'[11]

Harry Wulfsohn's widow, Trude Robins, recalls her late husband as a man of vision. 'He could see ahead. Some people could not. He had to fight for his views. He was usually right, but he would get very angry and upset with people who did not see his point of view.' 'He was totally honest – his name meant everything to him.' There is no doubt that he had a very strong sense of family and that he was driven by the desire to provide for their security, especially for the twins – his two younger daughters. Trude's brother, Freddy

Wiesenbacher, also sees him as a devoted family man, but acknowledges that he liked to get his own way. Edwin Wulfsohn disputes the view of his father as impetuous. He thinks, on the contrary, that he was a fundamentally risk-averse entrepreneur. He took risks, but only after sleepless nights and a very careful assessment of the downside.[12]

People who knew him socially found him an attractive person. Max Barnett's nephew, Richard Emdin, provides a string of generally favourable epithets. 'He was delightful, very unusual, a memorable character, charismatic. He had a real presence. He projected a sense of inner power. He was a rough diamond. He was one of a kind, intriguing.' Barnett's sister-in-law, Molly Emdin, recalled him as 'fiery, volatile, but a lovely man, a true personality'.[13]

Harry Wulfsohn was widely respected in both Northern and Southern Rhodesia. He was generous, contributing funds to Jewish and Zionist charities, for the History Gallery at the Rhodes–Livingstone Museum, which was furnished in 1956 and still bears his name, and for scholarships for medical students at the University of Rhodesia and Nyasaland. He was also public-spirited, serving as chairman of the Dairy Marketing Board in Southern Rhodesia. He remained loyal to the Federation until its end, and was awarded the OBE in the New Year Honours of 1964, on a list that was drawn up by Welensky to mark its dissolution. He was grateful to Northern Rhodesia for the opportunities that it had given him, and told Roy Welensky in August 1963: 'As you know I came to Northern Rhodesia over 33 years ago as more or less penniless young man without knowing a word of English. The country has been more than kind to me and my family.'[14]

It was, in all probability, his feeling that his talents were not fully appreciated by his partners, among whom he was often in a minority of one, that prompted him to think that he might be better off on his own. The break came close on two occasions, but never actually happened. The 'unscrambling' of the egg was certainly not made any easier by the effects of UDI. In the long run, this stopped the flow of goods, money and people between Zambia and Rhodesia. The two economies were so closely entangled that an immediate rupture was impossible. It is now surprising to see how long it took for contact to be broken. Residents of Zambia, though not Zambian citizens, were able to travel to Rhodesia until the closure of the border in 1973, but it became increasingly difficult for Rhodesian residents to travel to the north. Nobody imagined in 1965 that UDI would last for fifteen years. For the first few years Harry Robinson, and Harry Wulfsohn, hoped and expected that there would be a settlement that would allow for a quick

15 Harry Wulfsohn unveils the Wulfsohn History Gallery, Rhodes–Livingstone Museum, Livingstone, in the presence of the governor, Sir Arthur Benson, 1956.

return to 'normality'. The unexpected persistence of UDI, and the increasing complications that it caused, contributed to the postponement of plans for the distribution of assets.

The Succession: Edwin Wulfsohn

Harry Wulfsohn's sudden death raised the question of succession. David Susman had been able to work side-by-side with his father for five or six years before the latter's death. He had not only assumed the role of chief executive of Woolworths at the age of twenty-seven, but had also joined the boards of the main central African companies before his thirtieth birthday. Edwin Wulfsohn did not have the chance to serve this kind of apprenticeship, though he did spend some time in 1966 visiting the group's central African interests, and he helped his father to draw up a memorandum for the benefit of the trustees of his estate. This outlined the strengths and weaknesses of the various businesses, and of their managements. He was, nevertheless, plunged into the running of the central African businesses without preparation, and rather against his will.

Edwin was born in Livingstone in 1942 and left the town when his parents moved to Johannesburg in 1954. They moved again in the following year to Salisbury. He studied Economics at the University of Cape Town, and completed an MBA at Columbia Business School in New York in 1967. After deciding to make a career in international banking, he joined Chase Manhattan Bank, which seconded him to Standard Chartered Bank for some time. They had to get him out of America rather quickly as he had arrived in the country on a 'green card' and was in danger of being drafted for the Vietnam War. He worked with the American division of the latter bank in London and Johannesburg, acquiring in the process knowledge, experience, and contacts that were to be very useful in later years. At the time of his father's death, he was completing the Chase Executive Development Programme and was about to become a lending officer in the international division. He was living in an apartment on the Upper East Side of Manhattan with his wife, Dina Kahn, whom he had met at the University of Cape Town and had married in 1966. She was brought up in Bulawayo and worked for the United Nations in New York in 1965–6.

At a meeting on the day after his father's funeral in Salisbury, Maurice Rabb and Harry Robinson made it clear to Edwin that they expected him to return to Africa and to succeed his father in the management of the business. He thought that this would be a retrograde step and he was not keen to comply with their wishes. Taking into account the deteriorating macro-economic environment, the effects of UDI, international sanctions, the beginning of guerrilla warfare by ZAPU and ZANU, and the Mulungushi Reforms in Zambia, he did not think that the prospects in central Africa looked good. He asked for time to consider the question. His father's partners suggested that he make a quick visit to Zambia to assess the situation for himself. On this visit he discovered that Werners and the ranches were making losses, and the stores business was threatened with the loss of its licences. He decided that he would have to return to Africa in order to protect his father's legacy and the interests of his mother and sisters. He committed himself to spending a maximum of two years in Africa and travelled to Zambia with his wife in November 1968. His partners asked him to base himself on the Copperbelt and to take special responsibility for Werners. His role in relation to that company has been recounted in an earlier chapter.[15]

Maurice Rabb gave nearly two years' notice of his intention to leave Zambia in March 1971. He hoped and expected that Wulfsohn would take over from him as the representative of the controlling families in Zambia. Wulfsohn was equally determined not to take over this role. He recalls that David Susman asked him in 1968 whether he intended to 'build a business or carve out a sphere of influence'. This was a reference to the earlier discussion of the division of the assets. Edwin said that he saw his role as to build a business. He thought that this could be done better in London than in Kitwe, Lusaka or Livingstone. He did not think that the group's remaining interests in Zambia had much potential for growth. Edwin left Kitwe with his family in June 1970 and moved to London. Maurice and Peggy Rabb remained in Livingstone until November 1971. They were the last representatives of the founding families to leave Zambia. Maurice was also the last president of the Livingstone Hebrew Congregation. Before leaving the town he closed the synagogue, sold the building and sent the *sefer torahs* to Lusaka. Peggy Rabb, who had been in poor health for some time, died less than two years later.[16]

Concorde Investments

Edwin Wulfsohn was confronted in London with two businesses. These assets had been acquired in 1962 in response to the federal government's imposition of exchange controls in the previous year. The group had always reinvested its profits in the countries in which it worked. It was the imposition of exchange controls that prompted it to look for the first time for investments outside central Africa, but its first overseas investments were closely linked to the central African business. The acquisition of Vigers Brothers, and of Stevens and Adams – both London-based flooring businesses – has already been described. At about the same time the group bought two other London-based businesses with central African connections. These were Stenham and Company and T. A. Crombie Ltd. Both were shippers, and were closely associated with companies in the group. Stenham was the shipper for Northern Rhodesia Textiles, as well as for Kaufman Sons and Company, the Southern Rhodesian wholesalers, and for about forty other small businesses in central Africa. The company's owner and manager, David Yager, had helped Maurice Rabb find sources of yarn in Italy for the Livingstone blanket factory. T. A. Crombie was the shipper for Rhodesian Mercantile Holdings and for a small number of other businesses. Both these companies were 'confirming houses'. Their activities included the discounting of bills of exchange, and the guaranteeing of letters of credit. The group paid just over £50,000 for Stenham and £10,000 for Crombie. The companies were bought through an offshore company, Stenham and Crombie Holdings Ltd, which was set up in the Bahamas in February 1962. The purchases were financed by a loan of £70,000 from the Ngamiland Trading Company. It was funded in this way because Bechuanaland did not have exchange controls, and the Ngamiland Trading Company had unused overdraft facilities.[17]

Among Edwin Wulfsohn's first moves, together with Major Bobby Campbell, the group's chief accountant, who moved to London from Livingstone, was to plan the establishment of an offshore holding company for all the group's interests. This resulted in 1973 in the formation of Concorde Investments (Jersey) Ltd. Wulfsohn was determined to avoid the conflicts which had earlier brought the business to the brink of dissolution, and to work harmoniously with the other partners. The name of the new company may have symbolised that aspiration. Over the next thirty years he was to play the leading role in the management and development of the group's assets. He was able to establish a harmonious working relationship with David Susman, but was never close to Maurice Rabb, who remained chairman of Concorde Investments until shortly before his death in 1995. He was, however, able to establish a good working relationship with Rabb's son, John, who attended the annual meetings of directors and shareholders from the beginning. John Rabb had come to Livingstone as a small child. After taking a degree in Agriculture he had worked for a short time at Chambishi Farm on the Copperbelt. He then joined Woolworths in Cape Town, becoming a director, and, ultimately, managing director of the holding company Wooltru. Edwin Wulfsohn also established a good working relationship with 'Sonny' Emdin who had been on the board of Werners and joined the board of Concorde Investments as the representative of Max Barnett's family. He remains grateful to Emdin, and to Maurice Gersh, for impartial advice and counsel.[18]

The establishment of a holding company allowed for the centralisation of administration and the establishment of a single board of directors, which could supervise all the activities of the group. It also made possible a fair distribution of overhead costs. Bringing all the assets under one umbrella was not a simple matter. In his instructions to his trustees Harry Wulfsohn had insisted that they should not abandon the system of voting and non-voting shares which had given the Susman and Wulfsohn families the means of blocking all decisions in the stores and butchery companies. The original plans for the new company envisaged the retention of this system, but Maurice Rabb was strongly opposed to this. Wulfsohn eventually agreed to recommend to his family's trustees that the voting shares should be placed on a par with the non-voting shares. At the same time there were problems that arose from the slow externalisation from Zambia of the Rabb family's share of the assets. The Susman family's assets had been held externally for many years, and the Wulfsohn family's assets were also externalised in the early 1970s, with the help of advice from Oliver Irwin. The dividends owed by the Zambian companies to those members of the Susman and Robinson families who were resident in Rhodesia were also blocked for many years. It was not until after the independence of Zimbabwe in 1980 that all these problems could be resolved. It also took time to achieve a redistribution of assets in Zambia between Susman Brothers & Wulfsohn – which became the local holding company for Zambia Textiles – and Werners, later known as Concorde Agricultural Development Ltd, which became the holding company for the farms and ranches.[19]

Edwin Wulfsohn came under renewed pressure from his partners in 1980 to return to central Africa and take on the role of resident director for the Concorde group. He asked for time to think about it, but did not give way to this pressure. Denton Pitt was appointed as general manager in January 1981, and was later described as the group's chief executive in Africa. He was himself under pressure to move to Zambia, but remained in Harare. He took over responsibility for the group's accounts shortly before the death of Bobby Campbell, a long-serving director, in 1983. Edwin Wulfsohn emphasises the important role played by Campbell in the setting up of Concorde, and in unravelling and simplifying the complexities of its ownership structure.[20]

Rhodesia/Zimbabwe

Although the main focus of Edwin Wulfsohn's work in the 1970s and 1980s was on the British companies, there was unfinished business in two other areas: Rhodesia/Zimbabwe and Botswana. As a result of UDI the group's most important Southern Rhodesian business, H. Robinson and Co., was cut off from much of its market, and from its ultimate owner, Susman Brothers & Wulfsohn. An informal report on H. Robinson and Co. for the year ending in March 1966 indicated that two-thirds of the company's net profits had been earned in Zambia, though the bulk of its employees were based in the south. The report was written in July 1966, nine months after UDI, but its author, Ralph Herzstein, took a remarkably relaxed view of the consequences of UDI. He commented: 'With relations between Zambia and Rhodesia being as they are, one cannot entirely rule out the possibility of a final break at least temporarily. This could well mean that Robinson's in Salisbury (together with Gutu) will have to manage on their own.' He was confident that the 'southern' business could be run successfully as an independent enterprise. With the help of Herzstein, Denton Pitt and Colin Arnott, the company survived the period of UDI, making steady, though unspectacular, profits. It was a stable and conservative business, and a source of some frustration to more adventurous souls. Harry Wulfsohn deplored its low return on capital, and thought in 1966 that it should move away from the system of sales through commercial travellers to something closer to the 'cash and carry' format. In the end the business survived in much the same shape and form until the mid 1990s. A new holding company was set up for it in 1971, which separated it from its Zambian parent, Susman Brothers & Wulfsohn. There was some discussion in 1980 of the possibility of a merger with Kaufman Sons and Company, the Bulawayo-based wholesalers, who always had a rather larger share of the market, but nothing came of the proposal. Harry Robinson remained at the helm until his death in January 1989 at the age of eighty-eight. He had always taken a hands-on approach to the business and participated personally in stock-taking until the time of his death.[21]

Botswana

The Ngamiland Trading Company had suffered a major blow in February 1965 with the death of its long-serving managing director, 'Chobo' Weskob. He had been the dominant figure in the trade of Ngamiland for thirty years. O. Jackson, his long-serving deputy, succeeded him and remained in charge of the business until 1974. Weskob's death was followed by some major changes in the Ngamiland cattle trade. In the following year a partnership was formed between the Ngamiland Trading Company and the Greek Cypriot traders, Spiro Christos and the Deaconos brothers, operating as the Bechuanaland (later Botswana) Trading Association. The partnership formed a buying pool in an attempt to keep the price of cattle down. Prices had been driven up by a shortage of stock following an outbreak of foot-and-mouth disease. The partnership lasted for some years, but there seems to have been some doubt as to whether it achieved its primary purpose. There was evidence that the buyers for both sides continued to compete and that the Botswana Trading Association was getting more than its fair share of the cattle on offer. Within a year of Botswana's independence in 1966, the export of live cattle from Ngamiland across the Zambezi at Kazungula, which had been revived in 1961, came finally to an end. The new government decreed that all Ngamiland cattle should be sent to Lobatse for slaughter by the Botswana Meat Corporation. This was in spite of protests from the Ngamiland traders about the disadvantages, including loss of weight and condition, of trekking cattle to the Line of Rail for export to the south.[22]

The Ngamiland Trading Company continued, however, to engage in the cattle trade for a decade after the closure of the northern route. The network of retail stores and the cattle trade were so closely tied to each other that it was impossible to carry on one without the other. By the late 1970s the trading business had become loss making, apparently as a result of retail price controls, which seem to have taken no account of the difficulties of trading in remote areas such as Ngamiland. The cattle trade was also affected by a new outbreak of foot-and-mouth disease. In the last year or two of the decade the company withdrew from the cattle trade and closed or sold its outlying stores. The Ngamiland Trading Company then concentrated on wholesale trade in Maun, while a number of retail outlets remained open there and traded as Riley's Stores – numbers I–IV. The wholesale business was sold to Sefalana sa Botswana Ltd, a milling company, in 1982. At the same time Riley's Hotel was sold to Marakanelo Hotels Ltd. Ronnie Kays, who had been a partner with the Ngamiland Trading Company in the hotel and the garage business, took over Riley's Garage and Filling Station in 1983. In the last twenty years he has developed it into a thriving business and a major landmark for visitors to Ngamiland – better-known to international tourists today as the Okavango.[23]

Vigers, Stevens, and Adams

During the 1970s most of Edwin Wulfsohn's energies were devoted to the affairs of Vigers, Stevens, and Adams. The two companies were old-established businesses, with their roots going back into the late nineteenth century. Their leading directors had been with them for forty or fifty years. The companies had both undertaken prestigious contracts. Vigers Brothers had done the floors for the Royal Festival Hall and the refurbishment of 10 Downing Street, while Stevens and Adams had done floors for the Bank of England and for the Ashmolean Museum and Sheldonian Theatre in Oxford. Supervision from central Africa proved difficult, and the merging of the two companies was not easy. The nationalisation of Zambesi Saw Mills, and its subsequent decline, meant that the original reason for buying the business fell away. It had in any case become clear that the company could not be tied to central African sources of hardwood, as it had to compete in the market with cheaper West African suppliers. There was intense competition in the flooring market in the late 1960s, not only between firms supplying wood flooring, but also with cheaper vinyl tiles and low-cost carpeting.[24]

Although Vigers used new kinds of seals for its wood strips, blocks and mosaics, and also experimented with new types of plastic flooring, it was described in 1970–1 as 'a slightly old-fashioned, highly competent, expensive wood block manufacturer, not willing or able to advise on modern floor finishes'. At a meeting in July 1970 the group's shareholders made it clear that 'they wanted to cut their losses and either liquidate or sell the company'. Wulfsohn offered to investigate further and to advise the shareholders on what do next.

> When I arrived ... I discovered a technically highly-skilled but production-orientated management, most of whom had been with the company all their working lives. There was no real communication or discussion of vital issues and the company was riddled with interdepartmental quarrels and jealousies. The organisation was top-heavy – key executives had become desk-bound and secluded from the market. Moreover, efficiency was lowered by interference from management who had nothing to do and looked for work at head office instead of in the field.[25]

In August 1970 he received a memo from a newly appointed marketing executive confirming his own view that Vigers had not adapted itself to the changes in the marketplace and that it was 'a dying company in a declining market'. It was clear that hardwood was no longer viable as a staple product, and it was necessary to develop other revenue-producing commodities and services. Wulfsohn concluded that the company had a good team of middle managers and that, with better internal communications, and simpler decision-making processes, it would be possible to turn the company around. It was possible and desirable to save the business, but time was short and action must be swift if the shareholders were to be mollified. His strategy was to cut prices, promote sales of African teak aggressively and go for growth. The improvement of marketing and distribution placed the company in a strong position to benefit from the speculative housing boom of 1971–2, and two of the company's competitors were soon forced to close down. By March 1974 the company controlled three-quarters of the wood-flooring market, sales had doubled, and a loss in 1970 had been turned into a profit of £165,000.[26]

In the following year, however, the company began to suffer from the effects of the worldwide recession. Diversification into the DIY market had proved successful, but the company was compelled to withdraw from the contract-flooring business. A later diversification into cork flooring was also successful, but this was a period of high inflation and the company was affected by price controls within the United Kingdom. The company was involved in a labour-intensive business, and it was difficult for it to compete with products from South-East Asia and Eastern Europe. There was also a shortage of capital for the modernisation of plant and machinery. The last straw for the company was the imposition of tight fiscal policies by Mrs Thatcher's government in 1979. These produced the sharpest recession in Britain's post-war history. During the last nine months of 1980 the company made losses of over £300,000 which wiped out its accumulated, but undistributed, profits. Attempts were made to sell the company in the early months of 1980, but by the beginning of the next year it was threatened with liquidation. The National Westminster Bank placed the company in receivership in October 1981. Harrison & Crosfield, the commodity traders, bought the business, and the four-acre factory site was eventually sold for £700,000, but the shareholders got nothing. Edwin Wulfsohn had made heroic efforts to save Vigers, but there was little that he could do in the hostile economic environment of the late 1970s. The original investment was made in the wrong place and at the wrong time. Its primary purpose had been the creation of a market for Zambian teak, but that soon fell away. Its secondary purpose was to build up an overseas asset in the context of central African exchange controls. Timber flooring in Britain in the 1970s was not the ideal sector in which to do that.[27]

Stenham Ltd

The unfortunate demise of Vigers allowed Edwin Wulfsohn to spend much more of his time on the affairs of Stenham and Company, which had become Stenham Ltd in 1972. This had been a relatively small business, with a paid-up capital of only £40,000, which made profits of less than £3,000 in that year. Its capital was increased to £250,000 in the mid 1970s, but it was, like Vigers, an old-fashioned company in a declining sector. Edwin Wulfsohn was aware that all confirming houses were threatened by changes in the nature of world trade and in the relationships between newly independent states and their former colonial rulers. They were also threatened by competition from the commercial banks, which were financing the higher-quality importers, while the confirming houses were forced downmarket. He saw the need for the business to move into new sectors and find new ways of doing business. One of his first moves on coming to London was to invite Alan Grieve, a non-executive director of a number of British companies, to join the board, and to secure the retirement of David Yager, the former proprietor, from his position as chairman and managing director of the company. They appointed Mark Gould as managing director. He had joined the company in his twenties and had been with it for twenty-five years. Yager had regarded him as too young to assume the responsibility of management. Gould was to remain with the company until his retirement at the age of seventy in 1986.[28]

All confirming houses were adversely affected by the oil crisis and the world recession that began in 1973–4. Houses like Stenham, which specialised in the African market, were affected by the emergence of new states, by political instability and economic uncertainty. UDI in Rhodesia and subsequent sanctions had cut the company off from the majority of its customers, and it had become more heavily exposed to the Zambian market. It was the main shipper there for two related companies, Zambia Textiles and Susman Brothers & Wulfsohn's successor, Zambesi Trading. Wulfsohn had been aware of the vulnerability of the company as a result of its exposure to Zambia before the recession struck. This became a serious problem in 1976 when bills became overdue. In the late 1970s Zambia was unable to pay for accumulated imports and built up large debts to suppliers, which were placed in a queue for foreign exchange allocations. As was shown in an earlier chapter, Stenham was in 1979 waiting to receive more than £2,000,000 that had been placed in the 'pipeline' by Zambia Textiles. Although ninety per cent of the risk of exporting to Zambia was then insured through the United Kingdom's Export Credit Guarantee Department, there was a danger that the company's exposure in Zambia could wipe out its capital and reserves. In the end Stenham was saved by Wulfsohn's good relationships with the Chase Manhattan and Standard Chartered Banks, as well as by his determined lobbying with the Bank of Zambia. He once waited for two days for a meeting with its governor, eventually meeting him late at night, and persuading him to release vital funds.[29]

Although Stenham continued to be largely dependent on African business throughout the 1970s, finding new business in Botswana and Malawi, a process of diversification began during that decade. Research indicated that as Britain's manufacturing base declined, imports from Europe increased and there was a gap in the market for import finance. Wulfsohn was able to organise funding for this through his contacts with the Standard Chartered Bank, and also with Barclays, and the Hong Kong and Shanghai banks. The company began the process of applying for a licence as a secondary bank. The licence was not yet granted when the bursting of a speculative property boom wiped out most of the businesses in this sector in 1973–4. Wulfsohn feels that Stenham had a lucky escape as, if it had become a secondary bank, it would probably have gone down with the rest. The development of the import finance side of the business was intensified in the early 1980s through the acquisition of the British business of one South African confirming house, Trade and Industry Acceptances Corporation, and the Italian and Irish business of another South African house – Brown Brothers Shipping. The clients of Brown Brothers included a large number of old-established industrial businesses around Venice and Bologna. They included furniture and paper manufacturers, leather tanners and musical-instrument makers. Stenham eventually took over the residual customers of this firm in Britain and South Africa. Their manager, Steve Cogswell, became operations manager of Stenham's trade finance business in 1986.[30]

The company aimed in the early 1980s to do the bulk of its business outside Africa, but the independence of Zimbabwe in 1980 did allow it to re-open links with some of its former customers in that country. Most of its competitors had continued to do business with Rhodesia through South African and Swiss subsidiaries in defiance of sanctions. In the mid 1980s Stenham used a Zimbabwean subsidiary of the Concorde group, Mercantile

Investments Ltd, to take over the local branch of Anglo African Shipping, and set up Mercantile Trade Finance. At an earlier date the company had taken over the South African customers of a British confirming house, Balfour Williamson, and had established its own South African subsidiary, Stenham (Pty) Ltd. Maurice Gersh and Maurice Rabb, who had both retired to South Africa in 1971, continued to run this business for many years. They used blocked funds, derived from the sale of Zambesi Flooring, the former subsidiary of Zambesi Saw Mills, and Redwood Investments to finance the South African end of this business. David Samuels eventually took over the management, and a half share in this part of the business, though Gersh and Rabb remained as non-executive directors of the company. Gersh had also taken a ten per cent stake in the British parent company.[31]

In spite of its narrow capital base Stenham was in the mid 1980s able to undertake a great deal – up to £80,000,000 worth – of trade finance. It was able to do this safely as a result of credit insurance against potential losses, and with the help of low-cost finance from discount houses. Wulfsohn was, however, determined that the business should diversify out of trade finance into other activities. The most important of these diversifications was into offshore trust and asset management. This was a natural outgrowth from the trade finance business, as overseas clients had often asked Stenham to act as unofficial trustees of their offshore affairs. The company's client base in Southern Africa provided much of the business for these new developments. Errol Rudnick, son-in-law of Benny Gelfand, joined the company in 1983 and was largely responsible for the development of this branch of the business in subsequent years. This was done through a number of new subsidiaries – Concorde Advisors Ltd, an investment research company registered in the United Kingdom, Concorde Asset Management, registered in the British Virgin Islands, and Dubarry Trustees, which was run from Alderney in the Channel Islands. The founding boards of these companies included Wulfsohn himself, Alan Grieve, Errol Rudnick, David Susman and Barbara Kalman. Funds were invested in bonds, equities and through external managers, including George Soros's Quantum Fund. After the stock market crash of 1987, it was decided to abandon reliance on stocks and bonds, to employ a variety of fund managers, and to concentrate on hedge funds and alternative investment strategies. This approach proved beneficial through the prolonged stock market decline that began in 2000 with the collapse in IT stocks, and was intensified following the events of 11 September 2001. By 2000 funds under management had reached $600,000,000.

Following the departure of Errol Rudnick, Kevin Arenson took over management of this division.[32]

A further diversification was into property acquisition and development. This began in 1975 with the purchase by a syndicate, representing the Susman, Rabb, Wulfsohn and Gersh families, of 25 John Street, a Georgian house in Holborn, London. This was chosen as a suitable location for the office for Stenham Ltd because it was conveniently situated half-way between the City and the West End of London. The house was later sold for a substantial profit, and the same group of families, with the additional participation of the Zukas family, bought three further houses at 34–6 John Street through another syndicate. Stenham has used two of these houses as offices, and one of them also houses Edwin Wulfsohn's collection of photographs and other memorabilia relating to the history of the central African businesses. The success of these investments inspired the establishment of a property subsidiary which was set up to administer properties bought for clients in central London. By the late 1990s this company, Rightsector Ltd, was administering £250,000,000 worth of mainly commercial property in London and the provinces.[33]

With the establishment of Trans Zambezi Industries in 1993, which is described in the next chapter, Wulfsohn found that he was unable to devote much time to the management of Stenham. At about the same time the company was able to recruit Michael Fienberg, who had been managing director in London of Gerber Goldschmidt, the South Africa-based international trading group. Fienberg worked at first with Concorde Advisors, but soon became managing director of the Stenham group of companies. Among other new recruits – both came from the London office of the South African legal firm, Sonnenberg Hoffman and Galombik – were Ivan Kapelus, who became managing director of Dubarry Trustees, and Paul Arenson, who became managing director of the property division. In order to attract and retain high quality staff, it was necessary to offer them a share in the equity of the business. As a way of achieving this objective, without losing control of its other interests, Concorde Investments sold its financial services business to a new holding company, Stenham Investments Limited. The shareholders in the new company included members of the management team, as well as members of the old controlling families. Edwin Wulfsohn became chairman, and its directors included David Susman, John Rabb, Errol Rudnick, Ivan Kapelus, Michael Fienberg and Paul Arenson. Among the first moves of the new holding company was the sale of Stenham Trade Finance Limited, the original core business, to a Dutch financial institution. The sale excluded the African trade finance operation, which was retained and transferred to Cape Town.

In spite of earlier diversifications, Stenham Investments was still closely tied to southern Africa where many of the clients of its trustee, asset management and property subsidiaries were based. As a result of the emigration of wealthy families the flow of new business from this source tended to decline. With a view to future growth, Stenham acquired in 1998 two European businesses, Gestinor AV in Switzerland, and Sanne et Cie in Luxembourg. The name of the company and its subsidiaries was changed to Stenham Gestinor. These purchases were financed through Securities Investment Bank, a newly listed South African private bank, which bought a twenty-two per cent stake in Stenham – an investment equal to the price paid for the new acquisitions. Following a collapse in confidence in the small bank sector in South Africa, this bank was unable to exercise the option that it had to buy the balance of Stenham's shares. It was itself taken over by one of its major shareholders, Investec Bank, which thus acquired, by accident rather than design, a minority stake in Stenham. As Investec was a major competitor of Stenham, this was an unsatisfactory state of affairs. Stenham Investments found a new partner in BoE (formerly the Board of Executors), an old-established South African bank. It took control of Stenham Investments in September 2001 – the deal was completed on 14 September, three days after the attack on the World Trade Center. With the sale of the company to BoE, David Susman and John Rabb severed their link with the business, though Edwin Wulfsohn remained with the company as chairman. Over thirty years the business had grown in size from one office, a manager and two clerks, to eleven offices in nine countries with a multi-disciplinary team of bankers, accountants, lawyers and an actuary. The value of the business, about two-thirds of which belonged to the original shareholders, had multiplied a thousand-fold, and it was then worth close to £40,000,000. In the following year BoE was itself taken over by Nedcor, which is controlled by Old Mutual, South Africa's insurance and banking giant.

Edwin Wulfsohn had set out in 1970 to build a business in the United Kingdom. He devoted most of a decade to an attempt to rescue Vigers, but his best efforts were thwarted by global and, latterly, domestic economic and political forces. Stenham Ltd began as a small business in a declining sector, but in what was clearly case of the right man in the right place, at the right time, he was able to use it as the base for the development of a diverse and successful financial services business. Edwin Wulfsohn's academic training in Economics and Business Administration was a rarity in the City of

London in the early 1970s. He was able to use this, together with the contacts that he had acquired in banking in the United States and South Africa, and his inherited links with Southern Africa, to create an almost entirely new business, taking advantage of the abolition of exchange controls in 1979, and of financial deregulation, which followed the 'Big Bang' of October 1986. In terms of the production of wealth for its shareholders, Stenham Ltd was undoubtedly the most successful of all the various investments that formed part of the Concorde Group.

CHAPTER 21

Emerging Markets?
Trans Zambezi Industries (TZI)

The establishment of Trans Zambezi Industries – TZI – in 1993 was, at least in part, the consequence of political and economic changes in Zambia and in the wider world. The collapse of the Soviet Union coincided with, and possibly triggered, the end of apartheid in South Africa. The release of Nelson Mandela in February 1990 and his visit two weeks later to the ANC in Lusaka contributed to the movement for political change in Zambia. President Kaunda's government was discredited after years of economic mismanagement and decline. Two attempts at Structural Adjustment, including attempts to remove food subsidies, brought the people out on to the streets of the major cities in 1986 and 1990. It was in the latter year that Kaunda bowed to the inevitable and yielded to the demand for the end of the one-party state and a return to multi-party democracy. He was defeated in elections in October 1991 and a new party, the MMD, led by Frederick Chiluba, came to power. The government had the backing of business interests as well as the trade unions and moved quickly to embark on a policy of liberalisation. This included the abolition of foreign exchange controls, the reduction of tariffs, and the privatisation of parastatal companies.

Among the founders of the MMD was Simon Zukas, chairman of Zambesi Ranching and Cropping. He had been one of the first people to raise questions in public about the future of the one-party state. He was not only aware of events in the Soviet Union and South Africa, but he was also conscious of the implications of a World Bank report, *Sub-Saharan Africa: from Crisis to Sustainable Growth*, which was published in 1989. This drew attention to problems of governance and made it clear that economic and political reform was going to be a condition for future aid. He attended the meeting at the Garden House Hotel in July 1990 from which the MMD emerged, and was later elected deputy chairman of the new party. He had not originally intended to stand for parliament, but was eventually persuaded to offer himself for election in the remote constituency of Sikongo in the Western Province, west of Kalabo and on the Angolan border. After the election in October 1991 he became a minister of state in the president's office. On his promotion to the cabinet as minister of agriculture in the early months of 1993, he resigned as chairman of Zambesi Ranching and Cropping, though he remained a director of the company until 2002.[1]

The election of the MMD was greeted with great enthusiasm in Zambia and abroad. There were great hopes for the recovery of the economy. It was expected that the privatisation of the mines and other industries would be rapidly achieved and that this would stimulate economic growth. At the same time political change in South Africa held out the promise of the development of regional trade and investment. Some countries in Southern Africa, including Zambia and Mozambique, began to be seen as 'emerging markets' – a phrase which was more usually applied to the countries of Eastern Europe and Asia that were emerging from Soviet control. A report by John Taylor, a former Zambian and a researcher with the London stockbrokers, James Capel, borrowed the title of the earlier World Bank report, and added a question mark: 'Africa: from Crisis to Sustainable Growth?'. The report, which was published in November 1991, highlighted President Chiluba's inaugural speech. He had then said, with more prescience than he probably knew: '... we are like a country awakening from a coma. We are weak and ill, but still alive and determined to get well again. The economy's ills came over decades. And we won't solve them in several weeks or even months. For this we need discipline, hard work, honesty and determination.'

John Taylor's report referred to Zambia as one of a number of southern African countries in which there might be investment opportunities. It pointed out that countries like Zambia provided adventurous investors with the opportunity to acquire assets cheaply and there was the potential for high rates of return. He took the view that southern Africa was experiencing a second 'wind of change' with the movement towards democracy in South Africa, the abandonment of the one-party state in Zambia, widespread moves towards economic liberalisation, and the encouragement of foreign investment. He acknowledged that these African states were not yet 'emergent' in the fullest sense of the word, but he saw them as having the potential to become so.[2]

Edwin Wulfsohn had always taken the view that Zambia's experiment with what he describes as 'state socialism', though it has also been described as 'state capitalism',[3] would not last. While he, and the other directors of the Concorde Group, had sought local partners for their major asset, ZRC, they had also been interested in the possibility of finding international partners and of 'reversing' the shares of ZRC into an internationally quoted company. This would involve an exchange of shares rather than an outright sale, but would increase the marketability of the assets. He had been thinking along these lines since the late 1960s but he had to wait twenty-five years before it became possible to put his ideas into practice. Among the companies with whom there had been preliminary talks were Aberfoyle plc and the African Lakes Corporation, both companies with listings on the London Stock Exchange. Wulfsohn discussed his ideas with Joseph Marffy, a former Zimbabwean, and a corporate adviser in London, as well as with John Taylor and Mark Donegan of James Capel. With the new interest in 'emerging markets' they began to think in terms of using Concorde's Zambian assets as the base for launching a new company that would tap these funds for investment in Africa. Wulfsohn told a journalist a couple of years later: 'for us the beginning of the 1990s was the African equivalent of the Berlin Wall coming down. Quite suddenly, African socialism crumbled, and governments in the region began to think and now to act to deregulate and privatise. We decided there were real opportunities to build a broadly based industrial holding company.'[4]

Hillary Duckworth, who had first met Wulfsohn some years previously, while working for Robert Fleming and Company, the merchant bankers, had come, independently, to a similar conclusion. They got together and Duckworth offered his services as chief executive in Africa for a new company that they would launch. He came from a British family that had lived abroad for several generations. He was born in Singapore, but spent parts of his childhood in Zimbabwe and Zambia, where his parents farmed. He spent ten years in the British army before beginning to work as a merchant banker in the City, and now he was anxious to move back to Africa with his young family. Duckworth recalls: 'With some luck, great timing and a whirlwind tour around the USA and UK, Edwin and I raised some $11,000,000 to launch TZI.'[5]

Trans Zambezi Industries (TZI) was incorporated in the British Virgin Islands on 5 August 1993 with a nominal capital of $7,500,000 divided into 75,000,000 shares. Wulfsohn became the chairman of the new company. He ceased to be an executive in 1997, but continued as non-executive chairman until 2002. Duckworth became the chief executive officer and moved to Harare where he set up an office. Denton Pitt became the company's

16 Trans Zambezi Industries, board of directors, *circa* 1995.
Seated from left: David Phiri, Hillary Duckworth (CEO), Edwin Wulfsohn (chairman), Mario dos Remedios; standing from left: Simon Jones, Anthony Williamson, David Susman, Albert Rau, John Rabb, Peter Moyo (company secretary).

secretary and remained in the post until his retirement in 1996. The first non-executive director was David Susman, who remained on the board until January 1999. John Rabb served at first as his alternate, but became a full member of the board in 1997. Other people who joined the board as non-executive directors included Albert Nhau, a Zimbabwean accountant and banker, who succeeded Wulfsohn as chairman in 2002; David Phiri, a former managing director of Roan Consolidated Mines, and governor of the Bank of Zambia; Anthony Williamson, a former chief executive of Wooltru; and David Gemmill, chartered accountant, barrister, banker and businessman in the United Kingdom and Zimbabwe. Apart from Duckworth, executive directors included Mario dos Remedios, a Zimbabwean lawyer and accountant of Goan descent, who joined the company in 1994 from the Standard Chartered Bank in Zimbabwe and left in 1998, and Simon Jones, a British economist and accountant, who joined from Lonrho in Zimbabwe in 1996 and became a non-executive director in 2002.[6]

The company's first move was to take control of ZRC through an exchange of shares. Concorde Investments received 3,000,000 shares in TZI for its shares in ZRC. The price paid for over eighty per cent of the shares – a minority was retained by Chibote Investments Limited – was equivalent to $3,000,000, as the shares were offered to the public in the first issue at $1 a share. This represented a small proportion of ZRC's asset value of just over $11,000,000. The previous year had been an exceptionally difficult one as a result of hyperinflation, astronomical interest rates and wild fluctuations in the kwacha's exchange rate with the dollar. These fluctuations made the valuation of assets difficult and a large discount was inevitable. The low price for these assets was, however, intended to encourage institutional investors to subscribe.[7]

New capital for the acquisition of further businesses was provided by the issue of 11,000,000 shares at a price of $1 each to a number of investors, including Morgan Stanley Asset Management, Fleming Emerging Markets Trust, Mercury Asset Management, as well as the Rockefeller Foundation, and Yale, Harvard and Columbia University foundations. In May 1994 the issued share capital was increased to 28,000,000 shares. A further 16,000,000 shares were placed at a substantial premium in the course of 1996. This new issue of shares raised $36,000,000 and brought in about thirty new institutional investors from the United States and Europe. This brought the number of shares in circulation close to 50,000,000. In the following year the nominal capital of the company was increased to $30,000,000. A bonus issue of four shares for one, and the sale of shares to the general public in connection with the flotation of company on the stock exchange in Harare, brought the number of shares in circulation to more than 250,000,000. By that date the total capital invested, or available for investment, was more than $70,000,000. The shares were originally quoted on the Luxembourg Stock Exchange, but were listed on the Harare and Lusaka stock exchanges in 1997. Almost a third of the shares changed hands in 1997 and the bulk of these remained in local ownership. By 1999 it was reported that seventy per cent of the shares were owned in southern Africa, mainly Zimbabwe. Large regional investors included Hannover Re, the German-backed reinsurance company, and the Zimbabwean branch of the Old Mutual.[8]

The prospectus issued by James Capel prior to the incorporation of TZI indicated that the company planned to acquire two other companies in the Concorde Investments group. The first of these was Mercantile Investment Company (MIC), the holding company for H. Robinson and Co., which had recently entered into a partnership with another Zimbabwean company, Metro International. The deal was not finalised until June 1996 when Concorde Investments exchanged its half share in the business for shares in TZI. The other half of the business remained with Chris and David Peech. Edwin Wulfsohn had come to know the Peech brothers well during the 1980s when they became customers of Stenham. The original basis for an alliance between them and MIC had been their desire to take over the ground floor of the company's office, Harrob House, in Harare. Once the alliance was formed the two sides worked together to establish a wholesale superstore, the Metro Megacentre.[9]

This was a giant wholesale store and was opened in Harare in October 1995. It was based on the Dutch Makro concept, for which Wooltru Holdings had the franchise for Southern Africa. The Megacentre was set up with the co-operation and technical support of Wooltru's subsidiary, Massmart, which provided help with the design of the store, assistance with the computerised stock control system, and with the training of staff. It also provided a manager to supervise the establishment of the business. Wooltru, of which David Susman and John Rabb were directors, did not initially subscribe capital for this venture, and did not permit the use of the Makro logo, but it did grant a franchise to MIC. The new store had a selling area of almost 5,000 square metres and proved to be a great success. It had a turnover of US$8,000,000 in its first six months of trading.[10]

Some of the funds for this development came from the sale of Harrob House. This sale marked the end of H. Robinson and Company, which had survived as a traditional wholesaler for sixty years. It was a sad day for Colin

Arnott and Denton Pitt when, at the end of March 1996, they closed the office for the last time and walked away. The business was sold to Crown Clothing and some of the company's employees stayed on with the new owners.[11]

A second Megacentre was opened in Bulawayo in October 1997. Massmart then took minority share in MIC and allowed it to use the Makro name. It became the sole owner of MIC in 1999, when it bought the shares of TZI and the Peech brothers. There had been plans to build a Megacentre in Lusaka, but these were abandoned owing to continued uncertainty as to the future of the Zambian economy. There had also been a suggestion in 1993 that TZI might seek to reclaim Susman Brothers & Wulfsohn's store sites in Zambia and re-establish its trading network. People in western Zambia would have welcomed such a move, but it was always a remote possibility.[12]

According to the original prospectus, TZI expected to take over a second company – Zambia Textiles – from Concorde Investments. It was thought that TZI would pay $1,500,000 for this business. This acquisition was linked to the purchase of two unnamed Zimbabwe-based textile and clothing manufacturers. The three companies would have formed the basis of a textile division, but these plans were shelved. The management of TZI looked at no less than fifty businesses in the first year of its existence, but only bought five of them. The most important of these was the central African business of the British company, Chloride Group plc. TZI paid about $6,000,000 for the four subsidiaries, which were all involved in the manufacture or distribution of automotive and industrial batteries. Two of these subsidiaries were in Zambia, while the other two were in Zimbabwe and Malawi. Substantial funds for reinvestment were raised through the floating of Chloride Zimbabwe on the Harare Stock Exchange, and the sale of about one-third of the shares in the company to the public.[13]

Other early acquisitions were in the field of financial services. They included two insurance companies operating in Zimbabwe, IGI Insurance, which specialised in credit insurance for shops selling electrical goods such as cookers and refrigerators, and a life insurance company of the same name. TZI also took control of Zambia's largest private insurance company, Madison Insurance. This company had been a subsidiary of the Meridien Bank, and was sold by the liquidator following the failure of the bank in 1995. TZI also bought a substantial minority interest in Bard Discount House, a Zimbabwean business, whose other shareholders included the Anglo American Corporation, Old Mutual and Barclays Bank plc. TZI assumed management control of this company in October 1995. Within a few years it had taken complete control of this business, but sold the banking division in 1999.[14]

In the next few years TZI took over a number of other businesses, most of which were based in Zimbabwe. These included the lighting and telephone manufacturing subsidiaries of the Telemetrix Group, a British company. It also took a minority share in a low-cost housing construction company, and in Zimbabwe Express Airways. This company ran two aircraft on the Johannesburg–Harare–Victoria Falls, and Harare–Kariba–Victoria Falls routes. It took a half share in Howesco, a packaging, distribution and food commodity trading business, based in Botswana. Amongst the commodities it dealt in were tobacco, salt, beans, mopane worms and 'cools' – soft drinks sold in plastic packets.[15]

Paper and Newsprint in Zimbabwe

TZI's most important single acquisition was made in 1996. It bought a controlling interest in ART Corporation Ltd and its associated company, Baringa Corporation, for about $25,000,000. This gave it a dominant position in the fine paper, newsprint and cardboard industries in Zimbabwe. The share structure and financial affairs of these companies were very complex, as was the means through which TZI took control. The companies had substantial debts, were making losses and were under threat of foreclosure by the banks. Some of the problems of ART Corporation had been caused by losses in its plastics division. The acquisition of these businesses involved separate agreements with the shareholders and the banks. The raising of additional capital on the international market was necessary for this takeover and was also a condition of the banks' agreement to it.

Although these companies were financially embarrassed, there was no doubt that the underlying assets were of high quality. They included the Kadoma Fine Paper and Tissue Mills, the Mutare Board and Paper Mills and associated forests. The Kadoma mills were modern and capable of producing 7,000 tons of fine paper and 5,000 tons of tissue paper a year. The raw material for these mills was wastepaper, which was collected from all over Zimbabwe, and imported from Zambia and Malawi. The paper was strengthened with linter from the local cotton industry. The bulk of tissue paper production went to a subsidiary, Softex, which was Zimbabwe's leading manufacturer of toilet tissues. The Mutare mills produced 17,000 tons of newsprint and 10,000 tons of cardboard a year. They supplied Zimbabwe's newspapers with newsprint, and Lion Match in Zimbabwe and South Africa with board for matchboxes. TZI took complete control of the company through the acquisition of the minority shareholdings in 1997.[16]

Zambesi Ranching and Cropping

In terms of historical continuity, TZI's most interesting investments were in commercial agriculture in Zambia. Hillary Duckworth estimated in 1998 that the company had invested $15,000,000 in this sector in the previous five years. New investment began in 1994 with the injection of $1,000,000 into Zambesi Ranching and Cropping. This was used to pay off its kwacha debt, which threatened the survival of the company at a time of exceptionally high interest rates. A contribution to the reduction of this debt was also made through unusually high cattle sales. A reduction of 3,000 head in the cattle herds was made necessary in 1993–4 by serious drought in the Southern Province.

In the next few years ZRC greatly increased its land and cattle holdings. In 1996 it paid the Anglo American Corporation (Central Africa) Limited $2,400,000 for its 56,000-acre Chisamba Ranch with 7,200 cattle. The acquisition of ranching land north of the Kafue River was seen as providing some protection to the company against restrictions on cattle movements that might arise from outbreaks of cattle diseases such as foot-and-mouth. In the following year ZRC took over the agricultural assets of Lonrho. These included Kalangwa Estates, near Chisamba, and Rietfontein Ranch east of Lusaka. These purchases brought ZRC's land holdings to about 300,000 acres and its cattle herds to about 35,000.

The re-acquisition of Rietfontein brought back to ZRC a highly developed farm, which it had lost to Lonrho nearly twenty years previously. Rietfontein did not stay long with its new owners. It was an outlying farm and was sold again three years later. The Chisamba Ranch and Kalangwa Estates were run as a separate division, ZRC (North), under the general management of Craig Shiel. Substantial investments were made at Kalangwa in the development of a new feedlot and in the intensive cultivation under drip irrigation of crops such as baby corn, mange tout and green beans for export to the European market. Investments were also made in the development of dairy farming.[17]

Zambeef

ZRC had been selling two-thirds of it output of slaughter cattle to the Chibote Meat Corporation, which had its own ultra-modern, and Danish-funded, abattoir near Lusaka. As a result of the failure of Andrew Sardanis's Meridien Bank, to which it was closely linked, Chibote was unable from April 1995 onwards to buy cattle or to meet its outstanding obligations. Not long before the collapse of the bank, control of Chibote had been transferred from Andrew Sardanis to B. Y. Mwila, then minister of defence. As a result of this transfer Mwila became the minority shareholder in ZRC. He had little interest in the shares, but he was interested in the re-acquisition of Mendham Farm at Mazabuka, with its feedlot. This had been transferred to ZRC in 1991–2 as the only positive result of otherwise unsuccessful negotiations for a merger between Chibote and ZRC. The main attraction of Mendham Farm for ZRC had been the feedlot. It had not previously had its own facilities for fattening stock and had sold cattle for finishing and slaughter to Galaunia Farms, Kyundu Ranch, and Lendor Burton at Chisamba. Mendham Farm, which had been developed in the 1950s and 1960s as one of the agricultural projects of Sir Ronald Prain and Rhodesian Selection Trust, was eventually handed over to Mwila, and the minority shareholding was eliminated.[18]

In the course of 1995–6 ZRC found a new outlet for its cattle output in Zambeef Limited, a retail butchery business, which had been formed in August 1994 by Carl Irwin, son of Oliver Irwin, in partnership with Francis Grogan. Zambeef obtained the franchise to run butcheries in the Shoprite stores, branches of a South African chain, which had recently opened in Lusaka and the Copperbelt towns. Shoprite had moved into premises that had belonged to the now defunct and privatised parastatal stores, ZCBC, NIEC and Mwaiseni. ZRC, financed by TZI, took a half share in Zambeef for a price equivalent to $3,400,000 in March 1996. This deal involved the transfer by ZRC to Zambeef of the abattoir and feedlot at Chisamba, which it bought from Lendor Burton. ZRC undertook to supply 600 cattle a month to Zambeef, which in turn guaranteed a minimum price for cattle fixed at just under $1 per kilo.

Two years later Zambeef took over the newly built abattoir at Mongu and began to buy and slaughter large numbers of cattle in the Western Province (formerly Barotseland). It began to truck large quantities of beef from Mongu to Lusaka and the Copperbelt. By 1999 it was slaughtering 56,000 head of cattle a year, the bulk of which came from so-called 'traditional' herds in the Western Province. Most people in the province, including the Litunga, welcomed the revival of the cattle trade, which had been in serious decline since the collapse of Cold Storage Board purchases in the 1970s. Although the ownership of cattle in the Western Province is somewhat unequally distributed, there is no doubt that Zambeef's purchases put relatively large amounts of money into one of Zambia's poorest provinces. There were, however, some complaints about what were seen as the low prices paid for cattle and the high prices charged for beef, but these were thought to reflect a universal tension over prices between farmers and butchers. Commercial farmers on the Line of Rail were not so enthusiastic about this new development. They saw the flow of beef from the Western Province as providing unwelcome competition with their own production and as lowering Line of Rail prices – something that was in the interests of urban consumers though, ironically, not in the interests of ranchers like ZRC.[19]

Zambeef rapidly assumed a dominant position in the Line of Rail and Copperbelt butchery business. It was able to make good profits and reduce, or stabilise, prices through efficient distribution, using its own refrigerated trucks to supply Shoprite stores and its own butcheries. Diversification into the production and processing of milk and chickens allowed it to fill its trucks and achieve further economies. In the course of 2003 it moved into the production and distribution of eggs and cheese. Its interventions into new markets have brought new competition and lower prices in real terms.

At the same time there was talk of opening new abattoirs in smaller centres such as Kalabo and Senanga. Schemes for the provision of veterinary services to cattle producers in the Western Province through out-grower cooperatives were also under consideration, as was the possibility of establishing livestock disease-free zones from which beef could be exported to Europe, Japan and South Africa. Zambeef was in partial line of descent from Susman Brothers & Wulfsohn, and its involvement in the Western Province cattle trade was a return to the roots of the business. In the urban areas it seems to have achieved an even greater dominance of the butchery business than its other ancestor, Werners.[20]

Agriflora

In May 1997 TZI bought a controlling interest in Agriflora Zambia Limited, a producer and exporter of vegetables and flowers. Neil Slade had founded the company on a farm at Chelston, Lusaka, in 1993. He had been brought up in Kenya, where his family farmed at Laikipia, on the slopes of Mount

Kenya, and he trained in agriculture in the United Kingdom. He came to Zambia in the late 1980s to work for Lendor Burton at Chisamba and began producing vegetables for export there. Soon after setting up Agriflora, he entered into a partnership with Iqbal Aloo, the proprietor of Sable Transport and Sable Farms, businesses that had their origins at Sinda in the Eastern Province. In 1997 Agriflora's main activity was the growing, packing and shipping of fresh vegetables and flowers to the British and South African markets. Ninety per cent of the vegetables were bought from outgrowers, including ZRC, but the company produced roses for export to the same markets in nine hectares of greenhouses. The company expected to produce 20,000,000 stems for export in that year. The basis for the relationship between Agriflora and TZI was Agriflora's ownership of a modern pack house near the airport and TZI's access, through ZRC, to a great deal of land. TZI put farms and cash into the business and took a three-quarters share in it. Among the farms transferred to Agriflora were the Kalangwa Estates, which had recently been bought from Lonrho.[21]

By 2002–3 the business had expanded enormously. It had spearheaded the rapid growth of horticultural and floricultural exports from Zambia to the European, especially the British, market. These exports had grown in value to $60,000,000 a year, nearly half of which came from Agriflora. The company had 7,000 workers on the pay roll – about half the number of people employed in this sector. In terms of foreign exchange earnings and employment, this was, at the turn of the millennium, one of the largest growth areas in the Zambian economy. As a leading 'non-traditional' export, horticultural products had gone some way towards filling the gaps in exports and employment that were caused by the steady decline of the mining industry. Although wages were low by international standards – at about $1 a day – the entire labour force was unionised and there were regular negotiations on terms and conditions of employment. The success of Agriflora and other horticultural exporters inspired the Zambian government to place great emphasis in its Poverty Reduction Strategy Paper on the possibilities for the expansion of horticultural exports, and on partnerships between agribusiness and out-growers, as ways of reducing poverty in the country.[22]

By 2002–3 eighty per cent of Agriflora's exports were vegetables and only twenty per cent flowers. Ninety per cent of production came from the company's eleven farms. The company had a total of about 2,000 hectares of vegetables under irrigation on its different farms. As well as growing vegetables for export in the cool winter months, the company produced 100 hectares of winter maize on land in the Zambezi valley that was leased from the liquidators of the Gwembe Development Company. This was at a time of threatening famine and the harvest brought an official visit from President Mwanawasa. The company was conscious of environmental issues and some of the vegetables produced for export were internationally certified as organic.

In 2002–3 the company was exporting about 100 tons of vegetables a week to the British market. Vegetables were sold to all the leading British supermarket chains, with the single exception of Tesco. They were sold through import agents, but the company had a three-way relationship with the agents and the supermarkets. It received regular inspection visits from the agents, accompanied by representatives of supermarket chains such as Sainsbury and Waitrose. Agriflora's managers also made regular visits to their overseas customers. Maintaining a relationship with the British supermarkets required the ability to deliver large quantities of high quality produce on a regular and reliable basis. The economics of the business depended on filling up cargo aircraft that would otherwise return from South Africa to Europe half empty. Airfreight costs were roughly equal to production costs.

The balance of production had swung away from out-growers towards own production in the years since 1997. This was largely a consequence of the enormously expanded volume of production and exports. The company set up an out-growers' subsidiary, Agriflora Smallscale Ltd, under the management of David Harvey, grandson of Sir Stewart Gore-Browne, builder of Shiwa Ngandu, the now famous mansion in Zambia's Northern Province. This company had 500 out-growers organised in ten co-operatives scattered around Lusaka. Each depot had a collection centre with a refrigeration unit from which fresh vegetable were collected every day. There was also an extension worker attached to each co-operative, whose job was to travel around on a motorbike to advise farmers in the group on methods of cultivation.

Agriflora was said in 2003 to be the largest exporter of horticultural produce in Southern Africa. In Neil Slade's view the main constraint on the further expansion of the business was not the market, but the availability of capital. Its requirements for capital had outstripped the resources of TZI, but the company had benefited from relatively soft loans from the European Union. In the course of 2001 South Africa's Industrial Development Corporation, a parastatal company, invested $4,000,000 in the business. As a consequence of this investment, TZI's share of the equity was reduced to just over fifty per cent. At the beginning of 2003 Slade remained optimistic about the company's prospects, but it had grown too rapidly for its capital base, and had cash-flow problems that may have dated back to the serious drought of 2001. The company became insolvent in the middle of 2004 when loans from the major local banks were called in. It was unclear what impact this failure would have on what had appeared to be a promising and dynamic sector of the Zambian economy.[23]

Downturn in Zimbabwe and Unbundling

TZI as a whole grew rapidly in the years to 1997 when it recorded a net profit of over US$11,000,000. In 1998 it was adversely affected by a dramatic downturn in the Zimbabwean economy. Interest rates went above fifty per cent and the Zimbabwe dollar was devalued by over sixty per cent. An operating profit of more than US$6,000,000 became a loss of US$6,000,000 after a write down of US$12,000,000 in the value of assets and goodwill. The value of shares was adversely affected by events in Zimbabwe, as well as by a general collapse in emerging market stocks, following Russia's default on its international debt. The value of investments in Zimbabwe was later further undermined by the government's threat to seize white-owned farms, and then by actual seizures and hyperinflation.[24]

A number of the major international investors had sold their shares somewhere near the top of the market in 1998, with the possibility of making a threefold gain on their investments. The shares held by Concorde Investments were distributed to the individual shareholders and many of these were also sold. With the bulk of shares now held in Zimbabwe, a process of 'unbundling' or 'demerging' was begun. In 1999 the company distributed its shares in ZRC to its shareholders as a dividend *in specie*. A consortium including Hillary Duckworth, John Rabb and David Susman bought the shares from those institutional and other investors who did not wish to hold them. In the same way that ZRC had been taken over by TZI in 1993 at a heavy discount, the price paid for its shares by the consortium also represented a large discount on the asset value of the company. ZRC had represented a large capital asset in the books of TZI, but, owing to the collapse of beef prices, was making losses.[25]

After the distribution of ZRC's shares, there was a further reorganisation. This involved the merging of ZRC with Zambeef on a fifty-fifty basis. In order to achieve the right balance of assets within ZRC between Zambeef and the ranches, the Choma and Mazabuka blocks of farms were detached from ZRC and taken over by shareholders. Hillary Duckworth's family trusts took over the Choma farms, while John Rabb and David Susman, or their family trusts, took over the Mazabuka farms. As a result of these moves Carl Irwin and Francis Grogan became owners of half of the reconstituted company and became its managing directors. Hillary Duckworth's family trusts owned one-quarter of the shares, and the Susman and Rabb trusts held smaller stakes. In a further development, in March 2003 shares in Zambeef were distributed to ZRC's shareholders and the company was listed separately on the Lusaka Stock Exchange at a market valuation of just under $15,000,000. A number of Zambian institutions, including the Bank of Zambia's pension fund, bought shares, as did Roddie Fleming, a scion of the London banking family.[26]

In what may turn out to have been a beneficial consequence for Zambia of events in Zimbabwe, and of the distribution of the farming assets of ZRC, new developments were taking place on the Choma farms and at Kala Ranch, in 2003. A number of Zimbabwean tobacco farmers were being resettled on the farms in a series of joint ventures with Universal Leaf and other investors. New barns and dams were being constructed. It was anticipated that these farmers would make a substantial contribution to Zambia's tobacco production and non-traditional exports. They were also expected to plant maize, and to produce more than 10,000 tons within two years.[27]

The process of unbundling TZI continued with management buy-outs, or straight disposals, of Bard Discount House, Madison Insurance and the Botswana distribution company. In August 2002 the industrial division of TZI, including ART Corporation and Chloride, was listed on the Zimbabwe Stock Exchange as ART Limited with Hillary Duckworth as chairman and Simon Jones as chief executive. At the same time TZI sold some of its shares in this company and distributed the balance to its shareholders. TZI had now become an investment company with a reduced management structure.

Writing from Harare in March 2003, Hillary Duckworth, then still the chief executive, made the following assessment of the company's history:

> Over its life TZI assisted the creation of 7,000 jobs in Agriflora, and 3,000 jobs in ZRC/Zambeef. It saved and turned around Madison Insurance, the largest Zambian insurer ... It saved and turned around ART in Zimbabwe which employed 3500 people in paper production. We are developing the largest pan-African health delivery system through Strategis in East and Central Africa ... Over time it has made me and a large number of people good money from their investment although if you had chosen the wrong time to either buy or sell the record is different. The demerged companies are all

doing well and I have kept a shareholding and involvement in all of them. TZI remains profitable if much smaller. We are looking at the local situation to see if the structure has value and relevance to the times we live in. At present TZI has a valuable offshore structure and good business assets concentrated in the export horticulture industry. From a personal point of view I remain convinced that it is possible both to make money and contribute to society in this part of the world and I have no plans to move.[28]

By the end of 2003 the process of unbundling the company was almost complete with the sale of Strategis, a Zimbabwe-based medical insurance company, and Mars, a regional medical evacuation and insurance company. Duckworth and all but one of the other members of the board, including Albert Nhau and John Rabb, then stood down. A Zimbabwean businessman, Edwin Moyo, who had built up a substantial stake in the business, took over as chief executive, with the apparent support of Old Mutual, another major shareholder. Both of the company's remaining subsidiaries faced serious problems. Fresca, the Zimbabwean dried vegetable export business, was adversely affected by the disruption of commercial agriculture through farm seizures. By mid 2004 it appeared likely that the insolvency of Agriflora would bring down TZI, which had guaranteed its bank loans.

It may be too early to judge the contribution of TZI to the economies of central Africa in the decade of its active life. It certainly made through its investments in ZRC, Zambeef and, at least for a time, Agriflora, a positive contribution to the development of commercial agriculture in Zambia. Agriflora played a major role in the development of what appeared to be a dynamic sector of the Zambian economy. Zambeef has played a major part in the streamlining of food distribution in Zambia's urban areas, and recreated the market for Zambian cattle producers in the Western Province. TZI also played a positive role in many sectors of the Zimbabwean economy, and many of the companies that it financed continue to do so in very difficult circumstances.

CHAPTER 22

Conclusion

Edwin Wulfsohn is sometimes asked whether the Susman and Wulfsohn families are related. His standard reply is: 'No. We're closer than that. We're partners.' Among the underlying themes of this book have been entrepreneurship, religion, kinship and partnership, and the links between them. This book has told the story of the origins, growth and survival of what has always been primarily a family business. This began with a partnership of two enterprising brothers, who were joined for a while by a third. It evolved into a partnership between two unrelated families that had little in common initially except their Jewish roots in the Baltic provinces of the Russian Empire. This book tells a story not only of partnership within families, and between families, but also of many other kinds of partnerships: with kings, chiefs and occasionally governments, with entrepreneurs and managers, as well as with employees, clients and customers. In the course of a century Susman Brothers & Wulfsohn, with its various offshoots, became one of the largest and most extensive family-based businesses in southern Africa – certainly the largest of its kind in south-central Africa. It has operated in various forms and over a wide geographical area. It has flourished in logistically difficult, physically challenging and politically problematic environments. Beginning during the Scramble for Africa and the heyday of imperialism, it came through the colonial period, and the triumph of African nationalism, and has survived into the era of Structural Adjustment, emerging markets and the new globalisation. It has over the years shown a high degree of flexibility and resilience, as well as an unusual commitment to the place of its origins, which is now Zambia.

Although direct family control is now limited to a block of farms in the Mazabuka District of Zambia, companies that are in descent from Susman Brothers & Wulfsohn through Trans Zambezi Industries continue to play an important part in commercial agriculture and food distribution in Zambia, and have a continuing role in Zimbabwe. Edwin Wulfsohn stepped down as chairman of Trans Zambezi Industries in 2002, and Concorde Investments was wound up in the same year, but he continues as chairman of Stenham Gestinor plc, the London-based financial services group that grew out of a pair of shipping companies with links to central Africa. David Susman recently stepped down as president of Woolworths, one of South Africa's largest and most successful retail chains, but his son, Simon, continues to run that business as managing director. John Rabb, another grandson of Elie Susman, continues as managing director of the related company, Wooltru Ltd. He retired from the board of TZI in January 2004, but continues to be involved with the Zambian farms and ranches.

The story of Susman Brothers & Wulfsohn provides a vivid demonstration of the historian Eric Hobsbawm's observation that 'international trading, banking or finance, fields of sometimes physically remote activities, large rewards and great insecurity, [have] been most successfully conducted by kin-related bodies of entrepreneurs, preferably with groups from special religious solidarities, like Jews, Quakers or Huguenots'.[1] When the Susman brothers crossed the Zambezi in April 1901 they had very few assets apart from their youthful energy, their limited experience as traders and their membership of 'a special religious solidarity'. As Jews from the Russian Empire, they were able to attach themselves to a network with access to credit and global reach. They had the backing of Landau Brothers, of Bulawayo, who in their turn had backing from Julius Weil and Company of Mafeking, and Mosenthal Brothers of Port Elizabeth. Landau Brothers was in the process of establishing its independence from these backers by setting up its own office in the City of London, the epicentre of a global network that revolved around international banks. These included N. M. Rothschild and Company, a firm with a special interest in the gold and diamonds of Southern Africa, which had given vital support to Cecil Rhodes and Alfred Beit in their establishment of the British South Africa Company.[2]

The Jewishness of the Susmans and Wulfsohns gave them membership of important global and regional networks. It also exposed them to discrimination and persecution in their birthplaces and to anti-Semitic prejudice on the colonial frontier. There is not space here to examine in detail the role of refugees, whether religious, political or economic, as entrepreneurs, but there can be little doubt that anti-Semitism was a force that not only drove people out of their homes, but also helped to turn a few of them into overachievers. There were, of course, many others who were unable to cope with persecution, and forced migration, and sadly fell by the wayside. Anti-

Semitism on the frontier in southern Africa was at its strongest in the early decades of the twentieth century. The Susman brothers had to work hard to overcome this prejudice and to establish a position for themselves as respected members of colonial society. It seemed to fade a little in the 1920s, but it revived in reaction to the Depression of the early 1930s, and to the arrival of German Jewish refugees later in the decade. Harry Wulfsohn also had to contend with prejudice on the part of some members of the colonial establishment in the 1930s and 1940s, though he did have some support from members of the provincial administration. Nevertheless, anti-Semitism remained an issue in the 1950s. There was at least one occasion in that decade when Maurice Rabb had to intervene with the colonial government at the highest level when an apparently anti-Semitic district officer refused to issue store licences. Neither the Susman brothers nor Harry Wulfsohn were especially religious, but their Jewish identity meant a great deal to them. They were supporters of the Livingstone Hebrew Congregation and of the Zionist movement. Both the Susman brothers acted as president of the Livingstone Hebrew Congregation, as did Elie's son-in-law, Maurice Rabb. The Susman brothers had close links with Palestine through their parents, and continued to own property in Israel. Members of the Wulfsohn family had also moved from Latvia to Palestine in the 1920s.[3]

Although a number of the early partnerships of the Susman brothers were with fellow Jews, they also developed important partnerships with people who were not Jewish. Perhaps the most important of these, though it is difficult to document fully, was with King Lewanika and his son, Prince Litia. The Susmans would not have been able to establish a dominant position in the trade of Barotseland without the Lewanikas' support. Their links with Chief Letsholathebe Sekgoma were important too, for the establishment of a new sphere of influence in Ngamiland. They also formed partnerships in Barotseland with traders, like Jimmy Dawson, who were not Jewish, and were saved from bankruptcy after the collapse of the Barotseland cattle trade, through the intervention and backing of a colonial Scot, Tom Meikle. The Ngamiland venture involved them in a partnership with Charles Riley, who came from the island of St Helena, and was regarded as not quite 'white'. The racial status of Jews in Southern Africa was also ambiguous until after the First World War. It was only then that they began to lose their special status as 'Hebrews' and to be fully accepted as 'European' and 'white'.

The Susmans formed a number of new partnerships in the 1920s. The most important of these was with 'Bongola' Smith, another emigrant from the Russian Empire, who provided an important market in the Congo for Ngamiland cattle. Other new partners included two Scots, Robert Sutherland, with whom they started a transport and trading enterprise in Barotseland, and George Buchanan, with whom they became involved in the export of cattle from Barotseland to Angola. They also formed a partnership with Charlie Knight and W. E. Tongue, of Zambesi Saw Mills, as transport contractors, and as suppliers of timber from their own concessions in Southern Rhodesia and Bechuanaland. In the transport business they were in partnership with an Afrikaner, A. T. Dreyer. They employed a number of other Scots and Afrikaners as transport supervisors and farm managers. At the same time they began to be recognised by the governments of Northern Rhodesia and Bechuanaland as partners in the management of the cattle trade. The brothers established a special relationship with an outstanding civil servant, John Smith, Northern Rhodesia's chief veterinary officer and director of agriculture, and were later to establish a similar relationship with one of his successors, John Hobday.

Not all their partnerships were successful. Their early partnership with Messrs Sprinner and Monckts, in the adventurous hunt for King Lobengula's treasure, is a conspicuous case in point. A later failure was their partnership with Willie Hepker in the newly developing Copperbelt. Their partnership with the Sussmans, an unrelated family of Lithuanian Jewish origin, was more successful and resulted in the establishment of two new companies: Copperfields Cold Storage and Northern Caterers. Of even greater long-term significance was the partnership that they formed with their own nephews, Maurice and Harry Gersh, on the Copperbelt in the early 1930s. This resulted in the establishment of Economy Stores and, in the following decades, of African Commercial Holdings, and a wide range of other commercial and industrial enterprises on the Copperbelt. They formed another important partnership in Bechuanaland in the 1930s. This was with 'Chobo' Weskob and resulted in the establishment of the Ngamiland Trading Company. Weskob was to be their representative in Ngamiland for thirty years.

The Susman brothers were not always the senior or dominant partners. In the Congo cattle trade they had to take second place to 'Bongola' Smith. In the Copperbelt butchery and hotels business, they took second place as investors to the Sussman brothers, and yielded first place in management to Isadore Kollenberg. In their very important investment in Woolworths in the mid 1930s they were at first junior partners with Max Sonnenberg and his family, although Elie Susman established his own sphere of influence in the Transvaal and the Orange Free State. The Susmans eventually replaced the Sonnenbergs as the dominant family within the business. The Sonnenbergs and Susmans had jointly formed an important new alliance with Simon Marks and Israel Sieff, the promoters, with others, of Marks & Spencer in the United Kingdom. The philosophy and management techniques of the latter company were, perhaps surprisingly, to percolate down through Woolworths to the extremities of the central African business.

Their most important central African partnership – with Harry Wulfsohn – was formed in the late 1930s and early 1940s. Although the origins of this relationship are a little obscure, it seems to have begun with the Susmans' sale of the Livingstone butchery business to him in 1939 and was cemented through the joint purchase of Kala Ranch in 1942. The Susmans had clearly identified Wulfsohn as an exceptionally talented young entrepreneur and as someone who could help them solve the problem of succession in their central African businesses. This arose from Elie Susman's move to Johannesburg, Harry Susman's readiness to retire and his sons' lack of enthusiasm for business. It was not until the mid 1950s that Elie's son, David, was ready, willing and able to take over the management of Woolworths, and a supervisory role in relation to the central African businesses.

Meanwhile, Harry Wulfsohn had played the major part in the post-war creation of an essentially new business, the Susman Brothers & Wulfsohn stores network, and in the development of Werners, the Copperbelt butchery business. Susman Brothers & Wulfsohn was only loosely related to the Susman brothers' earlier Barotseland business, though it exploited their links with the Lozi royal family, and their own good name and reputation. Harry Wulfsohn was primarily responsible for bringing two new partners into these twin businesses. They were Maurice Rabb, Elie Susman's son-in-law, who played a major role in the management of the stores business, and Max Barnett, who became the main driver of the butchery business. He also brought in Robert Boyd as manager of the ranches and, together with the Susman brothers, formed a short-lived farming partnership with Geoff Beckett and Stewart Green. The expansion of the butchery business also involved an uneasy partnership with Abe Galaun in Lusaka.

The Susman brothers and Harry Wulfsohn were involved with different partners in a variety of other post-war enterprises. Abe Gelman, son-in-law of 'Bongola' Smith, and a key player in the cattle trades of the Congo and Southern Rhodesia, was an important partner in the takeover of Zambesi Saw Mills and in the establishment of Northern Rhodesia Textiles. Elie Susman's involvement in a Mozambican timber project was not a success, but

Harry Wulfsohn demonstrated his entrepreneurial talent when he took over the Mozambican project in partnership with Henry Victor Riva, and developed new timber and forestry interests in South Africa in partnership with Tom Robson. These enterprises were of great importance to him as they enabled him to establish sources of wealth that were independent of his partnership with the Susman family.

The structure of the partnership between the Susman brothers and Harry Wulfsohn was a hybrid between an old-fashioned partnership and a limited liability company. The fifty-fifty split in the voting shares in the two main companies proved to be a recipe for conflict. Although consideration was given to breaking up the partnership in the early 1950s and again in the mid 1960s, this never happened, and the tensions between the partners were, in a sense, creative and did not prevent the businesses from growing rapidly. The greatest achievements of the partners in these years were the building up of the two core businesses, Susman Brothers & Wulfsohn and Werners. The first of these achieved a dominant place in rural trade over much of Northern Rhodesia, always retaining a power-base in Barotseland. There is no doubt that this business provided a high standard of quality and service in an exceptionally difficult environment. It played an important role in creating a market for produce as well as in meeting, and possibly helping to create, a demand for goods. More than thirty years after its demise, it retains the loyalty of a now diminishing band of former employees and customers, for it has never been replaced. It was years ahead of its time in its application of advanced, though simplified, management systems, and its use of modern technology, including aircraft, in remote and inaccessible places. Werners was a more conventional business that operated cold stores and retail outlets in urban centres, but it also achieved a remarkable dominance of the market at the wholesale and retail levels, and did so through efficient organisation and good service.

The support given by the main partners in the Susman Brothers & Wulfsohn Group to the Federation of Rhodesia and Nyasaland was not beneficial to the group in the long run. The establishment of Rhodesian Mercantile Holdings involved a new partnership with Harry Robinson, a son-in-law of Harry Susman, but the extension of the business into Southern Rhodesia was not a great success. The shift of the headquarters to Salisbury proved to be an embarrassment after the break-up of the Federation and Zambia's independence in 1963–4, and a major handicap after Rhodesia's UDI in 1965, which had a toxic effect on regional relationships.

There was some irony in the fact that the Susman Brothers & Wulfsohn Group enjoyed at this time a special relationship, amounting to a partnership, with the Northern Rhodesian government, which looked to it for the management – through private enterprise – of the cattle and beef markets. As a consequence the group became the major protagonist in a battle with Southern Rhodesia's Cold Storage Commission for control of the regional markets. This was really a battle between Northern and Southern Rhodesia and between two different models for the management of the markets for cattle and beef. The Northern Rhodesian model allowed for control by private enterprise in alliance with the government through a regulatory board. The Southern Rhodesian model allowed for control through what was in effect a state monopoly. The federal government backed the Southern Rhodesian Cold Storage Commission against Werners, but the Commission's victory was short-lived. The Susman Brothers & Wulfsohn Group's activities were also adversely affected by the intervention in the regional cattle trade of another parastatal organisation – the Colonial (later Commonwealth) Development Corporation. Its involvement in Bechuanaland resulted in the beginning of the end of the northward export of Ngamiland cattle, though this trade did not come to a complete halt until after Botswana's independence in 1966.

The Susman Brothers & Wulfsohn Group's profitable partnership with the colonial government of Northern Rhodesia, and its less satisfactory attempt at an alliance with the federal government, meant that it was not well placed to respond to the rise of African nationalism. Max Barnett showed a degree of flexibility in his response to the threat of butchery boycotts on the Copperbelt, but Maurice Rabb underestimated the force of African nationalism in Barotseland, and his attempt to mobilise Lozi 'traditionalism' against the UNIP was doomed to failure. It demonstrated, however, the continuing importance to the group of the relationship with the Litunga of the Lozi – in this case Sir Mwanawina III. The group asked for, and welcomed, the fifty-one per cent takeover of Zambesi Saw Mills by Indeco, but vainly resisted the takeover of the stores business. Neither of the unequal partnerships that it formed with the new government of Zambia – Zambesi Saw Mills (1968) Ltd and Zambesi Trading Ltd – lasted long, nor were they successful commercially. Maurice Gersh proved more adept at managing the transition from colonial rule to independence. He entered into partnerships with Bookers and Lonrho, both multi-national companies that had developed their own ways of dealing with African nationalism, and he eventually sold the bulk of his group's interests to them.

After the loss of control of the stores business, and of Zambesi Saw Mills, and the running down of the butchery business, the Susman Brothers & Wulfsohn Group's main surviving interests in Zambia were the farms and ranches, which were brought together in Zambesi Ranching and Cropping, and the Livingstone blanket factory. There were other remnants of the business in Rhodesia and Botswana, and a few small businesses in the United Kingdom, which had been acquired because of their links to central Africa. The latter businesses had been bought after the imposition of exchange controls by the federal government in 1961. Until that time the companies in the Susman Brothers & Wulfsohn Group had reinvested almost all their profits in the expansion of existing businesses, and the development of new ones within the region. Within the Federation the group had represented national rather than international capital. It never did take capital out of the region, though it used its central African assets as security for loans that funded these small investments in the United Kingdom. The Susman brothers had used their central African assets in the same way in the 1930s as collateral for loans that helped to finance their investment in Woolworths. Even the new nationalist government of Zambia seems to have recognised that the group represented national capital. It took over Zambesi Saw Mills because it was asked to do so, and its takeover of the stores network seems to have come about as much by accident as design.

Following his father's death in 1968, it was Edwin Wulfsohn who carried the main burden of managing these varied business interests. He succeeded in bringing them all together under the umbrella of a single offshore holding company, Concorde Investments, and in working harmoniously with his partners. He tried hard to save Vigers, the British timber-flooring business, which had been purchased in connection with Zambesi Saw Mills, but was defeated by an extremely hostile economic environment, and by Vigers's place in a declining market. He was able, on the other hand, to build a large and successful financial services business on the basis of two small confirming houses, Stenham and Crombie, which had been acquired because of their role in the financing of central African trade. This involved new partnerships and was a remarkable achievement as Stenham had been brought close to bankruptcy in the late 1970s through guarantees made to Zambian companies. There is a kind of circularity in the latter-day history of the group. At the beginning of the twentieth century, the Susman brothers had built a business on the periphery of the world market, and at the end of a long chain of credit, which began in London. At the end of the twentieth century, Edwin Wulfsohn moved to London and used African connections to build a large business, which was primarily involved in the provision of credit, and the financing of world trade.

An equally remarkable achievement was Edwin Wulfsohn's establishment, in partnership with Hillary Duckworth, and with the support of David Susman and John Rabb, of Trans Zambezi Industries (TZI) in 1993. Taking advantage of political changes in Zambia, and the new interest in emerging markets, they were able to raise large sums of international capital for investment in central Africa and to use the Zambian farms and ranches as the basis for a new regional enterprise whose slogan was 'Business knows no boundaries'. This was a second new beginning for the group, and matched Elie Susman and Harry Wulfsohn's re-launching of the central African business after the Second World War. It also marked a major reversal of roles. The Susman Brothers & Wulfsohn Group had been built up over most of a century through the reinvestment of profits which had been generated from local production and trade. This new enterprise involved the mobilisation and import of international capital – about $70,000,000 in all – for investment in central Africa at a time when it was difficult to raise capital locally and investment was badly needed. The bulk of this capital went into commercial agriculture in Zambia and forestry and paper production in Zimbabwe. TZI played a major part in the development of two important new businesses in Zambia. It backed the growth of Zambeef, which became the dominant player in the butchery business in the country in the late 1990s – achieving a degree of dominance by the early years of the new millennium that was greater than that of Werners fifty years earlier. It also backed the development of Agriflora, which played a leading role in the development of horticultural and floricultural exports from Zambia – a significant new source of exports and employment in an otherwise declining economy. While Zambeef has survived and appears to be growing from strength to strength, opening branches in Malawi and the Congo, Agriflora appears to have overextended itself, outgrowing its capital base, and becoming insolvent in the middle of 2004. From 1998 onwards TZI was adversely affected by events in Zimbabwe. It had been largely dismantled by the beginning of 2004, though many of its former subsidiaries survived as independent businesses.

The Susman and Wulfsohn families produced in the course of a century five remarkable entrepreneur/managers. They were, in order of seniority: Elie Susman, Maurice Gersh, Harry Wulfsohn, David Susman and Edwin Wulfsohn. They were, and are, all very different people, with differing proportions of entrepreneurial and managerial talent. They have all shared a capacity for hard work, resilience in the face of difficulties, an ability to spot gaps in the market and new opportunities, as well as to identify enterprising partners and effective managers. Above all they have shared the ability to make things happen, to create businesses, employment, and wealth, in some of the poorest and most inaccessible places in the world. They have created assets that can be, and sometimes have been, run down, but which cannot be removed. Their role as entrepreneurs demonstrates the inestimable value of the knowledge, experience and relationships of people and of groups. Their membership of global and regional networks has given them the ability to mobilise expertise, credit and resources. Nothing is more remarkable to the historian than the indefatigable way in which they have continued to take new initiatives and to launch new enterprises – often at apparently inauspicious times. Entrepreneurship involves innovation and risk taking. In areas where the risks are in any case high, survival can best be assured by the spreading of risk. It is probably awareness of this fact that has led these entrepreneurs to launch so many new enterprises and to involve themselves in so many activities from cattle trading to ranching, from butcheries to retail trading, from timber to textiles, from garages to cinemas, and from farming to financial services. Cattle have, however, remained one constant theme in a kaleidoscopic scene.

The entrepreneurs who made Susman Brothers & Wulfsohn have displayed an exceptional degree of commitment to the region in which they have worked for more than a century. The involvement of several generations of the founding families has provided continuity, underpinned this long-term commitment, and ensured the survival of the business in the face of considerable political, economic and logistical difficulties. A business based on two families, with a shared religious background and ethos, has been better equipped to take the long view than some more conspicuous multi-national conglomerates, including rivals and partners such as Bookers and Lonrho, which have faded from the scene in recent years. Although the degree of family control is now reduced, there is still family involvement, and the businesses in central Africa that are in descent from Susman Brothers & Wulfsohn share a tradition of commitment to good quality and service. These businesses continue to display remarkable dynamism and may continue to act as economic catalysts in the Southern African region for a long time to come.

Acknowledgements and Note on Sources

I am very grateful to David Susman, Edwin Wulfsohn, John Rabb and Simon Zukas for inviting me to write this book, and for their generosity and patience. They have allowed me unrestricted access to personal and company papers and have given me complete freedom to interpret the evidence in my own way. I am also grateful to David Susman and Trude Robins (Wulfsohn) for allowing me to quote from their memoirs, to John Rabb for allowing me to use his father's 'Recollections' and to Edwin Wulfsohn for writing for me a number of memoranda on his own involvement in the business. I am also grateful to Marian Payne for writing a memoir for me of her and her late husband's experiences of twenty years' employment with Susman Brothers & Wulfsohn. I would like to thank David Susman and Edwin Wulfsohn, Professors Shula Marks, Ian Phimister and Andrew Roberts, and an anonymous reader, for their perceptive comments on the manuscript of this book. I hope that they will notice some changes for the better, but, needless to say, I remain responsible for all errors of omission and commission, and for infelicities of style.

I would like to thank my wife, Monica, and son, John, for their encouragement and support, and for their patience during my occasional physical absences, and almost continuous mental absence, in central Africa over the last three years. I would like to pay tribute to the memory of my mother who took a great interest in the research and writing of this book, and who died in July 2003, soon after the completion of the first draft of the manuscript.

I am grateful to the librarians and staff of all the libraries and archives where I worked, especially the National Archives of Zambia, Lusaka, the Livingstone Museum, Livingstone, the National Archives of Botswana, Gaborone, Rhodes House Library, Oxford, the British Library Newspaper Library, Colindale, and the Standard Bank Archives, Johannesburg.

I am especially grateful to the Litunga, His Highness Imwiko II, and to Senior Chief Inyambo Yeta, for receiving me at Limulunga and Mwandi, in the Western Province of Zambia.

I owe a particular debt of gratitude to the friends who provided me with hospitality and help on my travels in Africa, most especially to Geoffrey and Shirley

Mee in Lusaka, and to 'Rama' Rama Krishnan in Mazabuka, Mike and Gillian Beckett in Choma, Murray and Eva Sanderson in Kitwe, Neil Parsons in Gaborone, Eira Kramer, and Denton Pitt, in Harare, Sarah Clark and Dan Krige in Durban, and the Barben family in Cape Town; also to the staff of the Ngulu Hotel, Mongu; the Zambia Textiles Guest House, Livingstone; Riley's Hotel, Maun; the Brontë Hotel, Harare; Fairview Apartments, Cape Town; and the Johannian Club, Johannesburg.

Note on Sources

The most important private papers used in the writing of this book were the Susman family papers, which are divided between Edwin Wulfsohn's collection in London and David Susman's in Cape Town. These include a few early documents from 1901 onwards, an almost complete set of balance sheets for the Susman Brothers' business, and associated businesses, from 1907 until the late 1920s; a transcript of Elie Susman's diary for 1920, and a broken series of his diaries from 1931 to 1957; papers relating to the Susman brothers' involvement with Woolworths; and correspondence between Elie and David Susman, and partners, from 1946 to 1957, and between David Susman and partners, from 1955 until 1966. The papers of Maurice Rabb, held by John Rabb in Cape Town, are also an important source. They include a run of letters between Maurice Rabb and Elie Susman from 1946 to 1957, which provide a very detailed account of the central African businesses, and other letters between Rabb and various partners from 1946 to 1966. Harry Wulfsohn does not appear to have kept papers, but Edwin Wulfsohn has accumulated a large collection of documents relating to the history of the business. Max Barnett also does not appear to have retained documents, but I was able to see some papers relevant to the history of Werners by courtesy of the late Abe and Vera Galaun in Lusaka, and of Mike Beckett in Choma.

Company minute books have been an important source for this book, especially for the post-war period. These are listed below, with an indication of their locations, at the head of the list of private manuscript sources. The most important of these were the Rhodesian Mercantile Holdings minutes, and the Concorde Investments minutes, both of which I was able to see in Harare by courtesy of Denton Pitt. The former provide an exceptionally detailed account of the stores business in Northern Rhodesia/Zambia from 1955 until 1965, and also shed light on other aspects of the business in Southern Rhodesia and Bechuanaland/Botswana until a later date. The Concorde Investments minutes provide an overview of all aspects of the business from the early 1970s to 1990. The Zambesi Saw Mills Minute Books – two huge volumes – provide a detailed account of the history of that business form 1945 until its nationalisation in

1968. These were found at the offices of Zambesi Ranching and Cropping at Sikalozia Ranch, Mazabuka, Zambia, together with minute books for the individual ranching companies, beginning with those for Kala Ranch from 1942. I also had access there to the minutes of Zambesi Ranching and Cropping from 1968 to 1987, with a gap, and to the minutes of Susman Brothers & Wulfsohn itself from 1955, and for Werners from 1968. I was unable to find the first volume of minutes for Harry Wulfsohn Ltd/Susman Brothers & Wulfsohn Ltd, from 1944 to 1955, or the Werners minutes from 1937 to 1968, but some of the Werners minutes for the late 1950s survive with the records of related ranching companies.

The Northern Rhodesia/Zambia Textiles minute books are split between Edwin Wulfsohn's collection in London and the company office in Livingstone. I was able to consult the minute books of the Gersh brothers' companies, African Commercial Holdings and Central African Motors at the offices of Lonrho Africa in Lusaka by courtesy of Mr Luhanga. I was also able to consult minute books for Copperfields Cold Storage and Northern Bakeries at the Nkana Hotel, Kitwe, by courtesy of the Phiri family. Unfortunately, the first volume of the Copperfields minutes, as well as the Northern Catering minute books, appear to have been accidentally destroyed.

Among public archives, the National Archives of Zambia proved to be the richest source of information for this book. The KDE series of files on Barotseland is surprisingly rich in references to the Susman brothers' activities in the first three decades of the twentieth century. Other series shed light on Harry Wulfsohn's career in the Southern Province in the fourth decade of the century, and on many aspects of the business from the early years until the late 1960s. Some reference has also been made to files in the Zimbabwe National Archives, where access was restricted by bureaucratic obstacles, and in the Botswana National Archives, where a longer stay would have shed more light on the Ngamiland side of the story. There are also a few references to files in the South African National Archives in Pretoria and Cape Town.

The Welensky papers at Rhodes House, Oxford, have been another important source in a public archive. This collection provides an alternative government archive for the federal period and contains a mass of documentation on the negotiations between Werners and the Southern Rhodesian Cold Storage Commission. A search of the catalogues of the Public Record Office in London suggested that its collections would not add much to what was found in the relevant regional archives.

The most important published primary source for this book has been the *Livingstone Mail*. This provided a week-by-week account of the movements and other activities of the Susman brothers from 1906 until after the Second World

War and filled in many gaps in the manuscript record. I read the paper dating from 1906 to 1948, and for some later years, using files at the British Newspaper Library at Colindale and at the Livingstone Museum in Zambia. The paper survived until 1965, but became less useful in the post-war period.

Interviews have been a very important source for this book. I am very grateful to the seventy or eighty people who agreed to be interviewed, some of them on several occasions. It may be invidious to single out individuals, but I must make special mention of some exceptionally well-informed former employees of Susman Brothers & Wulfsohn and its subsidiaries: the late Geoffrey Kates, at Wentworth Estate, Job Haloba in Livingstone, Benson Kamitondo in Mongu, Denton Pitt, Colin Arnott and Steve Kuzniar, in Harare, Peter Green at Choma, and Tony Serrano in Johannesburg. The names of all the interviewees are listed below.

I Interviews

* Telephone interview. + Interviewed more than once.

Arnott, Colin, Harare
Barnett, Michael, Johannesburg*
Barnett, Timothy, Cape Town+
Beckett, Michael, Choma, Zambia+
Bligh-Wall, Alison, Lincolnshire, England*
Byrne, Phyrne, Livingstone, Zambia
Chick, Keith, Durban
Clyde-Anderson, Rodney, Mazabuka, Zambia+
Cohen, Victor, Harare
Diamond, Molly, Kitwe, Zambia+
Dorsky, Morris, Durban*
Emdin, Molly, Johannesburg*
Emdin, Richard, Cape Town*
Faerber, Esther, Cape Town+
Falk, Josephine (née Wulfsohn), Rochdale, Lancashire*
Fonseka, F., Livingstone, Zambia
Fuller, Arthur, Johannesburg
Gadsden, Bernard, Lusaka
Galaun, Abe and Vera, Lusaka.+
Gersh, Bernard, Washington, USA*
Gersh, Revée, Worcester, Mass., USA*
Green, Peter, Choma, Zambia
Haloba, Job, Livingstone+

ACKNOWLEDGEMENTS AND NOTE ON SOURCES

Hart, Robert, East London, South Africa*
Imwiko II, His Highness the Litunga, Limulunga, Zambia
Irwin, Carl, Lusaka
Irwin, Oliver, Lusaka
Kamitondo, Benson, Mongu, Zambia+
Kashita, Andrew, Dorchester on Thames, Oxford
Kates, Geoffrey, Wentworth Estate, Virginia Water, Surrey+
Kays, Ronnie, Maun, Botswana
Kollenberg, Gerald, Johannesburg
Kutoma, Ernest Mukwendela, Mongu, Zambia
Kuzniar, Steve and Patsy, Harare
Lewanika, Akashambatwa Mbikusita, Lusaka
Liswaniso, Joel Mubiana, Mongu, Zambia
Lowenthal, Hessie (née Wulfsohn), Johannesburg
McCarter, Peter, Lusaka
McKillop, Mrs L., Livingstone
Mee, Geoffrey, Lusaka
Molver, Neil, Lusaka
Mubitamwinda, Induna, Mwandi, Zambia
Muliata, Joseph, Mongu, Zambia
Mwaanga, Vernon, Mongu, Zambia
Myburgh, Chris, Durban
Neethling, Edwardina, Lusaka
Omei, Induna, Mwandi, Zambia
Pinshow, Len, Durban+
Perreira, Mr, Livingstone
Pitt, Denton, Harare+
Rama Krishnan, 'Rama', Mazabuka, Zambia+
Riva, Victor, Lisbon, Portugal*+
Robins, Trude (née Wiesenbacher, widow of Harry Wulfsohn), Johannesburg+
Robinson, Ella, Harare*
Robson, Tom, Johannesburg*
Sardanis, Andrew, Lusaka
Serrano, Tony and Marie, Johannesburg
Shamwana, Edward, Lusaka
Silishebo, Reverend Elizabeth M., Mwandi, Zambia
Slade, Neil, Lusaka
Smith, T. Bagnall, Oxford
Susman, David, Cape Town, London, Highclere+
Susman, Joe, Victoria Falls, Zimbabwe, tape of undated BBC interview, by courtesy of his widow, Alison Bligh-Wall
Teeger, Isa (née Lowenthal), Johannesburg+

Tilasi, Charles, Livingstone
Vlotamas, Alex, Maun, Botswana
Vos, Ronnie and Poppie, Boksburg, South Africa
Weskob, Cid, Johannesburg
Wiesenbacher, Freddy, Harare
Wolffe, Hymie, Cape Town+
Woolf, Ronald, Durban+
Wright, Trevor, Mazabuka, Zambia
Wulfsohn, Edwin, London+
Wulfsohn, Wulfie, London+
Yeta, Senior Chief Inyambo, Mwandi, Zambia
Zacks, Bruna (née Susman), Johannesburg
Zinn, Bella (née Kominsky), Israel*
Zukas, Cynthia, Lusaka+
Zukas, Simon, Lusaka+

II Manuscript Sources

A Public Archives

Companies Registry, Lusaka
Werner and Company File, 1937–

National Archives of Botswana, Gaborone
DCMA8/8 Ngamiland Cattle Exporters Association, 1954–61
S1/18 Sekgoma Letsholathebe, 1912
S178/6 Credit System of Ngamiland Traders, 'Good-Fors', 1930–60
S244/8 J. Riley and Trekking Cattle from Francistown to Kazungula, 1931–2
S282/7-17 Susman Timber Concession, 1932–7

National Archives of Zimbabwe, Harare
A/11/2/47 King Lobengula's Treasure
S1882, B. Susman, Correspondence re Naturalisation, 1919
S456/712/22 Gwaai Farms, Nos 82–3, 1911–19
S2279/836, Harry Susman Naturalisation Papers, 1908–48
Oral/236, Nathan Zelter interviewed by I. Johnstone, 1986

Livingstone Museum, Livingstone, Zambia
Paris Mission Papers
Elie Susman, Trade Licence, 1901
J. H. Venning Papers
R. Sampson Papers
F. V. Worthington Papers

National Archives of Zambia, Lusaka
A3/1/4 Colin Harding, Personal File, 1902–6
A3/22/3 List of Proclamations in Force, 1906
A3/23/1 Livingstone Church Council, 1909
A3/31/3 F. W. Dawson Personal File, 1903–5
A5/1/1-11 NWR Departmental Reports, 1907–11
A5/2/1-6 NWR District Annual Reports, 1908–11
A5/2/9 NWR Rifle Association, 1909–11
A5/3/1 NR Rifle Association, 1910–11
A6/1/1-2 Administrator, Matabeleland, 1898–1902

B1/1/4 Death of Lewanika, 1916
B1/2/1 Administrator's Meetings with Paramount Chief, 1909–21
BS2/227 High Commissioner to Administrator, 1904
BS3/242 Lobengula's Treasure, 1917

H1/1/1/1 Bankruptcies, 1905–8
H1/2/1/2-3 Bankruptcies, 1905–8
H1/2/2/3 Appeal Court, 1909
HC1/2/1-56 Administrator, NWR, 1901–11
HM7 CU/1/11/1, Boyd Cunninghame Papers

IMA1/1/3 Magistrate, Kalomo, General Correspondence, 1902–6
IMMI/1/K/322, 1948, Immigration File, G. Kates

KDB6/1/1/1-7 Batoka/Southern Province, Annual Reports, 1921–34

KDE1/1/1-5 Mongu-Lealui Out Letters, 1902–9
KDE1/2/1 Mongu Judicial Out Letters, 1907–10
KDE1/3/1 Miscellaneous Letters (Hazell), 1907–8
KDE1/4/1-9 Letters to Lewanika, 1905–9
KDE2/11/1-2 Bovine Pleuro-pneumonia, 1915–18
KDE2/21/1 Record of Military Service, 1914
KDE2/34/1-2 Magistrate, Mongu, Correspondence with Lewanika
KDE2/41/1-3 Trading in Barotseland, 1908–29
KDE3/2/4-5 Criminal Cases, 1908–9
KDE7/11/2 Barotseland Cattle Trade, 1916–18
KDE8/1/3-20, Barotse Annual Reports, 1911–28
KDE10/1/1 Vols 1–2, Barotse District Notebook

KSF1/8/4 Namwala Township Plot, 1934–7
KSF3/2/7 Annual Reports Namwala, 1934–7
KSX4/1 Mankoya District Notebook
KTO1/1 Sesheke Confidential Correspondence, 1912–18

KTO/3 Sesheke District Notebook

MAG2/2/32 Cattle Marketing and Control Board Minutes, 1955–9
ML1/9/4 Kafue Polder Pilot Scheme, 1961
ML1/14/15 Zambesi Saw Mills, 1961
ML1/17/50 Lochinvar, 1962
ML1/17/87 Lochinvar, 1965–6
ML4/5/2 Livestock Cooperative Society of NR, 1935–50

RC 579 Veterinary Conference held at Livingstone 1926
RC 625 Import of Cattle from Ngamiland, 1920–6

SEC1/949-50 Zambesi Saw Mills.
SEC1/1520/1 Closed Townships Commission Report, 1948
SEC1/1760-6 Post-war Problems
SEC2/282 Five Year Plans, Barotse Province, 1943
SEC2/283 Five Year Plans, Southern Province, 1943
SEC3/500/1-3 Proposed Zambesi River Transport Scheme, 1945–8
SEC3/547/1-2 Cattle for Mining Areas, 1929–33
SEC3/548/1-2 Import of Cattle 1932–8
SEC3/560 NR Cold Storage Board Works, 1940–5
SEC3/565/1 Bovine Pleuro-pneumonia, 1934–45
SEC4/1334-51 Price Controls
SEC4/1446 Groundnuts Scheme, 1946–50

W41 Minutes of the Agricultural Lands Board, 1914–15

ZA1/9 Paramount Chief's Accounts, 1915–25
ZA1/14 Visiting Commissioner (H. C. Marshall), 1913–19
ZA7/1/12-17, Barotse Annual Reports, 1929–34
ZP15 Cost of Living Enquiry Commission, Verbatim Record of Evidence, 1947
ZP18 Closed Township Commission, Verbatim Record of Evidence, 1948

Rhodes House Library, Oxford
M. G. Billing, 'The Crest of the Wave'
C. W. Catt Papers
Edward Garraway Diaries
Jules Ellenberger Papers
Vivian Ellenberger Papers
J. H. Venning, 'Memories'
Sir Roy Welensky Papers

South African National Archives, Cape Town
PIO 25 no. 2698E Behr and Taube Sussmanovitz Immigration File, 1913

South African National Archives, Pretoria
GG1536-50/69 Sekgoma Letsholathebe, 1911
GG2277-2/296 Governor-General's Visit to Northern Bechuanaland, 1929
MHG62561 Estate of Samuel Lesser, 1927
MHG 92641 Estate of Julius Monckts
WLD/238/1910 Julius Monckts, Criminal Case, 1910

South African National Library, Cape Town
Eric Rosenthal Papers

University of Cape Town Library, Cape Town
G. E. Nettleton Papers

University of the Witwatersrand Library, Johannesburg
Lobatse Cold Storage Papers

B *Company Minute Books cited in the text with an indication of their location*
African Commercial Holdings, 1949–73, Lonrho Motors, Lusaka
Agricultural Enterprises, 1946–70, ZRC, Mazabuka
Central African Motors, 1951–67, Lonrho Motors, Lusaka
Chambishi Farms, 1961–83, ZRC, Mazabuka
Copperfields Cold Storage, 1951–69, c/o Northern Caterers, Nkana Hotel, Kitwe
Concorde Investments, Board of Directors, 1974–90, Executive Committee, 1973–87, in care of Denton Pitt, Harare
Forsyth's Estates, 1964–75, ZRC, Mazabuka
Kala Ranching Company, 1942–58, ZRC, Mazabuka
Kaleya Estates, 1949–67, ZRC, Mazabuka
Kansuswa Farms, 1955–72, ZRC, Mazabuka
Livingstone Jersey Farm, 1956–63, ZRC, Mazabuka
Nanga Estates, 1961–5, ZRC, Mazabuka
Northern Bakeries, 1951–63, c/o Northern Caterers, Nkana Hotel, Kitwe
Northern Rhodesia Textiles, 1946–54, Edwin Wulfsohn Papers, London
Northern Rhodesia/Zambia Textiles, 1954–64, Annual Reports, 1965–86, Zambia Textiles, Livingstone
Redwood Investments, 1969–86, ZRC, Mazabuka
Rhodesia Meat and Provisions Company, 1955–86, ZRC, Mazabuka
Rhodesian Mercantile Holdings, 1955–89, in care of Denton Pitt, Harare
Stores Holdings, 1963–83, ZRC, Mazabuka
Susman Brothers & Wulfsohn, 1955–85, ZRC, Mazabuka
Susman Brothers & Wulfsohn, Meetings of Shareholders, 1972–3, in care of Denton Pitt, Harare

Susman Brothers & Wulfsohn and Werners, Joint Meeting of Shareholders, 1969, with Werners, see below
Werners, 1957–9, with Kansuswa Farms, see above
Werners, 1968–86, ZRC, Mazabuka
Woolworths, 1931–6, Woolworths House, Cape Town
Zambesi Ranching and Cropping, 1968–76, 1981–7, Sikalozia Ranch, Mazabuka
Zambesi Saw Mills, 1945–68, ZRC, Mazabuka

C Private Collections

Michael Beckett, Choma, Zambia
Geoffrey Calvert, Plumtree, Zimbabwe
Walter Dobkins, Brisbane, Australia
Abe and Vera Galaun, Lusaka
Lonrho Motors, Lusaka
Northern Caterers, Nkana Hotel, Kitwe
Northern Rhodesia Pioneer Settlers' Association Papers, in care of Heather Chalcraft, Lusaka
Roy Parkhurst, Durban
Denton Pitt, Harare
John Rabb, Cape Town
Trude Robins, Johannesburg
Denise Scott Brown, Philadelphia, USA
T. Bagnall Smith, Oxford
David Susman, Cape Town
Standard Bank Archives, Johannesburg
Westminster, His Grace the Duke of, Eaton Hall, Chester
Edwin Wulfsohn, London
Zambesi Ranching and Cropping, Sikalozia Ranch, Mazabuka
Zambia Textiles, Livingstone
ZCCM Archives, Ndola, Zambia

III Official Publications

Annual Reports on African Affairs, 1947–63 (Lusaka: Government Printer, 1948–64)
Annual Reports on Native Affairs, 1929–38 (Livingstone/Lusaka: Government Printer, 1930–9)
Annual Reports, Department of Agriculture, 1934–60 (Lusaka: Government Printer, 1935–61)
Annual Reports, Forest Department, 1947–72 (Lusaka: Government Printer, 1948–73) (reports on Forestry included with Agriculture until 1947, and with Lands and Natural Resources from 1959)
Annual Reports, Department of Veterinary Services, 1930–63 (Livingstone/Lusaka: Government Printer, 1931–64)

Busschau, W. J., *Report on the Development of Secondary Industries in Northern Rhodesia* (Lusaka: Government Printer, 1945)
Cape of Good Hope Government Gazette, 1899
Colonial Office, *The Financial and Economic Position of the Bechuanaland Protectorate* (Cmd. 4368, 1933, (Pim Report))
Northern Rhodesia Government Gazette, 1911–64
Official Gazette of the High Commissioner for South Africa (published with *Transvaal Government Gazette*), 1900–10
Poverty Reduction Strategy Paper (Draft) (Lusaka: Government Printer, 2002)
Reports on the Administration of Rhodesia, 1900–2 (no place: British South Africa Company, n.d.)
Report of the Commission of Inquiry into the Beef Cattle Industry in Northern and Southern Rhodesia (Horwood Report) (Salisbury: Government Printer, 1963)
Report of the Commission of Inquiry on the Marketing of Cattle for Slaughter and the Distribution and Sale of Beef in Southern Rhodesia (Turner Report) (Salisbury: Government Printer, 1956)
Ten Year Development Plan for Northern Rhodesia (Lusaka: Government Printer, 1947)
Walker, H. S., and J. H. N. Hobday, 'Report on the Cattle Industry of the Bechuanaland Protectorate with Recommendations for Improving its Organisation and Assisting its Future Development' (Bechuanaland Protectorate: typescript, n.d. [1939])

IV Periodical Publications

A Newspapers and Journals

Livingstone Mail (Livingstone), 1906–48, 1952, 1954, 1958–60, 1962
Zionist Record (Johannesburg), 1911–50

B Annual Reports of Companies, Parastatal Boards and Commissions

Cold Storage Board of Zambia, 1969–74
Cold Storage Commission (Salisbury), 1960–3
Southern Rhodesia Cold Storage Commission, 1938–59
Trans Zambezi Industries, 1993–2003

V Books and Articles

Anon., 'Barotseland: Whigs and Royalists, a Detailed Analysis of the Situation on the Plain', *The Central African Examiner* (Salisbury), October 1962
Anon., 'Extracts from the District Notebooks – No.3. Lobengula's Treasure', *Northern Rhodesia Journal*, 2: 3 (1954)

Anon., *Kafue Flats: a Development Plan* (produced on behalf of the Kafue Flats Pilot Polder Trust by the Public Relations Department of the Rhodesian Selection Trust Group of Companies, n.d. [1962])

Anon., *Lochinvar National Park* (Lusaka: map and brochure published by the Survey Department, 1986)

Anon., 'Northern Rhodesia's Oldest Industry', *Shell in Industry*, 1 (1960)

Anon., 'Profile of Elie Susman', *South African Jewish Times*, 29 February 1952

Anon., 'The Strangest Railway in the World', *Horizon* (RST House Magazine), August 1964

Anon., 'Trans Zambezi Industries, A Sub-Saharan Blue Chip in the Making' (London: ING Barings, 1996)

Anon., 'TZI, Information Memorandum' (London: Deutsche Morgan Grenfell, 1996)

Anon., 'TZI, Prospectus' (London: James Capel, 1993)

Anon., 'Zambesi Sawmills', *Z Magazine* (Lusaka), March 1972

Aronson, I. M., *Troubled Waters: The Origins of the 1881 Anti-Jewish Pogroms in Russia* (Pittsburgh: Pittsburgh University Press, 1990)

Baldwin, R. E., *Economic Development and Export Growth: A Study of Northern Rhodesia, 1920–60* (Berkeley: University of California Press, 1956)

Bancroft, J. A., *Mining in Northern Rhodesia* (no place: British South Africa Company, 1961)

Barty-King, H., *Girdle Round the Earth* (London: Heinemann, 1979)

Bertrand, A., *Au pays des Ba-Rotsi Haut-Zambéze* (Paris: Hachette, 1898)

Blond, Elaine (with Barry Turner), *Marks of Distinction* (London: Valentine, Mitchell, 1983)

Bookbinder, P., *Simon Marks: Retail Revolutionary* (London: Weidenfeld and Nicolson, 1993)

Braudel, F., *The Mediterranean and the Mediterranean World in the Age of Philip II* (London: Collins, 2 volumes, 1972)

Calvert, G. M., 'The Zambesi Saw Mills Railway, 1911–64', in *The Zambezi Teak Forests: Proceedings of the First International Conference on the Teak Forests of Southern Africa, Livingstone, March 1984* (Ndola: Zambia Forestry Department, 1986)

Campbell, J. S., 'I Knew Lewanika', *Northern Rhodesia Journal*, 1: 1 (1950)

Caplan, G., *The Elites of Barotseland, 1878–1969* (London: C. Hurst, 1970)

Chileshe, J. H., *Abe Galaun* (Lusaka: Walpole Park Development Ltd, 2000)

Chilvers, H. A., *The Seven Lost Trails of Africa* (London: Cassell, 1930)

Clark, P., *Autobiography of an Old Drifter* (London: George Harrap, 1936)

Clay, G., *Your Friend, Lewanika, Litunga of Barotseland, 1842–1916* (London: Chatto & Windus, 1968)

Cohen, M. I., 'The Jewish Communities of Rhodesia and the North', in *The South African Jewish Year Book* (Johannesburg: SA Jewish Historical Society, 1929)

Coillard, F., *On the Threshold of Central Africa* (London: Hodder & Stoughton, 1897)

Comay, J. (ed.), *Who's Who in Jewish History* (London: Routledge, 1974)
Cooke, C. K., 'Lobengula: Second and Last King of the Amandabele [*sic*]: His Final Resting Place and Treasure', *Rhodesiana*, 23 (November 1970)
Croxton, A. H., 'Rhodesia's Light Railways', *Rhodesiana*, 13 (1965)
Darling, F. Fraser (ed. J. M. Boyd) *Fraser Darling in Africa* (Edinburgh: Edinburgh University Press, 1992)
——, *Wild Life in an African Territory* (London: Oxford University Press, 1960)
Davis, J. M. (ed.) *Modern Industry and the African* (London: Frank Cass, 1967 (first edition, 1933))
Debenham, Frank, *Kalahari Sand* (London: G. Bell and Sons, 1953)
——, *The Way to Ilala: David Livingstone's Pilgrimage* (London: Longmans, Green, 1955)
Denny, S. R., 'Leopold Moore Versus the Chartered Company', *Northern Rhodesia Journal*, 4: 1 (1959), and 4: 4 (1960)
D'Hendecourt, R., *L'Élevage au Katanga* (Brussels: Desclée de Brouwer, 1953)
Dubnow, S. M., *History of the Jews in Russia and Poland from the Earliest Times until the Present Day* (Philadelphia: Jewish Publications Society of America, 2 volumes, 1916)
Ferguson, N., *The House of Rothschild: The World's Banker, 1849–98* (Harmondsworth: Penguin, 2000)
Franklin, H., *Unholy Wedlock: The Failure of the Central African Federation* (London: George Allen & Unwin, 1963)
Galbraith, J. S., *Crown and Charter: The Early Years of the British South Africa Company* (Berkeley: University of California Press, 1974)
Gann, L. H., *The Birth of a Plural Society: The Development of Northern Rhodesia under the British South Africa Company, 1894–1914* (Manchester: Manchester University Press, 1958)
——, *A History of Northern Rhodesia: Early Days to 1953* (London: Chatto & Windus, 1964)
Gersh, M., 'The Susman Saga', *Northern Rhodesia Journal*, 6: 3 (1965)
Gibbons, A. St H., *African from South to North Through Marotseland* (London: John Lane, 2 volumes, 1904)
——, *Exploration and Hunting in Central Africa* (London: Methuen, 1898)
Goy, M. K., *Alone in Africa* (London: J. Nisbet, 1901)
Harding, C., *In Remotest Barotseland* (London: Hurst and Blackett, 1905)
Hobsbawm, E., *Age of Extremes: The Short Twentieth Century, 1914–91* (London: Abacus, 1995)
Hobson, D., *Show Time* (Lusaka: Agricultural and Commercial Society of Zambia, 1979)
Hole, H. M., *The Passing of the Black Kings* (London: Philip Allan, 1932)
——, *Lobengula* (London: Philip Allan, 1933)
Hubbard, M., *Agricultural Exports and Economic Growth, a Study of the Botswana Beef Industry* (London: KPI, 1986)

Hubbard, W. D., *Ibamba* (London: Victor Gollancz, 1963)
Huxley, J., *The Conservation of Wild Life and Natural Habitats in Central and East Africa* (Paris: UNESCO, 1961)
Jacobson, D., *Heshel's Kingdom* (London: Hamish Hamilton, 1998)
Jalla, A. and E., *Pionniers parmi les Ma-Rotse* (Florence: Imprimerie Claudienne, 1903)
Kaplan, M. (with the assistance of M. Robertson), *Jewish Roots in the South African Economy* (Cape Town: C. Struik, 1986)
Kaunda, K. D., *Towards Complete Independence* (Lusaka: Zambia Information Services, 1969)
——, *Zambia Shall be Free* (London: Heinemann, 1962)
——, 'Zambia Towards Economic Independence', in B. de Gaay Fortman (ed.), *After Mulungushi* (Nairobi: East African Publishing House, 1969)
Knowles Jordan, E., 'Mongu in 1908', *Northern Rhodesia Journal*, 2: 4 (1954)
Kosmin, B., *Majuta: A History of the Jewish Community of Zimbabwe* (Gwelo: Mambo Press, 1980)
Kynaston, David, *The City of London, a Club No More, 1945–2000* (London: Pimlico, 2001)
Lessing, Doris, *Going Home* (St Albans: Panther, 1973, first edition 1968)
——, *Under My Skin* (London: HarperCollins, 1995)
——, *Walking in the Shade, Volume Two of My Autobiography* (London: HarperCollins, 1997)
Levin, D., *The Litvaks: A Short History of the Jews in Lithuania* (Jerusalem: Yad Vashem, 2000)
Levite, A. (ed.), *A Yizkor Book to Riteve, a Jewish Shtetl in Lithuania*, revised edition edited by D. Porat and R. Stauber (Cape Town: Kaplan-Kushlick Foundation, 2000)
Livingstone, D., *Missionary Travels and Researches in South Africa* (London: John Murray, 1857)
Mackintosh, C., *Yeta III, Paramount Chief of the Barotse* (London: Pickering and Inglis, 1937)
Macmillan, A., *Rhodesia and East Africa, Historical and Descriptive, Commercial and Industrial, Facts, Figures and Resources* (London: W. H. and L. Collingridge, 1930)
Macmillan, H., and F. Shapiro, *Zion in Africa: The Jews of Zambia* (London: I. B. Tauris, 1999)
Macpherson, F., *Anatomy of a Conquest: the British Occupation of Zambia, 1884–1924* (London: Longman, 1981)
Makasa, K., *March to Political Freedom* (Nairobi: Heinemann, 1981)
Mann, Barbara, 'Tel Aviv's Rothschild: When a Boulevard Becomes a Monument', *Jewish Social Studies*, 7: 2 (1998)
Martin, A., *Minding Their Own Business: Zambia's Struggle Against Western Control* (Harmondsworth: Penguin, 1975)

Martin, J. D., 'The Baikiaea Forests of Northern Rhodesia', *Empire Forestry Journal*, 19 (1940)

Meebelo, H., *African Proletarians and Colonial Capitalism* (Lusaka: Kenneth Kaunda Foundation, 1986)

Michelson, V. D. (ed.), *Central African Who's Who for 1953* (Salisbury: Central African Who's Who (Pvt.) Ltd, 1953)

Mills, E. C., 'Memoirs of a "White Hunter"', *Northern Rhodesia Journal*, 3: 3 (1957)

——, 'Overlanding Cattle from Barotse to Angola', *Northern Rhodesia Journal*, 1: 2 (1950)

Mulford, D., *The Northern Rhodesia Elections, 1962* (Nairobi: Oxford University Press, 1964)

——, *Zambia: The Politics of Independence, 1957-64* (Manchester: Manchester University Press, 1967)

Mulongo, A. H., 'Land Use Conflicts on Lochinvar National Park: an Example of Contradictions in Environmental Policy, 1950–75', *Zambia Journal of History*, 1 (1981)

Murray-Hughes, R., 'Demo Estate', *Northern Rhodesia Journal*, 3: 5(1958)

——, 'Kafue-Namwala in 1912, Part II', *Northern Rhodesia Journal*, 5: 2 (1962)

Mwaanga, V. J., *An Extraordinary Life* (Lusaka: Multimedia Publications, 1982)

Nell, L., *Images of Yesteryear: Film-making in Central Africa* (Harare: HarperCollins, 1998)

Nidlog [Goldin], B., 'Early Days in Northern Rhodesia', *Rhodesian Jewish Times*, January 1948

Oginski, M., *Memoires de Michel Oginski sur la Pologne et les Polognaises depuis 1788 jusqu'à la fin de 1815* (Geneva: Barbezat et de la Rue, 2 volumes, 1826)

Olsberg, Beverley, 'Marcus and Faiga Grill Family History' (produced for the Grill Family Reunion, Victoria Falls, 9–11 August 1996)

Perham, M., *Lugard: The Years of Adventure, 1858–1898* (London: Collins, 1956)

Perrings, C., *Black Mineworkers in Central Africa* (London: Heinemann, 1979)

Prain, R., *Reflections on an Era* (Letchworth: Metal Bulletin Books Ltd, 1981)

——, *Selected Papers, 1958–60* (London: privately printed, 1961)

Prins, G., *The Hidden Hippopotamus: Reappraisal in African History: the Early Colonial Experience in Western Zambia* (Cambridge: Cambridge University Press, 1980)

Ramsey, J., B. Morton, F. Morton, *Historical Dictionary of Botswana* (London: Scarecrow Press, 1996)

Rey, C. (eds N. Parsons and M. Crowder), *Monarch of All I Survey: Bechuanaland Diaries, 1929–37* (London: James Currey, 1988)

Roberts, A., *A History of Zambia* (London: Heinemann, 1976)

Roth, J., *The Wandering Jews* (London: Granta Books, 2001)

Sampson, R., *The Man with a Toothbrush in His Hat: The Story and Times of George Copp Westbeech in Central Africa* (Lusaka: Multimedia Publications, 1972)

——, *They Came to Lusaaka's* (Lusaka: Multimedia Publications, 1982)

Sardanis, A., *Africa: Another Side of the Coin, Northern Rhodesia's Final Years and Zambia's Nationhood* (London: I. B. Tauris, 2003)

Saron, G., and L. Hotz, *The Jews in South Africa* (Cape Town: Oxford University Press, 1955)

Schoenburg, N. and S., *Lithuanian Jewish Communities* (New York: Garland Publishing, 1991)

Smith, J. (ed. with commentary by T. B. Smith), *Vet in Africa, Life on the Zambezi, 1913–33: Selected Letters and Memoirs of John Smith* (London: Radcliffe Press, 1997)

Sonnenberg, M., *As I Saw It* (Cape Town: Howard Timmins, n.d.)

Stokes, E., 'Barotseland: The Survival of an African State', in E. Stokes and R. Brown, *The Zambesian Past: Studies in Central African History* (Manchester: Manchester University Press, 1966)

Storry, J. G., 'John Jacobs: A Peculating Treasure Seeker', *Rhodesiana*, 26 (1972)

Sutherland, R. F. (ed. June Lawson), *The Memoirs of 'Katembora' Sutherland* (Bulawayo: privately printed, 1956)

Taylor, John, 'Africa: from Crisis to Sustainable Growth?' (London: James Capel Emerging Markets Research, 1991)

Tlou, T., *A History of Ngamiland, 1750–1906* (Gaborone: Macmillan Botswana, 1985)

Trapnell, C. G. (ed. P. Smith), *Ecological Survey of Zambia: The Traverse Records of C. G. Trapnell, 1932–43* (London: Royal Botanic Gardens, Kew, 3 volumes, 2001)

Van Horn, L., 'The Agricultural History of Barotseland, 1840–64', in R. Palmer and N. Parsons, *The Roots of Rural Poverty in Central and Southern Africa* (London: Heinemann, 1977)

Vickery, K., 'Saving Settlers: Maize Control in Northern Rhodesia', *Journal of Southern African Studies*, 11: 2 (1985)

Weinthal, L., *The Story of the Cape to Cairo Rail and River Route* (London: Pioneer Publishing Company, 5 volumes, n.d. [1922–3])

Wulfsohn, Dina, 'Cattle Ranching in Zambia', *Livestock International*, February 1981

Zukas, S., *Into Exile and Back* (Lusaka: Bookworld Publishers, 2002)

VI Dissertations and Unpublished Papers

Baylies, Carolyn, 'The State and Capital Formation in Zambia' (Ph.D. dissertation, University of Wisconsin, Madison, 1978)

Dziewiecka, C. M., 'Transformation of an African Village, a Case Study of Maun, Botswana', Maun, 1996

Rhoderick-Jones, R., 'Westminster, Orange Free State, South Africa: an Imperial Adventure', October 2000, by courtesy of the Duke of Westminster, Eaton Hall, Chester

Robinette, W. L., 'Biology of the Lechwe and a Proposed Game Management Plan for Lochinvar Ranch', Lochinvar, January 1963, ML1/17/50

Notes

Unless otherwise stated all file references below are to documents in the National Archives of Zambia (NAZ), Lusaka.

1 From Lithuania to Barotseland

1. C. Harding, *In Remotest Barotseland* (London: Hurst and Blackett, 1905), 8–9.
2. F. Debenham, *The Way to Ilala: David Livingstone's Pilgrimage* (London: Longmans, Green, 1955), 73.
3. A. Sampson, *The Man With a Toothbrush in His Hat: the Story and Times of George Copp Westbeech in Central Africa* (Lusaka: Multimedia Publications, 1972).
4. Ibid., 78; A. St H. Gibbons, *Africa from South to North Through Marotseland* (London: John Lane, 1904), Vol. I, 121–2.
5. G. Prins, *The Hidden Hippopotamus: Reappraisal in African History: the Early Colonial Experience in Western Zambia* (Cambridge: Cambridge University Press, 1980).
6. J. S. Galbraith, *Crown and Charter: The Early Years of the British South Africa Company* (Berkeley and Los Angeles: University of California Press, 1974).
7. A. and E. Jalla, *Pionniers parmi les Ma-Rotse* (Florence: Imprimerie Claudienne, 1903), 236; L. H. Gann, *The Birth of a Plural Society: the Development of Northern Rhodesia under the British South Africa Company, 1894–1914* (Manchester: Manchester University Press, 1958).
8. Livingstone Museum (LM), Worthington Papers, 'Journal of Trip to Letebe, with Litia, to Settle Border Dispute between Tawana and Lozi Nations', 19 May–30 July 1902; L. H. Gann, *A History of Northern Rhodesia: Early Days to 1953* (London: Chatto & Windus, 1964), 65.
9. Debenham, *The Way to Ilala*, 73–4.
10. D. Livingstone, *Missionary Travels and Researches in South Africa* (London: John Murray, 1857), 254.
11. A. Levite (ed.), *A Yizkor Book to Riteve, a Jewish Shtetl in Lithuania*, revised edition edited by D. Porat and R. Stauber (Cape Town: Kaplan-Kushlick Foundation, 2000); M. Gersh, 'The Susman Saga', *Northern Rhodesia Journal*, 6: 3 (1965), 266.
12. Levite, *Riteve*, 19.

13 Ibid., 41–2, 87–8, 91–2. For the history of the Oginski family see also: M. Oginski, *Memoires de Michel Oginski sur la Pologne et les Polognaises depuis 1788 jusqu'à la fin de 1815* (Geneva: Barbezat et de la Rue, 2 vols, 1826).
14 Levite, *Riteve*, 54.
15 D. Levin, *The Litvaks: A Short History of the Jews in Lithuania* (Jerusalem: Yad Vashem, 2000), 25–7, 88.
16 Levite, *Riteve*, 2–22; S. M. Dubnow, *History of the Jews in Russia and Poland from the Earliest Times until the Present Day* (Philadelphia: the Jewish Publication Society of America, 1916), Vol. I, *passim*. For the career of the Vilna *gaon*, see entry for Elijah ben-Solomon Zalman in J. Comay (ed.), *Who's Who in Jewish History* (London: Routledge, 1974), 119–20.
17 Susman Papers (SP), Maurice Gersh, 'Background', n.d. [*circa* 1989]; Ber Susman [Behr Susman], Last Will and Testament, 12 July 1935 (certified translation from Hebrew).
18 I. Michael Aronson, *Troubled Waters: The Origins of the 1881 Anti-Jewish Pogroms in Russia* (Pittsburgh: Pittsburgh University Press, 1990), *passim*; Levin, *The Litvaks*, 88.
19 G. Saron and L. Hotz, *The Jews in South Africa* (Cape Town: Oxford University Press, 1955), 59–104.
20 Levite, *Riteve*, 70–1; N. and S. Schoenburg, *Lithuanian Jewish Communities* (New York: Garland Publishing, 1991), 308–9; F. Braudel, *The Mediterranean and the Mediterranean World in the Age of Philip II* (London: Collins, 1972), Vol. I, 199, 286; interview with Bruna Zacks, daughter of Elie Susman, Johannesburg, 2001.

2 Barotseland Beginnings

1 *Cape of Good Hope Government Gazette*, 28 February 1899.
2 Zimbabwe Archives (ZA), S1882, Bernard Susman [Behr Susman], Cape Town, to Administrator, Southern Rhodesia, 6 March 1919; P. H. Kirk, CID, Livingstone, Minute, 20 March 1919; B. Susman, Affidavit before J. Tuohy, Commissioner of Oaths, Cape Town, witness F. B. Aronson, 3 April 1919; Profile of Elie Susman, *South Africa Jewish Times*, 29 February 1952; SP, M. Gersh, 'Background'; interview with David Susman.
3 *South Africa Jewish Times*, 29 February 1952.
4 Interview with Michael Beckett, Momba Farm, Choma, Zambia, 2001.
5 LM, E. Susman File; LM, Richard Sampson Papers, notes of interview with Elie Susman, Lusaka, 1 August 1955. This interview is the source of the date of April 1901 for the Susman brothers' first crossing of the Zambezi.
6 A. and E. Jalla, *Pionniers parmi les Ma-Rotse*, 245; Gibbons, *Africa from South to North*, Vol. I, 113; National Archives of Zambia (NAZ), Lusaka, A3/22/3, List of Proclamations in Force, includes High Commissioner's Proclamation

number 18 of 1901, 31 August 1901; A6/1/2, Harding to Administrator, 5 July 1900. (Unless otherwise stated all file references below are to documents in the National Archives of Zambia.)

7 A. St H. Gibbons, *Exploration and Hunting in Central Africa* (London: Methuen, 1898), 373.
8 M. Perham, *Lugard: The Years of Adventure, 1858–1898* (London: Collins, 1956), 584.
9 Prins, *The Hidden Hippopotamus*, 85–7.
10 F. Coillard, *On the Threshold of Central Africa* (London: Hodder & Stoughton, 1897), 382, 401; Gibbons, *Exploration and Hunting in Central Africa*, 196.
11 Prins, *The Hidden Hippopotamus*, 79.
12 Ibid., 87.
13 A6/1/1, Secretary, BSA Company, to Lewanika, 13 March 1900; C. Harding to Secretary, BSA Company, 15 July 1900; R. Granger to H. Marshall Hole, Administrator's Office, 21 July 1900; A6/1/2, Harding to Administrator, 5 July 1900.
14 A6/1/1, Harding to Secretary, BSA Company, 25 June 1900; A6/1/2, C. Harding, 'Report on North Western Rhodesia for 1900', 16 February 1901.
15 A6/1/1, R. Coryndon to H. Marshall Hole, 23 September 1900.
16 Standard Bank Archives, Johannesburg (SBA), Bulawayo Inspection Report, 19 October 1901; Wulfsohn Papers, Stenham Gestinor Plc, London (WP), Elie Susman, Last Will and Testament, 29 July 1902.
17 Rhodes House Library, Oxford (RHL), Jules Ellenberger Papers, Diary of a Journey 'From Gaberones to Tsau', 1908, includes an account of the route and a sketch map of the Old Hunters' Road. For information on the Grossberg, Kollenberg and Braude families, see Eric Rosenthal Papers in SA National Library, Cape Town. The partnership of Grossberg and Kollenberg may have been dissolved in 1899, but the Kollenbergs appear to have remained at Plumtree.
18 *South Africa Jewish Times*, 29 February 1952; Gersh, 'The Susman Saga', 266; B. Nidlog (Goldin), 'Early Days in Northern Rhodesia' (based on an interview with Harry Susman), *Rhodesian Jewish Times*, January 1948.
19 Ellenberger Papers, 'From Gaberones to Tsau'.
20 Gibbons, *Exploration and Hunting in Central Africa*, 353.
21 Ibid., 354–5.
22 M. K. Goy, *Alone in Africa* (London: J. Nisbet, 1901), 3–4.
23 Gibbons, *Exploration and Hunting in Central Africa*, 205.
24 LM, Worthington Papers, F. Worthington, Journal, 2 June 1902.
25 WP, F. Sykes to E. Susman, 11 October 1901.
26 For more information on A. B. Diamond and his family, see H. Macmillan and F. Shapiro, *Zion in Africa: the Jews of Zambia* (London: I. B. Tauris, 1999), *passim*; LM, Worthington Papers, 'Journal of Trip to Letebe' (MS version), 19 May–30 July 1902, f. 9.

27 For more information on the Landau brothers, see Eric Rosenthal Papers, SA National Library, Cape Town, and B. Kosmin, *Majuta: A History of the Jewish Community of Zimbabwe* (Gwelo: Mambo Press, 1980). On wholesalers, see Macmillan and Shapiro, *Zion in Africa, passim*.
28 WP, R. Coryndon, Lealui, 'For Blackwater Patient', 1 August 1902.
29 KDE1/1/1, F. Aitkens to Administrator, Kalomo, 1 December 1902.
30 G. Clay, *Your Friend, Lewanika, Litunga of Barotseland, 1842–1916* (London: Chatto & Windus, 1968), 123–9; KDE1/1/1, Aitkens to Administrator, 1 December 1902, 15 January 1903.
31 KDE1/1/1, Aitkens to Administrator, 17, 18 October, 10 November, 1 December 1902.
32 KDE1/1/1, Aitkens to Administrator, 7, 15 January 1903.
33 KDE1/1/1, Aitkens to Administrator, 1 December 1902.
34 WP, Partnership Agreement between E. Susman and J. Austen, 14 July 1903; lease in the name of E. Susman of hotel and store site, Sebakwe, 5 February 1904.
35 For the membership of the football team, see Rosenthal Papers, Cape Town. F. Sykes, in 'North Western Rhodesia: Report of the Administrator, 1901–2', in *Reports on the Administration of Rhodesia, 1900–2* (no place: BSA Company, n.d.).
36 LM, Worthington Papers, 'Journal of Trip to Letebe' (typescript version), 1 June 1902; Worthington to father, 10 October 1903.
37 Worthington Papers, 'Journal of Trip to Letebe' (MS version), 2 August 1902; 'Journal of Trip to Letebe' (typescript version), 29 July 1902.
38 Worthington Papers, 'Journal of Trip to Letebe' (typescript version), f. 82.
39 Obituary of John Austen in *East Africa and Rhodesia*, 2 April 1942.
40 P. Clark, *The Autobiography of an Old Drifter* (London: George Harrap, 1936), 148–9; KDE1/1/1, Aitkens to Administrator, 31 August 1903; Aitkens to Lesser, 24 September 1903; *Official Gazette of the High Commissioner for South Africa*, 19 May 1905, Announcement of Special Meeting in the Insolvent Estate of S. Lesser and Company to be Held at Mafeking, 20 May 1905; SA National Archives, Pretoria, MHG62561, Estate of S. Lesser: he died 28 March 1927, leaving £3,000 gross and £300 net.
41 WP, Partnership Agreement between E. Susman and J. Austen, 14 July 1903; Inventory of Stock taken over from R. Gordon, Sheake (Sesheke), 21 July 1904; SBA, Gwelo Inspection Report, December 1903.
42 *Livingstone Mail*, 27 March 1907, notice of change of name as from 1 January 1907.

3 Settled at Sesheke

1 Interview with Senior Chief Inyambo Yeta, Mwandi, December 2001.
2 Interview with the Rev. Elizabeth Mulonda Silishebo, Mwandi, December 2001; sadly, she died in a car accident on the Sesheke road in 2003.

3 Interviews with Indunas Omei and Mubitamwinda, Mwandi, December 2001.
4 Gibbons, *Africa from South to North*, Vol. I, 113–15; *Livingstone Mail*, 16 September 1931 (retirement of Dr Reutter); Mwandi Hospital, Sesheke Hospital Diary, *circa* 1920–67 (kept in French).
5 BS2/227, Coryndon to High Commissioner (HC) Lord Milner, 13 October 1904; A3/31/3, Coryndon to HC, 19 August 1905.
6 BS2/227, HC, Lord Milner, to Coryndon, 14 November 1904; A3/31/3, Coryndon to HC, 19 August 1905.
7 C. W. Mackintosh, *Yeta III, Paramount Chief of the Barotse* (London: Pickering and Inglis, 1937), *passim*; A. Bertrand, *Au pays des Ba-Rotsi Haut Zambéze* (Paris: Hachette, 1898), 142; Goy, *Alone in Africa*, 35; Clark, *Autobiography of an Old Drifter*, 140–3; *Livingstone Mail*, Christmas Supplement, 1910; Louis Nell, *Images of Yesteryear: Film-making in Central Africa* (Harare: HarperCollins, 1998), 66–70; *Livingstone Mail*, 13 July 1932.
8 Gibbons, *Africa from South to North*, Vol. I, 114.
9 Ibid., 112.
10 Ibid., 112–13; interview with Chief Inambao Yeta.
11 Gibbons, *Exploration and Hunting in Central Africa*, 190.
12 *Livingstone Mail*, 2 January 1909; interview with Bella Zinn, daughter of Max Kominsky.
13 *Livingstone Mail*, 31 March 1906; A3/1/4, Lewanika to Harding, 8 June 1904; C. K. Cooke, 'Lobengula: Second and Last King of the Amandabele [*sic*]: His Final Resting Place and Treasure', *Rhodesiana*, 23, November 1970, 6; *Livingstone Mail*, 21 August 1909; A5/2/3, A. G. Willis, Annual Report, Sesheke District, 1908–9.
14 *Livingstone Mail*, 12 December 1908.
15 For the career of Dreyer see below. *Livingstone Mail*, 6 October 1906; Cooke, 'Lobengula: Second and Last King of the Amandabele', 6–9; *Livingstone Mail*, 22 June 1907; A5/2/3, A. G. Willis, Annual Report, Sesheke District, 1908–9.
16 IMA/1/1, Vol. III, Landau Brothers, Bulawayo, to Magistrate, Kalomo, 18 November 1904; H. Rangely, Magistrate, North-Western Rhodesia, to Messrs Frames, Coghlan and Welsh, Bulawayo, 19 January 1905; Messrs Frames, Coghlan and Welsh to Rangely, 30 January 1905.
17 IMA/1/1, Vol. III, Rangely to R. Gordon, 18 January 1905; Rangely to E. Susman, 10 February 1905.
18 KDE/1/4/1, Aitkens to Morena Mukwae, Nalolo, 1 May 1905; KDE/1/1/3, Aitkens to Assistant District Commissioner, Sesheke, 8 May 1905; WP, E. Susman, Trade Licence, Sesheke, 4 January 1906.
19 KDE/1/1/3, Aitkens to E. Susman, 9 May 1905.
20 A3/31/3, W. F. Dawson to Under-Secretary, Colonial Office, 19 November 1905.
21 A3/31/3, Coryndon to HC, 19 August 1905.

22 LM, Paris Mission Papers, E. Béguin, Monthly Report, Sesheke, June 1905.
23 H1/1/1, Vol. I, High Court of Barotseland, North-Western Rhodesia, Petition of L. Braude, C. Goldberg and L. Fedderman *versus* F. Levitz and R. Gordon, 1 September 1906; Agreement between S. Jacoby and L. Braude, and F. Levitz and R. Gordon, 5 July 1905; Temporary Injunction restraining F. Levitz and R. Gordon from selling 250 cattle in charge of E. Susman, Sesheke, Order to be Served on E. Susman, 7 September 1906; L. Braude, Francistown, to E. Susman, Sesheke, 1 August 1906 (in Yiddish).
24 H1/2/1, Vol. II, Gordon and Levitz, Bankruptcy Proceedings, Evidence of F. Levitz, 8 January 1908; D. Wersock, 11 February, 15 May 1908; S. Peimer, 15 May 1908; H1/2/1, Vol. III, Affidavit by E. Snapper, enclosed with W. Hazell, District Commissioner (DC), Mongu, to Registrar, High Court, Livingstone, 14 March 1908; C. Roberts, Trustee, to Acting-Secretary, Government, Livingstone, 20 February 1908; H1/2/2, Vol. II, Fishel Levitz, Application for Discharge from Bankruptcy, Report by C. Roberts, Trustee, 12 March 1909.
25 Evidence of F. Levitz, D. Wersock, S. Peimer, E. Snapper, as above.
26 SBA, Inspection Reports, Bulawayo, April 1907, February 1908.
27 For the early career of Leopold Moore, see S. R. Denny, 'Leopold Versus the Chartered Company', *Northern Rhodesia Journal*, 4: 3 (1959), 219–30, and 4: 4 (1960), 335–46.
28 See the *Livingstone Mail*, 10 February 1927, for an interview with the then Mrs Moore, reprinted from the *Cape Argus*.
29 Interview with Bella Zinn.
30 *Livingstone Mail*, 21 December 1907.
31 Reference to Sir Ronald Storrs *Orientations* (1939) in Gann, *A History of Northern Rhodesia*, 282, fn. 2.
32 B1/2/1, 'Administrator's Meetings with Lewanika', Meeting of Sir Drummond Chaplin with Yeta III, 9 April 1921.
33 *Livingstone Mail*, 21 December 1907.

4 Life at Lealui

1 Gersh, 'The Susman Saga', 267; LM, Worthington Papers, Worthington to his father, 10 February 1904; Clay, *Your Friend, Lewanika*, 130.
2 WP, Litia Lewanika to E. Susman, 3 September 1906, with note by E. Susman, 19 September 1906.
3 Jalla, *Pionniers parmi les Ma-Rotse*, 241 (author's translation from French).
4 J. S. Campbell, 'I Knew Lewanika', *Northern Rhodesia Journal*, 1: 1 (1950); RHL, J. H. Venning, 'Memories of My Life in Southern Africa from 1893 to 1962' (MS), f. 127.
5 KDE1/1/4, Hazell to J. Finkelstein, 31 July 1908; KDE1/1/1, Aitkens to Administrator, 1 December 1902.

6 A5/2/3, D. E. C. Stirke, Annual Report, Lukona, 1908-9.
7 KDE1/1/2, Aitkens to Lewanika, 7 November 1903; J. de C. Dillon to Aitkens, 6 November 1903.
8 KDE1/1/2, Dillon to Aitkens, 6 November 1903.
9 KDE1/1/2, DC to traders (circular letter), 1 June 1904.
10 B/1/2/1, Coryndon to Secretary, BSA Company, 13 October 1904.
11 Harding, *In Remotest Barotseland*, *passim*; HC1/2/4, Coryndon to Milner, 20 October 1904; A3/1/4, Coryndon to Imperial Secretary, Johannesburg, 21 March 1906.
12 Summary of correspondence in Harding's personal file, A3/1/4.
13 BS2/227, Milner to Coryndon, 14 November 1904, and further correspondence in Harding's personal file, A3/1/4, as above.
14 HC1/2/1, Harding, 'Report on Patrol to Lealui, Shalenda ...', 19 September 1905; Harding, *In Remotest Barotseland*, 31.
15 HC1/2/23, Vol. I, Coryndon to HC, 19 December 1905.
16 Gann, *A History of Northern Rhodesia*, 139, 156.
17 KDE1/4/7, Hazell to Katema, 6 September 1907.
18 *Livingstone Mail*, 5 January 1907; F. Macpherson, *Anatomy of a Conquest: the British Occupation of Zambia, 1884–1924* (London: Longman, 1981) 116, 161–3; *Livingstone Mail*, 14 April 1916.
19 KDE1/1/4, Hazell to Susman Brothers (SB), 17 January, 6, 11, 13 February 1908; KDE1/3/1, Hazell to SB, 18 February 1908.
20 KDE1/4/3, Hazell to SB, 13 February 1908. Copper coinage was not legal tender in Northern Rhodesia until the mid 1930s.
21 KDE1/4/3, Hazell to Lewanika, 22, 24 February 1908.
22 KDE1/4/3, Hazell to Lewanika, 29 February 1908; KDE3/2/4, Criminal Case number 6, Lealui, 29 February 1908.
23 KDE3/2/4, Evidence of Muishebela.
24 KDE3/2/4, Criminal Cases, Barotse District, 1908. Horn, a well-known hunter, was killed by a lion, or lions, at the junction of the Zambezi and Njoko rivers later in the year (*Livingstone Mail*, Christmas Number, December 1908).
25 KDE3/2/5, Criminal Cases, Barotse District, 1909.
26 KDE1/2/1, Hazell to Acting-Secretary, Law Department, Livingstone, 21 April 1908.
27 KDE1/1/4, Hazell to SB, 16 April 1908.
28 KDE1/4/7, Hazell to Lewanika, 5, 20 January 1909.
29 KDE1/1/4, Hazell to SB, 6 August 1908 (two letters on the same day and a third appears to be missing from the letter book); Hazell to D. Wersock, 6 August 1908; Hazell to H. A. Jacobson, 6 August 1908.
30 KDE1/1/4, Hazell to Secretary, BSA Company, Livingstone, 18 August 1908 (parentheses in original document).
31 KDE1/1/4, Hazell to G. Buchanan, 28 January 1909, to G. Smith, 6 August 1908; A2/5/1, Annual Reports, Barotse District, 1908–9; Proclamation 64 of

1908, *Official Gazette of the High Commissioner for South Africa*, 25 September 1908, 'It shall be lawful for the Administrator to refuse to issue or to renew any licence ... and it shall not be necessary to assign any reason for such refusal'.

32 A5/2/1, Annual Reports, Barotse District, 1908–9; KDE1/1/1, Aitkens to Administrator, 18 January 1903; KDE1/1/4, Hazell to W. H. Diamond, 6 August 1908.

33 KDE2/21/1, Record of Military Service of Residents of Barotseland, 1914; WP, R. Goode, Secretary to the Administration, Northern Rhodesia, to Secretary for the Interior, Pretoria, South Africa, 28 December 1916. Elie Susman was naturalised on 6 April 1903. ZA, S2279/836, Harry Susman was naturalised on 21 April 1908. A copy of the certificate was issued on 19 August 1948.

34 KDE2/41/1, H. Susman to Hazell, 25 November 1908; Hazell to C. J. Hebblethwaite, 27 November 1908; Hebblethwaite to Hazell, 2 December 1908.

35 B1/2/1, 'Administrator's Meetings with Lewanika', Administrator to HC, 10 September 1909, enclosing summaries of discussions, 30 July, 11 August 1909; and see below.

36 KDE1/1/4, Hazell to G. Epstein, 6 July 1908; *Livingstone Mail*, 13 February 1909.

37 H1/2/1, Vol. III, E. and H. Susman, trading as Susman Brothers, *versus* A. B. Diamond, 1910. Writ of Summons issued 30 September 1910. Case withdrawn, 11 November 1910. HM7, CU/1/11/1, Cunninghame Papers, Tom King to Boyd Cunninghame, 28 October 1912. The Susman brothers' acquisition of cattle at Elisabethville in connection with this debt may be one of the reasons for their establishment of a butchery in Elisabethville during 1912.

38 *Livingstone Mail*, 13 June 1908. Theodore Haddon was the father of Michael Haddon, a leading opponent of UDI in Southern Rhodesia in 1965. He was imprisoned by Ian Smith, the leading proponent of UDI, who was the son of J. Smith of Selukwe. Both Haddon and Smith were acquaintances of Elie Susman from his time at Sebakwe.

39 *Livingstone Mail*, 18 January, 1 February, 13 June 1908.

40 A5/2/3, Annual Reports, Barotse District, 1908–9.

41 SBA, Inspection Report, Bulawayo, 25 October 1909.

42 KDE2/34/2, C. McKinnon, Resident Magistrate (RM), Mongu, to Acting-Assistant Magistrate, Sesheke, 21 November 1911, enclosing copy of agreement between Lewanika and SB, dated 23 September 1909.

43 KDE2/34/2, J. Beringer, Acting Native Commissioner, to RM, Mongu, 29 December 1911; Acting RM, Mongu, to Lewanika, 14 February 1912; RM, Mongu (C. McKinnon) to C. Coxhead, 5 January 1912; S. Saperstein, (SB, Sesheke), to RM, Mongu, 11, 25 March 1912.

5 King Lobengula's Treasure

1. Gersh, 'The Susman Saga'; interviews with and communications from David Susman. It is difficult to resolve this discrepancy, though it is possible that in later life Harry was more willing than Elie was to talk about this episode.
2. *Livingstone Mail*, 2 January 1909.
3. *Livingstone Mail*, 23 January 1909.
4. ZA, A11/2/12/7, 'Lobengula's Treasure', H. M. Hole, Memorandum to Directors, BSA Company, 24 October 1907; Willson to Hole, 14 January 1908 (copy); Hole to Holland, 15 January 1908; Civil Commissioner to Willson, 25 January 1908; Willson to Civil Commissioner, 27 January 1908; F. Newton, Minute, January 1908.
5. BS3/242, 'Lobengula's Treasure', Criminal Investigations Department to Administration, Livingstone, 28 August 1917; J. G. Storry, 'John Jacobs: A Peculating Treasure Seeker', *Rhodesiana*, 26 (1972), 41–2. This article is largely based on a police file on Lobengula's treasure, S.903, in ZA.
6. ZA, A11/2/12//7, Hole to Holland, 5 November 1907; Hole to Holland, 15 January 1908; H. M. Hole, *The Passing of the Black Kings* (London: Philip Allan, 1932), 254–6.
7. H. M. Hole, *Lobengula* (London: Philip Allan, 1933), 194–6; Storry, 'John Jacobs', 37–42.
8. Ibid., 37–8; H. M. Chilvers, *The Seven Lost Trails of Africa* (London: Cassell, 1930), 107.
9. Hole, *The Passing of the Black Kings*, 254–62; *Lobengula*, 191–7.
10. Hole, *The Passing of the Black Kings*, 254–62; *Lobengula*, 195–6, 210–11.
11. KDE 1/1/4, W. Hazell to E. C. Monk (*sic*), 7 April 1908.
12. KDE 1/1/4, W. Hazell to E. Spinner (*sic*), 6, 8 August 1908.
13. 'Extracts from the District Notebooks – No. 3. Lobengula's Treasure', *Northern Rhodesia Journal*, 2: 3 (1954), 71–2; RHL, J. H. Venning, 'Memories', 179–80.
14. KDE/3/2/4, Criminal Cases, Mongu-Lealui, Case 34/1908, Rex *versus* J. Monckts and E. Susman. Quotations below are from the same source, which is not foliated.
15. E. Knowles Jordan, 'Mongu in 1908', *Northern Rhodesia Journal*, 2: 4 (1954), 64.
16. H1/2/2, Vol. III, 'In the matter of the appeal (Criminal) of Eli [*sic*] Susman against the decision of the Acting Assistant Magistrate Barotse District in the case of Rex v Eli Susman', 24 April 1909. This file includes a typescript copy of the original court record. *Livingstone Mail*, 27 January 1932.
17. 'Extracts from the District Notebooks', 71–2.
18. LM, G58A, J. H. Venning to Editor, *Northern Rhodesia Journal*, 19 September 1954.
19. Venning, 'Memories', f. 179.
20. LM, Venning to Editor, *Northern Rhodesia Journal*, 19 September 1954.

21 Gersh, 'The Susman Saga', 268. Gersh's account is also incorrect in stating that Harry Susman escorted Sprinner and Monckts. BS3/242, 'Lobengula's Treasure', Memorandum, J. H. Coxhead, September 1917. This account suggests a loss of £500.
22 BS3/242, Criminal Investigations Department to Secretary, Administration, 28 August 1917; J. Coxhead, Memorandum, September 1917; Storry, 'John Jacobs', 38–40; Chilvers, *The Seven Lost Trails of Africa*, 106–7.
23 SA National Archives, Pretoria, WLD/238/1910 (Criminal case); MHG 92641, 'Estate of Julius Monckts'.
24 Information from Professor Ray Roberts, Harare, who is working on a life of Lobengula, and from Marieke Clarke, Oxford, who has done a study of Queen Losikeyi.

6 From Sesheke to Livingstone via Palestine

1 See C. Perrings, *Black Mineworkers in Central Africa* (London: Heinemann, 1979).
2 *Livingstone Mail*, 27 February, 6 March 1909.
3 WP, Elie Susman, Last Will and Testament, 7 March 1909; Macmillan and Shapiro, *Zion in Africa*, 32, 36, 52, 57. See Chapter 2, above, for Elie's first will.
4 *Livingstone Mail*, 28 October 1931.
5 Interviews with David Susman; SP, M. Gersh to D. Susman, 24 September 1993; Barbara Mann, 'Tel Aviv's Rothschild: When a Boulevard Becomes a Monument', *Jewish Social Studies*, 7: 2 (1998).
6 Interview with Bruna Zacks; SP, M. Gersh to D. Susman, 24 September 1993.
7 WP, Elie Susman, Last Will and Testament, 7 March 1909; SB Accounts, 1914–20.
8 M. I. Cohen, 'The Jewish Communities of Rhodesia and the North', in *The South African Jewish Year Book* (Johannesburg: SA Jewish Historical Society, 1929); interviews with Zena Zinn (daughter of Max Kominsky) and David Susman.
9 *South Africa Jewish Times*, 29 February 1952; *Livingstone Mail*, 7 May 1910.
10 *Livingstone Mail*, 16 April 1910.
11 SP, M. Gersh to D. Susman, 24 September 1993; interview with Bruna Zacks.
12 SA National Archives, Cape Town, PIO 25 no. 2698E, Behr Sussmanowitz (*sic*), Immigration Act – Declaration by Passenger, London, 12 September 1913; Toybe (*sic*) Susman, Immigration Act – Declaration by Passenger, Cape Town, 16 September 1913; Standard Bank, Cape Town, to Chief Immigration Officer, 17 September 1913; E. Susman to O. Susman (telegram), 22 September 1913; Oscar Susman to Chief Immigration Officer, Cape Town, 24 September 1913; Under-Secretary for the Interior to Principal Immigration Officer, Cape Town, 8 October 1913; Principal Immigration Officer, Cape Town to Secretary for the Interior, 14 October 1913; Toybe Susman, Temporary Permit, 16 October

1913. For the engagement of Marcia Susman, see the *Livingstone Mail*, 12 February 1915.
13 A/3/23/1, E. Susman to Committee, Livingstone Church Council, 15 May 1909; R. Goode, Secretary to the Administration, to E. Susman, 21 May 1909, and other correspondence.
14 *Livingstone Mail*, 24 April, 3 July 1909, Christmas Number, December 1909, 24 February 1940.
15 *Livingstone* Mail, 25 October, 13 November 1909.
16 A5/3/1, Annual Report of Northern Rhodesia Rifle Association, 1910–11; A5/2/9, Annual Reports of North-Western Rhodesia Rifle Association, 1908–10; *Livingstone Mail*, 29 January 1910, Christmas Number, December 1910, 13 May 1911, 18 July 1913.
17 HC1/2/56, Administrator to HC, 11 March 1911; *Livingstone Mail*, 25 February 1911.
18 *Livingstone Mail*, 2 July 1910.
19 Beverley Olsberg, 'Marcus and Faiga Grill Family History', produced for the Grill Family Reunion, Victoria Falls, 9–11 August 1996. See also Macmillan and Shapiro, *Zion in Africa*, 44–7.
20 *Livingstone Mail*, 1 June 1917, 26 May 1931.
21 *Livingstone Mail*, 4 September 1909, 16 January 1914, 19 October 1917, 9 August 1918.
22 Nidlog, 'Early Days in Northern Rhodesia'.
23 *Livingstone Mail*, 25 April 1913, 29 August 1913, 16 January, 27 March, 25 May 1914; communication from David Susman.
24 *Livingstone Mail*, 2 July 1914.
25 WP, R. Goode, Secretary to the Administration, to Secretary for the Interior, South Africa, 28 December 1916; Leo Weinthal, *The Story of the Cape to Cairo Rail and River Route* (London: Pioneer Publishing Company, n.d. [1922–3]), Vol. III, 175; interviews with Bruna Zacks, David Susman and Cid Weskob.
26 *Livingstone Mail*, 31 July 1909, 15 May, 22 May 1909.
27 *Livingstone Mail*, 16 April, 19 February 1910; A5/2/4, Annual Report, Livingstone, 1910.
28 *Livingstone Mail*, 22 July, 19 August 1911.
29 *Livingstone Mail*, 22 June 1912. WP, SB Accounts, 1912–16.
30 ZA, S456/712/22, 'Gwaai Farms, nos. 82 and 83', SB to J. C. Jesser Coope, Manager, Estate Office, BSA Company, Bulawayo, 20 April 1911; Inspection Report, 2 May 1911; Director of Land Settlement, Approval, 9 May 1911; J. A. Chalmers to Director of Land Settlement, 21 January 1915, and further correspondence; *Livingstone Mail*, 14 January 1919. See also WP, Elie Susman Diary, 1920.
31 ZA, S456/712/22, SB to Director of Land Settlement, 18 March 1919, and further correspondence; SP, M. Gersh to D. Susman, 24 September 1993.

32 A5/1/1-11, Department of Mines and Lands, Annual Reports, 1908–9; *Livingstone Mail*, 17 April 1909, 9 July 1910, 18 February 1911.
33 WP, Chief Surveyor to SB, 14 October 1911 and subsequent correspondence; SB to Secretary, Lands Department, 22 February 1927 and subsequent correspondence; W41, 'Minutes of the Agricultural Lands Board', 23 March 1914, 1 April 1915.
34 E. C. Mills, 'Memoirs of a "White Hunter"', *Northern Rhodesia Journal*, 3: 3 (1957), 239.

7 Sesheke, War and the Barotseland Cattle Trade

1 *Livingstone Mail*, 13 February 1909.
2 WP, SB Accounts, 1911–14; *Livingstone Mail*, 13 October 1916, 10 October 1919.
3 *Livingstone Mail*, 13 February 1909, 23 December 1920, 23 September 1923.
4 J. H. Venning, 'Memories'; J. Smith (ed. T. B. Smith), *Vet in Africa, Life on the Zambezi, 1913–33: Selected Letters and Memoirs of John Smith* (London: Radcliffe Press, 1997), 148–50.
5 *Livingstone Mail*, 2 October 1914. See also KDE8/1/6-7, Barotse District Annual Reports, 1914–15.
6 *Livingstone Mail*, 2 October 1914.
7 SP, O. Susman, 'Proceedings on Discharge', 2 December 1916; *Livingstone Mail*, 27 August 1915, 2 February 1917.
8 KTO/1/1, C. R. Bennie to Legal Adviser, n.d.; P. J. Macdonell to Bennie, 7 February 1913; McKinnon to J. H. Venning, 13 October 1914; Macdonell to Venning, n.d.; WP, SB Accounts, 31 May 1912.
9 *Livingstone* Mail, 31 August, 19 October 1912.
10 KDE10/1/1, Barotse District Notebook, Vols I and II; WP, SB Accounts, 1911–12; Hole, *The Passing of the Black Kings*, 220, 242, 262; *Livingstone Mail*, 9 November 1912, Christmas Number, December 1921.
11 Cape Town, Rosenthal Papers, notes of interview with Olga Hilda Epstein, n.d.
12 *Livingstone Mail*, 3, 24 April, 8 May, Christmas Number, 1909.
13 Moss Dobkins, MS Autobiography and Transcript of Diary, copy in the author's possession, by courtesy of Walter Dobkins, Brisbane, Australia. Nidlog, 'Early Days in Northern Rhodesia'.
14 WP, SB Accounts, 1912; SBA, Livingstone Inspection Reports, 1912–14.
15 Venning, 'Memories'.
16 *Livingstone Mail*, 2 November 1912.
17 *Livingstone Mail*, 2, 9 November 1912.
18 Smith, *Vet in Africa*, 206.
19 Venning, 'Memories'.
20 Gersh, 'The Susman Saga', 267; Venning, 'Memories'; KDE10/1/1, Barotse District Notebook, Vol. I, note by J. H. Venning, 14 April 1915.

21 *Livingstone Mail*, 20 August 1915.
22 KDE10/1/1, Barotse District Notebook, Vol. I.
23 Smith, *Vet in Africa*, 216–23.
24 Ibid., 217.
25 *Livingstone Mail*, 9 April, 18 June 1915; KDE2/11/1, J. Smith to Secretary, Administration, 16 June 1915; R. Goode, Secretary to Administration, 'Outbreak of Pleuro-Pneumonia (Lung Disease) in Northern Rhodesia', 18 June 1915.
26 R. F. Sutherland, *The Memoirs of 'Katembora' Sutherland* (Bulawayo: privately printed, 1956), 101. Reference by courtesy of the late Dick Hobson.
27 Sutherland, *Memoirs*, 101; KDE2/11/1, Chief Veterinary Officer (CVO) to Rhodesian Hide and Skin Syndicate, 10 December 1915.
28 *Livingstone Mail*, 25 June 1915.
29 *Livingstone Mail*, 7, 14 January 1916.
30 SBA, Livingstone Inspection Report, 30 June 1915.
31 SBA, Livingstone Inspection Report, 1916.
32 SP, H. S. Whitehead to E. Susman, 28 May 1955.
33 Sutherland, *Memoirs*, 101; *South Africa Jewish Times*, 29 February 1952.
34 *Livingstone Mail*, 8 October 1915, 11 February 1916; ZA1/14, Memorandum of Meeting with Litia, H. C. Marshall, Visiting Commissioner, 27 July 1915.
35 L. Van Horn, 'The Agricultural History of Barotseland, 1840–64', in R. Palmer and N. Parsons, *The Roots of Rural Poverty in Central and Southern Africa* (London: Heinemann, 1977); B1/1/4, 'Death of Lewanika', 1916; ZA1/9, 'Paramount Chief's Accounts', 1925.
36 KDE10/1/1, Barotse District Notebook, Vol. I; *Livingstone Mail*, 21 January 1916.
37 KDE2/11/2, SB to CVO, 6, 8 October 1917; CVO to RM, Mongu, 12 December 1917; E. Susman to RM, Mongu, 14 December 1917; RM, Mongu, to SB, 22 January 1918; *Livingstone Mail*, 23 January 1918; KDE10/1/1 Barotse District Notebook, Vol. I.
38 Cape Town, Rosenthal Papers, Olga Epstein interview; *Northern Rhodesia Government Gazette*, 1916; *Livingstone Mail*, 21 October 1915; 2 July 1915; 17 May 1918; Christmas Number, 1921; KDE10/1/1, Barotse District Notebook, Vol. II.
39 *Livingstone Mail*, 26 December 1919, 16 January 1920.
40 KDE10/1/1, Barotse District Notebook, Vols I and II; KDE8/1/14-18 Barotse Annual Reports, 1922–6; E. C. Mills, 'Overlanding Cattle from Barotse to Angola', *Northern Rhodesia Journal*, 1: 2 (December 1950), 53–63; *Livingstone Mail*, 30 July, 6 August 1925.
41 KDE10/1/1, Barotse District Notebook, Vol. II.
42 KDE8/1/12, Barotse Annual Report, 1920–1.
43 KDE8/1/13, Barotse Annual Report, 1921–2; ZA7/1/13, Barotse Annual Report, 1930; *Livingstone Mail*, 4 August 1921, 21 June 1923, 14 June 1928; C. G.

Trapnell, (ed. P. Smith), *Ecological Survey of Zambia: The Traverse Records of C. G. Trapnell, 1932–43* (London: Royal Botanic Gardens, Kew, 2001), Vol. I, 57–8.
44 WP, Elie Susman Diary, 24 May–2 June 1920.
45 *Livingstone Mail*, 13 August, 12 November 1925, 19 August, 20 September 1930, 26 May, 8 July 1931; ZA7/1/14-15, Barotse Annual Reports, 1931, 1932.
46 SBA, Livingstone, Inspection Report, 1933; *Livingstone Mail*, 19 October 1917, 20 January 1927.

8 From Ngamiland to the Congo

1 Perham, *Lugard: The Years of Adventure*, 561–620; T. Tlou, *A History of Ngamiland, 1750–1906* (Gaborone: Macmillan Botswana, 1985), 90–1.
2 RHL, Jules Ellenberger Papers, Diary, 1908; J. Ramsey, B. Morton, F. Morton, *Historical Dictionary of Botswana* (London: Scarecrow Press, 1996).
3 SA National Archives, Pretoria, GG1536-50/69, Imperial Secretary to Governor-General (GG), 28 February 1911; Louis Botha, PM, Minute, 3 March 1911; *Livingstone Mail*, 10 September 1910.
4 Boswana National Archives (BNA), S1/18, S. Letsholathebe to SB, Sesheke, 13 October 1912, SB to S. Letsholathebe, 19 October 1912, S. Letsholathebe to RM, 26 October 1912, in RM to Government Secretary (GS), 4 November 1912.
5 BNA, S1/18 Panzera to Assistant Commissioner, Francistown, 1 October 1912; SB to Eason, 12 October 1912; Eason, Monthly Report to Resident Commissioner (RC), 23 December 1912; Stenham Papers, Eason to SB, 23 October 1912; WP, SB Accounts, 1912; RHL, E. Garraway Diary, 20 June 1917.
6 University of Cape Town Library, G. E. Nettleton Diary (transcript), 15 June 1916.
7 This is the man who was reputed in 1908 to be the Susmans' bitter commercial opponent at Nalolo in Barotseland.
8 Nettleton Diary, 17 June 1916.
9 Nettleton Diary, 29 July 1916.
10 *Livingstone Mail*, 30 January 1916; WP, SB Accounts, 1924, 1925.
11 *Livingstone Mail*, 3 February 1921.
12 C. M. Dziewiecka. 'Transformation of an African Village, a Case Study of Maun, Botswana' (unpublished paper, Maun, 1996), 74; RC 579, J. Smith to Governor, Northern Rhodesia (NR), 13 April 1926, enclosing report by W. H. Chase to Bechuanaland Protectorate (BP) Government on Veterinary Conference.
13 Nettleton Diary, 4 June 1925.
14 Nettleton Diary, 15 July 1925.
15 Nettleton Diary, 16 June 1925; *Livingstone Mail*, 27 December 1921.
16 Tape recording of BBC interview with Joe Susman (n.d.) by courtesy of Alison Bligh-Wall.

17 *Livingstone Mail*, 3 July 1924.
18 Aeroplanes associated with Dr A. L. Du Toit's Kalahari Reconnaissance Survey – an investigation of Professor Schwarz's ideas about diverting rivers and reclaiming the Kalahari for agriculture – reached Kachikau in 1925.
19 RHL, V. Ellenberger Papers, Ngamiland Annual Report, 1931; V. Ellenberger, Diary, 28 August 1931.
20 Ngamiland Annual Report, 1931.
21 *Livingstone Mail*, 28 January 1926, 21 October 1926, 27 January 1927, 2 February 1928, 27 September 1928, 1 November 1928; SA National Archives, Pretoria, GG2277-/2/296 Chief Secretary (CS), Livingstone, to Imperial Secretary, Cape Town, Telegram, 31 July 1929.
22 Quoted in C. Rey (eds N. Parsons and M. Crowder), *Monarch of All I Survey: Bechuanaland Diaries, 1929–37* (London: James Currey, 1988), 243 n. 50.
23 BNA, S178/6, G. E. Nettleton, Memorandum, 21 October 1931.
24 SP, Ngamiland Trading Company (NTC), Audited Accounts by H. Wolffe, 10 June 1947.
25 Macmillan and Shapiro, *Zion in Africa*, 30–2.
26 Ibid., 33, 133, 147, 149; R. d'Hendecourt, *L'Elévage au Katanga* (Brussels: Desclée de Brouwer, 1953), 45–51, 70–1.
27 *Livingstone Mail*, 13 February 1920; Macmillan and Shapiro, *Zion in Africa*, 32–4.
28 *Livingstone Mail*, 28 October 1920; WP, E. Susman Diary, 22 October 1920; SEC3/547, Vol. I, J. Smith, 'The Present Position of the Cattle Trade', 8 June 1932.
29 *Livingstone Mail*, 14 July 1921; RC 625, 'Import of Cattle from Ngamiland, 1920–6', especially correspondence and telegrams between Governor, NR, and HC, April–June 1924.
30 RC 625, J. Smith, Memorandum to Governor, 'Ngamiland Cattle', 31 July 1925; Dziewiecka, 'Transformation of an African Village'; SP, E. Susman Diary, 1933, 1934; BNA, S178/6, R. F. Sutherland to RM, Kasane, 10 May 1933; NAZ, RC 579, J. Smith to Governor, 13 April 1926.
31 SEC3/565/1, Director of Veterinary Services, J. Smith, to CS, 27 August 1929.
32 WP, J. Smith to E. Susman, 22 November 1932, 17 October 1933; interviews with T. Bagnall Smith and David Susman.
33 *Livingstone Mail*, 6, 27 December 1923; WP, SB Accounts, 1923.
34 *Livingstone Mail*, 13 December 1923.
35 *Livingstone Mail*, 24 April, 8 May, 20 November 1924; *Bulawayo Chronicle*, 3 May 1924; J. Smith, unpublished chapter of memoirs, copy in author's possession, by courtesy of Tony Bagnall Smith; interview with Tony Bagnall Smith.
36 Smith, *Vet in Africa*, 288, 292.
37 SEC3/548 Vol. I, 'Record of Proceedings of Victoria Falls Conference, 18–19 December 1932'; J. P. A Morris to CS, 10 January 1933.
38 SEC3/548, Vol. II, 'Record of Meeting between CS and H. Susman', 11 October 1933; H. Susman to CS, 17 October 1933; CS, NR, Confidential

Memorandum for Prime Minister, SR (n.d.); Minutes of Meeting, Governor Storrs and PM Huggins, 28 December 1933; J. P. A. Morris to CS, 11 January 1934.

39 Colonial Office, *The Financial and Economic Position of the Bechuanaland Protectorate* (Cmd. 4368, 1933, (Pim Report)), 126–7.

40 Rey, *Monarch of All I Survey*, 92, 99; BNA, S244/8, J. Riley, Report to CVO, Mafeking, 2 December 1931; Memorandum by C. Rey on meeting with H. Susman, 25 November 1931.

41 Rey, *Monarch of All I Survey*, 89.

42 BNA, S244/8, C. Rey, 'Note of Interview with Mr Susman', 28 November 1931.

43 Rey, *Monarch of All I Survey*, 131–2, 154.

44 SP, E. Susman Diary, March 1933, March 1934.

45 SP, E. Susman Diary, 1936; Rey, *Monarch of All I Survey*, 218; University of the Witwatersrand Library, Lobatse Cold Storage Papers, Government Secretary, BP, to Administrative Secretary, HC, 26 May 1943; H. S. Walker and J. H. N. Hobday, *Report on the Cattle Industry of the Bechuanaland Protectorate with Recommendations for Improving its Organisation and Assisting its Future Development* (typescript, n.d., [1939]), 2–3.

46 BNA, S282/7-17, Susman Timber Concession Files, 1932–7.

9 From Livingstone to the Copperbelt via South Africa

1 E. Stokes, 'Barotseland: the Survival of an African State', in E. Stokes and R. Brown, *The Zambesian Past: Studies in Central African History* (Manchester: Manchester University Press, 1966), 297–301; Gann, *History of Northern Rhodesia*, 183–4; G. Caplan, *The Elites of Barotseland, 1878–1969* (London: C. Hurst, 1970), 119–41.

2 Macmillan and Shapiro, *Zion in Africa*, 48, 183–4, 225; Stokes, 'Barotseland', 297–301. At an audience with the present Litunga Imwiko II in September 2001 he did not say that there were no archives at Limulunga, but referred in passing to 'piles of documents'. Akashambatwa Mbikusita Lewanika says that he has a trunk full of documents relating to the career of his father, Litunga Lewanika II. There is a particular problem relating to the archives of the Litungas and that is the fact that the title has not passed from father to son since the death of Lewanika I in 1916.

3 Gann, *History of Northern Rhodesia*, 245–50, 267–79. Letter from E. Susman to the Secretary, Hilton Young Commission, 20 March 1928. Reference by courtesy of Robin Palmer.

4 *Livingstone Mail*, 12 September 1919, 15 November, 27 December 1918, 9, 23 May, 31 October 1919, 30 January 1920.

5 Interviews with Bruna Zacks and D. Susman; D. Susman, unpublished memoir.

6 *Livingstone Mail*, 31 January 1924; interviews with Bruna Zacks and Ella Robinson.
7 J. Roth, *The Wandering Jews* (London: Granta Books, 2001), 25.
8 *Livingstone Mail*, 11 May 1922; interview with Bruna Zacks.
9 *Livingstone Mail*, 5 July 1928; *Zionist Record*, 5 October 1928.
10 *Livingstone Mail*, 30 March 1932; *Zionist Record*, April 1932.
11 *Zionist Record*, 21 April 1920, quoting obituary in *Zionist Bulletin* (London), 24 March 1920.
12 *Livingstone Mail*, 10 October 1919, 26 March 1920; WP, E. Susman Diary, 23–5 March 1920.
13 *Zionist Record*, 21 April 1920; SP, Oscar Susman, Last Will and Testament, 23 August 1915.
14 WP, E. Susman Diary, 8 February, 24, 25 March 1920; interview with David Susman.
15 *Livingstone Mail*, 14 May, 25 August, 1921; SP, M. Gersh to D. Susman, 24 September 1993; NR Pioneer Settlers' Association Papers, Application Forms, Maurice and Harry Gersh (by courtesy of Heather Chalcraft, Lusaka).
16 *Livingstone Mail*, 21 September 1917, 26 April, 1925, 6 July 1912, 7 September 1917, 12 May 1920, 25 August 1921, 24 January 1929.
17 *Livingstone Mail*, 16 July 1925; Smith, *Vet in Africa*, 276.
18 *Livingstone Mail*, 14 April 1916.
19 Macmillan and Shapiro, *Zion in Africa*, 114.
20 Smith, *Vet in Africa*, 272–6; *Livingstone Mail*, 17 May 1918, 9 June 1921, 1 April 1924.
21 WP, E. Susman Diary, 1920, *passim*; *Livingstone Mail*, 3 November 1927, 19 January 1928; 24 October 1929.
22 *Livingstone Mail*, 5 March, 29 July 1920; WP, E. Susman Diary, 5 March, 21 July 1920.
23 *Livingstone Mail*, 3 July 1924, 26 August 1926, 22 November 1928; KDB6/1/1 Batoka Province, Annual Reports, 1927, 1928.
24 Macmillan and Shapiro, *Zion in Africa*, 54–5; interview with Hymie Woolfe; SP, E. Susman Diary, 1935, 1936; *Livingstone Mail*, 9 May 1929, 8 July 1936, 13 September 1940; V. D. Michelson (ed.), *Central African Who's Who for 1953* (Salisbury: Central African Who's Who (Pvt.) Ltd, 1953).
25 *Livingstone Mail*, 26 April, 27 December 1923 (Annual Retrospect), 31 January 1924; interview with Molly Diamond.
26 *Livingstone Mail*, 26 August, 2 December 1926, 24 January, 16 May 1929; SEC 3/548, Vol. I, J. P. A. Morris to CS, 11 January 1934; *Livingstone Mail*, 19 May 1921; 11 June 1930; A. Macmillan, *Rhodesia and East Africa, Historical and Descriptive, Commercial and Industrial, Facts, Figures and Resources* (London: W. H. and L. Collingridge, 1930), 343.
27 *Livingstone Mail*, 24 February, 18 May 1932.

28 R. Murray-Hughes, 'Kafue-Namwala in 1912', Part II, *Northern Rhodesia Journal*, 5: 1 (1962), 111; SP, E. Susman Diary, 1920, *passim*; SEC3/548, Vol. I, J. Smith to CS, 7 September 1932; Verbatim Record of Meeting on Cattle Trade, Mazabuka, 22 February 1933, and other correspondence.

29 *Livingstone Mail*, 3 November, 1 December 1921, 3 December 1931, 5 May 1937; interviews with D. Susman and Edwardina Neethling.

30 WP, Correspondence about Extension of Leopard's Hill Ranch, including SB to Secretary, Lands Department, 22 February 1927, J. Moffat Thomson, DC, Lusaka, to CS, 28 March 1927, and SB to Secretary, Lands Department, 30 July 1927, and map.

31 *Livingstone Mail*, 1 December 1921, 30 December 1931, 13 October 1927.

32 SP, E. Susman Diary, 1932.

33 WP, SB Accounts, Mapanda Transport Company, 1924–5; A. T. Dreyer, 1925–6; Macmillan and Shapiro, *Zion in Africa*, 47–8; communication from David Philip, Cape Town.

34 *Livingstone Mail*, 20 January 1931; KDB6/1/1/2-4, Southern Province, Annual Reports, 1929–31.

35 *Livingstone Mail*, Annual Review, December 1921, 30 October 1924.

36 KDB6/1/1/3-7, Southern Province, Annual Reports, 1930–4.

37 G. M. Calvert, 'The Zambezi Saw Mills Railway, 1911–64', in *The Zambezi Teak Forests: Proceedings of the First International Conference on the Teak Forests of Southern Africa, Livingstone, March 1984* (Ndola: Zambia Forestry Department, 1986), 474–505; A. H. Croxton, 'Rhodesia's Light Railways', *Rhodesiana*, 13 (1965), 65–6.

38 Calvert Papers, A. H. Croxton, 'Notes on Susman Bros' Light Railway into Forests on South of Zambesi – Compiled from Letters from Bob Cooke to A. H. Croxton', 14 November 1964; Robert Beaton, copy of talk on Zambesi Saw Mills to Rotary Club, Livingstone (n.d. [*circa* 1963]), copies by courtesy of G. M. Calvert.

39 As above and Bob Cooke to G. M. Calvert, received 7 November 1966; BNA, S282/17, O. Miller, Forest Officer to GS, 21 September, 20 October 1936.

40 J. A. Bancroft, *Mining in Northern Rhodesia* (no place: British South Africa Company, 1961), 66, 145; WP, SB Accounts, 1918–19; SP, E. Susman Diary, 24 June 1936; interview with D. Susman.

41 *Livingstone Mail*, 22 March 1928, 3 May, 1, 29 November 1933; SEC3/547, Vol. I, Minutes of Interview, the Governor, Sir J. Maxwell, H. C. Werner, CS and CVO, 30 May 1929; SB (L. Hochstein) to CVO, 4 September, 16 October 1929; CVO to CS, 4 September 1929; CS to CVO, 11 September 1929; CVO to CS, 14, 20 September, 3, 11, 16, 23 October, 6 November, 12 December 1929, 7 January 1930, 21 March 1930; H. C. Werner to CVO, 4, 19 October 1929, 14 March 1930; R. Parker (Rhodesian Selection Trust) to CS, 2 November, 12 December 1929.

42 *Livingstone Mail*, 5 January, 12 March 1930; Scott Brown Papers, Philadelphia, Phyllis Lakofski-Hepker, 'Memories of My Childhood and Youth', ff. 17–20 (copy in author's possession by courtesy of the late P. Lakofski-Hepker and of Denise Scott Brown); SP, M. Gersh to D. Susman, 24 September 1993.

43 Macmillan and Shapiro, *Zion in Africa*, 85–6;

44 Bancroft, *Mining in Northern Rhodesia*, 152–3.

45 SEC3/547, Vol. I, 'Minutes of Interview', 30 May 1929; Macmillan and Shapiro, *Zion in Africa*, 86–7; ML4/5/2, 'Livestock Cooperative Society of NR', H. Forsyth to R. S. MacDonald, Veterinary Department, 11 July 1935.

46 Macmillan and Shapiro, *Zion in Africa*, 87, 92–3; SP, E. Susman Diary, 20 February 1931, 27 February 1934, 25 June 1936; Economy Stores Ltd, Minutes of AGMs, 2 January 1933, and 10 July 1934.

47 J. M. Davis (ed.) *Modern Industry and the African* (London: Frank Cass, 1967 (first edition 1933)), 136–74; SP, E. Susman Diary, 19 February 1932, 19 July 1933, February–March 1934. For notes on investments see E. Susman Diary, 1931–6.

48 M. Sonnenberg, *As I Saw It* (Cape Town: Howard Timmins, n.d.), *passim*; M. Kaplan (with the assistance of M. Robertson), *Jewish Roots in the South African Economy* (Cape Town: C. Struik, 1986), 343–59.

49 SP, 'Memorandum of Agreement between SB, Woolworths, M. Sonnenberg and E. Susman', 15 December 1934; E. Susman, Contract with Woolworths, 20 August 1936; Cape Town, Woolworths Archives, Woolworths Minute Book, 20 June 1935; WP, H. Susman to E. Susman, 31 July 1941.

50 SP, 'Statement of Account Elie Susman & Susman Brothers [with Woolworths]', 13 December 1934–30 September 1936; SBA, Inspector's Report, Livingstone, 16 March 1939.

51 *Livingstone Mail*, 23 February 1922.

52 Quoted in D. Hobson, *Show Time* (Lusaka: Agricultural and Commercial Society of Zambia, 1979), 86.

53 RHL, M. G. Billing Papers, unpublished memoir, 'Crest of the Wave', f 77.

54 Interview with Abe Galaun.

55 SEC3/547, Vol. II, CVO (J. P. A. Morris) to CS, 7 November 1934; KTO/3, Sesheke District Notebook, Interview of H. P Read with Governor, Sir Hubert Young, 12 June 1936; SP, E. Susman Diary, 21 March 1935; *Annual Reports on Native Affairs*, Barotse Province, 1935, 1937–8; *Annual Reports of Veterinary Department*, 1935–9.

56 *Livingstone Mail*, 8 July 1936, and see below.

10 Harry Wulfsohn: From Latvia to Livingstone

1 Most of the material relating to the Wulfsohn family in this section comes from interviews with Wulfie Wulfsohn, the late Josephine Falk, the late Hessie Lowenthal, brother and sisters of Harry Wulfsohn, Isa Teeger, his niece, and

from autobiographical fragments written by his widow, Trude Robins. I am also grateful for a communication from Delice Levenson, the widow of Harry's cousin Stan Levenson, and I have referred to the transcript of an interview with Hessie Lowenthal by Barbara Meyerowitz.

2. Saron and Hotz, *The Jews in South Africa, a History*, 378–80.
3. Macmillan and Shapiro, *Zion in Africa*, 14, 99.
4. Ibid., 14, 65.
5. Ibid., 63. Interview with W. Wulfsohn.
6. Trude Robins, unpublished memoirs, two versions.
7. SBA, Lusaka Inspection Report, June 1933.
8. SBA, Lusaka Inspection Reports, 1932–4. See also R. Sampson, *They Came to Lusaaka's* (Lusaka: Multimedia Publications, 1982).
9. KSF1/8/4, 'Namwala Township Plot, 1934–7', H. Wulfsohn to DC, Namwala, 20 November 1934; interviews with M. Dorsky and W. Wulfsohn.
10. KDB6/1/1/7, Annual Report, Southern Province, 1934.
11. KSF1/8/4, J. Gordon Read, DC Namwala, to T. F. Sandford, PC, Lusaka, 20 December 1934 and other correspondence.
12. KSF3/2/7, Annual Reports, Namwala, 1934–7; KDB6/1/1/4, Annual Report, Southern Province, 1931; KSF1/8/4, 'Namwala Township Plot, 1934–7', L. S. Diamond to DC, Namwala, 21 May 1937 and subsequent correspondence.
13. KSF3/2/7, Annual Report, Namwala, 1936.
14. Ibid.
15. Wynant David Hubbard, *Ibamba* (London: Victor Gollancz, 1963), passim.
16. Ibid., 25.
17. T. Robins, unpublished memoirs; K. Vickery, 'Saving Settlers: Maize Control in Northern Rhodesia', *Journal of Southern African Studies*, 11: 2 (1985).
18. *Central African Who's Who for 1953*; ML4/5/2, R. A. S. MacDonald to G. Beckett, 9 April 1937; interview with Mike Beckett, Choma, Zambia.
19. Eaton Hall, Cheshire, Duke of Westminster's Archives, Correspondence between Sir Herbert Baker and St G. Clowes on recruitment of Robert Boyd, May–June 1937 (by courtesy of His Grace the Duke of Westminster).
20. RHL, M. G. Billing, 'Crest of the Wave', ff 41–2.
21. Interviews with W. Wulfsohn and J. Falk.
22. Billing, 'Crest of the Wave', ff 41–2.
23. Macmillan and Shapiro, *Zion in Africa*, 103–19.
24. T. Robins, unpublished memoir; interviews with T. Robins and F. Wiesenbacher.
25. Macmillan and Shapiro, *Zion in Africa*, 116–19.
26. Interviews with W. Wulfsohn and M. Dorsky; *Northern Rhodesian Government Gazette*, 2 February 1940; *Livingstone Mail*, 12 August, 28 October 1939.
27. Interview with T. Robins; *Livingstone Mail*, 3 February 1940.
28. Interview with H. Wolffe; BNA, S282/17, H. Wulfsohn to O. Miller, Forestry Officer, 4 May 1937.

29 *Livingstone Mail*, 5, 30 July, 2 September 1939; J. W. A. Parkhurst, 'Lucky Me!', unpublished memoir, by courtesy of Roy Parkhurst, Durban.
30 Zambia Consolidate Copper Mines (ZCCM) Archives, Ndola, WM A 24, Minutes of Meeting of Mines Meat Contractors and Bechuanaland Cattle Traders, 1941.
31 Interviews with Trude Robins; T. Robins, unpublished memoirs.
32 Kala Ranching Company Minute Book, May 1942.
33 SEC3/560, 'Northern Rhodesia Cold Storage Board Works', Report by K. Tucker, Chairman, Cold Storage Control Board, 15 May 1945, f. 1; *Livingstone Mail*, 6 April 1940. Harry Wulfsohn is not named in the report quoted above, but it appears from internal evidence that the reference is to him.
34 SEC3/560, 'NR Cold Storage Board Works', Report, 15 May 1945, f. 1; J. H. N. Hobday, Veterinary Department, Annual Report, 1943.
35 SEC3/560, H. Wulfsohn to Secretary for Native Affairs, 22 August 1941.
36 SEC3/560 'NR Cold Storage Board Works', Report, 15 May 1945, 2–3; Veterinary Department, Annual Report, 1943.
37 SEC3/560, 'NR Cold Storage Board Works', Report, 15 May 1945, ff 15–16.
38 Lusaka, Companies Registry, Werners File; SP, Mortgage Agreement between Mrs H. A. Werner and E. and H. Susman, 3 April 1944; Cape Town, Rabb Papers (RP), H. Wulfsohn and Company, Minutes of Second AGM, 9 August 1946.
39 *Livingstone Mail*, 24 September 1943. This is an interesting though not strictly accurate historical document. Susman Brothers came into existence as a legal partnership under that name in 1907, not 1901, though a *de facto* partnership may have existed from the earlier date.
40 Interview with T. Robins; *Livingstone Mail*, 30 July, 20 August 1943, 31 March, 6 April, 28 July, 18 August 1944.
41 Communication from David Susman.

11 Susman Brothers & Wulfsohn: The Development of the Stores Network

1 A. Roberts, *A History of Zambia* (London: Heinemann, 1976), 206–11.
2 SEC4/1334-51, 'Price Controls'.
3 SEC1/1760-6, 'Post-War Problems'; SEC2/282, Five Year Plans, Barotse Province; SEC2/283, Five Year Plans, Southern Province; *Ten Year Development Plan for Northern Rhodesia* (Lusaka: Government Printer, 1947).
4 *Submission of Case for the Expansion of Livingstone Northern Rhodesia to Accommodate the Federal Capital of the Federation of Rhodesia and Nyasaland* (Livingstone: Livingstone Municipal Council, 1952.)
5 Trude Robins, 'Memoir'; interviews with and communications from Trude Robins and Edwin Wulfsohn.

6 Caplan, *Elites of Barotseland*, 165–90.
7 Gersh, 'The Susman Saga'; *Livingstone Mail*, 29 June, 6 July 1945, 16 January 1952; interview with Alison Bligh-Wall, widow of Joe Susman, and tape of BBC interview with Joe Susman, Victoria Falls, Zimbabwe, n.d.
8 SP, E. Susman to M. Rabb, 21 March 1951; *Livingstone Mail*, 12 September 1952.
9 RP, Harry Wulfsohn Ltd, Minutes of AGM, 9 August 1946.
10 Maurice Rabb, 'Recollections' (copy in author's possession, by courtesy of John Rabb).
11 Rabb, 'Recollections'; RP, Rabb to M. Barnett, 24 December 1951.
12 Information in this and subsequent paragraphs comes from Rabb, 'Recollections'.
13 RP, E. Susman to Rabb, 26 March 1946, 13 January 1947.
14 RP, E. Susman to Rabb, 13 January 1947, 5 February 1947; interviews with D. Susman and Tony Serrano.
15 Rabb, 'Recollections'.
16 Interviews with Esther Faerber, Wulfie Wulfsohn and Tony Serrano.
17 ZP15, Cost of Living Inquiry Commission, Verbatim Record of Evidence, Jack Faerber, 17 July 1947, 1399–1406; *Annual Report on African Affairs*, Barotse Province, 1947.
18 Rabb, 'Recollections'; interview with Tony Serrano.
19 Interviews with Tony Serrano, Geoff Kates and Andrew Sardanis; *Annual Reports on African Affairs*, 1949–52.
20 F. Fraser Darling (ed. J. M. Boyd), *Fraser Darling in Africa* (Edinburgh: Edinburgh University Press, 1992), 84; Rhodesian Mercantile Holdings (RMH) Minutes, 5 February, 15 July, 4 September 1963.
21 SEC3/500/1-3, 'Proposed Zambesi River Transport Scheme', 1944–6; RHL, Welensky Papers, 6/5, 'Zambesi River Transport Enquiry, March 1950. Report and Notes of Statements by Witnesses', evidence of M. Rabb and H. Wulfsohn; interview with Tony Serrano; Rabb, 'Recollections'. The government-backed Zambesi River Transport Service came into operation from 1 October 1944.
22 Interview with Tony Serrano.
23 *Annual Reports on African Affairs*, 1949–51; RP, Rabb to E. Susman, 17 November 1951.
24 *Annual Report on African Affairs*, 1950; RP, Rabb to E. Susman, 16 August 1950, 17 November 1951.
25 RP, Rabb to E. Susman, 16 August 1950; interview with Rob Hart.
26 Interview with Ronnie and Poppie Vos.
27 KSX4/1, Mankoya District Notebook.
28 Ibid.
29 Interview with Geoffrey Kates.
30 Interviews with G. Kates and Job Haloba; IMMI/1/K/322, 1948, Immigration File, G. Kates.

31 Interview with G. Kates; Rabb, 'Recollections'.
32 RP, Rabb to E. Susman, 12 December 1951.
33 RP, E. Susman to Rabb, 5 September 1952, 26 May 1952, 20 March 1953.

12 The Susmans, Woolworths and Marks & Spencer

1 Interviews with H. Wolffe and D. Susman; Kaplan, *Jewish Roots in the South African Economy*, 349–51.
2 SP, Chairman's Statement, Marks & Spencer, 26 September 1947; copy of Minutes of Meeting of Directors, Marks & Spencer, 26 September, 1947; Joint Information Statement Issued by the Directors of Marks & Spencer Limited and Woolworths Holdings Limited, 21 October, 1947; D. Susman, unpublished memoir.
3 D. Susman, unpublished memoir.
4 P. Bookbinder, *Simon Marks: Retail Revolutionary* (London: Weidenfeld and Nicolson, 1993), 138.
5 D. Susman, unpublished memoir; interview with Hymie Wolffe.
6 D. Susman, unpublished memoir.
7 Ibid.
8 Elaine Blond (with Barry Turner) *Marks of Distinction* (London: Valentine, Mitchell, 1983), 139.
9 SP, E. Susman to R. Sonnenberg, 30 May 1950.
10 Blond, *Marks of Distinction*, 140.
11 D. Susman, unpublished memoir.
12 SP, D. Susman to R. Sonnenberg, 4 September 1951.
13 SP, E. Susman to D. Susman, 13 June 1955; Blond, *Marks of Distinction*, 140.
14 D. Susman, unpublished memoir.
15 SP, E. Susman Diary, 1954–7.
16 SP, E. Susman Diary, 1955.
17 SP, E. Susman Diary, 22–9 April, 16 July 1957; Susman Brothers & Wulfsohn (SB & W) Minutes, 2 August, 1957; WP, Lochinvar Ranch Visitors' Book, 15 August 1957; ZSM Minutes, 17 September 1957; D. Susman, unpublished memoir.
18 SP, E. Susman Diary, 16 January 1956.

13 Susman Brothers & Wulfsohn: Partners and Politics

1 Welensky Papers, 476/2, H. Wulfsohn to Welensky, 24 July 1953; Welensky to Wulfsohn, 28 July 1953; A. Galaun to Welensky, 25 August 1953; M. Barnett to Welensky, 26 August 1953; interview with Simon Zukas.

2 RP, E. Susman to Rabb, 20 October, 2 November 1950; Rabb to E. Susman, 10, 11 September, 3 October 1952; E. Susman to Rabb, 15 October 1952; Rabb to E. Susman, 10 September 1952; interview with W. Wulfsohn.
3 RP, E. Susman to Rabb, 16 September, 3 October 1952; M. Barnett to H. Wulfsohn (copy), 17 September 1952; interviews with Wulfie Wulfsohn.
4 RP, E. Susman to Rabb, 15 March, 12 April, 29 June 1954. SP, E. Susman to D. Susman, 23 September 1954.
5 SP, M. Barnett to E. Susman, 22 January 1955; E. Susman to M. Barnett, 27 January 1955.
6 SP, D. Susman to M. Barnett, 27 January 1955.
7 SP, D. Susman to E. Susman, 14 June 1955. Interviews with D. Susman, D. Pitt, C. Arnott, Simon and Cynthia Zukas.
8 WP, N. Zelter, 'Meeting with Edwin Wulfsohn at Stenham's', 9 June 1980.
9 SP, E. Susman Diary, 7 March 1955; H. Wulfsohn to D. Susman, 15 April 1955; E. Susman to D. Susman, 4 April 1955; 'Minutes of a Meeting of Directors and Shareholders of Werner and Co. Ltd. and SB & W Ltd. held at the Chairman's Residence on Sunday 3 April 1955'.
10 SP, E. Susman to M. Barnett, 10 June 1955.
11 SP, D. Susman to E. Susman, 14 June 1955.
12 SP, D. Susman to E. Susman, 21 June 1955.
13 RMH Minutes, 29 July 1955.
14 RMH Minutes, 17 March 1956, 20 June 1958; interviews with Ronnie Kays and Alex Vlotamas.
15 SP, E. Susman to D. Susman, 23 August 1955; Kenneth Kaunda, *Zambia Shall be Free* (London: Heinemann, 1962), 73–4; K. Makasa, *March to Political Freedom* (Nairobi: Heinemann, 1981), 47–50; RMH Minutes, 17 March 1956.
16 RMH Minutes, 30 September 1955.
17 SP, 'Minutes of the Meeting to Decide on the Mechanics of the Move to Salisbury Held at Livingstone on 18 February 1956'. See also RMH Minutes, 16 March 1956, 29 August 1958, and 18 September 1959.
18 ZA, Transcript of Interview with Nathan Zelter by I. J. Johnstone, 17 November 1983; WP, N. Zelter, 'Meeting with Edwin Wulfsohn at Stenham's', 9 March 1980. See also Doris Lessing, *Under My Skin* (London: HarperCollins, 1995), 260, 384–9; *Going Home* (St Albans: Panther, 1957, first edition, 1968), 83–5; *Walking in the Shade, Volume Two of My Autobiography* (London: HarperCollins, 1997), 172–89.
19 RMH Minutes, 30 April 1962, 4 March 1960; interviews with D. Pitt and C. Arnott.
20 RMH Minutes, 4, 22 March, 20 June 1958; interviews with D. Susman, D. Pitt and C. Arnott.
21 SP, E. Susman to D. Susman, 28 May [*sic* – probably April], 1955; ZA, Oral/236, interview with N. Zelter by I. Johnstone, 1986.

22 SP, E. Susman to Directors, RMH, SB & W (Stores) and Associated Companies, 3 May 1957.
23 Rabb, 'Recollections'; interview with D. Susman.
24 SP, Managing Directors, African Stores Ltd to Chairman and Directors African Stores Ltd and RMH Ltd, 4 July 1959; R. M Campbell, 'African Stores Ltd: Notes on the Effect of the Disposal of Assets', 9 July 1959; D. Susman to Rabb, 21 July 1959; RMH Minutes, 22 December 1959, 7 January 1960, 4 March 1960, 29 June 1960; Rabb, 'Recollections'. See also RMH Minutes, 30 September 1955.
25 RMH Minutes, 11 April, 20 June, 25–6 October 1958, 28 July 1960; Minutes of 4th AGM, 30 December 1959; Rabb, 'Recollections'; interview with G. Kates, Keith Chick and Job Haloba.
26 RMH, Reports to and Minutes of AGMs, 1958–63; RMH Minutes, 8 May 1956.
27 SP, D. Susman to Rabb, 29 April 1958.
28 Interview with D. Susman.
29 SP, D. Susman to Rabb, 16 April 1956.
30 RMH Minutes, 4 July 1961, 25 November 1963; interviews with Wulfie Wulfsohn, Isa Teeger and Hessie Lowenthal.
31 Rabb, 'Recollections'; RP, Rabb to E. Susman [draft, n.d.]; E. Susman to Rabb, 10 November 1953.
32 D. Mulford, *Zambia: The Politics of Independence, 1957–64* (Manchester: Manchester University Press, 1967), 280–5; D. Mulford, *The Northern Rhodesia General Election, 1962* (Nairobi: Oxford University Press, 1962), *passim*.
33 Welensky Papers, 468/1, Malcolmson to Welensky, 17 May 1962; Welensky Papers, 468/2, Secret Memorandum on UFP–ANC Co-operation, 21 November 1962.
34 Caplan, *Elites of Barotseland*, 191–228; H. Franklin, *Unholy Wedlock: The Failure of the Central African Federation* (London: George Allen & Unwin, 1963), 217–22; Anon., 'Barotseland: Whigs and Royalists, A Detailed Analysis of the Situation on the Plain', *Central African Examiner*, October 1962, 32–3.
35 *Rhodesia Herald*, 12 May 1962.
36 RMH Minutes, 12 May 1962.
37 *Central African Post*, 2 May 1962.
38 Welensky Papers, 221/4, J. M. Greenfield to L. Dix, 1 February 1962, enclosing Welensky to Mwanawina; Dix to Greenfield, 6 February, enclosing Mwanawina to Welensky; Prince Ngombala Lubita and H. M. Kutoma to Organising Secretary, UFP, Lusaka, 6 June 1962.
39 Welensky Papers, 637/2, G. Mbikusita Lewanika to RC, Barotseland Protectorate, 27 November 1962; *Rhodesia Herald*, 26 May 1962; Welensky Papers, 221/4, Prince Ngombala Lubita and H. M. Kutoma to Litunga Sir Mwanawina III, 4 June 1962, and to Organising Secretary, UFP, Lusaka, 6 June 1962.
40 Welensky Papers, 508/2, Adams to Welensky, 4 June 1962.
41 Welensky Papers, 508/2, Welensky to Adams, 7 June 1962.

42 Ibid.; Secret Memorandum, 'Operation Elephant', 18 June 1962; Welensky Papers, 221/4, G. Mukande and L. M. Lipalile to Welensky, 12 June 1962.
43 *Livingstone Mail*, 12 October 1962.
44 Mulford, *The N. R. General Election*, 72; Welensky Papers, 468/2, Rabb to Permanent Private Secretary, Welensky, 3 December 1962.
45 Welensky Papers, 637/2, Lewanika to RC, 27 November 1962; Mulford, *Zambia: The Politics of Independence*, 280–1; Welensky Papers, 221/4, Lewanika to J. M. Greenfield, 17 August 1962; Anon., 'Barotseland: Whigs and Royalists', 33; *Daily News*, 10 July 1962; *Northern News*, 1 August 1962.
46 Welensky Papers, 514/3, 'UNIP Report on General Election Outcome'.
47 F. Suu, Y. Mupata, L. Mufungulwa to the Litunga, 27 November 1962, quoted in Caplan, *Elites of Barotseland*, 200.
48 Welensky Papers, 468/2, 'Secret Memorandum on UFP–ANC Co-operation', 21 November 1962.
49 Mulford, *The N. R. General Election*, 173; *Livingstone Mail*, 14 December 1962.
50 *Livingstone Mail*, 7 November 1962.
51 *Livingstone Mail*, 21 December 1962.
52 Caplan, *Elites of Barotseland*, 200.
53 Ibid., 200–22.
54 Interview with David Susman; *Livingstone Mail*, 5 October 1962; RMH Minutes, 12 July 1961; *Livingstone Mail*, 26 October 1962; Welensky Papers, 635/11, Rex L'Ange to Welensky, Memorandum of Meeting with Sir Frederick Crawford and Harry Wulfsohn on 7 November, 10 November 1962.
55 Interview with Benson Kamitondo; RMH Minutes, 17 May, 14 October, 11 November 1963.
56 RMH Minutes, 2 April 1963 and Appendix A 'Reconstruction of RMH Group'; SP, H. Wulfsohn to D. Susman, 16 September 1963; interviews with D. Susman and G. Kates.
57 RMH Minutes, 23 November 1965, 10 December 1965.
58 SP, Rabb to H. Wulfsohn and H. Robinson, 29 October 1966.
59 WP, H. Wulfsohn, Memorandum, 27 February 1967.
60 K. D. Kaunda, 'Zambia Towards Economic Independence', 34–74.
61 Interview with Andrew Sardanis.
62 Interviews with W. Wulfsohn, E. Wulfsohn, T. Robins and G. Kates; T. Robins, unpublished memoir; RP, H. Robinson to Rabb, 1 June 1966.
63 A. Sardanis, *Africa: Another Side of the Coin, Northern Rhodesia's Final Years and Zambia's Nationhood* (London: I. B. Tauris, 2003), 189. Interviews with Andrew Sardanis, Andrew Kashita and Simon Zukas. Sardanis is wrong to suggest that Gersh left the country in 1967. He did not do so until 1971. Simon Zukas, who remained on the board of Indeco, also had links with the Susman family, but there is no evidence that he was consulted on the takeover.
64 Rabb, 'Recollections'; interviews with J. Haloba, G. Kates and E. Wulfsohn.

65 Interviews with Job Haloba and Geoff Kates.
66 Rabb, 'Recollections'; interview with and communication from E. Wulfsohn.
67 Stores Holdings Minutes, 19 February, 1 March, 27 May 1969, and 19 January 1970.
68 Stores Holdings Minutes, 11 February, 30 March 1967, 10 November 1967, 25 November, 18 December 1968, 19 January 1970; SB & W/Werners Minutes, 24–5 June 1969.
69 SB & W/Werners Minutes, 24–5 June 1969; interviews with G. Kates and J. Haloba; Marian Payne, 'Memoir'.
70 RHL, Catt Papers, 'Experiences in Zambia, 1970–2'; 'Results of a Study of the Possible Causes of Shrinkage within the Four Main Trading Companies of Indeco Trading Ltd', enclosed in C. W. Catt to J. Cowan, 14 August 1970.
71 Interviews with A. Kashita, S. Zukas and A. Sardanis.
72 Interview with G. Kates, M. Payne, 'Memoir'; Stores Holdings Minutes, 30 July 1971, 18 November 1973; SB & W Minutes, 12 September 1975, 29 November 1976.
73 K. D. Kaunda, *Towards Complete Independence* (Lusaka: Zambia Information Services, 1969), 14.
74 Interview with E. Wulfsohn.
75 Interview with A. Sardanis. For a different account of this takeover see Sardanis, *Africa: Another Side of the Coin*, 216. It would not have been as easy as Sardanis suggests for a member of the Susman or Wulfsohn families to take out Zambian citizenship and assume personal ownership of the business. Nor is it the case that they made no effort to transfer stores to Zambian traders.
76 Interview with A. Kashita.

14 Susman Brothers & Wulfsohn Stores: People

1 WP, N. Zelter, 'Meeting with E. Wulfsohn'; interviews with D. Susman, E. Wulfsohn, G. Kates, D. Pitt and C. Arnott.
2 Interview with Steve and Patsy Kuzniar.
3 Interviews with D. Pitt and C. Arnott; M. Payne, 'Memoir'.
4 Interview with Keith Chick.
5 M. Payne, 'Memoir'.
6 M. Payne, 'Memoir'; interview with Job Haloba.
7 A. F. Serrano at Balovale seems to have been an exception to this rule.
8 M. Payne, 'Memoir'; RMH Minutes, 17 May 1961, 3 February, 12 May 1962.
9 M. Payne, 'Memoir'; Caplan, *Elites of Barotseland*, 216–17.
10 Ibid., 212–22.
11 The *Times of Zambia*, 13 December 1968, carried a report of the Indeco takeover of SB & W.
12 RMH Minutes, 12 November 1960, 2 April 1963, 10 April 1956.

13 RMH Minutes, 10 September 1956, 12 November 1960.
14 RMH Minutes, 10 September 1956, 17 May 1961, 11 November, 25 November 1963, interviews with G. Kates and Joel Mubiana Liswaniso.
15 RMH Minutes, 2 April, 17 May, 10 June, 11 November 1963, and 16 January 1964.
16 Interview with Mrs L. McKillop, and her daughter, Phyrne Byrne.
17 L. C. Dix, 'To Whom it May Concern', 31 October 1958.
18 Interview with Joel Mubiana Liswaniso.
19 Interview with Ernest Mukwendela Kutoma.
20 Interview with Benson Kamitondo.
21 RMH Minutes, 21–2 August 1960.
22 RMH Minutes, 26 July 1962.
23 RMH Minutes, 25 January, 17 May, 10 June 1963.
24 RMH Minutes, 15 July 1963, 29 November 1966.
25 Stores Holdings Minutes, Chairman's Report on the year to 31 March 1966, 28 October 1966.
26 Stores Holdings Minutes, Chairman's Report on the year to 31 March 1966, 28 October 1966.
27 Interview with Job Haloba.
28 Author's experience of fieldwork for Oxfam in Senanga West in January 1985. It was then that I first heard laments for the demise of the Susman Brothers & Wulfsohn stores network. Interviews with Simon Zukas and Akashambatwa Mbikusita Lewanika.

15 Werners: The Copperbelt and the Central African Cattle Trade

1 Werners's minutes are available for only a few years in the late 1950s, when there were sometimes joint meetings with the ranching companies, and from the late 1960s. The minutes of Northern Rhodesia's Cold Storage Board are supposed to be in the National Archives of Zambia, but have been misplaced. The minutes of the Cattle Marketing and Control Board (CMCB) are also incomplete. About half the minutes for the 1950s appear to survive. Some are in the Zambian Archives and some in the Welensky Papers.
2 NR Pioneer Settlers' Association, Questionnaires: E. Speck and W. Speck; interview with A. Galaun.
3 Rabb, 'Recollections'; *Livingstone Mail*, 25 July, 15 August, 19 September, 3, 10, 24 October, 7 November 1947.
4 Interviews with T. Barnett, M. Barnett, L. Pinshow and G. Kollenberg; Rabb, 'Recollections'.
5 Interviews with T. and M. Barnett; See also Macmillan and Shapiro, *Zion in Africa*, 88–92.

6 Interviews with G. Kollenberg, L. Pinshow, T. Barnett and D. Susman. See also Macmillan and Shapiro, *Zion in Africa*, 146–7, 232–3.
7 Ibid., 182–93; J. H. Chileshe, *Abe Galaun* (Lusaka: Walpole Park Development Ltd, 2000); interviews with Abe and Vera Galaun.
8 As above, and RP, Rabb to E. Susman, 16 March 1949, and E. Susman to Rabb, 2 August 1949; interviews with Abe and Vera Galaun.
9 Interviews with C. Weskob, A. Vlotamas and R. Kays.
10 *Annual Reports of the Veterinary Department*, 1939–51 (Lusaka: Government Printer, 1940–52); Welensky Papers, CMCB Minutes, 47/1, 1950–1; SP, NTC Balance Sheet, 31 March 1947.
11 Welensky Papers, 46/7, P. D. Morley-Fletcher to Welensky, 19 March 1951. See also F. Debenham, *Kalahari Sand* (London: G. Bell and Sons, 1953), and M. Hubbard, *Agricultural Exports and Economic Growth, a Study of the Botswana Beef Industry* (London: KPI, 1986), 118–42.
12 Welensky Papers, 46/7, 'Minutes of a Meeting held at Lusaka on Friday 7th September 1951 with Representatives of the CDC'; *Annual Reports of the Veterinary Department*, 1953–7 (Lusaka: Government Printer, 1954–8); Hubbard, *Agricultural Exports and Economic Growth*, 125–37, 232; *Livingstone Mail*, 23 April, 19 October 1954.
13 Welensky Papers, 46/7, 'Record of a Meeting held … on 17 March 1952 to Consider … the Administration of the Cold Storage Facilities at Livingstone'; SB & W to the Economic Secretary, 27 March 1952; Acting-Economic Secretary to SB & W, 6 June 1952; Acting-Economic Secretary to Private Secretary, Roy Welensky, 23 October 1952.
14 *Annual Reports of the Veterinary Department*, 1938–44 (Lusaka: Government Printer, 1939–45).
15 Welensky Papers, 47/1, CMCB Minutes, 1950–1; MAG2/2/32, CMCB Minutes, 1955–9; *Report of the Commission of Inquiry into the Beef Cattle Industry in Northern and Southern Rhodesia* (Horwood Report) (Salisbury: Government Printer, 1963), 17.
16 *Annual Report of the Veterinary Department*, 1953; MAG2/2/32, CMCB Minutes, 17 May 1956.
17 Southern Rhodesia (SR) Cold Storage Commission, *Annual Reports*, 1938–59; Welensky Papers, 589/1, G. Beckett to Welensky, 13 August 1957.
18 R. E. Baldwin, *Economic Development and Export Growth: A Study of Northern Rhodesia, 1920–60* (Berkeley: University of California Press, 1956), 157–9; Horwood Report, 'Extract from Evidence Submitted by the Northern Rhodesian Government', 134–7.
19 Welensky Papers, 589/1, G. Beckett to Welensky, 5 February 1954; MAG2/2/32, CMCB Minutes, 17 May 1956; Horwood Report, 19–20.
20 *Annual Report of the Veterinary Department*, 1954, 4.

21 Copperfields Cold Storage Minutes, Annual Report, 1953; Horwood Report, 20; *Annual Reports of the Veterinary Department*, 1954–5.
22 MAG2/2/32, CMCB Minutes, 23 March 1955, 26 August 1955, 21 December 1955, and 8 November 1956; interview with L. Pinshow.
23 RP, E. Susman to Rabb, 29 June 1954; Copperfields Minutes, Annual Report, 1954; ZCCM Archives: NCCM/RC/HO 522/2 O. B. Bennett to D. A. Etheredge, 19 January 1959; interview with L. Pinshow.
24 SP, E. Susman to D. Susman, 23 August 1955; D. Susman to E. Susman, 16 September 1955.
25 Welensky Papers, 157/2, 'Valuation of Fixed Assets etc', in Minister of Commerce and Industry to Cabinet Economic and Development Committee, 10 March 1959; MAG2/2/32, CMCB Minutes, 16 August 1955; SP, E. Susman Diary, August 1955.
26 *Annual Reports of the Veterinary Department*, 1957–9 (Lusaka: Government Printer, 1958–60); MAG2/2/32, CMCB Minutes, 30 April 1957, 9 October 1957; Welensky Papers, 589/1, Minister of Finance (D. Macintyre) to Welensky, 22 August 1957.
27 *Report of the Commission of Inquiry on the Marketing of Cattle for Slaughter and the Distribution and Sale of Beef in Southern Rhodesia* (Salisbury: Government Printer, 1956.); Hubbard, *Agricultural Exports and Economic Growth*, 131, 236; Welensky Papers, 589/1, G. Beckett to Welensky, 13 August 1957.
28 Horwood Report, 19.
29 Macmillan and Shapiro, *Zion in Africa*, 144–6, 187–9.
30 RP, E. Susman to Rabb, 19 September 1957; Galaun Papers, M. Barnett to A. Galaun, 21 November 1957, and copy of contract between Werner Group and Cold Storage Commission, 16 December 1957; Welensky Papers, 589/1, G. Beckett to Welensky, 13 August 1957; RP, D. Susman to M. Rabb, 11 October, 1957.
31 MAG2/2/32, CMCB Minutes, 11 March, 24 April, 19 August 1958; Welensky Papers, 157/2, Cabinet Economic and Development Committee Minutes, 23 March 1959.
32 MAG2/2/32, CMCB Minutes, 24 April, 19 August 1958, 12 February 1959.
33 Welensky Papers, 129/4, Werners to SR Cold Storage Commission, 'Proposed Purchase by Cold Storage Commission of Southern Rhodesia of Cold Storages in Kitwe, Livingstone and Lusaka', 31 July 1958.
34 Welensky Papers, 129/4, Cold Storage Commission, Memorandum, 'Acquisition of Certain Assets of Werner Group in Northern Rhodesia', 3 September 1958.
35 Welensky Papers, 129/4, Minister of Agriculture, Memorandum to Federal Cabinet, 'Proposed Purchase by the Cold Storage Commission of Cold Storages in Kitwe, Livingstone and Lusaka', 24 September 1958.
36 Welensky Papers, 130/2, Cabinet Conclusions FGC (59) 4, 15 January 1959.

37 Welensky Papers, 130/2, Cabinet Conclusions FGC (59) 4, 15 January 1959; Memorandum, Minister of Agriculture, 12 January 1959; FGC (59) 21, 1 June 1959; 157/3, Chairman, Cold Storage Commission (A. L. Bickle) to Minister of Agriculture (J. C. Graylin), 1 April 1959, 10 April 1959; 131/2, 'Minutes of a Meeting to Discuss the Purchase of Cold Storages in NR', 22 June 1959; Galaun Papers, 'Record of a Meeting Held in Bulawayo on … 19th March 1959 between Representatives of the Werner Group and the Cold Storage Commission'; interview with D. Susman.

38 Galaun Papers, 'Record of a Meeting', 19 March 1959.

39 Welensky Papers, 131/2, Werners to Minister of Agriculture, 20 April, 1959; 157/3, Minister of Agriculture, Memorandum to Cabinet Economic and Development Committee, 20 April 1959; 131/2, 'Minutes of a Meeting to Discuss Purchase of Cold Storages in NR', 22 June 1959; 133/1, Minister of Agriculture, Memorandum to Cabinet, 17 September 1959; 133/3, Copy of Contract between Werners and Cold Storage Commission, signed and dated 30 October 1959; Cabinet Conclusions, 2 October 1959; 157/2, Cabinet Economic and Development Committee Minutes, 30 April 1959; Werners Minutes, 31 May 1959; interview with D. Susman.

40 ZCCM Archives, NCCM/RC/HO 522/2, O. B. Bennett to D. A. Etheredge, 19 January 1959; Werners Minutes, 31 May 1959; Copperfields Cold Storage Minutes, Annual Reports, 1960–4.

41 Rabb, 'Memoirs'; Horwood Report, 50–1; WP, 'Report to Werners Shareholders Committee', 1970.

42 J. Chileshe, *Abe Galaun*, 80; interviews with Abe Galaun and D. Susman.

43 SP, M. Barnett to H. Wulfsohn, 24 April 1963.

44 WP, 'Report to Werners Shareholders Committee', 1970.

45 Ibid.; interviews with E. Wulfsohn, O. Irwin and L. Pinshow; Cold Storage Board of Zambia, *Annual Reports*, 1969–74.

46 WP, Werners Papers; ZRC, Mazabuka, Werners Rent Book, 1974–83; interviews with E. Wulfsohn, O. Irwin and L. Pinshow. See below Chapter 22.

16 The Gersh Brothers

1 Macmillan and Shapiro, *Zion in Africa*, 92–3.

2 NR Pioneer Settlers' Association Papers, courtesy of Heather Chalcraft.

3 Macmillan and Shapiro, *Zion in Africa*, 173–4, 214–15; D. Jacobson, *Heshel's Kingdom* (London: Hamish Hamilton, 1998).

4 SP, M. Gersh to D. Susman, 12 November 1994; interview with Revée Gersh.

5 ZP15, Cost of Living Inquiry Commission, Evidence, Vol. X, M. Gersh, Kitwe, 31 July 1947.

6 Welensky Papers, 32/3, Association of Chambers of Commerce and Industry of Northern Rhodesia, Report on Discussions with the Chairman of the Unofficial Members, Kitwe, 1 February 1951; SP, E. Susman Diary, 5 July 1945.

7 ZP18, Closed Townships Commission, Verbatim Record of Evidence, Vol. II, Kitwe, April 1948; SEC1/1520/1 Closed Townships Commission Report.
8 Macmillan and Shapiro, *Zion in Africa*, 174–7.
9 African Commercial Holdings (Afcom) Minute Book, 12 March 1951, 6 April 1952; Central African Motor Services (CAMS) Minute Books, 27 March 1951, 10 July 1951, 15 September 1953, 1 September 1956.
10 CAMS Minutes *passim*; Welensky Papers, 43/4, M. Gersh, 'Memorandum on the Suspension of Duties on British Motor Vehicles Imported into Northern Rhodesia from the United Kingdom', 31 March 1952 and subsequent correspondence.
11 Interview with Bernard Gersh; Baylies, 'The State and Capital Formation in Zambia', 974.
12 Macmillan and Shapiro, *Zion in Africa*, 152; Afcom Minutes, 12 March 1952, 16 March 1954.
13 Kaleya Estates Minute Book, *passim*.
14 Interview with Revée Gersh; communication from chairman, Electra Trust; H. Barty-King, *Girdle Round the Earth* (London: Heinemann, 1979), 311–20.
15 Afcom Minutes, Statutory Report, 30 November 1949.
16 Interview with Revée Gersh; Welensky Papers, 87/1, M. Gersh to Welensky, 26 June 1952.
17 Afcom Minutes, 29 September 1956, 25 September 1961; interview with Neil Molver, and communication from Bernard Gersh.
18 Afcom Minutes, 19 June 1952, 9 July, 17 November 1953, 8 June 1954, 18 November 1954; communication from D. Susman.
19 Baylies, 'The State and Capital Formation', 292; Afcom Minutes, 9 July 1953, 30 September 1960, 21 March 1964.
20 Interview with A. Fuller; see also Northern Bakeries Minute Book.
21 Interview with A. Fuller; Afcom Minutes, 15 September 1958.
22 Afcom Minutes, 16 March 1954, 11 February 1958, 2 August 1960, 25 September 1961.
23 Afcom Minutes, 9 July 1953.
24 Afcom Minute Book, 11 February, 11 June 1958, 21 May 1963, 24 June 1965.
25 Interview with and communications from Ron Woolf.
26 Interview with and communications from Ron Woolf; Afcom Minute Book, 8 June 1966; CAMS Minute Book, 8 June 1966.
27 Welensky Papers, 476/4, M. Gersh, 27 July, 12 November 1953.
28 Welensky Papers, 44/1, M. Gersh to Welensky, 5 September 1953, and M. Gersh, Memorandum, 'Is Taxation Really Low in Northern Rhodesia?', n.d. [late 1953].
29 Welensky Papers, 205/11, M. Gersh, 'Memorandum to the Monckton Commission', paragraph 3, enclosed in Gersh to Welensky, 10 March 1960.
30 Welensky Papers, Memorandum to the Monckton Commission, paragraph 8.

31 Ibid., paragraphs 10–30.
32 Welensky Papers, 347/6, M. Gersh, 'Memorandum on Industrial Policy Presented by the Kitwe and District Chamber of Commerce and Industry to the Committee on Industrial Policy', 9 November 1959, f. 1.
33 'Memorandum on Industrial Policy', f. 1.
34 Ibid., ff 1–4.
35 Ibid., ff 4–8.
36 Welensky Papers, 220/3, Gersh to Welensky, 7 February 1962; interviews with Edward Shamwana, Andrew Kashita and Bernard Gersh; Afcom Minutes, 2 March 1967.
37 Afcom Minutes, *passim*; interviews with Revée Gersh and Ron Woolf.

17 Primary Industry: Zambezi Saw Mills

1 Interviews with D. Susman, Victor Riva and Tom Robson.
2 SP, E. Susman Diary, 16–19 July 1945; RP, E. Susman to Messrs Frões and Portela, 29 June 1948 and Zambesia Holdings (Pty) Ltd, Minutes, 29 June 1948.
3 *Annual Reports of Department of Agriculture*, 1940–6 (Lusaka: Government Printer, 1941–7), these include reports on forestry; J. D. Martin, 'The Baikiaea Forests of Northern Rhodesia', *Empire Forestry Journal*, 19 (1940), 8–18.
4 H. Meebelo, *African Proletarians and Colonial Capitalism* (Lusaka: Kenneth Kaunda Foundation, 1986), 142–9.
5 SEC1/950, Zambezi Saw Mills (ZSM) to CS, 10 August 1940 and C. J. Lewin, Minute on above, 12 September 1940.
6 SEC1/950, C. Duff, 'Proposed Sale of Rhodesian Teak in Barotseland to ZSM under a Ten-Year Lease', n.d.; Memoranda by J. D. Keet and W. A. Robertson; ZSM Minutes, 'Precis of Meeting' with C. J. Lewin etc., 22 September 1946.
7 Duff, 'Proposed Sale of Rhodesian Teak'.
8 SEC1/949, C. E. Duff to Development Secretary (F. Crawford), 16 April 1947 (private).
9 Rabb, 'Recollections'.
10 SEC1/949, 'Minutes of Meeting with Governor, etc.', 12 May 1947; ZSM Minutes, 'Note on Discussions held at Government House', 12 May 1947.
11 SEC1/949, Duff to Crawford, 16 April 1947.
12 ZSM Minutes, Minutes of Meetings of Directors of the Old Company, 21 February, 14, 30 April, 17–20 May, 15, 30 November 1948; Meetings of Directors of ZSM (1948) Ltd, 22 September, 10 December 1948; Rabb, 'Recollections'.
13 ZSM Minutes, 9 July 1948; RP, E. Susman to M. Rabb, 19 July 1948; Rabb, 'Recollections'.
14 ZSM Minutes, 6 August 1947, 23 June 1952, 20 September 1954, 7 February 1964.

15 ZSM Minutes, 21 February, 30 April, 17–20 May, 10–11 June, 9 July, 22 September, 10 December 1948, 5 September 1949, 23 June 1950.
16 ZSM Minutes, 28 February 1949, 23 June 1950; RP, Rabb to E. Susman, 5 January 1951.
17 ZSM Minutes, 20 July, 1 October, 2 December 1951, 14 March 1952.
18 ZSM Minutes, 24 June 1952.
19 ZSM Minutes, 14 March, 10 May, 24 June, 6 November 1952; RP, E. Susman to Rabb, 26 May, 26 August, 5 September 1952.
20 Beckett Papers, Correspondence with Rhodesia Railways, 1957–8; interviews with Victor Riva, son of H. V. Riva.
21 Interviews with Victor Riva, and see below.
22 WP, H. Wulfsohn, 'Memorandum to the Trustees of the Harry Wulfsohn Estate', November 1966.
23 Interviews with E. Wulfsohn, D. Susman and T. Robins.
24 ZSM Minutes, 17–20 May, 10–11 June 1948; *Annual Report of Forest Department*, 1948 (Lusaka: Government Printer, 1949).
25 ZSM Minutes, 17–20 May 1948, 6 November 1952, 17 September 1953, 30 April 1961; *Annual Reports of Forest Department*, 1948–60 (Lusaka: Government Printer, 1949–61).
26 ML1/14/15, ZSM to Minister of Land and Natural Resources, 31 May 1961; *Annual Report of Forest Department*, 1949, and subsequent reports.
27 ZSM Minutes, 26 May, 12 July 1961 and 'Underwood Committee Report', copy included with minutes.
28 ML1/14/15, ZSM to Minister of Lands and Natural Resources, 31 May 1961; Consultant's Report and Annexures, 8 February 1962.
29 ML1/14/15, 'Record of a Meeting … in the Ministry of Land and Natural Resources on 29 August 1961 to Discuss Future Operations of the Zambesi Saw Mills in the Barotse Teak Forests'; SP, D. Susman to W. Simpson, 6 October 1961; M. Rabb to D. Susman, 18 October 1961.
30 Government of the Republic of Zambia, *Annual Reports of Forest Department*, 1964–8 (Lusaka: Government Printer, 1965–9).
31 ZSM Minutes, *passim*; Rabb, 'Recollections'.
32 ZSM Minutes, 23 June, 28 September 1955; Rabb, 'Recollections'; interviews with T. Robson and T. R. Robson.
33 ZSM Minutes, 18 May 1962, 6 September 1963, 18 September 1964, 19 February 1965.
34 SP, W. Simpson to all Directors, ZSM, 13 July 1962, 'Purchase of the Share Capital of Vigers Brothers Limited: London'.
35 Rabb. 'Recollections'; SP, R. M. Campbell to D. Susman, 25 May 1962, Memorandum, 'Reasons for the Requirement of Exchange Control Permission for the Purchase of the Share Capital of Viger [*sic*] Bros. Ltd. London', n.d. [May 1962].

36 ZSM Minutes, 14 August, 16 September 1956, 21 March, 17 September 1957, 7 March, 30 September 1958, 20 January 1959, 6 September 1963. Much of the information about the railway and its staff in these paragraphs comes from the following sources: Anon., 'The World's Longest Private Railway Serves Giant Mill', *Rhodesia Herald* (n.d.); Anon., 'Northern Rhodesia's Oldest Industry', *Shell in Industry* (Shell Company of Rhodesia), 1 (1960), 8–12; Anon., 'The Strangest Railway in the World', *Horizon* (RST House Magazine), August 1964, 16–21; Anon., 'Zambezi Sawmills', *Z Magazine*, March 1972. I am very grateful to G. M. Calvert of Plumtree, Zimbabwe, for information on the history of the railway.
37 Interview with Rob Hart.
38 Interview with Rob Hart; Calvert, 'The Zambesi Saw Mills Railway from 1911–64', 484; ML1/14/15, Consultant's Report, 8 May 1962.
39 Calvert Papers, Bob Beaton, MS of Speech to Livingstone Rotary Club, 1963–4.
40 ZSM Minutes, 23 June, 16 October 1950; Calvert, 'The Zambesi Saw Mills Railway', 480–1.
41 Anon., 'Northern Rhodesia's Oldest Industry', 8–12.
42 ZSM Minutes, 18 June 1965.
43 ZSM Minutes, 19 February, 18 June 1965.
44 ZSM Minutes, 7 June 1963, 7 February 1964, 19 November 1960.
45 ZSM Minutes, 19 February 1965, 18 November 1965, 11 January, 12 April, 29 June, 26 October 1966; SP, Bill Olds to M. Rabb, 30 December 1965.
46 ZSM Minutes, 18 November 1965, 11 January, 20 December 1966; WP, 'Record of Discussions between Representatives of Ministries and Directors of ZSM, Livingstone', 7 January 1967; interview with Andrew Sardanis.
47 ZSM Minutes, 23 March 1967; ZSM Minute Book, copy of Wulfsohn, Rabb and Gersh to Griffiths, 25 January 1967, Griffiths to Ministry of Labour, 27 January 1967.
48 K. D. Kaunda, 'Zambia Towards Economic Independence', in B. de Gaay Fortman (ed.), *After Mulungushi* (Nairobi: East African Publishing House, 1969), 63; ZSM Minutes, 19 January, 21 February, 4 July 1968; Redwood Investments Minutes, 13 November 1968; WP, Memorandum, 'Zambesi Saw Mills (1948) Ltd (Now known as Redwood Investments Limited)', 1968; Redwood Investments, Annual Report, 1971–2; Minutes of Meeting of Shareholders in SB & W, 19–20 August 1972. For a different account of the takeover, see Sardanis, *Africa: Another Side of the Coin*, 218.
49 Interviews with Edwin Wulfsohn, and Peter McCarter, Provincial Forestry Action Programme, Lusaka; and information from G. M. Calvert, G. Roberts and John Fynn.

18 Secondary Industry: Northern Rhodesia/Zambia Textiles

1. W. J. Busschau, *Report on the Development of Secondary Industries in Northern Rhodesia* (Lusaka: Government Printer, 1945), 40; *Livingstone Mail*, 1 June 1945.
2. Northern Rhodesia Textiles (Nortex) Minutes, 26 October 1946, 23 April 1957, 12 June 1965; Rabb, 'Recollections'; Carolyn Baylies, 'The State and Capital Formation in Zambia' (Ph.D. dissertation, University of Wisconsin, Madison, 1978), 291.
3. RP, List of Shareholders in Nortex, *circa* 8 May 1950.
4. Interview with Chris Myburgh; Rabb, 'Recollections'.
5. Macmillan and Shapiro, *Zion in Africa*, 99–100; Nortex Minutes, 11 May 1947; RP, E. Susman to Rabb, 23 April 1947; Rabb to H. Wulfsohn, 25 February 1950; Rabb to E. Susman, 25 February 1950.
6. RP, Rabb to E. Susman, 25 May 1950; Rabb, 'Recollections'; Nortex Minutes, 10 July 1956.
7. Nortex Minutes, 17 April, 17 July 1955.
8. Nortex Minutes, 26 May 1960, 25 September 1959, 17 July 1963.
9. *Livingstone Mail*, 28 September 1962; Nortex Minutes, 25 September 1962; Beckett Papers, J. de Haas, 'Report on Year to June 1964'.
10. Nortex Minutes, 25 September 1962, 7 March 1963; Rabb, 'Recollections'; Beckett Papers, J. de Haas, 'Report on Year to June 1964'; interview with Chris Myburgh.
11. Nortex Minutes, 23 December 1963, 29 May 1964; interview with C. Myburgh.
12. Beckett Papers, Rabb to J. de Haas, 22 September 1964; J. de Haas to Rabb, 25 September 1964; J. de Haas to Rabb, 15 September 1964; J. de Haas, 'Report to Directors', 31 August 1964; interview with C. Myburgh.
13. Beckett Papers, W. J. van der Merwe to Directors, Nortex, 14 April 1965.
14. Zambia Textiles, Annual Reports, 1971–2.
15. Concorde Investments, Executive Committee Minutes, 1972–4; Zambia Textiles, Chairman's Reports, 1975–6.
16. Concorde Investments Minutes, 20 March 1976, 4 February 1978.
17. Zambia Textiles, Chairman's Reports, 1979–81.
18. Concorde Investments Minutes, 17 February 1979, 15 January 1980.
19. Zambia Textiles, Chairman's Reports, 1981–3; Concorde Investments Minutes, 20 March 1984, 17 April 1985.
20. Interviews with Chris Myburgh and Charles Tilasi, a former weaver; Concorde Investments, Annual Report, 31 March 1987.
21. Concorde Investments Minutes, 5 July 1989.
22. Concorde Investments, Executive Committee Minutes, 24 October 1987, 5 July 1989; interviews with V. Cohen and E. Wulfsohn; communication from E. Wulfsohn.
23. Interviews with F. Fonseka, MD, Mr Pereira, Production Manager, Simon Zukas, Chairman, 2001.

24 Interviews with S. Zukas and Bernard Gadsden, Provisional Liquidator, and communication from S. Zukas, 2003.

19 Farms and Ranches

1 SP, E. Susman Diary, 22 June 1945; interview with Edwardina Neethling, Morester Farm, Lusaka.
2 SP, E. Susman Diary, 7 July 1945; RP, H. Wulfsohn Ltd, Minutes of Second AGM, 9 August 1946; Memorandum of Agreement between E. Susman, H. Wulfsohn and M. Rabb, 10 August 1946.
3 L. J. Vaughan to W. L. Robinette, 12 May 1962, quoted in Robinette, 'Biology of the Lechwe and a Proposed Game Management Plan for Lochinvar Ranch', January 1963, unpublished paper, copy in ML1/17/50.
4 Robinette, 'Biology of the Lechwe'; ZNA (no file reference), Annual Report, Southern Province, 1938; Marianne MacDonald, 'King of the Blockbuster', *Sunday Times: Inside Magazine* (Johannesburg), 11 May 1997; Rabb, 'Recollections'.
5 Robinette, 'Biology of the Lechwe'; A. H. Mulongo, 'Land Use Conflicts on Lochinvar National Park: an Example of Contradictions in Environmental Policy, 1950–75', *Zambia Journal of History*, 1 (1981), 61–75; Welensky Papers, Barnett to Welensky, 20 March 1952; RP, Rabb to E. Susman, 31 October, 17 November 1951; WP, Lochinvar Guest Book.
6 Fraser Darling, *Fraser Darling in Africa*, 102–3.
7 F. Fraser Darling, *Wild Life in an African Territory* (London: Oxford University Press, 1960), 37–8.
8 J. Huxley, *The Conservation of Wild Life and Natural Habitats in Central and East Africa* (Paris: UNESCO, 1961), 48–51; Robinette, 'Biology of the Lechwe'.
9 *Livingstone Mail*, 27 September 1946; Rabb, 'Recollections'; R. Rhoderick-Jones, 'Westminster, Orange Free State, South Africa: an Imperial Adventure', October 2000 (unpublished paper, by courtesy of R. Rhoderick Jones and the Duke of Westminster).
10 Sir R. Prain, *Selected Papers, 1958–60* (London: privately printed, 1961), 75–7; Sir R. Prain, *Reflections on an Era* (Letchworth: Metal Bulletin Books Ltd, 1981), 122–5; Anon., *Kafue Flats: a Development Plan* (produced on behalf of the Kafue Flats Pilot Polder Trust by the Public Relations Department of the Rhodesian Selection Trust Group of Companies, n.d. [1962]); ML1/9/4, 'Kafue Polder Pilot Scheme', C. W. Lynn to Permanent Secretary, Ministry of Agriculture, 18 December 1961.
11 Robinette, 'Biology of the Lechwe'; interview with Len Pinshow.
12 BNA, DCMA8/8, 'Minutes of the General Meeting of the Ngamiland Cattle Exporters Association held at Riley's Hotel, Maun, 22 February 1957'; Hubbard, *Agricultural Exports and Economic Growth*, 144–5.
13 Nanga Estates Minutes, 22 June 1962.

14 ML1/17/50, 'Purchase of Lochinvar', Memorandum on History of Lochinvar by Hungerford, 20 February 1962.
15 SP, M. Barnett to D. Susman, and Lochinvar Estates to Commissioner of Lands, 26 June 1964; ML1/17/87, E. L. Button, Memorandum to President Kaunda, April 1965; D. Talmage, Private Secretary to President Kaunda, to Permanent Secretary, Ministry of Lands, enclosing Minute by President Kaunda, 22 April 1965.
16 ML1/17/87 'Record of Meeting ... with Representatives of Nanga Estates Ltd, the Proprietors of "Lochinvar" Ranch', 29 June 1965.
17 ML1/17/87, Minutes of Meeting with H. Wulfsohn, 8 November 1965; M. Rabb to President Kaunda, 14 December 1965; Draft Memorandum to Cabinet, 1 February 1966; Nanga Estates to Permanent Secretary, Ministry of Lands, 20 April 1966; Permanent Secretary, Ministry of Lands to Nanga Estates, 30 June 1966; Lochinvar Lodge Visitors' Book, 17 October 1966; *Lochinvar National Park* (Lusaka: map and brochure published by the Survey Department, 1986).
18 Chambishi Farms Ltd Minutes, 1961–75; Kansuswa Farms Ltd Minutes, 1955–72; Livingstone Jersey Farm Ltd Minutes, 1956–63; Rabb, 'Memoirs'.
19 Agricultural Enterprises (AE) Ltd Minutes, Memoranda of Meetings 26 September 1946, 15 February 1947; Minutes of Statutory Meeting, 8 March 1947; Minutes of Meeting of Directors, 8 March 1947; Beckett Papers, Ellis and Co. to J. W. A. Parkhurst, 27 November 1946, preliminary agreement on AE Ltd.
20 Beckett Papers, Beckett to Wulfsohn, 20 August 1949; Beckett to Boyd, 11 September 1949; Beckett to Wulfsohn, 8 October 1950; interview with Peter Green.
21 Beckett Papers, Beckett to E. Susman, 30 January 1951.
22 AE Ltd Minutes, Beckett to Chairman and Directors, AE Ltd, 5 June 1949; AE Minutes, 1 August 1951, 10 July 1952, 11 April 1953, 22 February 1954; AGM, 15 October 1953.
23 Interview with Peter Green.
24 Interview with Mike Beckett.
25 SP, E. Susman Diary, 31 July 1955; *Central African Post*, 20 April 1956; Werners Minutes, 10 August 1957; RP, D. Susman to H. Wulfsohn, 13 August 1957; SP, M. Barnett to H. Wulfsohn, 12 November 1963.
26 SP, M. Barnett to D. Susman, 26 June 1964; interview with E. Wulfsohn.
27 WP, ZRC, 'Report to Shareholders', *circa* 1969; R. Murray-Hughes, 'Demo Estate', *Northern Rhodesia Journal*, 3: 5 (1958), 435.
28 WP, ZRC, 'Report to Shareholders', *circa* 1969; SB & W Minutes, 17 November 1967; Concorde Minutes, 20 March 1984; SB & W, 'Management Report to Shareholders', August 1972.
29 Concorde Minutes, 20 January 1983; ZRC Minutes, 28 February 1983; interviews with E. Wulfsohn and R. Clyde-Anderson.

30 ZRC Minutes, 1968–76, *passim*; SB & W, 'Management Report to Shareholders', August 1972 (with Concorde Investments Minutes); Concorde Executive Committee Minutes, 21, 25 October 1977; interviews with R. Clyde-Anderson and E. Wulfsohn.

31 ZRC Minutes, 10 September 1975, 2 June, 23–4 November 1982; Concorde Executive Committee Minutes, 21, 25 October 1977 (Annexure 1), L. A. Tuffin, 'ZRC and Forsyth's Estates Ltd: Intensification of Beef Production', 2–3 March 1981; Concorde Directors Minutes, 14–15 November 1981; Cold Storage Board of Zambia, *Annual Reports*, 1973–4.

32 Concorde Minutes, 11 January 1975, 14–15 November 1981; ZRC Minutes, 2 June, 23–4 November 1982, 10 December 1983; interview with E. Wulfsohn.

33 Interviews with E. Wulfsohn and Edwardina Neethling; Concorde Minutes, 4 February 1978; Concorde Executive Committee Minutes, 17 October 1984.

34 Dina Wulfsohn, 'Cattle Ranching in Zambia', *Livestock International*, February 1981, 8–10.

35 Concorde Executive Committee Minutes, 9, 10, 19 October 1973.

36 Concorde Executive Committee Minutes, 9 November 1978; Concorde Directors Minutes, 20 March 1976, 13 November 1976; Executive Committee Minutes, 18 October 1977; Rabb, 'Memoirs'; V. J. Mwaanga, *An Extraordinary Life* (Lusaka: Multi-Media Publications, 1982), 273–4; interviews with E. Wulfsohn and V. Mwaanga.

37 Concorde Directors Minutes, 13 November 1976, 4 February 1978, 13 February 1979, 15 January 1980, 5 March, 14–15 November 1981, 17 April 1985; interview with E. Wulfsohn.

38 Concorde Directors Minutes, 20 January 1983; for the career of Simon Zukas see S. Zukas, *Into Exile and Back* (Lusaka: Bookworld Publishers, 2002), and Macmillan and Shapiro, *Zion in Africa*, 239–46, 255–8.

39 ZRC Minutes, Concorde Investments, Directors and Executive Committee Minutes, *passim*.

40 SB & W, 'Management Report to Shareholders', August 1972; ZRC Minutes, *passim*.

41 Interviews with 'Rama' Rama Krishnan.

42 Concorde Directors Minutes, 5 July 1989, 21–4 February 1990.

20 From Conflict to Concorde

1 SP, D. Susman to B. Gelfand, 11 July 1962; Gelfand to Susman, 20 July 1962; D. Susman, Memorandum, 31 August 1962.

2 SP, H. Wulfsohn to D. Susman, 16 September 1963.

3 SP, D. Susman to H. Wulfsohn, 20 September 1963.

4 SP, D. Susman to H. Wulfsohn, 15 October 1963; M. Barnett to Susman, 23 September 1963; Rabb to Susman, 25 September 1963.

5 SP, H. Wulfsohn to D. Susman, 25 March 1964, and enclosure; Schwartz. Fine Kane and Company, Memorandum, 9 March 1964; N. Werksman to D. Susman, 6 March 1964.
6 RP, D. Susman to Rabb, 22 June 1964, 15 July 1964; Rabb to D. Susman, 7 August 1964; SP, H. Robinson to D. Susman, 11 August 1964; D. Susman to Rabb and Barnett, 20 August 1964.
7 RP, H. Robinson to M. Rabb, 17 May, 1 June 1966; D. Susman to H. Robinson, 31 May 1966.
8 Interviews with T. Barnett and Molly Emdin, and see above.
9 Communication from D. Susman.
10 Interview with G. Kates.
11 Interviews with D. Pitt.
12 Interviews with T. Robins and Freddy Wiesenbacher.
13 Interviews with Richard Emdin and Molly Emdin.
14 Trude Robins Papers, Johannesburg: Sir Arthur Benson to H. Wulfsohn, 19 May 1956; H. Wulfsohn to Sir Roy Welensky, 9 August 1963..
15 Interviews with and communications from E. Wulfsohn.
16 SB & W, and Werners, Meeting of Shareholders, 25 June 1969; Rabb, 'Memoirs'.
17 SP, 'Notes on Stenham and Crombie Holdings Ltd', n.d. [1962].
18 Interviews with and communications from Edwin Wulfsohn.
19 SB & W, Meeting of Shareholders, Minutes, 10 March 1973; Concorde Directors Minutes, 9 March 1974; communications from and interviews with E. Wulfsohn.
20 Concorde Executive Committee Minutes, 15 February 1979, 15 October 1980, and 24 October 1983.
21 SP, R. Herzstein to D. Susman, 7 July 1966, enclosing annual report; WP, Harry Wulfsohn, 'Memorandum to Trustees of the Harry Wulfsohn Estate', November, 1966; interviews with D. Pitt and C. Arnott.
22 SP, 'Report on Cattle Meeting', 7 October 1966; H. Wulfsohn to O. Jackson, 22 November 1966.
23 RMH Minutes, 18 March 1968, 1 March 1969; Concorde Executive Committee Minutes, 8 March 1974, 2 February 1978, 24 October 1983, Directors Minutes, 17 April 1985; interviews with R. Kays and A. Vlotamas.
24 ZSM Minutes, 7 June 1963, 18 November 1965; RP, Press Statement, Merger of Vigers Brothers and Stevens and Adams, 1963; Sue Birley, 'Barnes and Ward Ltd', (pseudonym for Vigers, Stevens and Adams).
25 Ibid.
26 Ibid.
27 Ibid.; Concorde Directors Minutes, 5 March, 14–15 November 1981, Executive Committee Minutes, 9 November 1978, 15 October 1980, 3 March 1981, 13 April 1982, 13 February 1985; interview with E. Wulfsohn.

28 SB & W, Minutes of Meetings of Shareholders, 19–20 August 1972, 10 March 1973; E. Wulfsohn, Memorandum on the History of Stenham Gestinor Limited; interviews with E. Wulfsohn.
29 SB & W, Minutes of Meetings of Shareholders, 20 August 1972, 10 March 1973; Concorde Executive Committee Minutes, 2 February 1978, 14 February 1979, 12 January 1980; Directors Minutes, 11 January 1975, 20 March 1976.
30 Wulfsohn, 'Memorandum'; Concorde Executive Committee Minutes, 8–9 May 1986.
31 Concorde Executive Committee Minutes, 12 January 1980, 24 October 1983; Wulfsohn, 'Memorandum'; Rabb, 'Memoirs'.
32 Most of the information in this and the next three paragraphs comes from Edwin Wulfsohn's Memorandum on the History of Stenham Gestinor, and from interviews with him.
33 Concorde Executive Committee Minutes, 3 June, 7 July 1975; Directors Minutes, 21–4 February 1990.

21 Emerging Markets? Trans Zambezi Industries

1 Zukas, *Into Exile and Back*, 176–97; interviews with Simon Zukas.
2 John Taylor, 'Africa: from Crisis to Sustainable Growth?' (London: James Capel, November 1991).
3 Anthony Martin, *Minding Their Own Business: Zambia's Struggle Against Western Control* (Harmondsworth: Penguin, 1975), 203.
4 Interviews with and communication from E. Wulfsohn; *International Herald Tribune*, 11 September 1995.
5 Communication from Hillary Duckworth.
6 Information from Trans Zambezi Industries (TZI) Annual Reports, 1993–2001.
7 James Capel Emerging Market Research, TZI, Prospectus, 1993; Deutsche Morgan Grenfell, TZI Information Memorandum, 15 July 1996.
8 Deutsche Morgan Grenfell, Information Memorandum, 15 July 1996; TZI Annual Reports, 1997–9.
9 James Capel, Prospectus, 1993; communication from E. Wulfsohn.
10 Deutsche Morgan Grenfell, TZI, Information Memorandum, 1996; ING Barings, Sub-Saharan Research, 'Trans Zambezi Industries, A Sub-Saharan Blue Chip in the Making', 12 June 1996.
11 Interviews with D. Pitt and C. Arnott.
12 TZI Annual Report, 1997; communication from E. Wulfsohn.
13 James Capel, Prospectus, 1993; Deutsche Morgan Grenfell, TZI Information Memorandum, 1996.
14 Deutsche Morgan Grenfell, TZI Information Memorandum, 1996; TZI Annual Report, 1999.
15 Deutsche Morgan Grenfell, TZI Information Memorandum, 1996.

16 Ibid.; ING Barings, Sub-Saharan Research, 1996; TZI Annual Report, 1997.
17 Deutsche Morgan Grenfell, TZI Information Memorandum, 1996; ING Barings, Sub-Saharan Research, 1996; interviews with R. Clyde-Anderson, 'Rama' Rama Krishnan and Patrick Wright.
18 Communications from S. Zukas and E. Wulfsohn.
19 Interviews with Carl Irwin, Jospeh Muliata (Manager, Zambeef, Mongu), the Litunga, Imwiko II, Geoffrey Mee.
20 Deutsche Morgan Grenfell, TZI Information Memorandum, 1996; TZI Annual Report, 1998; interviews with R. Clyde-Anderson and Carl Irwin.
21 TZI Annual Report, 1997; interview with Neil Slade.
22 Government of the Republic of Zambia, 'Poverty Reduction Strategy Paper' (draft), 2002.
23 TZI Annual Reports, 1997–2001; interview with Neil Slade; *Financial Gazette* (Harare, website), 3 June, 1 July 2004.
24 TZI Annual Report, 1999.
25 TZI Annual Reports, 1998–2001; communication from Hillary Duckworth.
26 WP, Circular letter from David Phiri, Chairman, ZRC, to Shareholders, 29 November 1999; communication from Hillary Duckworth.
27 Communication from Hillary Duckworth.
28 Communication from Hillary Duckworth.

22 Conclusion

1 E. Hobsbawm, *Age of Extremes: The Short Twentieth Century, 1914–91* (London: Abacus, 1995), 338.
2 N. Ferguson, *The House of Rothschild: The World's Banker, 1849–98* (Harmondsworth: Penguin, 2000), 351–68.
3 Interviews with Hessie Lowenthal and Isa Teeger; WP, Wulfsohn family trees.

Index

Aberfoyle plc, 397
Aberman, Isadore, 92
Abrahams, Maurice, 146
Adams, Alf, 240
Africa, Klaas, 22
'African advancement', 271–4, 313, 337
African Commercial Holdings, 209, 307–11, 369, 414
African Lakes Corporation, 118, 397
African nationalism 221–3, 235–45, 262, 417
African Stores Ltd, 226, 231, 232–4
Afrikaners, 14, 38–40, 170, 280
Agricultural Enterprises Ltd, 362–5
agricultural/horticultural produce: barley, 98; beans, 175; cassava, 199, 205; chickens, 405; cotton, 371; eggs, 405; flax, 10; grain, 11, 33, 38, 41–2, 47, 116, 199, 205, 254, 271; flowers, 405–6; groundnuts, 199, 205, 323; maize, 38, 47, 98, 153, 173, 175, 204–5, 274, 362, 364, 367; milk and dairy, 98, 361, 405; millet, 38,199, 205; pigs, 297, 361; rice, 199, 204–5, 254, 258, 274; sugar, 358, 360, 367; tea, 2; tobacco, 2, 306, 362–4, 371, 409; vegetables, 7, 98, 125, 403, 405–7, 410; wheat, 98, 153
Agriflora Ltd, 405–10, 419
Air transport, 37, 91, 117, 125, 145, 149, 190, 266, 306, 325, 451 n.; aircraft: Piper Cherokee, 262–3; Beaver, 264, 271; Vickers Vimy, 149; airfreight, 367, 407; airlines: Central African Airways, 264, 271, 306; Imperial Airways, 306; Thatcher Hobson Airways, 306; Zambesi Airways, 306; Zambia Airways, 264; Zimbabwe Express Airways, 402
Aitkens, Ferdinand, 27–9, 32, 41
Akafuna, Daniel, 139
Akanangisa Atangambuyu, see Mulena Mukwae, Sesheke
Alexander II, Tsar, 12
Aloo, Iqbal, 406
Amato Frères, (brothers), 304, 342
Amato, Ruben, 342
Amery, Leopold, 210
ANC (NR), 229, 235, 237–8, 243–4, 265, 290

ANC (SA), 82, 395
Anglo American Corporation, 158, 160, 222, 276, 279, 287, 295, 368, 370, 401, 403
Angola, 2, 43, 53, 72, 78–9, 102, 114–16, 149, 198–9, 330
Anti-Semitism, 12, 14, 21, 27–8, 32, 61, 77, 122, 131, 148, 167, 168, 176–7, 235, 328, 364, 412–13
Antonopoulos, George, 110, 114, 116
Arenson, Kevin, 391–2
Arenson, Paul, 392
Arnot, Frederick, 36
Arnott, Colin, 230, 256, 259, 385, 400–1
ART Corporation, 402–3, 409
Athlone, Earl of, 126
J. A. Austen and Company, 33
Austen, John, 30–3, 158
Baden-Powell, Lord, 191
Bakeries, 95–7, 309
Balovale (Zambezi), 68, 73–4, 76, 78–9, 198–201, 256
Bancroft (Chililabombwe), 306, mine, 311
Bancroft, J. A., 160
Bancroft Trading Company, 311
Bank of Zambia, 348, 350, 390, 399, 409
Barclays Bank, 170, 208, 223, 263, 324, 390, 401
Bard Discount House, 401–2
Barnett, Max, 197, 219, 221–38, 277–98, 312, 359–65, 373–9, 415, 417
Barnett, Sylvia, née Emdin, 197, 278
Barotse National Party, 238–45
Barotse National School, 53
Barotse Transport Company, 200–1, 204, 262–4
Barotseland (later Western Province), 1–8, 16–82, 101–19, 164–5, 168, 196–208, 212, 235–45, 261–71, 416
Barotseland Agreement, 265, 271
Barotseland Saw Mills Ltd, 331–3, 337
Bata Shoe Company, 372
Batoka, 198, 256
Beaton, Bob (and Donald), 335
Beaufort, Sir Leicester, 107

INDEX

Bechuanaland, 1–2, 16–17, 19, 71–2, 102, 120–38, 156–7, 168, 181–2, 238, 359, 386–7, 414, 417, and see Ngamiland
Bechuanaland Trading Association, 29, 123, 386
Becker, Miss, 143
Beckett, Geoffrey, 175, 184, 228, 236, 284–5, 289, 323, 333, 341, 362–4, 415
Beckett, Mike, 176, 364
Beef (see also cattle), 19, 96, 165, 284, 286, 288, 367
Béguin, Reverend Eugene, 35, 42
Beit, Alfred, 5, 412
Beit, Sir Alfred, 356
Beit Trust, 171
Ben-Gurion, David, 213
Bernhardt, Prince, 361
Berry, Hugh, 310, 316
Bickle, A. L., 293
Bicycles, 37, 99, 170, 198, 206
Bihé, 20, 43
Billing, Malcolm, 164, 176–7
Bissett, S., 39
Bloch, M., 89
Blond, Anthony, 219
Blond, Elaine, 211, 216, 218
Blond, Neville, 211, 218
Blue Lagoon Ranch, 356
Blumenthal brothers, 63, 128
Board of Executors (BoE), 393
W. Bolus and Company, 106
Booker Brothers, McConnell Ltd, 248, 369, 417, 420
Botha, General Louis, 194
Botswana, see Bechuanaland.
Botswana Meat Corporation, 386
Botswana National Archives, 181–2
Bowood Farm, 98, 153
Boycotts, 29, 41–2, 53–4, 222, 244, 268, 290, 302, 417
Boyd, Robert, 175, 184, 358, 362–4, 415
Brand, Captain, 149
Brander, Bishop S. J., 81
Brattle, Louise, 95, 143, 147
Lewis Braude and Co., 22, 42, 92
BSA Company, 1–140, *passim*; 157, 226, 232, 244, 360, 375, 412
British West Charterland Company, 120
Broken Hill, 84, 97, 163
Brown Brothers Ltd, 390
Brunapeg Ranch, 98
Buchanan, George, 39, 61, 105, 115–16, 118, 152
Buffé, Charles, 336
Bulawayo, 16–17, 19, 21–2, 44, 70, 72, 92, 169, 315, 341–2, 350, 401
Bulozi, see Barotseland

Burton, Lendor, 371, 404, 406
Bushman Pits Ranch, 359
Busschau, W. J., 340
Butcheries, 95–7, 181–4, 276–99
Button, Errol, 360
Bwana Mkubwa, 157–9, 161, 169
Cable and Wireless (Holdings) Ltd, 307–8
Cable and Wireless Ltd, 307
Cairo Road (Lusaka), 170–1, 175, 178–9, 280, 305, 369
Caldicott, J. M., 286, 293
Campbell, Sir Jock (later Lord), 248, 250
Campbell, R. M., 231, 247, 268, 272, 383–5
Cape Town, 1, 16–17, 87, 92, 143, 146–7, 162, 209–12
James Capel Ltd, 396–7, 400
Capel, Major, 103
Capital: accumulation, 30–1, 44, 64–5, 106–7; investment, 46, 121, 130, 142, 159–60, 163–4, 185, 210, 232, 288, 313, 324–30, 337, 346, 354, 373–4, 383, 399–400; shortage, 106–7, 208, 288, 407
Caprivi Strip, 2, 38, 102–3, 182, 290, 331
Carden, Lt Colonel J., 89
Cars, see motor transport
Catt, C. W., 251–2
Cattle breeds: Afrikander, 164, 367; Barotse, 18–19; Boran, 367–8; Hereford, 367–8; Hereford/Afrikander, 368; Ila-Tonga, 18–19; Ngami, 18–19; Sanga, 18–19; South Devon, 153; Sussex, 367–8; Sussex/Afrikander, 364, 368; Zebu, 18–19
Cattle diseases: anthrax, 106; bovine pleuropneumonia, 108–16, 122, 130, 165, 183–4, 201; corridor disease, 370; East Coast fever, 98; foot-and-mouth, 134, 138, 359, 370, 403; rinderpest, 18–19; 'Sesheke sickness', 107–8; trypanosomiasis, 98, 107–8, 124
Cattle prices, 19–21, 30, 43, 47, 54, 64, 107, 129, 173, 197, 283–5, 290, 404
Cattle trade from: Balovale, 199; Barotseland, 18–21, 28–32, 42–4, 47, 53, 63–4, 98–9, 101–19, 106, 165, 169, 182, 183–7, 201–3, 275, 288–9, 404–5; Bechuanaland (Line of Rail), 184, 282–3; Caprivi Strip, 290; Namwala, 172–4; Ngamiland, 120–38, 158–9, 182–4, 281–3, 285, 289, 291, 359, 417; Southern Rhodesia, 133–4, 289–97
Cattle trade to: Angola, 19, 43, 114–16; Congo, 106, 127–36, 291–4; Copperbelt, 158–61, 276–99; South Africa, 122–3, 137–8, 163; Southern Rhodesia, 20–30, 47, 63–5
Cattle Marketing and Control Board, 152, 175–6, 189, 283–93
Messrs. Cavadia and Nephews, 172–4

Cavadia, Pangos (Pete), 172
CBC, 203, 247–8, 251, 259, 271, 301, 304–5, 311, 316, 341, 343, 369
CDC, 276, 281–6, 292, 359, 367, 417
Central African Cold Storages Ltd, 219, 287
CAMS, 305, 311, 316
Chalinga, Gore-Browne Mopani, 241, 243
Chalmers, J. A., 39, 40, 97–8
Chamberlain, Joseph, 95, 334
Chambishi Farm, 296, 361
Chapman, Sir Henry, 323–4
Charter Holdings Ltd, 226
Chase Manhattan Bank, 381, 390
Chavuma, 73, 78
Chawama Stores Ltd, 229
Chenga Farm, 362–5
Chibote Investments Ltd, 399
Chibote Meat Corporation, 404
Chikwanda, Alex, 369
Chiluba, Frederick, 395–6
Chilvers, Hedley, 71–3, 81
Chimba, Justin, 239
Chisamba Ranch, 370, 403
Chloride Group plc, 401
Choma, 175; Hotel, 175
Choma Farms, 362–5, 368, 409
Christians, Dougie, 202, 258
Christos, Spiro, 386
Cinemas, 93, 117, 168, 306
Clark, Percy, 32, 36
Clarke, F. J., 83, 129, 142, 150, 152, 174–5, 365
Clay, Betty, 191
Clay, Gervas, 191, 192
Cloete, Hermanus, 364
'Closed townships', 279–80, 301, 303–5
Clutton-Brock, Guy and Molly, 230
Clyde-Anderson, Rodney, 366, 368, 371
Coca-Cola, 304–5, 308
Codrington, Robert, 55–6, 61
Cogswell, Steve, 390
Cohen, Reverend Moses, 26, 85, 90, 144, 145
Cohen, Sam, 215
Cohen, Victor, 351
Coillard, François, 4
Cold Storage Board (NR), 201–2, 286
Cold Storage Board of Zambia, 298–9, 367, 405
Cold Storage Commission (SR), 284–98, 417
Collins, Frank, 288
Commission Reports: Bledisloe, 142; Closed Townships, 303–4; Cost of Living, 302–3; Federal Tariff, 314; Federal Review (Monckton) 235, 313; Hilton Young, 140; Horwood, 289–90, 296; Native Reserves, 153; Southern Province Land, 367; Turner, 289
Concorde Agricultural Development Ltd, 384

Concorde Asset Management, 391
Concorde Investments Ltd, 369, 373, 382–5, 387, 392, 397, 399, 401, 412, 418
Congo, 2, 26, 32, 44, 63, 83, 95, 97, 106, 111, 127–36, 149, 169, 234, 260, 283, 285, 291–5, 311, 342, 343, 344, 414, 419
Congo–Rhodesia Ranching Company, 98, 128, 354
Connaught, Duke of, 89, 90
Connaught, Prince Arthur of, 147
Continental Timber Products Ltd, 321
Consolidated Textiles, 340, 342, 344–6, 351
Cooke, R. T., 157
Co-operatives, 189–91, 205, 249, 254
Copper: price, 165, 189, 253, 275, 310; production, 184, 189, 314
Copperbelt, 127, 129, 142, 148, 157–61, 171, 183, 219, 276–317, 361, 382, 404, 414
Copperbelt Bottling Ltd, 316
Copperfields Cold Storage Ltd, 160–1, 182, 183, 186, 226, 276–99, 300, 355, 357, 366, 414
Corah's of Leicester Ltd, 211
Coryndon, Sir Robert, 6, 21, 27, 32, 35–6, 42, 54–7, 60, 83
Court cases, 40–3, 58–9, 73–8, 120, 131–3, 153, 277
Cranko, John, 219
Crawford, Sir Frederick, 244
Credit, 26, 40, 104, 111–12, 126–7, 170, 181, 303
Critchley, Colonel R. A., 356, 359–60
T. A. Crombie Ltd, 383
Currie, D., (transport rider), 39
Currie, Sir Donald, 13
Daniell, W. T., 40
Danzig, B., 39
Darling, Frank Fraser, 199, 355–6, 360
Darling, Major H. F., 358
Davidson, Basil, 230
Davis, C. J., 277
Davis, Fred, 95–6
Dawson, F. W., 35, 41–2
Dawson, James, 105, 110, 114, 413
De Beer's, 159
de Haas, Joe, 345–6
de Hemptinne, Monsignor, 128
de Kock, Dr, 203
Deaconos brothers, 123, 130, 396
Deaconos, L. G., 124–5, 137
Debenham, Frank, 2
Dechow, E. W., 161, 183–5, 277, 280
Demo Estate, 175
Dempster, William, 114
Development Bank of Zambia, 348

Diamond, A. B., 25–7, 29, 43, 61–3, 88, 92, 106, 110, 114, 118
Diamond, Harry, 61–2,
Diamond, Louis Solomon, 61, 63, 172
Diamond, Molly, 151
Diamond, Sid, 151, 248, 301, 304
Dix, Lionel, 239, 246–7, 251, 257–8, 262, 268–70, 272
Dobbin, John, 266
Donegan, Mark, 397
Messrs. Dorsky and Wulfsohn, 171, 173, 179–80
dos Remedios, Mario, 399
Drake, Paddy, 153
Dreyer, A. T. 'Braam', 40, 151, 154–6, 414
Drought, 122, 125, 138, 403, 408
Duba Training School, 371
Dubarry Trustees, 391
Dublon, Dr, 302
Duckworth, Hillary, 397, 399, 408–10, 419
Duff, Colin, 320–2, 339
Dunell, Ebden and Company, 106
Eason, Captain H. V., 121–2
Economy Stores Ltd, 161, 186, 209, 300–5, 310, 316, 341, 414
Edward VII, King, 27, 51
Edward VIII, King/Prince of Wales, 147–8, 151
Elakat, 128, 159, 283, 354
Elderkin, W. F., 152
Electra (North) Ltd/(South) Ltd, 307
Electra Trust, 328
Elisabethville, 63, 84, 97, 128–9, 234, 444 n.
Ellacombe, Dr, 143
Ellenberger, Vivien, 125
Ellenbogen, H. B., 31
Embakwe, 30–1, 33, 63
Emdin, Molly, 379
Emdin, Richard, 379
Emdin, 'Sonny', 197, 228, 384
Epstein, David, 105
Epstein, Gabriel, 62, 89, 101, 105, 109–14
Epstein, Hilda, née Crowngold, 105
Etoile du Congo (Star of the Congo) Mine, 32
Export Credit Guarantee Department, 347, 390
Faerber, Esther, née, 196–7, 341
Faerber, Jack, 196–8, 341
Falk, Josephine, née Wulfsohn, 168, 177
Farms and ranches, 97–100, 152–4, 353–72, 403–8
Federation of Meat Distributors, 287
Feinberg, Michael, 391
Field, H. H., 341
Financial services, 389–94, 401–2
Findlay, George, 39–40, 92, 105
Findlay, James, 39

Finkelstein, Joseph, 22, 49–50, 60
Finkelstein, Mr, 168
Fischer, Sergeant, 103
Fisher, J. T., 89
Flax, Meyer, 140
Fleming, Roddie, 409
Fleming Emerging Markets Trust, 399
Robert Fleming and Company, 397
Fletcher, L. A., 309, 341
Fonseca, W. T. S., 346
Forest Products Ltd, 332
Foreign exchange, see money
Forsysth, Hamish, 161, 357
Forsyth's Estates, 357, 366
Fort Rosebery, 257–62
Fox, Louis, 257
Fox-Pitt, Thomas, 197
Frame, Phillip, 340–2, 344–6, 351
Francistown, 1, 16–17, 21–2, 33, 40, 42–3, 72, 121
Messrs. Freedman and Grossberg, 92
Frões, Antonio, 318, 325
Frost, J. A., 117, 125, 126
Fuller, Arthur, 309
Fuller, Austin, 360
Fuller's Bakery, 309, 313, 316
Galanos (Greek trader), 64
Galaun, Abe, 164–5, 200, 221–2, 280–1, 293, 296, 415
Galaunia Farms, 370, 371, 404
Gelfand, Benny, 231, 373, 391
Gelman, Abe, 159, 285, 322–3, 325, 328, 340–2, 415
Gemmill, David, 399
George VI, King, 37, 191
Germany, 1–2, 102–3
Gerber, Mr and Mrs Jack, 170
Gerber Goldschmidt and Company, 207, 392
Gersh family: Bernard, 302, 316; Brenda, 302; Dora, née Susman, 84, 85, 87, 47; Errol, 302; Gertie, née Baron, 301–2, 316; Harry, 87, 147–8, 161, 221–3, 300–2, 310, 316, 414; Jacqueline-Wendy, 302; Maurice, 12, 22, 81, 147–8, 159, 161, 219, 249, 278, 300–17, 337–8, 341, 365–6, 384, 391, 414, 417, 419–20; Rayna, 302, 316; Revée, née Melamed, 219, 302, 312, 316
Gesowitz, A. L., 117
Gibbons, A. St Hill, 4, 23–4, 37
Girshowitz, Rabbi Emmanuel, 86
Gladstone, Lord, 93
Glass, Solomon, 81
Glasstone, Mr and Mrs Reuben, 179
Glennie, A. F. B., 203
Globe and Phoenix Mine, 30, 63
Goldberg, Jack, 92

Goldreich, Arthur, 235
Gonçalves, Antonio, 200
Goodman, Bruce, 209–10
Goode, Durrant and Murray, 226
Messrs. Gordon and Levitz, 40, 42–3, 52, 61
Gordon, Robert, 21, 28–9, 33, 39, 40, 42–3
Gordon, Robert (rancher), 354
Gore-Browne, Sir Stewart, 407
Gosman, Charlie, 335
Gould, Mark, 389
Goy, Auguste and Mathilde Keck, 23
Gramsci, Antonio, 45
Granat, Robert, 128
Granger, Robert, 20–1
Green, Peter, 351, 363–4
Green, Stewart, 341, 362–4, 415
Messrs. Greenberg & Kriegler, 159
Grenfell, Harry, 240, 375
Grieve, Alan, 389, 391
Griffiths, J. W., 337
Grill, Annie, see Susman
Grill, Faiga, 92
Grill family, 148
Grill, Marcus, 90, 91, 92
Grill, Solly, 93
Grogan, Francis, 404
Grossberg, Abraham, 22, 31
Grossberg, S. S., 31, 181
'Groundnuts Scheme', 323
Guest, Sir Ernest, 307, 310, 328
Gutu, 233–4, 261–2
Gwaai River, 97–8
Gwembe Development Company, 407
Haddon, Michael, 444 n.
Haddon, Theodore, 63
Haggard, Rider, 68
Haloba, Job Kanenga, 249–50, 269, 273–4
Hamelitz newspaper, 13
Hannover Re, 400
Hantche, J. J., 96–7, 128
Harare, 400–1, and see Salisbury
Harding, Colin, 1, 20, 54–6
Harrington, A., 110, 118–19
Hart, Rob, 202, 334
Harvey, David, 407
Haskins, George, 121
Haslett, Sam, 39, 110, 152, 170, 280
Hazell, William, 49, 55, 57–62, 68, 72–4, 77–8
Heale's Estates, 358, 359, 366
Health: 1, 8; blackwater fever, 25–7, 30, 34, 39, 46, 84, 103, 146; hospitals, 34–5, 84, 103; malaria, 35, 44, 143, 266, 281; smallpox, 105; tuberculosis, 87
Hebrew Congregations: Bulawayo, 20, 26, 85; Elisabethville, 26; Nkana-Kitwe, 170, 302, 308; Livingstone, 88, 144, 413; Lusaka, 179

Heenen, Gaston, 128
Henry, John, 325
Hepker brothers, 168–9
Hepker, Hermann, 29, 168–9
Hepker, Willie, 31, 159, 169, 415
Hereford's Ranch, 158
Herzl, Theodor, 86, 95
Herzstein, Ralph, 230, 385
Hirschberg, A., 96
Hitler, Adolph, 87, 177
Hobday, John, 184, 284–5, 288, 414
Hobsbawm, Eric, 412
Hobson, J. D. H., 309
Hochstein, Lewis, 147, 150, 186
Hodges, Colonel John, 233–4, 261,
Hole, H. M., 70–72
Holland, H. B., 204
Holub, Emil, 4
Hong Kong and Shanghai Bank, 390
Horn, John, 59, 443 n.
Horton, George, 98, 152
Horton, George (younger), 164
Hotels: Bwana Mkubwa, 157–9; Garden House, 396; Grand Hotel, 179; Nchanga, 160; Nkana, 160; North-Western, 90; Victoria Falls, 94; Windsor, 151, and see Riley's
Houghton, Roy, 263
Hubbard, David Wynant, 173–4, *Ibamba*, 173
Huggins, Sir Godfrey (Lord Malvern), 134, 222
Human, N. M., 25–7
Hunt, Leuchars, and Hepburn Ltd, 332
Huxley, Sir Julian, 356–7, 360
Ibamba Ranch, 173–4
Imperial Cold Storage Company, 285
Imwiko, Litunga, 38, 112, 117, 140–1, 191–2, 238, 239
Imwiko II, Litunga, 452 n.
Industrial Development Corporation (NR/Zambia), 247–54, 265, 313, 316, 337–9, 417; South Africa, 407
International Monetary Fund, 348
Investec Bank, 393
Irwin, Carl, 404
Irwin, Oliver, 298, 370, 384, 404
Isdell, Neville, 308
Israel, 85, 210, 213, 214, 225, 413
Jabotinsky, Vladimir, 145
Jacobs, Aaron, 92, 111–12
Jacobs, Jehiel, 140, 280
Jacobs, John (alias Witbooi) 67–82
Jacobs, Lewis and Michael, 92, 154
Jacobs, M. J., 102, 145
Jacobson, Dan, *Heshel's Kingdom*, 302
Jacobson, H. A., 61, 62, 122, 450 n.
Messrs. Jacobson and Kiehl, 62
Jacoby, Sabrin, 42

Jager, Tom, 320–4
Jaipur, Maharajah of, 210
Jalla, Reverend Adolphe, 6, 52
Jameson, Dr L. S., 68, 71, 72, 111
Jews, 9–15, 38–41, 61–2, 130, 167, 176, 235, 280, and see refugees and traders
Joffe, Elton, 230, 246–7, 251, 270, 272–3
Joffe, Esmée, 230
Johannesburg, 16, 122, 209–10, 224, 322–3, 324
Johns, Harris, 102
Jones, Sir Glyn, 203
Jones, Simon, 399, 409
Judaism, 11–12, 144, 167–8, 413
Jutzen, E. F. R., 310
Kabulonga Farm, 153
Kafue Flats, 354–8
Kafue Flats Pilot Polder, 358
Kala Ranch(ing Company), 183, 362, 366, 368, 415
Kalabo, 53, 405
Kalangwa Estates, 403, 406
C. Kaldis and Company, 295, 306
Kaleya Estates, 306, 316, 365–8
Kalman, Barbara, 391
Kalomo, 35, 40, 57, 98, 169
Kalonga, Chief, 108
Kalue, Edward, 139
Kalufwelu, James, 257, 272–3
Kalulu, Solomon, 360
Kamitondo, Benson, 245, 270–1
Kansanshi, 32, 234, 314
Kansuswa Farm, 296, 361, 366
Kantor, Jimmy, 235
Kanyonyo, 61, 62
Kapelus, Ivan, 392
Kapenta (dried fish), 265
Kapwepwe, Simon, 239
Kashita, Andrew, 252, 254
Katema, Induna, 57
Kates, Geoffrey, 205–7, 230, 245, 246–7, 251–3, 259–62, 267–73, 344, 378
Katilungu, Lawrence, 222
Kaufman family, 343
Kaufman, Basil, 343
Kaufman, Sons and Company, 205, 229, 383, 385
Kaunda, President Kenneth, 222, 229, 235–6, 242, 244, 247–8, 253, 265, 290, 298 306, 337, 348, 360, 361, 367–8, 395
Kavindele, Enock, 351, 369–70
Kays, M. T. (Old Tom) 123, 228, 281
Kays, Tom (Young Tom), 228
Kays, Ronnie, 228, 386–7
Kazungula, 1–4, 7–8, 18–19, 20, 51, 64, 281–3, 359
Kee's (Lusaka), 175, 305

Keet, J. D., 320–1
Kenya, 95, 405–6
Khama, King, 3, 28, 36, 52, 105
King, Eric, 366–7
King, Tom, 114, 129, 158
Kisch, Colonel Frederick, 145
Kitwe, 161, 226, 276–9, 287–8, 291–5, 300–15, 361
Knight & Folkestad Ltd, 155
Knight, Charles S., 155, 318–19, 323–4, 414
Knight family, 323
Knight, Sidney, 324
Knutzen, Sofus, 155
Knowles Jordan, E., 77
Kollek, Teddy, 214
Kollenberg, David, 172
E. Kollenberg and Sons, 301
Kollenberg, Edward, 21–2, 160, 172
Kollenberg, Gerald, 299
Kollenberg, Henrie, 160, 172–3, 178
Kollenberg, Isadore, 159–60, 172, 183–4, 277–8, 287, 300, 359, 415
Kominsky, Max, 38–9, 42, 45, 86, 88
Kopelowitz, Elias, 198
Kopelowitz, Paul, 92
Kossuth, Fred, 216
Kruger, President Paul, 13, 71
Krystallnacht, 178
Kuomboka ceremony, 265
Kunda, Dr Rajah, 274
Kutoma, Ernest Mukwendela, 270
Kutoma, Henry Makiti, 239–40
Kuzniar, Patsy, 258–9
Kuzniar, Steve, 258–60
Kyundu Ranch, 370, 404
Labour, 127, 153, 266–75, 280, 310, 319, 329, 336–8, 344, 350, 352, 363, 406
Labour migration, 47–8, 112, 116, 118, 140, and see WNLA
Labuschagne, Barend C. 'Rooi', 40, 114
Banque Lambert, 128
Lambert, Baron Henri, 128
Land tenure, 127, 153, 312, 367
Landau Brothers, 26, 40, 92, 106, 114, 412
Landau, David, 26,
Landau, Dr J. L., 195
Landau, Morris and Louis, 26
Lane, A. J., 109
L'Ange, Rex, 244, 312
Languages, 4–5, 14; Afrikaans, 14, 17; Damara, 281; English, 14, 17, 85, 140, 170; San, 281; Silozi, 4, 17, 40, 202; Sesotho, 4, 40; Setswana, 202, 281; Yiddish, 14, 167–8, 170, 219
Laski, Ann, see Susman.
Laski, Norman, 211, 218
Laski, Simone, 219

INDEX

Laski, Viola, 218
Latvia, 167–8, 172–3, 177, 181, 196, 413
Law, F. D., 59, 151
Lealui, 1–5, 27, 31–8, 51–66, 67, 68, 73, 74, 205–6, 238
Lechwe, Kafue or Red, see Wildlife
Lee, William, 157
Leon, Joe, 233–4
Leopard's Hill Ranch, 99–100, 147, 150, 152–3, 182, 186, 280, 353–4
Lesser, Levitz and Co., 21, 31
Lesser, Samuel, 21, 33, 43
Lessing, Doris, 230
Levenson, Delice, 456 n.
Levenson, Miriam, 168
Levenkind, Julius, 231
Lever Brothers, 342
Levin, Wolf, 22
Levitz, Fishel, 21, 29, 33, 39, 43, 54, 88, 101, 118
Levy, Leon, 293–4
Lewanika, Akashambatwa Mbikusita, 452 n.
Lewanika, Godwin Mbikusita, 189, 238–42, 265
Lewanika II, Litunga, see Lewanika, Godwin
Lewanika, King (Lubosi), 3–9, 15, 18–21, 24–5, 27–30, 32, 37, 38, 40, 43, 49, 51–66 81, 93, 104, 105, 108, 112, 121, 139, 189, 239, 413
Lewin, C. J., 320
Lewison, Bertha, see Susman
Lewison family, 94–5
Lewison, Jack, 116
Libonda, 5, 34, 61
Line of Rail, 47–8, 83, 95–9, 109, 113, 117, 175, 405, and see Railways
Lion's Kop Ranch, 98, 152
Lion Tile Ltd, 313
Lipalile, Mufana, 240
Liswaniso, Joel Mubiana, 269–70
Litia, Prince, see Yeta III
Lithuania, 9–15, 39, 167, 370
Livestock Cooperative Society, 152, 175, 280
Livingstone, 35, 56, 83–100, 142–52, 163–6, 181–6, 190–1, 236–7, 245–6, 251, 262, 266, 268–9, 273, 306, 324, 341–2, 374
Livingstone, Dr David, 7, 19, 365
Livingstone Cold Storage Ltd, 181, 183
Livingstone Cold Storage Works, 183–5, 283, 288–9
Livingstone Industrial Holdings, 345
Livingstone Jersey Farm, 361
Livingstone Mail, 36, 44–7, 63, 64, 67–9, 84, 86, 89, 90–1, 95–7, 101, 107, 109, 112, 131–3, 151–2, 153, 181, 185, 192, 195, 344

Livingstone Railway Museum, 333
Livingstone Saw Mills, 154
Lobatse Abattoir, 137, 185, 282–3, 286, 359
Lobengula, King, 3, 39, 40, 67–82, 105, 414
Lobito Bay, 43, 63
Loch, Sir Henry, 72
Lochinvar Ranch, 128, 219, 354–7, 359–61
Lochner Concession, 5
Lock, R. B., 123
Locusts, 172
Loebenberg, Ernst, 217
Logie, A. A. 195
London Metal Exchange, 189
London Missionary Society, 36, 71, 155
Lonrho Ltd, 311, 316, 351, 369, 399, 403, 406, 417, 420
Losikeyi, Queen, 72
Louw, J. J., 122
Lowe, Chris, 366–7
F. H. Lowe and Company, 181, 182
Lowenthal, Abe, 168, 177
Lowenthal, Conrad, 168
Lowenthal, Hessie, née Wulfsohn, 168, 177, 236
Lowenthal, Marlie, née Wulfsohn, 168
Lowenthal, William, 168
Lozi people, see Barotseland
Luanshya, 160, Roan Antelope Mine, 162
Lubita, Prince Ngombala, 239–40
Lubombo Ranch, 128
Luezi Ranch, 161
Lugard, Lord, 120
Lukona, see Kalabo
Lukolwe River, 78
Lukulu, 198
Lungwebungu River, 7, 73, 79, 198, 200
Lusaka, 153–4, 169–72, 178–9, 279–81
Lusaka Cold Storage Ltd, 222, 280–1, 288, 294, 296, 370
Lyashimba, Induna, 31, 34
Lynwood's Farm, 97–8, 153
Lyster, Mike, 263
Macaulay, F. C., 36, 39, 41
Macintyre, Sir Donald, 289, 333, 375
MacKnight, Dr D. S., 84
Macleod, Iain, 237, 238
Macmillan, James, 241
Madison Insurance Ltd, 401
Mafeking, 22, 44
Mafisa (cattle loaning), 19–20, 53
Maize Marketing and Control Board, 175, 189
Makue, John, 81
Malan, Dr D. F., 168
Malawi, 2, 319, 343, 401, 419
Malcolmson, Rodney, 237
Malevris (Greek trader), 63

Managers/management, 150, 152, 186, 195–7, 202–5, 215, 229–31, 251–3, 256–76, 310, 324, 337, 342, 364–7, 371, 382, 386–9, 419
Mandela, Nelson, 235, 395
Mankoya, 203–5, 256–8
Mannsbach, Fritz, 202
Mapanda Mill, 155
Mapanda Transport Company, 154, 155–6
Marakanelo Hotels Ltd, 386
Mark, R. J. N., 203–5
Marks, Sammy, 13
Marks, Sir Simon, 210, 211–19, 232, 415
Marks & Spencer, 209–20, 225, 229, 415
Masons, 277, 310
Matabeleland Trading Association, 92, 106, 111–12
Matauka, see Mulena Mukwae, Nalolo
Matero Reforms, 253
Mathiba, Chief, 120, 126
Maun, 122–6, 228, 281–2
Marxism, 230, 235
Massmart Ltd, 400–1
Maxwell, Sir James, 145
May, Dr Aylmer, 91
Maybank, Frank, 303–4
Mazabuka, 176, 411
Mazabuka Farms, 365–6, 409
Mbeki, Govan, 235
McDowell, Sir Henry, 333
McKee, Hugh, 175
McKillop, Mrs L., 268–9
McKinnon, Charles, 59, 62, 65
Meikle Brothers, 59, 105, 112
Meikle, Tom, 92, 112, 413
Menashe, B. I., 304
Mendham Farm, 404
Merber, Gertie, née Grill, 93
Merber (or Rabinowitz), Jacob, 93
Mercantile Investments Company (MIC), 391, 400
Merchandise, 32, 41, 53, 62–3, 206–7, 216–17, 229–30, and see trade goods
Mercury Asset Management, 399
Meridien Bank, 401, 404
Metro International Ltd, 400
Metro Megacentres, 400–1
Metzger, Cantor Feivel, 179
Michello, Job, 243
Millar, H. J. 'Jock', 192, 195
Mills, E. C. 'Anzac', 99–100, 115–16
Milner, Lord, 35, 55
Mitchell, Jimmy, 319
MMD, 351, 395–6
Molema, Dr S. M., 82
Molema, Chief Silas, 82
Momba Farm, 175

Monckts, J., 67–82, 414
Money: bills of exchange, 40–1, 111–12, 181, 303, 383; cash, 55, 127, 260, 263, 268; copper, 58, 88, 443 n.; exchange controls, 189, 303, 347–52, 368, 372, 389–90, 394, 417; gold, 20–1, 42, 58, 88; gold standard, 162; silver, 42, 88, 183; Sterling, 303
Mongu-Kanyonyo, 41, 51, 62, 73, 74, 77, 116–19, 202–3, 256, 262–6, 275, 404
Moore, (Sir) Leopold, 36, 44–5, 67, 69, 78, 84–5, 89, 91, 94, 131–3, 140, 148
Morgan Stanley Asset Management, 399
Morris, J. P. A. 'Seamus', 134, 165, 184
Mosenthal and Company, 26, 106, 412
Motor transport, 125–6, 148, 149–50, 200–1, 174; assembly plants: Land Rover, 311, 313; Willis Jeep, 311; franchises: Fiat, 305, Hudson, 303; Rootes (Commer, Hillman, Humber), 305, Rover, 305; Volkswagen, 311; types: Bedford, 262; Caterpillar, 319, 335; Chevrolet, 126; Dodge, 126; Ford Model T, 150; Fordson, 119; General Motors, 200; Land Rover, 240–2, 260, 262, 274, 311; Toyota Land Cruiser, 311
Moyo, Edwin, 410
Mozambique, 2, 318, 319, 322, 324–8, 343, 396, 415–16
Mozambique Company, 318
Mufulira, 160, 162, 171, 227, 276–9, 295, 316, 361
Mukande, Griffiths, 239, 240, 242
Mukobela, Chief, 173
Mulena Mukwae, Sesheke, 24, 32, 35, 36–8; Nalolo, 24–5, 27, 41, 43, 49, 51, 53–4, 57, 60, 104, 105
Mulobezi, 156, 165, 196, 319, 321, 329, 334, 336, 337, 338
Mulungushi Reforms, 247–50, 253, 338–9, 382
Mundia, Nalumino, 265
Mungaila, Chief, 173
Murray, Charles, 164
Mussolini, Benito, 195
Muwi-Muwi (Moi-Moi), Induna, 29–30, 51
Mwaanga, Joshua, 370
Mwaanga, Vernon, 369
Mwaiseni Stores, 248, 252, 404
Mwanawasa, President Levy, 506
Mwanawina III, Litunga, 139, 191, 205–6, 238–44, 264–5, 417
Mwandi, see Sesheke-Mwandi
Mwanza, L. P., 360
Mwila, B. Y, 404
Myburgh, Chris, 342, 345–6, 350
Mzilikazi (Umsiligaas), King, 3, 56
Nakambala Sugar Estate, 154, 358, 367
Nalolo, 5, 24–5, 27, 31, 34, 38, 51, 52, 53, 61–2

INDEX

Nalubuto, John, 344
Nalumango, Nelson, 139–40, 189
Namayamba, Induna, 29, 57, 60
Namibia, see South West Africa
Namwala, 172–4, 176
Nanga Ranch, 176, 357–8, 366
Naparstock, Shmerl, 102, 117, 124
National Westminster Bank, 388
Nchanga, 160–1, 171, 276, 300
Nchanga Trading Company, 300
Ndola, 63, 97, 161, 168–9, 301
Nedcor Bank, 393
Neethling, Edwardina, 353
Nell, Steve, 244, 251–2, 257–8, 269, 272–3
Nettleton, G. E., 122, 124
Ngamiland, 8, 20, 120–38, 163–4, 234, 281–3, 285, 289, 359, 386
Ngamiland Cattle Exporters Association, 359
Ngamiland Trading Company, 138, 182, 184, 227–8, 257, 281–3, 383, 386–7, 414
Nhau, Albert, 399, 409
Nicolai, P. C., 118, 192, 196
NIEC Ltd, 253, 274, 275, 404
Nkana, 157–8, 161–2, 301–2, 162, 301–2
Nkobo, Benford, 364, 371
Nkomo, Joshua, 368
Nkumbula, Harry, 189, 222, 235, 244, 290, 306
Norris, Wilfred, 210–11, 218
Northcote, H. A., 144
Northern Bakeries Ltd, 219, 309
Northern Caterers Ltd, 159, 161, 186, 197, 219, 231, 300, 304, 414
Northern Cattle Exporters' Pool, 283
Northern Produce and Livestock Company, 172–3
Northern Rhodesia (NR), *passim*
NR Association of Chambers of Commerce, 301
NR Cattle Owners' Association, 147
NR Defence Force, 302
NR Congress, 189,
NR Farmers' Union, 175
NR Municipal Association, 301
NR Rifle Association, 89
NR/Zambia Textiles Ltd, see Zambia Textiles
Northern Suppliers Ltd, 159
Northern Theatres Ltd, 306
NWR Commercial Association, 89
NWR Farmers Association, 114, 129, 147
NWR Rifle Association, 89, 103
Ntyekwa, Induna, 65
Nyasaland, see Malawi.
Nyirongo, D. J., 344
O'Connor, A. S., 39
Oginski family, 10–15
Oil crisis, 253, 275, 388–9

OK Bazaars, 215, 219, 247, 252
Okavango River/Delta, 7–8, 387, and see Ngamiland
Old Drift, 31, 44–5
Old Mutual, 393, 400–1, 410
Olds, Bill, 324, 337
Oliver, John, 355
Oppenheimer, Sir Ernest, 158, 159, 232
Oppenheimer, Harry, 222, 235
Orphanides, George, 130, 137
Ossewa Brandwag, 202
Osterlick, T. C. H., 309
Palestine, 84–7, 145–6, 169, 213, 301–2, 413
Palestine National Fund, 146
Panzera, F. W., 121
Paoli, Mauro, 343
Papenfus, L. N., 107
Paper and newsprint, 402–3
Paris Mission, 4, 18, 23–4, 36–7, 40, 42, 105, 192
Parkhurst, J. W. A., 182, 192, 228
'Partnership', 223, 237, 243
Partnerships, *passim* and 411–20
Payne, Marian, 259, 261–6, 273
Payne, Tim, 251, 257, 261–6, 268, 273
Peech, Chris and David, 400
Pentopoulos, M. S., 198
A. F. Philip and Co., 155, 321
Philip family, 155, 323
Philip, Dr John, 155
Philip, J. B., 337
Peimer, Samuel, 43
Pelletier, Godfrey, 341
Peregrino, F. Z. S., 121
Perlman, Jeff, 211–12
Pepsi-Cola, 308
Phiri, David, 399
Phiri, H. M., 351
Photography, 36–7, 52
A. & I. Pieters and Co., 86, 92
Pieters, I., 106
Pinshow, Len, 277–9, 298–9, 360–1
Pioneer Butchery and Bakery, 95–6, 151, 182
Pioneer Trading Company, 200
Pires, Alex, 200
Pitt, Denton, 230, 256, 259, 346, 352, 378, 384–5, 397–401
Plaatje, Solomon T., 120
Plumtree, 21–2
Poniatowski family, 10
Portela, Victor, 318, 325
Port Elizabeth, 26, 155
Potocki family, 10
Prain, Sir Ronald, 222, 358, 404
Premier Caterers Ltd, 181,
Premier Milling Company, 309, 342

Pretorius, Attie, 334
Pretorius, Mike, 201, 257, 269–70, 334
Price, Jack, 308
Price controls, 277, 284, 298, 303, 346–7, 388
Private enterprise, 292–7
Profit and loss, AE, 362, 364; Afcom, 311; Agriflora, 408; NTC, 127, 282, 386; ranches, 358–9; RMH, 232, 234, 253; SB, 30–1, 44, 64–5, 106–7, 157; SB & W, 195, 207–8; Stenham, 389–90; Vigers, 388–9; Werners, 294, 298; Zamtex, 346, 350, 352; ZSM, 321, 327, 329–30; TZI, 408; ZT, 252–3
Rabb, John, 383–4, 392–3, 399–400, 408–9, 412, 419
Rabb, Maurice, 165, 193–6, 201–2, 208, 222–8, 236–50, 253, 262, 264, 270, 272, 277, 293, 312, 330–1, 337, 341–7, 355, 359, 361, 368, 374–8, 381–4, 391, 413, 415, 417
Rabb, Peggy, née Susman, 98, 165, 192–5, 236–7, 382
Rabinowitz, Jacob, see Merber
Rabinowitz, Joseph and Golda, 194
Rabompo, Chief, 55
Racism, 32, 45, 49–50, and see anti-Semitism
Radziwill family, 10
Railways: Benguela, 198, 315; Central African, 318; Rhodesia, 155, 277, 315, 321–34; Shire Highlands, 318; South African, 332; Susmans', 138, 157; Tazara, 339; Trans-Zambezia, 318; Uganda, 95; Zambesi Saw Mills, 155–6, 165, 196, 200, 244, 319, 320, 329, 330, 333–8; Zambia, 333, 339, and see Line of Rail
Raine, E.R, 341–2
Raine Engineering Ltd, 309, 316, 341
Rama Krishnan, 'Rama', 371
Rand Cold Storage Ltd, 194, 288
Rangely, Henry, 40, 57,
Ratau, Induna, 37
Read, J. Gordon, 172, 173, 176
Redwood Investments Ltd, 339, 391
Refugees: Herero, 120; Jewish, 148, 177–9, 190, 302; Polish, 190, 258
Reutter, Dr, 35
Rey, Colonel Charles, 136–7
Rhodes, Cecil, 5, 6, 17, 68, 412
Rhodes–Livingstone Museum, 236–7, 379
Rhodesia and Nyasaland, Federation of, 164, 191, 220–3, 245, 283, 312–15, 343–4, 416–17
Rhodesia Congo Border Concession Co., 157
Rhodesia Congo Oil and Soap Industries, 304
Rhodesia Meat and Provisions Company, 295
Rhodesian Aviation Company, 117
Rhodesian Bottling Company, 308
Rhodesian Front, 222
Rhodesian Land and Cattle Company, 354

RMH, 218, 228, 230–4, 246, 248, 258, 344, 373, 383, 416
Rhodesian Native Timber Concessions Co., 169, 321, 325
Rhodesian Selection Trust, 158, 160, 222, 279, 287, 358, 404
Rice, E., 323
Rietfontein Ranch, 219, 353–4, 362, 364, 369, 403
Rightsector Ltd, 391
Riley, Aidan, 228,
Riley, Charles, 120–2, 413
Riley, C. H. de B., 'Harry', 122, 125, 130, 228
Riley, Jim, 122, 123–4, 136
Riley's Hotel/Garage, 122, 228, 282, 386–7
Riteve (Lithuania), 9–15, 45, 98, 167, 220
Riva, Henry Victor, 326–8, 330–1, 337, 416
Riva, Victor, 326
River transport, 14, 23–5, 53–4, 122; barges, 118–19; *mokoros* (canoes), 262, 263; *Nalikwanda* (royal barge), 265; steel barges: *Nangweshi*, 262, 263–4, *Iron Duke*, 262
Roads, 149–50, 200; Great East, 140; Kazungula–Maun, 125; Missionaries', 3; Old Hunters', 3, 22–3; Pedicle, 260; Riley's, 123–4; Susman's, 124; Westbeech's, 3
Roan Consolidated Mines, 399
Robertson, W. A, 320–1
Robinette, Dr W. L., 357, 359, 361
Robins, Sir Ellis (later Lord), 232, 240
Robins, Trude, née Wiesenbacher, also Wulfsohn, 177–81, 183, 190, 378
Robinson, Ella, née Susman, 142, 144, 165, 226
Robinson, Harry, 165, 225–30, 232–3, 245, 260, 370, 374–6, 381, 385, 416
H. Robinson and Company, 226, 230, 260–1, 266, 385, 400–1
H. Robinson (Northern) Ltd, 246
Robinson, Julius, 226–7, 370
Messrs. Robinson & Schwarz, 226, 230
Robson, Tom, 332, 416
Rockefeller Foundation, 399
N. M. Rothschild and Company, 412
Rothschild family, 128, 136
Roxburgh Smith, Captain, 117
Rollnick, J. R., 84
Roth, Jacob, *Wandering Jews*, 144
Rothkugel, Herbert, 151
Rowland, Tiny, 311, 316, 369
Rubinstein, Louis, 87
Rubinstein, Marcia, née Susman, 84, 87, 94
Rudnick, 391–2
Rudge, B. P., 199
Rural Development Company, 366
Russia, 1, 9–15, 84–5, 87, 92, 167, 411
SAAR Foundation, 351

INDEX

Sable Transport Ltd, 406
Sabzwari, A. A., 346
Sacher, Harry, 218
Sacher, Michael, 211
Sakala, General, 274
Saldus (Latvia), 167–8
Salisbury (town), 227, 229, 245–6, 266
Salisbury, Lord, 237
Salmon, Elijah ben-Solomon, 11
Salomon, Charelik., 106
Samuels, David, 391
Sandford, T. F., 172, 176, 184
Sandys, Duncan, 238, 239
Saperstein, S. H., 89, 101–2, 103
Sardanis, Andrew, 248, 252–4, 337, 404, 462 n., 463n.
Savage, Charles, 307, 310
Scaw Metals/Scaw-Tow Foundries Ltd, 309, 316
Schatz, Mrs, 171
Schenk, H. A., 196
Schulman, Nathan, 197, 304
Scots, 4, 14, 39–40, 280
Secondary Industry, 312–15, 340–52
Sefalana sa Botswana Ltd, 386
Sekgoma Letsholathebe, Chief, 6, 102, 120–2, 126
Selborne, Lord, 56, 89
Selous, F. C., 4, 22
Senanga (see also Mulena Mukwae and Nalolo), 405, 464 n.
Serracões da Machave, 327
Serracões da Zambesia, 318–19, 322, 324–8
A. F. Serrano Ltd, 198–201, 248
Serrano, Antonio F., 198–201, 257
Serrano, Marie, 203
Serrano, Tony, 196, 200, 203
Sesheke-Mwandi, 3–5, 19, 24, 31–3, 34–52, 65–6
Sesheke (new), 34
Settler nationalism, 45, 188–9
Shapiro, David, 153, 169, 236
Shelmerdine, William, 118
Shelton, Eric and Thelma, 202
Messrs. Shelton & Whitehead, 117–18
Shenton, R. J., 365
Shiel, Craig, 403
Shoprite Checkers, 275, 352, 404
Sicaba Party, see Barotse National Party
Sieff, Israel, 210, 213, 415
Sieff, Marcus, 211–13, 217
Sieff, Rebecca, 213
Sikalozia Estate, 365, 368
Sikongo, 275, 396
Silishebo, Reverend Elizabeth M., 34
Silley, Ted, 270

Simpson, Walter, 324, 326, 337
Simpson, W. B., 53
Sipopa, King, 3
Sisulu, Walter, 235
Slade, Neil, 405–8
Smith, Barnett 'Bongola', 97, 98, 113, 127–36, 159, 176, 285, 322, 325, 354, 413–14
Smith, George, 61, 95
Smith, Herbert, 355
Smith, Ian, 223, 444 n.
Smith, John, 108, 109–11, 127–34, 152, 414
Smith, J. (Selukwe), 63
Smith, Maurice, 325, 328
Smith, Wilbur, 355
Smuts, General J. C., 353
Snapper, Egnatz, 43, 61, 118
Sombart, Werner, 13
Sokolow, Nahum, 145, 146, 151
Solanki Brothers, 248, 253
Sonnenberg, Cecilia, 213
Sonnenberg, Hoffman and Galombik, 392
Sonnenberg, Max, 162, 195, 210, 212, 414–15
Sonnenberg, Richard (Dick), 210, 212–16
Sossen, Harry, 251
South Africa, 16–17, 82, 87, 94, 122–3, 162–3, 168, 209–20, 416
South African Jewish Times, 14, 86
South West Africa, 2, 35, 168
Southern Rhodesia, 16–18, 30–3, 93, 98, 134, 136, 159, 168–9, 226, 245–6, 257–8, 289–97, 395–6, 417, and see Zimbabwe
Speares, D. E., 204, 257, 273
Speck, Eric, 276–7
E. Speck and Company, 296
Sprinner, A., 67–82, 414
Standard Bank, 30, 44, 64–5, 87, 106–7, 111, 163, 170, 208, 324
Standard Chartered Bank, 381, 390, 399
Standard Trading Ltd, 247–8, 301, 304
Stanley, Sir Herbert, 133, 176
Stenham and Company/Ltd, 343, 347, 383, 389–94, 418
Stenham and Crombie Holdings Ltd, 383
Stenham Gestinor plc, 393
Stenham Investments Ltd, 392–3
Stenham Trade Finance, 392–3
Sterling, George, 106
Stevens and Adams Ltd, 333, 383
Stevenson, R. L., 68
Stores Holdings Ltd, 246, 248, 250–1, 253, 273
Storrs, Sir Ronald, 49, 134
Streitwolf, Captain, 102
Strikes, 319, 344
Structural Adjustment, 347–8, 372, 395–6, 411
Strudwick, N. J., 365
Messrs. Sturrock and Robson, 332

Summerton, F. J., 355
Summit Trading Ltd, 230
Supermarkets, 266, 408
Susman family: Ann, née Laski, 211, 213; Annie, née Grill, 90–4, 142, 143, 153; Behr, 12, 18, 85, 87, 92, 144, 146, 302; Bertha, née Lewison, 93–5, 142, 143, 149, 218; Bruna, see Zacks; David, 142, 149, 165, 186–7, 193, 209–20, 224–9, 234–6, 244–5, 246, 256, 271–2, 293, 295–6, 300, 309–10, 329, 333, 336, 360, 364, 369, 373–7, 382, 391–3, 399–400, 408, 412, 415, 419–20; Dora, see Gersh; Ella, see Robinson; Elie, 1, 12, 16–17, 22–5, 27, 29–30, 41–3, 63–4, 67–89, 129, 131, 136–7, 140, 142–7, 161, 163, 208, 220, 223–4, 227–8, 231–3, 277, 288, 300, 318–19, 322–4, 328, 353, 362–4, 374, 376, 413, 415, 419–20; Harry, 1, 12, 16–17, 30, 44, 50, 58–60, 64, 67, 81, 87, 89, 90–4, 123, 132–4, 136, 163, 192, 226, 282, 415, 419; Joe, 93, 125, 142, 150–1, 165, 186, 192, 244; Joel, 12; Marcia, see Rubinstein; Oscar, 84–5, 89–90, 103–4, 145–6; Oscar (younger), 142, 165, 191; Osna, see Wilton; Peggy, see Rabb; Simon, 213, 412; Taube, 12, 87, 144, 146, 302; Zelda, 142
Susman Brothers & Davis, 95–6
Susman Brothers Ltd, 185, 193
Susman Brothers (partnership), 44, 57, 62, 63, 64, 65, 97–8, 101, 104, 111, 114, 121–5, 159, 162, 163, 185–6
Susman Brothers & Riley, 122–3
Susman Brothers & Wulfsohn Ltd, 34, 128, 188–208, 227, 248, 251–5, 342, 344, 362, 366, 373, 376–7, 401, 405, 411, 416
Susman Brothers & Wulfsohn (Stores) Ltd, 227, 246, 251
E. and H. Susman Ltd, 193
E. Susman and Company, 33
Sussman, Philip, 31, 159, 415
Sussman, Willie, 159–60, 415
Sutherland, Robert F., 110, 112, 117–18, 130, 186, 414
R. F. Sutherland Ltd, 118–19, 123, 154, 186, 199–200, 203–4, 207, 267, 341, 343
Suu, Francis, 240, 242
Suzman, Helen, 235
Swaziland, 55, 219
Sykes, Frank W., 25
Tailors, 267–8
Tara Siding, 173, 175–7, 179, 181, 196
Tariffs, 303, 314–15, 343, 344, 345, 351
Tate & Lyle Ltd, 358
Taube, Max, 92, 151, 280
Taxation, 42, 55, 112, 127, 312, 329
Taylor, John, 396–7

Teeger, Isa, 455 n.
Tel Aviv, 85, 146
Telemetrix Group, 402
Textile manufacturing, 215–16, 340–52
Thatcher, Margaret, 388
Thom, John, 229
Thomson, C. M., 39
Messrs. Thomson and Bissett, 39, 64
Tiger Oats Ltd, 309, 342
Timber: barges, 118–19; furniture, 151–2, 331; flooring, 329, 332–3, 387–9; mining, 323, 328–9; *mukwa*, 152, 331; *mukusi* (redwood, teak), 159, 320–1, 332; plywood, 331; railway sleepers, 318, 320, 321, 327–9, 339; royalties, 320–1, 323, 338
Todd, J., 39
Tongue, W. E., 155, 318–19, 322–4, 414
Tracey, Leonard, 358
Trade: retail, 31–2, 62–3, 116–19, 161–3, 188–220, 229–34, 250–75, 302–5; wholesale, 21–2, 31, 63, 92, 111–12, 197–8, 204, 226, 246, 271, 385–6, 400–1
Trade cycle: booms: 1900s, 43; late 1930s, 300; late 1940s and early 1950s, 201, 245, 303, 358; late 1960s, 253; depressions/recessions: 1880s, 12; 1910s, 106–8; early 1920s, 131; 1930s, 118, 136–8, 142, 159, 161–2, 169–72, 177; 1950s, 231–2, 290–1, 311, 329; 1970s, 253, 275, 347, 388–9; 1980s, 275
Trade goods (and see merchandise): alcohol, 11–12, 199, 260, 264; agricultural implements/machinery, 33, 36, 47, 206; arms and ammunition, 3, 20–1, 27–8, 39, 41, 57–8, 60; beads, 33, 206–7; beeswax, 199, 205, 258; bicycles, 198, 206; blankets, 33, 200, 259, 340–52; boots and shoes, 33, 63; cloth, 20, 206–7, 259, 268; clothing, 33, 35, 121, 179, 197–8, 206–7, 215, 217, 229, 244, 265, 268, 273–4, 303; crockery, 33; curios, 116; electrical goods, 306; fish, 7, 199, 234, 258–9; flour, 197; groceries, 63, 206–7, 229, 264; hardware, 63, 151, 229; hides and skins, 33, 110, 116, 198–9, 201–2, 205, 208, 258, 274; hippo strips, 116; ivory, 5, 53, 69, 78, 116, 205–6, 264; maize meal, 121, 205; piece goods, 33, 197, 303; rhino horn, 274; salt, 33, 197–200; sewing-machines, 206; soap, 31, 197–8; sugar, 31, 121, 197; tea and coffee, 121; textiles, 206–7, 215, 217, 229, 340–52; tobacco, 63; wax prints, 33, 207, 244
Trade licences, 16, 18, 25, 29–30, 32, 38–9, 41, 46–7, 56–7, 61–2, 65–6, 81, 104, 192, 248–9, 264, 266, 301, 303–4, 444 n.
Trade Unions, 222, 303, 336; African Mineworkers, 287; Commercial and Industrial Workers, 344; United TUC, 268

Traders: African, 5, 28, 41, 197, 204–5, 251, 275, and cafes, 306; Asian, 234, 254, 259, 264, 295, 301, 302, 343; Greek/Cypriot, 63, 96, 102, 123, 130; Jewish, 21–9, 38–9, 41, 61, 63; Portuguese, 5, 19, 198–9
Trapnell, Colin, 117
Trollip, Jack, 203
TZI Ltd, 351, 372, 392, 395–412, 419
Troumbas, Hippocrates, 154
True, Jack, 262
Tshombe, Moise, 244, 311
Tuffin, Jack, 298, 346, 361, 365–70
Tully, Reg, 327, 337
UDI, 223, 246, 254–5, 337, 345, 351, 361, 367, 375, 379, 381–2, 385, 389, 416
UFP, 222, 236–44, 293, 299
Uganda Scheme, 85–6, 95
Ullmann, W., 61
Ullmann brothers, 95
Underwood, Bill, 307, 329–30
Union Minière du Haut Katanga, 128, 136, 311
United Africa Company, 323
UNIP, 34, 222, 235–6, 238–9, 241–5, 264, 370, 417
van Blerk, H. E., 86
van der Merwe, W. J., 342, 345–6
van der Post, Laurens, 282
van der Spuy, Chris, 181
van der Westhuizen, J., 341
van Rensburg, Fanie, 280, 353
van Rensburg, Mr, 270–1
van Ryneveld, Pierre, 149
van Staden, J. F., 335
van Zyl, B. L., 257, 269
van Zyl, Bennie, 203
van Zyl, 'Van', 355
Vaughan, L. J, 354–5
Venning, J. H., 52, 73, 75, 76, 79, 81, 103, 108
Victoria, Queen, 6, 89
Victoria Falls, 2, 8, 25, 83, 145, 192
Vigers, Fred, 332
Vigers Brothers Ltd, 332–3, 383
Vigers, Stevens and Adams, 333, 339, 374, 375, 387–9, 418
Villa Elisabetta (Lusaka), 153
Vincent, Judge, 78
Vlotamas, Alex, 281
von Frankenberg, Herr, 102–3
Vos, Hester (Poppie), 203
Vos, Ronnie, 202–3, 207
Vulfsohns, see Wulfsohn
Wacks, Abraham, 152
Waddington, Sir John, 322
Wages, 47; Agriflora, 406; NTC, 127; SB & W Stores, 267–8; ZSM, 319, 328, 336–7

Wagon transport, 3–4, 14, 21–3, 38–40, 47, 53, 64, 73, 102, 123–5, 174
Wallace, Lady, 148
Wallace, (Sir) Lawrence, 62, 89, 103, 113, 143
Wars: Anglo-Boer, 16, 19, 26, 40, 61–2, 128; Korean, 201, 303; First World, 33, 93, 102–4, 167; Second World, 131, 188–90, 258, 302–3, 419; Vietnam, 253
Waters, A., 98,
Weber, Max, 14
Julius Weil and Co., 22, 412
Weil, Sam and Roselle, 178
Messrs. Weil & Ascheim, 178
Weinberg, Reverend A., 144
Weizmann, Chaim, 145, 146, 210, 213
Welensky, Sir Roy, 188, 197, 222, 236, 239–41, 293, 299, 308, 312, 315, 323, 379
Werner, Henrietta Alberta, 161, 185, 281
Werner and Company, 161, 182, 183, 185–88, 190, 193, 222, 248–9, 276–99, 355, 357, 374–6, 382, 384, 405, 416–17
Werner, H. C., 114, 130, 152, 160–1
Wersock, David, 43, 61
Messrs. Wersock & Peimer, 92
Weskob, A. D. 'Chobo', 138, 228, 257, 281–2, 359, 373, 384, 414
Weskob, Cid, 281–2
Weskob, Mary, née Kays, 281
Wessell, Bobby, 211
Westbeech, George, 3–4, 31, 105
Westminster, Duke of, 176, 358
Wetherell, Marmaduke, 365
Whitehead, H. S., 111, 117
Wienand, R. H., 152
Wiesenbacher, Adolph, 178–9, 190
Wiesenbacher, Freddy, 379–80
Wiesenbacher, Klara (Claire), née Weil, 178, 190
Wiesenbacher, Trude, see Robins.
Wildlife, 354–7, 360–1; birds, 356; crocodiles, 8, 79, 122, 173–4, 185; elephants, 185, 334; hippos, 8, 40, 103, 122; hyenas, 185; Kafue lechwe, 354–7; leopards, 153, 160; lions, 8, 106, 124–5, 160, 173–4, 185, 353, 443 n.; predators, 127, 368; snakes, 8, 160; wild dogs, 106
Williams, Ralph, 120
Williams, Theodore, 57
Williamson, Anthony, 399
Willis, A. A., 89
Willson, Sidney Paxton, 70
Wilshaw, Sir Edward, 307–8
Wilson, George, 334
Wilson, Harold, 246
Wilton, Jack, 214
Wilton, Osna, 142, 214,

INDEX

Wina, Arthur, 239, 242, 243, 245, 249, 337, 346
Wina, Kalonga, 239
Wina, Sikota, 239, 242
Winnicott, H. C., 157
WNLA, 197–8, 202, 265
Woest, Ben, 129, 353, 358
Wolffe, Hymie, 150, 181, 212, 229
Wolpe, Harry, 235
Wolverton, Frederick Glyn, Lord, 153
Wolverton Ranch, 153–4, 182, 186
Woolf, Ron, 311, 316
F. W. Woolworth Ltd, 162
Woolworths Ltd, 161–3, 165–6, 186, 209–20, 229, 377, 383–4, 412, 414–15, 418
Women, 105, 179, 198, 207, 257, 263–4, 268
Wooltru Holdings Ltd, 384, 399–400, 412
World Bank, 395–6
World Wildlife Fund, 361
World Zionist Federation, 145
Worthington, Frank, 24, 31–2, 41, 51, 88, 89, 91
Wroth, Peter, 365
Wulfsohn family: Chaya, 167–8, 177; Dina, née Keet, 367, 381; Edwin, 190, 248, 250, 253–4, 256, 298–9, 339, 361, 367–71, 374, 379, 381–5, 387–94, 396–400, 412, 418–20; Floretta, née Glasstone, 169, 178–9; Harry, 166, 167–87, 223–9, 245–6, 248–9 298, 361, 376, 249, 259, 270, 272, 276–7, 281, 288, 293–4, 300, 322–33, 337–9, 340–1, 358–9, 361–4, 373–81, 385, 413, 415–16, 419–20; Hessie, see Lowenthal; Isaac, 167–8, 177; Lena, 177; Marlene, 190; Miriam, 190; Paul, 177; Rosalind, 190; Samuel Barnett, 169, 172, 178–9, 280; Trude, née Wiesenbacher, see Robins; Wulf, 168, 177, 181, 224, 236, 248
Harry Wulfsohn Ltd, 185, 188, 193, 354
Wylie, Doug, 361
Yager, David, 343, 383, 389
Yeta III, Litunga (Prince Litia), 18, 21, 24, 31–8, 41, 49, 51–2, 104, 112, 118, 139–40, 141, 191–2, 238–9, 319, 413
Yeta IV, Litunga, 34, 270–1
Yeta, Inyambo, Senior Chief, 34
Zacks, Bruna, née Susman, 95, 98, 142–3, 146–7, 219
Zacks, Sidney, 219

Zaloumis, Paul, 175, 341
Zambeef Ltd, 299, 404–5, 408–9, 419
Zambesi Cold Storage and Export Company, 288–9
Zambesi Flooring Ltd, 331–2, 339, 391
Zambesi River Transport Service, 200, 262, 331
Zambesi Saw Mills Ltd, 130, 138, 152, 155–7, 159, 165, 188, 318–24, 414–15
Zambesi Saw Mills (1948) Ltd, 219, 243, 248, 304, 311, 324–39, 373–5, 387, 391, 417–18
Zambesi Saw Mills (1968) Ltd, 274, 338–9, 417
Zambesi Saw Mills Railway, see Railways.
Zambesi Trading Association, 83, 150
Zambesi Trading Company, 250–4, 265, 269–71, 274, 389, 417
Zambesi Transport Syndicate, 118, 154
Zambesia Holdings Ltd, 319, 326
Zambezi River, 1–8, 22–5, 86, 118–19, 155–6, 199–200, 262, 265, 331
Zambia, *passim*
Zambia National Archives, 58, 78
Zambia Spinners Ltd, 347, 367
Zambia Sugar Company, 367
Zambia Textiles Ltd, 188, 285, 304–5, 340–52, 373, 375, 384, 401, 415
Zambianisation, 247, 266, 371
ZANC, 222, 389–90
Zangwill, Israel, 85
ZANU, 382
ZAPU, 353, 368, 382
Zaremba, Sarah Taylor, 303
ZCBC, 251–2, 404
ZCCM, 372
Zelter, Nathan, 228–30, 232–3, 245, 256, 259, 271–2, 344, 376
Zeppelin, Count von, 103
Zimbabwe, 2, 261, 342–3, 347–8, 385, 397–403, 408–10, 419
Zimbabwe National Archives, 71
Zionism, 11–12, 26, 85–6, 95, 140, 145–6, 168, 213, 379, 413
ZRC, 316, 351, 365–72, 395–9, 403–4, 408–9, 418
Zukas, Cynthia, née Robinson, 370
Zukas, Simon, 222, 252, 275, 352, 370–1, 395–6
Zusmanowitz, see Susman.